PROBLEMS OF THE
PACIFIC, 1931

THE UNIVERSITY OF CHICAGO PRESS
CHICAGO, ILLINOIS

THE BAKER & TAYLOR COMPANY
NEW YORK

THE CAMBRIDGE UNIVERSITY PRESS
LONDON

THE MARUZEN-KABUSHIKI-KAISHA
TOKYO, OSAKA, KYOTO, FUKUOKA, SENDAI

THE COMMERCIAL PRESS, LIMITED
SHANGHAI

0

PROBLEMS OF THE PACIFIC
1931

Proceedings of the Fourth Conference of the
Institute of Pacific Relations, Hangchow and
Shanghai, China, October 21 to November 2

EDITED BY

BRUNO LASKER

ASSISTED BY

W. L. HOLLAND

Acting Research Secretary

THE UNIVERSITY OF CHICAGO PRESS
CHICAGO, ILLINOIS

MANUFACTURED IN THE U. S. A. BY
THE PLIMPTON PRESS
NORWOOD, MASS.—LA PORTE, IND.

PREFACE

The Fourth Biennial Conference of the Institute of Pacific Relations was held in Shanghai, China, from October 21 to November 2, 1931, with two sessions in Hangchow, the place originally announced as the conference site.

This volume is a record of the round-table discussions of this Conference with extracts from the materials prepared for them and from addresses delivered at general sessions. A handbook, prepared primarily for the guidance of conference members, and outlining the history, philosophy, and methods of the Institute, is reproduced in Appendix II.

That the Institute weathered the troubled circumstances in which it was held has widely been acclaimed as a remarkable achievement in itself. The world-wide economic depression and the financial crisis in some of the participant countries, famine and flood disaster in China, and, finally, the " Manchurian incident " which capped a long series of controversies between China and Japan had made the holding of the Conference at the scheduled time and place well-nigh impossible. The credit for overcoming all these handicaps belongs particularly to the Chinese and Japanese members of the Institute whose personal courage and devotion to the Institute braved opposition in their own countries and who came to Shanghai to spend two weeks together in close personal contact, to study with the nationals of six other countries the outstanding problems that faced the peoples bordering the Pacific. When the Pacific Council, the governing body of the Institute, met in Shanghai in the week preceding the Conference, the tension in both countries was so great that it was considered inadvisable to hold the regular Conference, as scheduled. Plans were made for a " modified Conference," consisting in the main of expanded sessions of the organizational committees of the Institute, charged with the conduct of its ongoing activities. But after a week of working together in the business meetings of the Pacific Council, the International Research Committee, and the International Program Committee, the members were ready for more extended discussions; and on October 21 it was possible for Dr. Hu Shih, the president of the Conference, to open its first regular session with the words: " This *is* the Fourth Biennial Conference." A part of his address is here quoted as indicating the temper of the subsequent conference sessions:

" This Conference has been made possible by a tardy realization on the part of its Japanese and Chinese members that, whatever calamities may have befallen their respective countries through the folly of their political leaders, some good may yet result from the coming together and the thinking together of the enlightened men and women of the various nations, and the application of scientific method both in research and discussion in international affairs.

" We may now congratulate ourselves that so far the Institute has successfully passed a severe test and has courageously met a powerful challenge. The challenge, as I look at it, has been this: Dare we give up thinking in the face of great emotional upheavals, in times of national crises? Is the ideal and method of the Institute only good for peaceful times when people can afford to be polite to one another? It is not saying too much that the opening of this Conference today will long be remembered, not only in the annals of our own Institute, but also in the history of all sister institutions of an international nature, as having set up a splendid precedent that all those who in peaceful times pride themselves as being internationally-minded must not desert the ideal of calm thinking, patient research, and open-minded discussion at a time when folly reigns and passions carry the day. . . . .

" We have many thorny problems waiting for our analysis and, if possible, our solution. We shall still fail in our spirit and methodology if any of us approaches these problems with the erroneous attitude of proselyting the rest to his biased views. We shall fail if we allow our passions and prejudices to blind us from seeing the other fellow's point of view. We shall fail if we enter this hall in the spirit of the defender of a particular creed or the apologist for a particular cause.

" Let us, on this first day of our labors, try to have a clear understanding of the nature of our problems and the nature of our work. The problems are problems of nations and peoples. And our job is to think for nations and peoples. To think for a nation or nations is a sacred trust and a perilous task. It is a task in which, in the words of a Chinese sage, one word may build up a nation, and one word may ruin an empire. We can only qualify ourselves for the performance of this sacred duty by religiously guarding ourselves against our private biases and provincialisms, and reverently resolving not to allow our prejudices and feelings to influence our thinking and color our judgment. We are here neither to laugh nor to cry, but to understand. We are here not to teach, but to think together and exchange our ideas with one another. It is only in the spirit of the humble seeker after truth that we may hope to achieve at least a small measure of success."

The following official greetings, read at the opening meeting, testify to the understanding of the Institute's mission and methods in the governments of the participant countries:

From the President of the National Government of China:

" On behalf of the Chinese people and the National Government of the Chinese Republic, I take pleasure in extending to you our sincere greetings and a hearty welcome. We have looked forward to your coming and believe that through the deliberations at your Conference an important step will be taken toward the improvement of international relations among the Pacific countries. It is my personal opinion that world peace and international good-will will forever remain empty words until men and women like yourselves are willing to give time and energy to study, and to seek to understand, the complex problems existing among nations. Indeed, world events today are so much shrouded with ignorance and ill-will that there is little reasonable hope for peace of a permanent nature. In such an atmosphere of suspicion and misunderstanding, the Institute of Pacific Relations fills an urgent need. The knowledge of facts which it spreads and the intelligent sympathy which it promotes will surely build a foundation on which a more promising future rests."

From the British Prime Minister:

" I shall be glad if you will convey to the Conference of the Institute of Pacific Relations my hearty good wishes for the success of their meeting. I followed the proceedings of the Honolulu and Kyoto Conferences with interest and pleasure. The Institute has done and is doing admirable work in the all important field of promoting international understanding, and I confidently hope that they will long continue to carry through their great task with an equal measure of success."

From the Prime Minister of the Commonwealth of Australia:

" In conveying best wishes to the Fourth Conference of the Institute of Pacific Relations, I sincerely trust that your efforts for the preservation of peace and the welfare of the people will be crowned with success."

From the Prime Minister of Canada:

" On behalf of government and people of Canada I extend most cordial greetings to Fourth Biennial Conference of Institute of Pacific Relations meeting at most critical time. I trust your deliberations may result in promoting the cause of peace and of mutual understanding among the peoples of the Pacific. Canada's interests in the Pacific are rapidly developing, and her earnest desire is to maintain most cordial relations with all peoples. Canada firmly believes that international disputes should be settled by peaceable means, and she has evidenced this faith by participation in and support of the League of Nations, the Permanent Court of International Justice, the Kellogg-Briand Peace Pact, and the General Act Providing for Peaceable Settlement of All International Disputes. We are therefore deeply interested in work of the Conference and earnestly hope it may be successful in achieving its objects."

From the Prime Minister of New Zealand:

" It gives me much pleasure to express my good wishes for the success of the Conference of the Institute of Pacific Relations that is to be held in China this year. I sincerely trust that useful work will be accomplished, and that the Conference will assist in still further strengthening the growing spirit of good-will that animates the peoples of the Pacific."

From the Prime Minister of Japan:

" I deem it a privilege, as well as a pleasure, to offer a few words of congratulation at the opening of the Fourth Conference of the Institute of Pacific Relations.

" The world, today, is confronted with a series of highly important problems, social, economic and political, upon the solution of which depends the future welfare and harmonious co-existence of the human race as a whole. All of these problems reveal in a marked degree their international character and the close interdependence of all the nations. Without international co-operation none of them could be satisfactorily solved.

" It is especially gratifying to know that the Institute is devoting its efforts to a scientific and impartial study of the facts pertaining to several Pacific countries, as well as to their mutual relations. It is my firm conviction that the accurate knowledge of the Pacific countries obtained by such a method and in such a spirit will prove to be highly useful in bringing about real mutual understanding and good-will among the peoples bordering on the Pacific.

" Taking this opportunity, I desire to express my sincere wishes that the deliberations of the present Conference will contribute to the betterment of the existing relations among the different nations represented at the Institute."

From two eminent Japanese statesmen, Viscount Shibusawa and Baron Sakatani:

" It is a source of profound gratification to us that the Institute of Pacific Relations is able to open today its Fourth Biennial Conference in an atmosphere of friendly and harmonious co-operation notwithstanding the fact that the political horizon in this part of the world is at present unfortunately threatened by a serious depression. We therefore offer you our most hearty congratulations and at the same time wish you all success."

From the President of the Philippine Senate:

" The Philippine Islands, in token of our appreciation of your recognition of the Philippines as an autonomous national unit in the Institute of Pacific Relations, pledges increased support to the purposes and program of the Institute."

From the President of the United States of America:

" In the conduct of international relations government policies rest in last analysis on public opinion. That opinion is bound to reflect the degree to which the public is informed and the extent to which it seeks to understand. It is therefore highly desirable that private citizens study and seek to understand the problems with regard to which governments have to act. Among the instrumentalities for such effort, the Institute of Pacific Relations has attained a recognized position. It is free from official inspiration. Its members have no official representative capacity. Its deliberations are not directed by any government.

" Please convey to the assembled members of the Institute my best wishes. I trust that from their efforts in the present as in previous sessions the members will derive increasingly accurate knowledge of essential facts and factors in the life and intercourse of nations, and, studying and interpreting in the spirit of mutual respect and reciprocal good-will, will be able to make new contributions to the cause of harmony in international relations."

During the course of the Conference, further greetings were received from the chairman of the newly constituted U.S.S.R. Council of the Institute, Dr. Fedor N. Petrov.

The cordial attitude of the National Government of China and of the outstanding provincial and local officials was further manifested on several occasions when members of the Conference were received by them, in Nanking, Shanghai, Peiping, and Hangchow.

In accordance with the recommendations of the members of the 1929 Conference, the size of the conference was reduced, 132 members being present as compared with 214 attending the Kyoto Conference. Groups from Australia, New Zealand, the Philippines, China, Japan, Great Britain, Canada, and the United States were present as members. Observers attended from the Dutch East Indies, the League of Nations, and the International Labour Office.

During the twelve days of the Conference, thirty-one round tables met in fifty sessions, discussing thirteen major topics. In addition, there were seventeen forums or general sessions.

In preparation for this Conference, the national councils and the central secretariat published and distributed in advance eighty-four data papers. Sixteen studies, most of which had a direct bearing on the topics under discussion at the Conference, had been carried on at the instigation or under the auspices of the International Research Committee.

The agenda of the Conference was drafted at a meeting of the International Program Committee held in New York in December, 1930, on the basis of official recommendations submitted by the different national councils to the headquarters office at Honolulu. The day-by-day program of the Conference was determined by this committee, which met for nine days prior to the opening of the Conference and held almost daily meetings during its progress.

The present report of proceedings, although as one of a series it will make possible a study of the developing international situation and thought in the Pacific area, differs in a few particulars from the preceding reports. Naturally, as the conference membership changes, there is an increasing and unavoidable repetition of arguments at round-table sessions; often ground already amply covered at a previous conference is briefly gone over again to insure a full understanding of the problem under discussion. To avoid such duplication in the printed report, the editors have endeavored to reproduce important new information and to indicate the trend of thinking on a given subject rather than to present a rounded statement of *all* significant facts and opinions. They have kept to the form of actual reporting even though, in many instances, this method leaves unstated facts and considerations presumably in the minds of conference members that have been stated elsewhere. The chapters of this volume are not, therefore, inclusive or exhaustive treatments of the subjects with which they deal but are intended to be supplemented by the individual reader and student from data given in previous conference reports (particularly *Problems of the Pacific,* 1927 and 1929) and in other available literature.

On the other hand, in order to reproduce more faithfully the actual integration of research and discussion characteristic of the Institute, of data papers, addresses, and round tables, these different types of contribution are no longer dealt with in separate sections of the volume of proceedings but have here been used as materials for chapters on major-subject fields. This treatment has further led to the inclusion of significant extracts from a much larger number of individual contributions than can be used when the reproduction of whole conference papers necessitates a rigorous choice and the entire exclusion from the volume of most of the data papers and addresses which actually have implemented the conference discussions.

The Fourth Biennial Conference of the Institute had the advantage of carefully prepared syllabi on nearly all of the major subjects on the conference program. These pamphlets, edited by Dr. J. B. Condliffe, W. L. Holland, Stephen A. Heald, and F. M. Keesing, not only proved very useful in the preparation of the final round-table agendas, but have also been drawn upon for important materials in the present report of proceedings.

In order to reduce somewhat the size of this volume, organizational reports and minutes, previously included in these proceedings, have been omitted. Those interested in that type of information can secure it from the office of the Central Secretariat in Honolulu or from that of any of the national councils. It is, however, important to mention here that in the China sessions of the Institute the Pacific Council admitted two new groups into its membership, which now constitute national councils: the Philippine Council was represented and took an active part in the China Conference; the newly formed Pacific Committee of the Institute in the U.S.S.R., though not represented at Shanghai, will in the future participate actively in studies and conferences.

The Pacific Council received a report from its representative at the Copenhagen Conference of Institutions for the Scientific Study of International Relations, which revealed that several European leaders were inquiring whether the time had not come to organize an Institute of Europe or an Institute of the Atlantic on lines similiar to those of the Institute of Pacific Relations.

In view of the reference made above to the necessary limitations of the present volume of proceedings, it may also be mentioned here that, by action of the Pacific Council, the Institute's journal, *Pacific Affairs,* is to be continued, under the editorship of Miss Elizabeth Green, as an integral part of the organization's machinery of uninterrupted reporting and discussion — an essential supplement of the biennial reports of conference proceedings for all serious students of Pacific problems. Furthermore, several of the larger contributions to this last Conference — among them some of the most important — are or will be available in the form of separate publications; and all the data papers referred to in this volume and listed (p. 508) are available in limited printed or mimeographed editions until the supply is exhausted. In its library at Honolulu the Institute has a further resource for aiding students and for disseminating information on Pacific affairs in the periods between conferences. Readers who desire information on the present research projects of the Institute are referred to an article in the February, 1932, number of *Pacific Affairs.*

CHARLES F. LOOMIS
Acting General Secretary

HONOLULU, HAWAII
March 5, 1932

TABLE OF CONTENTS

PART I

ECONOMIC RELATIONS IN THE PACIFIC

CHAPTER I

TRADE RELATIONS IN THE PACIFIC

DATA PAPERS

1. G. L. Wood. *Trade in the Pacific* (reprint of five articles from *The Argus*, Melbourne, July, 1931).
2. G. L. Wood. *The World Depression and the Australian Standard of Living* (mimeographed; Australian Council).
3. Norman Mackenzie. *Canadian Tariff Policy* (Canadian Council).
4. Tetsujiro Shidachi. *The Depression of 1930 as It Affected Japan* (Japanese Council).
5. Member of the Japan Economic Committee. *The Recent Customs Tariff Revision in Japan* (Japanese Council).
6. Zenichi Itani. *The Export of Japanese Capital to China* (Japanese Council).
7. Downie Stewart. *New Zealand's Pacific Trade and Tariff* (New Zealand Council).
8. Philip G. Wright. *The American Tariff and Oriental Trade* (American Council).
9. Lewis L. Lorwin. *The Need for World Economic Planning* (American Council).
10. International Secretariat. *Syllabus on Trade Relations.*

REFERENCES

1. League of Nations. *The Course and Phases of the World Economic Depression* (Economic and Financial Section, 1931), IIA, 21.
2. D. B. Copland (ed.). "An Economic Survey of Australia," *Annals of the American Academy of Political and Social Science*, November, 1931.
3. Allen and Others (eds.). *New Zealand Affairs* (Christchurch, 1929), chaps. vii and viii.
4. Carl F. Remer. *Foreign Investments in China* (International Research report, mimeographed), pp. 10–16 and 31.
5. H. D. Fong. *China's Industrialization: A Statistical Survey* (China Council), p. 41.
6. Harold G. Moulton. *Japan: An Economic and Financial Appraisal.* Washington: Brookings Institution, 1931.
7. John E. Orchard. *Japan's Economic Position..* New York, 1931.
8. D. B. Copland. "The Australian Problem," *Economic Journal*, London, December, 1930.
9. Dorothy Orchard. "China's Use of the Boycott as a Political Weapon," *Annals of the American Academy of Political and Social Science*, November, 1930.
10. Percy W. Bidwell. "The New American Tariff: Europe's Answer," *Foreign Affairs*, New York, October, 1930.
11. H. B. Elliston. "The Silver Problem," *ibid.*, April, 1931.
12. Charles P. Howland. *Survey of American Foreign Relations, 1930* (New Haven, 1930), chap. iv.

INTRODUCTORY NOTE

When members of the Fourth Biennial Conference of the Institute of Pacific Relations embarked for China, a dark cloud hung over their respective countries. Some of them saw half-starved men scramble for jobs at the docks; others took leave from colleagues whose heavy responsibilities in a time of general business depression had frustrated their plan to attend this Conference. On the ships that carried the members to China there was talk of bank failures, of the recent war-debts moratorium called by the President of the United States to prevent an imminent financial collapse in Germany, of the political crisis, and of the suspension of the gold standard in Great Britain. Unemployment had grown to alarming proportions in most of the Pacific countries for which statistics are available; wholesale and export prices of the great staple commodities of international trade had fallen precipitately with disastrous effects on those nations, like Australia, New Zealand, and Japan, whose national welfare depends in large measure on overseas trade; the trade between the Pacific countries had declined with prices, bringing severe losses to Pacific shipping, which was already suffering from a spell of international competition not yet ended. To aggravate the difficulty, four of the Pacific countries, Canada, the United States, Australia, and New Zealand, had raised their import tariffs to considerably higher levels; China had introduced her new national tariff early in 1930; and India, slightly outside the Pacific basin, had raised her tariff, resulting in an appreciable reduction of her imports from Japan.

There have been few periods in history that serve so well as the two years passed since the Kyoto Conference of the Institute — concluded only a day or two after the slump on the New York stock exchange had dramatically announced the onset of the world economic depression — to illustrate the intimate connection between economic forces and the political relations of peoples. The fall in the price of silver, with its immediate effects on the growing Chinese market, had made itself most felt in the trade of those Pacific countries with which China conducts most of her foreign commerce. In Australia a similar fall in foreign exchanges had been brought about by the necessity of making payments on overseas loan obligations at a time when the export commodities which alone could provide the means of payment were declining in value. Japan, after determined and successful efforts to abolish the embargo on gold exports in January, 1930, had been obliged to undergo a painful financial deflation as the drain on her gold reserves proceeded, involving hardships which were intensified in her case by the partial collapse of her market for silk in the United States. The unusually abundant rice harvest at home afforded some relief to the consuming public but so reduced prices as to inflict acute distress on her agricultural population. More serious was the plight in the wheat-exporting countries on the other side of the Pacific, in Canada and the United States, where huge surplus stocks accumulated and depressed the buying power of the farming population.

It was not by accident, then, that " Trade Relations of the Pacific Countries " appeared as the first subject for round-table discussion on the agenda of the Conference. Out of the twenty or so foodstuffs and raw materials whose world-prices had declined most seriously in the depression, no less than three-quarters were commodities that form the principal products for consumption or export in Pacific countries and India — wool and butter in Australia and New Zealand; tin and rubber in Malaya and the Dutch East Indies; rice in India, Indo-China, Java, China, and Japan; sugar in Java, the Philippines, Formosa, and Hawaii; wheat in India, Canada, Australia, and the United States; silk in China and Japan; cotton in India, China, and the United States; silver, zinc, and copper in North America; and petroleum in the United States, Mexico, and the Dutch East Indies.

Meanwhile, in these two years the world-markets had begun to feel, though as yet not seriously, the effect of competition from a newcomer in international commerce, as Soviet Russia's export trade, notably in wheat, lumber, and petroleum, began to recover from its post-war eclipse. The repercussions were immediately felt in the wheat and lumber industries of Canada and the United States, the former of which used the fact that the Soviet Union was not a signatory of the Versailles Treaty to take the drastic step of imposing a ban on all Russian imports. In an appreciable although much slighter degree, the Soviet Union began to make its influence felt also in certain markets of the Far East.

The Canadian ban upon Russian trade was only one example among several of the manner in which economic tendencies reacted upon international political relations. Even between the sister British dominions, New Zealand and Canada, the imposition of the latter's new tariff, with its prohibitive duty which effectively destroyed a profitable butter trade from the former, resulted in considerable ill feeling and ultimately in a retaliatory action by the New Zealand Government under which the preference given to imported automobiles of Canadian manufacture was abolished. The protests which were submitted by thirty-six nations, including several Pacific countries, against various provisions of the United States Tariff of 1930 provide another illustration of the effect of perfectly legal and domestic action by a state upon international relations in a world so knit together by the ties of economic intercourse.[1] So also in the Sino-Japanese dispute in Manchuria a Marxian theorist might find abundant illustrations for an economic interpretation of contemporary history in the decline of prices for Manchurian bean products in European countries and Japan, or in the slump in silver — both of which events combined to reduce the revenues of the South Manchuria Railway and to add a new economic irritation to the existing political tension. Moreover, it was in the realm of trade relations that the subsequent international resentment between the two countries manifested itself most aggressively, as the anti-Japanese boycott in China became more and more stringent in its application, affecting not only overseas trade but commerce with Japanese manufacturing, financial, and shipping enterprises domiciled in China itself. The depression had already shown its influence on immigration policies in the English-speaking countries of the Pacific, all four of which

[1] See paper read by Philip G. Wright at the meeting of the American Political Science Association in Washington, D.C., December 29, 1931.

by legislation or special administrative orders had practically stopped their characteristic intake of immigrants from European countries. China was similarly affected, in the south by the drastic restrictions placed upon the immigration of her nationals into British Malaya, and in the north by the slump in the bean trade of Manchuria, which acted as a deterrent to the enormous volume of migration ordinarily taking place from Hopei and Shantung provinces.

The four round tables, therefore, met to consider problems which were by no means remote or academic, but close home to all their members and of deep concern in each of the countries from which they came. An analysis of the records of their discussions shows that the attention was mainly centered upon three problems: first, the tariff situation in the Pacific countries; second, the effects of the trade depression; and third, the silver problem in relation to China's foreign trade. As was natural, there was a tendency to turn toward the problems of China for concrete illustrations, with the result that several incidental discussions took place on such matters as the effect of China's new tariff on her industrial development or on the import of foreign capital into China, and on the economic effectiveness of boycotts, as compared with tariffs, as means for restricting commerce.

The following pages, then, represent a discussion definitely affected by the immediate situation; they do not systematically cover even all the more important problems of Pacific trade relations, and within the scope of the questions faced it would be easy to point to gaps that were not bridged.

Owing to the limitations of the present volume of proceedings, it is not possible to present here more than a fraction of the information which members of the Conference had before them. Mr. Wright's thorough study of the United States tariff in its effect on Pacific trade has in the meantime been separately published;[2] and with the decision of the International Research Committee to co-ordinate the separate studies by other national groups on tariffs and trade in the Pacific (see p. 37), the future publication of their contribution to knowledge seems assured. On some of the subjects brought up in discussion, reliable data were not available; and the analysis of many problems was incomplete on the theoretical side also. In this as in other chapters of the present volume, the editor has not considered it his function to supply missing information or arguments.

[2] *The American Tariff and Oriental Trade.* University of Chicago Press.

TABLE I *

FOREIGN-TRADE DECLINE OF PACIFIC COUNTRIES

(Million dollars gold)

Country		1929	1930	Decrease	Decrease Per Cent
Canada...............	Imports	1,299	1,008.5	290.5	22.4
	Exports	1,208.3	905.4	302.9	25.1
	Total	2,507.3	1,913.9	593.4	23.7
United States...........	Imports	4,399.4	3,060.9	1,338.5	30.4
	Exports	5,241	3,843.2	1,397.8	26.7
	Total	9,640.4	6,904.1	2,736.3	28.2
China.................	Imports	820	611	209	25.5
	Exports	660	420.1	239.9	36.3
	Total	1,480	1,031.1	448.9	30.3
Japan (proper)..........	Imports	1,021.7	763.6	258.1	25.3
	Exports	990.5	726	264.5	26.7
	Total	2,012.2	1,489.6	522.6	26
Chosen (Korea)..........	Imports	195	181.3	13.7	7
	Exports	159.4	131.6	27.8	17.4
	Total	354.4	312.9	41.5	11.7
Taiwan (Formosa)........	Imports	29.8	22.3	7.5	25.2
	Exports	15.3	11.3	4	26.1
	Total	45.1	33.6	11.5	25.5
Netherlands East Indies...	Imports	431	335.1	95.9	22.3
	Exports	581.4	483.6	97.8	16.8
	Total	1,012.4	818.7	193.7	19.1
British Malaya..........	Imports	497.8	399.6	98.2	19.7
	Exports	518.6	369.6	149	28.7
	Total	1,016.4	769.2	247.2	24.3
French Indo-China........	Imports	102	......	.....	....
	Exports	102.4	......	.....	....
	Total	204.4	......	.....	....
Philippines	Imports	147.2	123.1	24.1	16.4
	Exports	164.4	133.2	31.2	19
	Total	311.6	256.3	55.3	17.7
Australia................	Imports	706.5	452.1	254.4	36
	Exports	600	444.9	155.1	25.8
	Total	1,306.5	897	409.5	31.3
New Zealand.............	Imports	237.1	207.6	29.5	12.5
	Exports	264.8	215.8	49	14.7
	Total	501.9	423.4	78.5	15.6
India....................	Imports	900	666.5	233.5	25.9
	Exports	1,190.6	927.3	263.3	22.1
	Total	2,090.6	1,593.8	496.8	23.3
U.S.S.R.................	Imports	453.5	545.3	91.8	20.2
	Exports	475.7	533.7	58	12.2
	Total	929.2	1,079	149.8	16.1

* Source: *Commerce Yearbook* (1931), Vol. II: "Foreign Countries," table on pp. 724–27 and tables in chapters on the different countries. *Ibid.*, Vol. I: "United States," table on p. 79. U.S. Department of Commerce, Bureau of Foreign and Domestic Commerce, Washington, D.C., United States Government Printing Office, 1931. The figures of imports and exports for New Zealand, Australia, and British Malaya include bullion and specie. No statement is made as to whether or not bullion and specie are included in the Netherlands East Indies

EXTRACTS FROM DATA PAPERS

I. CAUSES OF THE ECONOMIC DEPRESSION IN JAPAN [3]

By Tetsujiro Shidachi

DOMESTIC CAUSES

Maladjustment of capital and heavy debts. — It is evident that the present depression in Japan is the result of a combination of domestic and worldwide factors which have caused a condition in the country of equal, if not in some respects greater, distress to that in other countries. Turning first to the domestic causes, we may dismiss the ever-present problems of population and scarcity of natural resources, and proceed immediately to those special economic conditions which seem to have led to the depression. Except during a very few years, Japan was, up to 1914, a nation with an adverse balance of trade; but during the five years which followed the outbreak of the European war this balance turned in her favor to such an extent that it almost took the nation's breath away. During this time the total excess of exports over imports amounted to 1,400 million yen. As the result of this excess together with invisible exports the national stock of gold at one time reached 2,100 million yen. This was a time of unprecedented economic expansion. Public finances, both central and local, prices, wages, cost of living, note-circulation, capital — everything — increased to an extent hitherto unknown. But from 1919 we observe an abrupt change in the situation. The balance of trade once more became adverse, and the gain of 3,600 million yen acquired during the war by the visible and invisible trade balance was totally lost. In spite of this change the same high standard of living was maintained in all walks of life throughout the country. This resulted in a maladjustment of capital which naturally led up to the gradual increase of debts, until, at present, the entire country, including business enterprises and private individuals, is gasping under a burden of debt. With a few exceptions, the industrial corporations established or enlarged during the boom have not reduced their

figures. Bullion is included in the figures for French Indo-China but specie is excluded. Bullion and specie are excluded from the remaining figures.

These figures are not estimates but are based on actual data received from the respective countries. In the case of Australia, New Zealand, and the Netherlands East Indies, the 1929 figures as given in the 1931 edition of the *Commerce Yearbook* differed slightly from the 1929 figures in the 1930 edition. This was also true of the export figures for Japan and India for 1929. One may assume that similar minor changes may occur in the 1930 figures which will appear in the 1932 edition. The changes in the 1931 edition in the 1929 figures are as follows (in million gold dollars):

Country		1930 Edition	1931 Edition	Change
Japan (proper)..............	Exports	988.5	990.5	2 inc.
India.......................	Exports	1,191	1,190.6	.4 dec.
Netherlands East Indies........	Imports	435.9	431	4.9 dec.
	Exports	578.4	581.4	3 inc.
Australia....................	Imports	708.1	706.5	1.6 dec.
	Exports	661.5	600	61.5 dec.
New Zealand.................	Imports.....	237.2	237.1	.1 dec.
	Exports	270.5	264.8	5.7 dec.

[3] Extract from *The Depression of 1930 as It Affected Japan* (Japanese Council).

capital to meet the present conditions, so that the very root of the domestic distress is undoubtedly this same maladjustment of capital and the resultant burden of debt.

Another factor not to be overlooked is that during the boom the Japanese people overestimated their true financial power, which led them to resort, sometimes with disastrous results, to such ventures as the unsound use of call-money for exchange, the over-stimulation of uncertain enterprises, and the encouragement of doubtful foreign loans. This desire for expansion was abused by speculators, adventurers, and even by the Government, and greatly aggravated the subsequent difficulties.

During the critical years between 1919 and 1930 the problem of re-adjustment was further aggravated by the earthquake of 1923 and the bank panic of 1927. These two disasters completely upset certain industries and financial institutions which might have pulled through under ordinary circumstances.

The lifting of the gold embargo. — A more recent factor in the depression is the return to the gold standard. The exchange rate on New York rose from 44 in June, 1929, when the Hamaguchi Cabinet came into existence, to 49⅜ in January, 1930, as the result of the lifting of the gold ban according to pre-war parity.[4] It is believed by some that this return to pre-war parity is the major cause of the depression. But I cannot support this view. I am convinced that, belated though it was, there was no other policy for the Government to adopt. There is no doubt, however, that this raising of the money value by nearly 10 per cent has worked great hardship in industrial circles by rendering it difficult for debtors to discharge their obligations and by further increasing the adverse balance of trade. It was most unfortunate for Japan that the crash on the New York stock market occurred in the autumn of 1929 just as the return to the gold standard was in the course of preparation.

Heavy taxes. — Another outstanding cause of the present depression is the heavy burden of taxation. During the years of prosperity, expenditures for government activities expanded, entailing a corresponding increase of taxation. But with the shrinkage in income, taxation was not adjusted; and the Government, both central and local, continued to levy exorbitant taxes, especially for defense and education, until we have reached a point where taxation from all sources amounts to 19 per cent of the national income. When we compare this to the figures given in the report of the National Industrial Conference Board of the United States which places the proportion of all taxes (government, state and local) to the total income in 1929 at 11.6 per cent,[5] we can form some idea of the burden under which the Japanese people are groaning. The actual cost of national defense, not including pensions, annuities, and other auxiliary costs, comprises 26.8 per cent of the national budget, an expenditure in excess of that of France, Great Britain or the United

[4] Par exchange is 49.846.
[5] *Bulletin of the National Industrial Conference Board*, March, 1931.

States. What Leroy-Beaulieu, the French economist, wrote regarding the limitation of taxes in the latter part of the nineteenth century still holds true. He said that if the total of national, provincial and communal taxes does not exceed 7 or 8 per cent of the revenue of private individuals, the burden is very moderate; that it is still bearable when it does not exceed 10 or 12 per cent of the revenue of citizens, but that beyond 12 or 13 per cent it is exorbitant; and that the progress of national wealth will certainly be retarded, and the liberty of industry and of citizens will be menaced and restrained by the vexations and inquisitions necessarily resulting from the complication and heightening of taxes.[6]

Unusually abundant rice harvest. — As might be expected, the agrarian population has suffered exceedingly during the present depression; the decline in the price of silk, which will be discussed later, caused serious hardships to a large portion of agricultural Japan; and the phenomenal drop in the price of rice has made the lot of the farmer well nigh hopeless. In 1920 rice was sold at 54 yen per *koku* (4.9629 bushels). Between 1920 and 1929 the price fluctuated between 30 and 40 yen per *koku*. But after the unprecedented crop of 1930 the price of the best rice dropped to 20 yen at the end of the year. Since the cost of production of rice, according to the government report, is 21.35 yen per *koku*, it is obvious that the farmers can under no circumstances afford to sell rice at such a low price.

It might be supposed that we would welcome a bumper crop of rice since Japan proper is obliged to import large quantities every year not only from Korea and from Formosa but from Siam and even from the United States of America. But the crop of 1930, which exceeded any ordinary good crop by 6 million *koku* in Japan proper and 4 million *koku* in Korea, so reduced the price that it plunged the farmers into deepest distress. It is hard to imagine the conditions of agrarian Japan. Burdened with debts, the farmers are not only unable to reduce their obligations but find it increasingly difficult to obtain necessary implements and fertilizers. Thus their purchasing power has been reduced, resulting in a nation-wide decrease in the demand for manufactured goods, and aggravating to no small degree the general depression. . . .

INTERNATIONAL CAUSES DIRECTLY CONCERNING JAPAN

The fall in the price of silver. — The fall in the price of silver will perhaps be discussed separately at this conference. So it is not necessary to go into that matter in detail here. Suffice it to say that, in-so-far as it has reduced the purchasing power of the Chinese people, it has affected Japanese trade and consequently must be regarded as a cause of economic depression. But it is difficult to say how much of the decrease in trade with China proper, which amounted to 25 per cent in exports and 23 per cent in imports during 1930 compared with 1929, is due to the decline in silver, and how much to other causes — such as the Chinese political unrest and the boycott of Japa-

[6] Leroy-Beaulieu, *Traité de la science des finances* (8th ed.), Vol. I.

nese goods. Since, however, our trade with China proper comprises an average of 17 per cent of our exports and 10 per cent of our imports, any serious decrease in this trade is not to be treated lightly. The question of the decline in the price of silver is one that must be adjusted in one way or another, for, since the savings of the Chinese people are mostly in silver, the present condition which decreases their purchasing power must be remedied. But this decrease of the purchasing power of China has been exaggerated by superficial observers. R. S. Tucker's scholarly criticism of the report of the Senate Committee of the United States on the silver problem [7] and the able address of Sir Arthur Salter before the Academy of Political Science, London,[8] are to my mind fundamentally sound. Sir Arthur, in examining the proposal for a world conference on silver, says most aptly that such conferences without due preparation and reasonable prospects of result put the cart before the horse. As he suggested, the causes of the depression should be tackled first.

Political unrest in China and India, the Chinese boycott of Japanese goods, and the increase of tariff in India, Australia, and America. — While it is beyond doubt that political unrest in China and India and the Chinese boycott of Japanese goods have been responsible to no small degree for the decrease in Japanese trade, it is exceedingly difficult to estimate to what extent these factors have directly contributed to the present depression. A few words should be said regarding the increase of tariff in India, Australia, and the United States in 1930. Needless to say, this has had a detrimental effect upon the foreign trade of Japan; but it is a question whether this was as serious for Japan as the reaction in those countries themselves. For instance, the increased tariff on cotton goods in India not only raised the price of cotton goods but was the cause of the decreased demand for raw cotton from that country; while the United States is suffering from retaliative tariffs to such an extent that it is doubtful whether she has gained any real advantage from raising her duties, which were already too high in 1929.

The crash on the New York stock market. — The crash on the New York stock exchange in the autumn of 1929 had a very serious effect upon Japan. This can be easily understood when it is remembered that the United States buys 95 per cent of all the raw silk exported by this country. During last year the raw silk exported to the United States decreased 47 per cent in value and 18 per cent in quantity. This was a tremendous blow to our foreign trade. Before 1929 the price of raw silk had been maintained at a comparatively uniform level of about 1,300 yen per 100 *kin*. But the New York crash, combined with the lifting of the gold embargo, brought the price down from 1,345 yen in September, 1929, to 1,100 yen in March, 1930. The merchants in a panic appealed to the Government for aid; and a law, which had never before been resorted to, was put into force. By the operation of this law, banks making loans to silk merchants may be compensated by the

---

[7] *The Annalist*, February 27, 1931.
[8] A review of the address is in *The Economist*, July 4, 1931.

Government against loss to the amount of 190 yen per bale (100 *kin*) up to 150,000 bales. This resulted in the congestion of 200,000 bales of silk at Kobe and Yokohama and in a sharp drop in the price of silk to 540 yen in the autumn of 1930. This is an outstanding illustration of the futility of artificial stimulation — a lesson, it is hoped, that will be remembered in the future. Thus the fall in price of silk was due to a combination of circumstances, namely, the crash of 1929, the lifting of the gold embargo, and the attempt of the Government to peg the price. But it was undoubtedly the New York crash which gave it its downward impetus. . . .

II. RECENT DEVELOPMENTS IN CHINA'S FOREIGN TRADE [9]

With the appearance of industrial development on her soil, China like every other country has been drawn into a world economy. Her economic prosperity affects and is affected by the prosperity of America, Russia, Japan, Great Britain, France, and Germany. Foreign trade and the " Great Industry " are inseparable companions in China, and the money value of trade is but an imperfect measure of its economic and social significance. But that is not all. Chinese agriculture no less than Chinese industrial production is concerned in overseas trade. Contrary to a widespread belief, much of Chinese agriculture is not subsistence farming but production for a market, and often a foreign market. A striking example of this is to be seen in the agricultural economy of the Four Eastern Provinces, with its emphasis on the export of beans, millet, other cereals, and timber; but it is equally true of the northwest frontier with its exports of wool, and of central China with its export trade in cotton, silk, tea, vegetable oils, and egg products, and its imports of tobacco, sugar, flour, and kerosene. . . .

A great part of the revenues of the Chinese Government is derived from the duties levied on imports and exports, and these customs revenues form the security on which most of her foreign loans have been floated and the fund out of which payments on interest and retirement are being made. Thus it is as necessary for Chinese Government finances as it is for the banks and shipping companies that the volume of overseas trade should be maintained.

As regards the value, composition, distribution, and trends in Chinese foreign trade, the statistics compiled by the Maritime Customs are more satisfactory than most others published in China, but they are not complete, and in certain respects they are inaccurate. They do not include a considerable volume of trade carried in junks not under the control of the Maritime Customs. The valuations of the large volume of goods which pay specific duties are published "with reserve " — inasmuch as the Customs authorities have not the right to demand certified invoices; one result is that exports

[9] Extract from the Conference syllabus on *China's Economic Development*. A few minor revisions of the original syllabus have been made in this extract in order to bring the statistics up to date.

are appreciably undervalued. Finally, there is a considerable amount of smuggling along the southeastern coast, and in the neighborhood of Hong-kong, Macao and Kwangchowan. Hongkong, though a free port like Dairen, has no branch of the China Maritime Customs stationed there, and its own statistics are so unsatisfactory — they were discontinued entirely from 1925 to 1929 — that its great entrepot trade constitutes a source of endless confusion in all questions of China's trade.

Table I shows the recorded values of China's merchandise trade for pre-war, post-war, and recent years, and the same values converted into gold dollars.

Expressed in terms of percentages, these figures show that the silver value of China's imports had increased 33 per cent above pre-war by 1920, and 122 per cent by 1929. Exports increased in the same degree to 1920, and by 152 per cent to 1929. The gold values show a different trend: In 1920, import and export values had increased by 128 per cent above pre-war; in 1929 they had fallen to 95 and 121 per cent respectively above the 1913 level.

TABLE I

NET IMPORTS AND DOMESTIC EXPORTS

YEAR	MILLION HAIKWAN TAELS *		MILLION U.S. DOLLARS	
	Imports	Exports	Imports	Exports
1913.....	570	403	416	294
1920.....	762	542	945	672
1925.....	948	776	797	652
1926.....	1,124	864	854	657
1927.....	1,013	919	698	634
1928.....	1,196	991	850	704
1929.....	1,266	1,016	810	650
1930.....	1,310	895	603	412

* The haikwan (customs) tael is a money of account equivalent to 557.33 grains of chemically pure silver, 1,000 fine. It is equal to 1.114 Shanghai taels, or roughly 1.5 Mexican dollars. Its gold values have fluctuated as shown below:

1913   36½d. .... $0.66 gold
1920   81½d. 1.24
1928   35 1/16d. 0.71
1929   31 3/16d. 0.64
1930   22 1/16d. 0.46

The differences between the gold and silver values are, of course, due to the post-war increase and the present day decline in the gold value of silver. Neither set of figures can give us a true picture of the changes in the actual volume of goods entering into China's trade, for both gold and silver prices have fluctuated widely. We are obliged, therefore, to consider the changes in the volume of certain commodities which bulk large in the imports and exports. Some of these changes are shown in Table II in the form of percentages based on 1913 as 100.

These crude indices reveal several interesting tendencies in the commodity composition of trade. In the imports there is a steady increase in the

TABLE II

PHYSICAL VOLUME OF IMPORTS

	1913	1920	1925	1928	1929	1930
Rice......................	100	21	233	233	200	365
Sugar.....................	100	55	168	194	204	174
Flour.....................	100	20	108	231	458	200
Kerosene *................	100	125	196	205	167	118
Tobacco..................	100	141	345	667	565	568
Raw cotton...............	100	503	1,340	1,420	1,863	2,561
Cotton yarn..............	100	49	23	9	8	5.5
Shirtings (plain gray)......	100	60	40	28	24	17.5
Shirtings (plain white).....	100	79	63	71	73	46
Silk (white steam filature)...	100	79	132	154	160	132
Silk piece goods.	100	95	79	88	69	61
Yellow beans..............	100	110	245	483	553	386
Bean cake	100	161	175	180	158	166
Wood oil.................	100	117	193	237	231	252
Tea......................	100	21	57	64	66	48
Raw cotton...............	100	51	108	150	128	112
Egg albumen and yolk †.....	100	272	366	260	298	265
Coal	100	132	171	218	232	201

    * Imports from America only.   † Not including "whole eggs moist and frozen."

volume of foodstuffs.   There is a phenomenal post-war growth in the imports of raw cotton, together with a great increase in imports of cotton yarn and a marked decrease in imports of the plainer cotton piece goods — striking evidence of the development of the Chinese cotton industry which now supplies a great part of the home demand for plain piece goods and has even developed an appreciable export trade in yarn and piece goods.   A similar tendency is revealed by comparison of the volume of decreasing cigarette imports and increasing imports of raw tobacco to be used in Chinese factories.   In the exports table, the eye is immediately drawn to the prodigious growth of the trade in beans and bean products (from Manchuria and North China), and the trade in egg products (from Central China).   With the exception of tea and silk piece goods, the important exports listed above have all shown a steady increase in volume up to 1929.

When some commodities are increasing while others are declining in volume and importance, and while differences of quality are disguised under the same name in the records, it is no easy matter to compile an average which may be taken as an index of the total volume of trade.   This difficulty applies with especial force to the imports table where these divergent tendencies are most apparent.   For exports, however, the evidence of several different sources [10] seems to suggest that, taking 1913 as 100, the volume of exports

[10] See *Memorandum on International Trade, 1913–1927* (League of Nations, 1928), in which the figures are based partly on the calculation printed in the *Chinese Maritime Customs Report and Abstract of Statistics, 1923*, pp. 19 and 26.   See also Franklin L. Ho, " An Index to the Physical Volume of Foreign Trade in China," *Problems of the Pacific, 1929*, p. 300.

rose to about 135 at the close of the war, fell to about 115 in 1920, rose again to about 135–140 in 1925 and to 150–160 in 1929. It is almost impossible to speak with certainty on the imports, since the figures vary greatly according to the method of calculation followed, and because obviously no average, however well computed, can tell the whole truth when some imports are declining, some increasing, and some nearly stationary. It seems fairly probable, however, that the total volume of imports fell away, as was to be expected, during the war to 20–25 per cent below pre-war, rose to about 110 by 1925, and to perhaps 125–130 by 1929.[11] As a result of these changes, the composition of China's trade now differs appreciably from that of pre-war days, as may be seen from Table III, where the value of the several commodities imported and exported is expressed as a percentage of the total trade.

TABLE III

	1913 Per Cent	1920 Per Cent	1929 Per Cent	1930 Per Cent
Imports:				
Rice......................	3.2	0.70	4.66	9.26
Sugar.....................	6.4	5.12	7.80	6.60
Kerosene..................	4.5	7.12	4.36	4.19
Cotton goods..............	19.53	22.06	13.76	11.44
Raw cotton................	0.5	2.36	7.20	10.10
Cotton yarn...............	12.5	10.32	1.13	0.62
Flour.....................	1.8	0.30	5.06	2.44
Fishery products..........	2.3	2.26	2.08	1.97
Metals and minerals.......	5.11	8.08	5.60	5.79
Machinery................	1.40	3.05	2.36	3.38
Cigarettes................	2.20	2.89	1.64	1.97
Tobacco..................	0.62	1.69	2.12	2.37
Paper.....................	1.30	1.85	2.70	2.85
Timber...................	0.87	1.58	2.20	1.77
Coal......................	1.65	1.88	1.51	1.90
Exports:				
Raw silk, etc.............	20.62	14.21	16.26	13.30
Silk piece goods...........	5.17	4.49	2.07	2.19
Beans and products.......	12.94	15.68	22.62	20.66
Eggs and products........	1.42	2.20	5.09	5.72
Hides, skins, leather.......	5.90	4.03	4.48	3.84
Tea......................	8.41	1.64	4.06	2.94
Metals and ores..........	3.67	4.70	3.31	3.82
Seeds and seed-cake.......	4.78	3.36	3.26	3.97
Coal.....................	1.63	2.25	3.04	3.03
Raw cotton...............	4.03	1.70	2.92	2.96
Cereals..................	2.36	6.76	2.59	3.40
Wood oil.................	1.00	1.24	2.32	3.41
Peanuts and products	1.95	2.83	1.63	4.19
Cotton yarn..............	....	0.53	1.81	2.12

As long as a large proportion of China's imports and exports continues to be credited in the statistics to Hongkong when in reality they should be credited

[11] Professor Ho's figures range much higher and indicate that the 1928 volume was 50 to 60 per cent above the 1913 level.

to India, Java, Japan, the United States, Great Britain, and other European countries, it will be impossible to give accurate figures on the distribution of trade. The figures in Table IV are taken from the Customs returns and indicate that Japan now holds first place in both the import and the export trade, with Hongkong and the United States next in importance.

TABLE IV

	1913 Per Cent	1920 Per Cent	1929 Per Cent	1930 Per Cent
Imports from:				
Hongkong.................	29.27	19.91	16.74	16.44
Japan....................	20.36	28.64	25.22	24.63
United States...........	6.04	17.90	18.02	17.50
Great Britain...........	16.53	16.46	9.30	8.15
India...................	8.24	4.06	4.25	9.95
Germany.................	4.83	....	5.23	5.20
Exports to:				
Hongkong.................	29.04	25.20	17.09	17.66
Japan....................	16.25	26.21	25.25	24.20
United States...........	9.34	12.39	13.57	14.74
Great Britain...........	4.05	8.46	7.32	7.00
Russia and Siberia......	11.14	2.67	5.51	6.19
France..................	10.10	3.88	5.54	4.77

If, however, allowance is made for the transhipment trade at Hongkong, Dairen, and Japanese ports, or if the trade statistics of Japan and the United States are also consulted, there is good ground for believing that the United States is the principal buyer of China's exports, and that she probably holds first place in the total trade of China, with Japan a close second. There is also reason to believe that the United States now buys more from China than she sells to China, though the Chinese statistics convey the opposite (and generally accepted) impression.

It is equally instructive to turn to the internal distribution of China's trade. Again the statistics are not adequate for a thorough analysis of the question, but on one important aspect they shed light. As is well known, China has a characteristic excess of merchandise imports, and this " unfavorable " balance, instead of being compensated by an export of treasure, is increased by large imports of silver coin and bullion. So much is undoubtedly true. What is often forgotten is that this condition is not characteristic of all China, and that the regions of which it is characteristic have a much more " unfavorable " balance than the figures show. The reason is, of course, that the trade of Manchuria, amounting to 25 or 30 per cent of China's total trade, shows a regular excess of *exports*, and that if Manchurian trade is excluded, the figures for the rest of China reveal a still heavier import excess. In 1928, for example, import values were about 70 per cent of export values for Manchuria; for the rest of China, on the contrary, export values were about 68 per cent of import values. Yet, reading from the crude statistics of trade for all China, one would suppose that exports were about 80 per cent of imports for the whole country.

The ratio or difference between merchandise imports and exports seldom warrants the attention it attracts in popular discussion of China's trade. There are many other so-called " invisible " items to be considered before anything can be known of the terms on which China trades with the outside world. Few of these items can be measured with accuracy, but they are sufficiently well known to be appreciated. First must be reckoned the great net import of bullion (mostly silver), amounting in 1913 to 35 million haikwan taels, in 1920 to 75 million, and in 1928 and 1929 to about 105 million, and tending to aggravate the " unfavorable " merchandise balance; next are the imports of capital in the form of investments in real estate and buildings, by foreigners and foreign companies; then the great sum sent home to China by her eight or nine million nationals living abroad in Malaya, Java, Hawaii, on the American continent, and elsewhere — a sum which amounts perhaps to more than 150 million taels annually, most of it going to the provinces of Kwangtung and Fukien, where, as many observers have noted, whole towns and communities are developing mainly as a result of funds sent home from abroad.

In anticipation of the subsequent section on currency and finance in China, it may be well to say something of China's position in the present world trade depression, if only because she is not affected in precisely the same manner as most other countries. Silver and not gold is the basis of China's several chaotic currencies; and silver, being a commodity in the rest of the world, has shared in the present fall of commodity prices, though it must be recognized that the decline in silver has been intensified by the increased production of silver as a by-product from other mines, by the demonetization of silver in the coinages of European countries, and by the adoption of a gold bullion standard of currency in India and Indo-China. For China the result is revealed in a sharp rise in the price of all imported goods with the falling silver exchange. To buy a given foreign article requires a constantly greater outlay of Chinese dollars, and in consequence there is a tendency for the volume of foreign imports to decrease. Figures published by the U.S. Department of Commerce indicate that American exports to China, Hongkong, and Kwangtung in 1930 were valued at $112,192,000 gold, or 28 per cent less than in 1929. Imports into America were $133,338,000 gold, or 38 per cent less than in 1929. Some of the principal items in the China trade are shown below. In theory, export prices being little changed, the favorable exchange should encourage foreign buyers to purchase increased quantities of China's exports, but in the present depression this tendency has been offset by the reduced demand and reduced purchasing power of the outside world which has thus not taken full advantage of the opportunity to buy cheaply in China. The reduced volume of imports is therefore not compensated, as it theoretically should be, by a corresponding increase in the volume of exports.

A second result of the decline in the value of silver in the West is the evident desire of the outside world to unload its surplus silver on China, which remains the only large market for the consumption of silver for currency purposes. Net imports of silver into China have increased greatly since 1927, up to the end of 1929; but owing to the insecurity of political conditions in the interior, most of it remained for some time (particularly before the end of 1930) in the principal treaty-port cities. In consequence, the inflation of prices which normally follows the inflow of specie has been restricted. It must, nevertheless, be remembered that Chinese wholesale prices are rising, and not falling like those of the outside world, as is shown in Table V of wholesale price indices for Tientsin, Shanghai, Tokyo, and the United States, all of which are converted to a 1913 base.

TABLE V

INDEX NUMBERS OF WHOLESALE PRICES

Year	Tientsin (Nankai)	Shanghai (Bureau of Markets)	Japan (Bank of Japan)	United States (Bureau of Labor Statistics)
1913..............	100	100	100	100
1920.............	132	152	259	221
1925..............	145	159	202	148
1929..............	166	164	166	138
1930 (first half)....	170	175	146	131
1930..............	173	180	137	124
1931 (March)......	185	...	119	108

While it is true that prices in Tientsin and Shanghai do not necessarily reflect conditions in the interior of China, the fact that prices are steadily rising in the principal ports of China is of considerable significance. It ought in theory to mean a definite if temporary stimulus to business enterprise despite the difficulties of buying from abroad; it has probably much to do with the great volume of building construction and real estate speculations of Shanghai; it should mean a lightening of the burden of private and public debts contracted in silver currencies. On the other hand, insofar as the rise in prices merely reflects the fall in exchange, China must suffer from the contraction of her import trade and from a great increase in the burden of her foreign public debts, payments on which must be made in gold, taking ever increasing amounts of silver for a given amount in gold currency. It is mainly this latter factor which led to the adoption of a gold unit for the collection of customs duties in February, 1930.

Finally, it is necessary to emphasize once more the vital connection between the development of China's internal communications and her foreign trade. From lack of communications, producers are often unaware of changes in demand, slow to adjust their production to changes in price, and thus seldom reap the profits they might reap with better facilities for putting their products quickly on the market. What has happened again and again, as the customs reports bear witness, is that, with an increased foreign demand for China's exports, dealers could not quickly bring new stocks on to the market and instead resorted to adulteration and substitution of goods of inferior quality, to their own immediate profit, but to China's ultimate loss. Communications and the establishment of export testing and conditioning houses, with which the Chinese Government has already made a useful beginning, are indispensable to the rooting out of this evil.

QUESTIONS FOR ROUND–TABLE DISCUSSION

The following questions were recommended by the Program Committee after consultation with the round-table chairmen, as an outline for discussion:

1. Through what forms of international co-operation may trade relations be improved? Consider such subjects as statistics, communications and transport, finance, tariffs, and discriminative laws and regulations.
   a) In what way do the domestic policies of the Pacific countries affect the international trade of the area?
   b) In what way might it be desirable to modify these domestic policies?
2. What has been the experience of Pacific countries in regard to external trade, particularly during the recent depression?
3. What has been the effect of the fluctuation of silver on Pacific trade?
4. Which of the following subjects should be recommended for consideration by special groups at a later stage —

                    Pivotal industries,
                    Control of raw materials,
                    Boycotts and embargoes?

SUMMARY OF ROUND–TABLE DISCUSSIONS

I. THE DEPRESSION IN THE PACIFIC COUNTRIES

The subject of the economic depression in the Pacific is treated first in this chapter, not because it was the first to be taken up in any of the round tables, for in fact there was little concentrated discussion of the depression as a phenomenon in itself, but because it pervaded all the more specific discussions of tariffs, silver, and the like and provided a theme for illustration and reference on many different occasions, not only in this but in later round tables of the Conference. In particular, there was a marked tendency to examine suggestions for the development of Pacific trade or the increase of production in China in the chilly light of the present breakdown of the economic machine in the Western world. Thus it was in the course of a discussion of public opinion in relation to modern tariff policies that a Canadian member chose to state a fairly representative Western opinion on the fundamental economic dilemma of the modern world. He said:

" We know that there is no lack of production in the Western world. Yet we cannot supply ourselves with adequate goods. In Canada we have produced in one year 300 million bushels of wheat when we needed 50 million, and there are now people dying of starvation in our country. That is the condition of an over-producing world; we produce more than we need, more than we consume, and are not allowed to consume it."

For Australia and New Zealand, as for Canada, the greatest economic hardships were the products of forces that came from without and were uncontrollable. No one in those countries could have stayed the fall of prices on the world-markets of the raw materials and foodstuffs which comprise the bulk of their trade — wheat, wool, meat, and dairy products. Admitting, as an Australian member pointed out, that there were certain internal conditions in his country which intensified the effects of the slump in overseas trade, it is nevertheless accepted by Australian economists that "the fundamental cause of the unfavorable developments was not the false policy of Australia in the past but the onslaught of a sudden disaster for which the country was not responsible." [12]   In both countries the general effect of the depression was remarkably similar.   A New Zealand member reported that exports in that country had declined in value by about 19 per cent and imports by about 21.8 per cent during the year ending March, 1931, and that after a severe decline had already occurred since 1929.   He went on to show that the bulk of this loss was due to reduction in export prices and not in quantities — a fact which aggravates the hardship in that it means New Zealand must exchange more and more of her products in order to purchase the essential imports of manufactured goods whose prices have failed to decline in the same degree with those of foods and raw materials.   The same considerations apply with increased force to the condition of Australia where prices tumbled even more seriously, [13] but where the burden of economic distress was made the heavier because of a loss of credit on the foreign capital markets, entailing a cessation of the overseas loans with which Australia's prosperity has been so closely linked in the past.   Her borrowings which, according to a member from that country, had reached the huge sum of £550 million over a period of seventy years, were made in times of normal price levels, and required annual remittances of £30 million to £40 million for payments on interest and principal.   But after the slump in world-markets, to make these remittances now means that she exports from one and one-third to twice the physical quantity of goods as in 1928 or 1929.   Within the country itself it has been possible to lighten some of the burden of the national indebtedness by providing for a 22½ per cent reduction of interest to domestic bondholders and to ease the strain on production by drastic cuts in wages and salaries, but for the overseas loan obligations such adjustments are not possible.   In consequence of the obstacles in the way of making the necessary remittances in the face of falling prices, the exchange has turned more and more against the Australian pound, with the result that by the middle of 1931 Australian currency was at a discount of approximately 30 per cent in London.

It might be supposed that Japan, like Australia, suffered principally in the depression from purely external and uncontrollable forces, notable among them being the contracted demand for raw silk in the United States.   But Japanese members were at some pains to qualify if not to refute this view by laying stress on the influence exerted by purely internal conditions in Japan on the course of business and trade.   Naturally they did not deny the

[12] D. B. Copland (ed.), "An Economic Survey of Australia," *Annals of the American Academy of Political and Social Science,* November, 1931, p. 262.

[13] *Ibid.,* p. 30. It is estimated that between December, 1929, and December, 1930, Australian export prices fell 30–40 per cent for wool, 60 per cent for wheat, 30 per cent for meat, and 30 per cent for butter.

blow which Japan's most valuable export commodity had received in the fall of raw-silk prices in America; but they maintained that local conditions, such as the raising of the gold embargo at the beginning of the world-depression, the lower price levels in Japanese agriculture, and the drastic policy of financial retrenchment imposed by the Government, had been equally important contributory factors; and furthermore certain other incidental causes, such as the silver slump and the raising of the Indian, American, and Australian tariffs, though admittedly not domestic, were not wholly the product of the general world-depression.[14]   But however the underlying causes may have differed, the results of the depression showed themselves in Japan as elsewhere in the same forms — receding prices, surplus stocks, agricultural distress, wage reductions, declining trade, and increased un-employment.

The discussions of the depression in China revealed a very different set of conditions.   One round table indeed found itself asking the question: Is there really an economic depression in China, and, if so, by what phenomena is it to be judged?   A similar idea ran through several of the subsequent round tables on China's economic development and found expression still later in a round table on the silver problem, where a Chinese member urged the need for unification and reform of China's internal currency system, partly in order to dispel the present-day bewilderment concerning the real trend of economic welfare in the country.   "At the present time," he said, "nobody can say whether we are in a period of deflation or inflation."   The problem is a difficult one, for, as was revealed at one round table, some of the usual symptoms of a trade depression have been manifest in China but not others.   Despite the decline in the silver exchange, which ought to have been a considerable inducement to foreign buyers to purchase Chinese products, exports had declined appreciably even in silver values, and still more when expressed in terms of gold currencies.   China more than most countries had suffered from political disorder, extortionate taxation, and natural catastrophes; yet the general trend of prices in China was upward, and in certain ports at least there was evidence of increasing business activity, amounting in Shanghai to the dimensions of a small boom at least in building and real estate.   No certain reasons for these phenomena could be offered while statistical or other information on business conditions in China is not to be had, but certain Chinese members of the round table were inclined to attribute China's apparent immunity from some forms of the world-depression to the unfortunate fact that low purchasing power and unemployment or chronic underemployment were the normal state of affairs.   One of them summed up the matter in these words:

"China has not become sufficiently industrialized to feel the pulse of the world.   The depression has made itself felt only in the few things in which we are industrialized.   We are *always* below the point of depression for other countries. Everybody is underemployed except in a few highly organized industries."

[14] See Tetsujiro Shidachi, extract from *The Depression of 1930 as It Affected Japan*, above, pp. 8 ff.

As might be expected, there was an apparent difference in point of view between foreign and Chinese members, though it was not brought out very clearly. While one of the former quoted a statement by a prominent Shanghai business man to the effect that China had been "living on a silver island isolated from the economic upheavals of the rest of the world," a Chinese pointed to the steadily mounting cost of living in China — a fact which is made the more significant by the large proportion of essential foodstuffs and fuel which the country imports from abroad and pays for in gold prices. That Chinese should complain of the hardships inflicted by rising prices at a time when the rest of the world is stricken by the economic paralysis brought on by falling prices is an important commentary on the difference in the situations of the two areas.[15]

One illuminating example which was used by a round-table chairman to lend support to this view that China has in some measure been able to shelter from the depression behind the depreciation of her currency standard was found in the present economic condition of Manchuria. There is a region which, as was pointed out, is in many ways more economically developed and more closely linked to external economic forces than the rest of China. Yet, because of that very fact, it had been more severely hit by the collapse of foreign markets than other regions of the country. The merest accident, such as the occurrence of a mild winter in Western Europe, could reduce the demand for bean-cake as fodder for livestock and so disorganize the prices of beans and bean products as to plunge a great part of Manchuria into keen economic distress during 1930 despite an abundant harvest.[16] To quote the speaker:

"The Manchurian farmer has been the sufferer from a condition that was beneficial for the European farmer, and we have had the unhappy history of falling bean prices for which no one is to be blamed. It has had its effect on the railway problem, on the port of Dairen, on Manchurian currency, and not least on the state of mind of everyone in Manchuria. The instance brings home in a most vivid form the close relation between economic and political questions."

Not the least puzzling of the problems created by the depression for China's foreign trade has been its effect on the balance of trade. The characteristic import excess, which has always been something of a mystery in China, increased in 1930 to about 415 million haikwan taels [17] (roughly

[15] A foreign economist questions whether the difference between the domestic price levels in China and world-prices is explained chiefly by inflation or is due to monetary causes. See below, p. 24.

[16] See *China Maritime Customs Report and Abstract of Statistics* (1930), p. 60, where it is estimated that, at the end of 1930, surplus stocks amounting to some 20,000,000 piculs (1,333,000 short tons) of beans lay stacked between Harbin and Changchun, awaiting sale.

[17] Merchandise trade only. If figures for trade in gold and silver be included, the imports are 1,415 million, exports 950 million, and the import excess 465 million haikwan taels. See *ibid.*, p. 73, for notes regarding the accuracy of the statistics of specie movements.

$190 million gold) — a divergence never before equaled, even in the depression of 1921, and one which has come about, as was mentioned in these round tables and that on silver, in spite of greatly reduced imports of silver and unusually heavy exports of gold. One group which gave its attention to the problem made use of a recent attempt to calculate on approximate balance of payments for China [18] in order to ascertain the amount of the various invisible items of China's trade balance, and was led to surmise, though the figures are not available, that one factor in the phenomenal amount of the import excess was a probable reduction in the volume of remittances sent or brought back by Chinese nationals abroad, many of whom — especially in America and Malaya — had been hard hit by the general slump in business, and thus unable to invest savings in China as the low silver exchange would normally have encouraged them to do. An American economist, on the other hand, suggested that fear of continued depreciation probably was the principal factor.

II. THE SILVER PROBLEM

Each of the four round tables devoted time to the silver situation in relation to China's trade and Pacific trade generally, and one of them to the world-problem of silver prices and production. In the interests of logical continuity, however, discussions on this last-mentioned aspect of the problem, or on silver in its special relation to Chinese currency reform, are not dealt with here but are incorporated in a later chapter on silver and currency (chap. vii). What follows is, therefore, an attempt to weld together a number of scattered and somewhat unrelated remarks made by various round-table members, first on the effect of the silver slump on China's foreign trade, and second on its effect on the development of competitive industries within China.

As to the first of these two points, there was general agreement that the effects of silver fluctuations have not been quite as might have been expected, and that practically they have been less serious than popular opinion has been led to believe. It was realized, of course, that it is impossible to disentangle the effects of the silver slump from the effects of the general depression; but nevertheless there was some evidence to suggest that trade with China had not suffered a contraction any more serious than world-trade in general. American exports to China, for example, fell off less in 1930 than did American trade with Canada or certain countries of Europe. Japan's exports to China, Hongkong, and the Kwantung leased territory dropped from 532 to 403 million yen between 1929 and 1930, a decrease of about 24 per cent as compared with the decrease of 31½ per cent for her whole export trade or of 46 per cent for her sales to the United States which comprise the largest single item in her trade and which dropped from 914 million yen in 1929 to 506 million in the following year and have probably fallen still

---

[18] C. F. Remer, *Foreign Investments in China* (International Research report, mimeographed), p. 31.

further in 1931.[19] It should be observed in passing that the Chinese statistics record a slight increase in imports from Japan and America — a fact which is quite misleading and solely due to the depreciated silver unit in which the statistics are computed. Certain Japanese members, however, while they acknowledged the tendencies revealed in the foregoing statistics, stated that the effect of the silver decline had been felt quite definitely in Japan, and that it had shown itself in an increasing competition from Chinese factories or foreign (often Japanese) factories on Chinese soil in supplying a variety of articles hitherto bought from Japan. It was partly to the silver situation (taken in combination with the imposition of the new Chinese tariff and the desire to take advantage of low labor costs in China) that they attributed the recent influx of Japanese capital for industrial enterprises in Shanghai and other Chinese cities.[20]

There were repeated allusions in the discussions to the rapid growth of small factories in China under the stimulus afforded by the rising internal price level, as well as the encouragement afforded by the anti-Japanese boycott in 1928–29 and again in 1931. Reliable information on the extent to which this development has proceeded was unfortunately not available in the round tables, but it was pointed out in one Japanese data paper that, according to an investigation made by the municipality of Osaka, a sum of about $5 million silver had been invested in new Chinese enterprises around Shanghai during 1929 alone.[21] Though some doubt was expressed as to the ability of such mushroom enterprises to stand on their feet when the temporary protection given by low silver had disappeared, it was felt by some that their growth had important elements of permanence in it and indicated what one member characterized as an increasing tendency for China to become an industrial center independent of Europe and European markets. Others were disposed to question the ultimate value of such artificial stimulation as that generated by the present silver situation, for, on the one hand, the present sheltered position of these new industries would gradually vanish as internal prices rise, if indeed their profits were not already offset in large measure by the increased cost of imported raw materials and machinery and the increased import duties which become proportionately more burdensome as silver declines; and, on the other hand, the changes which had brought stimulus to these small industries had brought hardship to many of the poorer classes who had to pay higher prices for the necessities of existence without

[19] For more detailed figures see Shidachi, *op. cit.*, p. 21, or *Economic Statistics of Japan, 1930* (published by the Bank of Japan, Tokyo, 1931).

[20] See Zenichi Itani, *The Export of Japanese Capital to China* (Japanese Council), p. 13, where it is estimated that new investments in Japanese cotton spinning and miscellaneous industries in Shanghai amounted to about 10,457,000 yen for the period June, 1930 — June, 1931.

[21] See *ibid.*, p. 11. See also *Report and Abstract of Statistics* (1930), p. 67, where a useful description is given of such products as tooth powder and paste, toilet soaps, enameled ware, paint, soap, candles, leather, and matches, in which domestic production is expanding and in many instances displacing imported articles.

being able to any considerable extent to make effective a demand for higher wages. For the national finances of China, of course, the fall in silver has had very definite effects, tending to lighten some of the burden of domestic indebtedness through the rise in prices, but increasing the burden of foreign obligations contracted in gold currency, except in so far as these were secured on the customs revenues and thus safeguarded since the adoption of the gold unit for the collection of duties. Many loans, however, particularly outstanding railway loans, as a Chinese railway expert emphasized, are not thus secured; and for them the fall in silver has entailed a vast increase in the payments which will be necessary when obligations must be met.

No certain answer could be given to a question that was asked concerning the effect of the silver decline in the interior and on the standards of living in the country districts. It was admitted that one effect would probably be to raise the prices and reduce the consumption of such imported articles as kerosene and tobacco, though here again it was revealed that in China such extraneous factors as local taxation often bulk largest in the determination of prices in the interior of the country; and one foreign member, familiar with conditions in Honan, said that kerosene, since taxes on it had been consolidated, was now lower in price in that province, despite the fall in silver exchange, than it was five years ago.

Similar considerations were found to apply when another round table addressed itself to the examination of the effect of the silver situation on China's export trade. Several foreign members were at a loss to understand the considerable reduction of exports which occurred in 1930, at a time when all the evidences suggested that China would have provided a most attractive market for foreign buyers. The explanation given by the Chinese member who presided over this group was that internal conditions in China were such as to counteract the normal tendency for exports to expand: bad conditions of transport, internal disorder, combined, of course, with the falling-off in demand from the outside world, had conspired to prevent China from taking advantage of the low value of silver to develop her overseas markets. The decline, moreover, was accentuated by the special conditions which led to the contraction of the Manchurian bean export trade. Extending the argument in another direction, he went on to show that these same conditions of disorganization at home had prevented the country from using more of its domestic supplies — of cotton and wool, for example — in place of the imported article. Instead of that, China had imported more rice and raw cotton than ever before — only in small part accounted for by increased industrial activities — though these are precisely the commodities she is exceptionally well fitted to produce herself.

III. TARIFFS

As was pointed out in the introduction to this chapter, the effects of the trade depression in the Pacific have been intensified by tariff increases in

China, India, Australia, New Zealand, Canada, and the United States. In Australia and New Zealand these increases were partly the result of the depression, for in the latter country they were introduced largely in order to secure revenue, and in the former to ease the exchange situation by putting a drastic check upon the import trade. China also was compelled partly by the fall in silver to place her new tariff upon a gold basis, in order to safeguard the revenues needed for foreign loan obligations. Japan is remarkable among the Pacific nations during the depression for not having raised her tariff but having abolished duties on a few commodities no longer judged to be in need of artificial protection, and lowered them on a few others.[22]

It is thus a little surprising to find that almost no active discussion occurred on the known effects of these tariff increases on particular countries and particular industries, even though there had been definite expressions of dissatisfaction or resentment when the increases were made. On the contrary, there was a marked tendency for discussion to revert to fundamental, almost academic, phases of the whole problem of free trade and the difficulties of giving proper weight to considerations of international co-operation in commerce, in the face of the multifarious vested interests and group pressures which sway the legislative bodies of modern states. Nevertheless, there was some incidental comment on certain tariffs, notably those of the United States and China. It was acknowledged that the Smoot-Hawley Tariff of 1930 had not fallen with special severity on the trade of either China or Japan, but, on the other hand, as an American data paper showed:

> The fact that Japan's greatest need is for a market for her manufactured products, while the American tariff bears heavily on many of them, and the further fact that Japanese merchants, with the apparent sanction of their Government, entered a lively protest against certain increased rates proposed for the present tariff act, are evidence that possible sources of friction are far from absent.[23]

More inevitably still, as the following extract indicates, the raising of the United States tariff has tended to provoke ill will in Australia, where it added an understandable irritation to an already difficult trade situation.

> Mr. Herbert Brookes, lately Commissioner-General to the United States, recently declared that the opportunity of exporting Australian products to the United States had become so restricted as to make the trade position hopeless. The Smoot-Hawley Tariff has excluded the agricultural products which form Australia's chief exports. . . . In the last recorded six-year period, Australia's adverse balance with the United States has aggregated £169 million, or an average of £28 million a year, imports for the period being £214,400,000 and exports only £43,600,000. . . . Butter now carries a duty of 7d. a lb., cheese 3½d. a lb., beef 3d., mutton 2½d., lamb 2½d., and eggs 5d. a dozen. . . . Hides and skins are loaded with a duty of 10 per cent, and the trade in sausage casings has been given to Russia. For wool, Aus-

[22] See *The Recent Customs Tariff Revision in Japan* (Japanese Council). Duties have been abolished, subject to approval of the 58th session of the Diet, on millet, cotton yarns, cement, iron pipes, and tubes; and rates have been revised on artificial silk and wood.

[23] Philip G. Wright, *The American Tariff and Oriental Trade*, p. 168.

tralia's main export, the astounding duty of 17*d*. a lb. has been imposed upon greasy and 18½*d*. upon scoured fleeces, an impost which represents more than the market value of the commodity.   In consequence, purchases of Australian wool by the United States have fallen away from £6 million in 1925–26 to £1 million in 1929–30. Short-sighted and provocative tariff policy of this kind, in which Australia is equally at fault, must in the final analysis be detrimental to all countries concerned.   Apart altogether from the deplorable effect on international relations, the interposition of higher and ever higher trade barriers cannot be justified by other than national emergency.   International trade, as all the evidence shows conclusively, becomes more and more imperative as national income increases and standards of living rise. The great commercial nations are not only rich because they trade; they trade because they are rich.[24]

The Canadian reaction to the American tariff of 1930 and to the dispute with New Zealand is briefly summed up in the following extract from a Canadian data paper:

The effects of the American tariff increases have been to arouse resentment in Canada against that country, to incur tariff reprisals against American goods, and to increase the spirit of economic nationalism within the country.   Other effects have been a decrease in trade between the two countries in certain industries and primary products and the establishment in Canada of a number of branch factories of American manufacturing companies in order to escape the Canadian tariffs, and incidentally to take advantage of the Empire preference on Canadian exports.
The tariff on New Zealand butter has not been in effect long enough to enable one to draw other than the most obvious conclusions, but these are that it has destroyed, temporarily at least, a very profitable trade between Canada and New Zealand.   For, New Zealand, failing in its attempt to induce the Canadian Government to remove or reduce this tariff, has retaliated by increasing the tariff against her (by removing her from the Empire preferred list and placing her on the general list).   Incidentally, it is interesting to note the suggestion that the butter tariff against New Zealand was necessary, in part at least, in order to provide Canadian dairymen with a market for the cream they had exported to the United States before American tariff changes had made this impossible.[25]

All four round tables gave some attention to the new Chinese tariff enforced in January, 1931.   It was agreed that, though it represents a large increase over the old rates on certain commodities, its level is still fairly low, and that it is very doubtful whether any appreciable part of the blame for China's reduced import trade can be assigned to it.   In the opinion of most Chinese members who spoke on the matter, the tariff has been framed in the main for revenue rather than protective purposes, protection being confined to such commodities as matches, cigarettes, woolen goods, tea, and silk goods. Even there the rates are not excessive.

This schedule [of the new tariff] introduces for the first time the protective principle, raising the duty to the maximum of 50 per cent *ad valorem* for those articles whose import may inflict serious competition upon home industries, but reducing the duty to the minimum of 5 per cent for other articles whose import helps, directly or indirectly, China's industrialization.   With respect to cigarettes,

[24] G. L. Wood, *Trade in the Pacific* (Australian Council), p. 4.
[25] Norman Mackenzie, *Canadian Tariff Policy* (Canadian Council), pp. 3–4.

the specific duty for some brands is actually higher than the maximum *ad valorem* rate. For cigarettes whose value is over 21.88 gold units [26] per thousand, the specific duty is 16 gold units. For silk goods the tariff is fixed at 35 to 45 per cent; for woolen goods at 30 per cent (35 per cent for carpets); for matches at 40 per cent; for tea at 30 per cent. For cotton piece goods and cotton yarn, which are still needed despite China's rapid development, the tariff varies from $7\frac{1}{2}$ to 15 per cent. For metals and machinery, which are indispensable to China's industrialization, the tariff is rather low, being 5 per cent for ores and agricultural machinery and $7\frac{1}{2}$ per cent for electrical machinery, engines and steel. For railway and tramway supplies, as well as for aeroplanes, the tariff is 5 per cent. Other instances may be cited, but the above sufficiently illustrate the protective nature of the new tariff, aside from the revenue features.[27]

Among the Japanese members the opinion was generally expressed that the new Chinese tariff had had appreciable though not serious effects on Japanese trade and had served as an added stimulus to the export of Japanese capital and the establishment of Japanese industries behind the tariff wall in China.

At the moment, the Japanese cotton industry is not affected by this tariff reform as it is protected by the Sino-Japanese Tariff Agreement. This Agreement will have expired in three years' time, and it is difficult to hope for a postponement of the expiration. Therefore, in order to cope with the situation, capital is being exported to support Japanese enterprise in China, which has Shanghai as a center. This, in short, is a counter-measure to the tariff reform. Industries in general commodities are important in our trade with China, but only a small series of these was included in the Tariff Agreement. It has been said that the majority of them were not included because the smaller industrialists were able to exercise but little political influence. The effect of the new tariff has been considerable. The already existing Chinese enterprises were protected indirectly by the decline in the value of silver, and directly by the new tariff. Consequently, Japanese exports decreased, and they are even losing the South Seas market. The manufacture of umbrellas, electric equipment, rubber goods, woolen materials, and sea products were most affected by the change which was responsible for some increase in unemployment.[28]

It was significant that two of the four round tables on trade relations opened with a plea from Japanese members for greater international co-operation in trade, more especially in raw materials, and a franker recognition of the principle of international division of labor in the Pacific countries, where, as one of them maintained, there is already a large measure of specialization and where accordingly there is less excuse for perpetrating the tariff follies of Europe. Further development of this specialization, he continued, might well lead to a radical modification of tariff policies in this part of the world, with an increasing recognition of national and international social good as a criterion, rather than the special interest of a particular group of producers. American members in each of these two round tables pointed out the enor-

[26] One customs gold unit is equivalent to 40 cents United States currency.

[27] H. D. Fong, *China's Industrialization: A Statistical Survey* (China Council), p. 41.

[28] Zenichi Itani, *The Export of Japanese Capital to China* (Japanese Council), p. 20.

mous practical obstacles in the way of such a policy. It is an impossible task, one of them said, to decide what country should specialize in the production of any given product. No one can say which country shall or shall not produce wheat, for example, or say that China shall not produce silk because at present Japan is far ahead of her in the silk trade. Competitive production and the possibility of avoiding some of the wastes it entails by co-operative international planning had been discussed at some length in the Amsterdam Conference of the World Social Economic Congress (August 24–28, 1931),[29] but the difficulties had shown themselves to be very great, since national economies and needs differ so greatly and the social system of one country may make it essential to protect a particular class within it on non-economic grounds. By way of illustration he alluded to the peasant class in countries like France or Switzerland, for whom it is judged best to maintain a system of protection in the interests of national welfare though it is recognized as unjustifiable on purely economic grounds. A parallel difficulty arose in another round table where a Chinese economist supported the principle of protection for some of China's basic industries, and provoked a query from a British member as to the criterion with reference to which an industry should be judged basic or not. If the criterion is economic self-sufficiency in time of war, for instance, the definition of basic industries must be made much more inclusive than if the criterion is maximum economic welfare.

With the increasing intricacy of the economic mechanism today, there seems to be no limit to the lengths to which tariff protection is coming to be demanded. Two American members, basing their remarks on a data paper prepared by their group, showed that the whole tendency in the United States appeared to be for manufacturers to demand high duties not only on imported commodities which came into direct competition with their own products, but also on any commodity which might conceivably be used at some time as a substitute. Thus a cotton growers' conference will indorse a tariff on all vegetable oils that compete in any shape or form with cottonseed oil.

In this sense, Japanese pottery is competitive with American earthenware, and so is Chinese hand-made lace with American machine-made lace, and so, indeed, are all the items mentioned in the Japanese merchants' protest, competitive with some articles made in the United States. Just how far this definition of a " competitive product " can be stretched before it breaks may be a matter for debate. It certainly can be stretched far. It has been seriously proposed to place a duty on imported bananas in order to protect American apple-growers.[30]

One American member expressed doubt as to whether any such thing as a completely non-competitive product or industry existed any more, since there is no end to the substitutes that are possible in a modern economy. " For example," he said, " when the price of wool is high, people may tend to avoid the need of warm clothing by using more fuel or better household

[29] See Lewis L. Lorwin, *The Need for World Economic Planning* (American Council).

[30] Wright, *op. cit.*, p. 169.

heating arrangements. Expenditure on food, clothing and shelter is flexible in such a way that when the satisfaction of one of these needs is barred by high prices, one of the other needs can be increasingly enlarged." His remarks find an interesting confirmation in an Australian data paper [31] where the progressive decline of Australian wool exports to the United States is attributed in part to the development of central heating in the latter country, enabling lighter fabrics to be used for clothing even in winter.

To this difficulty must be added another to which both Canadian and Australian members were able to testify. It arises from the fact that tariffs once imposed, perhaps for emergency purposes, are difficult to remove when vested interests have already developed. The Australian situation was thus described:

" Australia has been a high-tariff country with high protection for industry for some years. There has been a growing belief among the professed protectionists that the policy required some rational survey instead of going ahead with the protection of industries in a haphazard way. In 1928 a group of economists, not in any official capacity but with the approval of the Government, made a report in which they indicated that Australia has probably reached a stage at which further application of protection could not be carried out without certain risks to the sound economic development of the country itself. The report was published, but shortly afterwards a general election occurred in which the Government in power was displaced. By the end of 1929 the economic depression, coupled with financial embarrassments at home, began to fasten upon Australia, and one of the first things to be done by the new Government was to impose an emergency tariff, the purpose being first of all to check imports in view of the exchange situation, and in the second place to provide some additional outlet for employment.

" As the situation has developed since 1929, there have been three or four revisions to this emergency tariff, all in the direction of raising duties, and to quite a considerable extent prohibiting the import of certain commodities. The result is, as Canadian members have suggested, that while provisions of this kind are introduced as emergency measures, you create some sort of vested interest; and consequently it may be difficult to get rid of them. On September 3, 1931, a group of economists and treasury officials made another report to the Government to the effect that there was urgent need for a thorough survey of the whole tariff question, and that the country could not carry on for any length of time under such emergency regulations. However, between the establishment of a conviction of that kind and a political achievement of any result there is naturally a wide gap."

Not the least of the obstacles in the way of an effective tariff truce is to be found in the constitutional limitations imposed by certain states on their legislative and treaty-making bodies. This difficulty, which was discussed at length in one group, was first raised by a member from Canada. The Government of this country, he stated, cannot lay down a fixed tariff policy for a number of years in advance, inasmuch as one Parliament is constitutionally prevented from committing its successors to a predetermined fiscal policy. This fact had seriously militated against attempts to conclude reciprocal trade treaties with other countries, in particular with the United States where the same limitation is to be found. Proposals which had been put

[31] G. L. Wood, *Trade in the Pacific*, p. 2.

forward for such treaties had repeatedly been opposed not only on the ground that they would bind one Canadian Parliament, but on the ground that there was no assurance that such a treaty would not be revoked with a change in the American Government. It was stated by a student of the problem that on one occasion a treaty of this type had been upset by the Congress of the United States even though in theory treaty provisions are supposed to take precedence over legislation in that country.

The importance of this difficulty was obvious to all members, but a representative of the International Labour Office with considerable experience in the negotiation of agreements on tariffs and labor legislation strongly challenged the view that it was an insuperable barrier. He said:

" The suggestion of a tariff holiday is so important that it is worth while spending a little more time on it. It would be unfortunate if this suggestion were brushed aside simply because these constitutional difficulties have been brought forward. It may be recalled that this and similar difficulties have had to be faced many times in Geneva; and a number of ways have been devised for circumventing them in some measure. Some ten or twelve years ago, when the section of the Versailles Treaty dealing with the International Labour Organization was drafted, the authorities foresaw the difficulties that would be imposed on countries like the United States, Canada, and Switzerland which are not in a position constitutionally to ratify an international convention or able to bind themselves for a number of years to an international agreement. Nevertheless, conferences have gone on, and agreements have been concluded in spite of that fact. The International Labour Conferences every year issue their draft conventions. Of these there are now more than thirty; and several hundred ratifications of them have been registered, all of which indicate a definite step toward international co-operation. I take it that countries around the Pacific are likewise prepared to adopt measures which will promote peace in the Pacific and perhaps eventually around the world. Of these measures a tariff holiday must certainly be considered a major one.

" In the agreements concerning labor legislation, draft conventions are sent to the various countries for ratification after the conferences; and in the case of countries like Canada which cannot ratify in the ordinary way, the Government recognizes that the convention embodies a world-standard adopted after careful deliberation and designed to promote a better understanding in the world, and they therefore recognize the necessity of conforming to these requirements. If a government cannot formally adhere to the agreement, it can at least take steps to see that the standards laid down in the agreement are put into force in their own country.

" It should also be pointed out that a tariff truce is not necessarily shorn of all its value because it cannot be concluded for a long period of years. It is much better to have an agreement made for one or two years with the possibility of renewal than to persist in the competitive and retaliatory tariff policies which at present seem to be most in vogue."

Others felt likewise that the possibilities of improvement are not so remote as had been suggested by frequent references to the difficulties. American members stated that in their own country the apparently close connection between the 1930 tariff and the business depression, however illusory or fallacious the connection may have been in reality, had begun to have a definite effect in shaking the faith of the people and of some important business interests in the supposed benefits of high tariffs. It was reported by one member that the interests of the consumer were being represented more and more in the Congressional lobbies, while another stated that certain interests that depend largely on a foreign market for their products, such, for instance, as the lumber industries of the American Pacific Coast, were showing signs of less willingness than in the past to support a tariff policy which, by checking imports from the Orient, might destroy their market in that part of the world. The formation of a " tariff-for-revenue " movement with fairly influential backing was quoted as an illustration of the tendency to turn away from traditional policies; and the belief was expressed that the next Presidential election campaign would reveal a considerable revival of anti-tariff agitation. But even for the present, the following extract from an American study would suggest that there are definite hopes of improvement if the right avenues of approach are used:

There will be less waste effort when those who would order the tariff with reference to some principle of public welfare or international amity, instead of appealing to the conscience of Congress, appeal directly to the interests of the constituencies. Members of Congress are for the most part doing what they conceive to be their duty as " Representatives." Convert the constituency, and there will be little difficulty in modifying the tariff. The case is far from hopeless. . . . Tariff making is an adjustment among conflicting interests. In every region there are interests, and generally powerful interests, that would benefit by a reduction of duties as well as interests that would benefit by an increase. Those who, motivated by such idealistic objectives as the public welfare or international peace, believe that their ends can be promoted by a policy of tariff reduction, should organize the forces whose business interests lie in the same direction. Prominent among these forces are the great majority of the farmers, professional men, manufacturers whose products are on a substantial export basis, and the majority of laborers. In proportion as these forces prevail tariff reform will proceed automatically.[32]

The possibilities of a tariff holiday in the Pacific countries were explored in three of the four round tables. Little hope was entertained of very great reductions in tariff levels, partly because of the fact that many of the smaller Pacific countries depend on their tariffs for much of their national revenues, although on this point Japan might be quoted as a country which has made provision in a special commission for the removal or reduction of duties on products when the industries in question are no longer judged to be in special need of tariff protection. It was recognized in one group that little is yet known of the exact effects which might attend the complete abolition of tariff barriers or a large reduction of duties in the Pacific countries, and a recommendation was made that a study along such lines should be considered by the International Research Committee. The matter is closely connected with, and in fact arose in this group from, the related question posed by several members of the British group as to how far the Pacific area could be reckoned an economic unit for trade purposes. Theoretically, if that area is taken to include all the countries whose shores touch the Pacific

[32] Wright, *op. cit.*, p. 173.

Ocean, it is possible to conceive that the region might form an almost self-sufficing unit.   But at the present time, it was answered by others, a very large percentage of the total trade of these so-called " Pacific " countries is conducted with parts of the world outside of the Pacific basin.   Canada and the United States still do an enormous business with Europe; Australia and New Zealand find their principal markets both for buying and for selling in Great Britain, despite the gradual growth of their Pacific trade; and even China and Japan depend on non-Pacific countries for an important percentage of their imports and exports.

These facts were recognized as constituting important limitations upon two other suggestions put forward at the round tables, one of them a proposal for a tariff conference of the Pacific countries, attended by leading business men as well as government officials; and another a suggestion, urged with some emphasis by a Japanese member, for an extension of trade and tariff agreements among Pacific countries.   Some of the remarks made by the latter are reminiscent of arguments advanced by Japanese members in the discussion of food and population problems at the Kyoto Conference in 1929. He said:

" I wonder whether the prosperity of a great nation like the United States is not due in great measure to the fortunate chance of its early occupation of a rich, undeveloped country.   The same thing is true of other English-speaking countries in the Pacific.   Peoples other than the Anglo-Saxons arriving later in the world arena found themselves compelled to be content with their own smaller areas of territory.   This fact and certain unhappy prejudices which create political barriers to trade and migration are important factors in the present economic depression. A national economic unit in Asia would be highly desirable; but immediately we try to make it possible we bump into political obstacles.   The present economic and political situation in this Asiatic area is unnatural, and political thinking is here far behind economic actualities.   Japanese opinion is beginning to ask whether the more fortunate nations of the Pacific are going to perpetuate their present narrow economic nationalism which is comfortable for them but exceedingly distressing for a small country like Japan.   High-sounding phrases about world peace will be of no use until we can harmonize our political with our economic concepts."

With these views a Chinese economist agreed, but he argued that China was in a parallel if not worse situation than Japan, in that she was the last to enter on the race for industrial development.   Foreign countries had gone far ahead of her in the development of trade, and to ask China at this time to continue a system of practically free trade would mean an impossible sacrifice.   A British member voiced a doubt as to whether the undisputed need for better co-operation in trade and tariff arrangements among the Pacific countries necessarily involved changes in political status as had seemed to be implied in the remarks of the Japanese speaker, and asked whether the conclusion of a series of separate commercial agreements with various countries would not achieve the desired end.   In addition, there was the obstacle arising from the fact that several large non-Pacific nations had large interests or large colonial possessions in the Pacific and would be unlikely, in consequence, to look with favor on any proposal that would tend to make the Pacific a closed or partially self-contained commercial area. The Japanese speaker said:

" But that need not prevent us from dealing first with the relations of the independent Pacific nations, such as China and Japan. A ' closed ' Pacific trade region would be no more unnatural than the present situation brought about by European nations coming into the Pacific and closing certain territories, economically and politically, to those peoples who from time immemorial have dwelt in the Pacific. Let us begin with China and Japan, coming into some agreement on broad economic principles, and later if it is found practicable extend the idea to the Philippines, Java and other territories. At the moment I have had no thought of including Australia and New Zealand within the scope of such an agreement, for they seem to be more closely linked with the other side of the Pacific, if not the other side of the world. My purpose is merely to suggest a plan to get us out of the deadlock existing in the western Pacific."

IV. DUMPING

Two other matters which engaged the attention of different round tables are introduced at the close of this chapter following on the discussion of tariff problems, first because they have a place in the development of trade in the western Pacific and second because they may be taken as illustrative of an extreme form of economic nationalism which is not far removed from the spirit of tariff-making. They are dumping and boycott.

In regard to the first, as members of a round table discovered, there is an initial difficulty of definition. The subject came up when a Japanese referred to dumping from the U.S.S.R. in connection with trade rivalries between that country and Japan in northern Manchuria. It was found that the usual definition of dumping — as selling over a period of time in a foreign market at a price cheaper than that of the domestic market — is not accepted in the Soviet Union, where it is considered that dumping proper must have in it an element of state policy. Under this conception no individual concern can be accused of dumping unless it is a large national syndicate or a trust important enough to exercise political influence. Definite figures on the amount of recent competition from Soviet sources in Manchuria were not given, and it is therefore of interest to note the remarks of the China Maritime Customs,[33] namely, that the statistics of trade as a whole lend no support to the view that there was dumping of Russian goods during 1930, except perhaps in a few commodities, notably timber, in which there seems to be clear evidence of a policy of dumping in the usual sense of the word. In the subsequent round tables on China's economic development, statements were made by Chinese members — to the effect that evidences of dumping from other foreign countries were to be seen in certain lines, such as matches, cigarettes, and tobacco. The subject was judged to be of some importance, and a recommendation was made that the International Research Committee consider the possibility of initiating a study of the whole question of dumping in the Pacific countries and of legislation concerning the practice.

[33] *Report and Abstract of Statistics* (1930), pp. 41 and 49.

V. BOYCOTT

In the short discussion which took place on boycotts as an obstacle to Pacific trade — in this instance to Sino-Japanese trade in particular — considerable doubt was expressed by both Chinese and foreign members as to the ultimate effectiveness of boycott as an economic weapon, quite apart from its effects as an expression of popular resentment or an instrument of policy. Evidence was brought forward to show that many boycotts have resulted mainly in raising the prices of goods for the Chinese consumer, or in merely diverting direct trade with Japan to indirect routes through Hongkong, and after the boycott had subsided, in a sudden spurt of trade in order to replenish stocks. A foreign member resident in China quoted a well-known Chinese banker as saying that he would consider a boycott justified and would willingly support it if he thought that local industries in China were really prepared to consolidate their position permanently and make something out of the situation, but that he knew of no case in which that had really happened.[34]

QUESTIONS FOR RESEARCH

In each of the round tables members discovered that certain matters could not profitably be discussed for lack of definite information — in some cases because there had been no assembling of the existing materials, and in others because no study of the problem had yet been attempted — so that a number of requests were transmitted to the International Research Committee, asking that studies be undertaken whenever possible.

The first of these was a recommendation for a study of the trade statistics of the Pacific countries with a view to discovering the important errors and biases to which many of them are known to be subject, and to accounting for some of the marked discrepancies between the figures of one country and those of another. For example, it was found difficult to understand the huge discrepancies between the Canadian and the Chinese figures of Chinese-Canadian trade, even when all the ordinary allowances had been made. But the dilemma, as most students of Pacific trade have found, is much more widespread. Much Oriental trade with the United States is credited to Canada in the statistics; methods of valuation in Chinese export statistics are known to be defective; there is a large amount of smuggling on the coasts of southeastern China; the existence of such large transshipment ports as Kobe, Dairen, Singapore, and Hongkong, especially the latter with its most unsatisfactory system of recording, adds greatly to the difficulty of knowing the real origin and destination of much Pacific trade. The International Research Committee, after considering the matter, decided to bring the problem to the

[34] At the Kyoto Conference a research project for a comparative study of boycotts was authorized by the International Research Committee and placed under the direction of Professor Kenzo Takayanagi of Tokyo Imperial University. A report on progress was made at the 1931 Conference, and it is expected that the final report will be available well before the 1933 Conference.

attention of the International Statistical Association, and also, through the medium of members of the national councils of the Institute, to responsible officials in the Pacific countries and Great Britain.

A second request has already been mentioned, namely, a proposal for a study of dumping and regulations concerning it in the Pacific area. No project on this was framed by the Research Committee; but it is possible that studies on the matter will be initiated by certain national councils, and that some attention will be devoted to it in the study of Pacific trade which is mentioned below.

A third suggestion was that an attempt should be made to collect information showing possible connections between tariffs and employment or unemployment in the principal Pacific countries. A fourth was a request that a fairly theoretical study should be undertaken by competent economists to estimate the effects on trade in each of the Pacific countries which would follow from (a) an abolition of all tariffs in the whole region, and (b) a very drastic reduction of the present tariff — in short, an attempt to estimate the economic effects of the present tariff situation in the Pacific upon the development of each country and on the nature, growth, and direction of Pacific trade as a whole. Conference members had before them several brief reports and one very thorough investigation of tariffs and trade in Canada, New Zealand, Australia, Japan, and the United States, as well as a syllabus prepared by the Secretariat of the Institute and containing an outline of a possible study of Pacific trade developments as a whole. The proposal is quoted below:

"In order to carry this out, it would be necessary to devise a co-operative research project somewhat upon the lines worked out in the Institute's investigation of foreign investments in China. Comparable studies made in each of the Pacific countries, brought together and supplemented by a comparative analysis of the facts revealed, would be a most useful basis for intelligent discussion in future. The problems involved in these studies would include such questions as the following:

" 1. A record of the post-war course of imports and exports, compared with the statistics of 1913, indicating the economic background for outstanding changes in
    a) The commodity composition of trade;
    b) Its distribution among the various markets, with special reference to the Pacific markets.

" 2. In analyzing this record, the methods and degree of accuracy of the statistical source material should be carefully described.

" 3. Allowance should be made both for increasing population and for changes in the price-level, of both imports and exports.

" 4. A study of movements of capital should supplement the statement of the balance of trade, and any changes in the nature or direction of the capital movements should be noted.

" 5. The effects both of tariffs and of boycotts on the volume and direction of international trade should be studied.

"A series of studies of this character would provide material for a discussion of the possibilities of developing new and extending old markets. They would necessarily lead also to consideration of the effects of secular movements in the price-level, and particularly of the recent severe fall in gold prices. No such international discussion based upon comparable studies made in different [Pacific] countries has been held, and, as indicated above, such a study might yield significant theoretical as well as practical results."

The Research Committee, after examining the material before it, decided to authorize a study of tariffs and trade in the Pacific which would endeavor to co-ordinate the shorter studies already completed and, when necessary, have them amplified by suitable persons in each national council. A grant for publication and other expenses was approved for this purpose. A grant was also made for a study of the silver situation and its effect on Pacific trade, as described later in chapter vii.

CHAPTER II

CHANGES IN STANDARDS OF LIVING

DATA PAPERS

1. KOKICHI MORIMOTO. *The Efficiency Standard of Living in Japan* (Japanese Council).
2. L. K. TAO. *The Standard of Living among Chinese Workers* (China Council).
3. G. L. WOOD. *Memorandum on the World Depression and the Australian Standard of Living* (mimeographed, Australian Council).
4. *Syllabus on Problems of Food and Population*, Secs. I and II.
5. INTERNATIONAL LABOUR OFFICE. *The Possibilities and Limitations of International Comparisons of Cost of Living and Family Budgets.*
6. G. L. WOOD. "Growth of Population and Immigration Policy," *An Economic Survey of Australia* (Australian Council).
7. C. DELISLE BURNS. *The Standard of Living in China and Japan: An Essay on Policy* (mimeographed, British Group).

REFERENCES

1. R. H. TAWNEY. *A Memorandum on Agriculture and Industry in China*, Sec. III, v.
2. J. L. BUCK. *Chinese Farm Economy* (University of Chicago Press, 1931).
3. H. D. LAMSON. "The Standard of Living of Factory Workers," *Chinese Economic Journal*, November, 1930.
4. TETSUJIRO SHIDACHI. *The Depression of 1930 as It Affected Japan* (Japanese Council).
5. INTERNATIONAL LABOUR OFFICE. *Some Labour Problems in Pacific Dependencies.*
6. K. MATSUOKA. "The Peasant Worker in Japan," *Pacific Affairs*, December, 1930.
7. J. B. TAYLER, ELEANOR M. HINDER, H. D. LAMSON, WARREN THOMPSON, D. Y. TSIEN, PHILIP CHEN, ANTSON WONG, and OTHERS. *The People's Livelihood: Proceedings of a Conference Held at Shanghai, February 21–28, 1931.* Shanghai: National Christian Council, 1931.

INTRODUCTORY NOTE

A realistic view of international economic relations will conceive them in volitional as well as quantitative terms: not only as currents of trade and services directed by an invisible censor called "market," but also as means by which individuals and classes try to improve their livelihood. Thus across the Pacific, fleets under many flags carry consignments that cannot be measured in tonnage: in hold and steerage, and even on the upper decks, they bear cargoes of common human wants and hopes — silk to buy grain without which a people must starve, lumber to build new homes, drugs from some distant inland plain to relieve suffering; and also the only son of a poor peasant family, whose savings will pay off the mortgage on the farm, the craftsman whose skill will transplant an industry, the merchant. The material and human resources of two hemispheres here interweave a rich pattern of intercourse, as yet too largely guided by personal and national purposes without concern for social and international interests.

The dynamic quality of modern life, if left unregulated, is likely to become more pronounced. New technical processes, geographical shifts in industry, changes in habits of consumption, in the relative economic power of nations, in the distributions of population, and in the character and growth of national and world markets loom ahead as increasingly complex forces, less and less likely to work out an automatic and stable equilibrium.[1]

Increasingly, the conferences of the Institute of Pacific Relations, by bringing its members into personal relations with those from other countries who know intimately the human realities behind published statistics, have given recognition to psychological factors in economic relations. Increasingly also they have learned that trade agreements and political treaties are fragile instruments of world-peace unless they express the degrees to which the desires of the peoples have become integrated in common purposes. These desires find their embodiment not only in social institutions and traditions but also in the habits of life that seem so individualistic when seen close at hand, yet clearly distinguish in the large one nation from another. Thus differences in habits of consumption are important to the statesman no less than to the student of human nature. This subject was discussed at Kyoto under the general heading of " Food and Population." Desires for a higher standard of living and, more often perhaps, fear that the established standard may be undermined by the demands of a growing population on limited natural riches were seen to underlie both economic and political movements. Territorial expansion, on the one hand, quests for a more effective use of the existing wealth in materials and labor, on the other, were seen to derive a common dynamic from this source. But as yet there were few evidences in the world of concerted action among nations to secure the needs of one people in the willing guaranty of others that it might live and prosper.[2]

The very concept " standard of living " is vague; and the efforts of several contributors to the documentation of the Institute's Fourth Conference to arrive at a satisfactory definition show that much co-operative study is yet required before the problem implied in the slogan " Live and Let Live " can be said to be fully understood.[3] Scientific inquiry has played havoc with some of the older established norms: it has been found, on the one hand, that for the great masses in our Western lands, and in those that have adopted the ideals of Western civilization, a life sustained on what physiologists tell us is a bare minimum standard of existence is not preferable to extinction; and, on the other hand, that in every country there is a margin, and in some a very large margin, of people who actually live on less than we have been assured is necessary for survival. The reason for these discrepancies is, of course, that no human want is of fixed dimensions:

[1] Lewis L. Lorwin, *The Need for World Economic Planning*, p. 4.
[2] *Problems of the Pacific, 1929*, pp. 46 ff.
[3] See also J. B. Condliffe, *New Zealand in the Making* (London, 1930), p. 389.

not only climatic differences and differences in human physiology but custom and other, more fluctuating influences upon the desires of peoples and classes decree what in any one place and at any one time they will consider a possible minimum standard of comfort or an unbearable privation.

It is now recognized that neither minimum nor optimum standards of living can be transferred from one country to another or from one region to another; and that under the impact of modern change the standards of yesteryear may be wholly ruled out of practical consideration today. Thus, it may theoretically be possible for American workmen to live in homes heated by wood-burning stoves and lighted with oil lamps; but in the cities at least no one would consider such heating and lighting arrangements part of the present minimum standard. It would be possible for the Chinese to do without kerosene or for the Japanese to do without Western hats; but no practical person would consider such economies either possible or desirable. Our consuming habits are no less in flux than our processes of production and exchange; and in this flux the economic relations between peoples are both cause and effect. Demand follows supply; but supply — and less than that, the example of distant peoples' consuming habits as seen in individual representatives, in literature, and in moving pictures — creates new desires and requirements.[4]

Not only economically backward but highly advanced countries have again and again been stimulated, even in recent years, by standards established in another part of the Pacific. Thus, for example, labor standards in America have been influenced by those in Australia, and the older sections of the British Commonwealth have copied or at least aspired to the social legislation of New Zealand. It is not impossible, therefore, that a " normal " standard of living over a large part of the world will ere long include as part of its elements social provisions that are already recognized ingredients of that standard in Australia and New Zealand. One of the data papers says:

New Zealand can only be compared with other countries when its social legislation, arbitration system, and their effect on the standard of living are fully understood. The standard of living in New Zealand includes a better chance of long life after birth than in any other country in the world.[5]
[The author proceeds to enumerate some of the social welfare provisions which the New Zealand worker enjoys: family allowances, free education and a school medical system; hospital treatment; widows', blind, and old-age pensions; low-interest state advances of capital for housing.] New Zealand provides its children with a better chance of living, with opportunities for a freer life than is available in many other countries.

But even New Zealand, according to this author, lags behind other countries in *some* of the factors that make up a high standard of living. He mentions the unprecedented unemployment of recent years for which until

---

[4] See, e.g., *Filipino Immigration*, chap. xv; A. D. A. de Kat Angelino, *Colonial Policy*, I, 41 ff.; L. K. Tao, " Social Changes," *Symposium on Chinese Culture*, pp. 347 ff.

[5] Walter Nash, " New Zealand Labour and the Pacific," chap. ix of *New Zealand Affairs*, pp. 167 ff.

recently there was no adequate system of insurance comparable with that of England and Germany. He might have added that a new country necessarily does not share an older one's treasures of great art and fine buildings or the traditions of artistic production as part of its standard of life; that many elements in a stable social system are the deposit of centuries of effort, so that, for example, in a new country there are no old-established universities and no great corporate social enterprises with accumulated funds.

A more searching inquiry might have revealed that in some things the standard of living in Peiping is higher than that in Liverpool, and that the villager in the Philippines has enjoyments denied to the strap-hanger of the New York subways. In the economics of trade it is realized that all peoples do not desire the same material goods, but that what is a valueless waste product in one place may be highly esteemed in another. In the comparison of standards of living there has been too much of an assumption that while, for example, clothing and dietary habits differ, the proportion in which people desire the satisfaction of what is regarded as elementary wants is the same. These desires tend to become somewhat standardized, as has been stated, under the impact of cultural contacts; but the outstanding fact today is their difference. Tastes and consuming habits do not vary in an arbitrary fashion from some ideal norm but are determined to a large degree, on the one hand, by the physical requirements of different regions upon food and protection and, on the other, by the natural resources available to meet these requirements, and the technologies and economic institutions which they produce. Both wants and scales of value are therefore part of a larger situation which may be described as the joint expression of heredity and environment in terms of the total culture of a people.[6]

The Program Committee evidently recognized that, while it is possible to discuss the larger aspects of international economic relations in the Pacific area on the basis of ostensible facts, the roots of most of the problems in that field lie in greatly diversified needs, demands, tastes, and aspirations, and are as yet too largely hidden from the statistician's eyes. Therefore, in its original agenda[7] it suggested a general round table on " Trade Relations in the Pacific " but three different technical round tables to deal, in part, with their causes: on " Food and Population," on " Migration," and on " Labor Problems and the Standard of Living." In the actual program, the proposed round table on " Food and Population " dropped out, although a syllabus had been prepared for it, because research on this subject had not yielded sufficient new data since its full discussion at Kyoto.[8] The subject was, however, fully discussed by the Research Committee. In the round tables it was discussed, not as a separate problem area, but in its bearing upon two related subjects: " Migration " and " The Standard of Living." As the syllabus states:

[6] See *The Possibilities and Limitations of International Comparisons of Cost of Living and Family Budgets* (data paper, International Labour Office), p. 6.

[7] *Conference Handbook*, pp. 41–44.   [8] *Problems of the Pacific, 1929*, chap. ii.

The effect of population pressure, and especially of varying pressures in different countries, is not usually discerned as a phenomenon in itself. It works rather by increasing the stresses and strains, adding a persistent dragging influence, working against the settlement of issues arising from migration controversies, trade conflicts, aspirations for higher standards of living, competition for markets, struggles toward industrial development, rivalries for the control of important raw materials. All of these aspects of conflict are present in the Pacific area. They are surrounded by local and temporary influences, all of them important in themselves and claiming attention as the proximate causes of difficulty. But to concentrate attention on such proximate causes while ignoring the element of population pressure behind them would be equivalent to studying aviation without any recognition of the force of gravity [pp. 15–16].

In both the round tables on " The Standard of Living " and on " Migration " population pressure was discussed. But while there have been studies of the part which it plays in the flow of labor, there have not as yet been incisive inquiries into the influence of changes in the density of population upon local standards of living. The scientific study of these changes themselves is relatively recent and therefore necessarily descriptive.[10]

The scheduled " technical " round tables on " Labor Problems and the Standard of Living " and on " Migration and Race Problems " were in fact carried on as general round tables. As a result, these subjects were discussed as questions of experience in which the observations of laymen as well as the findings of specialists were used to implement more theoretical considerations. Since the round tables on these subjects were separated in time, there was an unavoidable overlapping in subject matter. Therefore, in the present volume the materials resulting from the earlier round table which have to do with the influences of migration upon standards of living in the sending and receiving areas have been added to the chapter on " Migration " (chap. xiii, pp. 454 ff).

Further overlapping occurred through the tendency of Conference members to take their examples of labor problems in relation to standards of living from the recent experience of China, thus continuing the threads of previous discussions on China's economic development. In this connection also, therefore, a transference of materials from the records of the later round tables to the chapters on the earlier discussions (but in these proceedings given in reversed order) has seemed advisable for the sake of simplicity.

The present chapter, in these circumstances, is made up almost entirely of extracts from data papers dealing specifically with changes in standards of living in the Pacific area and their study, followed by a few extracts from the proceedings of this round table that do not fall logically either under the heads of " Migration " or of " China's Economic Development." [11]

[10] Examples of this type of study are the data paper by Kokichi Morimoto, *The Efficiency Standard of Japan* (extract below, pp. 44 ff.), and parts of L. K. Tao's *The Standard of Living among Chinese Workers* (extract below, pp. 52 ff.).

[11] Perhaps because it was anticipated that the discussion of the Conference would bear more fully upon the relation of living standards to those two areas of major interest than upon the direct causes and consequences of changes in these standards, or upon pos-

EXTRACTS FROM DATA PAPERS
I. RISING STANDARDS OF LIVING IN JAPAN [12]
By Kokichi Morimoto
AS TO DIET

The national diet, which means the average diet of a nation, is obtained by dividing the total amount of the food destined for the consumption of the nation by the number of the total population reduced to the equivalent number of the adult population.

One should remember that food consumption is a matter which differs according to different individuals, localities, climates, customs, and manners. Such being the case, the intensive method of investigation based upon the data of limited numbers often results in an erroneous conclusion with regard to the actual status of the national diet as a whole.

The first step of this method is to find out the total amount of the food produced in the year to be investigated; the next, to add all imports of food; the third, to subtract all exports and also such parts of food produce which will not be used for food; and the fourth, to divide the sum by the number of the total population reduced to the equivalent of adults. For the sake of convenience, the regular scale of equivalent has been reduced to the following simplified scale:

        A man or woman over 15 .... 1.0
        A child of 10–15 .... 0.8
        A child of 5–10 .... 0.6
        A child under 5 .... 0.4

By the adoption of these equivalents the total population of 62,938,200 is equivalent to 53,375,999 adults. In dividing the total net amount of the yearly produce of food by the adult population, the quotient is the amount of the national diet per capita per annum. The national diet obtained in such a way necessarily cannot be very exact; but the results are suggestive and valuable in the study of the national standard of living, provided we consider them in co-ordination with the results of the intensive studies of food consumption.

i) *Consumption of grains.* — The most important grain in Japan is rice. The first use of rice is as the principal food item. Generally speaking, the principal food in Japan is exclusively composed of polished rice. Every day plain boiled rice without milk or sugar, in such a large quantity as about three bowls, on an average, is consumed at each of the three meals. The second use is in the brewing of the national strong drink called *sake*. The

sible means of affecting them directly without relation to larger economic issues, no special syllabus was provided for the guidance of this round table.

[12] From chaps. vi–xii of *The Efficiency Standard of Living in Japan* (Japan Council).

third is for manifold purposes, such as the making of confectionery, starch, and barm (*koji*). Also seed for the next year's crop is stored away. The second and the third uses, however, are minor compared with the first. To be more exact, 1.095 *koku* (5.07 bushels) per annum, or 3 *go* (450 grams) per diem, is the average amount of rice consumption.

The general belief that the Japanese principal food consists entirely of rice is true of the urban population only. The rural population use naked barley and other grains mixed and boiled with rice for their principal food. The poorer the farmer, the greater a proportion of grains other than rice is used. The consumption of naked barley is 0.55 bushels per capita per annum. Ordinary barley and wheat are cultivated in Japan, but the former is chiefly used for making beer and feeding horses, and the latter for making flour.

ii) *Consumption of vegetables.* — The Japanese consume more vegetables than any other people in the world, and there are two most important kinds, namely, sweet-potatoes and *daikon* (garden radishes). The daily average consumption of sweet-potatoes and *daikon* are 131 grams and 124 grams respectively. The total of these two, amounting to 255 grams, consists of 53 per cent of the total consumption of vegetables, which is 476 grams in all. Such an enormous consumption of sweet-potatoes is due to the fact that they are used in the southern part of Japan as a part of the daily principal food and also as a kind of sweet eaten between regular meals. Garden radishes are most extensively used as pickles which are known by the name of *takuwan-zuke*.

iii) *Consumption of legumes.* — The soy bean (soja bean, *daizu*), which is very rich in proteins and fats, is the most essential legume in Japan. It is a good substitute for meat, though its nutritive value, especially in its digestibility and its vitamin contents, may be inferior to that of meat. In comparison with its market value, however, the nutritive value is very high. The essential element of the most common dishes in daily use, such as *miso*, *shoyu*, and *tofu*, is the soy bean, and the numerous soy bean recipes are the favorite relishes of the people.

iv) *Consumption of fruits.* — Generally speaking, fruits are consumed by most Japanese as a refreshment between meals, and have little value as a regular foodstuff. One exception, however, is plums (*ume*); the quantity of the consumption of plums is not so large as that of oranges and persimmons, but it is the only kind of fruit which is consumed as regular foodstuff. This preparation is called *umeboshi*, which is made by first drying the fruit and then pickling in plenty of salt. As a consequence of its being inexpensive and appetizing, it is consumed extensively throughout the country, especially among the poorer classes of people. The *umeboshi* and pickled radish (*takuwan-zuke*) are unexcelled as appetizers, giving a relish that otherwise would be lacking in the plain boiled rice.

v) *Consumption of animal food.* — In Japan, animal protein, which is the most important nutrient, is chiefly obtained from fish. More than four hundred kinds of fish are caught in Japanese waters and they are consumed by the Japanese in the same way as meat is used by the Americans. The total consumption per capita per diem is 65 grams. The price of fish is much cheaper than that of meat, and the cost of fish consumption per capita per diem is only 2.2 sen. Besides fish, shellfish is a popular food in Japan but it is minor in comparison with fish.

The habit of eating meat is not very old in Japan. Formerly some of the Buddhists were forbidden to eat animal food of any kind, and only the outcast class could enjoy animal meat. This has now changed, but still the consumption of meat is limited to a certain class of people though it is increasing steadily year by year.

vi) *Consumption of sugar and salt.* — In order to make the most of the nutrients contained in food, it is necessary to have good cooking with proper seasoning. Sugar and salt serve as most important elements in seasoning. Sugar is important not only as a nutrient but also as an indispensable condiment. One may probably relate the consumption of sugar to the progress of civilization. Owing to a heavy protective tariff in the interests of native sugar, the price of sugar in Japan is scarcely exceeded anywhere in civilized countries. This fact is naturally a barrier to the free use of sugar. In Japan as a whole, sugar is used most commonly for confectionery, and is not yet in as much demand for cooking purposes as it ought to be. In the poorer rural districts sugar is not used at all except a very little in the form of sweets.

The consumption of salt is large partly from the fact that the habitual taste of the majority of the Japanese is inclined to salt. Such national food articles as *shoyu, miso, tsukemono,* which are used everywhere in great quantities for almost every meal, have plenty of salt for their essential ingredient. The sale of salt is a government monopoly in Japan, and its price is not so low as it should be. The function of salt as a food is contrary to that of sugar, and the greater use of the former means a smaller consumption of the latter. Until a certain limit is reached, as human taste advances, it craves more and more for sugar in cooking.

vii) *Consumption of liquor, tea, and tobacco.* — Liquor, tea, and tobacco are not strictly food articles, yet they have a close relation to food consumption. They have little value as nutrients; at best they serve only as stimulants. Their cost is disproportionately high, and they should be considered as belonging to the class of luxurious consumption. *Sake,* which may be called the national drink of Japan, is brewed from rice and contains 15 or 16 per cent of alcohol. Besides the native drinks, we have the imported liquors. The consumption of these foreign liquors is not important because their use is limited to a few of the richer classes.

NATIONAL DIET

Summing up all the food consumption, the national diet of Japan is as shown in Table I.

I have been keeping up the study of the national diet so far in five different years, namely, 1916, 1918, 1921, 1925, and 1929. In comparing these

TABLE I

KIND	PER CAPITA PER ANNUM			PER CAPITA PER DIEM	
	Quantity	Cost	Per Cent	Quantity	Cost
	Kg.	Yen		Gr.	Sen
1. Grains...................	221.5	31.71	32	607	8.7
2. Vegetables..............	174.4	6.44	7	478	1.8
3. Legumes.................	14.2	2.05	2	39	0.5
4. Fruits...................	20.7	1.83	2	57	0.5
5. Animal foods............	43.4	21.57	22	119	6.0
6. Sugar and salt...........	31.8	7.05	7	87	1.9
7. Liquor, tobacco, and tea....	....	27.45	28	...	7.5
Total..................	....	98.10	100	...	26.9

studies, it is interesting to discover that some changes with a certain regularity are occurring from time to time in the consumption of food materials in Japan at large. To state some of the striking features:

In grains, there is a tendency toward a gradual decrease of consumption in the grains other than rice. This is because the standard of living of the rural population has recently risen to a higher level, and now they use more rice and less of other grains as their principal food.

In vegetables, we notice the great decrease of sweet-potato consumption. This also may be due to the fact that those people in the southern part of Japan who used to eat sweet-potatoes as their principal food are now consuming more rice as do their brothers in the urban districts.

There is a noteworthy increase of consumption in all kinds of fruits. Then, a steady and gradual increase of consumption in meat and milk is conspicuous. The consumption of sugar has been unchanged since 1918, but the use of salt has greatly increased.

Sake consumption increased rapidly up to 1921 and then greatly dropped. Beer, though the amount of consumption is very little compared to that of *sake,* shows a gradual increase in its use. In the consumption of tobacco, the use of cigarettes is increasing and that of *kizami* (chopped) has decreased. The consumption of tea has been the same at all periods, probably always approximating the point of saturation from the olden time up to this date.

Table II (p. 48) shows the change in the national diet per capita per diem for all classes of food between 1916, when the first of these studies was made, and 1929.[13]

AS TO CLOTHING

The study of clothing from the view of economic consumption is a subject exceedingly complicated because it changes greatly according to the taste, income, fashions, climate, social classes, etc. Naturally, there are as yet only a few publications which are available for the study of clothing in Japan. My work on this line of study dealing with clothing is based on the data of

---

[13] Summarized from the author's more detailed tables.

TABLE II

CHANGES IN THE NATIONAL DIET, 1916–30

KIND	QUANTITY (GRAMS)		COST (SEN)		PER CENT OF TOTAL COST	
	1916	1929	1918	1930	1918	1930
1. Grains.................	577.4	606.4	15.9	8.7	61	32
2. Vegetables..............	615.0	476.3	2.1	1.8	8	7
3. Legumes................	33.8	39.2	0.6	0.5	3	2
4. Fruits..................	41.3	56.6	0.4	0.5	2	2
5. Animal foods............	86.3	120.0	2.0	6.0	8	22
6. Sugar and salt...........	52.5	86.3	1.4	1.9	5	7
7. Liquor, tobacco, and tea...	....	....	3.3	7.5	13	28
Total.................	....	....	25.7	26.9	100	100

1914–15.[14] Owing to the scarcity of more recent investigations and also to the fact that on the whole the use of clothing and its expenditure have not changed much since that time, I use the same data, but with changes in price. The figures are the average of seven hundred and forty-three schedules, and those enumerated here are the average for Tokyo, Nagoya, and Kyoto (Table III).

TABLE III

FAMILY EXPENDITURE FOR CLOTHING OF THE INCOME GROUP, 960–1,679 YEN

	Value of Clothing (Yen)	Expenditure per Annum (Yen)*
Father:		
Japanese clothing..........	171.20	41.25
European clothing.........	151.24	52.90
	322.44	94.15
Mother....................	282.71	59.19
Boy (average age, 7).........	47.36	23.40
Girl (average age, 8).........	119.11	38.84
Total..................	771.62	215.58

* Owing to the fact that clothing is generally worn for a longer period than here estimated, the real expenditure per year would be about 20 per cent less.

The leading features of the expenditure for clothing in the Japanese cities are as follows:

1. The fabric most used is cotton; the consumption of cotton fabrics per capita per annum is 31 yards, entailing an expenditure of about three yen.

2. The materials next in importance are silk fabrics and silk mixtures. The consumption per capita per annum is 6 yards, an expense of three yen.

3. Woolen fabrics and woolen mixtures are used only to a small extent;

[14] For details see Morimoto, *Standard of Living in Japan* (Baltimore, 1918), pp. 71–114.

their consumption per capita per annum is 1.2 yards, a value of eighty-eight sen. The use of these fabrics is generally limited to the urban population.

4. The expenditures for clothing is greater in the large cities than in the small ones.

5. The percentage of expenditure for clothing decreases with the increase of income.

6. In the apportionment of expenditure for clothing among the different members of the family, the father uses 54 per cent, the mother 38 per cent, the girl 18 per cent, and the boy 12 per cent.

7. The use of European clothing is limited chiefly to the father and the children. The use of European clothing results as a whole in a greater expenditure for clothing on the father's part, but for the children it frequently means some saving in cost over their native clothing.

8. The Japanese dress varies greatly in style, form, and material. At least three different kinds of both overcoats and garments (padded, medium weight, and light weight) must be provided according to the change of the seasons.

9. The costly Japanese costume can be worn for a comparatively long time. Generally, silk costumes which are worn by the majority of people are not so durable, but since they are worn on only a few special occasions, probably not more than one or two dozen times a year among people of the middle classes, they may last over a period of ten years or more. For this reason, the yearly expenditure for clothing is not so heavy in spite of its high price.

Recently, men and children have come to use European costume to a great extent. European clothing is necessarily worn as the street and working dress, and the Japanese, as the house and ceremonial dress. It would be a convenient custom to adopt both the Japanese and the European dress if it were not necessary to consider the expense. The expense of two kinds of clothing is somewhat of a waste and can hardly be justified in an efficiency standard of living.

For the improvement of clothing, the use of only one set, either European or Japanese, is fundamentally necessary. As for women's apparel, the use of the European costume is limited to a small number.

In comparing European and Japanese clothing, the following points should be observed:

1. The Japanese dress is not serviceable for active work.

2. The making of the Japanese dress requires a greater expenditure of time and labor than that of the European garment.

3. The main materials used for the Japanese dress — namely, silk and cotton — are not so satisfactory as wool, which is the main material used for the European dress.

On the other hand, the Japanese costume has the following points which surpass the European:

1. The European dress fits too tightly and is not so comfortable as the

Japanese dress, especially for those who are unaccustomed to the European kind.

2. Making men's European clothes at home is generally impracticable.

3. Mending European clothes is difficult, while the Japanese dress is easily mended and is commonly remade.

Taking all these factors into consideration, there is a tendency for the European costume to become an integral part of the native dress in Japan, at least for men and children. As for women, the use of European clothes is almost insignificant. The reasons why Japanese women do not adopt the European clothes may be enumerated as follows:

1. Japanese women, generally speaking, have comparatively short legs in proportion to the rest of the body, and on them the Japanese dress is more becoming.

2. In the moral training of Japanese women, even at present, great stress is placed on the virtues of gentleness and meekness to the point of sacrificing modern conveniences.

3. The Japanese women as a whole are not required to enter such an active life as the men, and the inconvenience of wearing Japanese costume is not so great as with men.

4. For the sake of economy, women keep to the use of one set of Japanese clothing. The fashions of the European dress change much oftener, and it would be quite expensive to follow those ever-changing fashions.

Taking the foregoing points into consideration, the simplification and the economy of clothing are of the first importance for improvement. Japanese custom tends to lavishness and waste in expenditure for clothing. Too many different kinds of suits are required to appear properly on different occasions. First, three different kinds of garment in weight — " wataire," " awase," and " hitoye " — in both *kimono* (coat) and *haori* (overcoat) — are used for the different seasons. Then the garments for each season must include an every-day dress, a visiting dress, and a ceremonial dress. The ceremonial dress and the visiting dress are very costly, but their use is greatly limited. They are simply hoarded and are often used as little as once or twice a year. Under the circumstances, a lavish custom, such as to make a woman feel it is necessary to change her visiting dress at each social call in order to display her large store of clothing, is still prevailing in ladies' society.

AS TO HOUSING

During the last decade or two, a number of new-style houses have been built, and housing conditions seem to have made a great change. On the whole, however, such changes in buildings have occurred only in limited localities, mostly in the large cities. The housing conditions in Japan which I published in *The Standard of Living in Japan* will not be far from the present housing conditions in the rural districts.

Out of the 863 schedules which were used in my former study[15] in the

[15] For details see Morimoto, *Standard of Living in Japan* (Baltimore, 1918), pp. 115–26.

survey for both clothing and housing in the cities, 680 have been used for this study. Some of the leading facts as to housing conditions for the middle class, which is supposed to maintain the efficiency standard of living in the large cities, are as follows:

A typical family of the income group of 960–1,679 yen lives in a house of 1,504 square feet in the small cities and of 1,058 square feet in the large cities. The number of rooms is about seven in both cases. The size of rooms is 115 square feet in the small cities and 90 square feet in the large cities. The 1930 rate of house rent is 13.46 yen in the small cities and 23.39 yen in the large cities. This fact means that about 20 per cent of the family income is spent for rent in the large cities.

The principles of expenditure for housing which are deduced as a result of the investigation are as follows:

1. The expenditure for housing in the family budget increases with the severity of the climate.

2. The expenditures for food, clothing, and housing stand in correlation in the family budget.

3. The expenditure for housing tends to increase rapidly as the family income increases.

4. The expenditure for housing in the family budget is much greater in the city than in the country; also, the larger the city, the greater the expenditure.

5. The proportion of rent per month paid by poor families is greater than that by families of the middle and high classes. . . .

It is calculated that a man inspires from 16 to 18 cubic feet of air in an hour, and at the same time expires from 0.5 to 0.7 cubic feet of carbonic acid gas. Air which contains more than six ten-thousandths of carbonic acid gas is injurious to life. Based upon these figures, the minimum space which is physiologically necessary for one man has been estimated at 600 cubic feet for an ordinary living room, 1,000 cubic feet for dormitories or other buildings designed for group life, and 1,300 cubic feet for hospitals or other buildings where fresh air is especially needed.

The rooms most commonly used in Japan are the six-mat room, which is 9 by 12 feet, or 108 square feet, and the eight-mat room, which is 12 by 12 feet, or 144 square feet. The usual height of the ceiling from the floor is 8½ feet. Thus a six-mat room, which has a spatial area of 918 cubic feet, is large enough for one and a half adult persons, and an eight-mat room, which contains 1,214 cubic feet, is large enough for two grown-ups. This means that 72 square feet of floor space are necessary for one person's sleeping place. In the ordinary Japanese house, the room area is about 50 per cent of the whole house area. According to this calculation, the necessary house area for an adult is 144 square feet and for a family of four adult members, 576 square feet.

II. FOOD CONSUMPTION IN THE CHINESE STANDARD OF LIVING [16]
By L. K. TAO
STUDIES OF THE COST AND STANDARD OF LIVING

Although the working class budgetary inquiry of a nation-wide scope has yet to be made in China, it is nevertheless satisfactory to note for the present that no less than 82 inquiries into the cost of standard of living among Chinese laborers and peasants, each, it is true, being of a local character, have been conducted since 1917 by various persons or institutions. It goes without saying that these inquiries differ from one another in many important respects; not only they were conducted at different times, but the scope, the period of time covered, methods of investigation, computation and analysis and even the use of terms often vary among them. While only a few inquiries were conducted with the painstaking method of keeping daily accounts for the families under investigation, a method, which, if carefully used, yields accurate and reliable results, yet many were simply arbitrary estimates for a limited number of households which may have some practical value but are inadequate for any accurate measurement of the standard of living. It will thus be seen that the value of the inquiries varies greatly. Nevertheless it may be maintained that the data these inquiries yielded may at least supply some notion of the living standard of a section of the working population of the country.

A review of the cost-of-living inquiries so far conducted in this country may now engage our attention. They may appropriately be grouped as urban families, 48; rural urban families, 5; rural families, 16; and individuals, 13. Some important results of the first three groups will be summarily presented in the subsequent pages, while the last group, given merely as reference, will not be dealt with in this paper.

First of all, it is of interest to know the average income together with the average cost of living of the working households that were covered by the inquiries. It is necessary to know the average family earnings or income because they are the means whereby the standard of living of the members of a family is maintained or the need of necessaries to which they are accustomed is supplied; and it is the earnings that transform themselves into family expenditure. It has been found that the family earnings in 43 (or about 74 per cent) of the 58 inquiries in which the family earnings were ascertained (or 62 per cent of the total inquiries) fell in the range of $100 and $400. And the cost of living in 53 (or about 80 per cent) of the 66 inquiries in which living expenses were ascertained (or 77 per cent of the total inquiries) fell in the same range; in fact one-third of the inquiries confined themselves to families with an annual living expenditure of between two to three hundred dollars. If we leave aside the extreme cases, whose average annual income and expenses are exceedingly low or high, it may be presumed that for the majority of the working families the average annual income and living expenses amount to from $100 to $400 each.

[16] Extract from *The Standard of Living among Chinese Workers* (China Council).

It should be remarked that living expenses just referred to can hardly be used to judge the standard of living, as the purchasing power of money changes with time and space. They are given here because in the mind of the ordinary person it is the money income and money expenses that are used for comparing living conditions. In terms of the currency of the United States of America and Great Britain at the present rate of exchange, it is noteworthy, the range of the average annual income and the average annual expenditure of Chinese working families under investigation is incredibly low, being between G. $25 and G. $100 or between £5 and £20. In this connection it should be observed that a family with an annual income and an annual expenditure of from $100 to $400 in China by no means represents the poorest class, as it still has a narrowly sufficient income to cover its living expenses. There is no doubt that, as is to be shown later, the quality of its living leaves much to be desired, and compares extremely unfavorably with that of the family of a similar occupation or standing in other countries. But it should be borne in mind that the earnings are in general low throughout all classes in China, and to earn a bare livelihood is all the great majority of her population can do. As there must be millions of families which are unable to earn even a bare livelihood, the $100–$400 class may therefore rightly claim to rise above the line of poverty and belong to the low-income group of the country.

Regarding the geographical distribution of the inquiries, it appears that while many of them were concentrated in Peiping and its environs and in Shanghai — the former claimed 18 and the latter 12, both together amounting to more than two-fifths of the total number of inquiries — those devoted to other parts of the country were unhappily few in comparison. On the whole it may be said that, while the towns and country districts lying along, or within a reasonable distance to, the seaboard have been fairly well covered by the inquiries, localities in the interior were relatively neglected.

It is evident that tremendous and important local differences must occur in the standard of living in various parts of China. On the one hand climates vary in different latitudes while on the other hand economic resources, such as soil fertility and mineral production together with transportation facilities, are unequally distributed in the country. It is also well known that the town and the country as a rule offer distinct living conditions. Incomplete as the inquiries are as a nation-wide survey, nevertheless a cursory examination of them reveals that on the whole there are decided local differences of a prominent kind in the standard of living. . . . On the average the general standard of living is inferior in the north to that in the south in China. . . .

A comparison of the standard of living among the farmers and peasants in different regions is illustrated by a series of surveys made by Buck of Nanking University. It is shown that the average of the food percentage for eight surveys in districts in the northern region (namely, in northern Anhwei, Hopei, Honan, and Shansi) which is 62.1 per cent is distinctly higher than the same for five surveys in the central and southern regions (namely, southern Anhwei, Fukien, and Kiangsu) which is 53.8 per cent. The average of the miscellaneous expenses is 13.6 per cent for the former and 20.3 per cent for the latter, which also shows the superiority of the standard of living among the farming population in the south.

When the vocational distribution of the workers included in the various inquiries is considered, it is found that they are heterogeneous in character and may be grouped in a broad way under the following classes: factory workers, handicraft and skilled workers, rickshamen, servants, postmen, and peasants and farmers. It is evident that the selection of the families in various inquiries was not made on a uniform plan, and the classification of their vocations was far from being consistent with one another. Consequently no valid generalization can be made with regard to the relation between the vocation and the living conditions of various families. Nevertheless, it is possible for us to find from an examination of the data that, generally speaking, factory and skilled workers are superior to handicraft workers and coolies, and farmers are superior to agricultural laborers, in the cost of living. As the cost of living is not necessarily the same thing as the standard of living, a higher amount in the family expenditure does not therefore always mean a higher living level.

It is important to examine the distribution of the living expenditure among the working families as disclosed by the various studies. The percentages of the living expenses of the 69 inquiries, classified in the usual manner under the five principal groups of food, clothing, house rent, light and heat, and miscellaneous, are shown in Table I.

TABLE I

EXPENDITURE IN PERCENTAGES OF THE 69 INQUIRIES

PERCENTAGE GROUP	NUMBER OF INQUIRIES				
	Food	Clothing	Rent	Light	Miscellaneous
0– 4.9%	..	13	17	6	7
5.0– 9.9	..	37	26	39	9
10.0–14.9	..	13	17	17	15
15.0–19.9	..	3	6	7	20
20.0–24.9	..	1	2	..	9
25.0–29.9	..	2	..	..	8
30.0–34.9	..	..	1	..	1
35.0–39.9	1	..	..	..	..
40.0–44.9	4	..	..	..	..
45.0–49.9	8	..	..	..	..
50.0–54.9	16	..	..	..	..
55.0–59.9	16	..	..	..	..
60.0–64.9	12	..	..	..	..
65.0–69.9	6	..	..	..	..
70.0–74.9	4	..	..	..	..
75.0–79.9	2	..	..	..	..
Total	69	69	69	69	69

It will be found that the percentages for the five principal groups are distributed in the following manner:

Food .... 50%–60% in 40% of the 69 inquiries
Clothing .... 5%–10% in 54% of the 69 inquiries
House rent .... 5%–10% in 38% of the 69 inquiries
Light and heat ...... 5%–10% in 57% of the 69 inquiries
Miscellaneous .... 10%–20% in 51% of the 69 inquiries

FOOD CONSUMPTION IN CITY AND COUNTRY

Having reviewed briefly the 69 inquiries of the cost of living, let us now examine more closely " the standard of living " of the Chinese working families, as revealed by a few studies. We shall deal in this section with food consumption for which detailed data are now available.

Food. — It has been shown that food costs more than half of the living expenses of a Chinese family. And of this food expenditure, cereals, that is, rice in the south of the Yangtze and corn flour and millet flour and rarely wheat flour and rice in central and north China, always constitute more than half. The proportion of expenses for various kinds of food among the working families in Shanghai and Peiping has been found as shown in Table II.

TABLE II

Locality	Cereals %	Vegetables %	Fish Meat, Eggs, Etc. %	Others %	Average Total Food Cost per Family per Year
Shanghai..............	53.2	10.9	13.2	22.7	$218.52
Peiping...............	80.0	9.1	3.2	7.7	144.50

It may be concluded that the main characteristic of the Chinese diet is the superabundance of cereals over all other classes of food.

It is also interesting to note that the Chinese diet bears resemblances of an important character to that of Japanese and Indians. It appears that the three peoples, the Japanese, the Indian, and the Chinese, all use rice or wheat or some other cereal product as their principal food and other edibles like meat, fish, green vegetables, condiments, as subordinate food or appetizers. Because of the sparing use of meat as food, the three peoples are usually considered as essentially " vegetarian." At any rate, the expenditure on food among the three peoples is unequally distributed between cereals and meat and fish to the advantage of the former (see Table III, p. 56).

That cereals should constitute such a high percentage in food expenses deserves our attention. It was found that among the 136 items of food articles consumed by Peiping working families, no less than 42 items were cereals or their products. The variety of foods consumed by Shanghai working families appeared to be greater in number, being 340 kinds of food articles, of which only about 16 articles definitely belonged to the cereal group. If any generalization may be drawn with regard to food consumption among the Chinese,

TABLE III

PERCENTAGES OF EXPENDITURE FOR PRINCIPAL AND SUBORDINATE FOODS
— A COMPARISON AMONG THE EASTERN COUNTRIES

CLASSES OF FOOD	JAPANESE				LABORER IN BOMBAY	LABORER IN SHANG-HAI (1927–28)	LABOR IN PEIPING		FARMER IN PEIPING (1927)	PEAS-ANT IN PEIPING (1926)
	Tokyo Farmer (1915)	Country Farmer (1913)	Laborer (1914)	Prisoner (1913–14)			A (1926–27)	B (1927)		
Percentage expenditure for cereals and products.........	59.9	61.9	84.5	86.5	59.6	53.2	80.0	86.5	89.0	84.0
Percentage expenditure for other foods	40.1	38.1	15.5	13.5	40.4	46.8	20.0	13.5	11.0	16.0
Total.........	100.00	100.0	100.0	100.0	100.0	100.0	100.0	100.0	100.0	100.0

it seems that northern Chinese subsist mainly on a greater variety of cereals
and their products, including rice, wheat, millet, Indian corn, buckwheat, wild
oats, sorghum (kaoliang), while southern Chinese subsist on a greater variety
of edibles except rice and wheat of the cereal group; they do not eat the
other cereals mentioned above, either because they are not grown in the
lower latitudes or because they are too coarse for the southern palate. In
other words, the Chinese lives principally on cereal plants: rice and wheat in
the south and wheat and other varieties of grain in the north. . . . .

It has been found from an analysis of the various kinds of food consumed
by Chinese working families in Shanghai and Peiping that their respective
values per equivalent adult per day are as shown in Table IV. It may be

TABLE IV

Locality	Proteins (Grams)	Fats (Grams)	Carbohydrates (Grams)	Fuel Value (Calories)
Shanghai.................	88.00	48.52	531.01	2,913.41
Peiping..................	75.88	29.61	505.27	2,595.14

asked whether these values for Chinese workers and peasants are sufficient.
To answer the question, we must first of all know the standard requirement of
nutrients for an average person. Now the energy required in the bodily
system of a person of course varies with his or her age, sex, conditions of
health, height and weight, kind of activities or occupations, and so on. As to
what the dietary standard in terms of nutrients ought to be for an average
adult, even specialists often differ. It seems, however, that 3,000 calories per
adult per day or 100 grams of protein, 60 grams of fat, and 500 grams of carbohydrates, per adult per day may be taken as the standard requirements.
Judged by this standard, workers of both Peiping and Shanghai, one finds, are
short of fuel value in their daily rations by calories, though the latter is not
far from meeting the standard. One finds further that protein is 25 per cent
below the standard among the Peiping working families and 12 per cent be-

low the standard among Shanghai families; fat is 40 per cent below the standard among the former and almost 12 per cent below the standard among the latter.   In both cases, however, carbohydrates are higher in quantity than the standard requirement.   This reflects well the disproportionately high cost of cereals in food expenses as shown in the foregoing pages.

Food consumption conditions in country districts appear also to be below the standard requirements.   As the variety in the diets of farming families is usually restricted, it is of necessity that a few articles are consumed in large quantities.   It has been reported that the articles supplying 10 per cent or more of the total food energy are, according to localities, only kaoliang, wheat, millet, corn, beans or peas, sweet potatoes, and rice. But in rice growing districts, as a rule, rice supplies 75 per cent of the food energy.

The sources of food energy in farming families, as found from a study of 1070 farm households in six localities in four provinces, are mainly derived from cereals and leguminous products, chiefly beans.   It appears that the former constitute about 70 per cent and the latter about 15 per cent of the total energy for all foods.   A comparison of the percentages of the sources of food energy for families in China and in the United States shows clearly the inferiority of the diet of the former.   It will be observed from Table V that,

TABLE V

Sources of Food Energy	1,070 Farm Households in China	124 Representative Urban and Rural Dietaries for a Period of Several Years, U.S.A.
	%	%
Seeds and their products (including cereals, legumes, and vegetable oil).............	89.8	38.7
Animal products........................	1.0	39.2
Vegetables (and roots, chiefly sweet potatoes)	8.9	9.0
Sugar...................................	0.2	10.1
Fruit...................................	0.1	3.0

as compared with only two-fifths in the United States, about nine-tenths of food energy in Chinese family households is from seeds and their products. Further, the Chinese farmer receives only 1 per cent of food energy from animal products as against the American farmer's 39 per cent; while his consumption of fruits is hardly noticeable, being only one-thirtieth of that of the American farmer, his consumption of sugar is but one-fiftieth of the latter.   The food energy derived from vegetables and roots, however, is nearly the same for both groups.

Regarding the fuel value, it is found that it amounts on the average to 3,461 calories per adult per day in the Chinese farming families, ranging from 2,176 to 4,559 calories.   It may perhaps be said that on the whole the fuel requirement of the Chinese farmer is sufficiently supplied.   It is further found that the food energy from protein amounts to 113 grams per adult per day, which is 12.7 per cent of total food energy and compares favorably with the accepted standard of 10.15 per cent.

To sum up, it appears that in calories and protein, the diets of mill workers in Shanghai and of farmers in six localities are either almost sufficient or abundant, while those of the workers in Peiping are sorely deficient. Whereas the carbohydrate is about sufficient for the Peiping group, it is over-abundant for the Shanghai group. Fats are insufficient for both groups, in particular more so for the former. The nutrition of the Chinese worker and farmer, so far as our limited data go, may be said, then, to be on the whole inadequate.

A closer investigation into the Chinese diet reveals most of its shortcomings. For instance, the quality of the proteins in the Chinese diet, it has been maintained, is decidedly inferior. Taking quality into consideration, " what is a moderate allowance in the American diet becomes a bare minimum in the Chinese diet." This contention is supported by the fact that the coefficient of digestibility is much lower with cereals and legumes than with animal foods, in particular when the former two form the bulk of the diet. Only about 80 per cent, it appears, of the intake of proteins of a plant origin is available for nutrition. Looked at in this light, it is evident that the Chinese diet, even though it meets standard requirements, has still little margin of safety with regard to the protein factor.

Another remark that may be made here is that apart from the insufficient quantity of vegetables and fruits consumed by Chinese, there are lacking entirely in the Chinese diet, dairy products, such as milk, butter, and cheese, which are mostly valuable in supplying the important mineral of calcium for bodily growth. The adequacy of calcium in the Chinese diet, owing to the absence of dairy products, has been seriously questioned.

With regard to vitamins, it has been stated that as the quantity of green vegetables that enter into the Chinese diet is hardly as much as that in the American diet, the supply of vitamin A is therefore reduced in proportion to the total food. It is consequently doubtful whether the vitamin factor in the Chinese diet is sufficient.

It has also been stated that in view of the sparing use of eggs, of whole wheat, and the less polished rice, which are all-important sources of vitamin B, there is every reason to believe that the Chinese diet is deficient in vitamin B.

We have dealt at some length on food consumption of Chinese workers and farmers because the dietary, more than any other necessaries of life, is of fundamental importance to their health and well-being. It has been shown that Chinese diet is inadequate in many respects; at best it represents only the minimum of subsistence, below which the health of the worker and the farmer would be undermined.

QUESTIONS FOR ROUND–TABLE DISCUSSION

The following questions were recommended by the Program Committee as an outline for discussion:

FIRST SESSION

1. To what extent is migration a means of raising the standard of living? Consider in its temporary and permanent aspects.[17]
2. What influences would be effective in raising the standard of living in Oriental countries? How far is increasing money income a factor in this?
3. What validity is there in the popular argument based on standards of living which is made the basis of tariff and exclusion policies? [18]

SECOND SESSION

4. What are the most effective ways of promoting the application of protective labor legislation in China and other Oriental countries? [19]
5. What other influences for improvement of conditions may be usefully employed at this time?

PARTIAL SUMMARY OF ROUND–TABLE DISCUSSIONS [20]

Of the four round tables on " Labor Problems and Standards of Living," three started with question 1 of the agenda, and one with question 4. Since neither the title nor the suggested agenda provided a clue to a possible connection between migration and labor legislation, no attempt was made to round out the discussion of the two sessions in an effort to assess the relative importance of the major causes or means of rising standards; and the last question on the agenda — " What other influences for improvement of conditions may be usefully employed at this time? " — was variously interpreted as referring to standards of living or to industrial labor conditions.

In one round table a distinction was made between the direct influences of migration and improved labor conditions on living standards, and their less direct and slower influences through their tendency to increase the vitality of the people and to change the composition of the population. A Japanese member gave it as his view that the effect of emigration upon the birth-rate is more important than upon the death-rate because the former can be more easily controlled. The lengthening of human life that comes with improved living conditions is almost automatic, but these conditions have no direct effect upon the birth-rate except by way of voluntary control. Japanese and foreign members agreed that any attempt to relieve population pressure through emigration cannot be expected to produce the same permanent result as an attempt to relieve it through industrialization: even with enlarged opportunities for emigration the permanent influence would probably be less pronounced than the influence of new attitudes derived from higher

[17] Reported in chap. xiii.
[18] Reported in chaps. i and xiii.
[19] Reported in chap. v.
[20] See explanation in Introductory Note, p. 42.

standards of life in town and country. A decreasing death-rate does not produce a decrease in the birth-rate, but it is a stimulant to birth control. This tendency works too slowly to show early results but can be accelerated by appropriate means.

In another round table, the same question was raised in a somewhat different form in relation to the vital statistics of China. A medical missionary reported that the peasant people of Honan are spontaneously inquiring for information on birth control. A Chinese member agreed that there is no need today to convince either farmers or industrial workers of the need for smaller families, but that they are ignorant of methods to effect such limitation. There was some doubt whether the establishment of birth-control clinics is against the law, and even whether the teachings of Dr. Sun Yat-sen permit of interpretation in favor of their operation; but in practice there had been no interference with medical advice in that direction when given in forms inoffensive to folkways.

An ethnologist thought that the question in China and in other parts of the Pacific area was attacked in too negative a spirit: there is not sufficient evidence, he said, that a reduction in births by itself actually raises standards of living; but a more eugenic attitude, making for a strengthening of the race, undoubtedly does.

There was a spirited discussion at the same round table concerning the relation of income to the standard of living. A Chinese member essayed the remark that over great parts of China " it is absurd to speak of a standard of living at all "; the people live and die in a state of permanent destitution below any minimum standard even to insure bare subsistence.[21] A foreign member, closely associated with movements for improving industrial labor conditions in China, had expressed the view that the standard of living could materially be raised even without a considerable rise in the national income, through wise public administration, reinforced by organized public opinion and social work. To this the objection was made that educative influences cannot at present reach more than that small minority of the population which lives in cities and industrial centers; in a country like China it would take hundreds of years before their influence could permeate the vast rural areas; more drastic measures were therefore needed.

In this connection, a Japanese member drew attention to a measure which, while not directly effective in raising income, nevertheless had in other countries substantially contributed toward the improvement of standards of living, namely, the legal provision of greater security of tenure for tenant farmers. In Japan, the tenants, through organized action, had produced considerable improvement in this respect, and the Government had recently passed a draft act with the same end in view.

One of the data papers, submitted by the British group,[22] contained a strong plea for further study of such subsidiary methods of raising standards

[21] On this subject see also the paper by C. C. Chang, pp. 75 ff. of this volume.
[22] C. Delisle Burns, *The Standard of Living in China and Japan: An Essay on Policy* (mimeographed).

of living as are particularly capable of employing international co-operation. In Great Britain itself, not only a rising economic prosperity and a better distribution of the national income, due to various causes, but the spread of education and state action for public health (though these in themselves are partly a result of increasing national wealth) have been among the principal factors in improved living conditions. International intercourse, likewise, has played its part, not only through the economic effects of foreign trade but also through " the transit of ideas across frontiers." The same was true of the rapid rise of standards in France during the eighteenth century.[23]

On the same general theme, the Conference heard a member of the technical staff of the League of Nations at one of its general sessions. While giving a general outline of the technical structure of the League to co-operate with member countries, where these desire it, in the development of their financial and economic development, communications, public works, and education, Dr. L. Rajchman was able to refer to substantial achievements already brought about by this form of international co-operation. At first there was a tendency for experts to draw attention only to the experience and methods of their own countries when facing the problems of the country which they had been sent to advise. More recently there had grown up a more real pooling of experience in a general body of knowledge and methodology and a corresponding larger emphasis on attention to the specific conditions and needs of the country to be helped. The active relations between the League and the Government of China, with the inclusive aim of raising standards of living, he described as follows:

" At the end of last April, the National Government of China addressed to the Council of the League a request for the collaboration of its technical organization. The Government stated that a new organ had been set up in this country to co-ordinate all efforts at national reconstruction, particularly in the field of economic development. The Government asked the co-operation of the League for the National Economic Council in six different ways:

" First, an arrangement by which the Council of the League would from time, for a period to be further agreed upon, send to China an official who would act as a liaison officer between the League organization as a whole and the National Economic Council, to advise the Council of any technical facilities which the League might have available for aiding the Council in the study of the problems it was facing;

" Second, the despatch to China from time to time of experts representing the League's technical commissions, to study subjects agreed upon;

" Third, the formation of special commissions for such studies in cases where the League had not yet set up a permanent commission to deal with a particular problem of interest to the Chinese Government;

" Fourth, facilities for the training of Chinese technical officers and civil servants to carry into effect the plan of reconstruction as gradually elaborated by the National Economic Council;

" Fifth, facilities for increasing in various ways, and specifically through exchange professorships, the intercourse between centers of intellectual activity in China and in other countries;

" Lastly, assistance in the convocation, at the initiative of the Chinese Govern-

[23] *Ibid.*, pp. 14–15, 21.

ment, from time to time of technical international conferences if such should be found necessary to remove some obstacle to the normal economic development of China.

" This request was considered by the Council of the League in May and unanimously acceded to. . . . At the present time, five services of the technical organization of the League have been placed at the disposal of the Chinese Government. . . . The health work was the first in the field. For two years we have had the privilege of collaborating with our Chinese colleagues covering almost every one of the specific fields enumerated in the Chinese request for League co-operation.

" For instance, since the Government had decided to have a central health station in Nanking, which would provide the headquarters staff for a national sanitary organization, we discussed the organization of this institution with the directors of similar institutions all over the world and placed at the disposal of the Chinese Government one of our experts for the initial period.

" We also were able to offer the Chinese Government specialists experienced in quarantine practice all over the world. And particularly there has been collaboration in connection with the recent flood. Five weeks ago, an appeal was issued to all nations for co-operation with the National Flood Relief Association, and, although this form of co-operation has remained small, we have already had one sanitary mission sent over by the Netherlands East Indies, one by French Indo-China, a third by Spain. Two specialists have been sent from Geneva, and a number of governments have sent supplies."

This illustration from the actual practice of international co-operation in the raising of living standards outside the larger area of international economic co-operation was in a sense an answer to those who in the course of the round-table discussions doubted the value of other influences than those of a radical economic reconstruction. Palliatives, it was stated, may be important if they provide a breathing space during which more permanent changes can take place. In Japanese experience, particularly, according to the testimony given, new levels of well-being, no matter how established in the first instance, tend to build up a force of resistance to later depressive influences. In a case such as that of China, several members felt, the immediate need is for psychological aids to optimism and ambition, whether these aids themselves are permanent or not. A higher money income, in China as elsewhere, has not in itself been found sufficient to raise living standards; unless it is accompanied by a new outlook, it may — and in certain cases among Chinese factory workers whose wages rose suddenly was actually found to — do more harm than good by leading to detrimental forms of expenditure.

This part of the discussion may be said, then, to have led to a more general recognition of the complexity of the problem, and also of the variety of ways in which international co-operation, quite apart from that incident to trade relations, can help to raise the whole level of human welfare in the Pacific area. To quote Professor Burns:

Such an institute as the Institute of Pacific Relations is a good instrument for that intercourse upon which the raising of the standard of living depends. International intercourse, however, is not only a cause of the rising in the standard; it is also the result of such a rising. In proportion as the standard in any country rises, the dependence of that country upon other countries increases. New tastes arise, new goods and services are desired. Localism gives place to experimentalism, and a new vitality displaces the fear of foreigners and the too great affection for the village group. The final purpose of a policy of raising the standard of living, therefore, is the establishment of a world order.[24]

[24] *The Standard of Living in China and Japan,* pp. 21–22.

PART II

CHINA'S ECONOMIC DEVELOPMENT

CHAPTER III

RURAL RECONSTRUCTION

DATA PAPERS

1. R. H. TAWNEY. *A Memorandum on Agriculture and Industry in China* (International Research report).
2. C. C. CHANG. *China's Food Problem* (China Council).
3. AKIRA NAGANO. *Development of Capitalism in China* (Japanese Council), pp. 86–102.
4. L. K. TAO. *The Standard of Living among Chinese Workers* (China Council).
5. R. FENG. "Agriculture," *Symposium on Chinese Culture* (China Council), chap. xiv.
6. FRANKLIN L. HO. *Population Movement to the Northeastern Frontier in China* (China Council), pp. 40–51.

REFERENCES

1. J. LOSSING BUCK. *Chinese Farm Economy.* Chicago: University of Chicago Press, 1931.
2. J. LOSSING BUCK. "Agriculture and the Future of China," *Annals of the American Academy of Political and Social Science*, November, 1930.
3. LEONARD M. OUTERBRIDGE. "Seeds for China's Arid Areas," *ibid.*
4. W. C. LOWDERVILLE. "Forestry in Denuded China," *ibid.*
5. WALTER H. MALLORY. "Famines in China," *ibid.*
6. *Symposium: The People's Livelihood.* Shanghai: National Christian Council, 1931.
7. K. A. WITTFOGEL. *Wirtschaft und Gesellschaft Chinas.* Leipzig, 1931.
8. J. SION. "L'Asie des Moussons: Chine-Japon," *Géographie universelle* (Paris, 1928), Tome IX.

INTRODUCTORY NOTE

The Program Committee, in drafting the questions for the three days of round-table discussion on China's economic development, chose as the general theme of the whole topic the question: " In the light of China's background and resources and the experience of other countries, on what lines should China's economic development proceed? What part may foreign co-operation play in this? " In view of this general framework of reference, it is therefore of some significance to find how large a proportion of their time the different round tables chose to spend on the discussion of rural as distinct from industrial and commercial problems in China, more especially since the number of data papers on rural and agricultural questions was small. One of the four groups gave practically the whole three days to the question, and even in the others where discussions on such matters as transportation or investment played a part, it was usually a minor rôle, ancillary to the central topic of the possibilities of rural reconstruction. Whether in examining the need for railway development, the possibilities of large-scale industries, or plans for foreign investment and currency reform, there was in each of the round tables a well-defined tendency to take as the criterion by which all these schemes were evaluated, their immediate and ultimate effects upon the fifty million or more farm families whose standard of life constitutes the key economic problem of China.

Thanks, largely, to the stimulus given by the principal data paper made available to these round tables and to the lead taken by a good many members of the British and Canadian groups who held a number of preliminary meetings on the way to the Conference, there was a widespread interest in these rural problems among the general Conference membership, and there was accordingly a fairly lively interchange of opinion among Chinese and foreign members in the discussions, colored by the tendency on the part of the latter to seek analogies and comparable problems from the history of other countries, differing as widely as Ireland, Japan, the Philippines, Java, Australia, the United States, and Mexico. Members in each of the groups were disposed to take fairly much for granted the undeniable skill of the Chinese peasant in adapting his business to the conditions into which the pressure of his environment has forced him.

Spontaneously, unaided by science or theory and without guidance from above, by an effort which seems at first sight as instinctive as that of the beaver, but which in reality is the expression of habits formed and experience accumulated during many centuries, the Chinese farmer has elaborated a technique which enables him, though with heavy losses and recurrent defeats, to keep starvation at bay. Cut off by his environment from the easy triumphs of extensive farming, he has acquired an ingenuity which has rarely been surpassed, in wringing from the land at his disposal not, indeed, the most that it can yield — for the output could be increased by the use of modern methods — but the utmost possible with the resources that he has hitherto commanded.[1]

Recognizing the truth of this, the groups gave their attention to some of the weaknesses of the traditional agricultural technique in China and to the possibilities of changing the system on which that technique is based rather than of modifying the technique alone. Of the improvements discussed, two stood out prominently. There was little agreement on the possibility of developing a much more extensive and scientific system of animal husbandry in China, and, related to this problem, the better use of hilly country now utilized principally for the provision of fuel. More prospect was seen for an early and great expansion of the existing rural and handicraft industries in China as a supplementary employment for agricultural families who are at present obliged to remain idle during long periods in winter, especially in the harsher climatic conditions of North China and Manchuria, and in the introduction, where possible, of new industries as well as improved methods of production and marketing for the existing crafts. The two of them served as the focusing points for a number of other problems which arose in the course of discussion — the extension of rural education and the rural co-operative movement, the application of simple machinery to Chinese agriculture and

---

[1] R. H. Tawney, *A Memorandum on Agriculture and Industry in China* (International Research report), p. 35.

village industry, the improvement of agricultural credit and marketing arrangements, and the closer settlement of frontier regions in the northwest and northeast. Finally, the importance of the development of village industries was recognized by the International Research Committee of the Institute which in its final report recommended that a study of a selected number of these industries in North China, already contemplated by the Nankai Institute of Economics, Tientsin, should be considered as pertinent to the Institute's research program for the ensuing two years. The problems relating to the utilization of hill country and the development of animal husbandry are already subjects for investigation in the Institute's research on land utilization in China, which is now being carried on at the University of Nanking and will be continued during the years 1932 and 1933.

EXTRACTS FROM DATA PAPERS

I. CHINA'S AGRICULTURAL RESOURCES [2]

China's is an agricultural civilization. While it is true that her mineral resources (notably of coal) are considerable, they are as yet largely unexploited, and her wealth is pre-eminently the wealth of the soil. The opinion of most observers is that from three-quarters to four-fifths of her huge population is directly engaged in winning a livelihood from its land, and that probably over nine-tenths of it is dependent in some way on her agricultural wealth for a living. It is accordingly not surprising to find that she is the world's largest producer of rice, tea, rapeseed, soya beans, the second largest exporter of sesamum seed, the third largest producer of cotton, and an important producer (though her exact ranking cannot be ascertained) of millet, peanuts, wheat, maize, and tobacco.[3] She dominates the world-market as supplier of soya beans, and of the wood oil on which the modern paint and varnish industries have become so dependent. Figures are not available, but it is fairly certain that she leads the world in the production of silk, which is indirectly an agricultural industry. She is one of the largest exporters of eggs and egg products which form the basis of an important subsidiary industry to Chinese farming.

Facts such as these have little meaning until they can be expressed in terms of human wants and satisfactions. It is useful to know that China is the world's leading producer of rice; but it is equally important to know that her production is not sufficient to fill the mouths of her people, and that she must annually import millions of bushels of rice from Indo-China and Burma. While it is true that she ranks first in tea production, it is equally true that her export trade in tea has dwindled to a poor shadow of its earlier fame in the middle of the nineteenth century when American and English tea-clippers raced between China and Europe with their fragrant cargoes. Today, however, China is far outstripped by India and Ceylon. Almost the same may be said of the silk export trade, in which Japan has largely captured the position once held by China. It yet remains to be seen whether a like fate is to befall two more of her characteristic products, when the introduction of the soya bean and the tree which produces the wood (*tung*) oil, into the United States and other countries, will have proceeded a little farther than at present.

How, then, are the agricultural resources of China to be appraised? In their present condition of utilization they are clearly not sufficient even to maintain the incredibly low standards of life of a great part of her population. If proof of this is demanded one need only point to the volume of foodstuffs annually imported into the country — foodstuffs which are for the most part

---

[2] Extract from the Conference syllabus on *China's Economic Development*, pp. 9 ff., slightly revised.

[3] See *Population and Natural Resources* (League of Nations [1927], II, 38; C.E.I. 39), p. 32, where a useful tabulation of China's principal resources and products is shown.

products already grown in China [4] — and to the further fact that these imports are still not enough to remove the almost chronic conditions of famine which obtain over large areas of North China. It must, of course, be remembered that these conditions are aggravated by the continuance of civil war with its resultant disorganization of existing means of communication; given peace, it is certain that a great improvement could be quickly effected. Nevertheless, only a small part of the evil can be attributed to internal disorder; banditry and civil war are as much effects as causes of the economic malaise.

The question to be answered is whether these facts are evidence that China has already more mouths than she can feed even on present standards, or whether there are still considerable opportunities for the expansion and improvement of her agricultural and food production, when allowance is made for the probably steady growth, however slow, of her population.

The facts are less encouraging than a cursory inspection of the map of China might suggest. Of the 4,282,000 square miles usually credited to China in the atlases, an area which may be compared with the 2,975,000 square miles of Australia, or the 3,620,000 of the United States, more than a quarter are in the desert or semi-desert areas of Mongolia, Chinese Turkestan and Tibet. If the areas of mountainous and arid lands be also subtracted the figure is further reduced by nearly one-half. The result, as Professor Cressey has shown,[5] is that " agricultural China " which supports probably nine-tenths of the population is confined to an area of about 1,460,000 square miles, and that if the 1926 Post Office estimate of population (485 millions) be accepted, the density of population on cultivated land (about 22 per cent of the total) averages about 1,480 persons to the square mile, which means that the average area of cultivated land per person, for all agricultural China, is a little more than two-fifths of an acre.

No one will insist that what has just been said precludes the possibility of further advances, both extensive and intensive, in Chinese agriculture. The Chinese peasant has deservedly been famed for the skill with which he contrives to produce the greatest possible yield from a niggardly soil with the crude methods at his disposal. Yet careful investigators have shown [6] that

---

[4] In 1929, imports of four basic foodstuffs — all of them indigenous to China — were valued at 237 million haikwan taels, or about 152 million U.S. dollars. The items are shown below:

Wheat	5.7 million piculs	21.43 million haikwan taels
Flour	11.9	62.90
Sugar	13.9	93.71
Rice	10.8	58.98

(Figures from *Report and Abstract of Statistics, 1929.* Shanghai: China Maritime Customs, 1930.) One picul equals 133⅓ lbs.

[5] In *The Annals,* November, 1930, p. 3.

[6] See Buck, *Chinese Farm Economy* (University of Chicago Press, 1930). See also " Chinese Rural Economy," *Journal of Farm Economics,* July, 1930, p. 440; " Agriculture and the Future of China," *The Annals,* November, 1930, p. 109 — both of which give excellent summaries of the larger book.

his farming methods are often inefficient, that his crops are not always well diversified, that farm labor (both human and animal) is badly distributed over the year, resulting in long periods of idleness, and that crop yields are not as high as is commonly believed, despite the great expenditure of human labor. Considerable improvement is still possible from the adoption of new seed varieties, new methods of cropping, the use of simple means of controlling insect pests and, above all, the improvement of education and internal communications.

The possibilities of extreme advance are less promising. The only large areas of undeveloped agricultural land are in northern and eastern Manchuria and in the northwestern districts of Suiyuan and Shensi. In the latter area, rainfall is extremely light and irregular, and although irrigation schemes — such as that recently completed in Suiyuan by the Famine Relief Commission [7] — may do much to open up new areas for settlement, the majority of those observers competent to judge are inclined to discount the chances of any important development on the northwestern border. In the meantime, this is precisely the region in which famines are commonest. Judged by its natural resources, Manchuria offers and has furnished a more attractive field. The fertility of the northern Manchurian plains is undoubted; they have already provided a home for many millions of emigrants from Shantung, Hopei and Honan. It is thus all the more to be deplored that the possibilities of this pioneer belt should have been so largely frittered away, and that so little has been done to initiate a rational policy of settlement.

Manchuria forms a fascinating geographic laboratory of huge proportions, with potentialities somewhat similar to those which faced the Pilgrims. Nature has provided a favorable environment; will the Chinese use the opportunity to develop a new and better civilization, or will the land become as overcrowded and famine-threatened as old China? The world may well judge the fundamental ability of the Chinese race by what it accomplishes here.[8]

To sum up, China has rich agricultural resources, though they are less than they seem at first sight. Under the present conditions of exploitation, however, and because of a number of other factors, chief among which is civil disorder, they do not suffice to maintain her population. There is still some opportunity for extensive expansion, and considerable room for intensive improvements in agricultural production. The three great needs must depend in large measure on state action: they are the improvement of communications, provision for rural co-operation and rural credit, and the development of elementary and agricultural education. Whether, given these improvements, population will merely increase again up to the limit of its resources, is a fundamental question of great importance on which, however, further discussion at this stage is not possible.

[7] See China International Famine Relief Commission, *Annual Report, 1929* (Peiping, 1930).

[8] Cressey, "The Geographic Regions of China," *The Annals*, November, 1930, p. 5.

II. SOME BASIC PROBLEMS IN CHINESE AGRICULTURE

SUMMARY OF AN ADDRESS BY C. C. CHANG

The great agricultural problems of China may be divided roughly into two classes, namely, those that are caused by the forces of nature, and those that are due to economic and social conditions.

Under the class of natural forces I shall first mention the frequent occurrence of drought. As is well known, domesticated plants under ordinary cultivation need about 20 inches of annual rainfall to mature. But a glance at any rainfall map will show that a large part of China has an average annual rainfall of less than 20 inches. In that region, therefore, farming by ordinary methods is constantly in danger of drought. North of the Yangtze Valley where they do get more than 20 inches of rain, it does not always fall at the proper time. This uneven distribution of rainfall from year to year and season to season also threatens that region with flood in one year and drought in another. In this year and in 1929, reports were often received from the same farmers complaining of drought in the spring and flood in the fall.

The second natural force is flood, which occurs frequently in Central and South China. In the last three hundred years, floods of some importance have occurred almost every year in one place or another. One of the worst among them is probably that of this year. According to the inquiries made by the Directorate of Statistics at Nanking and the aerial survey of the National Flood Relief Commission, the present flood has affected nearly 37 million acres of farm land and 70 million of farm population. It has destroyed at least 60 per cent of the fall crops and rendered 20 per cent of the affected farm area unusable for winter planting. The map prepared by the commission clearly indicates that the most seriously affected areas are precisely those regions which are the most productive and densely populated.

The third natural force to be mentioned is insect pests, among which the locusts in the North and the rice borer in the South are the farmers' most deadly enemies. Locust attacks occur in dry years, although not as often as drought. But when they do occur they may destroy every plant in the field. The rice borer, while it is not as formidable as the locust, occurs every year in the rice regions. The annual losses to the farmers from these pests must be millions of dollars.

These and other natural forces not mentioned here have made farming in China an extremely risky business. It seems to me that the problems due to natural forces are the most fundamental obstacles to Chinese agricultural development, and their solution cannot be much effected without the generous co-operation of foreign scientific effort.

Let us now review some of the most important economic and social problems. Under this heading I mention, first, the uneconomical size of the average farm area. Exact statistics are not available, but the Bureau of Statistics at Nanking has made inquiries which show that the average crop area, including that of double crops, per farm is roughly nine acres in the

North East, six acres in the Yellow River region and four acres in the Yangtze Valley and South China. These are indeed small farms; yet even this small amount of land may not be all in one piece near the farm house. It may be in several small plots scattered all over the village. If one compares that situation with the 160 acres of farm land, all in one piece, in some parts of the United States it is easy to imagine the hardships under which the Chinese farmers have to work.

The second economic problem I may mention is the lack of transportation facilities. In the United States, I was told, the transportation costs of farm produce to the most distant consuming centers usually make up less than 10 per cent of the consumer's price. In China transportation of farm products may cost more than the goods themselves, even for comparatively short distances. Another important economic factor that limits the productivity of the Chinese farm population is the lack of supplementary industries which may occupy the farmer's leisure time. The reason is not that the farmers are lazy but that the credit and marketing facilities and raw material needed are lacking.

The last but not the least economic problem is foreign competition. I pass by the continuous decline of China's tea and silk industries which is too well known. Let me mention just one instance of the effect of foreign competition. In this year the Chinese cotton crop is about 65 per cent of the acreage for valuation. Last year it was 82 per cent. China produced 30 per cent more cotton last year than this year, but the cotton price this year at Shanghai is 6 per cent lower than that of the last year for the same month. It is because American cotton now sells cheaper than Chinese cotton and is much better in quality.

So much for the problems. Faced with them, the farmers in most cases have no other remedy than to adapt themselves to their environment as best they can. In adapting the crops and the methods of cultivation to the natural and economic conditions, the present-day farmers feel that their ancestors have pretty well fixed a standard for them. Any drastic deviation from that standard may cost them dearly. The Chinese Government has also from time to time set up organizations to attack these problems, but the work has not yet begun to show great results. Recently the Government has decided to organize a central agricultural experiment station which, in co-operation and co-ordination with other institutions, will undertake research projects on a national scale in plant and animal industries and also in agricultural economics. It is hoped that when this experiment station is properly furnished with men and funds, it will in due time contribute valuable facts to the planning of programs for improving farm technique, rural organization and rural education.

III. CHINA'S FOOD PROBLEM [9]

By C. C. CHANG

The purpose of this paper is to describe in quantitative terms China's supply and consumption of food by taking a sample of fourteen provinces for which some reasonably approximate statistics are available. The description confines itself to only fourteen provinces because even such approximate statistics are lacking for other parts of the country. It should be noted, however, that the fourteen provinces considered here include the greater part of China's most important agricultural regions and have a population totalling up to nearly 280 millions, which is certainly over one-half that of the entire country. Those included are:

Heilungkiang	Hopei	Kiangsu
Kirin	Shansi	Chekiang
Liaoning	Shantung	Anhwei
Jehol	Honan	Kwangtung
Chahar	Hupeh	

The principal omissions are therefore the western provinces of Suiyuan, Kansu, Shensi and Szechwan, with the southern provinces of Fukien, Kiangsi, Hunan, Kwangsi, Kweichow and Yunnan.

The information concerning food supply, crops and populations is based upon returns to questionnaires sent out since 1928 by the Bureau of Statistics, Nanking, to district magistrates, postmasters, school teachers and individual farmers in every district (*hsien*). In these schedules the number of farm households and the acreage of cultivated land refer to the time of filling in the schedule, but the crop acreage and crop yields refer to average years. Thus answers made in different months and years are fairly comparable. All the returns have been drawn up in such a way as to permit of an effective system of counter-checking the principal items for discrepancies and obvious errors.

The total area of these fourteen provinces is 8,836 million mow,[10] or approximately 1,000,000 square miles. The cultivated land totals up to 900 million mow, or 18 per cent of the entire area. The acreage of irrigated land, which is more productive than non-irrigated land, is about 18 per cent of the total cultivated area, while of the remaining 82 per cent, 65 per cent is on plains and the rest on hills. Details are shown in Table I, p. 76.

Taking these provinces by regions, the percentages of cultivated land to the total area are 9 per cent for the North East, 37 per cent for the North, 27 per cent for the Central regions, and 11 per cent for Kwangtung province, or an average of nearly 19 per cent for the whole.

In Table II, items for seed and feed requirements and milling wastes are subtracted from each of the food crops, and the remainder is considered as

[9] Summary of a data paper of the same title.
[10] One mow, in these tables, is taken as approximately one-sixth of an acre.

TABLE I

TOTAL AREA AND ACREAGE OF CULTIVATED LAND OF 14 PROVINCES

REGIONS AND PROVINCES	TOTAL AREA IN 1,000 MOW	ACREAGE OF CULTIVATED LAND IN 1,000 MOW			
		Total	Irrigated	Non-irrigated	
				Level Land	Hilly Land
Heilungkiang...........	962,844	49,407	377	45,854	3,176
Kirin.................	458,480	71,234	1,793	56,916	12,525
Liaoning..............	429,430	71,961	878	50,541	20,542
Jehol.................	283,631	18,147	242	8,069	9,836
Chahar................	409,418	16,839	1,855	7,515	7,469
North East region......	2,543,803	227,588	5,145	168,895	53,548
Shansi.................	278,796	60,560	3,629	27,540	29,391
Hopei.................	224,396	103,432	8,467	88,088	6,877
Honan.................	300,291	112,981	7,802	89,915	15,264
Shantung..............	238,017	110,662	2,395	93,672	14,595
North region..........	1,041,500	387,635	22,293	299,215	66,127
Hupeh.................	313,339	61,010	26,273	23,565	11,172
Anhwei................	235,433	48,812	19,219	25,939	3,654
Kiangsu...............	177,029	91,669	35,574	52,486	3,609
Chekiang..............	156,865	41,208	29,806	7,281	4,121
Central region........	882,666	242,699	110,872	109,271	22,556
Kwangtung...........	368,476	42,452	24,690	12,411	5,351
Grand total.........	4,836,445	900,374	163,000	589,792	147,582

available for human consumption, or net supply of food. In order to make the quantity of one crop comparable with that of another, each crop is expressed in terms of rice equivalent calculated on the fuel value of each crop in proportion to that of middle-grade rice.[11] According to the table, the total supply of food in all fourteen provinces amounts to 107,438 million catties (of 1.33 lbs.) or 143,216 million lbs. per year of rice equivalent. Rice, wheat, kaoliang, millet and corn make up about 85 per cent of the total supply.

For soya beans, which are not included in the table, we exclude all the production of the North East region where the proportion which is used for food is negligible in proportion to the huge amount which goes for export, seed, feed and industrial purposes. For the other provinces we arbitrarily take 40 per cent of the gross production as the portion used for food, which give an amount of 4,417 million catties with a rice equivalent of 5,192 million catties. Adding this to the amount of food from the other principal crops gives a total of 112,630 million catties of rice equivalent for the food supply from domestic sources. Imports of food from abroad for the period 1926–29 average about 2,538 million catties, and the excess of imports over exports, about 1,724 million catties of rice equivalent. Adding this last to the domestic food supply, we have a final total of 114,354 million catties. For the estimated population of 278 millions, this means a per capita supply of

[11] After the analysis of Dr. H. Wu in the *China Journal of Physiology* ("Report Series," 1928), No. 1, pp. 153–86.

TABLE II

ANNUAL NET SUPPLY OF FOOD FROM VARIOUS CROPS OF 14 PROVINCES

CROPS	PRODUCTION IN 1,000 CATTIES	SEED REQUIREMENT IN 1,000 CATTIES*	PRODUCTION LESS SEED REQUIREMENT IN 1,000 CATTIES	FEED REQUIREMENT IN 1,000 CATTIES†	PRODUCTION LESS SEED AND FEED IN 1,000 CATTIES	EDIBLE PORTION IN 1,000 CATTIES‡	EDIBLE PORTION IN RICE EQUIVALENT§		PER CENT OF TOTAL PRODUCTION SUPPLIED BY EACH CROP
							In 1,000 Catties	In 1,000 Pounds	
Rice............	41,097,782	1,180,800	39,916,982	......	39,916,982	25,946,040	25,946,040	34,586,071	24.15
Wheat...........	32,651,088	2,726,530	29,924,558	249,597	29,674,961	22,256,222	22,256,222	29,667,544	20.72
Kaoliang........	21,042,110	688,995	20,353,115	609,713	19,743,402	17,769,060	18,657,514	24,870,466	17.37
Millet..........	19,452,605	398,199	19,054,406	137,161	18,917,245	17,025,521	17,366,031	23,148,919	16.16
Corn............	9,776,421	250,036	9,526,385	24,347	9,502,038	8,741,876	9,266,389	12,352,097	8.62
Sweet potatoes..	15,496,749	1,494,400	14,002,349	......	14,002,349	12,602,118	4,158,699	5,543,546	3.87
Barley..........	9,394,976	694,710	8,700,266	4,882,755	3,817,511	3,435,760	3,195,257	4,259,278	2.97
Glutinous rice..	5,050,213	158,400	4,897,813	......	4,897,813	3,183,577	3,119,905	4,158,833	2.90
Other beans.....	1,033,840	71,575	962,265	39,211	923,054	283,055	867,672	1,156,607	0.81
Potatoes........	3,107,905	439,600	2,728,305	......	2,728,305	2,455,478	662,979	883,751	0.62
Peas............	592,197	36,883	555,314	9,380	545,934	545,934	513,178	684,066	0.48
Other millets...	548,160	17,060	530,500	......	530,500	477,450	482,225	642,806	0.45
Oats............	648,716	76,320	572,396	20,191	552,205	386,545	390,410	520,417	0.36
Broad beans.....	450,479	37,550	412,929	......	412,929	412,930	388,154	517,409	0.36
Buckwheat.......	174,736	14,148	160,588	......	160,588	120,443	118,034	157,339	0.11
Taro............	383,741	67,900	315,841	......	315,841	284,253	42,638	56,836	0.04
Yams............	61,520	3,000	58,520	......	58,520	52,668	7,374	9,830	0.01
Black beans.....	512,890	30,254	482,636	482,636	......	......	......	......	0.01
Total...	......	......	......	6,454,991	......	......	107,438,721	143,215,815	100.00

* Seed requirement is calculated at the following rates (catties per mow): rice 8; wheat 10; kaoliang 5; millet 3; corn 4; sweet potatoes 100; barley 10; other beans 7; potatoes 100; peas 7; other millets 4; oats 10; broad beans 10; buckwheat 6; taro 100; yams 100; black beans 7.

† Feed requirement is estimated at 500 catties of grain or legume seeds per work animal unit per annum. The number of animal units of a province is estimated at 100 mow of non-irrigated land and 30 mow of irrigated land per animal unit.

‡ Edible portion of a crop represents the quantity available for food less the wastes in processing.

§ Rice equivalent of a crop is calculated on the basis of fuel value produced by a catty of that crop compared with the fuel value produced by a catty of medium-grade rice.

about 411 catties or 548 lbs. The per capita supply from domestic sources is 405 catties or 540 lbs.

In order to calculate the average daily rice requirement of the country and city populations, we make use of the results of a sample study by C. M. Chiao and J. L. Buck [12] to obtain the age distribution of the farm population, and the results of two studies by the Bureau of Statistics for the age distribution of city populations in China and for the average daily rice requirement of country people and town people. The calculations yield the result shown in Table III.

TABLE III

Persons	Daily Requirement		
	Catties	Grams	Calories
Country male.......	1.373	823	2,906
Country female.....	1.200	720	2,542
City male..........	1.070	642	2,266
City female........	0.932	559	1,974

Certain inevitable difficulties and shortcomings have to be faced in estimating the population of the fourteen provinces. Eight of the fourteen have population census returns giving the number of males and females for 1928. The remaining six have returns for the number of households but not for the number of persons. The method used for these six is to multiply the number of households by the average number of persons per household of a neighboring province or provinces where conditions are similar. Thus the total number of persons in Kirin is found by multiplying Kirin's number of households, 1,260,907, by the average (6.67), which represents the number of persons per household in Liaoning, the next province. A similar procedure is used to determine the sex ratio of these six provinces. This is admittedly a rough method, but it is the best one available. In using it, however, we have had to assume that the average farm household is the same in numbers as the average city household, when in fact we have good evidence to suggest that it is distinctly larger. Our table will therefore show too large a city population and too small a country population, and as city folk eat less rice than country folk, our calculation of total food requirement based on these population estimates will give a total less than it should be. No attempt is made to correct this bias, but it is necessary to point out its existence. The results of the calculations are given in Table IV.

According to the table, the normal food requirement of the fourteen provinces should be about 124,564 million catties or some 83 million short tons of rice or rice equivalent per annum. For the estimated population of 278 million this gives about 448 catties or 597 lbs. per head. This amount is about 10,211 million catties or nearly 6.8 million short tons greater than the total estimated food supply of 114,354 million catties. In other words, food

[12] "Rural Population of China," *Chinese Economic Journal*, March, 1928.

TABLE IV

ANNUAL FOOD REQUIREMENT OF 14 PROVINCES

(In 1,000 catties of rice or rice equivalent)

REGIONS AND PROVINCES	REQUIREMENT OF THE FARM POPULATION †				REQUIREMENT OF THE CITY POPULATION †				TOTAL REQUIREMENT
	Farm Male		Farm Female		City Male		City Female		
	Population	Requirement	Population	Requirement	Population	Requirement	Population	Requirement	
Heilungkiang *.....	1,811,883	907,391	1,457,484	638,378	497,631	194,375	400,296	136,181	1,876,325
Kirin *..........	3,480,628	1,743,099	2,799,827	1,226,324	1,194,605	466,612	958,832	326,195	3,762,230
Liaoning.........	6,643,470	3,327,950	5,415,621	2,372,042	1,669,166	651,976	1,271,073	432,419	6,783,487
Jehol *..........	1,448,744	725,531	968,125	424,039	358,301	139,952	239,431	81,454	1,370,976
Chahar..........	922,847	462,162	643,804	281,986	253,638	99,071	176,945	60,197	903,416
Northeast......	14,307,572	7,165,233	11,284,861	4,942,769	3,973,339	1,551,986	3,046,577	1,036,446	14,696,434
Shansi..........	5,672,748	2,840,912	4,252,018	1,862,384	1,253,354	489,560	909,831	309,525	5,502,381
Hopei...........	13,266,702	6,643,964	11,031,714	4,831,891	3,915,139	1,529,253	2,925,272	995,178	14,000,286
Shantung *......	17,939,226	8,983,064	14,226,641	6,231,269	2,247,828	878,002	1,782,633	606,452	16,699,687
Honan *.........	15,342,799	7,683,074	12,107,554	5,329,388	2,932,228	1,145,328	2,325,395	791,099	14,949,489
North..........	52,221,475	26,152,514	41,677,927	18,254,932	10,348,549	4,042,143	7,943,129	2,702,254	51,151,843
Hupeh..........	10,101,669	5,058,916	8,214,363	3,597,892	4,621,865	1,805,300	3,758,358	1,278,593	11,740,701
Anhwei.........	8,645,189	4,329,511	6,728,226	2,946,963	3,566,392	1,393,033	2,775,589	944,255	9,613,762
Kiangsu.........	13,343,181	6,682,265	11,890,978	5,208,248	4,820,495	1,882,885	4,075,030	1,386,325	15,159,723
Chekiang........	7,866,150	3,940,870	6,149,403	2,693,439	3,725,178	1,455,055	2,879,336	979,550	9,068,914
Central and East..	39,959,189	20,011,562	32,982,970	14,446,542	16,733,930	6,536,273	13,488,311	4,588,723	45,583,100
Kwangtung *....	10,501,333	5,259,068	8,472,636	3,711,015	6,292,193	2,457,731	5,013,039	1,705,436	13,133,250
Grand total....	116,980,569	58,588,377	94,418,394	41,355,258	37,348,011	14,588,133	29,491,056	10,032,859	124,564,627

* Populations of these provinces are estimated by multiplying the number of households by average number of persons per household of the neighboring province or provinces. The multipliers used for several provinces are as follows:

Province	Multiplier	Neighboring Province
Heilungkiang.............	6.670	Liaoning
Kirin.................	6.670	Liaoning
Jehol.................	5.256	Chahar and Suiyuan
Shantung.............	5.575	Hopei and Shansi
Honan................	5.575	Hopei and Shansi
Kwangtung............	5.594	Kwangsi

† Farm and city population is calculated according to the ratio between the number of farm households and that of city households.

supply is some 8 per cent less than the estimated requirement. With the present inexact data and approximate methods of calculation, we cannot definitely infer from this result that the population of the fourteen provinces is permanently undernourished, but it seems at least safe to draw the tentative conclusion that in normal years the provinces have no more than enough, even when net imports of food are included. The conditions, however, vary greatly from one province to another. As Table V shows, the North East

TABLE V

COMPARISON OF ANNUAL FOOD PRODUCTION AND REQUIREMENT

(In million catties of rice equivalent)

PROVINCES AND REGIONS	TOTAL FOOD REQUIREMENT	PRODUCTION			SURPLUS OR DEFICIENCY
		17 Chief Food Crops	40% of Gross Soybean Products	Total	
Heilungkiang....	1,876	3,992	....	3,992	+ 2,116
Kirin...........	3,762	6,435	....	6,435	+ 2,673
Liaoning.......	6,784	8,145	....	8,145	+ 1,361
Jehol..........	1,371	1,728	....	1,728	+ 357
Chahar........	903	1,291	....	1,291	+ 388
North East...	14,696	21,591	....	21,591	+ 6,895
Shansi.........	5,502	5,341	126	5,467	− 35
Hopei..........	14,000	9,789	526	10,315	− 3,685
Shantung.......	16,700	12,522	693	13,215	− 3,485
Honan.........	14,950	10,985	1,638	12,623	− 2,327
North........	51,152	38,637	2,983	41,620	− 9,532
Hupeh.........	11,741	11,233	369	11,602	− 139
Anhwei........	9,613	6,437	504	6,941	− 2,673
Kiangsu........	15,160	14,043	1,079	15,122	− 38
Chekiang.......	9,069	7,130	163	7,293	− 1,776
Central.......	45,583	38,843	2,115	40,958	− 4,625
Kwangtung...	13,133	8,367	94	8,461	− 4,672
Grand total	124,564	107,438	5,192	112,630	− 11,934

region produces more food than it requires, while the provinces of Shansi, Hupeh and Kiangsu are about self-sufficient. All the other provinces do not produce enough for themselves, Kwangtung being at the bottom with a deficiency of more than a third. This conclusion is supported by the statistics of foreign trade in foodstuffs (rice, wheat, flour, kaoliang, millet, and corn), which indicate the crude weights of imports and exports in million catties shown, without regard to the different fuel values of the foods.

North East .... 1,000 million catties export excess
North .... 1,453 import excess
Central 38
Kwangtung 1,072

IV. SOME MAJOR PRODUCTS AND THEIR IMPROVEMENT [13]

By AKIRA NAGANO

The improvement and development of agriculture have an important bearing upon the expansion of industry in China. Failing that, China cannot hope to become a commercial and industrial country. Hitherto the agricultural products of China have been chiefly foodstuffs; in North China tall millet, Italian and Indian millet have come to be the principal crops, and in Central and South China, rice and other cereals; but the development of industry has compelled the realization of the necessity for the domestic production of the raw materials required, and has stimulated the production of wheat and soya beans, and the quality of wool is being improved. I propose to outline the actual condition of the principal products.

COTTON

The most important of China's new industries is the cotton industry. Much attention has been paid to the improvement of raw cotton and to the expansion of the area cultivated. Because of her climate and the vastness of her arable land, China is qualified to be the second cotton producing country in the world next to America.

The quality of a good deal of the Chinese cotton is not suitable for spinning, and production does not keep pace with the development of the spinning industry. On the one hand, cotton which is not fit for spinning is exported for use as quilt padding; and on the other, Indian, and some American, cotton for spinning is imported as shown in Table I.[14]

TABLE I

Year	Exports (Piculs) *	Imports (Piculs)
1913	738,812	133,255
1919	1,072,040	239,003
1920	376,230	678,297
1921	609,481	1,682,528
1922	842,010	1,780,618
1923	974,574	1,614,371
1924	1,080,019	1,241,881
1925	800,832	1,807,450
1926	878,512	2,745,017
1927	1,446,950	2,415,483
1928	1,112,000	1,916,000
1929	944,000	2,515,000
1930	826,000	3,457,000

* One picul equals 133.33 lbs. or 100 catties of 1.33 lbs.

Thus China was originally a cotton exporting country, but since she built spinning mills she has begun to import it. As will be seen from the list

[13] Extract from the data paper, *Development of Capitalization in China.*
[14] *Maritime Customs Annual Report.*

in Table I, the import of cotton increased suddenly after the European war, that is to say, from about 1921, when spinning mills in China showed a conspicuous development. The quantity of cotton for spinning consumed in 1929 is shown in Table II.

TABLE II

	Piculs
Japanese mills	3,003,000
British mills	300,000
Chinese mills	5,928,000
Total	9,231,000

The increase in the import of American and Indian cotton is attributable to the shortage of Chinese cotton, but at the same time it shows that spinning in China is turning from coarse yarns to fine. It is for this reason that the Japanese mills where technical skill is most highly developed consume a great quantity of American cotton.

Thus has arisen the question of extending the area under cotton and improving its quality. In order to increase the area under cotton, there are such schemes as the encouragement of planting, the reclamation of the Hwaiho basin and the cultivation of cotton on the waste salt-fields of Changlu. Shansi, for instance, which has hitherto imported the cotton it requires from other provinces, is now not only self-supplying but is also exporting to other provinces, thanks to the encouragement of General Yen Hsi-shan. In North China, if cotton is cultivated the profit is about twice that of common cereals; but as irrigation is necessary for the cultivation of cotton, planting in North China is determined by the rainfall in spring, and the area for the cultivation of cotton therefore varies according to the year. It follows that, in order to increase the cotton area, adequate irrigation facilities must be provided. It will not be difficult to increase the cultivated area in China, as there are extensive tracts of unreclaimed and waste land, as stated above, but the work of reclamation is now hindered by the present disturbances in China.

The next point is the improvement of the quality of Chinese cotton. The question of improvement has been under discussion for some time past, and American cotton has been introduced and has been gradually gaining in popularity in China. Of the cotton grown in Siho in Chihli in 1923–24 about 10 per cent was American cotton, and also in Shensi American cotton has been grown for some years. Considerable attention has been paid by China to the improvement of cotton, and the Tungnan University in Nanking has done excellent work. After it took over the cotton experimental stations established by the Association of Cotton Merchants in every province in 1921, it organized a committee for the improvement and extension of cotton cultivation, it established branch experimental farms in Kiangsu, Hupeh and Honan, it distributed publications and held exhibitions, it distributed improved seed, and it advised farmers on improved cultural methods. The university has increased its cotton experimental stations, made new agricultural implements, studied means of exterminating insect pests, and established educational institutes for young men for practical study. The quantity of improved cotton seed distributed in 1926 amounted to 51,928 catties, the number of households which received it being 805, and the area on which the seed was planted 9,769 mow. Although this is only a drop in the ocean compared with the whole of China, the good work is going on, and it is seen that Chinese raw cotton is gradually improving as the result. Hitherto Chinese cotton could not be spun into yarns finer than 20 count or less, but of late it can be used for 30 to 40 count. This improvement is, however, hindered by present conditions in China. As soon as this obstacle has been removed, the improvement of cotton will progress hand in hand with the development of the Chinese spinning industry.

SERICULTURE

The next most important material for industry in China after cotton is cocoons. Sericulture has been carried on in China from ancient times; but as the Chinese clung to old methods, they gradually lost their leading position, and the silk reeling industry is now not very active. Hence the improvement of raw silk is now regarded as most urgent. The Lower Yangtze Valley is the center of cocoon production, contributing 65 per cent of the total. According to investigations made in the autumn of 1929 by the Bureau of Commercial Affairs of the Japanese Foreign Office, the whole crop of cocoons throughout China is 3,700,000 piculs.

Taking the crop of cocoons in China as 3,700,000 piculs, 260,000 piculs of raw silk can be obtained. Exports from China are about 24,000 bales of re-reels and about 123,000 bales of steam filatures, totalling about one-fourth of Japan's export. Very few cocoons are exported from China, the most part being consumed in the country.

In China, spring silkworms comprise about 80 per cent, summer silkworms about 15 per cent, and autumn silkworms which have been recently developed only about 5 per cent. With regard to the quality of Chinese cocoons, these vary according to locality. There are large ones, as those of Shaohsing in Chekiang, and small ones, as those of Wusih in Kiangsu; but in general their filament is small and well-fitted for reeling. Only, as scientific study with regard to diseased silkworms and feeding is insufficient, undersized cocoons are mixed with good, naturally resulting in a great waste when reeling, and defective thread. Some ascribe this to the fact that unmatured silkworms are purposely transferred to cocoon-beds with the idea of making money.

Except in a part of Chekiang and Kwantung, there are many tainted silkworms, as they are hatched from home-made cards, and therefore the necessity of improving egg-cards is widely advocated. Chekiang and Kiangsu, which have their silk reeling factories at Shanghai, are especially keen for improvement. Improvement in Chekiang is systematically organized under the guidance of the Government, while in Kiangsu the girls' Sericultural School at Suchow and silk reelers there are the center of the movement; but the progress of improvement is hindered by want of uniformity, as there are many private egg breeders. Against about 12 million cards made in Kiangsu, Chekiang and Anhwei, improved cards are about 600,000 — that is, about one-twentieth. Silk from improved cards shows an increase in weight of about 40 per cent. It is estimated that, in Chekiang only, the crop of raw silk can be increased by about 200,000 piculs. Popularization of improved cards has been rapid, and many are now making them. In Kiangsu alone there are thirty places making such cards. Autumn sericulture began to be practised in 1926 and is gradually developing. As has already been stated, the Nationalist Government has recently established a silk conditioning house in Shanghai, with the object of securing uniformity of its quality. . . .

As the Chinese Government officials as well as the people are straining every nerve in their efforts to improve raw silk, and as America is intending to promote the development of Chinese silk, Chinese sericulture will show gradual development and progress.

LIVESTOCK

The improvement and development of livestock is also indispensable for the progress of modern industry in China. The industrial materials to be improved are wool, camel's hair and hides.

Wool and camel's hair are needed for the woolen textile industry of the future. The object of sheep breeding in China is to obtain the skin and the meat; the wool is quite unsuitable — it is so straight and coarse that it is not suited for woolen fabrics and is therefore used for mixed weaves or rugs. Consequently, the improvement of sheep breeding has been planned for some time past, and there is now an experimental station, established in Shansi, a suburb of Peiping, where a second cross from a merino almost identical with a merino is bred. It is impossible to popularize this breed as the people are not interested, and the necessary expense cannot be met under present political conditions in China. At Shansi, Marshal Yen Hsi-shan bought American merinos and planned sheep improvement on a large scale. The question of stock breeding is not regarded so seriously as that of cotton or sericulture; but the question of improvement has arisen and is likely to make progress. The quantity of the present crop of Chinese wool is not known, but the amount forwarded to Tientsin in recent years is as shown in Table III.

TABLE III

Year	Wool	Camel's Hair	Total
1925	554,301 piculs	51,733 piculs	606,034 piculs
1926	178,375 piculs	31,602 piculs	209,977 piculs

This amount is about 80 per cent of the total quantity of wool produced in the whole country. When the breed of sheep in China has been improved, the production of wool will greatly increase, and naturally the development of the woolen textile industry will be accelerated. The production of hides is also quite large. In the past ten years, the amount of raw ox hides exported ranged from two to three hundred thousand piculs per year. If improved the cattle could supply the leather industry. The quality of Honan cattle is good, whereas that of Mongolian cattle is very inferior, the hides being worm-eaten. At present no effective steps have been taken for the improvement and development of livestock, but the question has not been lost sight of.

OBSTACLES TO THE DEVELOPMENT OF AGRICULTURE AND THEIR REMOVAL

There are two chief forces which hinder the development of agriculture in China; one is political and the other technical. The political obstacle appears in various forms and in various directions, but chiefly in the two following ways. The first is the exactions of officials in times of disorder. Not only are heavy taxes imposed on the people, but their provisions and even their carts, horses and coolies are requisitioned, leaving them without all means of living. In such circumstances the improvement of farming is impossible; the area under cultivation goes to ruin, and reduced production follows. Again, as the result of civil wars, all state income is wasted on military funds, and nothing can be spared for the development of industry. Thus, though the importance of improving and developing agricultural products is recognized, nothing can be done. Although the people do their best, their influence is trifling and has no effect on the general situation. The second is the obstruction of traffic which accompanies civil wars. Every time a war breaks out, not only is transportation by land and sea hindered, but damage is done by bandits. Rolling stock is commandeered, freight rates are increased, heavy taxes are imposed, and illegal *likin* offices are set up on land and sea routes. Such being the case, no materials required in factories can be brought from distant localities. About half the modern factories are situated in Shanghai; those which can obtain materials from the neighborhood of Shanghai are fortunate, but those which depend on remote districts cannot pay, owing to the obstruction of heavy freight and other impositions. Consequently it does not pay to produce raw materials. This applies equally to farm produce destined for the factory, and there is therefore no incentive to improve it. Industry also has no option but to draw its materials either from the immediate neighborhood or from overseas. The condition in general can be seen from the fact that Chinese coal costs about one yen at the pit head, and yet it pays to transport Japanese coal, which is more expensive, from Shanghai to Hankow.

The next point is the progress in the technique of agriculture. Despite the fact that in China the technique of agriculture made good progress in early days, its subsequent progress has been very slow. We know from the Chingtien system that under the Chow dynasty the use of nightsoil as manure was known, and continuous cultivation was widely practised. Agricultural implements were quite well developed, and it is recorded that the plough was already in use. Under the Han dynasty also cattle were used for cultivation, but nowadays the old-fashioned implements are still retained. Though there was a period when improvements were introduced, the Chinese farmer is conservative and makes no effort to adopt new implements. The same is true of manure; they use as a basic dressing dried cattle manure mixed with earth, bean-cakes being used for the cultivation of cotton or other high-class crops only. It seems that chemical fertilizers are not yet used at all. This is due to the fact that Chinese farmers are more anxious to keep down expenses as much as possible rather than to increase the crop by applying high-priced fertilizers. The shape of the fields is very irregular, never having been adjusted, because farmers dislike to alter the original shape of their fields. As to the improvement of seeds, cotton is getting gradually better as the result of persistent efforts, but it is very difficult in the case of other crops. The next requirement in China is irrigation. Chinese farmers accept drought and floods as visitations of fate and make no effort to prevent them, saying that it is Heaven's retribution for the evil deeds of the people. Therefore, droughts and floods recur every year throughout the country, causing many to starve to death; but this causes no surprise. If irrigation equipment were installed, waste land would become fertile, and the area cultivated and the crop would be greatly increased; moreover floods and droughts would be largely averted. Having learned a lesson from the drought of 1917–18, the people of Hopei province dug irrigation wells which numbered over a million by 1923–24; and of late, it seems, Honan province has also begun to do the same. Drainage work has also been undertaken. As irrigation on a large scale involves great expense, such undertakings as the repair of the Yuantingho River in Hopei or the riparian work on the Hwaiho in Kiangsu can only be carried out by the Government. Again, the extermination of insect pests must be studied and a radical cure undertaken by the Government. For the prevention of flood damage it is widely recognized that afforestation is necessary, but at present, owing to the prevailing disturbances, no effective work can be carried out.

V. RURAL CONDITIONS IN THE COLONIZATION AREAS OF MANCHURIA [15]

By Franklin L. Ho

An understanding of land acquisition in Manchuria is indispensable to a study of the conditions of settlement of the Chinese immigrants. In the early days, land in Manchuria was practically all owned by the Imperial Govern-

[15] Extract from the data paper, *Population Movement to the Northeastern Frontier of China.* The choice of this extract, which may at first sight seem to belong rather to a subsequent chapter on migration, has been made for two main reasons. In the first place, agricultural conditions in the newly settled frontier districts of Manchuria have an intrinsic importance which is greater than can be measured in thousands of acres or thousands of settlers, since they provide at least a rough idea of the obstacles to be overcome in any attempt to relieve population pressure by colonizing other sparsely peopled regions of China. In the second place, the problems of tenure, of credit and of marketing, which are here described, are at bottom the same problems which the Chinese

ment in Peking. There have been several auction sales of public land by the Government since the latter part of the Tsing Dynasty, through which most of the land has passed from public to private ownership. At present, however, land acquisition by auction purchase is very rare, except in some of the frontier districts where the provincial governments of Kirin and Heilungkiang designate definite areas for sale. The buyers of public land at auction sales, in the early days as well as at present, are mostly absentee holders who form semi-official colonization companies of private syndicates and acquire large estates of arable land for speculation. It may be stated parenthetically that a greater portion of the arable land in the provinces of Kirin and Heilungkiang, particularly in the latter, is today in the possession of large absentee owners who are mostly retired civilian or military officials.

As a remedy of the situation, the provincial governments of Kirin and Heilungkiang have from time to time issued administrative acts authorizing " pre-occupation " of unreclaimed lands for cultivation by actual settlers. Under the Act of Kirin, issued in February, 1923, and that of Heilungkiang, issued in September, 1928, unreclaimed lands may be occupied by settlers who file an application with the magistrate of the district in which the land is located. A settler with one plough may occupy one fon or 540 mow [16] of land on the condition that he cultivates it within a time limit of three years. After the land is all cultivated at the end of the third year, 60 per cent of it belongs to him and 40 per cent goes to the original owner. The original owner as well as the settler then has to apply for a new deed at one dollar each to the district magistrate. We have, thus, another way of land acquisition by " pre-occupation " as different from that by auction purchase in Manchuria. But the absentee owners of unreclaimed lands are mostly retired officials or military lords whose influence in the district government is predominant. As a consequence, the administrative acts authorizing " pre-occupation " of unreclaimed lands by actual settlers have become practically dead letters. Land acquisition by " pre-occupation," like that by auction purchase, is now scarcely available in practice in Manchuria.

The prevalent method of land acquisition in Manchuria, however, is by alienation from individual owners or by cultivation through agreement with the owner. By the latter is meant that a man with sufficient capital or labor at his disposal arranges with some large absentee owner for the cultivation of his unreclaimed land, on the condition that a portion of the land thus cultivated goes to him as compensation. The proportion, however, varies in each individual case, ranging, usually, from 40 per cent to 60 per cent of the land cultivated. The market price of land in Manchuria depends on various factors, the principal ones of which are soil quality, location and accessibility to communication facilities. Usually, land in the unreclaimed areas

---

farmer in the home provinces must face, and the cruder conditions of exploitation on the frontier, where traditional social safeguards and controls have not yet been erected, serve to illustrate in bolder outlines the essential problems of Chinese rural organization.

[16] One mow equals about one-sixth of an acre.

in the interior sells at $10 to $16 per shan, or 12 mow. A newly arriving immigrant who wishes to buy ten shan of land for cultivation has to have a minimum capital of from $600 to $800 to begin with. Should he wish to obtain land through cultivation for some absentee owner, he would have to have a minimum capital of from $500 to $600, since the only item of expenditure that he can save in this case is the purchase of land which costs from $100 to $160 per ten shan. It is not without difficulty, however, that an immigrant can obtain the land for cultivation even if he is provided with the capital he needs, as landowners, usually, do not want to sell their land by small lots, nor care to arrange with individual immigrants for cultivation.

Driven out by civil wars and famine from their home districts, the newly arriving immigrants in Manchuria have, in most cases, neither sufficient money nor adequate implements for farming. Indeed, most of them have no money at all upon their arrival. To obtain land in freehold for cultivation under any one of the methods stated is practically impossible for them. As a rule, they settle down either as tenant farmers or as farm hands. Some of them are engaged as peddlers, lumbermen, or millhands, but these are relatively few in number and less permanent in settlement. In general, there are three ways through which Chinese immigrants in Manchuria may become employed as tenant farmers or farm laborers. In the first place, most of the new arrivals have friends or relatives from their home districts who have already settled down in Manchuria and upon whom they depend entirely for assistance and information. In many cases, these are themselves tenant farmers or farm laborers through whom the new arrivals get similiar employment. In the second place, landowners and colonization companies oftentimes have agents stationed in the principal distributing centers of Changchun, Harbin or Imeipo on the eastern line of the Chinese Eastern Railway, whose function is to select and to employ the immigrants as tenant farmers or farm laborers for their respective landowners and colonization companies. These agents are, in most cases, originally immigrants from Shantung. In the third place, " benevolent " bodies may make arrangements with landowners in Manchuria previous to the arrival of the immigrants. As a measure of famine relief, for instance, the Honan Relief Organization in Peiping requested the Provincial Government of Heilungkiang in 1929 to find employment for the famine refugees whom the organization took the responsibility of transporting to Manchuria. What the Heilungkiang Government did, then, was to order the magistrates of the frontier districts to solicit the landowners of their respective districts for employment. The landowners, then, made subscriptions in accordance with their capacity to employ. Upon the arrival of the immigrant refugees in Tsitsihar, they were divided upon among those subscribers who took them back to their respective farms.

The system of tenancy in Manchuria differs in accordance with the terms of tenure relating to payment of rent and other conditions. In general, two systems prevail in Manchuria. One system allows exemption of rent for the first five years. Beginning with the sixth year, the tenant is required to pay a rent the amount of which varies with the soil quality of land, distance from the market and supply of prospective tenants in the vicinity. In most cases, it amounts to two shih of cereals of three kinds (usually soy beans, kaoliang and millet) for one shan of land, which equals, approximately, one-third of the total value received by the farmer. Under this system, the landowner furnishes the land only, while the tenant provides everything else himself, including seeds, implements, livestock, building, and food for the crop season.

A second system requires an annual payment of rent beginning with the first year of cultivation. Usually, the annual rent for each of the first five years consists of one-fifth of a shih of soy beans for one shan of land; while beginning with the sixth year, it consists of two shih of cereals of three kinds per shan of land. Under this system the landowner furnishes not only the land but also a part of the expenses for the building. In some cases, he furnishes the tenant farmer with livestock as well as implements. In both cases the time for payment is after the harvest in November, called Shia Da Tsu. It may be mentioned that in well colonized districts near the cities or industrial centers, rent is sometimes paid in the autumn of the previous harvest year, called Shan Da Tsu, and is paid usually in cash instead of in kind.

There are several grades of farm laborers in Manchuria. (1) The foreman on the farm looks after the farm laborers, wagons, horses and cattle. On a large farm, his service is the most important and his work very difficult, as he supervises all the activities on the farm for his landowner. Usually, he is chosen from among the older immigrants who understand local farming conditions and possess some administrative ability. He is paid an annual wage of about $200 Harbin currency. (2) The farm hand follows the foreman and works according to his direction. His wage is about $170 Harbin currency per annum. (3) The assistant farm hand, recruited almost exclusively from the new arrivals from Shantung, assists the foreman and farm hand in all the manual work on the farm. He receives about $130 a year. (4) The sub-assistant farm hand helps the foreman, farm hand, and assistant farm hand, and learns at the same time. He is recruited from among those new arrivals who are young and not yet fully developed physically. His wage amounts to $80 Harbin currency per annum. (5) The night servant stays on watch in the Manchurian farmyard throughout the night, feeds the horses and cattle, and cleans the yard. He receives from $100 to $180 Harbin currency per year, largely in accordance with the size of the farmyard. A new arrival may become a night servant in a small farmyard, but a large farmyard requires the service of an older immigrant who understands the farming conditions in Manchuria. (6) The cook prepares the food for all farm laborers, especially during the sowing and reaping seasons. His wage is about the same as that of the night servant. (7) The horse driver is employed either by one farm or by several farms or by one village to herd the horses and cattle in wild areas not yet under the plough. He must be an expert horseman and know the adjoining territory well. His wage varies with the number of horses and cattle which he is taking care of. (8) The domestic-animal man looks after pigs, sheep and domestic fowls. Usually a boy of twelve to thirteen years of age can do this work and is paid a wage of from $30 to $60 a year. In all these cases, lodging and food are provided by the employer. In addition to these several kinds of laborers employed on the Manchurian farms, there are seasonal workers, engaged mostly during the sowing and reaping seasons, month — and day — laborers, and piece-work laborers. Their wage varies largely in accordance with the demand and supply of the prospective farm laborers in the locality.

There is another kind of farm labor which differs greatly from those enumerated in the preceding, and in which a great many of the Chinese immigrants are engaged. A landowner employs a man, usually together with his family, for the cultivation of his land. He furnishes him with seeds, implements, building, livestock and food for the crop year. In addition to the land which he cultivates for the landowner, he is given a certain amount of land which he cultivates for himself, and for which he provides his own seeds. The crops which he receives from the land constitute his wage for the year. The amount of land given varies in each individual case, ranging from two shan to four shan in the eastern region of the Chinese Eastern Railway. His term of employment is usually one year but can be renewed so far as both parties, the landowner and the laborer, are satisfied with each other.

While almost all the newly arriving immigrants are engaged as tenant farmers or farm hands and few of them are in the position to acquire land in freehold immediately upon their arrival in Manchuria, it is not infrequently the case that a number of them become small landowners in the course of time. A new arrival with some money himself or with friends or relatives upon whom he can depend for assistance usually settles down first as a tenant farmer, but after several years of hard work he may accumulate some savings and thus become a landowner. In Manchuria, a tenant farmer has the prior privilege to purchase the land from his landowner in case the latter desires to sell his land. On the other hand, those who settle down first as farm hands may gradually turn to be tenant farmers after they have acquired sufficient knowledge of the local farming conditions and have accumulated some savings through hard work and parsimony. But at present enormous obstacles stand in the way of the immigrant-settler's road to prosperity as promised by the productivity of the Manchurian soil. Some of the obstacles may be enumerated as follows:

There is, first of all, the obstacle of insecurity which tends to cripple the rapid economic development of most of the settlement regions in Manchuria. In places away from the large centers of habitation and protection, roving bandits frequently prey on the more industrious settlers. Indeed, the problem of banditry in Manchuria is a real one. While large colonization companies usually maintain their own police to protect their farms and warehouses, small farms are left almost entirely at the mercy of the banditry. It may be stated parenthetically that small farms of less than 30 shan of land constitute nearly 75 per cent of all the farms in North Manchuria, and occupy about 50 per cent of the entire area under cultivation at present.[17]

There is also the obstacle of high interest rates in the rural districts in Manchuria. Almost all the newly-arriving immigrants have little or no money at all. Most of those who are engaged in farming have to resort to borrowing for the crop season. In his investigation in Manchuria, the writer found very few cases where farmers did not have to borrow for the purchase of seeds, or for maintenance during the farming season. The credit facilities in the rural districts in Manchuria are provided invariably by pawnshops and moneylenders, who are usually landowners, grain merchants, or *Tsaho* firms, i.e., groceries. The rate of interest charged by moneylenders ranges from 40 per cent to 100 per cent per crop season (four to five months), either on the security of farm crops or on that of land deeds. Added to the implicit interest consisting of gifts or entertainments that are sometimes necessary to obtain loans from the moneylender, the total interest rate not infrequently amounts to more than 100 per cent for a crop season. The interest charged by pawnshops is much higher than that charged by moneylenders. In Hailun, the terminus of the Hulan-Hailun Railway, one pawnshop named T'ung Young charges an interest rate of 1 per cent per day, with 40 days' time limit for redemption of the articles pawned! The customers of the pawnshop are mostly farmers in the vicinity.

In the third place, farmers in Manchuria suffer immensely from the prevalent method of marketing agricultural products. Agriculture in Manchuria, particularly in the North, is characterized by the predominance of cash crops, such as beans and wheat. A recent study reveals that, on the average, 50 per cent of all the monetary earnings of the farming population in North Manchuria are derived from the sale of beans, and 30 per cent from the sale of wheat. The bean trade in Manchuria is exclusively handled by grain merchants, called *Liang-Pu, Liang-Hang* or *Liang-Teh,* who purchase the beans from the farmer and resell to the exporter or miller.

Usually, however, the number of intermediary firms between the farmer and exporter or miller is more than one. Even in the interior trading centers one may observe the concentration of beans in the hands of large grain merchants to whom the beans bought from the farmer are sold by the small grain merchants. The same process is repeated at railway stations and large distributing centers whither the beans are transported from the interior trading centers, and where consignments are given for export. Mention may be made that, in the interior trading centers, inns also perform the function of middlemen in the bean trade. Farmers arriving from remote places always stay in the inns. Being unacquainted with the marketing conditions, they entrust the sale of their beans to the inn in which they stay, paying the latter a commission the amount of which varies from 2 per cent up. Under such

[17] L. T. Lubimoff, "Crisis in the Sale of Beans and Losses of the Manchuria Farmer," *Manchuria Monitor,* January, 1930, p. 3. (In Russian.)

a method of marketing, a large portion of the price paid by the exporters or millers would have to go to the hands of the grain merchants who act as middlemen. It has been estimated that farmers receive on the average only 80 per cent of the price paid by the exporters or millers for the beans sold, whereas 20 per cent of the price goes to the middlemen. In the case of advance sales or " green sale," a practice which prevails among the small farmers in the rural districts in North Manchuria, the loss to the farmer is much greater.[18] By " green sale " is meant that, because of the lack of capital and because of the difficulty in obtaining credit, a farmer is sometimes obliged to sell his crops — in most cases beans and wheat — to the grain merchants before harvest time. A farmer suffers in a " green sale " from both the low prices and the underestimate of crops. Usually, the price of grain and the quantity estimate of the crop at a " green sale " average approximately one-third lower than the price and actual quantity produced at the harvest time.

In the fourth place, the diversity of the currency system as well as the magnitude of its inflation in Manchuria have imposed untold sufferings upon the ignorant and innocent agricultural settler. In Manchuria, each province has a currency by itself or attaches a different value to the same currency; and no port or city has a currency which is exactly the same as that of its neighbor. In addition to the many kinds of Chinese currencies, there are also various kinds of foreign currencies in circulation in the different parts of the country. The loss one suffers from this diversity of currency system in Manchuria is enormous. During one of my trips to the interior regions in Manchuria in 1930, I made an experiment to ascertain approximately how much people suffer through the absence of a uniform currency system. I took five dollar Tientsin currency and exchanged them into various kinds of currencies as I went from one place to another. Finally, I had the money exchanged into Tientsin currency again. I found that the original five dollars were reduced to two dollars and seventy-five cents. Two dollars and twenty-five cents disappeared in the process of exchange from one kind of currency to another for fifteen times altogether. The average rate of loss in each transaction of exchange was 3 per cent.

However much the people in Manchuria suffer from the diversity of their currency system, they suffer more from the violent depreciation of paper notes due to inflation. Take, for instance, the kuantieh which constitutes the chief, if not the only currency of the rural population of North Manchuria and serves as the monetary medium for the immense turnover of agricultural produce every year. The kuantieh are paper notes issued nominally against strings of copper cash by the Governments of Kirin and Heilungkiang. The kuantieh-tayang rate of exchange in 1911 was on the average 3.8 tiao of Kirin kuantieh and 4.6 tiao of Heilungkiang kuantieh for one tayang dollar. Twenty years later, in 1930, however, the rate of exchange between kuantieh and tayang was in the neighborhood of 211 tiao of Kirin kuantieh and 532

---

[18] In 1928 the quantity of beans sold through " green sales " in the western region of the Chinese Eastern Railway constituted about 20 per cent of all the beans sold (*ibid.*).

tiao of Heilungkiang kuantieh for one tayang dollar. The depreciation of Kirin kuantieh for tayang in 1930 was equivalent to that of 0.0000018 tiao of Kirin kuantieh in 1911; whereas the exchange value of one tiao of Heilungkiang kuantieh for tayang in 1930 was equivalent to that of 0.000-00086 tiao of Heilungkiang kuantieh in 1911.

In addition to its general depreciation, the kuantieh fluctuates seasonally, rising in autumn and winter when the demand for kuantieh for the settlement of grain transactions increases, and falling in the spring and summer when the demand slackens. The losses that an agricultural settler suffers from the general depreciation as well as from the seasonal fluctuations of kuantieh are enormous. He has to pay for the purchase of groceries and other necessaries of life with the depreciated currency, which he has to accept at a higher rate when he appears as a seller on the market.

Finally, mention may be made of the burden of heavy taxation in the rural districts in Manchuria. The burden of taxation in Manchuria becomes in many cases unbearable to the agricultural settler. In the eastern region of the Chinese Eastern Railway, for instance, taxes and levies of various designations on one shan of cultivated land amount to approximately $5.00 Harbin currency, which represents at least 5 per cent of the value of land. Of these the landowner pays $2.00 while the farmer pays $3.00 as contribution to the local police. In addition, the total sum of taxes and charges collected at the sale of grain amount to about 10 per cent *ad valorem*. There are, besides, a host of other commodity taxes and miscellaneous contributions, the incidence of which falls either directly or indirectly upon the farmer as a consumer. In addition, the tax collecting sub-offices, of which there are 641 in the rural districts of Manchuria, prey frequently on the ignorance and innocence of the farmers. Indeed, illegal fines and levies imposed on a farmer sometimes exceed the proper taxes and contributions.

That Manchuria constitutes probably the only outlet for the surplus population of the intra-mural provinces of China is generally admitted. Over five million Chinese immigrants have gone into Manchuria during the period of 1923–30, and about one million and a half have settled as permanent colonists in the various regions of the country in 1927, 1928 and 1929. But, for several decades to come, Manchuria will continue to have the " demand for men " — using the demand in the technical economic sense — which other parts of China can and have the prior right to supply. If the estimate of a Russian authority is correct, it will take at least forty years for Manchuria to reach a total population of 75,000,000 and a density of 187 persons to the square mile, which density represents only about one-third of that at present in Shantung, Hopei, or Honan.[19] While the effects of the present Chinese population movement into Manchuria — the effect on the immigrants, the effect on the land whence they come and the effect on the land whither they go — remain a subject for careful investigation, it may be

[19] E. E. Yashnoff, " Colonization Prospect in Manchuria," *Manchuria Monitor*, June, 1928, pp. 20–21.

said without fear of contradiction that such a movement should be a blessing to China as well as to the world at large.   But the movement will not, nor can it, result in maximum benefit to all parties concerned until definite measures for the establishment of a positive social policy of land acquisition and settlement are taken, until a uniform currency and a sound credit and distributing system are adopted, and, finally, until security and protection are assured.   While the problem of the Chinese population movement into Manchuria is a national as well as an international one, the responsibility for a proper solution of the problem cannot but be our own.

QUESTIONS FOR ROUND–TABLE DISCUSSION

In its suggested agenda for the discussion of " China's Economic Development," the Program Committee recommended the following questions for the consideration of rural aspects of that subject (questions relating indirectly to rural economy being, in the present volume, dealt with in later chapters):

1. In what respects do the traditional skills and techniques of the Chinese farmer need to be supplemented, and by what means can this be effected?
2. In what ways can the movement toward agricultural economic organization be hastened and extended?
3. What agencies and methods are needed to improve agricultural research and to relate it closely with the life of the farmer?
4. How far and in what ways does the improvement of peasant life depend on the development of rural industries?

SUMMARY OF ROUND–TABLE DISCUSSIONS

I. DEFECTS AND POSSIBLE IMPROVEMENTS IN CHINESE FARMING

One round table which took good advantage of the presence of several competent students of Chinese agriculture to consider weaknesses in the customary technique of the Chinese farmer began with the fundamental question of water control. This problem which, of course, arises partly from the natural climatic limitations of China, was well stated by a foreign member with a long experience of the matter in China. He said:

" We find that while the skill of the Chinese farmer undoubtedly needs supplementing in certain respects, there are a number of necessary improvements which he cannot be expected to undertake himself without special assistance. In the course of many years in this country, I have found that lack of proper water control constitutes one of the greatest limitations to the traditional technique of the farmer. In many parts of the country this factor is so important that it is practically futile to attempt improvements in seed selection or the introduction of new agricultural implements since the crops are continually subject to the risk of flood or drought. It seems to me that a great weakness in many schemes for agricultural development lies in their exclusive attention to schemes for crop improvement and their neglect of the more basic problems of too much or too little water. Problems of this sort naturally require some measure of co-operative action or centralized control either through the villages or through the central Government. For the purely local problems of irrigation, the responsibility may safely rest with the village or district authorities, as the International Famine Relief Commission has shown in its work of developing wells for irrigation purposes in North China. For the larger problems of flood prevention the assistance of national or provincial authorities is essential."

The comment which followed showed that a term like " irrigation " had widely differing meanings in the minds of various members. To an Australian member the term implied a highly organized and highly capitalized system, placed under the control of a governmental authority. For most

Chinese members it meant an intricate mass of local usages and individual practices, differing greatly in different regions of China. While in most parts of the country there is not much that could go by the name of co-operative effort or centralized administration in regard to supplying water for irrigation, it was shown that in some districts an informal type of co-operation is enforced upon the farmers by the natural requirements of different crops. In such cases those concerned would agree in advance on what parts of their scattered strips of land were to be planted in certain crops so that the water requirements of a particular area of ground could be arranged. But the whole question, it was stated, is one which has provided continual cause for disputes and even for armed conflict in many country districts. In Manchuria, where Koreans are involved in a dispute of this kind, it had even been cause for an international controversy.

> The cooperation — and quarrelling — which in the European village had their occasion in the maintenance of the common course of cultivation, and the regulation of the use of common pastures, meadows and woods by the Court of the Manor, in China finds its most striking expression in the control of water.[20]

The problem of water supply naturally differs in the various geographic regions, as a Chinese geologist showed. For the mountainous districts the problem is not serious, since each valley, as a rule, has its own natural supply; but for some delta lands and the northern plains where supplies have to be apportioned sparingly the difficulties may be greatly intensified. In southern and central China where supplies of water for rice culture are generally ample there is less need for governmental control than in the North and Northwest where water for irrigation purposes must in many cases be derived from wells and where, by a perverse trick of Nature, the risk of flood is ever present. But in both areas the difficulties are grave enough. Even in the rich rice-producing region of the Yangtze Valley, a series of dry years has so reduced the harvests as to necessitate huge increases in the importation of rice into China. For the farms on slightly elevated land lack of rain means crop failure; for those on the low-lying areas rain may mean the loss of crops through flood, as the year of 1931 has so tragically proved.

The converse aspect of water control is conservation or flood control. This aspect, as a Chinese member emphasized, is often of greater significance than the provision of water for irrigation. As a problem in administration it is certainly more important, involving, as it does, a vast amount of engineering and maintenance work, together with a complex system of financing and the difficult task of distributing responsibility for various functions among local and central authorities. For China, moreover, the problem is complicated by unique climatic peculiarities. A Chinese member said:

> " In this country about 70 per cent of the total annual rainfall usually comes in July and August. As this coincides with the period of highest temperature, it is all to the good. But unfortunately in many regions, especially in North China, the

[20] Tawney, *op. cit.*, p. 36.

rainfall is not constant from year to year. Worse than that, it often happens that half of the whole year's rainfall will come in two or three consecutive days, thus greatly increasing the chances of flood. Still another difficulty in the North is to be found in the huge volume of silt carried by the rivers. Attempts to build dams or reservoirs would only aggravate matters because they would silt up in a few years; and the raised bed of the river would merely increase the flood menace to the surrounding country. For this situation there is no exact parallel to be found anywhere else in the world; and there is consequently good reason for doubting the effectiveness in China of flood prevention methods adopted elsewhere."

Replying to a query as to whether a program of reafforestation of the denuded hillsides on the upper reaches of such North China streams as are most subject to flood was not an essential preliminary to flood-prevention schemes, he went on to say that it was doubtful whether such a program would prove as effective as is often believed or as it has been in other countries, on account of the loess country through which so many of these rivers flow. With the peculiar combination of the two factors — the soft loess soil with heavy rainfall concentrated in two or three days — it would be difficult to see how the delayed run-off and reduced erosion, which are the benefits normally to be expected from reafforestation, could have much effect.[21]

Apart from the question of water control, the denudation of hillsides is only part of a broader problem which engaged the attention of several groups in the Conference. This is the problem of the better utilization of hilly lands in China — a matter which was brought before the Conference as a whole in an address by a British geographer. Many foreign members visiting China for the first time expressed their surprise at the apparent neglect of upland cultivation in a country of such intensive cultivation as China. It is true, as a Chinese member stated, that in many parts of southern China these observations would not hold true, since mountainsides have been terraced up to great heights; but in much of central and northern China even low hills and broken country which cannot be used for the usual crops are left in rough grass which is cut and used for fuel. There was a generally expressed opinion among foreign members that some of this land could be effectively put under crops, and that the remaining portions would be of greater value if planted with trees than if left under grass. The former of these views is supported by scientific opinion. A student of the question has shown that in districts near Nanking, although the low hills are admirably suited to the growing of peanuts, sweet potatoes, and fruits, the supply of which is insufficient in the local markets, very few of the farmers are growing these crops.[23] Japanese members recalled that a similar discussion of the use of hilly country in Japan, where an excellent system of afforestation has been developed, had taken place at the Kyoto Conference in the round tables on food and

[21] See W. C. Lowdermilk, "Forestry in Denuded China," *Annals of the American Academy of Political and Social Science*, November, 1930, pp. 127–41, where a more optimistic view is taken.

[23] J. Lossing Buck, "Agriculture and the Future of China," *The Annals*, November, 1930, p. 111.

population.[24]   But in China, as in parts of Japan, the utilization of hill lands is bound up intimately with the fuel problem, the development of animal husbandry, and the improvement of communications, the last of which is fundamental for the modification of present conditions. Animal husbandry could undoubtedly be made profitable, it was urged, provided only a cheap fuel substitute could be found for the grass now gathered from the hillsides. These limitations have had a distinct effect on the cropping systems and again on the maintenance of soil fertility, since crops must be grown for their grain, leaf, and fiber products, and the hoarding up of all stubble and grass or stalks not only impoverishes the soil directly but prevents the keeping of livestock and, therefore, cuts off an important indirect means of soil improvement. The escape from this impasse, as shown by a specialist on the subject, lies either in railway and road developments which will permit coal to be transported cheaply to country districts at present without supplies or in a program of afforestation which will yield supplies of wood for fuel. Given these conditions, he felt that a great deal could be done to persuade farmers to make the necessary adaptations in the cropping systems and general farming practice.

Granting these serious limitations, it must still be recognized, as it was in another round table, that China already has in the northwestern districts a large pastoral industry where there is vast scope for improvement in feeding and breeding. Chinese members agreed that the wool industry of Suiyuan and the wool export trade of China have suffered great and often unnecessary losses through the absence of grading and testing of the products and the deterioration of flocks. The remarks contributed to the round table by Australian, New Zealand, and Japanese members showed that there is an ample store of practical and scientific knowledge, tried out under many different climatic and economic conditions, on which China might draw with profit if an organized attempt should be made to improve her pastoral industries. In Australia, remarkable increases in wool yields have been obtained from the use of small quantities of a newly developed protein substance — cystine — in feeding sheep; while in Japan, according to a member from that country, the use of the refuse of mulberry leaves (used in raising silkworms) for stock feed has resulted in decided improvement, both in the quantity and in the quality of the wool. Nearer at home for China are the results of the extensive researches in this field conducted by the experiment stations of the South Manchuria Railway, and the work done by the agricultural department of the Mass Education Movement in North China.

It was shown that outside of the pastoral regions of the Northwest, a great part of the animal population of Chinese farms is maintained for power purposes. Cattle and buffaloes are kept not for meat or milk but as beasts of burden, serving in place of the machinery which has superseded animal power in many sections of the Western world. In an industry as

[24] See *Problems of the Pacific, 1929*, p. 53.

seasonal as agriculture in North and Central China, with its long periods of winter idleness, the maintenance of unemployed animals on a farm is a serious drain upon the farmers' resources and constitutes at least one argument (out-weighed, however, by many opposing ones) in favor of a more general application of mechanical power to Chinese farming.

The animal labor on the farms is evidently not well planned, for while a man works an average of about 119 ten-hour days a year on productive enterprises, an animal works only about 63 ten-hour days, and it is a common sight to see a man toiling in the sun while his beast lies resting in the shade of a tree.[25]

Although the question of introducing modern machinery into Chinese farming was raised in this round table, no members expressed a belief that this would be an important factor in the immediate future. It was, of course, acknowledged that in newly opened country, where large holdings of agricultural land are common and farming is on a highly commercialized basis, tractors and other types of agricultural machinery may be used to advantage, as in fact they are in parts of Manchuria. For most of China, however, it was believed that only comparatively simple forms of machinery, such as cheap oil engines for pumping, and certain improved forms of agricultural implements as distinct from machines, which might be copied or manufactured without great additional cost in China, would lend themselves to widespread use. The great advantage of these simple forms of machinery was that they tended to relieve the demand for human labor at certain peak seasons of the year when all available man-power is needed in the fields for harvesting or transplanting. At such times, the use of mechanical power for working irrigation pumps or grinding grain would be very economical, more especially as a machine does not require to be fed, like a buffalo, when not working. Simple oil engines for such purposes, it was stated, are now beginning to have a fairly extensive market in the country districts where pumping is sometimes done by non-agricultural families at regular charges.[26] But in the main, there was agreement that no great progress can be expected in the application of Western machinery to Chinese farms, and that the absence of power machinery is perhaps one of the least of the obstacles to the amelioration of rural conditions.

" Progress in Chinese agriculture does not depend, as so many think, upon the introduction of the expensive farm machinery of the Occident. Farm machinery can only be well used to the extent to which it saves labor that might otherwise be profitably employed, or to the extent that it performs labor that the hand cannot do as well or cannot do quickly enough to enable operations to be carried out at the time most suitable for maximum production. Even then it will be found that much of the Western machinery is wholly unadapted to conditions in China, not only because of its expense in capital investment and operating costs, but because

[25] Buck, *op. cit.*, p. 112.
[26] See Chen Han-seng, " The Effect of Industrialization of Village Industry in Wusih," *The People's Livelihood* (Shanghai: National Christian Council, 1931), where it is estimated that over two-thirds of the families in the district use pumps for irrigation purposes.

of the small farms, the tiny fields, and the different practices. Possible exceptions to this are types of machinery for pumping water, particularly in rice-growing regions, and for threshing."

The fact that the small size and the scattered nature of the plots which compose them are among the chief hindrances to the introduction of even simple forms of machinery led the round tables by a natural transition to examine the possibilities of consolidating farm holdings, as has been done in Japan where similar conditions obtained in the past, and thence to the related questions of land tenure and the need for rural co-operation. The difficulties of abolishing the strip system, as described by a foreign member resident in China, are precisely those which had to be faced in Europe some centuries past. In a densely peopled area the system appears necessary to insure that the good land and the inferior land are fairly evenly distributed among all the farmers. Unless the process of consolidation were part of a broader plan for rural co-operation or communal or collective farming, it was considered that it would tend to disrupt the whole social organization of the countryside. Given these or similar safeguards and given careful advance preparation, however, a Chinese agricultural specialist gave his opinion that consolidation could be carried out in some areas. In Japan, according to an authority on the question, the process of consolidation has been effected under the provisions of the Land Readjustment Act, passed about thirty years ago, and the changes were only made in conjunction with carefully prepared plans for the provision of cheap credit to farmers, and engineering facilities for the improvement of drainage and irrigation. In spite of the difficulties, it was stated, and in spite of the great expense it involves, the practice is far from unknown in China. Foreign members with first-hand knowledge asserted that voluntary arrangements for consolidation of holdings are becoming increasingly common. Still more in the regions of West and South China, where the communist influence is strong, there have been many examples of land redistribution carried out on a large scale under local authority and sometimes involving the cutting-up of a large estate. A statement was made at another round table which touched on the matter, that definite experiments in collective farming have been made in some of the so-called soviet states in Central China.

While the round tables gave relatively little time to examining problems of land tenure, recognizing no doubt that the problem in China is dwarfed by the much greater one of credit and usury, there was an interesting connection traced in one group between conditions of tenure and the growth of the communist influence, already mentioned, in such provinces as Hunan and Kiangsi. Chinese members stated that these parts of the country have been remarkable for the high proportion of tenant farmers in their population and for the existence of a number of large landed proprietors, many of them absentee owners. In such a community where, with an extreme unevenness in the distribution of land and wealth, agrarian unrest had always been present, and which geographically had lain in the path of the northward advance of the

Nationalist movement when it was still strongly imbued with communist aims, the conditions were right for the development of the schemes of land redistribution and of collective agriculture which have since been put into force here and there. Such a connection between tenant farming and agrarian unrest is, of course, not peculiar to China, as was emphasized by a Japanese member who told of a similar condition in his own country. In Japan, however, the unrest has gradually crystallized into effective means of action and protest; and tenants have been able to organize farmers' leagues through which their demands can be voiced and which have been effective in some districts of Japan in securing rent reductions. Most members of the round table who recalled the agrarian history of Europe, while admitting the historical accidents which had made southern and central China good soil for communist propaganda, were disposed to the opinion expressed in one data paper:

The growth of counter-organization among peasants, with demands for a 25 per cent reduction in rents, the abolition of usury, establishment of provincial banks to make loans at low rates of interest, and freedom of combination — not to mention the more violent eruptions in Hunan and Kiangsi — is, in such circumstances, inevitable. In parts of the country the payment of rent is being refused; landlords have been driven from their homes; titles have been burned, as in 1381 and 1789; owners of holdings in excess of 300 *mow* [45 acres] have been required to hand over their property above that figure to the local peasants' association for distribution among poorer farmers. . . . No reference to communist propaganda is required to explain the no-rent campaign and peasants' revolts which have taken place in parts of the country. It is surprising, indeed, that they have not been more frequent.[27]

II. REMEDIAL MEASURES

Rural organization. — None of the round tables contented itself with a listing of the deficiencies in Chinese agriculture or of the grievances of the peasant. In all groups there was a consistent effort to take a constructive point of view and to examine practical possibilities of adopting new and reforming old systems and techniques. The numerous specific proposals considered may be summed up in the one phrase " improved rural organization," taking the words to include the social reforms of educational extension work and the development of co-operative movements as well as the more technical innovations of rural credit societies, marketing organizations, and schemes for the improvement of seed or livestock.

Of these schemes, the possibility of providing adequate credit facilities for the conduct of China's farmers was the first to challenge the notice of several groups. The problem here to be solved was recognized as one of the most burdensome that the peasant must endure. Indeed, it was shown that many of the disputes which appear on the surface to be concerned with land tenure are in reality disputes with a landlord who is primarily a moneylender. The appalling scarcity of capital and the tiny margin between the average

[27] Tawney, *op. cit.*, p. 54.

farm income and the basic requirements of subsistence are such as to plunge the farmer into debt upon the slightest misfortune. Even a wedding or a funeral may involve expenditures that will place the farmer in the hands of the moneylender for months or years. An instance was cited in one round table of a whole rich valley in which all the land had passed into the hands of three pawnshops in the town; and it was reckoned that for most of China all the land passed through the hands of the moneylenders on the average once in every thirty years. It was seen that the evil is rampant in almost every part of China, though it is to be found in its extremest forms in the frontier belts of Manchuria where the greatest need for capital tends to co-exist with the greatest scarcity in its supply.

As far as the poorer peasants are concerned, permanent indebtedness is the rule rather than the exception. They pawn their crops in summer, their farm implements in winter, and their household belongings throughout the whole twelve months. . . . An exceptionally good harvest is regarded as a doubtful blessing, since it is the occasion for the moneylender to call in his debts. The occurrence of forced sales is, in such conditions, inevitable. Next to drought, inability to meet the claims of the moneylender is said, in parts of the country, to be the principal cause of the ruin of peasant families.[28]

The remedy for the trouble, it was agreed, in China, is essentially that which has been found most efficacious in other parts of the world so afflicted, namely, the development of a system of rural co-operative credit. In this, it was shown, China has already made a promising if small beginning, thanks in large part to the energies of the China International Famine Relief Commission. According to a statement made by a foreign student of the movement, some 900 societies have been organized since the scheme was initiated in 1923, together with six unions. Of the societies, almost all of which are in Hopei province, 227 have been recognized as fulfilling the conditions laid down by the Commission, while the rest are still awaiting recognition. A total of $172,000 (Chinese currency) has been issued in loans to the societies by the Commission. As an example of the slight outlay needed to perform effective work, the speaker made reference to a loan of $5,000 on the basis of which 19 societies had been organized under the supervision of the Department of Agriculture at the University of Nanking, most of the credit being extended for productive and marketing purposes. In recent years the good example set by the Commission has induced some of the provincial governments to initiate similar schemes, notably in Chekiang and Kiangsu. Loans amounting to a large sum have been made, but the great difficulty has been to secure competent leaders for the societies. The same handicap has been mainly responsible, he said, for the failure of the newly established Farmer's Bank to do as effective work as might be expected. The bank has been set up by the Kiangsu Provincial Government with a capital of $3,000,000, but has not functioned altogether satisfactorily. Its loans have been made

[28] Tawney, p. 49. For conditions in Manchuria see the extract "Rural Conditions in the Colonization Areas of Manchuria," printed above, pp. 86–94.

at the relatively low rate of 10 per cent, in contrast to the more customary rates of 20–25 per cent; but the bank has taken the easier path of lending to merchants who not infrequently find it possible to re-lend at higher rates, rather than of dealing directly with the farmers or the credit society as was originally intended. The difficulty is not easy to avoid, since the contacts between banks and the merchant community are much better established than those between the banks and the agriculturalists who are completely unaccustomed to such a type of credit. A further difficulty, it was stated, is the danger of making interest rates low enough to be of real benefit to the farmer and yet high enough to prevent the re-lending which is encouraged by too low a rate. In spite of these and many other serious handicaps, some of which can be ascribed wholly to political disorder and banditry, the societies have been remarkably satisfactory. Losses on loans have been exceedingly slight, and interest payments have been maintained in the face of great handicaps.

Elsewhere the point was brought out that certain other banks and financial institutions in Shanghai are taking a much deeper interest in the possibilities of agricultural financing. The inevitable risks attaching to farming and the long period of waiting between sowing and harvest have everywhere made it difficult for ordinary commercial banks to engage in this type of work; for this reason, members of two round tables listened with special interest to the account given by Japanese members of the elaborate arrangements for the financing of the co-operative movement in Japan. There, it was said, something like 13,000 societies with a rural membership of nearly 4,000,000 are included under the system. At the top is a special Central Financing Institute of Co-operative Associations, set up about seven years ago and empowered, because of its financial standing, to borrow from other banking institutions and to lend to credit associations. In addition there are numerous philanthropic and voluntary credit organizations which provide funds for their members without interest. In the banking world the interests of the co-operative credit movement are the care of the Hypothic Bank with its subsidiary agricultural mortgage banks in each of the 47 prefectures.[29] The movement in Japan, according to the report given, is not merely concerned with the provision of cheap credit, but is designed to foster schemes for co-operative buying and marketing by rural communities and for the co-operative purchase and use of agricultural machinery.

The point was stressed in another group that co-operative organizations in China, whether for credit, for the purchase and use of implements, or for irrigation schemes, have this great advantage over many other schemes for rural improvement — that they are not absolutely blocked by the lack of transportation and the absence of educational facilities. It is true, as one member argued, that some forms of it, such as co-operative marketing schemes, must wait upon the development of roads and railways before they can grow to their full importance; but for other forms, as experience has already shown,

[29] For a recent concise account of the system see H. G. Moulton, *Japan: An Economic and Financial Appraisal,* pp. 173–74 and 186–91.

effective progress can be made, given only a little initial capital and organization. So too, it was acknowledged, the lack of elementary education in China has seriously inhibited the development of all those valuable social by-products which have so greatly enhanced the value of the movement in Japan, Denmark, and Germany, for example, and which many students consider indispensable for its success. Without education there is the danger, described by a Chinese member with some experience in the matter, that wealthier farmers or officials will exploit their neighbors in the name of co-operation, or that private and illegal concerns will spring up which borrow funds nominally for co-operative purposes but in reality for the purpose of re-lending at extortionate interest rates to ignorant farmers. Nonetheless, it was stated, the co-operative society is itself an important educational agency, and the success of the societies organized by the Famine Relief Commission has been largely due to the care that has been taken to explain to the farmer some of the broader aspects of co-operation.

The provision of cheap credit and the elimination of superfluous distributive charges are not the only benefits which cooperation confers. Its educative influence is more fundamental and far-reaching than the immediate financial and commercial advantages accruing from it. By organizing the rural population, it creates a temper of mutual confidence, a consciousness of common needs, and a habit of collective action. In time, it may be hoped, it will enable the peasants in China, as in other countries, to carry their proper weight in the public affairs which affect them and in the conduct of which they appear today to be sacrificed without compunction. There is no movement on which a group of men who desire to improve the life of the farmer can engage with greater certainty of producing permanent results.[30]

In contrast to voluntary co-operative movements, it may be asked whether large-scale collective farming has not many of the technical advantages and economies of co-operation. This question was raised in one group, but a foreign member who described the system now in force in parts of the Soviet Union felt somewhat skeptical as to the benefits which it might bring if it were applied to China, in spite of its undoubted successes at home where conditions in many districts are specially conducive to its application. For China, he believed, the only suitable part of the system would be that in vogue in some regions of Russia, where farmers combine to work land under contract for the state, although they own their own homes and tools. Information on the part of other members as to the working of the collective farms reported to have been organized in Hunan and Kiangsi provinces was unfortunately too scanty to be at all conclusive.

The problems of education which have been touched upon in the foregoing paragraphs on rural co-operation continued inevitably to occupy a great deal of attention in the round-table discussions of China's rural problems. A distinction was drawn between the educational needs that arise from the prevailing illiteracy and circumscribed experience of the greater part of

[30] Tawney, *op. cit.*, p. 77.

China's farming population, and those more specialized needs that call for the training of leaders, teachers, and scientific research workers, all of which are urgent if the basic problems of Chinese agriculture are to be tackled effectively. In addition to these two types of educational requirement, it was realized, there must be a means of linking them together, so that the results of training and research can be brought to bear upon the lives and work of the rural population. From the discussions which took place in the various groups it was apparent that agricultural education in its more specialized sense is far from sufficient to meet even a portion of the demands which it would have to meet if a determined effort were to be made for a program of agricultural reconstruction. Agricultural departments in some universities have made an excellent beginning but are inevitably handicapped by lack of support from the larger extension work which calls for governmental action. In the field of scientific research, a great part of the work on agricultural problems has been financed not from ordinary government revenues but from special funds, such as those of the China Foundation, or from private university funds. Such major pieces of agricultural research as the taking of an agricultural census, the carrying-out of a soil survey, the systematic recording of climatic data, are either not yet contemplated by the governmental agencies which will ultimately have to finance them, or are only beginning.

The present research work on Chinese agriculture is taken up by two kinds of organization, namely, the agricultural college and the agricultural experiment station. There are altogether twelve agricultural colleges in China, of which three are national, six provincial, one private, and two American missionary institutions. On account of political upheavals, the national and provincial colleges have had little chance to do research work, and if there is any, it is very elementary. With regard to the agricultural experiment station as an organization for agricultural research, the condition is not much better. At present the Ministry of Agriculture has under its direct administration eleven agricultural experiment stations; a general agricultural experiment station, four experiment stations, one tea experiment station, three farm animal experiment stations, and two experiment stations. These are all the important stations in China, not including those carried on by agricultural colleges.[31]

Recollecting the complaint so often laid at the door of scientific agricultural institutions in other countries, that they do not bring their work into direct relation with the ordinary practice of the farmers, the members of one round table felt strongly that great attention should be paid in China to the organization of farm demonstrations. In this connection, an American member gave an account of the system worked out in the United States. He said:

" This development began in the period 1905–10, at a time when farming in many parts of the country was still conducted along very primitive lines with poor seed selection, shallow ploughing and general carelessness in the improvement of crops. The agricultural farm demonstration which was then introduced at the initiative of the U. S. Department of Agriculture takes place on a typical farm on

[31] R. Feng, "Agriculture," *Symposium on Chinese Culture,* chapter xiv, p. 272.

which normal labor is employed, but to which the best technical advice is given with the consent of the farmer who however furnishes the labor and pays for all supplies. The effect in all the southern states has been extraordinary. It has been estimated that if the improvements produced by these farm demonstrations were uniformly applied throughout the southern states of America, an additional production worth $300,000,000 annually would be added to the present output. At first it was difficult to find farmers with sufficient imagination, but in a year or two the benefits became visible in doubled or tripled production, and the attention of neighbors was attracted. The more general instruction followed, and so the spread, especially in those states that were suffering from the cotton-boll weevil and had to learn how to protect themselves against it, mainly through crop rotation and variation. The technical knowledge on such schemes as this is available here in China. Clearly the best way to improve farming methods is to have good examples rather than exhortation. What is needed is not charity but advice. A remarkable effect can be produced by Government co-operation with private persons."

With these remarks there was general agreement. A Chinese member pointed out that the value of such schemes was being fully recognized in China. The Government had already instructed provincial authorities to establish at least one experiment station in each province, though this instruction had not yet everywhere been carried out. But even where experiment stations had been set up they did not always work well, particularly because so far they had gone along the wrong lines, such as introducing foreign seeds instead of helping farmers to experiment with a better selection from their own seeds. This was intended as a short-cut, but the results had not been satisfactory. Corn seeds were distributed that had been obtained in the United States, and the poor crops obtained were discouraging, as the officials had not sufficiently noticed differences in conditions. Last spring a delegation of visiting experts came to the experiment station in Suiyuan, headed by a graduate of the University of Nanking. In spite of the financial straits of that province, the results were good. Excellent work, according to the same speaker, was being done in a few other small centers, notable among them the Tinghsien experiment of the Mass Education Movement, the agricultural work of Lignan University of Canton, and the farm demonstrations set up under the auspices of various missions in Honan, Hopei, and Shantung provinces. But as this and other Chinese members repeatedly stated, the great need is for men with the necessary technical training and at the same time the necessary familiarity with conditions of Chinese farming. It is in research and the training of workers rather than in direct dealing with the farmers that foreign individuals and foreign scientific institutions can be of greatest assistance to China, and it was in this field, according to another Chinese member, that the foreign missions had rendered excellent service. Among these foreign institutions the University of Nanking, through its College of Agriculture and Forestry, has done more for agricultural research in China than any other. Hitherto the number of foreign agricultural experts in China had been regrettably small, but it was now reported that the Government contemplated making arrangements for such help under the auspices of the proposed Supreme Economic Planning Commission. Even with such assistance, however, a major problem was the working-out of a system of mutual co-operation between foreign and Chinese research workers. Without a basis of mutual confidence much of the value of such work would be lost. It was perhaps for this or a similar reason that the excellent research work conducted by the experiment stations of the South Manchuria Railway had not been put to the use it deserved.

Because of its remarkable attempt to co-operate intimately with the farmer, the work of the Mass Education Movement in Tinghsien, Hopei, attracted considerable attention. Here, according to the description given by two foreign members, a whole Chinese district with a population of 400,000 has been taken as a demonstration area, and many of the principles adopted in the United States farm demonstrations have been followed. Improved techniques and improved types of seed or livestock are demonstrated on the ordinary Chinese farms, great care being taken to see that the improvement invokes no additional cost for the farmer. Once the value of an improvement has been demonstrated to the satisfaction of the farmers, a process of extension is initiated, and instructions are broadcast through the district by an elaborate system of traveling schools and lecturers, in the process of which the active co-operation of thousands of peasants and their children is enlisted. Greater perhaps than the immediate economic value of the experiments is their fundamental educational significance.[32] A British member gave his impression of this phase of the work in these words:

" Most of all, I was impressed with the atmosphere and the methods of the whole enterprise. It is strictly practical — a living experiment going on all the time, not merely the expounding of dogmatic theory. The Mass Education Movement is in close touch with the people. It has many workers living in the surrounding villages or workers who visit these villages every day. Mr. Yen and his workers have taken the large point of view, namely, that they must make contacts with the people at all points — not in farming alone, but through education in many other things. The campaign for literacy was the starting-point, for it was realized that you cannot get far without it. Then there was worked out an improvement of tools so that farmers may make other improvements for themselves. The destruction of pests was co-operatively worked out. To do all this the farmers must be able to read and write. Small societies for chicken and pig breeding were started. The members of these also began to feel that they must be able to read circulars and keep records. In these societies the members are often provided with selected eggs on condition that they keep the fowls apart from others and keep egg-laying records. There is also much medical and general educational work going on together with the other. The whole problem of agricultural improvement is here seen as part of a general system of raising the standard of life of the agricultural masses."

Still another type of work in which foreign assistance of several kinds may be enlisted is the process of supplying fertilizers and improved seed varieties. Although the value of these activities was apparent, there was an inclination on the part of both foreign and Chinese members to stress rather the need for concentrating on the improvement of indigenous varieties and the perfection or modification of existing Chinese practices — things which can often be done without the expense which so often takes the foreign fertilizer

[32] For other principles adopted in the movement see R. Feng, *op. cit.*

or improved implement out of the ordinary poverty-stricken farmer's reach. The application of imported artificial fertilizer to Chinese soils which are systematically bared of all organic matter every year had not always been attended with good results, in the opinion of a student of the problem who cited the matter as an example of the need for scientific research before elaborate experiments are made for the improvement of crops or herds. On the other hand, a foreign member told of excellent work being done, admittedly not always out of disinterested motives, by foreign fertilizer concerns in South China, where agricultural demonstrators and instructors work in collaboration with salesmen of the firms, enlisting the interest of the farmers. Similarly, it was stated that a good beginning had been made in centers such as the University of Nanking, the Mass Education Movement, and the research organizations of the South Manchuria Railway, as well as in parts of the program of the Famine Relief Commission, with the development and distribution of improved seed varieties designed either to increase yields or to withstand unusual climatic conditions.[33] It was stated by Chinese members that one of the first large industrial enterprises which the Government plans to undertake under its new ten-year plan is a large concern for the manufacture of artificial fertilizer. The purchase and marketing of fertilizer, it was shown, is an activity which might lend itself well to rural co-operative action, as it has done in other countries.

The development of rural industries. — The bad distribution of human labor over the year was repeatedly shown to be an important reason for the low income and relatively inefficient organization of Chinese farming. Partly for that reason and partly because there was no great confidence among most members that large-scale industrial developments would prove to be the way of economic salvation for the country, the round tables devoted a great part of their time to examining how far and along what specific lines China might profitably attempt the development of the many handicraft village industries which are to be found in every province, and the introduction of useful new enterprises. The discussion was reinforced with an abundance of examples of parallel developments in other countries. A Chinese member stated the need for China as follows:

"We must try to develop types of rural industry that require skill and technique and for which raw materials are available. For such industries we hope to utilize not only the spare labor of farmers but unemployed labor throughout the year. A farmer may have members of his family who are not needed for the cultivation of the farm. Throughout the year part of the labor of the whole family is available. In the district of Kao-Yang in Hopei Province, for instance, cotton weaving has been developed as a home industry. There is native weaving in the home of almost every farmer throughout the year, though of course there is more in winter than in summer. In Shantung we have, in the same way, straw-hat-making, farmers using their own materials throughout the year with the aid of members of their family. So in the west suburb of Tientsin, artificial flower-

[33] See Leonard M. Outerbridge, "Seeds for China's Arid Areas," *The Annals*, November, 1930, p. 99; South Manchuria Railway, *Second Report on Progress in Manchuria, to 1930*, pp. 159–62.

making is a home industry. The Government should promote only those rural industries that require skill and local raw materials. But there still remain the questions of credit and marketing. In some rural industries in China, the farmers are
exploited by middlemen. In most cases, cotton is supplied by these, and the product
is sold in a distant market. Scarcity of capital means that the farmer must rely on
credit from the middleman. There are a few other credit agencies, among them
small loan shops where the rate of interest may be from 30 to 75 per cent monthly,
and where the product serves as security for the loan. This is only another element
of exploitation. Credit and marketing on a co-operative basis, therefore, are most
necessary for the growth of village industries."

A list of the various home industries mentioned in the course of the discussion may serve to show how great the possibilities for improvement are,
granted there be a suitable arrangement for credit and marketing. In addition to those mentioned in the above statement, other members referred to
pottery, basket-making, strawbraid-weaving, the making of hairnets and lace
in Shantung and Hopei, wool-weaving in Suiyuan. It was shown that such
industries have naturally developed most, and ought to be capable of most
extension, in those provinces of North China where the long winters make
the problem of seasonal unemployment on the farms more serious than in
South China where agricultural work can be carried on all the year round.
The problem in North China, it was stated, has already caught the attention
of various individuals and institutions, and formed the subject of an important paper and a discussion at the Conference on the People's Livelihood
held in Shanghai during February, 1931.[34]

A description of the steps that had been taken to revive home and rural
industries under wholesome conditions was given by a British member. He
said:

" There is little strictly co-operative work in the peasant industries of Ireland.
The peasant education department and private associations have trained people in
weaving, embroidery, and other crafts, but no big co-operative movement has
grown up in these products as it has in eggs and dairy products. The example of
England is more instructive; especially during the last few years we have had good
experience in combining governmental and volunteer action. The aim here is deliberately to develop and re-establish rural industries. The movement started
with the realization that in an industrial country men who are pivotal to rural life
are constantly being lost to the countryside. The village smith, for instance, has
almost disappeared. Hence a conscious effort has been made to develop crafts in
ironwork subsidiary to the regular work of smiths to make it possible for these men
to make a living. On the women's side, there is the development of weaving, embroidery, and similar crafts, largely due to women's institutions in close touch with
the Government. There is also a development of basket-making, saddlery, and
woodwork, very much like that of ironwork. A government bureau of rural industries operates with funds granted by the Development Commission under the Treasury Department, but quite independent of any other government bureau, engaged
partly in the organization of rural industries and partly in research. This bureau
particularly is endeavoring to improve designs and marketing facilities. It issues

[34] See J. B. Tayler, *A Policy for Small Scale Industry in China*. Shanghai: National Christian Council, 1931. An abstract is printed in *The People's Livelihood*,
pp. 52–58.

catalogues and forms guilds of producers for marketing purposes. English experience is not as developed, however, as Swedish experience, which is the most valuable model for China to study. There is a determined effort in that country to build up rural industries and to link up this work with efforts to strengthen the rural community life through village and county committees."

His remarks were supplemented by a Filipino member who spoke of the home weaving industries in Luzon which, however, had declined a great deal with the importation of cheap cotton cloth from China and Japan. In the vicinity of Manila, he stated, the making of embroidery by women had grown into an industry of quite important dimensions, maintaining an export trade with the United States. At the present time the importance of rural industry found recognition in the education system under which provision was made for instruction in basket-work and embroidery.

In view of the objections raised by some members to elaborate plans for the encouragement of these industries, on the ground that they would inevitably be short-lived and follow the fate of many existing crafts by succumbing before the competition of factory-made goods, considerable interest was shown in the statement made by a Japanese agricultural expert on the scheme worked out in Japan where competition from large-scale industry might be expected to be very severe. It was understood from his remarks that the strength of the movement in Japan derives from its close association with other forms of rural co-operation.

" With the advent of industrialization, all the industries carried on by peasants are taken out of their hands and taken to cities. Japan has been no exception in this historic development. So in rural districts where there are many people and not enough arable lands, our people too are underemployed. There is an abundant supply of labor, not only in winter but during the whole year. The average farm employs three persons, but two suffice to conduct the farm business. On an average, therefore, one man's labor on every farm is not sufficiently exploited. We already have an extensive cultivation which, with the law of diminishing returns, cannot easily be made more intensive. If more were produced from the farms, prices would be lower, so that the farmers would not benefit. Our Government, therefore, has thought it necessary to let the farmers have supplementary industries. A special division for this purpose was created in the Department of Agriculture. The amount of production through such supplementary industries is over 100,000,000 yen annually. There are two kinds of rural industries: (a) those that cannot compete with factory industries; (b) those carried on mainly on the ground that they can support themselves in competition with capitalistic industries. Many of our rural industries belong to this second class where the processes of manufacturing require artistic skill or where the raw material is easily supplied by farmers themselves, and where the cost of labor is lower than it would be in the cities, through the use of underemployed farm labor.

" Our experience suggests three possible systems of rural industry: first, let the peasants themselves make articles in their own homes and sell them through a co-operative agency; second, let them build their own factory and supply the labor from peasant farms. This has been accomplished in Japan in raw silk filatures. Formerly the farmers sold their cocoons to the capitalist factories, but the price fluctuated so much and the farms suffered so heavy losses that they gradually resolved to run these factories themselves. There are quite a number of these co-operative raw-silk factories staffed with farmers' daughters, where the profits are divided among the cocoon raisers. Because of the keen competition of these co-operative shops, the capitalist filatures are gradually changing their policy and trying to get the good will of the cocoon raisers through profit sharing. This method originated over thirty years ago. It has not developed into capitalist enterprise, and we firmly believe that these co-operatives can hold their ground. In fact, capitalist enterprise is losing ground and has been unsuccessful in efforts to buy these co-operative filatures which have a central office from which they sell to America. The factories run throughout the year as a rule, though in some districts the mill is closed in January and February. Labor is collected in one place, but the people are not forced to stay in dormitories as is the case in capitalist industries where the living conditions of farmers' daughters are often unsatisfactory. In these rural industries, the aim is not profiteering, but the co-operative industries are run by the fathers of these girls themselves. In the third place, there is a system of contract in which a portion of the goods made in large-scale industries is sent to farmers to be worked up, and then returned to be finished at the central factories. Such a contract system may be beneficial or it may be detrimental. It may exploit the labor of farmers or add to their income. The contract system is flourishing in certain parts of Japan. Some city manufacturers, disgusted with strikes and sabotage, thought it advisable to have part of the processes carried on in peasant homes. Particularly near Tokyo, in this way many rural families are supplied with goods to be worked up. This also is the old system which still exists near some weaving mills."

The statements made by various members familiar with conditions in China would nevertheless seem to indicate that the spread of factory industry has already meant the death or the crippling of formerly flourishing village industries. A Chinese member stated that the weaving of grass cloth and the making of shoes and stockings had declined greatly in the face of competition from machine-made articles. In other industries, of which the hairnet industry of Shantung is the outstanding instance, the failure to maintain standards of quality in conjunction with a sudden change in fashion in women's styles of hairdressing had had even graver effects. The view that this kind of fate was inevitable was, however, challenged by certain Chinese members who maintained that with reasonable assistance at first, preferably in the form of co-operative organizations for financing and marketing, there need be no fear of ruinous competition from the factory. They also insisted that experience had proved the possibility not only of maintaining existing crafts and of introducing new types of work but also of reviving defunct or decadent industries. They admitted that with world tariff policies in their present condition, the prospect of finding good foreign markets for such handicraft products was not encouraging, but pointed to the large and valuable market within China itself.

China would be badly handicapped in comparison with Japan, it was argued, since she would be unable for a long time to come to rely upon the inestimable benefits of the cheap electric power with which the latter country is abundantly supplied. For this reason it was believed that Chinese rural industries would not be able to compete effectively, as had apparently been possible in many Japanese village industries, with the products of the factory. Rather they would be obliged to center their activity upon comparatively simple products which can find a ready market among the farmers themselves, or on special articles which call for a high degree of skill and taste, and which it would not be profitable to imitate by machine methods.

A final objection, or rather a warning, which was urged upon the members of several groups concerns the social dangers which may arise in rural industries unless good safeguards are devised. Many members, recollecting the history of domestic industries in the early stages of industrialism elsewhere in the world, urged that great care would be necessary to prevent a rural industry from becoming surrounded by all the ills of sweated labor, exploitation of child labor, and the like, which are to be found today in the domestic and semi-industrialized industries of Tientsin and Shanghai. Parents, it was recognized, are likely to prove harsher employers than the ordinary industrialist; and since members were aware that hours and conditions of work for women and children are already bad in most Chinese agricultural life, there was some reluctance to encourage a system that might perpetuate those conditions under a new guise without bringing the compensations that are sometimes associated with them in large-scale industry.

To enumerate difficulties is easy. The round tables, while not denying their existence or their gravity, nevertheless concluded with a definitely expressed belief that along this road lay one of the most promising escapes from the present agrarian distress which affects all China. In the rural industries, it was perceived, the benefits of co-operation could find one of their best forms of expression, and in this field the difficulty which besets the plans for large industrial programs — namely, the provision of huge amounts of capital by the floating of foreign loans — is largely if not wholly absent.

Once cooperation is firmly established, it can be extended from agriculture to the crafts carried on in connection with it. In view of the long periods of enforced idleness to which the farmer is exposed — he is said, in parts of China, not to be employed for more than a hundred days in the year — by-employments which supplement his income ought obviously to be encouraged. In the majority of European countries, and particularly those with a large peasant population, rural industries carried on in the cottages of the workers still play a more important part than is commonly realized. In China the impression of a superficial observer is that hardly a district is without one or more of them. The dexterity, ingenuity, resourcefulness and, above all, sense of beauty of her common people are a social and economic asset of inestimable value. The course of wisdom, it may be suggested, is to build upon them. It is to retain, where possible, as Professor Tayler urges, the small productive units which are the traditional form of industrial organization in China, but to secure for them the advantages of large-scale methods in finance and commerce, by taking steps to promote the formation of cooperative societies for credit, marketing and the purchase of raw materials.[35]

In most of the round tables which considered this and similar channels of improvement for Chinese agricultural society there emerged at last an appreciation of the fact, at first rather queried by some foreign members fresh from the economic ills of an overproducing Western world, that for some

[35] Tawney, *op. cit.*, p. 76.

time to come China's problem is essentially that of increasing her production of goods and services, of growing more crops — and that notwithstanding the present glut in the bean markets of Manchuria — of weaving more cloth and building more roads, bridges, and railways.   China, it was admitted, has her problems of unequal distribution, but the inequality is founded not upon a surfeit but upon a scarcity of commodities.   For that and for other obvious reasons, her economic problem is the betterment of her country people rather than the vanquishing of foreign competitors in the markets of the world or the building of a new industrial machine to rival the nations of the West. It was with the realization that these rural needs are the paramount ones that members of the round tables took up the discussion of transportation and of those necessary forms of large-scale industry which are treated in the following chapters.

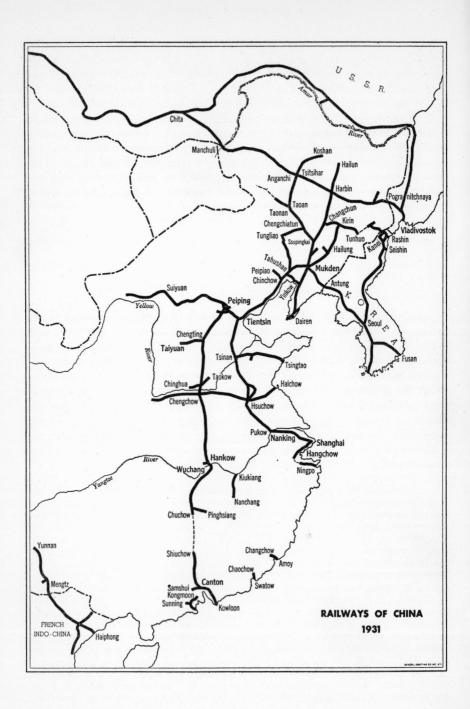

RAILWAYS OF CHINA
1931

CHAPTER IV

COMMUNICATIONS

DATA PAPERS

1. R. H. TAWNEY. *A Memorandum on Agriculture and Industry in China* (International Research report), pp. 68–70.
2. *Syllabus on China's Economic Development*, pp. 42–48.

REFERENCES

1. G. E. BAKER. "Transportation in China," *Annals of the American Academy of Political and Social Science*, November, 1930.
2. A. VIOLA SMITH. *Motor Highways in China*. Washington: United States Department of Commerce, 1931.
3. SOUTH MANCHURIA RAILWAY. *Second Report on Progress in Manchuria, to 1930* (Dairen, 1931), chaps. iii and v.
4. *Statistics of Chinese National Railways, 1915–1929.* Nanking: Ministry of Railways, 1931.

INTRODUCTORY NOTE

It requires no argument to show the essential significance of communications and transport as factors in the economic development of China, and it required but an hour or two of discussion in the round tables on China's economic problems for members to realize, sometimes with a sense of futility, that all large-scale attempts at reconstruction depend for their success upon either the attainment of political stability or the development of communications — each of which was waiting upon the other. Again and again in discussion members were forced to the conclusion that a particular improvement, say in agricultural technique or in industrial methods, can be achieved only with a better system of communications. The all-pervading character of the problem is well expressed in one of the data papers:

It is needless to dwell on the economic paralysis which such conditions produce. It was recently found that the cost of transporting 1,400 tons of wheat, for the purpose of famine relief, a distance of 233 miles in Shansi, by carts and pack animals, was 79 cents silver per ton-mile. If moved by tractors and trailers, it would cost approximately 13 cents; it could have been hauled by rail, had a railway existed, for just under two cents. Mass production is obviously impossible unless the output can be marketed, and, in the absence of communications, industrial development is necessarily strangled. The effects upon agriculture and rural life are equally serious: The farmer has no incentive to increase his production if he cannot be certain of disposing of it; owing to the impossibility of choosing his market, he is liable to be bound hand and foot to the local dealers; the specialisation of different regions to different types of farming, with the economies which it offers, is impracticable, as long as every district must grow its own supplies of food; the recurrence of local famine is inevitable, since the deficiency of one area cannot be supplemented by the surplus of another. Motor roads can be built piecemeal without the heavy capital expenditure required for railways, and are somewhat less liable to be rendered completely useless by civil disturbances. Hence, in the view of good judges, it is by the extension of roads, rather than of railways, that these evils are to be overcome;

and since unemployed labour, in the shape of soldiers, is abundant in China, the extension of roads should present no great difficulty. But what is obviously required today is the extension of both, the latter as trunk routes for mass traffic, the former as feeders. The urgency of the need can hardly be overstated. To the layman it appears that the most effective way of aiding China to attain both a larger measure of economic well being and political stability would be an international loan, with the necessary safeguards against undue interference in her internal affairs, for the purpose of enabling her to improve her means of communication.[1]

Yet again in many indirect ways the effect of communications or the lack of them makes itself felt on the political and cultural life of the people as well as on the economic organization. It was argued, for instance, that the better use of uplands in China for grazing purposes is not possible in some areas until cheaper coal for fuel is available for the farmers who now cut the grass from the hillsides. But cheaper fuel and a more efficient mining industry in China in many instances lie waiting for the fuller development of roads and railways or for conditions insuring a more efficient use of the existing ones. So, too, in the unification of language, of tastes, of currency, and of political control, the road, the motor bus, and the railway are the most potent forces known, as was in fact pointed out by a conference member with an extensive knowledge of the economic development of the Netherlands East Indies.[2] That the present Government of China is well aware of the fact is also evidenced by its efforts at modern road construction and by the Good Roads Exhibition held in Shanghai shortly before the opening of the Conference. At the Exhibition the benefits of good roads were given publicity in the following slogans:

1. Good roads reduce the hardships and increase the pleasures of travel, thereby enabling people to go about more freely.
2. Good roads save the time and energy of travelers, so that they will be able to accomplish much more in a given period of time.
3. They tend to lower the cost of transportation very materially by the use of trucks or wagons.
4. They encourage the development of trade and promote economic prosperity.
5. They facilitate the preservation of peace and order to the community, such as bandit suppression.
6. They expedite the dispatch of all forms of emergency relief, such as the transportation of medical and food supplies during famines and similar catastrophes.
7. They facilitate the exchange of ideas in education and commerce.
8. They tend to unify the spoken language, thereby removing misunderstandings and localisms by broadening the outlook of the people.
9. They encourage tourist trade.
10. They develop " auto-mindedness," which will materially assist in the unification of the country.

---

[1] R. H. Tawney, *A Memorandum on Agriculture and Industry in China*, pp. 69–70.

[2] See also A. D. A. de Kat Angelino, *Colonial Policy*, II, 269 ff.; F. V. Field and E. B. Field, " Methods of Marketing," *Filipino Immigration*, pp. 431 ff.; J. B. Condliffe, *New Zealand in the Making*, chap. ix; A. G. Whitlaw, " Control of Transport," *An Economic Survey of Australia;* Harold G. Moulton, *Japan — an Economic and Financial Appraisal*, chap. v.

EXTRACTS FROM DATA PAPERS
I. TRANSPORTATION IN CHINA [3]

The present status of communications in China may be summed up briefly by saying that the country now has rather less than 9,000 miles [4] of railways, of which over two-thirds are government lines; between 35,000 and 40,000 miles of roads, not indeed improved motor highways, but roads including caravan routes over which motor vehicles have been known to travel; a considerable length of excellent navigable rivers, and a vast network of canals whose length has been estimated at roughly 40,000 miles.

Table I (p. 118), which lists the principal Chinese railways with their mileages, gives too rosy an impression of the true conditions. It will be observed that about a quarter of the length of all lines is in the hands of concessionaries and private owners, and that two of these lines, the Chinese Eastern Railway — under joint Sino-Russian control — and the South Manchuria Railway — under Japanese control — have an importance which is greater than the mileage figures would suggest. About 43 per cent of the total mileage is in Manchuria. Still more significant is the fact that four out of the seven principal trunk lines in the rest of China, namely, the Peiping-Hankow, the Peiping-Suiyuan, the Lunghai, and the northern and southern sections of the uncompleted Canton-Hankow line, are in such a state of disrepair or have lost so much of their rolling stock, as a result of successive civil war and banditry, that their commercial utility is but a fraction of what it should and could be. Locomotives and cars have been commandeered by military officials and have not been returned. Those lines which have tried to maintain services have been crippled with exactions levied on them by local generals and corrupt officials. It was reported on official authority in 1929 that various armies were taking the huge sum of over two million dollars monthly out of the Government railways in the form of freight and protection charges.[5] The present Minister of Railways, speaking at a conference on railway transportation held during March, 1931, made the following statement, according to press reports:

The various railways are now on the verge of bankruptcy, the total obligations amounting to the staggering figure of more than $1,000 million. According to reports submitted by the Shanghai-Nanking Railway Administration, it has to provide almost $3,000,000 this year to meet loan obligations and several million dollars for the purchase of new rolling stock. The number of freight cars available on the Peking-Hankow line has dwindled from 4,000 to 1,000.

[3] Extract from the *Syllabus on China's Economic Development*. A number of minor revisions and additions have been made on the original *Syllabus* in order to bring the information more nearly up to date. The table of railway mileages has also been added.

[4] See note, p. 118.

[5] Quoted in *Economic Conditions in China to September 1st, 1929* (London: H.M. Stationery Office, 1930), p. 23.

TABLE I *

RAILWAYS IN CHINA, 1931

Lines in Manchuria	Miles	Kms.	Lines in China Proper	Miles	Kms.
A. Government railways:			A. Government railways:		
1. Ssupingkai-Taonan (including branch to Tungliao).........	264	465	20. Peiping-Mukden (Shanhaik-wan to Peiping).............	265	426
2. Taonan-Anganchi...........	139	224	21. Peiping-Hankow............	822	1,321
3. Tsitsihar-Anganchi..........	15	24	22. Tientsin-Pukow............	690	1,106
4. Tsitsihar-Koshan...........	98	158	23. Kiaochow-Tsinan...........	283	453
5. Hulan-Hailun..............	137	222	24. Peiping-Suiyuan...........	543	876
6. Kirin-Changchun...........	79	127	25. Taokow-Chinghua..........	95	152
7. Kirin-Tunhua..............	130	210	26. Lung-Hai (including Kaifeng-		
8. Kirin-Hailung..............	113	182	Honan line)...............	512	823
9. Taonan-Solun (portion already			27. Shanghai-Nanking..........	204	327
built)†.....................	62	100	28. Shanghai-Hangchow-Ningpo	178	286
10. Tahushan-Tungliao (branch of			29. Chengting-Taiyuan.........	152	243
Peiping-Mukden).........	156	251	30. Hupeh-Hunan (including Chu-		
11. Peiping-Mukden (Shanhaik-wan to Mukden including branches to Yinkow and Peipiao)...................	388	627	chow-Pinghsiang line).......	318	513
			31. Canton-Shiuchow (including Canton-Samshui line)......	171	274
12. Mukden-Hailung...........	202	326	32. Canton-Kowloon...........	90	143
			33. Kiukiang-Nanchang.........	79	128
			34. Swatow-Chaochow..........	26	42
			35. Changchow-Amoy...........	18	28
Total government railways...	1,793	2,876	Total government railways...	4,445	7,141
B. Concessioned railways:			B. Concessioned railways:		
13. Chinese Eastern...........	1,069	1,730	36. Yunnan (Chinese section)....	288	464
14. South Manchuria (including			37. Canton-Kowloon (British sec-		
branches).................	689	1,110	tion).....................	29	46
Total concessioned railways..	1,758	2,840	Total concessioned railways..	317	510
C. Private and light railways:			C. Private and light railways:		
15. Kaiyuan-Hsifeng...........	39	63	38. Sunning Railway...........	84	135
16. Muling Colliery............	37	60	39. Other industrial lines (ap-		
17. Tumen-Tienpaoshan........	68	110	proximate length)...........	93	150
18. Penchihu Ironworks........	9	15			
19. Chinchou-Chengtzutung.....	63	101			
Total private and light lines..	216	349	Total private and light lines..	177	285
TOTAL FOR MANCHURIA.....	3,767	6,065	TOTAL FOR CHINA PROPER..	4,939	7,936

All government railways....... 6,238 miles   10,017 kilometers
All concessioned railways...... 2,075   3,350
All private and light lines...... 393   634
GRAND TOTAL................ 8,706   14,001

* Statistics of mileage differ somewhat according to various definitions adopted and according to the inclusion or exclusion of double track and sidings. In this table these are excluded, and only main and branch lines are included. The figures have been compiled from *Statistics of Chinese National Railways* (Nanking, 1931); *The China Year Book* (1929-30); and Julean Arnold, *A Commercial and Industrial Handbook of China* (Washington, 1926), p. 317.
† Estimate. Construction still in progress.

With the exception of the Manchurian railways, the only lines which have maintained anything like an ordinary service during the last three years have been the Shanghai-Nanking, the Shanghai-Hangchow (not yet completed to Ningpo) — both of which have remained under the effective control of the National Government; the Peiping-Mukden — which, since October, 1929, has been under a unified administration at Tientsin; and the British section of the Canton-Kowloon line. And though they have maintained a service, it has often been far from efficient or profitable. The Manchurian lines have been relatively free from these evils, but inasmuch as they serve an exporting region which is more sensitive than the rest of China to the world economic depression, and as the finances of the two principal lines are based on a gold currency, their revenues for 1930 have declined seriously.

The tragedy of all this is that most of China's railways, given half a chance, are exceedingly profitable enterprises. As expert observers have often pointed out, their operating costs are low, and even with poor rolling stock and a permanent way in bad repair, they are capable of yielding a handsome profit, provided only that they are freed from the clutches of military officials.[6] More important still is the influence they exert on the economic progress of the districts which they serve, and on the whole of China's foreign and domestic trade.

The same things may be said of road development in China. It has, indeed, been urged by many people that China ought to concentrate on road building rather than on developing expensive systems of railway transport which have often proved uneconomical in other countries. They point out that motor roads are easily and quickly constructed in China and, unlike railways, do not require a huge outlay on capital equipment and on operation and repair. On the contrary, they provide an excellent opportunity for utilizing the services of many millions of unemployed or half-employed unskilled workers in China. It is hardly to be expected, however, that they will completely take the place of railways in a country of such long hauls as China, but they can undoubtedly be used to serve as feeders to trunk lines and save a great expenditure of capital on the construction of small branch railways. As long as great and populous regions like Szechwan, Kwangsi, Fukien, and Shensi provinces are wholly or almost wholly without railway communications, and as long as a glut of agricultural products can exist while famine is rife within five hundred miles, it is idle to minimize the urgent need for railway construction or to suggest that China can skip the railway age in her industrial revolution.

Outside of the four Eastern Provinces, there has been no important railway construction in China for a number of years. The only recent work has been the extension of the Lunghai line running west through North China. In Manchuria the principal construction has taken place on the Hulan-Hailun line, running north from Harbin; on the line running north and northeast from Tsitsihar to Koshan; on the line which now joins Kirin and Mukden, permitting a direct connection on Chinese railways between Shanghai, Peiping, and Kirin; and on the similar connecting line between Taonan and Anganchi on the Chinese Eastern Railway. It is possible that the next major piece of construction will be the completion of the 250-mile gap on the Canton-Hankow line, for which the greater part of the remitted British Boxer Indemnity funds may be used. It is clear, in any case, from the railway conference held in March, 1931, and the railway traffic conference held at Mukden in

---

[6] See, e.g., G. E. Baker, *Explaining China* (London, 1927); *China: A Commercial and Industrial Handbook,* pp. 273 and 309; *The Annals,* November, 1930; also below, pp. 126 ff.

February, 1931, that the National Government is directing serious attention to the improvement and extension of China's railway communications.

There is, indeed, no surer way to effect the political and economic stabilization of China. Roads and railways are the prerequisites for all other developments — as much for China as the former were for the Roman Empire and the latter for the Germany of the nineteenth century. They are the only escape from the Chinese vicious circle in which economic progress is barred by political leaders and civil war, and political stability is impossible while economic chaos and distress are rife. The improvement and extension of communications is at once a defensive weapon in the hands of the central Government, an opening for the employment of the vast floating population of soldiers, "communists," and bandits which have preyed so long on the peasants of China, and an instrument for enriching the material and cultural life of millions.

II. MODERN ROAD DEVELOPMENT IN CHINA

ADDRESS BY C. S. LIU
Former President, Chinese Eastern Railway

The Chinese have been a people that since time immemorial have appreciated the value of good roads. It has always been considered a great virtue for anyone to contribute to building good roads and bridges, but roads in the modern sense have not been built on a large scale until twenty years ago, at most. This is because modern roads require much greater organization and finance for construction.

Road development in our country today has definitely become a movement and carries all the features of a movement. It is of spontaneous growth. We have road activities all over the country. It is not evenly distributed, but in certain areas in the north, south, east, and west, and along the coast, developments are taking place. In the south we have Kwangtung, in the southwest, Kweichow; in the west, Szechwan; and in the north, Shansi. Around Shanghai, we have the roads of Kiangsu and Chekiang. To the movement as well as to the neighboring provinces, these provinces give stimulus and inspiration.

I will describe briefly, first, the road construction of the provinces, and, second, the plan of the central Government. We have never had a good system of collecting statistics, but we have been making efforts for a number of years, and according to our present information, the total mileage of roads is about 35,000 miles for the different provinces. These are not entirely new roads. They include old roads or postal roads. This figure includes all the roads on which a motor truck can be operated. Some are bad even for an old Chinese cart, but on most of them a motor truck can go at slow speed.

The road extensions carried out by the different provinces are all entirely modern roads. There are about 5,000 miles of these provincial roads, and many of them are in the process of being completed. These roads are scattered all over the country, either forming part of a national trunk line or serving local interests, perhaps connecting two towns twenty to thirty li apart, for instance.[7] The administration of these roads is centered in one department — the Department of Public Works. Each province since 1928 has a Bureau of Reconstruction, the commissioner being a member, usually, of the Provincial Commission.[8] Most of the roads are unsurfaced mud roads, though some have surfaces of gravel or stone. Inside the cities, 90 per cent are stone-paved or graveled roads. In Nanking, Shanghai, Hangchow, and Peiping you will find macadamized asphalt roads. The decision has been made to construct long country roads without a surface, for we cannot afford surfacing for the time being, and even gravel is too expensive.[9]

The construction usually is undertaken by human labor. Very little machinery has been used until within a year or two, when some American machinery, such as caterpillar tractors, has been introduced to a small extent.[10] Many roads have been built by the China International Famine Relief Commission, which has been said to be the earliest promoter of modern roads in our country. It has constructed roads in a number of districts and has stimulated local leaders to build roads.

Of the 35,000 miles of country roads, a very small percentage have been utilized for private motor traffic. The driver of any motor car can make his vehicle into a bus and put it on the highway, much as a ricksha, for hire. There is an immense unregulated competition, and the traffic is in confusion with nobody making any profit. This does not mean that the traffic would not pay: it is a highly paying proposition in such a densely populated country, provided the service is organized, centralized, and highly regulated.[11] That has been shown by the service of the Chekiang Highway Administration, which owns about 150 busses and 50 motor cars. The service is well organized, and even with a low fare it still pays a good maintenance charge and something besides.

The characteristics of our road traffic are rather different from those of other countries, following the differences which are to be noted in our railways. For instance, in America only part of the railways pay. Passenger traffic does not pay, while freight loadings do. In China the reverse is chiefly the case. In China the movement of goods on the highways is potentially important. The question for this country is not one of speed but of

---

[7] One li equals about one-third of an English mile.

[8] Some provinces, in addition, have a well-organized Highway Bureau, within the Bureau of Reconstruction, in charge of a special director of highways.

[9] [An authority on Chinese road construction comments: " This statement of policy is no longer quite representative. Highway officials and others have learned that it is wasteful to have a dirt road which is out of use for long periods of bad weather. Several provinces, such as Szechwan and Kiangsu, are therefore now endeavoring to surface the roads they have, even though it be only with a crude water-bound macadam, instead of extending the mileage of dirt roads." – Editor.]

[10] See below, p. 126.

[11] Further discussed below, p. 125.

low cost. A Fordson hauling a train of four trucks, going on a mud road at a speed of ten miles, about three times the speed of a horse car, carrying about a ton of cargo, would about meet the needs of our country, provided the rate was cheap.[12] The goods traffic is as promising as the passenger traffic, provided both services are well organized. . . .

In 1927 the central Government made a plan for the building of 23,000 miles of highways covering the whole country. These lines were divided into two categories: the first to be built were lines in China proper; and in the second period lines were to be built to the frontier. It was hoped to build these in twenty years. This is not much for twenty years, but we planned this with due regard for our financial resources. The total cost for gravel-surfaced roads will be 364,000,000 silver dollars. The immediate requirement for ten years in China proper will be 170,000,000 silver dollars. The Government has laid down specifications for these roads, as is done with the building of railways and purchase of rolling stock, so that they will follow a uniform standard. The two questions facing the Government are, first, that of finance; and, second, that of technical experience. It will require a large engineering force qualified in road engineering, and today we do not have very many skilled men. I am taking this first because what is being done is that the different provinces have sent students to America to be trained in the bureaus of public roads. Now we are also contemplating a plan of engaging an American road engineer to give engineering courses. For instance, we have three engineering colleges, Shanghai, Peiping, and Canton. Accordingly we want to train engineers representing these different parts of the country.

The question of finances is pertinent. At least we must have a revolving fund to start with. It would depend entirely on the increase of income from the roads themselves in the form of increased taxes, motor-car licenses, or tolls. These methods are all practicable but require time. But we need at once a fund to start road building. A plan for this has been suggested, namely, that the Ministry of Finance give for road building a part of the customs duties collected on gasoline and other motor-vehicle necessities. The amount of the revenue from these sources is now, I think, well over ten million dollars.

To build a provincial line which may be part of a trunk line, a province is expected to contribute a share — the other part to be given by the central Government. In this way, it is hoped, a practical financial program can be worked out on a minimum-requirement basis. For the present, the plan under the central Government is held in abeyance due to lack of funds. The practical system of co-ordination with the provincial governments has not yet been fully worked out; but in some sections progress has been made.

[12] [It may be pointed out, perhaps, that according to some authorities the high cost of gasoline in the more remote interior of China would go far to offset the advantages of tractors. — EDITOR.]

QUESTIONS FOR ROUND–TABLE DISCUSSION

The following questions were recommended for discussion as part of the Program Committee's agenda on " China's Economic Development ":

1. What should be the relation between the programs of railway and road development, and what is their place in the total scheme of communications in China?
2. What are the possibilities of concentration at this time on the development of internal waterways as the cheapest form of transport facility as far as initial capital is concerned?

SUMMARY OF ROUND–TABLE DISCUSSIONS

The three round tables which gave attention to the problem of communications in China did so on consecutive days, with the result that at least two members, one Chinese and one Japanese, who were thoroughly acquainted with the subject were able to be present and submit statements at two or more different round tables.

I. ROADS

By a fortunate division of labor, one round table at which no specialist on railways was present devoted most of its time on the third day of its meetings to a discussion of road construction in China and of the relation between road and rail communications. The subject was opened by a statement from a foreign member who had given a great deal of study to the problem and was familiar with the Government's plans of highway construction:

" A glance at a map of China's modern road system will show that so far the greater part of the highways are to be found in the northern provinces. There are certain historical and geographical reasons for this fact. Transport in the southern provinces is partly taken care of by a well-developed canal network. In the north the dry climate and flat ground and the existence of many old-style cart roads made it much easier to proceed with modern dirt-road construction. A map will also show a series of short roads radiating from many provincial capitals but as yet not linked up with a system of trunk highways, as much of the road building until the last few years has been done by various provincial authorities without reference to a national plan. There has thus been a lack of co-ordination; but it should be remembered that practically all road building in China belongs to the last decade, and it is therefore encouraging to find that over 35,000 miles have been constructed already. It is still difficult to get information even regarding the existence of roads in certain parts of China. Not many people know, for example, that with the exception of two small gaps, amounting to about 75 miles, there is now a motor road all the way from Nanking to Lanchow, the capital of Kansu Province in the far west of China." [13]

[13] See p. 132. There is not at present available a thoroughly reliable road map for the whole of China. However, in the preliminary mimeographed edition of *Motor Highways in China,* by A. Viola Smith, later published by the United States Department of Commerce as *Motor Roads in China,* Trade Promotion Series No. 120, the interested student will find almost complete materials for the mapping of China's road system.

It was shown that a great deal of the lack of co-ordination between local road systems is to be explained by topographical difficulties in some regions. Szechwan was quoted as a province in which there are some 1,500 miles of new roads but no connection by road between Chengtu, the capital city, and Chungking, the chief port. In such mountainous country, according to a Canadian member resident in China, the costs and engineering difficulties are such as to make it impossible for villages and local authorities to execute the work. For the completion of these roads special financial and technical aid would be required. Such aid, according to several members, is coming from a source which, in other respects, has been a cause of severe handicap to the development of China's system of communications: the military leaders. Thus, in Szechwan a highway has recently been laid by military engineers and military labor over a high mountain range to provide one of these missing connections. Similar road work has been undertaken by military leaders in Kweichow, in Kwangsi, and elsewhere, without financial or technical assistance from the central Government, but using such Chinese engineering assistance as they could get and, of course, military labor. Although theoretically a case could be made out for a system of " federal aid " as a necessity to speed up national road building on a commensurate scale, some members familiar with the conditions did not see much hope that the Government would soon be in a position to render such aid and pointed to the many examples of excellent roads built without it by local civil and military authorities as showing a possibility of progress in spite of the many existing difficulties.

In some cases roads have been constructed, for military purposes primarily, by chambers of commerce which agree to finance the building of roads at the request of the generals because it is less expensive to do this than to pay the levies which the military men will otherwise exact from them. Elsewhere roads have been built by contractors at the request of interested merchants and business men who are willing to pay for construction costs by a system of toll charges. The same thing applies, it was said, to the motor services which utilize the new roads: some are managed by private concerns under charter, others are operated by provincial authorities, while the province of Chekiang, through the Highway Bureau in its Department of Reconstruction, operates its own fleet of buses between the provincial capital Hangchow and the neighboring country.

Discussions in several groups of the methods used for the actual labor of road construction brought out the fact that the troops of local military men had been widely used in such provinces of North China as Shansi, Honan, and Hopei, and also in certain regions of South and West China. According to a Chinese member, it was the aim of the central Government and provincial authorities to make the fullest possible use of this source of labor and also to utilize road-building schemes as an effective way of overcoming the dangers incident to the disbandment of large numbers of soldiers. In other parts of China, where roads have been built under the auspices of the China International Famine Relief Commission, the labor of famine or flood refugees has been utilized. But recruitment of labor from the villages by the local authorities with varying degrees of compulsion has been one of the commonest methods employed. In this connection, a Chinese member chose to point out that road construction, at least in some regions, has been attended by a great deal of hardship inflicted (sometimes without good reason) upon the common people through whose villages new roads have been constructed. Provinces like Kweichow and Kwangsi in Southwestern China have often taken the able-bodied members (including, in some instances, women and children) of village families for compulsory labor on roads at places far removed from their homes, so that the farms suffer from the absence of necessary labor.[14] Moreover, in these cases the roads have been built without proper regard for the needs of the country. Kweichow was mentioned as an example of a province that has a great many miles of road but has only one motor vehicle, and is so completely cut off from the rest of China that the cost of gasoline is prohibitive. The example was stressed by the speaker as indicating the paramount need for a centralized system of road planning.[15]

Only little time was given by the round tables to a discussion of what a few of the members considered perhaps the outstanding reason why road transportation is not more developed in China, namely, the unreasonable and shortsighted taxation, on the one hand, of motor vehicles and, on the other, of commodities in process of transit. The chief difficulty of Kweichow, it was said, was the prohibitive cost of gasoline due to repeated taxation in transit on the Yangtze River before it reaches the terminal point of the provincial mountain road. Coal is brought to Peiping on camel backs, it was stated on another occasion, because this archaic mode of transportation avoids the exactions of military officials who control the highways. Such exactions were also given as an explanation why up-to-date bus services for passenger transportation are not more frequently found on Chinese highways: the smallest appearance of prosperity, it was suggested, under the present unstable conditions, invites heavy exactions. Toll fees, again, in some cases, are so high as to discourage the operation of private motor vehicles.

Associated with impositions that at least outwardly take the form of

[14] Under a national highway law, adopted at the suggestion of the Highway Planning Commission of the central Government, farm labor may be requisitioned, except during the harvest season, for new road building. Such compulsory labor may not, however, be employed for road maintenance.

[15] The statement made at the round table concerning Kweichow was subsequently disputed by an authority familiar with that region and its recent history: " Kweichow up to 1926 was an isolated mountainous province in Southwestern China, without outlet to either river or sea. An enlightened Chinese military governor set about building roads. These roads, though crudely built, have given the province an outlet to the Yangtze River, permitting quicker transportation than it ever knew before. The progressive governor was killed, and his program was abandoned. Military strife broke up some fifty motor vehicles that were in the province. Under a new régime established in recent months, a tax exemption was declared for the first one hundred motor vehicles to be registered in the province during 1931. By the end of the year there were about seventy motor vehicles in the province."

taxation, there is, according to one student of the subject, the widespread evil of petty graft. This was held responsible, in part, also for the small progress with the use of machinery in the building of roads.[16]

" Steam road rollers, usually of British or German make, were first introduced, followed by narrow-gauge industrial railways with dump cars. In a few instances, American tractors and road-building graders have been purchased; but much of this machinery is lying idle. The reason is that grafting officials cannot make as large a rake-off from its use as they can from operations with human contract labor."

The needs and the available resources of China, in short, are such as not to call immediately for an expensive system of metaled roads, but rather for extension and stability. Others agreed with the statement made by Mr. Liu in his address (see p. 121), that high speed for vehicles is not an essential in the interior of China. Nearly all the new roads are accordingly of a simple construction, which serves quite well for the great dry areas of northern and northwestern China, and has the advantage of being quickly constructed and easily repaired. Many more miles of such dirt roads, the introduction of motor vehicles with a low fuel consumption, and exemption of highway transportation from unreasonable taxation and exactions were seen as the outstanding needs in the near future.

II. RAILWAYS

The problems of railway development in China are not primarily economic problems, as was demonstrated by a Japanese member who opened one round-table discussion. The country's railway systems are not faced, like those abroad, with the constant threat of financial loss through competition from other forms of transport. He said:

" Railway enterprise in China is one of the most profitable business propositions in the world. There are several reasons for this. The first is the low cost of construction, as the existing railways run mostly through flat country and across only a few large rivers, a fact which incidentally serves to keep the cost of operation to a more or less low figure.

" Second, the general public does not make any serious complaint of poor service in railway traffic. For instance, goods are transported at the owner's risk, and a watchman is hired by the owner to travel with the goods in transit. In the winter time one often comes across a few watchmen in fur coats huddling together on a wagon, attending their job day and night, even when a blizzard is raging. They travel on the same wagon with the goods on the way out, and obtain third-class return tickets, free of charge, from the railway.

" Third, the wage of employees is also very low, the lowest monthly wage amounting to but $14. When the workers went on strike some time back to enforce demands for an increase in wages they asked particular consideration for those who had received no promotion whatsoever for the last ten years.

" Fourth, the mileage of the railway system in China is exceedingly small in proportion to her population as well as her area. A comparison with various countries is made in Table I.

[16] See p. 12.

TABLE I

RAILWAY MILEAGE

Country	Kilometers of Line per 100 Square Kilometers	Kilometers of Line per 10,000 Persons
Japan.................	4.7	2.9
Russia................	1.0	5.0
Germany..............	12.4	9.2
America..............	4.3	37.9
England..............	12.5	8.1
France...............	9.7	12.0
China................	0.1	0.3

" At present there are no parallel lines, outside of Manchuria, which compete with one another, and the only rival service is the steamship line on the Yangtze River plying between Nanking and Shanghai. To show how profitable the railway undertakings in China are, the Peking-Hankow Railway — 1,030 miles — realized in 1918 a revenue of \$23,822,621 — against an outlay of \$7,977,853, the latter representing only 33.1 per cent of the former. The net profit amounted to \$15,-844,767, which is about 15 per cent of the cost of road and equipment, \$100,250,927. In the same year the revenue of the Peiping-Mukden Railway — 806 miles — was \$20,853,532, and the expenditure was only \$6,903,148, the percentage being 33.5. The net profit amounts to \$13,950,384, and, the construction expense being \$61,-438,097, the percentage shows the pleasing figure of 22.7.

" As to the South Manchuria Railway which, though it has only 750 miles, gains the greatest profit in China, the revenue was 122,103,742 yen, and the expense was 47,213,508 yen in 1929, so that the percentage is only 38.7. The net profit amounts to 74,890,234 yen; this is 28.6 per cent against the construction expenditure of 261,882,378 yen. It must, however, be noted that in spite of its gain of large profits by the South Manchuria Railway, the second reason mentioned above regarding poor service must be excluded. The accommodations over the South Manchuria Railway are not inferior to those in Europe or America. But on account of the protection furnished by the Japanese army and the scientific management of its operation, the net profit, with only 750 miles, is much greater than the revenue of all the Chinese Government railways, with a total of 7,679 miles. This comparison is made on the basis of a conversion rate of 100 yen equal to \$100 Chinese currency, while the present actual conversion rate is nearer 100 yen equal to \$200.

" For these several years, however, the Chinese Government Railways Administration has not been able to avail itself of its facilities to the fullest extent. The fact that the revenue of the Chinese Government Railways in 1929 was less than the revenue of the South Manchuria Railway, which had only one-tenth of the mileage, was largely the result of the devastation brought about by disastrous wars. Twenty years ago the Manchu dynasty was overthrown by the republic of China. Since the organization of the present Government, however, civil war in China has never ceased. . . .

" Chinese generals, in order to obtain funds, took over the railways, which form the largest enterprise in China, confiscated the income, and used the funds which had been reserved for the purposes of construction and improvements of the railways in the future. The railway bridge on the Hwang Ho River, which is 2.5 miles long, was built with many difficulties and was guaranteed safety for only fifteen years. The Peiping-Hankow Railway, therefore, reserved \$1,000,000 every year for a reconstruction fund. This fund, however, was confiscated by one of the generals, and the fifteen years' safety guaranty term for the bridge expired eleven years ago, so that it can stand the running of trains only at a ricksha speed.

" The generals, not satisfied with the confiscation of the income and the reserve funds, levied special surtaxes on the passenger and freight fares of the railways under their jurisdiction. For instance, they levied on goods several kinds of taxes, totaling from 40 to 510 per cent of the freight rates, which differ according to lines. The average surtax on all railways is about 140 per cent of the freight rate. Sometimes generals undertake railway operation themselves and demand extra payments for supplying cars. They have paid no attention to repairs, so that the railways have deteriorated badly.

" The greatest loss to the railways in China proper was the carrying away of 6,212 units of rolling stock to the Three Eastern Provinces in 1927 by the order of Chang Yin-huai, Vice-minister of Communications at that time. . . . The total of 6,212 units of rolling stock consisted of 400 locomotives and 5,812 passenger and freight cars, and is estimated to comprise half of the rolling stock in the area north of the Yangtze River. 5,231 units of rolling stock are still retained in the Three Eastern Provinces, only 981 of them having been returned. . . . Later on, 25 locomotives, 24 passenger cars, and 500 freight cars were newly built; and though these newly built cars have superior efficiency to the rolling stock carried away, the difference in the number of cars is too big to cover the loss.

" The above facts will explain clearly how profitable the railway enterprise in China might be, given a strong central government. It would not be difficult to make the income increase to $200,000,000 if several million dollars were spent for rehabilitation and improvement under a stable government. The working expenditure is capable of being reduced to 50 per cent of the gross income, so that it would be very easy to gain a profit of one hundred million as a net profit. It may be added, however, that China has a debt of about six hundred million yen which, converted at the present rate, amounts to twelve hundred million dollars. Unless the Ministry of Finance devises ways and means to redeem half the debt through the general accounts, though the net profit amounts to $100,000,000, the redemption of the debt of principal and interest will remain quite a different question."

There was some questioning of the interpretation to be given a table of figures presented by the speaker which showed a gradually rising but still exceedingly low proportion of operating expenses to operating revenue. Certain members of the round table contended that if interest on debts or dividends to stockholders or adequate allowances for depreciation were included, it would be found that the financial position of most lines was decidedly precarious. More important than that, as another Japanese asserted, much of the revenue figures made known by the railways represent, not cash but merely cash entries, since payments due from military commanders have not been made in reality. The first speaker agreed that the figures did not tell the whole story. He maintained, however, that despite this fact his original remarks on the profitable nature of the railways would still apply in anything like normal times.

The round table in which this discussion occurred followed it by an examination of the layout and distribution of the main lines over China. Illustrating his remarks by reference to a map, a British member pointed out the three or four great trunk lines — first, the line running from Harbin in North Manchuria to Peiping and Tientsin in North China and connecting with the trunk line running south through Eastern Central China to Nanking and Shanghai.   To the west of this is the system connecting Peiping to Hankow, and designed to continue south to meet the line running north from Canton, though there is still a gap of 250 miles to be completed.[17]   It had been left unfinished not because of engineering difficulties, as had been suggested by another member, but because of lack of funds and of political disturbance. In a program of new construction, he suggested, the first obvious steps would be to close this gap, to link the trunk system with the existing short line from Kiukiang to Nanchang by building a line across from Changsha to Nanchang, as had long been proposed, and perhaps later to proceed with the construction of a third trunk system running through western China, which was without railways, into Szechwan, obviating the dangers and difficulties of river transport through the Yangtze gorges.

Reference was made in another group to this uncompleted section of the Canton-Hankow line, and certain members asked for information concerning the popular understanding that the British Indemnity funds would be applied to this purpose.   British members stated that the plan was not clear in certain details, but that out of the £3,000,000 which has already accumulated payments may be made for railway materials to be ordered in Great Britain.   One said:

" The Willingdon report contemplated some form of economic investment but really advocated the use of the funds for education.   The situation seems to be that the payments already accumulated can be used for rolling stock, and that of the annual instalments to come, one-half will be put under the control of the Purchasing Commission, and one-half will go to trustees in China ' for educational and other purposes,' whatever that phrase may mean.   It is clear, however, that some form of economic development is envisaged, though the funds should be regarded primarily as an endowment for educational purposes."

A Chinese member cognizant with the plan stated that the Government proposed to set aside two-thirds of the funds which would be at its disposal for rehabilitation and completion of the Canton-Hankow line.   Of the other third, 20 per cent would be used respectively for electric-power enterprises, irrigation schemes, and conservancy work in the Pearl River.   The remaining 40 per cent of this third part would go for the Hwai River conservancy scheme. According to the understanding of another member, the Government also had in mind using a part of the fund for the completion of the line between Hangchow and Ningpo.

The plan had not been devised as well as it might have been, in the opinions of some foreign members resident in China.   They stated that many people are unaware that the Chinese Government has over a period of years drawn up a fairly definite plan of railway building and of the order in which various lines should be started.   It was therefore very awkward to have the use of the Boxer Indemnity fund restricted by so many conditions.   It would be very difficult to apply the fund to the projects which came first on the Government's program, as long as the Government was tied by conditions

[17] See also below, p. 131.

obliging it to use the fund from any one country for railways already built by, or originally reserved for, construction with the capital of that country. Moreo·.er, the necessity of purchasing rolling stock in different countries would make it impossible to standardize the equipment on different lines in China.

In the minds of all those members competent to make comparisons, there was no doubt that the Government railways had deteriorated badly in the last twenty years, and that many lines were not far from going completely out of commission, owing to lack of attention to bridges and permanent way. One speaker, indeed, remarked that it was a tribute to the builders of the lines that these had been capable of use so long after effective maintenance work on them had ceased. He continued:

"I have travelled over most the railways of China, before the war in 1912 when they were in their heyday, in 1918, and again in 1931. In 1912 the Chinese railway system was in excellent shape: roadbeds were good, rolling stock was adequate, and the administration was efficient. It was an impressive sight to see the mountains of grain and other produce that lay awaiting shipment. The same conditions obtained fairly generally in 1918. But in 1931 there is practically no cargo to be seen; farmers have found that they cannot get their produce carried. Equipment has depreciated everywhere; sleepers [ties] are broken, bridges are dangerous, rolling stock and locomotives are old and out of repair. Yet, in spite of such conditions a fairly punctual service of sorts is maintained. There is no doubt that the Chinese have learned the technique of running railways even under the most trying conditions."

These opinions found a parallel in another group where a Chinese member with long experience in railway administration pointed out several interesting differences between Chinese and foreign railway problems: In other countries most lines earn the greatest revenue from freight traffic, but in China the third-class passenger traffic is all important and is alone sufficient to make the lines pay for themselves. It could hardly be otherwise when they serve such thickly populated regions. He said:

"Considering the nature of the traffic and the highly monopolistic position of most Chinese railways, it would easily be possible to enforce rate policies which would bring in a great deal of revenue and yet be exceedingly beneficial to the majority of the people. Almost any line which gets freedom from war conditions cannot help but pay."

He went on, however, to urge criticisms of some points of current railway policy. On most lines the freight charges on agricultural products were too high to correspond with the Government's ideas of agricultural development. For many such products, he thought, the interests of both the farming population and the railways themselves would be furthered if other lines followed the example of the Peiping-Mukden line in reducing such charges by 25 or 35 per cent. It had been found that the increased tonnage resulting from such a step more than compensated for the lower rates, so that net revenues were on the whole larger. Such a policy could be of great indirect benefit to mineral and agricultural production in the interior of the country and, as some foreign members of the group pointed out, had been widely adopted in other countries, like Australia and Canada, even when it involved some financial loss to the railways. Further discussion revealed that the Chinese Eastern Railway had also experimented successfully with rate reductions, inasmuch as the railway route became increasingly used for commodities that had previously been transported by boat or cart or caravan. Not the least of the benefits which might be expected from an enlightened policy concerning rates on agricultural produce would be the encouragement of direct dealings between farmers, or groups of farmers, and the railways, eliminating some of the expensive and oppressive system of middlemen and dealers who now robbed the farmer of much of his profits.

III. CO–ORDINATION BETWEEN ROAD AND RAIL COMMUNICATIONS

Notwithstanding the defects and lack of uniformity which were revealed in the previous discussions, it was shown that the National Government has in recent years drawn up a very farsighted set of principles for the future development of both roads and railways. It hopes to profit from the lessons learned in other parts of the world by avoiding unnecessary and wasteful competition between the two systems of transport. A Chinese member familiar with the recently formulated plans for China's national highways thus stated the main principles:

1. The highways should traverse the most populous and productive districts.
2. They should pass through the most important commercial centers of the provinces.
3. They should act as feeders to railway lines.
4. They should be the most economical, both in construction and in maintenance.
5. Provincial highways, either already built or definitely scheduled for construction, should be linked together to become national highways, whenever their importance warrants.
6. Projected railways, if not likely to be built in the near future, should first be built as national highways.

The last named of these principles was considered in the light of several examples. It is best illustrated, according to one authority on this subject, by the road over the projected Canton-Hankow Railway. There is a break at present between the Hankow-Changsha and the Canton-Shiuchow sections of this railway, of about 250 miles. The Hunan Highway Bureau has built a highway, which is now in use, from Changsha to the border of Kwangtung; the province of Kwangtung is now building, to meet it, a highway from Shiuchow. Another illustration is the highway constructed in Shantung on the railway bed originally surveyed for the Chefoo-Weihsien line; the Peking administration in the old days opened a bus service over this line which, it was said, is still running. There was reference also to a road running from Sianfu to Lanchow on a line projected many years ago for a railway. Parts of this line, it was stated, however, can hardly be described as available for traffic. A highway exists from Lingpao, the end of the Lunghai Railway, through Sianfu to Lanchow; but in several sections it has mountain grades of 25–30 per cent. Motor trucks have made this route, but usually they have to be pulled over these hills by bullock carts. The China International Famine Relief Commission has before it a project, it was reported, to cut down these grades.

In these and other projects the principle is recognized that new roads shall not parallel railways already in existence or likely to be constructed in the near future. Thus also the recently finished highway of 230 miles between Nanking and Hangchow will serve a rich section of the country without competing with any railway; and the new road planned to link Shanghai and Nanking will run through towns not at present touched by the railway.

Though little attention was given to the point, it was taken fairly much for granted by those who participated in the discussion that for a long time to come the development of railways, roads, and canals in China could proceed without serious overlapping. Rivers and canals would still be profitable for the transport of bulky and non-perishable goods; roads would serve as freight feeders to the railways and as special passenger routes; railways would be needed for the long hauls and for perishable and costly goods. At present, the high cost of gasoline in the interior, which is in itself a by-product of the poor development of rail communications, tends to make motor transport so expensive, it was said, that only a few commodities whose value is high in relation to their bulk can profitably utilize the roads.

Apart from the obvious benefits of improved roads and railways and of better co-ordination between the two, there is an incidental financial benefit which evoked some discussion in the round table. It was shown that the poor development of communications into the interior of China, with the consequent necessity for repeated transshipments of goods from railway to cart, to junk or barge and to porters or pack animals, has almost certainly encouraged the growth of a stifling system of local transit taxes. With the development of through traffic by railways and with the extension of trunk roads, these would be much easier to abolish, since goods could be examined and taxed once only, at the port of entry, with economies both in the tax administration and in the handling of the goods. The question was taken by the round table as an illuminating illustration of the ways in which, without conscious planning, the development of communications could overcome those political and social particularisms which have long beset the path of national unification in China.

It was further pointed out that, given political stability, road construction can be financed as it goes along out of the revenues which it makes possible; this important form of national development does not, therefore, compete with the railways, mines, and industries for foreign capital.

CHAPTER V

INDUSTRIAL DEVELOPMENT

DATA PAPERS

1. H. D. FONG. *China's Industrialization: A Statistical Survey* (China Council).
2. R. H. TAWNEY. *A Memorandum on Agriculture and Industry in China* (International Research report).
3. AKIRA NAGANO. *Development of Capitalism in China* (Japanese Council).
4. FRANKLIN L. HO. "Industries," *Symposium on Chinese Culture* (China Council), chap. xv.
5. C. F. REMER. *Foreign Investments in China* (mimeographed, International Research report).
6. *Syllabus on China's Economic Development*, Secs. III and VII.

REFERENCES

1. H. D. FONG. *Rayon and Cotton Weaving in Tientsin.* Tientsin: Nankai Institute of Economics, Nankai University, 1930.
2. H. D. FONG. *Hosiery Knitting in Tientsin.* Tientsin: Nankai Institute of Economics, Nankai University, 1930.
3. H. D. FONG. "Industrialization and Labor in Hopei with Special Reference to Tientsin," *Chinese Social and Political Science Review*, April, 1931.
4. TA CHEN. *Study of the Applicability of the Factory Act of the Chinese Government.* Shanghai: China Institute of Scientific Management, 1931.
5. C. YANG and L. K. TAO. *A Study of the Standard of Living of Working Families in Shanghai.* Peiping: Institute of Social Research, 1930.
6. *Report of the British Economic Mission to the Far East, Department of Overseas Trade.* London: H.M. Stationery Office, 1931.
7. MANCHURIA RAILWAY. *Second Report on Progress in Manchuria — to 1930* (Dairen, 1931), chap. ix.
8. *Manchuria Year Book, 1931.* Tokyo: East Asiatic Economic Investigation Bureau, 1931.
9. JULEAN ARNOLD. "The Commercial Problems of China," *Annals of the American Academy of Political and Social Science*, November, 1931.
10. HAROLD M. VINACKE. "Obstacles to Industrial Development in China," *ibid.*
11. O. S. LIEU. "Certain Vital Problems of China's Industry," *ibid.*
12. EVAN B. ALDERFER. "The Textile Industry of China," *ibid.*
13. WALTER VOSKAIL. "The Iron and Steel Industry of China," *ibid.*
14. TA CHEN. "Fundamentals of the Chinese Labor Movement," *ibid.*
15. FANG FU-AN. *Chinese Labour.* Shanghai, 1931.
16. *The People's Livelihood — Papers and Abstracts of the Proceedings of a Conference Held in Shanghai, February, 1931.* Shanghai: National Christian Council, 1931.
17. L. K. TAO. *The Standard of Living among Chinese Workers* (China Council).

INTRODUCTORY NOTE

The round tables were guided in their allotment of time more by the evident interest of the members than by a logical subdivision of the inclusive subject of "China's Economic Development." Hence more attention was paid to the problems of agriculture, of communications, and of finance than

133

to those of industrial growth.   In the national economy of Continental Asia large-scale industry is not yet revolutionizing the life of the people.   To many members the survival and development of rural handicrafts seemed more important as a potential element in China's welfare than the building of smokestacks.   Yet, in this modern age, the manufacture of staple crops (such as cotton), the generation and distribution of power, the production of means of communication, and other industrial processes are too closely linked with agricultural prosperity to permit their neglect in a general survey of the assets for economic reconstruction.   Hence a number of the data and reference papers before the Conference presented the results of recent industrial studies; and a discussion motivated in part by a desire to know what foreign co-operation might contribute to the upbuilding of the resources of China could not fail to dwell upon some of the special problems of her industries.   Nor could observers in the country's industrial centers fail to note that hitherto China has avoided few of those social evils that have marked the incipient stages of industrialization in the West, or economists fail to learn, from documents before them, that for reasons to be further explored the country has as yet failed to realize the material benefits that are supposed to flow from a more intensive manipulation of the natural resources.   Industrialization was discussed, then, in the main from three points of view: its relation to the improvement of agriculture, the social problems arising from its incomplete control in the interest of public welfare, the part played by manufacture in the country's general economy and more particularly in its present confused financial situation.   Some of these topics came up also in the discussions that centered upon China's financial structure, upon standards of living, and upon China's foreign relations, which to that extent have been drawn upon in the following pages. The present chapter may be regarded, therefore, as an introduction to, rather than a full presentation of, the conditions and problems that face the industrial development of China.   Like the chapter on " Rural Reconstruction," it reveals a need for searching inquiry at many points but also gives evidence of sound studies already under way and of a wholesome concern with the essential factors in the situation that promise well for the future.

ADDRESSES

I. INDUSTRIAL GROWTH IN CHINA [1]

By O. S. LIEU

The prevalent industrial system in China today is essentially that which predominated in most regions in the West till the nineteenth century. In parts of the country, however, this traditional order no longer stands alone. For about three-quarters of a century, that is, since the early sixties of the last century, a new type of economic technique and industrial structure has been developing on the fringe of a society based on handicraft methods and small productive units. This movement for industrialization owes its impetus primarily to the opening up of five ports in China to foreign commerce in 1861. Thus, we may note that in 1865 the first steamship was built by the Ammunition Bureau at Anching. Three years later, in 1868, the Kiangnan Construction Bureau, now the Kiangnan Dock and Engineering Works, was established. In 1872, the China Merchants Steam Navigation Company, the first and only large shipping enterprise, was organized. Four years later, in 1876, the first railway, the Woosung Railway, was built. The modernization of China's transport was accompanied by similar changes in her manufacturing and mining industries. The first rice cleaning mill was established in Shanghai in 1863; the first silk filature in 1873; the first coal mine in Kaiping in 1878; the first match factory in Shanghai in 1888; the first cotton spinning and weaving mill in Shanghai in 1890; the first iron and steel works in Wuchang in 1890; the first oil pressing mill in Newchang in 1895; the first flour mill in Shanghai in 1896.

Despite the early beginning in the development of modern industries in China, the opportunity for rapid industrialization did not present itself until the World War shut off the supply of European goods and, thus, gave native producers a new hold upon the home market. This rapid industrialization in China since 1913 may best be portrayed by Table I and Chart I taken from Dr. H. D. Fong's paper on *China's Industrialization*. We may note that the coal output increased from about 13 million tons in 1913 to about 21 million tons in 1920, an increase of 59 per cent; the iron ore output from about 959,000 tons in 1913 to 1,865,000 tons in 1920, an increase of 94 per cent; the iron output from 256,000 tons in 1913 to 428,000 tons in 1920, an increase of 67 per cent. As coal and iron constitute the two largest mining industries in China, the rapid increase in their output may be taken as an index of China's growth in mining industry. In the manufacturing industries the rate of growth is even greater. Taking 1913 as 100, the quantity for filature silk export reached 168 in 1919; that for bean oil export reached 480 in 1919; that for cotton spindles reached 372 in 1920; and that for tobacco import reached 140 in 1920. As silk and bean oil are largely for export, the

[1] This address, delivered before a general meeting of the Conference, is based throughout on the information given in the data paper by H. D. Fong, *China's Industrialization: A Statistical Survey* (China Council).

TABLE I

GROWTH OF CHINA'S INDUSTRIALIZATION, 1912–29

Year	Coal Output * ooo (Tons)	Iron Ore Output † ooo (Tons)	Iron Output ‡ ooo (Tons)	Filature Silk Export § ooo (Piculs)	Bean Oil Export § ooo (Piculs)	Cotton Spindles (Number) ‖ ooo	Tobacco Import § ooo (Piculs)	Export Quantity Index ¶ 1913 = 100	Import Quantity Index ¶ 1913 = 100	Railway (Mail Carrying Length) ** (Km.)	Post (Postal Route) ** (Km.)	Shipping (Steamers Entered and Cleared) ‡ (Million Tons)
1912	8,886	721	178	74	526	....	143	103.9	82.9	10,368	229,824	82
1913	13,379	960	257	70	492	837	162	100.0	100.0	10,944	264,384	88
1914	13,640	1,005	300	57	607	855	118	83.8	91.6	10,944	279,936	91
1915	14,480	1,096	336	87	1,018	977	77	96.5	92.1	10,944	283,738	85
1916	15,903	1,129	369	81	1,566	1,228	147	102.4	96.6	10,944	290,707	82
1917	17,300	1,140	358	87	1,891	1,281	154	108.3	103.1	11,232	299,578	80
1918	18,340	1,475	354	88	2,277	1,456	181	105.5	92.8	11,520	310,349	74
1919	20,055	1,861	447	118	2,362	2,367	160	140.1	105.9	11,695	344,407	90
1920	21,260	1,865	428	73	1,713	3,111	227	119.4	106.5	11,800	396,491	100
1921	20,459	1,403	403	119	1,148	3,192	221	127.0	132.9	12,259	424,874	109
1922	21,997	1,559	394	110	1,480	3,267	254	130.6	158.5	12,551	439,222	119
1923	24,552	1,733	343	107	2,127	3,380	315	137.4	155.0	12,901	445,707	127
1924	25,781	1,766	331	101	2,121	3,581	683	144.8	170.8	13,152	456,304	137
1925	24,255	1,519	370	136	1,989	3,588	552	140.9	157.0	13,480	463,891	125
1926	23,040	1,562	405	137	2,667	....	755	149.6	186.7	13,707	471,271	132
1927	24,172	1,710	411	127	2,470	3,675	633	163.4	157.2	14,199	462,237	112
1928	25,092	2,004	434	151	942	3,850	1,070	165.5	188.3	14,578	458,051	118
1929	....	....	....	152	1,115	4,223	911	....	....	14,921	466,548	150

* Geological Survey of China, *General Statement on the Mining Industry*, Special Report No. 1 (1921), pp. 26–27, 31; No. 2 (1918–25), Table II; No. 3 (1926–28), Table II. Coal output for 1912–15 and 1917, for which no statistics are given, is inferred from 1912–17 output for 16 large mines. In 1916 the output of these 16 mines amounts to 55 per cent of the total output.
† *Ibid.*, No. 2, Table XIV; No. 3, p. 298.
‡ *Ibid.*, No. 2, Table XIV; No. 3, p. 300.
§ China Maritime Customs, *Foreign Trade of China. Part I: Report and Abstract of Statistics* (1912–29).
‖ Chinese Cotton Millowners' Association, "A List of Cotton Mills in China, 1929, 1930," *Chinese Economic Journal*, February, 1926; April, 1928; *China Cotton Journal*, January, 1923, pp. 2–3.
¶ Franklin L. Ho: "Index Numbers of the Quantities and Prices of Imports and Exports and of the Barter Terms of Trade in China, 1867–1928" (Table VI), *Problems of the Pacific*, 1929, p. 312.
** C. W. Wong, "Chinese Postal Statistics," *Statistical Monthly*, October, 1930. (In Chinese.)

CHART I

CHINA'S INDUSTRIALIZATION, 1912–29

1913 = 100

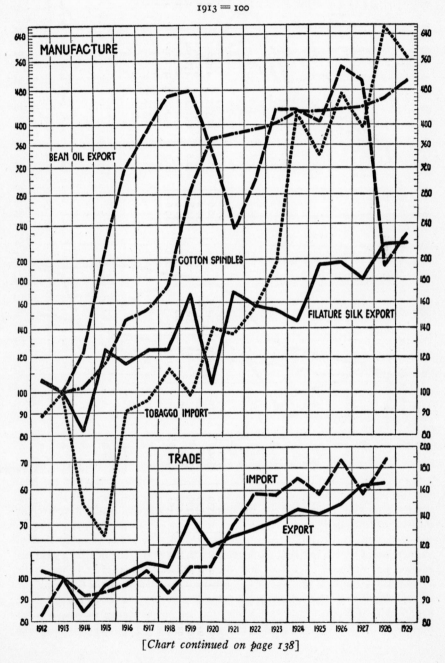

MANUFACTURE

BEAN OIL EXPORT

COTTON SPINDLES

FILATURE SILK EXPORT

TOBACCO IMPORT

TRADE

IMPORT

EXPORT

[Chart continued on page 138]

CHART I — *Continued*

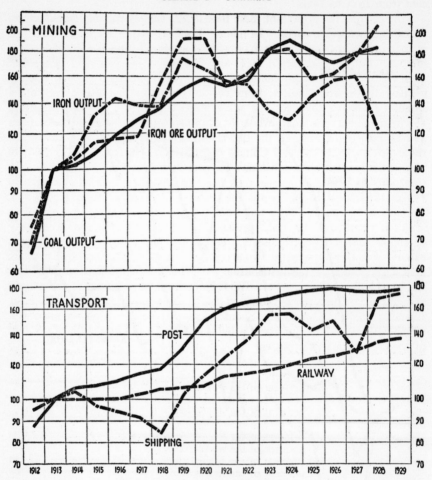

export statistics, in the absence of output statistics, may be taken as an index of growth. On the other hand, the import of tobacco, the raw material for the cigarette industry, serves also as an index for the growth of the cigarette making industry. In the trade and transport field, however, the increase during the period of the World War was not so great as that in mining or manufacture. In foreign trade the quantity of China's import showed an increase of only 6 per cent from 1913 to 1920, while that of China's export showed an increase of 19 per cent during the same period. As might be expected, the increase in exports was greater than that in imports during the time of the World War. In transport, the length of railways increased about 8 per cent from 1913 to 1920, while that of postal routes increased more rapidly — by 50 per cent during the same period. Meantime the tonnage of the steamers entered and cleared in the treaty ports increased by 12 per cent from 1913 to 1920.

After 1920 the growth of these four fields, namely mining, manufacture, trade, and transport, varies. In mining, the coal output increased from 159 in 1920 to 188 in 1928, while iron ore output increased from 194 in 1920 to 209 in 1928. For the iron output there was, however, a decrease over this period from 167 to 122. In manufacturing the increase from 1920 to 1929 was the greatest for tobacco import, from 141 to 564; and the second for cotton spindles from 372 to 505. For silk filature output, the increase was from 168 in 1919 to 217 in 1929, while for bean export, there was a decrease from 480 to 226, due chiefly to the depression in trade since 1927. In foreign trade the quantity index of China's exports increased from 119 in 1920 to 166 in 1928, while that of China's imports increased from 106 to 188. In transport the greatest increase took place in shipping, from 114 in 1920 to 171 in 1929; next to which was the increase in railways, from 107 to 136. The increase in postal routes was from 150 in 1920 to 176 in 1929.

The preceding " vertical " presentation of China's industrialization may be supplemented by a cross-section or " horizontal " analysis of its present extent. For this purpose the two accompanying tables prepared by Dr. Fong give a good idea of the distribution of China's industrialized regions (see Tables II and III, pp. 140–41). Among all the provinces in China, industrialization in the modern sense is confined chiefly to six provinces, namely Kiangsu, Liaoning, Hopei, Kwangtung, Shantung and Hupeh. These six provinces, which have a total area of about a tenth of China's territory and 36 per cent of the total population, possess

55 per cent of the mining industry,
65 per cent of the coal mining,
64 per cent of the iron mining,
93 per cent of the cotton spinning,
92 per cent of the silk reeling,
86 per cent of the oil pressing,
88 per cent of the electric power capacity,
84 per cent of the whole trade,
92 per cent of the foreign trade,
91 per cent of the transit trade,
53 per cent of the railways,
42 per cent of the motor roads,
42 per cent of the telegraph wires.

Among the six provinces Kiangsu is the most industrialized, leading in cotton spinning, silk reeling, electric power capacity, whole trade, foreign trade, transit trade and telegraph. It is the leading commercial and industrial province in China where Shanghai, the largest city in China, and Wusih, the most industrially developed city in the interior, are located. Liaoning ranks after Kiangsu in respect of trade and manufacture, but surpasses it in respect of mining. Here Dairen, the largest commercial port in North China, is located. Hopei, the second largest province in mining, ranks after Kiangsu and Liaoning, in trade as well as in manufacture, with Tientsin, the largest

TABLE II

PROVINCIAL DISTRIBUTION OF CHINA'S INDUSTRIALIZATION

Item	Kiangsu	Liaoning	Hopei	Kwang-tung	Shan-tung	Hupeh	Other	Total
Area (sq. miles) *	44,346	126,326	69,358	91,872	69,812	78,449	4,306,752	4,786,915
Population: *								
Total, 1930 (000)..........	35,511	15,275	31,242	34,877	32,500	26,724	309,034	485,163
Density per sq. mile, 1930..	801	121	450	380	466	341	72	101
Mining, 1927 (output 000 $): †.	6,606	87,311	45,979	4,565	14,939	5,255	134,196	298,851
Coal, 1928 (output 000 tons)‡	117	8,281	6,336	150	1,157	318	8,733	25,092
Iron, 1928 (ore output 000 tons) §	.....	655	.....	2	.....	634	713	2,004
Manufacture:								
Cotton, 1930 (spindles) (000)‖|	2,805	136	292	.....	371	324	296	4,224
Silk, 1929 (original export of filature, 000 hk. tls.) ¶	57,743	9,108	.....	48,523	5,635	141	9,470	130,621
Bean, 1929 (original export of oil and cake, 000 hk. tls.) ¶	44	68,788	2	1	241	74	11,262	80,412
Electricity, 1929 (power capacity, 000 kilowatts) **	259	132	67	32	24	24	77	615,000
Trade: ¶.................								
Whole trade, 1929, million (hk. tls.)	1,113	643	375	383	206	313	583	3,616,000
Foreign trade, 1929, million (hk. tls.)	1,003	495	206	264	95	63	172	2,298,000
Transit trade, 1929, million (hk. tls.)	84	5	61	5	3	4	5	167,000
Transport:								
Railway, 1924, kilometres ††	700	3,320	1,930	822	1,024	363	7,141	15,300
Motor road, 1930, kilometres ‡‡.................	3,207	3,136	3,011	4,217	5,440	1,397	28,248	48,656
Telegraph, 1928 (kilometres of overland wires) §§.....	19,557	6,875	15,855	8,279	17,061	8,149	104,773	180,549

* C. M. Chen, "A Study in China's Population Statistics," *Statistical Monthly*, June, 1930. (In Chinese.)
† Geological Survey of China, Special Report No. 3, Table XXI; *Nankai Weekly Statistical Service*, September 29, 1930.
‡ *Ibid.*, Table II.
§ *Ibid.*, pp. 295–98.
‖ *A List of Cotton Mills in China* (1930), by the Chinese Cotton Millowners' Association.
¶ China Maritime Customs, *Foreign Trade of China*, Parts I and II (1929).
** C. S. Chang, "Electric Light and Power Plants in China," *Statistical Monthly*, September, 1929. (In Chinese.)
†† *Statistical Monthly*, September, 1929, p. 28.
‡‡ *Nankai Weekly Statistical Service*, June 16, 1930.
§§ *China Yearbook* (1929–30), p. 475.

industrial, if not commercial, city in North China as its center. Among the other three industrialized provinces, Kwangtung, dominated by the city of Canton, leads in trade; Shantung, with the city of Tsingtao, leads in manufacture; and Hupeh, with the city of Hankow, leads in mining. In respect of transport, Liaoning and Hopei lead in railways, Shantung and Kwangtung in motor roads, Kiangsu and Shantung in telegraph. In Kiangsu also, the density of population is highest, 800 persons per square mile. Shantung, with a density of 466, is the second, after which may be mentioned Hopei (450), Kwangtung (380), Hupeh (341) and Liaoning (121).

A brief survey of the growth and the present degree of China's industrialization helps at least to dispel the common misunderstanding that China under the industrializing influence of the West has undergone a rapid process of economic modernization. Whatever industrialization there has been in China during the last three quarters of a century is confined chiefly to the six provinces whose area is but one-tenth of the total area of China. Such

TABLE III

PROVINCIAL DISTRIBUTION OF CHINA'S INDUSTRIALIZATION

(Per Cent)

Item	Kiangsu	Liaoning	Hopei	Kwangtung	Shantung	Hupeh	Other
Area..................	0.9	2.6	1.5	1.9	1.5	1.6	90.0
Population, 1930........	7.3	3.2	6.4	7.2	6.7	5.5	63.7
Mining, 1927 (value of output)...............	2.2	29.2	15.4	1.5	5.0	1.8	44.9
Coal, 1938 (quantity of output)............	0.4	33.0	25.0	0.5	4.6	1.1	35.1
Iron, 1928 (quantity of ore output).........	....	32.7	....	0.1	....	31.6	35.6
Manufacture							
Cotton, 1930 (spindles)	66.4	3.2	6.9	....	8.8	7.7	7.0
Silk, 1929 (export value of filature).........	44.2	6.9	....	37.1	4.3	0.1	7.4
Bean, 1929 (export value of oil and cake).......	0.1	85.5	....	....	0.3	0.1	14.0
Electricity, 1929 (power capacity).............	42.2	21.5	10.9	5.2	3.9	3.9	12.4
Trade							
Whole trade, 1929 (value)	30.8	17.8	10.4	10.6	5.7	8.7	16.0
Foreign trade, 1929 (value)	43.7	21.5	9.0	11.5	4.1	2.7	7.5
Transit trade, 1929 (value)	47.4	3.1	34.6	2.9	1.6	2.3	8.1
Transport							
Railway, 1924 (length)...	4.6	21.7	12.6	5.4	6.7	2.4	46.6
Motor road, 1930 (length)	6.6	6.5	6.2	8.7	11.2	2.9	57.9
Telegraph, 1928 (length)	10.8	3.8	8.8	4.6	9.5	4.5	58.0

industrialization again is very limited in scope and plays an insignificant rôle in international terms. In respect of mining, China produced in 1927 only 0.5 per cent of the world's iron ore, 0.02 per cent of the world's copper, 0.09 per cent of the world's lead, 0.09 per cent of the world's zinc, 6 per cent of the world's tin, 1.6 per cent of the world's coal, and an infinitesimal part of the world's petroleum. The cotton industry, the largest factory industry in China, possessed about 4,224,000 spindles in 1929, or only 2.6 per cent of the world's total; 29,272 power-looms, or 0.9 per cent of the world's total. The silk industry, for a long time the first staple industry in China, has also lost its leading position in the world to other nations. Silk power-loom weaving is still an unknown innovation, while Chinese silk reeling by machine processes is an industry which has been considerably surpassed by that of Japan. Of the total silk production that entered into the world's trade in 1925, 39,860,000 kilograms, China supplied only 8,120,000 kilograms, or 20.4 per cent, while Japan supplied 25,845,000 kilograms, or 64.8 per cent. Whereas in Japan almost all of the silk exported is reeled by machinery, in

China the machine-reeled silk amounts to only 80 per cent of the total export in 1929. In foreign trade China's share as compared with that of other nations is also insignificant. For the year 1929 the per capita foreign trade expressed in gold dollars was only 3.15 for China, which was considerably lower than that for other Pacific countries, namely 334 for New Zealand, 242 for Canada, 213 for Australia, 77 for the United States, 46 for Formosa, 31 for Japan, 25 for the Philippines, 19 for the Dutch East Indies, 18 for Korea, 9 for French Indo-China and 6 for Soviet Russia. In transport, China's international status is even lower. At the end of 1924, China had only 0.95 per cent of the world's railway mileage, while in respect of railway mileage per 10,000 population the figure for China, 0.2 miles, was the lowest in the world except 0.02 miles for Canberra, the Federal District in Australia. The figures for other leading nations are as shown in Table IV.

TABLE IV

The United States, including		European Russia	5.3 miles
Alaska	23.6 miles	Italy	3.3
France	8.5	Japan	1.7
Germany	6.0	British India	1.2
Great Britain	5.5	Asiatic Russia	1.0

I may conclude my brief discussion with a few remarks on the prospect of China's industrialization in the future. As a relief to the pressure of population and as a means to a higher standard of living, industrialization is undoubtedly very much needed in China. From an international point of view, too, China's industrialization is highly desirable as it offers one of the possible remedies to the problem of over-production in the Western countries. By means of industrialization, China would be in a position to absorb a larger quantity of the world's goods. But, for lack of natural resources, China will be industrialized only on an *Oriental* and not an *Occidental* scale, because she can scarcely aspire to the degree of industrialization that has been realized in the industrial nations of the West. As Chinese and foreign experts have often indicated, the reserve of basic minerals for industrialization in China is very limited. Her coal reserve, which is estimated to amount to 217,626 million tons, is only 4 per cent of the world's total. Her iron reserve, amounting to 980 million tons, is only 1.6 per cent of the world's total. In respect to petroleum, China's reserve, after making every allowance for the deficiencies in the present knowledge of the economic geology in China, is still probably less than 1 per cent of that of the United States. Without a sufficient supply of these basic minerals for industrialization, the prospect of ever raising China's industrialization to the same level as that which prevails in England or in the United States must remain exceedingly remote.

II. PROBLEMS OF FUTURE INDUSTRIAL DEVELOPMENT IN CHINA

By Franklin L. Ho

The industrialization of China is very limited in extent. For instance, the coal production of China, in terms of output, is only 1.6 per cent of the total of the world's output; in the cotton industry, which is the biggest manufacturing industry we have in China, in terms of spindles, we have a little over 2 per cent of the total of the world. Then again, our industrialization today is limited to six provinces, the area of which is only 10 per cent of the total area of China, and the population of which is only 30 per cent of the total population of this whole country. We can safely draw the conclusion that industrialization in China has not gone very far. What is responsible for the slow development and the small degree of success of modern industry in China?

There is, first of all, the insufficiency of capital and the difficulty of getting credit. In the cotton industry, for example, one of the few for which we have reliable statistics on capital return, the Chinese-owned mills, with 57 per cent of the total spindles in all cotton mills in China, possess only 28 per cent of the total capital invested in all the cotton mills in China; while on the other hand the Japanese mills, which possess only 39 per cent of the total spindles of all the cotton mills in China, have nearly 70 per cent of the total capital invested in the cotton industry in China. Correspondingly, the capital per spindle in Chinese cotton mills in only 39 taels, whereas in the Japanese cotton mills it amounts to over 137 taels. As a result of this scarcity of capital in Chinese industries, particularly in cotton mills, the capital of Chinese factories is always used as a fixed capital, while only a small amount is left for use as circulating capital. I know personally of quite a few cases where a factory is started with almost no circulating capital; in some extreme cases factories even have to buy machinery on credit. If these factories could get credit facilities the problem would not be so serious; but as a matter of fact, financial institutions in China are not in a good position to extend them. Even if they were, the interest charged would probably be too high. This, of course, is due primarily to the peculiar financial difficulties in which we as a nation are at present. I know of no case in North China where a factory can get credit at less than 10 per cent. In some cases the rate is more than 12 per cent. The banks do not consider such industrial business their responsibility because they have other channels of investment which yield a much more profitable return — particularly the bond market in which an investor today, if he is shrewd enough, can easily get an interest rate of 15 per cent and more.

The second factor of difficulty is that of management. While we have factories today in China that are properly managed, there are still larger numbers that are not. In my study in North China I found few cases where factories had proper methods of budgeting and of accounting, or a proper policy of dividends. I may illustrate this by one extreme case. I recently had occasion to analyze the balance sheets of a certain big cotton mill in North China for the past several years. In some years I found a net profit shown, but as I went into the matter in more detail, I found this to be a fiction, because in this particular mill nothing whatever had been allowed for depreciation. In another extreme case in which the lack of proper budgeting was evident: this particular factory started with a capital of $300,000, but discovered that it had to have a capital of more than $2,000,000 for operation. I may cite another extreme case with respect to dividend policy: during the war, when the cotton industry was growing fast in China, 100 per cent dividends were declared in certain factories without leaving reserves to provide for the natural growth of the industry.

Another factor which, I think, accounts for the slight degree of success is political instability. I need not dwell on this in detail, but I want to mention only two points connected with it. The first has to do with communications. The total length of railways in China amounts to about 9,000 miles; three-fourths of these were built from 1895 to 1915. Since 1915, due partly to the European War but principally to political instability, we have not done much in the development of communications. If one calculates the cost of transporting wheat in Shansi Province by cart or by pack animals, as compared with the cost by railway if railways were available, it is found that the cost per ton-mile by cart or pack animals is 79 cents silver, whereas by railway it would be less than 2 cents. This lack of proper transport greatly hinders the industrial development of the country. Second, there is the question of taxation — especially the multiplicity of taxes. Before the recent abolition of *likin,* the amount of taxation plus freight charges for transporting wool from the place where it was produced to Tientsin was more than 10 times the original cost. We have now abolished *likin,* but the substitute taxes, though an improvement, still constitute a great obstacle to trade. Political instability thus accounts to a large extent for the slight success achieved in our industrial development.

What have been the social effects of industrialization? In spite of the fact that it has not gone very far, the evils of industrialization have become evident in the matter of low wages, long hours of work and in the extent of child and woman labor. While statistics are scanty, I might mention by way of example the wages paid in one of the biggest cotton mills: here the maximum wage is $1.40 Chinese currency per day, while the minimum is 40 cents per day, with earnings averaging $15 to $16 per month. Then, as to hours of work — the ordinary practice is the twelve-hour two-shift system, though practice varies in the modern factories of Shanghai. In Tientsin certain factories have adopted the three-shift system. Child and woman labor is quite extensive. In Tientsin, 21 per cent of the total labor is child labor, and 6 per cent woman labor. In Shanghai, child labor under 12 years of age is 9 per cent of the total, while woman labor is 66 per cent. With the prevailing employment of children and women, it is particularly serious that many of our factories have not adopted proper measures for health protection and accident prevention.

For the improvement of these social evils we look to two influences: the labor movement and labor legislation. You may have heard of the organization of unions, of labor disputes that are becoming increasingly frequent; but in my own opinion this movement is so far more political than economic. The labor union in China is under the auspices of the Kuomintang; in every municipality there is a municipal Kuomintang headquarters, with a training department that has under its charge the organization of unions in the locality, as well as in each of the factories. The expenses for forming unions in the factories are paid not by the workers themselves but by the employers! We find here a phenomenon which contradicts itself and suggests that a great deal of improvement is still needed in the organization of our workers.

Then we expect help, of course, from labor legislation. The Government has already passed a Factory Act. On the question of how far it is applicable in its present form, I may refer you to a paper prepared by Dr. Ta Chen.[2] But before *any* factory act can be put in practice, one important problem has to be solved: the problem of contract labor which prevails in our industries today. I have not made a very intensive study of this subject, but I know that contract labor is very extensive in some of our industries; 80 per cent of the mining workers, for example, are hired and fired under the system. Where is prevails, it is practically impossible to put any factory act into effective operation.[3]

As regards the future of industrial development in China, it is clear that we do not have sufficient basic material for large-scale industrialization, particularly since our coal, iron, and petroleum supply is very limited. It is, therefore, quite unlikely that we can develop much heavy industry in China. For this reason, before we formulate a policy of industrial development from the economic viewpoint, we should first survey what particular raw materials we have for exploitation. After a survey of this kind has been made, we should concentrate our capital and resources upon those industries for which we have raw materials and for which our environment is especially adapted. Thus, among other industries, cotton and silk may perhaps deserve further development, but even in their respect there is need for a survey.

The concentration of capital and natural resources on those industries for which we have resources is the first step. Then we have to have a certain amount of protection in our tariff, for those industries which we are going to develop. This protective tariff will have to be carefully formulated and to be very selective. Moreover, the point should be stressed that, in the formulation of an industrial policy for China, careful consideration be given to the handicraft and other small industries which we already have and which can be further developed. In this connection, three things are essential — first, we should investigate what industries best lend themselves to further de-

[2] Ta Chen, *Study of the Applicability of the Factory Act of the Chinese Government.* Shanghai: China Institute of Scientific Management, 1931.

[3] The opinion here stated was subsequently challenged by other students of Industry. See below, p. 160.

velopment, and what improvements and modifications should be made; second, how the product may best be marketed; and third, how to provide these small rural and home industries with an adequate credit machinery.

EXTRACTS FROM SYLLABUS

I. CHINA'S MINERAL RESOURCES [4]

China has large reserves of coal, much of it anthracite of high quality, but little of it coking coal, and therefore not wholly suitable for metallurgical purposes; she has only moderate reserves of iron ore (about 950 million tons), much of which has a low iron content and is not profitable to work under present methods; her known reserves of petroleum are insignificant, and the structural conditions of most of China render further important discoveries unlikely, though she has at least one large deposit of oil shale at Fushun in Manchuria; she is the world's most important supplier of tungsten and antimony, and a large exporter of tin, most of which goes to the United States.

Estimates of China's coal reserves vary from a minimum figure of 23 billion tons to a maximum of 996 billion tons,[5] but little of these resources is yet exploited, and China's annual production, including the output of small mines under Chinese control, is estimated approximately at no more than 25 million metric tons, an increase of about 11 million tons over the 1913 output. Of these 25 million tons, an uncertain amount, usually estimated at about 7 million tons, is produced from small mines under local control, and by far the greater part of the remainder comes from the Fushun mine operated by the South Manchuria Railway Company and from the Sino-British Kailan Mining Administration near Chingwantao.[6] In 1928 the former mine produced some 7,198,000 long tons and the latter 4,583,000. Exports of coal ranged from 3½ million to 4 million tons in the last three years, most of them going to Japan from the Manchurian mines under Japanese control; imports (largely from Indo-China) are about 2½ million tons.

The iron and iron ore reserves of China are summarized by Tegengren [7] as shown in Table I.

[4] *International Economic Relations in the Pacific: B. China's Economic Development*, pp. 15–19, slightly abbreviated.

[5] Dr. V. K. Ting stated at the present Conference of the Institute that, in the light of the most recent study in China, a total of 200 billion tons should be regarded as the most reasonable estimate.

[6] Figures for Fushun are from the New York office of the S.M.R., and for the Kailan mine from *Economic Conditions in China to August 30, 1930.* London: Department of Overseas Trade, H.M. Stationery Office, 1930.

[7] "The Iron Ores and Iron Industry of China," *Memoirs of the China Geological Survey* (1923).

TABLE I

RESERVES

(In million tons)

	ACTUAL RESERVES		POTENTIAL RESERVES	
	Ore	Iron	Ore	Iron
Archean ores............	295.0	110.0	477.0	159.0
Sinian ores..............	28.0	15.0	64.0	36.0
Contact-metamorphic.....	73.0	41.0	9.6	4.8
Other types..............	....	....	5.1	2.4
Total..............	396.0	166.0	555.7	202.2

Total reserves: Ore.. 951.7 million tons
Iron.. 368.2

Over four-fifths of these reserves are in the Archean ores of South Manchuria and Hopei, ores which are of low iron and high silica content and require expensive preliminary concentration before they can be smelted. Equally significant is the fact that the iron and steel industry of China has not been a profitable business despite the heavy subsidies which most of the Japanese and part-Japanese enterprises have enjoyed. In recent years the annual output of pig iron has varied from 300,000 to 350,000 tons, the greater part of which comes from the Japanese-controlled Anshan works in Manchuria. The operation of this, the largest plant in China, has entailed an aggregate loss of some 24,000,000 yen for the first nine years since the works opened in 1919. Since 1928, for the first time, the enterprise has shown a profit, but this is probably due in large part to a writing down of capital.

The production of iron ore is correspondingly small. In 1927 the total output of modern mines was roughly 862,000 tons of which more than nine-tenths came from mines wholly or partly under Japanese control, more than half from the two Manchurian mines, and nearly all of which is exported to Japan either directly or in the form of pig iron.

Not much need be said of China's other mineral resources. The production of gold, silver, copper, lead, and zinc is small to the point of insignificance. Tin exports from Yunnan form an important part of the American supply, 7,000–9,000 tons being the usual volume, although for 1929 a reduced output of 6,500 long tons has been estimated.[8] China holds a strategic position as a world-supplier of tungsten (in the form of wolfram ore) and of antimony, both of which are of great importance to modern industrial civilizations. Table II (p. 148) will indicate the general conditions of production of the three minerals.[9]

[8] See *The Annals,* November, 1930, p. 123.

[9] China Maritime Customs, *Report and Abstract of Statistics,* 1920, 1925, 1929, 1930 (Shanghai). The above figures are converted from piculs to short tons.

TABLE II

(Short tons of 2,000 lb.)

Year	Tin Ingots and Slabs	Antimony Regulus	Wolfram Ore
1920............	12,663	10,721	....
1925............	9,782	18,754	6,574
1928............	7,876	18,137	8,116
1929............	7,592	22,116	9,776
1930............	7,261	17,663	9,620

II. CHINA'S RESOURCES OF INDUSTRIAL POWER [10]

China's greatest natural power resources are her coal reserves which have been discussed above. Definite knowledge of her water-power resources is lacking, and no judgment can be given in its absence. The present Director of the Geological Survey of China has expressed the opinion that a considerable utilization of water power for hydro-electric schemes will ultimately be possible in China, and has pointed out a number of probable sites where conditions are favorable.[11] Despite this possibility, however, many observers point out that several important factors — such as the great distance from the river gorges and regions of rapid flow to the sea-coast and the large centers, and the huge volume of sediment carried by many Chinese rivers — will combine to make the development of hydro-electric projects in China a difficult and costly business. Added to these is the economic obstacle. There will be little economic incentive to spend large sums to harness and utilize the powers of nature, so long as there is a cheap and inexhaustible supply of human labor.

Up to the present time, coal and oil have been the only sources of electric power for China. According to a recent estimate,[12] there were in 1929 some 645 electric light and power plants in the country. Figures given for the power capacity of 499 of them show that 418 independent plants had a capacity of 380,000 kilowatts, 40 plants attached to cotton mills a capacity of 121,000, and 9 plants attached to mines a capacity of 108,000. Of the provinces, Kiangsu claimed 42 per cent of the power output, Liaoning (South Manchuria) 21 per cent, and Hopei 11 per cent. The figures show that the development of electric power in China is on a small scale, and that it is concentrated in a comparatively few centers in Northern and Eastern China. The exploitation of China's mineral and power resources has been per-

[10] *Syllabus on China's Economic Development*, pp. 20–21, slightly abbreviated.

[11] See T. Shing and W. H. Wong, " An Outline of the Power Resources of China," *Transactions of the First World Power Conference* (London, 1924), Vol. I.

[12] Figures from *Nankai Weekly Statistical Service* (Tientsin) for March 30, 1931, where a comparison of two estimates by C. S. Chang and the Bureau of Reconstruction is made. The Bureau's figure for the total power capacity of independent plants is 477,000 kilowatts. The figure of 645 plants is difficult to reconcile with the estimate of 231 plants given in the *China Year Book* for 1927.

mitted to reside in the hands of private companies or concessionaires. It is a matter of some significance, however, that if the teachings of San Min Chu I are to be followed, the National Government would seem to be committed eventually to the ownership if not the operation of these resources.

III. THE HUMAN FACTOR IN CHINA'S INDUSTRIALIZATION [13]

SUPPLY AND EFFICIENCY OF FACTORY LABOR

Pending the discovery of an acceptable definition of a factory in China, the number of factory workers must remain a matter of speculation. Estimates range from 500,000 to 1,460,000.[14] What seems fairly certain is that the number of workers employed in establishments which at least have some resemblance to factories does not exceed 2,000,000, and that the total number of those employed in establishments using power and having 30 workers or more (the definition adopted in the new Chinese Factory Act) must be under 1,500,000. Neither of these figures would include quarrying and mining labor, which has been estimated by M. Torgasheff [15] at 1,042,000 for mineral mines, and at 1,247,000 for salt, clay, brick, tile, and cement works, including of course a great number of local enterprises which cannot be called modern.

In the absence of complete statistics, we can do no better than assemble the results of partial surveys which have been made in several important industrial centers. Table I shows the number of workers employed in the industrial concerns of Shanghai, Tientsin, Wusih and Hankow, as reported

TABLE I

ESTIMATES OF INDUSTRIAL EMPLOYMENT

	Men	Women	Children *	Total
Shanghai, 1928–29:				
Textile workers.............	41,828	113,540	15,154	170,522
All factory workers..........	76,248	125,785	20,637	222,670
Tientsin, 1928–29:				
Textile workers.............	24,676	2,314	7,274	64,264
All factory workers..........	35,183	2,606	9,730	47,519
Hankow, 1929:				
Spinning and weaving.......	407	1,231	313	1,951
All factory workers..........	5,204	3,336	1,810	9,720
Wusih, 1928–29:				
Cotton and silk factories......	3,619	28,448	5,909	37,976
All factory workers..........	5,997	32,065	6,500	44,562

* Under 12 years for Shanghai; under 16 years for Tientsin; other cities not defined.

[13] *Syllabus on China's Economic Development*, pp. 67–79.

[14] For some of the estimates see C. F. Ma, " Notes on China's Labor Population," *Chinese Economic Journal*, November, 1930.

[15] Torgasheff, " Mining Labor in China " (Shanghai: Bureau of Industrial and Commercial Information, 1930), p. 97.

to the Bureau of Social Affairs in each city.[16]   The figures are not exact and are generally underestimated, for in several instances the investigations, especially that conducted in Tientsin, are known to have omitted important enterprises; and the Hankow figures do not include the sister-town of Wuchang, which is a major industrial center.   But even with these defects, the table reveals the predominance of Shanghai as a center of factory labor, and the extent to which women and children are employed in the textile industries.

Scientific knowledge of the efficiency of Chinese factory labor is lacking, and even were it available it could not tell us much.   Labor efficiency is not an easy thing to measure; what is often called by that name and expressed in terms of labor cost per unit of production might better be described as the efficiency of capital.   Labor in China is so plentiful and capital often so scarce that human energy is used to perform tasks which in other countries are done by machinery; to make international comparisons of labor efficiency without recognizing this is to run the risk of serious error.   It must be recognized, for example, in reading Mr. Torgasheff's estimate that the average efficiency of labor in China's two largest and best equipped coal mines is only one-eleventh of the average American efficiency, and that for most semi-modern and native mines the average ratio is one-twentieth and lower, or about one-quarter of the average European efficiency.   Similar and lower ratios apply to China's iron mines.[17]   There is, moreover, another and more important qualification.   Labor efficiency, measured in terms of the volume of output, may be very low; but at the same time it may be economically profitable to employ such inefficient labor.   The efficiency which, according to the advocates of the high-wage doctrine in the West, is reported to arise from the increased output of highly paid labor may arise from low-paid labor in China where inefficient output is more than offset by the low rate of wages. In this fact lies, perhaps, the greatest obstacle to the application of automatic and advanced machine methods to Chinese industry.

A number of reasons combine to strengthen the view that the efficiency of China's factory workers is low and will remain low for some time.   The results of several investigations have shown that many families do not receive an income adequate to maintain their physical efficiency.   The amount of child labor, the high incidence of disease, the absence of elementary and technical education, the length of the working day, and the absence, until 1930, of effective factory legislation, all reduce the physical and mental efficiency of workers.

LABOR ORGANIZATION AND LABOR LEGISLATION

The trade-union movement in China is temporarily under a cloud.   Following its vigorous development and its support from the Communist factions in South China, it entered upon a period of restriction and suppression after

---

[16] The table is condensed from statistics reproduced in Tyau, *Two Years of Nationalist China* (Shanghai, 1930), chap. xii.   For other statistics compiled for factories of over 30 workers in 29 Chinese cities see appendix below.

[17] Torgasheff, *op. cit.,* p. 29.

the establishment of the National Government. Since the break between the Kuomintang and the Communists, it has been the policy of the Government to purge the labor movement of all undesirable " Red " elements, and to this end the party has sponsored the organization of "union labor purification committees." Both provincial and national legislation has been introduced with the object of restricting the right to strike and the right to combine under certain circumstances. Partly for these and partly for other reasons, the incomplete statistics of unions and union membership show a marked decline — from over 3,000,000 in 1927 to a little over 576,000 in 1930.

The Ministry of Industry, Commerce, and Labor in 1930 completed a survey of the trade-union movement during the year 1928. The survey recorded 1,117 unions with a membership of about 1,774,000, of which over a million members were asserted to belong to " provincial labor unions " in Kwangtung.[18] The latest survey by the Ministry relates only to 27 cities in 9 provinces for the 1930 survey and apparently excludes " labor unions " such as those mentioned above for Kwangtung. The following figures are taken from the report.[19] They cover the principal industrial centers of China, with the exception of Tientsin, which in 1928 was reported to have 76 unions with 21,580 members.

TABLE II

City	Unions	Members
Shanghai....................	129	18,133
Soochow....................	2	14,812
Wusih......................	29	20,886
Nanking....................	53	29,155
Hangchow..................	49	33,906
Wuhu......................	49	20,914
Hankow....................	21	57,125
Wuchang...................	7	28,084
Tsingtao....................	33	25,639
Canton.....................	35	108,334
Swatow.....................	30	45,186
27 cities.................	741	576,250
Tientsin (1928).............	76	21,580

The legal status of unions in China has been defined in several legislative measures, the first of which was a set of regulations promulgated by the National Government at Canton in 1924, and the last of which is the Trade Union Law put into effect on November 1, 1929. Space does not permit of any extended discussion of the provisions of the law; [20] it is sufficient to point

[18] For details see *Nankai Weekly Statistical Service*, Vol. III, No. 48 (December 1, 1930).

[19] *Ibid.*, Vol. IV, No. 10 (March 9, 1931).

[20] For the articles of the law see Lamb, *The Origin and Development of Social Legislation in China* (Peiping: Yenching University, 1930), p. 51; and for an examination of their significance see Tawney, *op. cit.*, chap. v.

out that while workers over 16 years numbering 100 in the same industry or over 50 in the same trade may form unions, the restrictions concerning the right to strike are so severe and the powers given to the local Kuomintang to dissolve or suspend unions for " violation of law " or " nuisance " or " impediment of public welfare " so extensive as to deprive the unions of what is regarded in most countries as their greatest strength.

Factory legislation, as distinct from the regulation of trade-unions and of industrial disputes, dates from 1914 when the first mining regulations were drawn up, and from March, 1923, when the Ministry of Agriculture and Commerce under the Peking Government drafted the " Provisional General Factory Regulations." These have since been supplemented by a number of other provisional laws promulgated by various provincial authorities. The political conditions of China up to 1928 were such that most of this legislation remained entirely provisional, and naturally little of it could be effectively enforced. It was not until December 27, 1929, that the National Government promulgated the National Factory Law. The date fixed for its enforcement was February 1, 1931, but in January an extension to August 1 was granted after representation by leading Chinese business men who urged that the immediate application of the somewhat drastic provisions of the law would seriously disorganize China's industries. The provisions of the Act include prohibition of the further employment of children under fourteen, and of night work or more than eight hours' day work for child workers (under sixteen years). It establishes the eight-hour day as the ordinary working time, with provision for extension to ten hours in certain circumstances, and prohibits women's work between 10 P.M. and 6 A.M. Provision is made for a weekly day of rest, for annual vacations, and for eight weeks' leave for women workers in case of childbirth. It provides for the setting-up of factory councils with employee representation, for minimum wage rates, equal rates for men and women on identical work, arbitration and conciliation machinery, and a number of regulations concerning workers' health, safety plans, and insurance schemes.

The law has been criticized — on the one hand, because no detailed provision for inspection of factories and enforcement of regulations accompany it and, on the other, because the reforms which it introduces are too sweeping to allow of its effective enforcement without disrupting industrial production. A more significant objection is that despite the severity of its standards, the term " factory " has been so defined (an establishment using power and employing thirty or more workers) that it will affect a comparatively small number of establishments — probably no more than 2,500 in all China — and will leave untouched the thousands of small workshops and craft enterprises in which conditions of health, safety, wage rates, apprenticeship, and employment are at their worst.

CONDITIONS OF LABOR

Many competent observers report to the effect that the conditions of industrial workers in most of China are with few exceptions bad, and in many cases atrocious, even by comparison with other Asiatic countries. Not many persons claim that the Chinese urban or industrial worker has reaped any of the benefits which ought to flow from the introduction of modern industrial processes. When allowance is made for the higher cost of living in the cities, for the unwonted rigor of factory discipline, and for the risk of industrial accidents and disease, there is little to suggest that the factory laborer fares better than his peasant brother. There is, indeed, definite evidence that he fares worse than the average craft worker. Studies made by the Japanese Chamber of Commerce in Tientsin for the period 1927–29 indicate that the average real wage per day for ten types of tradesmen was about 68 cents Chinese currency, while that for eight types of male adult factory workers was only about 45 cents.[21]

To generalize on the average rate of wages in China is an impossible task. All that can be done is to take note of representative rates which prevail in certain important enterprises. For ordinary mining workers M. Torgasheff has calculated a daily average wage of about 35 cents, with a range of 35–45 cents in the better and larger coal mines, and a much lower range — of 15–30 cents — in many local enterprises. For cotton-mill operatives in Shanghai, where wages and prices are relatively high, a recent study [22] shows an average daily rate of 51 cents for male general workers, 47 cents for female, and 33 cents for child workers. Actual monthly earnings, however, are only about $13.85 for male general workers, and $12.15 for females. In Tientsin, where rates are lower, the same type of worker earned on the average a daily wage of 45 cents for males and 34 cents for females during the period 1927–29, and a sample list of over 2,000 factory workers in that city were found to earn only about $9.00 per month. In the semi-modernized workshop industries of carpet-weaving, hosiery-knitting, rayon- and cotton-weaving, an average monthly wage of $11.28 was usual,[23] though it must be remembered that nearly half the labor in these industries is supplied by apprentices who receive little or nothing in wages during their first three years of employment. In Shanghai, during the second half of 1928, the Bureau of Social Affairs calculated that the average monthly earnings for male workers in thirty types of employment, both skilled and unskilled, was only $21.33.[24]

Working hours in China are everywhere long, whether in workshop or

[21] Fong, *Industrialization and Labor in Hopei,* a paper presented at the Conference on "*The People's Livelihood.*" Shanghai: National Christian Council, 1931.

[22] Yang and Tao, *A Study of the Standard of Living of Working Families in Shanghai.* Peiping: Institute of Social Research, 1931.

[23] Fong, *op. cit.,* p. 12.

[24] In making conversions from silver to gold dollars, it is on the whole better to attribute the silver dollar with a gold value of 40 or 50 cents United States currency rather than with its present depreciated value of 20–25 cents. Chinese prices and wages have not moved upward in proportion to the fall in the exchange.

factory industries. Tientsin factories average 12½ hours a day; 12 hours is the usual day in coal and iron mines; 11–12 hours with day and night shifts is the rule for most cotton mills in China; in many of the smaller workshops the hours run up to 14 and 15. Only in certain large cities is the Sunday rest at all frequent; elsewhere a few hours off once or twice a month is often the rule.

On the general conditions of labor no useful generalizations can be made. To the casual observer it often seems as if the conditions in the large factories are infinitely preferable to those in the tiny, unhealthy, and ill-lighted hovels which house the carpet, hosiery, and rayon workers of Tientsin and Peiping. Yet, it must be remembered that the strain and hurry of the factory where the machine is master are absent from the workshops with their leisurely and inefficient ways; and, on the other hand, it is difficult to say whether the child labor of the cotton mills is a greater social evil than the apprentice labor of the hosiery knitting shops. The evil is great enough in both cases. High mortality from preventable accidents and industrial diseases, unprotected machinery, bad ventilation, lighting, and sanitation, overcrowding, and housing conditions where even the best is deplorable and the worst is appalling — the conditions are such as to throw added luster on the few public-spirited employers who have attempted to rise above them.

APPENDIX

TABLE I*

FACTORIES WITH 30 OR MORE WORKERS IN 51 PRINCIPAL INDUSTRIAL
CITIES, EXCLUDING TIENTSIN

City	1911	1920	1930
Shanghai............	48	192	837
Wusih..............	8	43	153
Dairen.............	39	118	152
Hankow............	15	38	76
Canton.............	3	17	63
Harbin.............	5	26	57
Tsingtao............	...	12	44
Hangchow...........	4	19	50
51 cities.........	171	673	1,975

* Source: *Report of the Ministry of Industry* (Nanking, 1930).

TABLE II*

WORKERS IN INDUSTRIAL ESTABLISHMENTS OF 30 OR MORE WORKERS

CITY	MALES		FEMALES		CHILDREN UNDER 16		TOTAL
	Number	Per Cent	Number	Per Cent	Number	Per Cent	Number
Shanghai.......	82,341	23	258,500	71	22,053	6	362,894
Soochow........	41,043	70	13,286	22	4,485	8	58,814
Wusih..........	18,398	26	42,959	61	9,331	13	70,688
Hangchow......	10,770	17	6,016	31	385	2	16,171
Wuhu..........	11,996	76	2,309	15	1,530	9	15,835
Hankow........	149,089	87	17,330	11	3,473	2	169,892
Wuchang.......	11,348	48	12,626	52	.....	..	23,974
Tsingtao.......	23,332	88	2,797	11	299	1	26,428
Shunteh........	3,832	7	44,228	81	6,389	12	54,449
Foochow.......	5,078	32	10,654	66	300	2	16,032
28 cities....	448,038	46	449,578	47	67,337	7	964,953
Canton.........	....	..	....	..	......	..	239,365
Total......	....	..	....	..	......	..	1,204,318
Tientsin factories†	35,183	..	2,606	..	9,730	..	47,519

* From the report of the Ministry of Industry summarized in the *Nankai Weekly Statistical Service*, Vol. IV,
No. 9 (March 2, 1931).
† The incomplete figures reported by the Bureau of Social Affairs in Tientsin for 1928–29 are inserted
merely for purposes of rough comparison. They do not relate to establishments of 30 or more workers.

QUESTIONS FOR ROUND–TABLE DISCUSSION

The Program Committee, in its suggested agenda on " China's Economic Development," recommended the following questions for discussion:

1. In the light of (*a*) China's background and resources and (*b*) the experience of other countries, on what lines should China's economic development proceed? What part may foreign co-operation play in this?
2. How far and in what ways does the improvement of peasant life depend on the development of rural industries?
3. Can a practical program be devised for large-scale industries for particular areas in China? Under what auspices and by what means can they best be developed along financially sound and socially healthy lines?

SUMMARY OF ROUND–TABLE DISCUSSIONS

I. CHARACTERISTICS OF INDUSTRIALIZATION IN CHINA

In the round tables that dealt with the question of large-scale industry the members who participated did so after a series of prior addresses and arguments had impressed on them the facts, first, that China because of her rather limited natural resources (particularly of iron and coking coal) can never hope to parallel the industrial development of Germany or the United States, and second, that industrialization, however successful, would be no panacea for her chronic economic ills which are at bottom rural and must predominantly remain rural in so vast a nation of farmers. There was for the most part a tendency on the part of members to examine the possibilities of specific industries that seemed necessary or likely to foster the growth of particular forms of agricultural production, that is, particularly village industries, rather than to consider grandiose plans for the construction of factories and steel mills.

It was early realized in one group that the term " industrialization," and even the term " factory," cannot in China be used with their customary Western connotations, but require careful definition when used in discussion. The difficulty was well illustrated when an American member inquired whether the rug industry of Peiping and Tientsin had been industrialized. If by " industrialized " is meant the application of mechanical power to the processes of production then the industry is not industrialized, as a Chinese economist explained. He showed, however, that in other respects this industry, like the kindred hosiery-knitting and rayon-weaving industries of the same cities, has many of the characteristic marks and most of the characteristic social evils of factories in the early stages of industrialism. In some of them various types of machinery (usually operated by hand, however) are used; in some of them workers numbering more than thirty (the official number in the Chinese Factory Law) are assembled in one establishment; in others a great deal of work is farmed out to smaller establishments or to families. Such industries represent the transition between the domestic and factory economy and are modern counterparts of conditions that were common enough in the early stages of the Industrial Revolution in Western Europe.[25] That such intermediate types of industrial organization are wont to persist, however, even in modern economically advanced countries was clearly brought out in this and other round tables where American members cited various attempts on the part of large manufacturers in the United States to utilize the services of farmers, by the aid of cheap electrical power, for the manufacture of small articles, such as simple accessory parts for automobiles. Japanese members thereupon stated that the same practice which had been common in the Swiss watch industry was now being emulated in Japan by a few large foreign concerns — in particular motor and phonograph manufacturers — who were encouraging their employees to do additional work in their homes.

In this connection the need for cheap and widely distributed electric power was seen to be all-important, and members pointed to the great contrast between conditions of rural China, where men and beasts are the source of almost all power, and those of Japan, where thousands of villages are served from central power stations or from small local hydroelectric plants. It was seen that for this purpose alone — the provision of power-generating plants and equipment — China would probably need a certain amount of heavy industry. Similarly in the provision of simple forms of farm machinery and implements, such as pumps, threshing and winnowing machines, and the like, there would be need for engineering enterprises for the manufacture of iron and steel products.

A British member from Shanghai said:

" In a comparatively undeveloped country like China, industrial development proceeds under the influence of forces that are outside the control of governments. If there is peace and security China will be attractive to foreign capital because it has an abundant labor supply and excellent raw materials. In the early stages of industrialism in China the industries will concentrate on comparatively simple products of low quality, requiring little technical skill from both managers and workers. Such a development will undoubtedly have a harmful effect on the same industries in other, more highly industrialized countries; but on the whole there will be a net benefit. China will find her natural place in the world-economy as a manufacturer of less specialized goods, while the Western countries with better equipment and larger experience will devote themselves more and more to a trade with China in more highly specialized types of commodities which cannot be produced in China."

To this a Chinese member ventured the rejoinder that China, like other nations becoming conscious of their economic powers, might not be content for long with such a rôle. He mentioned the British Dominions as instances of countries which are eminently fitted by nature for the production of foods and raw materials but where public opinion has forced industrial developments even when these were possible only with the expensive aid of tariff protection. But in any event, as another member suggested, there is a growing appreciation on the part of foreign manufacturers of the fact that far-reaching changes are to be expected in the nature of their trade with China

[25] For details see H. D. Fong, *Hosiery Knitting in Tientsin, and Cotton and Rayon Weaving in Tientsin*. Tientsin: Nankai University, 1930.

during the next decade or so. The report of the British Economic Mission to the Far East had clearly stated that Great Britain must look for a permanent decrease in her market for plain piece goods in China, and that her manufacturers must make preparations for supplying a better quality and more specialized products.[26]

Despite what was said of the difficulty of subjecting the forces of industrialization to much rational control, it was stressed in some groups that the National Government had in fact drawn up certain principles concerning the development of basic industries in China and had even kept in fashion to the extent of formulating a ten-year plan.[27] In the opinion of one Chinese member, however, there has been a great deal of exaggeration in popular statements about the Government's plans for nationalizing industries. In the policies propounded by Dr. Sun Yat-sen, nationalization was intended to apply mainly to railways, mining, and similar basic enterprises where capital from private sources could hardly be expected to be adequate. He maintained that the present authorities have no intention of exercising any unusual control over industry in general, but in fact are desirous of encouraging private enterprises except in special cases. There is, nevertheless, a very real determination to care for the interests of labor in future plans of industrialization, and to nationalize all large businesses which have a natural tendency toward monopoly, or which have proved themselves incapable of being conducted by private initiative along socially healthy lines. It was also stated that the Government has in mind three main types of enterprise, varying from private ownership and management to state ownership and management with an

[26] A student of the industry in Shanghai declared that the English imports even of the better qualities will soon be challenged by Japanese mills in that city which recently have established automatic looms designed for the manufacture of cotton yarns of finer count.

[27] See *Pacific Affairs*, September, 1931, and *Chinese Economic Journal*, August, 1931, for a résumé of the plan, which includes the following principal objectives:

1. Construction of harbors, canals, railroads, etc., where urgently needed
2. Reclamation of undeveloped territory in the northwest and general improvement of the agricultural and pastoral industries throughout the country
3. Development of mines and quarries
4. Establishment of smelting works and mills for metallurgical industries
5. Production of iron and steel
6. Manufacture of bricks, cement, and other building materials
7. Building of locomotives
8. Building of merchant ships and fishing vessels
9. Manufacture of vehicles of all types
10. Promotion of the coal-tar industry
11. Establishment of works for making basic chemicals
12. Development of hydroelectric schemes and establishment of central power-stations
13. Manufacture of electrical machinery
14. Establishment of municipal waterworks

In addition to these proposals, the authorities contemplated the establishment of a large machine factory under Government auspices for the training of engineers and mechanics.

intermediate class of concerns owned by the state but operated under semi-private direction. No obstacles would be placed in the way of foreign participation in mining and other industrial ventures, subject only to the new laws to the effect that Chinese citizens should hold more than half the shares and constitute a majority of the directors.

Members in most of the groups took it fairly much for granted that China has an important career to shape for herself in the industrial world in spite of handicaps in her natural resources and in being a late-comer in the field. Discussion on specific lines of development was lacking in most round tables, but the following extract from a data paper may serve to give a point of view which was widely held and found expression in the Conference.

China will make a profound mistake if she is so much impressed by the industrial achievements of America and Europe as merely to ape them, instead of striking out her own line for herself. She must start from the foundations of economic enterprise which already exist, expand those industries which, because she is best suited for them, offer the best conditions, and develop the assets which she already possesses.

Nor are such aspects difficult to discover. China possesses a laborious and intelligent population, with unusual gifts for qualitative production; its most serious economic defect — a very grave one — is that, owing to its abundance, human labour is cheap, with the result that the introduction of machinery, which, had labour been dearer, would have taken place long ago, has been discouraged. She has valuable raw materials, which, owing to primitive methods of cultivation and preparation, are less valuable than they should be. Given the development of her coal industry, she may have cheap power. She already manufactures by modern methods a large output of goods which a generation ago were produced by hand, so that, as far as the immediate future is concerned, her problem is less to introduce new industries than to expand those of which the nucleus is already in existence. The character of her foreign trade, which — like that of most countries in the first phase of industrial development — is largely an exchange of raw materials and foodstuffs for manufactured imports, permits her, as her industry develops, to replace part of the latter by domestic products. She has a market at home which at present, owing to the absence of communications and to the low standard of life of the rural population, has a small effective demand, but which, given the improvement of transport and agriculture, is potentially large.

In such circumstances it is difficult to believe that she cannot, for example, work up her raw silk and raw wool at home instead of exporting them to be manufactured abroad; grow fruit and can it instead of importing canned fruit from California; deal with her eggs in her own egg factories instead of leaving the profits of exporting them to foreign concerns, and develop other industries based on agriculture; multiply her flour mills, oil mills, and cement works; supply her own railway materials and electrical plant; carry further the substitution, which she has already begun, of Chinese cottons for piece-goods imported from Great Britain and Japan, and create the nucleus, at least, of a Chinese mercantile marine. Since she is never likely to be industrialized in the same sense as the United States, Germany, or Great Britain, it is needless to inquire whether that type of civilisation possesses all the virtues with which Chinese politeness is accustomed to credit it. But it is paradoxical to suppose that, if she chooses to take the necessary steps — which at present she has not taken — she cannot greatly increase both her production of manufactures and the population employed in manufacturing industries.[28]

[28] R. H. Tawney, *A Memorandum on Agriculture and Industry in China*, pp. 108–10.

Several members in each of the round tables which discussed labor problems had had considerable experience with labor conditions and the recent factory law in China or were familiar with the development of the working-class movement in China. The discussions, therefore, were confined rather closely to the possibilities of enforcing that law effectively in the large industrial centers.

The discussions soon showed that the obstacles which confront the Government in the introduction of protective labor legislation are much the same as those which other nations have had to face in the early stages of industrialization. The whole conception, as a Chinese member indicated, is a new thing in China, whereas in Europe and America the fight against industrial evils was begun a century ago. So little of the problem has been studied that the difficulty of securing an adequate system of inspection is augmented by the lack of persons equipped to train inspectors. Again, the task is made harder by the fact that the large factory is comparatively rare in Chinese industry where the tendency has been for the growth of small enterprises with inadequate capital and often incompetent management. Such small concerns, it was said, in China as elsewhere, constitute a greater hindrance to real progress in the betterment of labor conditions than the large enterprise where a decision by one authority can affect conditions for thousands of employees immediately, and where a broader and more intelligent view of the value of labor regulation is usually to be found. A Chinese economist said:

" Most Chinese employers believe that cheap labor means economical production and greater profits. They have not yet realized that if they bettered the conditions of their employees they would improve the quality of the work performed, reduce the costs due to sickness and accidents, and ultimately make greater profits. Many employers, of course, are virtually prohibited from attempting any improvements simply because they have not the necessary capital. The ignorance of workers and parents, too, is a great hindrance to the improvement of working conditions in industry. When the general standard of living is as low as it is among the masses of our people, all members of a family must work, and children will be sent to work for the most paltry wage. Working mothers will often prefer to take their children with them to work in the factories for no wage at all, to avoid the necessity of having someone stay at home to care for them."

The widespread existence of the contract labor system was another serious obstacle emphasized by a foreign member, as it had already been by Dr. Franklin L. Ho in his address (see above, p. 145). While it was stated that the system was tolerable in cases where, as in parts of the United States, the labor union is itself the contractor, in China where the contractor is a special middleman, it has few redeeming features. Its great evil lies in the fact that the employer has no contact with the workers in any form and has no means of telling what their conditions are, or whether improvements and wage increases are really passed on by the contractor to the worker. The system, it was stated, is almost universal in the Chinese mining industry and common in the building industry. Thousands of miners are employed by a large enterprise through contractors with no system of registration, so that the responsible authorities are completly in the dark as to the real wages, hours, and working conditions of the mass of the employees. To effect a reform such as the eight-hour day with any assurance that it will effectively be carried out was considered by these members almost an impossibility under such circumstances. On the other hand, it was pointed out with reference to the experience of other countries that it is possible by appropriate legislation, first of all, to secure the keeping of records by employers which subsequently can become the basis for protective laws that place the responsibility for the treatment of employees upon the registered employer. An increasing severity of requirements later may contribute toward the substitution of direct employment for the contract system.[29] It was not admitted, therefore, that even a widely prevalent contract system must necessarily defeat labor legislation. Nevertheless, it was recognized that any labor system employing intermediaries between employers and employed, paid on a commission basis, constitutes a serious hindrance to labor reform; and it was pointed out that in European countries the evil was suppressed only after public agitation that lasted many years.

A more fundamental barrier, not merely to the enforcement of factory legislation but to the whole problem of raising standards of living in China by industrialization, was stressed by a British member of long residence in the country. The difficulty consists in the enormous reservoir of unskilled, unemployed, or semi-employed labor in the country districts, constituting an unfailing source of cheap labor for the industrial employer who chooses to take advantage of it. The evil, he showed, is, on the one hand, that the unscrupulous factory owner can recruit labor from the country to work for a pittance in the towns, simply because even a pittance is often better than the semi-starvation of many rural districts, and, on the other hand (and perhaps this is the more serious aspect), that even with the enforcement of laws on reasonable wages, hours, and conditions in the cities, the presence of this outside labor supply and its tendency to crowd into industrial areas would be a constant temptation to all kinds of indirect evasions of the law, and would increasingly tend to destroy the prospects of raising standards of living among the industrial workers and of developing an effective labor movement. Most Chinese students of the problem, however, while they would be the first to acknowledge its gravity, would not conclude thereupon that it gives any grounds for questioning the need and the value of protective legislation. Rather the reverse — they would support the author of one Conference paper who expresses the matter thus:

[29] It was reported that in India, where the contract system has proved as pernicious as in China, the first of these stages had been reached; California's administrative system under the state labor law for protecting seasonal farm labor may be cited as an effective example of the middle phase; while the industrial legislation of practically all industrially advanced countries has now ruled out the *compradore* or *padrone* system even in trades with highly fluctuating labor demands.

Whether urban poverty may not be preferable to the life of many villages in China is a matter of opinion. To that of some of them — since one cannot easily do worse than die of hunger — it certainly is; to that of others, it may be suspected, it is not. But the fact that peasants are starving in Shansi or Kansu is not a reason why factory operatives should be sweated in Shanghai or Tientsin. . . . . It is difficult to be patient with the casuists who plead in one breath for the industrialization of China on the ground that it will raise the standards of life in agriculture and, in the next, defend low standards in industry on the ground that those prevalent in agriculture are still lower.[30]

Remembering the rôle played by the trade-union movement in the application of protective labor laws in Western countries, foreign members in several groups asked for information on the growth of a trade-union organization. The answers, particularly that given by a Chinese student of the subject, revealed that so far the unions in China have been either too badly organized or too much under the thumb of the local political authorities to exert an effective influence on schemes for social legislation. He quoted extreme cases of unions in Shanghai which had given no consideration to the new Factory Law at all and were apparently unaware of its bearing on the whole labor movement if not of its actual existence. Not much else could be expected with the prevailing standards of literacy among the workers and the extreme youth of the whole labor movement in China. He continued:

" Some of the first unions were organized toward the end of the Manchu régime and during the first years of the Republic. In these remarks I do not include the various guilds, because it is difficult to state the relation between them and the new unions without much further investigation. The movement has grown, however, chiefly since 1920. In the five years following there was a great deal of social unrest, the symptoms of which are to be seen in a series of important strikes — the machinists' in 1920, the seamen's in 1922, that of railway workers in 1923, and of miners in 1922–23. In these five years, the movement was on the whole rather conservative, and the agitations were concerned in the main with economic questions — protests against wage reductions, demands for better social treatment, and so on. But from 1925, particularly after the May 30 incident of that year, the movement became quite radical, with strong elements of communism in it; and patriotic demonstrations and strikes over political issues became frequent. With the victory of the Nationalist party in 1927, the movement came very much under the control of the Kuomintang, with the suppression of much of the former activities. Radicalism still undoubtedly exists, but in secret, for the Government and the party have not allowed the workers much freedom."

Asked whether the control exercised by the authorities in China corresponded to the influence brought to bear in Italy by the Government, he stated that members of the party had been sent out to supervise the organization of unions, with the result that they could keep a firm hand on all union activities. In part, this cause of action had been dictated by the lack of competent leaders in the unions, and in part by the determination to stamp out communist agitation. Prior to 1927, most of the more radical leaders had their training in the unions of South China, where such groups as the Engineers' Union in Hongkong and the Machinists' Union in Canton really

[30] Tawney, *op. cit.*, p. 115.

constituted the backbone of the whole Chinese labor movement. In answer to a further question he said that, apart from the affiliations with the Communist International in Central and South China, there have been no important attempts at co-operation with overseas or international labor activities.

In considering the enforcement of the new Factory Law, the round tables were able to avail themselves of the results of a recently completed survey on the degree to which the law in its present form could be applied in the Shanghai area and on the modifications and postponements which were considered necessary for some time to come.[31] Attention was at first concentrated on the clause which had aroused most criticism from employers in China, namely, the eight-hour day regulation. There was something of a tendency on the parts of both Chinese and foreign members to accept the popular view that the clause expresses a worthy ideal but is at present impractical and too idealistic. To this, however, an American economist demurred. He argued that research in the United States and other countries had repeatedly shown that for many industries a working day of eight hours or less is not only practical but more profitable than a longer day because of the great reduction in fatigue with its accompaniments of accidents and spoiled work. In many cases, business men have refused to be convinced of the profits to be gained from a reduction of working hours until legislation or other pressure has forced them to make the changes on grounds of social welfare. There was, of course, no ground for asserting that an eight-hour day would prove most profitable for all industries in China, but it would almost certainly be found if scientific investigations were made that a reduction of the existing long hours in most cases would justify itself on pecuniary as well as on humanitarian grounds. A demonstration by one factory in China might well convince most employers that the idealistic provisions of the Factory Law embody some sound business principles. Chinese members said the practice was far from unknown in China. A number of Shanghai concerns work on an eight-hour system, and a large soda and alkali plant in North China has done likewise for years with good results. The experience of a Tientsin cotton mill, according to a Japanese member, has been inconclusive since the reduction of hours from two twelve-hour shifts to three eight-hour shifts has also been accompanied by wage reductions.

One member, familiar with industrial labor conditions in China, warned against a tendency among foreign students of this matter to consider in a too piecemeal fashion specific evils of the Chinese industrial system — such as long hours, child labor, and the like — and possible legislative remedies for them. Each reform of this nature represents cost features that make complete administration prohibitive without reference to other aspects of industrial management. To quote the experience of American employers with the eight-hour day, for example, was not relevant unless it were remembered

---

[31] See Ta Chen, *op. cit.* For a brief account of the main provisions in the Act see "The Human Factor in China's Industrialization," above, p. 152.

that this adjustment has for its background an intricate working system of factory regulation, the result of slow development during many years. The situation in China, in the matter of hours, would be comparable only if there had first been a period of years during which the more general provisions of the Factory Act had been in force.

On the basis of long experience in labor legislation in Japan, a member from that country urged the adoption of measures which make possible a more gradual transition from present practice to the conditions aimed at in the Act. He himself had been trying for ten years to bring about the adoption of the eight-hour day in Japan by stimulating public opinion and bringing pressure to bear on Government authorities; but even so, after ten years, only 30 per cent of the factories in Japan come under the provisions of the eight-hour law. Similarly, it had required twenty years of constant agitation to secure the abolition of child labor and of night work for women. Because of the great discrepancy between existing labor conditions in China and the provisions of the Act, he believed that, in the interests of effective enforcement, a number of temporary modifications were desirable.[32]

An interesting argument arose in two round tables on the merits of a law which provided moderate measures capable of immediate application and one which introduced highly desirable but far-reaching reforms not susceptible of or intended for immediate introduction. An official of the International Labour Office drew a distinction between the British conception of law as a set of rules for immediate enforcement and the Continental European conception of a law as something which states an aim and a plan of action.[33] It was his understanding that the Chinese Factory Law is an example of the latter type and might be parralleled by many similar measures in Europe. The Sunday Observance Act in France, for example, had not been

[32] See Ta Chen, *op. cit.*, p. 29, for a plan of such modifications. These provisions include:
  (a) For immediate enforcement: record-keeping, compulsory notification of accidents, twelve years as the minimum age of admission, two compulsory rest days per month without pay, ten-hour working day for women, compensation for injuries and specified industrial diseases, eight national holidays with pay, health and safety measures, bonus provisions, machinery for discussion between employers and workers.
  (b) For enforcement after one year: four-week maternity bonus.
  (c) For enforcement after two years: eight-hour working day for young persons and provision for educational opportunities.
  (d) For enforcement after three years: abolition of night work for women and young persons.
  (e) Clauses for indefinite suspension: wage agreements, annual leave, extra payments for periods of notice for dismissal, payment while absent because of sickness.
[33] See also p. 308. Members with special knowledge of French and German law challenged this statement — which on another occasion was also made by a Chinese member. They said that the British and Continental " conception " of law is exactly the same, even though the more pragmatic island people, who also have a longer history of popular government, are perhaps less disposed to pass laws which it is difficult to carry into effect.

fully enforced for a period of two years after its promulgation, in order to permit of adjustments being made gradually. Not only in Europe but in the United States, as an American pointed out subsequently in a general meeting of the Conference, similar laws might be found. The Seaman's Act passed in 1915 had been regarded as an extremely radical piece of legislation — so much so, in fact, that many shipowners had believed it would ruin their business. The Act had not been repealed or modified and was not yet completely enforced but was increasingly being enforced every year. There were also repeated references, in this connection, to the American experience with the prohibition of liquor.

Granting the contention of another foreign member that such laws had the advantage of indicating to industrialists exactly what the long-term plans of the Government are in regard to protective legislation and of thus allowing them to prepare in advance for the necessary adjustments, some Japanese and British still considered that there was need of framing the law more definitely in order to leave less doubt as to what measures were expected to be enforced at once, and consequently to obviate the danger of having the whole law become a dead letter. The same point was embodied in a more comprehensive criticism voiced by a Chinese. He said:

" Our Factory Law is essentially Western and not entirely in accord with Chinese conditions. The psychological effect of a law which cannot be properly enforced is bad. What we need is a less ambitious law which can really be applied. The present Act, moreover, applies only to a very small section of the population, namely, to those who come under its narrow definition of a factory, and it therefore excludes great numbers of handicraft workers who are urgently in need of protective legislation."

In view of the assertions commonly made on the difficulties placed in the way of introducing social legislation by the presence in the large industrial towns of foreign factories and of foreign-administered areas outside the jurisdiction of the Chinese Government, one group examined this problem in some detail. Constitutional difficulties, it was explained, preclude the functioning of officials of one administration in the territory of another: hence the Chinese inspectors in the service of the municipality of Greater Shanghai cannot directly inspect factories in the French Concession or in the International Settlement. Since the Factory Act had come into operation only on October 1, it was too early as yet to know whether co-operation in its administration would be effected in the three areas similar to that, for example, which had been established to enforce the Chinese governmental standards in respect of weights and measures. Similarly, it was reported that co-operation between the health administrations of the three municipalities had during the last two years resulted in a greatly improved control of certain communicable diseases, especially cholera. One speaker made a plea, therefore, that political constitutional difficulties as between different local administrations should not be allowed to interfere with the progressive application of essential social legislation. It was stated that among the foreign employers themselves there was no disposition to resist regulation but rather to welcome and even to invite it, provided its incidence were gradual and equitable; only recently, the Shanghai Employers' Federation, composed of fifty foreign firms, had requested the Municipal Council to indorse the principle of industrial regulation at the time of the declared enforcement of the Factory Act by the Government of China.[34] A Chinese member stressed the fact that foreign employers were in a position to make or mar the whole purpose of the Act. Any sign of a forward step on their part toward co-operation in its application would have an immense effect in breaking down the shortsighted opposition of many Chinese factory owners. For, rightly or wrongly, these men, as long as foreign employers do not abide by the Act, will plead the fact as an excuse for ignoring it also, on the ground of unfair competition. In reality, in the speaker's opinion, their troubles lay nearer at home and were to be found rather in faulty management and bad financing, but for these fundamental weaknesses the sweating of laborers was no solution. A progressive move by the foreign concerns would do much to expose the error of their arguments, and was the more to be desired because the foreign firms in many cases were better prepared (and often indeed more willing) to initiate reforms — some of these, in fact, having already been introduced. On the whole, the attitude taken by the Shanghai Municipal Council had been encouraging. The sacrifices which would be involved were less than might appear on the surface, since it was recognized quite frankly that certain parts of the law were experimental, and that the more advanced proposals would not be made effective for some time to come.

For these views a foreign member in business in China expressed his support. Whatever the faults of foreign business enterprises in China, they were unable to shut their eyes to social and labor questions if only because the problems they touched upon were so acute. There had been distinct signs of advance in recent years. There was the beginning of a movement for adoption of a nine-hour day; more and more attention was being paid to the position of women workers; and as employers were giving more attention to the quality of their labor, there was a growing tendency to have some concern for the children of their employees and for young employees under the age of sixteen.[35]

He went on to mention the need, already voiced in other round tables, for more scientific study of industrial problems. The recently founded Institute of Scientific Management was cited as an example which ought to be

[34] This the Council did, gazetting its support of the principle on August 1, 1931 (see below, p. 169).

[35] With the lack of birth certification, the reduction of child labor has been found particularly difficult. In 1925, the Shanghai Municipal Council tried unsuccessfully to introduce a by-law to limit employment of children progressively to those of ten, then of twelve years. (The Chinese law makes fourteen the limit.) No foreign-owned mills in Shanghai now employ children known to be under fourteen. All young employees in Japanese cotton mills are given a height test before employment — the minimum standard being 4 ft. 2 in.

matched by a Workers' Institute, since both were urgently needed to combat the ignorance and apathy which were characteristic of many employers no less than of workers. Akin to this was the need for a system of model or demonstration factories which could prove the economic as well as the human utility of protective legislation in ways that would appeal much more to the ordinary business man than the arguments of theorists or the pleas of social reformers. There was a keen realization of the fact that the appalling lack of both elementary-school education and practical social education in China constitutes a grievous handicap to all attempts at social advancement.

It was in this spirit that an American and a Chinese member at different round tables ventured some doubts as to the ultimate efficacy of social legislation in China and, indeed, of industrial progress in general unless these developments were accompanied by a determined effort on the part of the responsible authorities to urge the need and to provide the requisite teaching for conscious limitation of population. It was recognized, of course, that as a matter of history industrialization had commonly coincided with a reduction in birth-rates. None the less, to quote the Conference syllabus on the matter:

There are no natural laws of industrialization, and no one may speak with certainty of its social and political reactions in China. But this much is probable if history is any guide: industrialization in its first decades can do little to relieve the present pressure of population. It will do well if it can absorb the fresh expansion of population which it will itself bring in its wake. Provided it does so, and provided there is a considerable advance in elementary education, there is hope that within a generation, or perhaps two, the influence of new standards of comfort and new social ideas may begin to show itself in a reduction of the birth-rate through voluntary limitation of families. The realization of that hope depends mainly on whether the development of industry is left to run wild or is consciously regulated by some central authority. Industrialization in some form or other will proceed willy nilly. The crucial issue is whether it shall proceed in order or in chaos.[36]

Evidences of the same attitudes were to be seen in many of the remarks made by foreign members at the round table. Painfully conscious of the economic muddle into which the oft vaunted Western civilization has fallen, they were likely to look with doubting eyes on all plans that implied a too wholesale acceptance of the machinery of that order of society without a careful decision in advance as to the ends to be achieved.[37] The view found

[36] *Syllabus on China's Economic Development*, p. 25.

[37] At the final meeting of the Conference, a Japanese, speaking for some of the younger members of the Conference who had been meeting informally by themselves, said: " There exists a marked difference of opinion between the generations — those above and those below forty. Our younger people have grown up in a period of highly organized industry, of increasing international economic interdependence and of decreasing authority of absolute nationalism. We see in the last Great War, so called, an inevitable clash of capitalistic nations, and since then an untiring fight for peace. We have passed through a decade of relatively successful economic rehabilitation in a specific area which coincides with national governmental organization; but we find ourselves at present in a depressing chaos of world-economy. These experiences have made the mentality of our younger generation different from that of the older generation. . . .

expression in the conclusion of a Chinese paper which, after an examination of the cruelly low material standard of living on which the bulk of China's people is forced to exist, ended with these remarks:

It is not our purpose here to applaud what Russia has achieved so far; but what is suggested is merely that, in order to promote without waste and in the shortest time possible the industrial and economic development of this country that would contribute to the welfare of the population as a whole, some kind of planned economy undertaken by an efficient state organization appears to be highly desirable.[38]

The organization of such a planned economy, as was well perceived in the round tables which considered the point, is in China inevitably linked with the problem of securing adequate supplies of capital.

"When capital is as scarce as it is in China, it is of vital importance that it should not be diverted from industries whose development is an urgent national need into financial ventures which, if profitable to investors, are, from a public standpoint, at best of secondary importance and at worst mischievous. What is required, in fact, is a scheme of priorities under which the undertakings whose establishment or expansion is of most general moment will have the first call on the capital available for industry. The execution of such a policy would involve a relationship between the state and banking institutions sufficiently close to enable the former to exercise control over the proceedings of the latter, and to guide investment into the employments, whether the most immediately remunerative or not, in which its utility to China will in the long run be greatest."

It is scarcely necessary to add, since it was well brought out in subsequent discussions at the Conference, that such a policy also involves devising a new set of relationships between the state and those foreign banks and financial establishments which in the past have provided the main channel for the inflow of capital into China and which in future must continue to play a major rôle in the economic rebuilding of the country. These discussions, therefore, like those on the central problems of communications, treated in the previous chapter, lead on very naturally to the deeper and more involved (because more overlaid with political complications) questions of foreign investments and public loans in China, which are reported below in chapter vi.

We put more emphasis upon problems of distribution than upon those of production. We are more interested in the conquest of social vices than in the conquest of nature. . . .

"There has not been sufficient treatment of this problem of distribution. We have talked about peace and the machinery of peace; but we must remember that the problem of peace is that of a highly complicated economic situation. For this problem not only so-called international questions but also apparently internal questions have grave significance. We have at this Conference discussed, it is true, problems of land utilization, of labor and the standard of living in various countries; but we have only slightly touched upon the problem of reorganizing the whole economic system. We have got to face that cardinal issue. . . ."

[38] L. K. Tao, *The Standard of Living among Chinese Workers* (China Council), p. 28.

POSTSCRIPT

PROGRESS TOWARD INDUSTRIAL REGULATION, TO DECEMBER, 1931

By Eleanor Hinder

An important progressive step was taken when, in June, 1931, a Training Institute for Factory Inspectors was set up by the Ministry for Industries, and thirty-one students enrolled in a course to last three months. A second course for a group thirty-nine in number, this time sent from various provincial and municipal governments throughout the country, began in October. In the second group five were women.

One of the factors which has to be taken into consideration in attempting to secure regulation is the existence of other-than-Chinese governmental administrations in the country, such as those of concessions and settlements: and of the existence of extraterritoriality under which various nationals are subject, not to Chinese law, but to that of their own country. Hence there is importance in the fact that on August 1, the date upon which the Factory Law came into effect, the Shanghai Municipal Council gave publicity to a resolution taken two days earlier, indorsing the principle of industrial regulation, giving its opinion that application must be gradual, and outlining the scope (upon the suggestion of its Chinese members), of what it believed such regulation should ultimately cover. This step followed upon the request of the Employers' Federation, who, throughout, have shown no inclination to resist regulation as such, but rather to welcome it, provided its incidence shall be gradual and equitable. Perhaps in no other instance in history can it be recorded that organized employers have addressed authorities, requesting regulation. It is true that there is an amount of political expediency involved: it must not be said by the Chinese Government that it is prevented from the enforcement of its factory legislation through refusal of foreign factories to submit themselves to regulation.

In September, at the invitation of the National Government of China, a delegation of two from the International Labour Organization of the League of Nations arrived to advise upon the subject of inspection. It consisted of M. Camille Pone, head of the Diplomatic Section of the I.L.O., and Dame Adelaide Anderson, whose lifework and former experience in China amply fitted her for the task. These advisers significantly confined their attention to the question of enforcement from the point of view of the Inspection Law. That is to say, since this law specifies the duties of inspectors, they felt justified in considering as for the moment not to be enforced, those clauses of the main Factory Act which are not included within this range of duties. They have recommended to the National Government immediate application of more urgent clauses, such as those covering health and safety, and suspension of those other clauses to the Factory Act which are not, by law, subject to inspection. They have further recommended that for Shanghai there shall be one inspectorate under the Chinese authorities, members of which, as they enter either the French Concession or the International Settlement, shall be accompanied by officials of these administrations. These foreign authorities have agreed that forthwith Chinese inspectors may commence inspection of Chinese factories within the confines of their adminis-trations, provided they are drafted into the actual municipal service of either the International Settlement or the French Concession. This the Shanghai Municipal Council may do without constitutional change, and the French Consul-General may also decree such, for the Chinese citizens within the Settlement and Concession are subject to the Criminal and Civil Code of the Chinese Government, in addition to Municipal regulation. But as yet, the Shanghai Municipal Council has not power to cause inspection of all, including foreign factories, within the borders of the International Settlement.

In order, however, to indorse the principle of industrial regulation, the Employers' Federation, in November again addressed the Council, asking that steps be taken to call a special meeting of ratepayers for the purpose of altering By-law No. 34, applying to licensed premises, so as to include factories as premises for the operation of which a municipal license is necessary, as a prerequisite for permission to operate. Once in possession of this authority, the Council can impose on all factories in the Settlement any license conditions, such as health and safety features, and any sections of the Chinese Factory Act which are satisfactorily enforced in the Chinese administration. Once again it is unique that employers should take the initiative in requesting regulation. In Shanghai the task of getting out the more than one thousand ratepayers who represent a quorum is a very difficult one; and the Employers' Federation has assured the Council of its help in this matter. On December 9, the Council took decision to call a special meeting of ratepayers for this purpose on the occasion of the annual meeting in April. Thus another milestone of progress can be reported.

CHAPTER VI

FOREIGN LOANS AND INVESTMENTS

DATA PAPERS

1. CARL F. REMER. *Foreign Investments in China* (mimeographed, International Research report).
2. D. K. LIEU. *Foreign Investments in China* (China Council).
3. C. Y. HSIEH and M. C. CHU. *Foreign Interest in the Mining Industry in China* (China Council).
4. ZENICHI ITANI. *The Export of Japanese Capital to China* (Japanese Council).
5. MASUTARO KIMURA. *Problems of Financial Reforms and Readjustment of Public Loans in China* (Japanese Council).
6. KATSUSHI UCHIDA. *The Problem of China's Loan Readjustment* (Japanese Council).
7. F. V. FIELD. *American Participation in the China Consortiums* (American Council).

REFERENCES

1. A. N. HOLCOMBE. " Can the Nations Cooperate in the Economic Rehabilitation of China? " *Annals of the American Academy of Political and Social Science,* November, 1930.
2. A. N. COONS. *The Foreign Public Debt of China.* Philadelphia, 1930.
3. HERBERT M. BRATTER. *Financial Development in the Far East during 1929.* Washington: U.S. Government Printing Office, 1930.
4. U.S. DEPARTMENT OF COMMERCE. *American Direct Investments in Foreign Countries* (Trade Information Bull. 731). Washington, 1930.
5. SOUTH MANCHURIA RAILWAY. *Second Report on Progress in Manchuria — to 1930* (Dairen, 1931), chap. iii.
6. TOSHI GO. *Japanese Investments in China.* New York: Foreign Policy Association, 1931.
7. EAST ASIATIC ECONOMIC INVESTIGATION BUREAU (TOA-KEIZAI CHESAKYOKU). *Manchuria Year Book, 1931* (Tokyo, 1931), chap. xvii.
8. KYI ZUH-TSING. " Japan's Loan Operations in Manchuria," *Chinese Economic Journal,* November, 1931.

INTRODUCTORY NOTE

No special round table at the Conference was organized for the discussion of foreign investments and loans in China, and even in the discussions of China's economic development little mention was made of the more technical aspects of the country's foreign and domestic indebtedness or of future policies regarding large-scale investment in China. The reason is to be found in the marked preoccupation of the members with the possibilities of progress in agricultural techniques and rural economic organization.[1] Only one of the

---

[1] The suggested agenda of the Program Committee contained, among other questions implying concern with the financial side of China's economic development, the following specific queries: What modification of financial arrangements in China itself is needed to make capital more available for socially productive purposes? To what extent are both agricultural and industrial development in need of foreign co-operation and credits, and how can they be satisfactorily secured?

four groups came to grips with the matter. The Conference as a whole had the benefit of two valuable addresses — one by an official of the Bank of China on the subject of Chinese public finance in recent years, and another by a foreign banker in Shanghai on problems of finance and investment in Shanghai. In addition to these addresses, five or six data papers — supplied by the Chinese, Japanese, and American councils — dealt directly with the subject, and a preliminary report of one of the Institute's larger international research projects provided an up-to-date estimate of the amount and distribution of foreign investments in China. The present chapter is therefore mainly a compilation of addresses and extracts from a few of the data papers.

The subject, however, is important enough to warrant a few introductory remarks on those wider aspects which have to do with the economic reconstruction of China and the political future of the Republic. As will be seen from preceding chapters, the fact was impressed forcibly on the minds of Conference members that the obstacles in the way of economic progress in China arrange themselves in series of vicious circles unless attention is concentrated on possible ways of breaking these circles at their weakest point. It is fatally easy to show that rural development in China depends on better credit and marketing arrangements — that these in turn require a unification of the currency and improved communications — which are blocked by the shortage of capital — because new foreign loans are no longer forthcoming — while the question of outstanding foreign public debts remains unsettled — as a result of internal political disorder — which obliges the Government to squander most of its resources not already mortgaged upon maintaining its military machine and buying off rival military factions, and prevents its taking those steps necessary to balancing its budget and initiating the works of reconstruction — which would do much to rehabilitate its credit in foreign bond markets. Political stability and economic development are each held back by the defects of the other; yet a slight injection of outside stimulus to either might open the way to the advance of both.

For foreign nations directly to assist in the suppression of political disorder in China is no longer a course that seems within the bounds of practicability, although this is far from precluding certain indirect forms of assistance, as a British member forcibly stated at a general meeting of the Conference body. He said, addressing himself to foreign members:

"The key problem for China is how she can secure a strong government, and the question which, I suggest, we as foreigners should put quite bluntly to ourselves is this: do we or do we not want China to realize for herself a strong government? — and to answer it publicly when we return to our countries."

He went on to suggest that perhaps the first step for the foreign countries was to keep in closer touch with the Government of China.[2]

Possibilities of direct assistance in the economic sphere were not, however, overlooked. A brief interchange of opinion on the question took place

[2] See also proposals for additional diplomatic machinery, pp. 260 ff.

toward the close of one round table.   The subject was broached by a Japanese member who, in discussing the need for foreign credits in China's industrial development, advocated an international conference on the adjustment of public loans in China as the essential preliminary to the rehabilitation of China's financial status abroad, and drew attention to the chances of China repaying her outstanding loans without any great difficulty from the increasing surplus of the customs revenue.[3]   His remarks elicited support from a British member who referred to the discussions which the Chinese Government had opened with representatives of the principal creditor countries in November, 1930.

The conference adjourned, it was reported, after it had discussed only future procedure and agreed that the Chinese authorities should negotiate separately with representatives of the Powers, further meetings to be opened only when they were deemed necessary. Eight months have elapsed, but except that in the interval the Chinese Committee has met once or twice, and the representatives of Japan and China have had a few conversations, no substantial progress has been made.[4]

A Chinese economist, in reply, readily admitted the justice of the remarks made by the previous speakers but went on to suggest the possibility of new industrial loans which would not necessarily enter into the category of Government loans.

" The economic development of China needs foreign credit, and credit is desirable both from the Chinese standpoint and from that of foreign countries. Any fair-minded Chinese would not expect new governmental loans to be made without provisions for these existing obligations which have just been mentioned. Conditions so far have undoubtedly been adverse, and we must rest content with the recognition of the problem by the National Government. But the industrial loans of which I am speaking would be matters for negotiation directly between business concerns and not through the Government. It would be a question of co-operation between bankers' associations, chambers of commerce, and industrial firms for the development of particular industries."

Asked whether the banks who are members of the Consortium, which has reference only to loans for the National and Provincial Governments, would in practice try to discourage such outside loans for industrial purposes, a British member gave the opinion that the British banks at any rate would probably not discourage them, but that if all the banks were brought into a scheme they would keep to the principle that further loans could not be made without reference to existing Government and railway loans. More serious than defaults on general Government loans had been failures to pay for equipment purchased by certain Chinese railways, even though in some cases the lines had been earning profits. He agreed with the views expressed by the Chinese member as to the need for more co-operation in the financing of industrial enterprises between Chinese and foreign banks, maintaining that

[3] A detailed plan based on this principle was set forth in a data paper submitted by the Japanese Council (see Katsushi Uchida, *The Problem of China's Loan Readjustment*, pp. 9–13).

[4] *Ibid.*, p. 1.

the idea is an essential part of the policy of British banks in China, and of the Consortium itself. A great deal, he concluded, had already been achieved along those very lines, and certain Chinese banks were already working in close co-operation with foreign banks on loan operations, in this respect partly taking the place of the German and Russian groups of the old Consortium.

It was, of course, recognized that direct business investments by foreign concerns, as distinct from loans, have been increasing steadily in the treaty ports and concessions, and that of late a significant volume of Chinese capital has been invested in building and public utilities of cities like Canton and Amoy, which derive a great deal of wealth from their nationals living abroad in the United States and British Malaya.

The round-table members for lack of time did not push the discussion further. Yet it is pertinent to add a few points on a problem so basic for the economic future of China. For those bankers and bondholders whose interests are directly affected and whose dealings in certain Chinese Government loans have not always been fortunate, the question of outstanding debts naturally comes uppermost in all talk of further large investments. On the other hand, for the statesman and even for the financial concern which can afford to take a long view, it might be possible to contribute greatly to international good-will and ultimate material profit to insist rather less on such conditions as debt settlements and foreign supervision of new loan enterprises, and to take a more positive constructive view. They are in a position to initiate fuller co-operation with Chinese banking and commercial houses and to assist in the economic regeneration and thus in the political stabilization of the country. So far, to take even the first steps in this direction will bespeak an important psychological change.[5]

Such a policy, it was felt by many of the foreign members, would not be wholly visionary and impractical. Every member who had traveled in China mentioned that he was impressed with the fact that in many parts of the country things lie waiting to be done, wanting only the initial push of assistance from outside. For example, the construction of the 250 miles of railway to complete the Canton-Hankow line that would provide China with a trunk railway running right through the interior from Hopei to Kwangtung has waited for twelve years for lack of funds since work under the Kwangtung Provincial Government ceased in 1919, with the result that both north and south sections have suffered from the loss of revenue on the through traffic which ought to be the mainstay of the completed line. The short gap be-

[5] This positive, co-operative attitude is stressed in the conclusions of C. F. Remer's study of *Foreign Investments in China,* soon to be published in book form. It is, however, amplified and placed in a different light by a prominent British banker who writes to the editor: " It has been one of our cardinal tenets that further foreign capital will not be available in China until their large foreign undischarged debt is taken care of. This is not the laid-down condition of a harsh creditor clamoring for his money, but an indication to Chinese financiers and statesmen that their prime need is the restoration of credit, and that no restoration of credit is possible so long as outstanding debt with ever accruing interest is ignored. China's capital requirements are very large and will, when world conditions improve, tax the resources of the world's money markets."

tween the northern and southern sections of the Shanghai-Hangchow-Ningpo line has remained unclosed for years. Elsewhere in China surveys for lines have been carried out and roadbeds have even been partially constructed, and the work has been left unfinished. The machine stands ready to run; only the fuel for the furnace is lacking.

Chinese and foreign members agreed that much of this stagnation is the result of military operations and the illegal exactions of local military officials, and that railways, like other basic enterprises in China, must be freed from such interferences before they can perform their whole function in the reordering of China's social economy.[6] To say that, however, is but half the truth; for the assistance that will set the essential parts of the economic machine running will simultaneously and increasingly strengthen the hand of the central authority and weaken the forces of provincialism and local militarism which now clog its wheels. Reconstruction no less than deterioration proceeds with increasing momentum, and a movement for progress once started makes further steps both easier and longer. As Mr. Lieu points out in the concluding passage of his paper (see p. 192), the foreign financial institutions, both abroad and in the treaty ports, could without serious hazard to themselves adopt for a period the view of the statesman rather than that of the creditor. They could, it was felt, with the certainty of eventual gain give China slight but invaluable aid in taking those first steps toward achieving that station in the economic community of nations which she is by nature fitted to occupy.

[6] See p. 119. The British banker quoted in the previous note takes the uncompleted Canton-Hankow railway as an illustration of a view which he considers typical for Lombard Street and Wall Street: " This work of construction requires not less than £6,000,000, and it is a project which has no prospect of being carried out until China's credit in the New York bond market is restored. The £100 bonds issued for the first section of this particular line are in grievous arrears in the matter of interest, and can be purchased for £14½. It seems to me wrong to hold out any encouragement to the Chinese that there can be progress in the face of facts like these. . . . We have, during recent years and in a small way, supplied some of the better railways with new rolling stock, on easy terms of credit and upon the assurance that increased revenue will be immediately forthcoming. Locomotives and waggons are put in operation, but so long as no attempt is made to fulfill the bargain by payments in accordance with the terms of the agreement our action is frustrated."

ADDRESSES

I. FOREIGN CAPITAL IN CHINA

By G. E. HUBBARD

My subject presents many aspects. I have decided to take my line of approach from the round-table agenda on " China's Economic Development," and have tried to correlate my subject with the questions suggested for discussion in that agenda.[7] These questions center mainly round the development of agriculture and industry on " socially productive " lines, and I propose to discuss how far the importation of foreign capital to China has been in the past, and may be in the future, an active agent in this development. . . . .

With the help of the figures given in Professor Remer's data paper on *Foreign Investment in China* it is possible to present the following analysis of foreign capital invested in China at the present time. The figures, of course, contain a great deal of estimate, and it is better to take them only as providing a rough measure of the general order of magnitude of the items concerned and as a scale for judging proportions. Professor Remer, like other investigators, has divided foreign investment into two parts, " business investments " and " Chinese Government debt." The combined total is estimated at something in the region of Mex. $15,000 million. Of this more than three-quarters falls under the head of " business investment "; but here there are two important qualifying facts which should at once be stressed: first, the peculiar nature of much of the business investment in China due to the existence of what Professor Remer calls " foreign colonies " planted in China's internal economy. A large part of the capital is confined to the treaty ports. These stand in a peculiar economic relation to China on the one hand and to the rest of the world on the other, and for this reason a considerable part of the capital has only an indirect effect on the development of China as a whole. The other fact is that of the business investment one-third is in Manchuria alone, one-third in Shanghai, and the remaining one-third covers Hongkong as well as the rest of China.

As to the provenance of this capital, about three-quarters of the total business investments have been made by Great Britain and Japan in approximately equal parts. Whereas the British investment is spread throughout China, the Japanese is mainly centered in Manchuria. The two countries are far ahead of all others in business investment. The same is true of their share in Chinese Government loans, though the figures in this case are much less informative, being based merely on the localities where the loans were originally issued; as the bonds are freely salable, the distribution of present holdings may of course be very different from what it was at the time of issue. Professor Remer's figures for foreign investment in general give Great Britain 37 per cent of the whole, and Japan 34 per cent, Russia 10 per cent (also, of

[7] See p. 171.

course, concentrated in Manchuria), and the United States and France 5 per cent each.

The purposes for which the imported capital has been employed can be expressed — very roughly, it is true — in terms of percentage. The percentages are as follows, and I invite your particular attention to the first item:

Transportation, 27 per cent

Manufacturing, 13 per cent

Real estate (principally situated in Shanghai and the larger treaty ports), about 10 per cent

The machinery of import and export trade, about the same amount, 10 per cent

Of the remainder, about 13 per cent represents loans to the Government for so-called " general purposes " which have not, as a whole, been of productive character

There is one last division into distinctive categories to which it is important to refer, namely, the different sources of Chinese Government revenue which have been allotted as security for the existing foreign debt. The largest group of Government loans, aggregating nearly 40 per cent of the whole, is secured upon the railway revenues. The next, of approximately the same magnitude, is secured on the two public revenues which in the past have been looked on as the mainstay of Chinese credit, namely, customs and salt revenue. These are composed chiefly of war loans and indemnities,[8] together with the large £25,000,000 loan, known as the Reorganization Loan, made to Yuan Shih-kai in the early days of the Republic. The last category, accounting for 20 per cent, comprises the so-called " unsecured " loans made for various purposes and contributed mostly by Japan.

What part of this mass of imported capital has gone into " socially productive " developments? The answer to this question is greatly helped by Professor Remer's calculation to the effect that one-half of the outstanding foreign investment has behind it some form of industrial equipment. As I have already mentioned, transportation alone, including railways and river shipping, accounts for about a quarter. Of the balance, a great part is sunk in Shanghai; how to regard this partly " colonial " investment, in relation to the general development of China, it is difficult to say. The question is closely linked up with the future political status of this great city. Apart from the foregoing I can see only two productive fields of any great importance into which foreign capital has entered. The first is the development of mines, largely by Sino-foreign corporations, and the other the establishment of factories, especially cotton mills. Agricultural development has been little affected by foreign capital. The same is true, I think, of power generation except in two or three treaty ports.

Of the fields I have mentioned, transportation, and in particular railways, is far the most important historically. It seems likely to hold the same leading place in the future. Almost everyone accepts transportation as the

---

[8] " Remitted " Boxer-indemnity annuities are not herein included.

first step toward economic reconstruction on a large scale in China. It seems fairly certain that railway development cannot advance far without foreign financial assistance. Let us see, then, how this has been obtained in the past. For our present purpose we can ignore the so-called concession lines, comprising the Chinese Eastern Railway and its limb the South Manchuria Railway, the German-built Shantung railway, now returned to China, and the French-built railway in Yunnan. One important line, the Peking-Suiyuan, was built with purely Chinese funds, derived mainly from surplus earnings of other Government railways. Practically all the rest were financed on the uniform plan of raising a loan abroad against the issue of fixed interest bonds, marketed by a foreign bank or banking syndicate. The banks acted as underwriters; they lent their credit to the flotation of bonds and acted as the Government's agents for the service of the loans. By this means the Government obtained the necessary funds at an average rate of about 6 per cent, and built therewith the railways as their own property, though subject in some cases to a mortgage clause in the bondholders' favor. These mortgage clauses, I may mention, have never actually been invoked, in spite of defaults. The underwriting banks insisted on certain conditions to protect the interests of the bondholders, the principal being a Government undertaking to employ foreign technical men in certain key positions in the engineering and accounts departments. The nature of these conditions tended to relax with each succeeding loan contract signed with foreign banks, but the principles remained as an essential part of every railway loan agreement up to the time of the most recent, which was concluded just before the Great War.

If foreign capital is to flow again into China for railway purposes, one of the chief questions to consider will be whether the type of contract will be similar to that which I have just described or conceived along some quite different line. In considering this, there are two points which have an important bearing. When a railway is built with the help of long-term credit on a gold-currency basis, the Chinese Government assumes exchange risks over a long period, and until final redemption of the loan its liability remains an uncertain quantity in terms of Chinese currency. In the case of direct investments the risk, of course, is borne by the foreigners. A point on the other side is that under the old system the foreign bondholder bears what may perhaps be considered an undue share of the loss when things go wrong with the railway. Although his bond is nominally guaranteed by the Government, in practice he seldom gets paid once the revenue of the particular railway ceases to be sufficient to provide the service funds.

I have said so much about railways because the problem of transportation seems of preponderant importance in regard to foreign investment. What I now have to say is of general application. What are the principal barriers to the further flow of capital into China? The availability of investable foreign funds is at a time like the present a question on which I cannot venture to touch. But I may draw attention to Professor Remer's suggestion that the limiting feature for the future is likely to be what he describes as " China's capacity to receive," which apparently depends upon her degree of progress in a number of different fields, political and economic. A more specific barrier is China's silver currency which, by the instability of its exchange value with gold, puts a decided check on the import of short-term funds while adding great complications to longer-term credits. There is another ditch to be crossed, more especially in the case of Government borrowing, consisting of the heavy accumulation of overdue debt of which a very large part is in respect of the railway loans. It is generally recognized, and not least by the Chinese Government itself, that a funding settlement of some sort is a *sine qua non* to the resumption of Government credits on any considerable scale. A further difficulty which often obtrudes itself on the attention of the foreign banker in China is the gulf which exists between current interest rates in China and the West, reflecting a wide difference of view concerning credit security.

As to the agencies through which foreign investments have chiefly entered China: direct investment on a large scale is comparatively new, and the funds involved come through multifarious channels. Large corporations and big individual firms are doubtless responsible for a large proportion of the imported funds. As regards government loans, most of the borrowing has been made through banking groups of a single or several nationalities. The China Banking Consortium has behind it a long and complicated history covering the gradual development from cutthroat competition to a highly organized machine of international co-operation. Mr. Field has supplied us with an excellent summary in his book on the Consortium,[9] prepared for this Conference. The great practical difficulties of welding foreign banks into an organization suitable for tapping the money markets of the world smoothly and simultaneously for the purpose of loans to China have been gradually overcome; and machinery now exists which in its present or some modified form may eventually prove an exceedingly useful organ for mobilizing capital abroad for China's economic development.

On the more strictly practical side of the subject is the readiness of foreigners to subscribe to Chinese loans or to invest in industrial undertakings in China. It is a number of years since any important foreign loans have been issued by the Chinese Government. Money has been steadily pouring in, it is true, for industrial development, but this has been mainly limited to the treaty ports, and especially to Shanghai. This investment in foreign-controlled areas stands on a special footing and is hardly indicative of what China can expect in the wider sphere of economic development throughout the country. Supposing for the moment China were ready to borrow today, what would be the principal features in the situation from the foreigner's point of view? I will try to express it in the form of a balance sheet, and I will put the debit side first. There is, then, first, the somewhat sorrowful experience of holders of Chinese loan bonds and especially railway bonds. Many of these have for years past had to forego their interest and the re-

[9] F. V. Field, *American Participation in the China Consortiums* (American Council).

demption of their bonds. Besides this, and equally important from the point of view of the foreign banks who sign the loan agreements, is the fact that the Chinese Government has in at least one instance altered by unilateral action the terms of such an agreement, a procedure which has naturally tended to raise doubts about the practical validity of its loan contracts in general. Then there is the mixed experience of shareholders in mining companies. Some have done quite well, but others with investments in properties in the far interior of China have suffered severely from the results of local political disturbance. As regards investment in factories, there is an uncertainty in the outlook which is inevitably discouraging to present expansion. I refer to the uncertainty in regard to future taxation and to legislation in the form, for instance, of factory acts, for we are passing through a period when new laws and regulations are in process of frequent promulgation by the National Government. Investments may also be influenced, though on this point I speak without much certainty, by doubts as to eventual Government policy in regard to such essential matters as the socialization of industry. All these considerations find expression in stock-market quotations; and it is only necessary to look at the present level of Chinese bonds to realize how impossible would be the flotation of Chinese loans abroad at this particular moment. It is hardly necessary to add that the same remark might apply today to about nine-tenths of the nations of the world.

To turn to the credit side, I would put first the growth of modern Chinese banking. The development of great Chinese banks like the Bank of China has had a stabilizing effect on Chinese finance; and it is common knowledge that the leading Chinese bankers now form a very strong influence in this country which is exerted in the direction of solid and sane finance. Another point concerning the Chinese banks is the prospect of co-operation between them and foreign banks, which, I may add, is one of the standing principles of the International Consortium. A further credit item is the evidence of serious attempts by the Ministry of Finance, under the present minister, Mr. T. V. Soong, to unify the government finance and to bring it on to a solid and budgetary basis. I should like to add that Mr. Soong's work in this direction has received repeated recognition in the press of foreign countries during the last two years.

It would not be easy to strike the balance between these two contrary sets of influences on the mind of the investor, and I shall not attempt to do so. There is, however, one thing which I can confidently affirm. One of the greatest encouragements to the foreign investor to place his money in China will be if he sees the Chinese investing their own funds. If we may visualize the foreign investor in the guise of the " golden goose," I should say that what he particularly needs to stimulate his laying is a good nest-egg in the shape of Chinese investment.

II. PUBLIC FINANCE IN CHINA

ADDRESS BY PING-FANG HSIA

The most outstanding phase of the financial situation in China from the point of view of her future economic development probably is the condition of the Chinese Government's finance. This is so because a government always plays an important rôle in the economic development of any country, either by taking the initiative to establish commerce and industries or by giving encouragement to private undertakings through the provision of adequate laws, taxation and banking systems, and other favorable conditions. But, for economic development in China, sound government finance is perhaps even more necessary than in other countries, and the Government perhaps will have to act more as a leader than in other cases. Moreover, to a considerable extent, China will require the support and co-operation of foreign capital which is not likely to be attracted to China and participate in her economic development unless China as a nation is able to balance her budget and to improve her credit standing abroad.

For various reasons, the Chinese Government has found it difficult to limit her expenditures to the amount of her income. In his report on the national finances covering the eighteenth fiscal year of the Republic ending June 30, 1930, Mr. T. V. Soong, minister of finance, indicated a deficit of more than $100,000,000, which had to be made up through borrowings in the form of bond issues, bank loans, and bank overdrafts. Mr. Soong's report for the nineteenth fiscal year ending June 30, 1931, is not yet available; but it is known that during that period the Nanking Government issued domestic bonds to the amount of $350,000,000. We do not know how much of the proceeds of these bonds were actually required to balance the budget, but the amount must have well exceeded $200,000,000, which we may roughly take as the size of the deficit for that year. On the basis of this information and the current rates of taxation we may attempt to draw up as follows a rough budget of the country for the twentieth fiscal year and see what is going to be the difference between revenues and expenditures (Table I).

TABLE I

ESTIMATED BUDGET FOR THE TWENTIETH FISCAL YEAR

REVENUES		EXPENDITURES	
Customs.................	$350,000,000	Military expenses.......	$320,000,000
Salt....................	150,000,000	Loan service...........	364,000,000
Consolidated taxes.......	70,000,000	Other expenses.........	216,000,000
Other revenues..........	30,000,000		
Estimated deficit........	300,000,000		
Total...............	$900,000,000	Total..............	$900,000,000

As will be seen from the estimate, the military expenses of the Chinese Government are extremely heavy, amounting to over a third of the total expenditures. Unfortunately, frequent occurrence of civil war and the presence of communism and banditry in many parts of China have necessitated the maintenance of large military forces, not only causing a severe drain upon the Government's income which otherwise might have been diverted to more useful and constructive projects, but also destroying trade opportunities and hindering the economic growth of the country which will have to contribute to the Government's income. The situation is truly deplorable and may well be likened to burning the candle at both ends — which cannot be expected to last very long.

The second group of the Chinese Government's expenditures comprises the requirements for the payment of interest and principal on her outstanding loans. Figured at the present rate of exchange, the total amount of the Chinese Government's foreign loans that are yet unredeemed is about $1,200,000,000 (silver), whereas the total amount of her outstanding domestic loans, including both those issued by the old Peking administration and those issued by the present Nanking Government, is about $850,000,000. These are the loans for which payments must be regularly provided by the Ministry of Finance, and they do not include railway loans and other unsecured obligations of the Government. There has been practically no increase or new issue in China's foreign loans since 1922, but domestic bonds have been issued repeatedly in substantial amounts during recent years, primarily as the result of heavy military and other administrative expenses. On the basis of the loans now outstanding, it is estimated that the total amount of funds required for loan services during the present fiscal year will be about $364,000,000 — about $170,000,000 for domestic bonds and $194,000,000 for foreign loans. At this rate of debt repayment, it would be possible to redeem domestic bonds completely in less than ten years, provided that no new issues were floated from now on. Most of the foreign loans are of a longer maturity, but as existing loans are gradually paid off without incurring new ones at the same time, the burden upon the nation's finances should become progressively less in the future.

Of the $850,000,000 domestic bonds outstanding, $660,000,000 have been issued by the present Nanking Government since it came into power in 1927. This is a tremendous increase in Government debts; but the most notable thing about it is that there has not been a single default on either principal or interest payments on any of these new loans. The credit for this brilliant record in the face of trying difficulties in China's national finances should go entirely to the able finance minister, Mr. T. V. Soong, who has perhaps done more than anybody else in improving the nation's financial organization and strengthening her credit's standing during recent years.

Besides military expenses and loan-service requirements, the Chinese Government spends about $200,000,000 a year for administrative and miscellaneous purposes. Of this amount very little, if any, has been devoted to constructive projects that would aid the economic growth of the country. The

Government, faced constantly with military problems, has had little time and still less funds for productive and constructive projects.

Turning now to the revenues of the Chinese Government, we find that the principal sources of revenue are the customs, the salt, the consolidated taxes, and other small miscellaneous revenues. Customs revenues of China have been benefited by higher rates during the recent years when the conclusion of tariff autonomy treaties with other countries enabled her to exercise an important sovereign right and to adjust her tariff schedules in accordance with her economic needs. The collection of salt revenues in China has also been put on a new basis with the recent reorganization of the Salt Inspectorate for greater efficiency of administration and better collection of revenues.

The long-awaited abolition of likin was carried into effect in January, 1931, and in the place of likin a system of consolidated taxes was installed. This represents an important measure of reform which has not only meant the removal of an obstacle that for decades has hindered the free flow of trade in China, but has also brought the collection of taxes under the central control and supervision of the Government. Unsettled political conditions in China have no doubt retarded the growth of her trade. But as Mr. Chang remarked in his last annual report to the shareholders of the Bank of China, business goes on in this country under the most trying circumstances. The natural tenacity and perseverance of the Chinese people seem to enable them somehow or other to surmount their immediate difficulties. When war breaks out in one section of the country, trade goes to and prospers in another section, so that in spite of serious handicaps, there probably is a larger turnover of domestic trade today than there was two or three years ago. During the last year, two other factors have considerably affected China's trade conditions and government revenues, particularly her foreign trade. They are, first, the world-wide economic depression which greatly diminished the amount of goods that other countries normally would buy from China; and, second, the unprecedented decline in the value of silver which, while it has to some extent stimulated certain lines of native industries, has meant a sudden reduction in the purchasing power of the Chinese people in gold-standard countries.

There are also other forces operating that affect the Government's revenues. I have reference to the unusual flood which has destroyed numberless lives and an incalculable amount of national wealth. And how the unfortunate Manchurian situation will affect the Chinese Government's finances is yet to be known.

The combined total of the Chinese customs, salt, consolidated taxes, and other revenues now amounts to about $600,000,000 a year, but with total expenditures of $900,000,000 indicated above, there is a deficit of about $300,000,000.

Thus, there are tremendous difficulties in China's Government financial situation, and the most important and immediate problem is that of reducing her huge deficit and of balancing her budget. The successful solution of this problem will largely depend upon improved political conditions and the maintenance of peace in the country. Given peace, people will go to work with confidence, and trade and government revenues will naturally increase. If this should be accompanied by a general recovery of world-trade and systematic reduction of wasteful expenditures, the Government in a few years ought to attain a position where it will be able to devote real attention to the establishment of industries for the economic development of the country. The Chinese banks and other people who control the destiny of capital in China are hoping for peace, for increase in Government revenues, and for a sound budget. They are hoping not only that the Government may have sufficient revenues to cover its expenditures, but that it may be able to set aside a reserve that may be used for future constructive purposes.

Contrary to popular belief, the Chinese banks show in their published reports that they are holding not more than one-quarter of the outstanding Government bonds as reserves for note issues and investment needs. The banks could buy more Government bonds, deriving therefrom an exceedingly high return on their capital; but most of the banks are refraining from doing this and are reserving part of their resources for future investment in industries, when peace is established, and when the Government is ready to give real encouragement and protection to such undertakings.

Peace will not only direct domestic capital to the development of industries but, I am sure, will also open up the gate through which foreign capital may be expected to flow in large amounts to co-operate with the Chinese industrial developments. China welcomes foreign capital, as has been pronounced by Dr. Sun Yat-sen and often repeated by high Government officials in their public statements; and, I think, foreign capital would like to come to China, provided it is given adequate protection and is assured that it will be employed in ways that will add to the wealth and productive capacity of the country instead of being diverted to wasteful and unproductive channels. The advantage of foreign participation in the economic development of China, as I see it, is a mutual one. Chinese industries will have the advantage of cheaper capital from foreign sources, while foreign investors may hope to receive the benefit of higher returns from their investments.

There are, I think, at least three forms in which foreign capital may be invested in China to co-operate with the Chinese in the economic development of the country.

There is, in the first place, the opportunity for railway construction, as adequate transportation systems are urgently needed in China to facilitate the development of her natural resources and the movement and growth of her trade. Foreign financial groups can unite with Chinese banks on a joint commercial basis to extend long-term credits to Chinese railways for the purchase of materials and equipment.

In the second place, foreign capital may seek investment in China by participating in the development of her basic industries and by extending long-term credits to these industries in co-operation with Chinese banks for the purchase and installation of machinery.

Still a third form of foreign investment in China probably will be some kind of an administrative loan to the Chinese Government. This loan will perhaps best be made in the form of silver, since China annually requires and imports between 120,000,000 and 150,000,000 ounces of silver from foreign countries, and since there is an apparent surplus of silver outside of China. This silver loan may well take the place of some of the domestic bonds which will gradually be retired in the next few years, releasing a sufficient amount of Government revenue (probably chiefly customs revenues) to provide a security for meeting the services of the silver loan. I think we are going to see a fundamental difference between future foreign loans to China and the old foreign loans; and that is, future foreign investments and loans, even in the case of government loans, will be made more on a business basis, without question about security and without those political considerations that have characterized some of the existing foreign loans.

These three forms of foreign investment in China if properly carried out will doubtless make valuable contributions in developing China's industries and increasing her national wealth. But such foreign assistance and co-operation in China's economic development as I have just described will at the same time result in great benefit to the foreign countries themselves. The sale of foreign material and machinery to the Chinese for the development of their industries and the subsequent increase in China's wealth and the purchasing power of her people are certainly important and practical means to quicken the recovery of world-trade from the lack of which every country in the world has suffered severely during the last two years.

In conclusion, for the time being the Chinese Government is still struggling with an unbalanced budget. Most of the Government expenditures are used in wasteful and unproductive ways, and very little attention is given to industrial developments and genuine economic reconstruction of the country. But with the dawn of peace and settled political conditions, which we hope will soon be achieved, there are real opportunities for foreign financial groups to co-operate with Chinese banks in developing the country to the advantage of both.

EXTRACT FROM DATA PAPER

CHINESE ATTITUDES TOWARD FOREIGN INVESTMENT [10]

By D. K. LIEU

I. INTERNATIONAL DEVELOPMENT OF CHINESE RAILWAYS

The many proposals for the international development of Chinese railways brought up in 1918 and 1919, and the heated discussion that followed, culminating in the organization of the New Consortium, were so important in the history of China's foreign loans that they deserve a more detailed

[10] Extract from *Foreign Investments in China* (China Council), pp. 42–53.

account. Among them we do not include the plan of Dr. Sun Yat-sen, which is discussed below in connection with the policy of the National Government towards foreign investments.

Since the establishment of the Republic, many railway loans had been contracted from abroad which did not result in the construction of any line. The Tung-Chen, Pukow-Hsinyang, Nanking-Changsha, Shansi-Singyi, Chin-Yu, Harbin-Blagoveschensk, Siems Carey 1100 Mile, Kaomi-Hsuchow, Shunteh-Tsinan, Manchuria-Mongolia railway loans were all of this nature. Characterized even by foreign writers as representing merely a scramble for concessions,[11] they served to set up a dog-in-the-manger system under which the contracting firms either could not or would not build the lines contracted, nor would allow others to build them. More than anything else these contracts frustrated the economic development of this country; but it was not until the Japanese banking syndicates carried out the policy on a grand scale that the Western Powers saw the necessity of calling a halt to this vicious practice.

When one of the Chinese delegates to the Paris Peace Conference left Peiping, the writer of this paper submitted to him a detailed proposal for the restoration of all concessional railways to China under international administration, and the turning over of all foreign contracts for projected lines into the hands of an international pool, which should begin to build such lines as the Chinese Government desired to construct. Similar proposals were made by others, both Chinese and foreigners, without consultation of each other, which showed how the need of railways in this country as well as the evil effects of the dog-in-the-manger contracts were felt by those who gave any thought to the matter. At first such proposals were discussed in private circles, but by the beginning of 1919 a Chinese Government committee took the matter up, and the attention of the public was called to this important question.

Although conflicting opinions were expressed by the leading Government officials and such public bodies as the People's Diplomatic Association, the Chinese Railway Association, etc.; and although the final result was the shelving of all such proposals through the opposition of this or that political party to this or that particular scheme, it did not prove that Chinese public opinion was against further railway development or in favor of the existing system of railway contracts. Of course, a certain political party was in favor of the latter, because it enabled the party to raise political loans under the guise of railway contracts, but they were severely attacked by the public which finally brought about their downfall. So far as the public was concerned, they might be considered as in favor of railway development with foreign funds, provided it did not involve further infringements on China's sovereign rights.[12]

[11] Srinivas R. Wagel, *Finance in China* (Shanghai, 1914), p. 49.
[12] For a detailed account of the conflicting opinions see D. K. Lieu, *China's Industries and Finance*, pp. 154–96.

In spite of the shelving of the Chinese proposals by the political party then in power, the New Consortium was organized in Europe. All the rights and concessions which had been obtained by the Powers participating in the New Consortium, but which had not been carried into effect, were to be transferred to the New Consortium. According to press reports, this included all unexecuted railway contracts, except those for a few lines in Manchuria which were reserved by Japan. This arrangement served to stop Japan from making further loans to this country, but it did not bring about the importation of any capital from the Consortium Powers for the construction of the projected lines. It was stated by representatives of the Peiping financial administration that the New Consortium insisted upon certain terms concerning some former loans which the Chinese Government could not accept, and failing that it was unwilling to extend any more credit to this country.[13] From this it would appear that the political party in power in 1920 and 1921, after the pro-Japanese party had gone, was not averse to the pooling of the contracts under the Consortium, but objected to the conditions which the Consortium insisted on as *sine qua non* to further loans. At the same time, newspaper and magazine articles attacked the New Consortium on various grounds, chiefly because it was in a position to dictate terms to this country. If, however, the terms so " dictated " had been acceptable to China, the fundamental objection would have been removed. The negative effect of the Consortium in preventing promiscuous borrowing from abroad had the hearty support of the Chinese public, even though it failed to launch any positive program for the economic development of this country.

2. DR. SUN ON FOREIGN INVESTMENT

As stated in his own preface to his book bearing that title, Dr. Sun Yat-sen " began to take up the study of the international development of China, and to form programs accordingly, as soon as the armistice was declared in the recent World War." It was his idea that " the vast resources of China be developed internationally under a socialistic scheme, for the good of the world in general and the Chinese people in particular." He hoped that " as a result of this, the present spheres of influence can be abolished; the international commercial war can be done away with; the internecine capitalistic competition can be got rid of, and last, but not least, the class struggle between capital and labor can be avoided." The scope of his plans, which have since become some of the cornerstones of the Kuomintang policy, is therefore much broader than the mere importation of foreign capital into this country, but his reference to the abolition of the then existing spheres of influence had a direct bearing upon the various railway loan contracts.

The late leader of the Kuomintang believed that the Chinese people

[13] Discussion with the late Mr. Frederick Stevens, then representative of the Consortium in Peiping, did not confirm this statement, but the opinion expressed at other times by other foreigners concerned with the matter leads the writer to believe that the statement was not altogether groundless.

would " welcome the development of our country's resources — provided that it could be kept out of mandarin corruption and ensure the mutual benefit of China and of the countries cooperating with us." As a prerequisite to the execution of his plans he suggested that " the various Governments of the capital-supplying Powers must agree to joint action and a unified policy to form an international organization with their organizers, administrators and experts of various lines to formulate plans and to standardize materials in order to prevent waste and to facilitate the work." [14] Thus his view was different from that of those people who feared the monopolistic power wielded by international organizations such as the New Consortium. Inasmuch as this book was later translated and formed the second part of his Chinese work " Programs of National Reconstruction," which is read and followed by all Kuomintang members, this attitude may be considered as the official attitude of that party.

It would be very wide of the mark to suppose that Dr. Sun meant to entrust the whole development work to the international organization. On the contrary, the foreign experts were to be under Chinese employment.

During the construction and the operation of each of these national undertakings [referring to railways, highways, canals, telegraph and telephone lines, harbors, factories, etc., mentioned in the programs] before its capital and interest are fully repaid, it will be managed and supervised by foreigners; but these foreign experts have to undertake the training of Chinese assistants to take their places in the future. When the capital and interest of each undertaking are paid off, the Chinese Government will have the option to employ either foreigners or Chinese to manage the concerns as it thinks fit.

Four general principles were enumerated for guidance in formulating this scheme of international development of China:

The most remunerative field must be selected in order to attract foreign capital;
The most urgent needs of the nation must be met;
The lines of least resistance must be followed, and
The most suitable positions must be chosen. [15]

In a later connection Dr. Sun said:

Europe and America are a hundred years ahead of us in industrial development; so in order to catch up in a short time we have to use their capital, mainly their machinery. If foreign capital cannot be gotten, we shall have to get at least their experts and inventors to make for us our own machinery. In any case, we must use machinery to assist our enormous man-power to develop our unlimited resources. [16]

This shows that his emphasis was on foreign technical assistance, in the form of experts, inventors and machinery. But machinery is important, and to utilize large quantities of machinery to supplement our man-power, it

[14] Sun Yat-sen, *The International Development of China,* pp. 6 and 9.
[15] *Ibid.,* pp. 11 and 12.
[16] *Ibid.,* p. 198.

must be supplied to China in the form of loans. At one time he advocated the contraction of certain foreign loans entirely in the form of machinery and raw materials, instead of money.

As to mines, Dr. Sun did not welcome foreign financial assistance unreservedly:

Mining in general is very risky, and to enlist foreign capital in its development in a wholesale manner is unadvisable. Therefore, only mining projects which are sure to be profitable will be brought under the International Development Scheme.[17]

As Dr. Sun's English book was first published in April, 1921, after the New Consortium had come into existence, he had this to say about that international organization in his book:

Fortunately, however, soon after the preliminary part of my programs had been sent out to the different Governments and the Peace Conference, a new Consortium was formed in Paris for the purpose of assisting China in developing her natural resources. . . . Thus we need not fear the lack of capital to start work in our industrial development. *If the Powers are sincere in their motive to cooperate for mutual benefit,* then the military struggle for material gain in China could eventually be averted. For by co-operation they can secure more benefits and advantages than by struggle.

Again he said:

We, the Chinese people, who desire to organize China for peace will welcome heartily this new Consortium *provided it will carry out the principles which are outlined in these programs.*[18]

These quotations will serve to express Dr. Sun's and therefore the Kuomintang's attitude toward the New Consortium, if we do not ignore the conditions he set down in the lines italicised above.

In pursuance of Dr. Sun's policy of international development of this country, the Central Political Council passed a few resolutions at its 179th Meeting in March, 1929, which were to serve as guiding principles in the utilization of foreign capital. They were:

1. That, as long as the arrangements do not infringe upon the national sovereignty and prerogatives, the Government may, besides contracting ordinary loans, carry out constructive work with capital jointly supplied by itself and foreign firms, and the work may be carried on by a corporation. There must however be certain limitations to such arrangements, the principles governing which will be outlined elsewhere.
2. That corporations operated by the Government or by Chinese merchants may allow foreign merchants to invest their capital in them, or supply their capital and operate the corporations jointly with the former, provided,
    a) That the Chinese shares should constitute over fifty-one per cent of the total capital,
    b) That the Chinese directors should be in the majority,

[17] *Ibid.,* pp. 222–23.
[18] *Ibid.,* pp. 233–34. (The italics are mine.)

c) That the chairman of the board of directors and the general manager should be Chinese, and

d) That private concerns in such cases should be regulated and governed by the Chinese company law and other Chinese laws.

The above resolutions were the result of certain proposals brought forth by the then Ministers Sun Fo, H. H. Kung, Yi Pei-chi and Wang Po-chun, who were also members of the Central Political Council. Among the proposals was one by Minister Yi suggesting specially that the Government might, as long as the arrangements did not infringe upon its powers and prerogatives, either raise foreign loans for the operation of mines, or operate them with joint Chinese and foreign capital. As Sun Fo was then the Minister of Railways, H. H. Kung, the Minister of Industry, Commerce and Labor, and Wang Po-chun, the Minister of Communications, their proposal naturally covered these lines of national economic development. The resolutions, then, were also intended to cover the same scope.

Although these resolutions covered both foreign loans and business investments, the latter were limited to Sino-foreign companies and did not include purely foreign firms in China. Since the policy of the Kuomintang is in favor of encouraging private enterprise, there can be no sweeping condemnation of foreign private enterprises in this country. However, certain forms of enterprise, be they now in Chinese or foreign hands, are to be nationalized, according to the Program of National Reconstruction. As stated by Dr. Sun, " all matter that cannot be taken up by private concerns and those that possess a monopolistic character should be taken up as national undertakings." [19] These include coal, iron, oil and copper mines, iron and steel works, cement works, and many other basic industries. Some of them are to be taken over entirely by the Government; in other cases the Government will establish large enterprises of its own, at the same time allowing private individuals to engage in the same industries. The sugar refinery and the soda plant recently planned by the Ministry of Industries are of the latter category. Thus no projection is entertained by the Kuomintang towards foreign business enterprises as such, in spite of the occasional attacks hurled by some young party members at the foreign firms in China as being the representatives of imperialism. As to the Government's encouragement of national goods, it is what every other country is doing at present, and the only difference is that China does not use the protective tariff to discriminate against foreign products.

3. POSSIBLE FORMS OF INVESTMENT

The resolutions of the Central Political Council stated above open up a new form of investment by foreigners interested in the economic development of this country. The plan is in a way similar to the mixed companies of Soviet Russia, in which foreigners may invest their capital.

Some two years ago a discussion group of Chinese and foreigners in

[19] Sun Yat-sen, *The International Development of China*, p. 11.

Shanghai tried to evolve a system by which foreign loans might be made not to the Chinese Government directly, but to a board of trustees consisting of Chinese and foreign bankers appointed by the Chinese Government.   The Chinese members of the board should be in the majority, and the whole personnel of the board should not be subject to frequent changes, once the appointment was made.   Since the board must be acceptable to foreign financial interests before any loan could be made, unworthy members would not be likely to be appointed in the first instance, and the only danger would lie in changes of personnel later on.   The opinion was expressed by some foreign members of the discussion group that this system could apply only to smaller loans for the construction of municipal public utilities.   But if good securities are provided and if the system proves its value in small loans there is no reason why its application may not be widened to large investments.   Hundreds of millions of dollars' worth of domestic bonds are now managed under such a system.

Another suggestion came from a foreign firm interested in the operation of Chinese mines.   According to its representative, the firm would supply funds under Chinese management of the mines, provided its representative had control over the technical and engineering work.   If the same opinion were held by all foreign firms interested in mining, electricity, and public utility works, one form of foreign financial co-operation may evolve along this line.   It agrees with the Kuomintang policy as enunciated by Dr. Sun, and it affords, in the opinion of the present writer, sufficient protection to the foreign investors against possible losses due to inefficiency.

On account of the sudden slump in silver prices, a proposal was made by a foreign adviser to the Chinese Government that a loan of actual silver bullion be made by the United States to this country.   He actually went to America and consulted with the silver-producing interests of that country, and the amount proposed was reported as high up as one billion ounces.   Although the plan did not materialize, it indicated a new form of investment, namely, a loan of actual commodities (from the viewpoint of the creditor nation) instead of money.

Better than this would be the loaning to China of the commodities that she now imports regularly — rice, wheat flour, piece goods, metals, etc.   I do not mean all these commodities, or to the total quantity imported.   A large portion will be enough.   It will relieve the trade depression abroad on the one hand and improve China's foreign exchange on the other.   The latter will indirectly improve the silver situation.   To maintain high prices on their products in the home market, large producers abroad often dump a portion of such products on foreign markets.   Some would even destroy it rather than allow the superfluous quantity to depress the market.   Compared with destruction or dumping, the loaning of such products at reasonable prices would be more profitable to the producers, even though some risk might attach to such loans.   The foreign governments may back them up by export credit insurance, as Germany and England did for Russia.   At the same time, market are not attractive. To loan these to China certainly need not depend Chinese bankers and chambers of commerce may form some organization to facilitate such arrangements which would be beneficial to both parties concerned.

The writer has no intention of advocating foreign loans to the Chinese Government for political purposes. In the last few years the Government has relied entirely on domestic loans to cover its budgetary deficits. Although the available public revenues have been mostly pledged for such loans, there is yet no sure indication that native capital has been exhausted. In the interior, money is often so easy that the native banks pay no interest at all to depositors. Some arrangements may be made to tap this source of surplus capital, not for defraying the ordinary expenditures of the Government, but for carrying out the necessary constructive works. However, lack of statistics in this respect makes it difficult to estimate the quantity available, and whether or not it would be adequate to the needs. For rapid development of railways, mines, industries, etc., foreign credit, in the form of either money or materials and machinery, would be very useful to China.

Of course, much may be said for the attitude of foreign financial interests towards further loans to this country. Many issues of Chinese securities floated abroad, for default of principal and interest payments, command very low prices in the foreign markets. Under such conditions, they insist, it is naturally hard to talk about further issues. This is the ordinary business viewpoint on financial matters. But if the financiers find it hard to raise funds with Chinese securities it may not be so with manufacturers extending credit on their products to this country. The products are there, and in the business depression they are not readily disposed of. Their prices in the home upon any improvement in the prices of Chinese securities.

Even with the financiers, it may be a wise policy to increase China's capacity to pay by loans for constructive uses. Although China's natural resources are not as rich as was at first thought, their development along modern lines cannot but bring benefits to this as well as other nations. It will create a better market for their products. China at present is unable to amortize her railway loans because the railways need further funds for repairs and maintenance. The foreign financiers want her to amortize their former loans but will not supply her further funds to maintain the railways. In a few more years, the roadbeds, the rolling stock, and all the equipment will be in an even worse condition, the earning capacity of the railways will fall, and the prospect of amortization of former loans will be more remote. Either the financiers or the manufacturers of railway supplies must come to the rescue, but better both, since their co-operation will be necessary.

CHAPTER VII

SILVER AND THE CURRENCY PROBLEM

DATA PAPERS

1. W. F. SPALDING. *Memorandum on the Position of Silver and the Far East* (mimeographed, British Group).
2. HOU SHU-T'UNG. *Japanese Bank Notes in Manchuria* (China Council).
3. MITSUTARO ARAKI. *Report on the Currency System of China* (Japanese Council).

REFERENCES

1. COMMISSION OF FINANCIAL EXPERTS. *Project of Law for the Gradual Introduction of a Gold Standard Currency System in China.* Shanghai: Bureau of Industrial and Commercial Information, 1929.
2. E. KANN. "How Much Silver Is There in China?" *Chinese Economic Journal*, Shanghai, April, 1931.
3. SOUTH MANCHURIA RAILWAY COMPANY. *Second Report on Progress in Manchuria, to 1930* (Dairen, 1931), chap. x, pp. 182–99.
4. LEAGUE OF NATIONS. *The Course and Phases of the World Economic Depression: II. Economic and Financial* (1931), IIA. 21, pp. 241–46.
5. PINNICK. *Silver and China.* Shanghai, 1930.

INTRODUCTORY NOTE

The discussion of the silver problem at the Conference was not confined to the special round table on that topic, for the subject emerged in the course of the first day's round tables on trade relations in the Pacific and again at intervals in the discussions of China's economic development. The discussions, moreover, were conducted with reference to three fairly distinct problems: first, the international problem of silver as a commodity which, like other metals, has been affected by the collapse of world-prices since 1929; second, the effect of the fall in the price of silver on the trade of the other Pacific nations with China; and third, the effect of the depreciation of silver on the internal economy of China, with particular reference to the effects on prices in China and on the foreign-debt obligations of the Chinese Government. The discussion of this third question very soon broadened into a consideration of the general currency problem in China and the pros and cons of introducing some form of gold standard. In this chapter the aim has been as far as possible to report the discussions of the first and the third of these problems, while the discussions on the second problem have been relegated to chapter i, on "Trade Relations," where they more properly belong. The dividing line, however, is not clearly defined, and a certain amount of repetition or cross-reference is necessary in the interests of clarity.

The round table on silver differed from other Conference groups both in its composition and in its method of discussion. It was made up mainly of experts or persons particularly interested in the silver situation, many of whom were not full Conference members but members of the Shanghai banking and business communities specially invited to participate. The discussion was conducted along rather more formal lines than in other round tables; it did not seem to lend itself as much to brisk exchange of opinion as to extended arguments by specialists on the subject. The discussion may not unfairly be taken as representing the opinions of leading Shanghai bankers, Chinese and foreign, on the effects of silver depreciation on business in China, and their views on the desirability for reform in China's currency through the introduction of a gold-exchange standard.

In this as in other round tables which touched on the silver question, several fairly clear-cut conclusions appeared to emerge. First, the decline in the value of silver has had a much smaller effect on trade with China than was popularly supposed or than certain silver-producing interests in the Western Hemisphere suggest. Second, thanks to her silver standard, China has been sheltered, partially at least, from the full effects of the collapse of world-prices. Third, the questions of silver stabilization and of currency reform in China are inseparable from the problems of Government finance, so that a balanced national budget is a prerequisite for improvement in the currency situation. Fourth, in spite of the obvious advantages of some form of gold standard, it is wiser at the present time, when supplies of gold are barely sufficient for the rest of the world, to postpone any attempt to adopt a gold standard or to stabilize China's currency in a fixed relation with gold, the effect of which would be to link China's price system with world-prices which are now at an abnormally low level, and to plunge the country into a disastrous period of deflation and business depression. Fifth, in the meantime China should proceed with the essential task of unifying her existing chaotic currencies.

Whether these views coincide with those of the Chinese Government or the Chinese and foreign mercantile or industrial interests as distinct from the financial and banking interests is an interesting question to which in the circumstances no definite answer was given. The implied distinction is pertinent, however, and its significance is hinted at in the following quotation from a Japanese student of the currency problem in China:

Another point which may be regarded as a positive cause for the maintenance of the silver standard is the opposition of the financial interests to the gold standard. The ideal currency of a nation should be based on a unit which does not fluctuate in value. From this it is apparent that the silver standard which is controlled by the value of silver bullion quoted on the market is unsuitable for a national currency, for either domestic or international purposes. It goes without saying that the gold standard will remedy this shortcoming of the silver standard. The greatest opposition to the adoption of the gold standard is the personal interest of those who profit by taking advantage of this fluctuation in the value of silver.

The fluctuation in the value of commodities is for all business men a source of profit, but for a speculative business man it is the only source of profit. The silver standard, which is subject to great fluctuation in value, is a convenient standard for the financial broker whose business it is to take profit from those fluctuations. It is for this reason that the adoption of the gold standard which makes for the stability of the value of a currency means a fatal improvement for him. The objection against the gold standard on that ground must not be ignored. The fact that the reluctance to effect a reform on the Chinese currency in the past was based on the interest of the practical business man rather than on mere theory shows the existence of this close relation between the silver standard and the practical interest of the speculators. This is a less obvious reason why China is still unable to adopt the gold standard.[1]

Whatever the validity of these arguments, it was evident to outside observers at the round table that the Chinese bankers attending based their arguments fundamentally on the assumption that the economic welfare of China was the goal to be kept in sight in discussions of the currency problem. If there was any conflict between the general economic interests of the country and the financial and banking interests, it was not in evidence and did not affect the soundness of the arguments adduced by the representatives of the latter. In only one point was there a limitation: in their preoccupation with the puzzle of silver prices and the chances of a gold-exchange standard, the specialists gave little time to discussing practical steps toward the internal unification of China's present silver currency. In consequence, many important questions, such as the best form and fineness of China's metallic currency, the best measures to guard against counterfeiting of coins on the one hand or overissue of notes on the other, the future regulations concerning legal tender and convertibility when a gold-exchange fund is established, were passed over without the expert comment which many of those present were well fitted to make.

The international importance of the silver problem in the economic relations can hardly diminish as long as such a vast and developing nation as China continues to use the metal for its currency standard or even for its circulating coinage alone. It was mainly in recognition of this fact that the International Research Committee at the close of the Conference gave favorable consideration to a project of research submitted by the Japanese Research Committee, namely, a study of " Silver Fluctuations as Affecting Pacific Trade." The project will give special attention to the effect of silver fluctuation on China's economic development, on the development of international trade between China and the other Pacific countries, especially Japan and the United States, and on the relation between the silver problem and the present depression and the post-depression period in the Pacific countries. A grant for two years was authorized for this purpose from the international research fund of the Institute, and the work has been placed under the direction of Professor Mitsutaro Araki of the Tokyo Imperial University.

[1] Mitsutaro Araki, *Report on the Currency System of China*, p. 28.

DATA PAPERS

I. MEMORANDUM ON THE POSITION OF SILVER IN THE FAR EAST

By W. F. SPALDING

The decline in the gold price of silver from the high level of 89½d. touched in February, 1920, has attracted considerable attention. With but spasmodic upward movements, it may be said, speaking in general terms, that the price of the metal has moved steadily downwards since 1920, as is evidenced by the average price of the metal since that year.

The following are the average prices per standard ounce for each of the years in question:

1920	61⅛₆d.	1926	28¹¹⁄₁₆d.
1921	36⅞d.	1927	26½₂d.
1922	34⅞₆d.	1928	26¾d.
1923	31¹⁵⁄₁₆d.	1929	24⅞₆d.
1924	34d.	1930	17¹¹⁄₁₆d.
1925	32⅛d.		

The lowest price for silver touched in 1931, up to May 6, has been 12d. per standard ounce for spot silver, and 11 15/16d. per standard ounce for forward silver.

There seems to be no doubt that the prevalent business depression throughout the world and the fall of all commodity prices have been contributory factors to the depreciation in the price of silver. However, as has been pointed out by the London *Economist*, the market for silver is further distinguished from the markets for other commodities by the fact that the depreciation problem is some sixty years old. The demonetization of silver, first by Germany and then by a large number of other countries in continuous succession, began in the early seventies of last century, with a resultant steady decline in the ratio of the value of silver, to that of gold, from approximately 1:16 in 1871–75 to 1:36.6 during the quinquennium 1911–15. The recovery in the price of silver due to war causes culminated in the attainment of the record price of 89½d., above referred to, in 1920; then the decline was resumed, and the ratio by the time the price of 12d. had been reached (in February, 1931) had fallen to 1:76.6.

Actually, overproduction had not been altogether responsible for the decline in price. Special conditions increasing the supply of the metal, while reducing at the same time the potential demand for it, started the decline, and these factors may continue to exercise an influence after the present depression in world-prices is over and other commodities have recovered their values.

The point to be remembered is this: that although a case has sometimes been made to prove overproduction, yet silver is probably one of the few commodities the production of which is unaffected by its price. If the price of other metals falls to unprofitable levels they will not be mined, and this adjustment, in due course, will bring back an equilibrium between supply and demand. Silver, however, is essentially a by-product of a number of other metals — gold, tin, copper, lead and zinc. Whatever the price of silver, it must be brought to the world's markets as long as its allied metals continue to be worth mining. Though this might seem to encourage overproduction, yet in practice nothing of the kind has happened, and in the last 130 years the average increase per decade has been approximately 22.5 per cent as compared with the following percentages for other metals: lead 48.6; copper 52.48; gold 51.6; zinc 114.4.

The most that can be said at the moment is that, owing to the low price of silver, a number of the straight mines in Mexico and America (mines which produce silver only) have been closed down, owing to the uneconomic value of their production. It seems possible, therefore, that 1931 will see a fall in the total production of silver.

Table I, prepared by the eminent statistician, Mr. J. Kitchin, with the aid of other experts, gives, as comprehensively as possible, the supply of and demand for silver during each of the eleven years, namely, 1920–30.

TABLE I

(In millions of fine ounces)

	SUPPLY			DEMAND							UNAC-COUNTED FOR	PRICE (GOLD) PER FINE Oz.
Year	New Output	Extra Supplies	Total	Private	Govt.	Total	China	Industrial Arts	Known Coinage Purchases	Total		
1920.....	173	44	217	6	.....	6	113	45	40	204	− 13	50.0d.
1921.....	171	41	212	57	.....	57	39	53	69	218	+ 6	31.5
1922.....	210	50	260	71	1	72	48	58	56	234	− 26	33.9
1923.....	246	41	287	97	1	98	82	55	57	292	+ 5	32.4
1924.....	239	4	243	91	.....	91	32	53	71	247	+ 4	33.3
1925.....	245	6	251	105	.....	105	75	59	17	256	+ 5	34.7
1926.....	254	2	256	111	.....	111	65	57	31	264	+ 8	31.0
1927.....	254	25	279	108	.....	108	79	58	47	292	+ 13	28.1
1928.....	258	71	329	99	− 19	80	130	53	21	284	− 45	28.9
1929.....	262	53	315	87	− 19	68	129	60	36	293	− 22	26.4
1930.....	241	71	312	114	− 13	101	130	50	16	297	− 15	19.1
Total..	2,553	408	2,961	946	− 49	897	922	601	461	2881	− 80	
Average p.a.....	232	37	269	86	− 5	81	84	55	42	262	− 7	31.8

It will be observed in the table that quantities are given in fine ounces, and the price is in each case per fine ounce.

The period covered by the table immediately follows the year 1919, when the price of silver averaged 56.3d. (gold), the highest since 1882. The years 1918–19 were years in which the United States released from its silver stocks 197,000,000 ozs. to India and 12,000,000 ozs. to China, thus supplementing the ordinary supplies of new silver for those two years by 55 per cent. The high price of silver around 1919 due to war causes was undoubtedly the cause of considerable demonetization in the years 1920–23, and further demonetization after a pause of three years occurred on a rather larger scale in the period 1927–30. Roughly speaking, the supply of silver has been increased by about 25 per cent by the addition of some 60,000,000 ozs. a year of silver derived from coins. It would seem, then, that the main factor which induced a reversion from silver coinage to silver bullion in Europe was the high price of silver during the war and the years immediately following. In quite a number of countries the silver coins in circulation were more valuable as bullion than as currency, and it became necessary to take steps to prevent the exporting or melting of silver coins. In 1920, Great Britain reduced the fineness of her silver coin from .925 to .500. As supplies of the new coins became available, the old ones were withdrawn from circulation, melted down and sold as bullion. As a matter of fact, almost immediately after this step was taken, silver commenced to fall again, and the danger of coins being sold for their melting value passed. It was argued, however, that if silver had gone up once, it might go up again. Other European countries were quick to follow the example of England: France, Belgium, Germany, Italy and Greece all have called in their old full-weight silver coins and issued others of a much reduced silver content.

Europe was not the only place from which the supply of silver from demonetized coins emanated. With the adoption of the gold bullion standard by India in 1926–27, and the abandonment of the silver standard by French Indo-China in 1929–30, further supplies were added to the silver produced from the mines. This obviously had a weakening effect on an already over-burdened silver market. To take British India, it is estimated that from 1926 to 1930 the Government there sold approximately 90,000,000 fine ounces of silver. In the same period, the amount of rupee coins in the reserves have gradually increased from Rs.85 crores in 1926 to over Rs.120 crores by the end of 1930; that is to say, Rs.95 crores in excess of the 25 crores recommended by the Indian Currency Commission of 1926 as an ultimate maximum. This excess Rs.95 crores represents over 300,000,000 ozs. potentially ready for the market; and this in itself is a strong factor against any long-continued recovery in the price.

The supplies of silver from demonetized coins, apart from India, have now practically ceased, but it remains to be seen whether, when Spain stabilizes her currency, she will put on to the market any part of the large stock of silver which the Bank of Spain is known to hold.

PRODUCTION

Kitchin, in drawing up his statistics of the world's production of silver, maintains that it has shown three definite trends, as shown in Table II.

It is of interest to know that the greatest advance happened to come between Germany's demonetization of silver (1871) and the closing of the Indian mints to the free coinage of silver (in 1893), i.e., at the time when the price of silver was falling rapidly. The yearly average in 1871 was 60½d.

TABLE II

	Production per Annum	Annual Rate of Increase in Intervals
1821–30	14,800,000 oz.	....
1866–70	43,100,000	2.5 per cent
1893	165,000,000	5.5
1929	262,000,000	1.3

per standard ounce and in 1893, 35 ⅝d. Since 1893, the rate of increase of production has been 1.6 per cent to 1912, and 0.7 per cent between 1912 and 1922. This latter coincides roughly with the rate of increase of the world's population (0.8 per cent), and only about one-fourth of the rate of increase shown by any of the base metals.

The estimated production of silver for 1930 is 244,000,000 ozs.

Table III gives the production figures, together with the source and supply from 1919 to 1930 — the year 1912 being given as the pre-war record year.

TABLE III

SILVER PRODUCTION

(In millions of fine ounces)

Year	Mexico	United States	Canada	Elsewhere	World
1912 *	75	64	32	60	231
1919	66	57	16	41	180
1920	67	55	13	39	174
1921	64	53	13	41	171
1922	81	56	19	54	210
1923	91	73	18	64	246
1924	91	65	20	63	239
1925	93	66	20	66	245
1926	98	63	22	71	254
1927	105	60	23	66	254
1928	109	58	22	68	257
1929	109	61	23	69	262
1930 †	106	51	26	61	244

* Pre-war record.   † Estimate.

These figures are prepared in London, and differ somewhat from those prepared by the American Bureau of Metal Statistics. That institution makes the production from 1927 to 1930 as shown in Table IV, p. 200.

The above countries produced about 87 per cent of the world's production of silver in 1929.

In some quarters there has been a disposition to make very definite statements concerning the unprecedented disparity between the values of gold and silver. On one hand, it has been said to be due to a growing scarcity of gold and an increasing abundance of silver, or on the other hand to the overproduction of silver itself. Yet, on closer investigation, it has

TABLE IV

(In thousands of fine ounces)

Year	U.S.A.	Canada *	Mexico †	Peru ‡	Australia §	Burma	Total
1927......	59,412	20,761	104,575	18,381	9,296	6,005	218,430
1928......	56,149	20,328	108,536	21,818	8,132	7,404	222,367
1929......	60,180	21,587	108,701	21,163	8,969	7,280	227,880
1930......	50,234	23,447	105,204	16,634	8,854	7,055	211,428

* Incomplete; silver contained in blister copper and lead bullion exported is omitted.
† Total silver exported and delivered for coinage.
‡ Partly estimated in 1929–30.
§ Refined.

been proved that neither view is correct. An examination of the indices of the annual world production of gold and silver for each of the decades from 1879 to 1929 reveals the curious fact that production of silver has increased at approximately the same rate as that of gold. The truth is that, with an increase of the countries adopting one form or other of the gold standard, or that halfway house in the matter of currency, the gold exchange standard, and a diminution in those countries adhering to the silver standard, the disparity between the value of gold and that of silver was bound to widen.

It may be generally accepted that the more correct explanation of the reason for the depreciation of the price of silver is to be found in the abandonment, wholly or partially, of silver for coinage by European nations and, as a standard of value, by some of the Eastern countries. As we have pointed out earlier in this paper, large quantities of silver bullion from demonetized coins have been thrown on the silver market in recent years, and during 1930 India itself sold approximately 30,000,000 ozs. of silver on the London market, while France, although not selling silver from demonetized coins to the same extent during 1930, yet managed to place on the market some 23,-000,000 ozs.

Silver has thus suffered a double blow; nations that supported the market by purchases have not only withdrawn that support but have caused further depression by becoming sellers of silver.

With but a small consumption of silver by the great gold standard countries, it has been left for Asia (principally China) to absorb not only the annual production from the mines, but all the surplus silver that other nations have had to sell. That being so, there is little wonder that the price of silver has declined. In such circumstances, it might have been thought that the demand for silver from both China and India would have been seriously curtailed owing to falling trade, yet in 1930 China purchased no less than 140,000,000 standard ounces of the metal, while India purchased 102,585,000 ozs. These figures show very little falling off as compared with previous years; and but for the fact that the market had to absorb the large amounts released by India and European governments, Asia could have comfortably dealt with the production from the mines.

II. THE SIGNIFICANCE OF JAPANESE BANK NOTES IN MANCHURIA [2]

By Hou Shu-t'ung

The advantages which the Japanese banks derive from their activities in Manchuria may be divided into two groups, direct and indirect. On the direct side the first advantage is that which comes through the issuing of silver and gold notes. The total amount circulating in Manchuria in recent years has varied between fifty and sixty million. Thus a large sum in interest is earned annually from the Chinese. While it is lawful for banking houses to make profit through the use of their credits, it should be noted, however, that Japan so far has no treaty right to issue bank notes in Manchuria. Another direct advantage also coming through the issue of the notes is to be found in the difference in the value of the notes, varying between the time of their issue and the time for their redemption. The silver note is issued at a higher value and redeemed at a lower value in terms of the *kuei-yuan* tael of Shanghai. This is, to a certain extent, also the case with the gold notes. The circulation of *kin-piao* in Manchuria expands in winter when the grain traffic increases, and contracts in summer when the trade is over. Neglecting variations in the ratio between silver and gold, the *kin-piao* usually rises in terms of Chinese local currencies when it is most urgently needed in winter, and drops when its need relaxes in summer. Thus the Bank of Chosen is able to make profit from these fluctuations in the value of the note it issues, which variations under ordinary circumstances are practically regular.

According to the trade returns for recent years, Manchuria's annual foreign trade amounts, in round figures, to 700,000,000 *hai-kwan* taels. Among Chinese banks in Manchuria, the Bank of China is the only institution that does a little business in foreign exchange. The banks of other foreign nationalities do not have much business in exchange except with their own respective countries. Of the total business in exchange which arises from this annual trade of 700,000,000 *hai-kwan* taels, the large bulk is done by Japanese banks. This is the third important direct advantage which Japan gains through her financial activities in Manchuria.

As to the advantages derived indirectly, the first thing to notice here is the fact that all trade between the Japanese and Chinese in Manchuria, except the grain trade, is carried on in *kin-piao*. It is in this way that the risk involved in changes in the ratio between gold and silver is entirely shifted to the Chinese merchants, whereas in trade between the Chinese and other foreigners in other parts of China at least part of the risk is borne by the foreign merchants.

Japan's purchases of soya bean from Manchuria assume tremendous amounts every year during the winter. The purchases are invariably effected either through the issue of bank notes or the expansion of bank credits, but

[2] Extract from *Japanese Bank Notes in Manchuria*, pp. 17–28.

never have they paid any cash to Chinese merchants. This means that they defer the payment (without giving any interest) until the spring of the following year, when these notes and credits begin to be gradually returned or cancelled for the payment of imported goods from Japan. This device saves Japan a lot of interest, and such savings as are made may be counted as a second indirect advantage derived by the Japanese. But we must admit that this has only been made possible through the use of Japanese bank notes by the Chinese.

The several items specified above are obvious advantages gained by the Japanese from their note issue in Manchuria; many more may be added. The material acquisitions from the direct advantages may be calculated in terms of money, but how conducive to the advancement of Japanese interests in Manchuria the indirect advantages have been cannot be so readily seen. We may say, in short, that without her banking and monetary arrangements Japan's achievements in Manchuria would not have been as great.

FACTORS IN CIRCULATION EXPANSION

We have just spoken of the contribution of Japan's currency system to the development of her position in Manchuria. This is, however, only one phase of the situation. If we discuss the matter from another angle we see that Japan's position in Manchuria, in turn, has greatly aided the expansion of Japanese notes. In other words, the steady expansion of Japanese note circulation has been materially aided by certain advantages which Japan has been able to secure through the years. The first and foremost element which has helped in the expansion of Japanese bank notes has been the large trade between Japan and Manchuria. According to the trade returns of recent years, Manchuria's trade with Japan amounts to approximately 40 per cent of her total trade with the outside (including intra-mural China). Its volume occupies the first place, and exceeds even that between Manchuria and intra-mural China. As we know that all trade, both import and export, with the Japanese has to be effected in either *kin-piao* or *chao-piao*, we can easily see how the circulation of these notes must have been widened by such a trade situation. Moreover, a large volume of trade necessitates a large business in exchange. Thus, because of the increasing Japanese trade with Manchuria, the exchange business of the Japanese is correspondingly promoted.

Had currency exchange been mostly effected through some Chinese port, say Newchuang, and not through Dairen, Japan's trade with Manchuria, though large in volume, would not necessarily have favored the expansion of Japanese notes to such an extent. Had Newchuang held the first place in Manchuria's trade up to the present, it would have naturally resulted in a much wider use of its local currency — the so-called " transfer tael."

It would have given the more prosperous and influential position to the *yin lu* (" silver foundries," by which name banks in Newchuang are known) rather than to the Japanese banking institutions. But Dairen has risen to the third place among the ports in China, and the first in Manchuria. According to the trade returns for the year 1929, the Manchurian ports in volume of trade stand as shown in Table I.

From this table it will be seen that approximately 67 per cent of the total trade in Manchuria is effected through Dairen. This trade has all to

TABLE I

Ports	Total of Imports and Exports
Dairen	508,527,913 hk. taels
Antung	92,360,810
Newchuang	86,564,949
Harbin districts	58,960,000
Aigun, etc.	9,107,621

be made in Japanese currency. This not only leads to a wider circulation of *kin-piao* and *chao-piao*, but also makes them indispensable to every Chinese who desires to do business with the Japanese. As to the currency exchanges arising in connection with trade in Dairen, it goes without saying that they are exclusively the business of the Japanese banking houses. In view of the volume of this business, we find here another element which adds greatly to the financial position of Japan. Dairen, as the leading port in Manchuria, may therefore be regarded as another stone in the foundation upon which the Japanese financial influence in Manchuria has been built.

Besides the large trade between Manchuria and Japan, and the commercial ascendancy of Dairen, the South Manchuria Railway is a third important factor favoring the expansion of Japanese currency. As all payments for freight rates and passenger fares have to be made in *kin-piao*, scarcely a single person who resides or travels in Manchuria can dispense with the use of Japanese bank notes. This, of course, is another exceptionally effective way by which *kin-piao* are diffused among the Chinese.

Moreover, the South Manchuria Railway has maintained a number of settlements. Though having only an area of 25,760 acres altogether, these settlements have become the financial or commercial centers of South Manchuria. All imports coming by the railway have to be unloaded there before they are distributed to the surrounding country. All agricultural products for export are also transported there first before being carried to Dairen by the railway. In several of the settlements, money exchanges are maintained for the negotiation of *kin-piao* or *chao-piao* against local currencies. Many Chinese firms are established there, among whom we see *kin-piao* used as the principal medium. In short, these settlements are, in one sense, the places where the Chinese world meets the Japanese, and through them Japanese currency has been widely distributed among Chinese.

Owing to the existence of the three factors outlined above, Japan holds such a dominant financial position in Manchuria as cannot compare with what has been achieved by any Power in China (except perhaps the position formerly held by Imperial Russia in North Manchuria). Under the present circumstances it is hardly possible for any Chinese to escape the use of Japanese bank notes in Manchuria. All governmental banks on the Chinese side, despite their large capital and government support, find themselves constantly under the practical necessity of bowing before the supremacy of Japanese banking houses.

THE SCOPE AND NATURE OF JAPANESE FINANCIAL ACTIVITIES

Most of the foreign nations carrying on commercial pursuits in China are at the same time also engaged in some sort of financial business. There are banking houses of many foreign nationalities, and we see in circulation notes issued by many foreign banks. But although Japan has not been the only country which is financially active in China, yet we should like to point out that the banking and currency arrangements made by the Japanese in Manchuria are different in both degree and nature from those adopted by other nations in other parts of China.

In the first place, from the very beginning Japan's financial institutions in Manchuria were devised to promote Japanese colonization. The fields of financial activity are well divided between three specially chartered banks: the Bank of Chosen being the central institution to issue gold notes, the Yokohama Specie Bank the exchange bank to foster international trade, and the Oriental Development Company the investment agency to facilitate Japanese immigration in Manchuria. We do not forget that there are also banking agencies of other foreign nationalities in China, but they have no system whatever. Although most of them act on behalf of their respective governments in the case of making loans to China, yet they are predominantly commercial concerns charged with no special mission, as is the case with the Japanese banks.

Secondly, several banks of other nations also issue bank notes in China, but as far as standard and unit are concerned they make no deviation from the local currency system. Such notes are fused into the local currency as easily as those issued by private Chinese banks; but with the Japanese notes issued in Manchuria, an entirely different situation exists. While the silver note for the Yokohama Specie Bank is on a different unit, the gold note of the Bank of Chosen deviates both in unit and in standard from the local currency. This, under ordinary circumstances, tends to make the local currency system more confused. In days of political disturbance such notes become the objects of speculation.

At this point we should like to point out the fact that, while the silver notes are primarily designed for the Chinese, more than three-quarters of the gold notes circulating in Manchuria, which in recent years have amounted from forty to fifty million, are also circulating among the Chinese. While we have no statistics to verify this statement, still in view of the number of Japanese residents in Manchuria and their economic situation, we believe that this estimate would not be far from the fact. Consequently, the argument advanced that these notes are issued to circulate mainly among the Japanese nationals, and not for circulation among the Chinese, does not stand.

Thirdly, in addition to the Japanese banks, a number of money exchanges have been established in Dairen and the settlements. At these exchanges gold *yen* and silver *yen* are negotiated against the local currency. These exchanges are run under the auspices of the Japanese authorities and beyond the reach of Chinese jurisdiction. In times of financial crisis or political unrest they are centers of speculation. The fortunes of thousands have been lost there. Among the circle of conservative Chinese merchants they are known as the " spring of commercial vices."

In the case of the decline of the *feng-piao* (Mukden notes), in the last analysis we have only the Chinese provincial authorities to blame; but speculations in these Japanese exchanges helped to make the situation much worse, especially at the time when depreciation was most rapid, and when it was most difficult for the provincial government to make efforts to prevent it. The late Marshal Chang Tso-lin has been severely criticized for the execution of the three managers of Tien Ho Sheng, a big money house which was situated in the railway settlement and speculated heavily in Japanese *yen* at Japanese exchanges every time when the Chinese authorities were using every effort to check further depreciation of the *feng-piao;* but we must remember that at the time of their execution Marshal Chang had been driven to his wit's end.

THE FUTURE OF JAPANESE BANK NOTES

The currency arrangements in Manchuria are in a state of extraordinary confusion. In addition to the Japanese bank notes, each of the three Chinese Provinces has its own paper currency system. Such a state of affairs as is found in Manchuria is, of course, not desirable. It not only causes inconvenience to the public, but it also incurs unnecessary losses to trade. For instance, foreign merchants who come to Manchuria to purchase soya bean have to convert the money in their possession into *chao-piao* before they can get the products from native grain dealers. But the *chao-piao* is not the money obtaining in rural districts; the grain dealers in turn also are under the necessity of changing the *chao-piao* they receive into *feng-piao* or *kuan-tieh* which are acceptable to farmers. In most cases money exchange means a series of business dealings, and the expense thus incurred is usually heavier than a burdensome taxation. In order to put an end to this undesirable state of affairs, and also to reform the plan now contemplated by the central Government, a commission on Financial Readjustment was appointed in March, 1930, by the Mukden Provincial Government to formulate some working plan to reform the banking and monetary system in the Three Eastern Provinces. The commission submitted their report together with a reform project to the provincial authorities in December, 1930. The report suggested currency uniformity and the adoption of a gold standard. If peace can be maintained in the country for a few years some reform program, such as the recently proposed one, is bound to be carried out eventually.

If currency uniformity can be established in Manchuria then the following question would naturally arise: What would be the fate of the Japanese bank notes in Manchuria? A concurrent circulation of foreign bank notes would defeat the ends of reform; naturally they should be excluded from Chinese territory. We cannot deny the fact that the present Japanese financial arrangements have greatly aided legitimate Japanese commercial activities in Manchuria. Under the modern system of economic institutions, a sound banking and monetary system is absolutely essential for commercial enterprise of any kind. On the other hand, we must point out that the issue of bank notes is a sovereign right; no modern state would tolerate private or foreign bank notes on its territory. For the present, Japan may justify her acts on the basis of practical necessity; but as soon as currency reform is accomplished, no further arguments can be advanced. A simple uniform currency system on a certain standard would serve the interests of both foreigners and Chinese. Multiplicity would be detrimental to all.

With the abrogation of their right to note issue, the business activities of the Japanese banks would necessarily be curtailed to some extent, but their future development could be concentrated along the same lines as those taken by commercial banks of other foreign nations. Indeed, it is only by so doing that these banks could rightfully exist. A banking policy such as that adopted at present by Japan in Manchuria has far exceeded what is necessary for the pursuance of ordinary commercial activities. It can only be defended on the ground that it serves the Japanese business world in the absence of a sound Chinese financial system. When the reform, referred to above, is completed, the Japanese system would cease to serve any good purpose and would give rise to international misunderstanding.

QUESTIONS FOR ROUND–TABLE DISCUSSION

The following questions were recommended by the Program Committee as an outline for discussion:

1. Having regard to the widespread discussions for and against international governmental action for the purpose of stabilizing silver prices, what is the measure of importance of stabilization to (a) China's financial economy, (b) international trade with China?
2. What are the principal effects of a low level of silver prices on (a) China's internal economy, (b) China's foreign trade? How transitory are such effects likely to be? In this connection what account must be taken of the movement to put China's currency on a gold basis?
3. In any attempt to stabilize silver by international co-operation, what special part could and should be played by countries in the Pacific area?
4. What is likely to be the future development in the supply and demand of silver?
5. On the assumption that the present gold standard is not an entirely satisfactory monetary medium, is silver likely to play an important part in any reform of that medium?
6. What advantages and liabilities accrue to Chinese finance and economy from the retention of the silver standard?
7. What national or international action could be taken to affect the demand for silver in relation to the supply?

SUMMARY OF ROUND–TABLE DISCUSSIONS

I. STABILIZATION

It was a Chinese banker, but not a member of the Shanghai financial community, who opened the discussion in the special round table on silver, and because his opinions differed in marked degree from those expressed by most other speakers, and served to evoke certain arguments in rebuttal, they are here reproduced almost in full.

" It has been generally recognized that in view of the serious curtailment of the monetary uses of silver in different countries, the chief support for the white metal will have to come from China, which is the only country still on a silver basis. Should the economic development of China proceed apace without let-up or hindrance, the demand for silver will naturally increase, resulting in higher prices for the white metal; otherwise the future trend of silver prices cannot be hopeful. Speaking as a Chinese banker and publicist, I should not like to see China become the perpetual dumping ground for silver for two reasons: In the first place, the whole world with the exception of China has enthroned gold as the standard metal. The considerable fluctuations in the price of the white metal which we have witnessed during the past decade have caused not only dislocation of China's foreign trade but also retarded her normal course of industrial development. In other words, the capriciousness of silver has played havoc not merely in China, but also in those countries which are growing more dependent on trade with China. The only sensible course for China to follow is to adopt the gold standard as soon as possible. It will then not be necessary for China to absorb more silver, which would make her currency reform increasingly difficult. Secondly, the phenomenal fall of silver is due to the fact that the supply of the metal has far outstripped the demand for it, especially because of the existence of demonetized silver in the hands of certain currency authorities, which hangs as a dark cloud over an already depressed economic horizon. For China to consume all this continuous stream of silver and await a further fall in its price is almost suicidal.

" So by force of circumstances China will be compelled to reform her currency system at a quicker pace than would otherwise be the case. If I see correctly, public opinion in China favors the adoption of a policy leading to the limitation, if not the prohibition, of the importation of silver into China. Whatever the price of silver, China ultimately is bound to come into line with the rest of the world as far as currency standard is concerned — if only to facilitate international trade and to promote international co-operation in the development of China. Unless the nations of the world either increase the consumption of silver for monetary purposes or agree to control the disposition of surplus silver stocks and the further production of silver, so as not to exceed the normal demand, further depreciation of silver is still possible. In order to protect herself from ultimate ruin, China will be obliged to follow a course which will appeal to her self-interest.

" Before I close, I should like to correct two views which seem to me to be quite erroneous. One is that which adopts a pessimistic outlook regarding future economic enterprise in China on account of the low level of silver. It seems to me that depressed silver cannot but impel China to reform her currency, thereby redounding to the gain of international trade and commerce. The other view asserts that the Chinese people are hoping for an appreciation of silver. What we are really hoping for is the immediate reform of our currency. I am convinced that the occasional fluctuations of the price of the white metal will hardly have much effect on the course of China's industrial development if she nails her future monetary system to a gold standard."

The opinion which is implied in this statement, namely, that the fall in the value of silver and the depreciation of Chinese currency in terms of gold is the product of external forces over which China has no control whatever, is, of course, widely held. Nevertheless, a Chinese banker of high standing in Shanghai took it upon himself to urge a number of opposing considerations. It would seem, he maintained, that the fall in the price of silver is, in part at least, merely a reflection of the currency depreciation which is going on in China and is but another aspect of the internal inflation on which many authorities on silver have remarked. The inflation is the normal result of the financial operations of the Government in issuing domestic bonds during the last few years to make up the deficit in its budget. Bond issues to the amount of about $750 million have been floated by the Government since 1927, and the Chinese banks, which are often put under various forms of indirect pressure to purchase the bonds, have been compelled in turn to expand their note issues, bringing about a general inflation of currency especially in the large commercial centers. The proof of this is easily to be seen, he continued, by comparing the volume of notes issued three years ago with the present volume. As symptoms of the existence of currency inflation, he pointed first to the steady drain of gold from China over the past few years, amounting in his estimate to about $35 million gold for the period January, 1929, to October, 1931. A second symptom is the real-estate boom in Shanghai; a third the mushroom growth of small Chinese factories under the stimulus, of steadily rising prices; a fourth the rapid development of investment companies employing foreign capital in Shanghai; and a fifth the craze for speculation in gold bars, foreign exchange, and real estate. A second and less important contributing factor in the depreciation of China's currency was seen in the abnormally unfavorable trade balance for 1930 and 1931, which is itself caused by the reduced demand of the outside world for Chinese exports, and the increased demand in China for foreign imports to make up for shortages of domestic supplies arising from natural calamities and political disturbances.[3]

The speaker then directed the attention of his hearers to the possibilities and the desirability of stabilizing China's currency at some fixed relationship with gold, and in consequence laid down the lines for most of the subsequent discussion in the round table. He began:

" The first difficulty arises from the fact that the Chinese Government is still unable to balance its budget; and without that, we know, a country cannot have a stable currency. Then in regard to the desirability of stabilization, we may ask what advantages will accrue from fixing the value of silver. We stabilize silver in order to establish a definite relationship between silver and gold; but in doing so we have no assurances that we shall secure a stable or favorable price level in China. Fortunately for China, and because we have had a silver standard, we have had a gradually rising price level which has acted for the benefit of Chinese producers. But at present, while prices in China are relatively high and are rising higher, prices abroad are ridiculously low. If we stabilize silver now, we shall, as Irving Fisher has pointed out, inevitably link the internal price level of China with the international price level. This country must realize that by the very act of adopting a gold standard or fixing its currency in a definite relationship to gold, it has placed its economic destinies at the mercy of the government and banking policies of other nations. What the dollar will buy in America depends on whether European nations keep peace or war. There is no problem which is more international than monetary stabilization, for the action of any great national bank in one country will affect other countries almost immediately; and all gold-standard countries are so closely tied together that gold moves freely back and forth among them, tending to keep the exchange rates in equilibrium, but in doing so, to disorganize the price levels.

" Silver stabilization would therefore cause deflation in China. Our price level would collapse with disastrous results to our whole financial and industrial system. And for that reason I am inclined to think that, while we must eventually adopt a gold standard, we must postpone this until our Government is secure enough to have a balanced budget and until a time when world economic conditions will have settled sufficiently to make further violent changes in price levels unlikely. When that time comes we may safely connect China's currency with the international system of the gold standard."

Asked by a Japanese member whether the introduction of a gold standard into China would be very difficult at the present time, or whether it was not possible to proceed by gradually extending the gold-unit system already adopted in the Maritime Customs out into the provinces, the speaker gave his opinion that the practical difficulties were not so great as the fundamental theoretical ones already suggested. Practically it would be possible for large

[3] The trade statistics for 1930 show that China's imports increased from 1,266 million haikwan taels in 1929 to 1,310, while her exports declined in value from 1,016 to 895 million taels, thus increasing her characteristic unfavorable balance from 250 million to the unparalleled figure of 415 million taels, or nearly 191 million gold dollars.

mercantile houses to agree to quote in gold units, for the railways to calculate their revenues likewise, and for long-term contracts or loans to be made in gold, and thus to go far toward the effective working of a gold standard. But the real objection was that the gold standard itself in the rest of the world had been greatly hampered in its effective working — on account of reparation payments, war debts, tariffs, and the other economic dislocations of the post-war world. For China to adopt a system already laboring under such handicaps would be to plunge herself into very dangerous waters. Once she had adopted it, a sudden period of inflation or deflation in Germany or France or Japan would immediately affect prices and credit in China where the financial and industrial organization is still far too weak to withstand such unforeseen fluctuations from outside. Ultimately, of course, he recognized the necessity for China to adopt a gold standard, or more precisely a gold-exchange standard, in common with the rest of the world. Even at the present time, however, he pointed out, he would have less objection to plans for stabilization if it were done on the basis of prevailing prices of silver, or about 26 or 28 gold cents an ounce, since this would not involve any sudden disturbance of China's internal prices. But the object of most foreigners who argued for stabilization was for the fixing of the price of silver by international agreement at some artificially high rate, such as 40 or 50 cents an ounce. Stabilization at that level would mean acute deflation for China. Great Britain and Italy had both had sad experience of the difficulty of restoring or trying to restore their currencies after the war to their theoretical parity. For China to follow in their path would be folly. He concluded:

" If you artificially raise your currency standard, you are merely lowering your price level and altering the relationship between the savings class and the enterprising class. It will work an injustice on many people, and I think it would be ill-advised in China where the standard of living is already so low, to attempt such deflation. Dr. Kemmerer of the Commission of Financial Experts has, in fact, specifically mentioned the dangers of deflation and the futility of using it as a means of reaching the gold standard. We all know that most of the foreign powers, with the notable exception of France, returned to the gold standard by means of deflation. Britain has now abandoned it again, unable to stand the strain. Japan will probably follow the same course before long. China must stand firm and not attempt deflation. We need more of the capitalist and enterprising class rather than more of the savings or *rentier* class. We must encourage factories, merchants, and banks. For the time being, we can sacrifice the interests of the fixed-income class and the wage-earners, in order to accumulate some essential reserves of wealth."

The allusion to the concern of certain American interests led the round table to examine some of the arguments advanced by these proponents of silver-stabilization schemes, and thus to a consideration of the silver problem in its more international aspect — as a commodity which has suffered like others from the fall in world-prices and which might conceivably be made to supplement gold for currency purposes as the scarcity and maldistribution of the latter grows more acute. Despite the publicity which had been given to certain agitations and resolutions of interested American groups, American members believed that none of the proposals made had the effective backing of recognized authorities. One member, indeed, ridiculed the activities of this group, consisting mainly of silver-producing interests from Nevada, with some support from British and American investors in Chinese securities, and took it upon himself to refute the agreements advanced in the following preamble to a resolution passed by the Western Division of the United States Chamber of Commerce on December 8, 1930:

Whereas it is self-evident that the peace of the world depends on the prosperity and contentment of its peoples; that the political and economic conditions of all nations are closely interwoven; that the employment of labor in the United States is, in large part, dependent on the consumption of our products in foreign countries; that over half the peoples of the world use silver money exclusively in their domestic trade; that the depression in the price of silver has caused a tremendous decrease in the purchasing power of a large proportion of the world's population; that because of this our trade with the Orient and other silver-using countries has fallen off in an alarming degree. . . .

Such groups, he urged, have simply shut their eyes to the fact that China's trade has actually increased in many commodities; that the decline in American purchases from China has been much greater than the decline in China's purchases from America; that the loss of American trade has been much greater in other more important countries, such as Canada, Australia, Germany, and Italy, than in China; and, finally, that China, which is the only large trading country using a silver standard, has a trade which is only about $2\frac{1}{2}$ per cent of the world's trade and in which less than 4 per cent of the total trade of the United States is involved.

The view was later put forward that it is a mistake to assume, as is often done, that silver has fared unusually badly in comparison with other commodities in the world-depression. It was demonstrated that prices of other metals, such as tin or zinc, and primary commodities, such as wool, rubber, coffee, and silk, had suffered a greater fall than silver prices.[4] Similarly, it was shown that silver-mining as an investment had proved little or no worse than many other forms of enterprise, and that the holder of Chinese securities was no more in dire straits than the holder of United States Steel Corporation stocks.

In the light of these arguments, which were later reinforced by the remarks of other leading banking officials, it became increasingly apparent to members of the round table that the question of stabilization which was put first on the agenda was of less practical importance than had been supposed. For the two main points in arguments for stabilizing silver prices, as a British member stated, are, first, that some such step is needed to ease the world monetary situation which grows out of the increasing shortage and mal-

---

[4] A diagram which illustrates this point very clearly is given in *The Course and Phases of the World Economic Depression* (League of Nations, 1931), p. 160.

distribution of gold reserves; and, second, that stabilization will improve trade conditions between China and the rest of the world. He continued:

" It is well known that trade conditions depend in large measure on internal and political developments in China, and we have just been shown the disastrous effects which might be expected were China to adopt a gold standard or, what is in effect the same thing, to stabilize the value of her silver currency. In addition to this, an American member has just shown that silver has had less effect on foreign trade with China than we have been led to believe. If these views are sound, it would seem that several of the weightiest arguments for silver stabilization go by the board."

The general opinion of the round table thus appeared to turn away from the views put forward in the opening statement. One foreign student of Chinese currency, in fact, described these views as commendable for their patriotism but quite impracticable in the present state of affairs. In particular, he objected to the policy suggested by the opening speaker of restricting or prohibiting further imports of silver into China, the objection being based on the fact that China has insufficient silver to serve as cover for her note issues. His remedy for the admitted evils arising out of the present-day speculative trade in silver was to confer a monopoly for the import or export of silver upon the central bank or a small number of important banks who could be relied upon to pursue a wise policy.

Moreover, a prohibition on imports of silver would be particularly unwise at the present time when there is definite evidence that accumulations of silver in Shanghai are decreasing [5] despite large importations from abroad, as silver is moving more and more into the interior provinces of China and passing into the hands of farmers and small traders. He scouted the opinion that China had no need of more silver as long as great and rich areas like the Four Eastern Provinces were almost devoid of silver coins, and agreed with a British member that with the passage of time and the gradual absorption of silver into the interior, the silver problem in China would tend to solve itself — provided only that the export trade were given a chance to develop.

II. SILVER IN CHINA'S INTERNAL ECONOMY

Circulation. — The question of silver stocks and the movement of silver into the interior suggests the further question of how far silver in the interior is put into active circulation and how much of it merely goes into hoard. As was pointed out in the round table, the problem is one which has been significant for India as well as China. Foreign members asked for estimates of the amount of hoarding which takes place in China, but were told by Chinese specialists that the question is quite unanswerable since hoardings in many cases go back for generations. The head of a leading Chinese bank said:

[5] In the estimate of the speaker, the net decline of silver stocks in Shanghai amounted to about 20 million taels for the twelve months ending September, 1931.

" I have studied the question carefully, but it is impossible for anybody to say. There is no possibility of finding out how much money a man has in his pocket unless we steal his purse. I cannot put much confidence in estimates which are made of silver hoarded in India, since silver is put back into circulation and withdrawn again into hoard from time to time."

The most that could be assumed, in his opinion, was that silver would tend to be put into circulation again in time of distress, and that hoards must certainly have decreased in those parts of China which have been stricken by flood and famine. On the other hand, a foreign currency expert suggested that some information, at least, could be gained from a study of the imports and exports of silver over a long period of years. Such a study, in combination with an examination of the stocks held in the principal financial centers of China, had led him to the conclusion that there should be a minimum amount of roughly 2,500 million ounces of silver in China, as against the 4,500 million ounces estimated for India.[6] The portion of this total which was buried away in hoards could not be determined, and it was made clear that the total represents the amount of silver whose existence can be proved. The actual amount is possibly slightly larger, though not so large as that suggested by another member of the round table who had hazarded a total of 4 billion to 5 billion ounces.

Effect of depreciation. — Very little discussion took place in the round table on the actual and expected results of exchange depreciation from the mercantile and industrial point of view. In an earlier round table on trade relations, however, Chinese members referred occasionally to the development of small Chinese industries under the shelter of the depreciated silver exchange (or, from the Chinese viewpoint, the appreciated gold exchange), which acts as a kind of temporary protective tariff, encouraging Chinese producers to offer locally made goods which can thus compete favorably with foreign goods whose prices in silver have been abnormally enhanced by the exchange movements. From the standpoint of the foreign importer and distributor in China, this protective effect of the depreciation has been further accentuated since the early part of 1930 by the adoption of the gold unit in the collection of customs duties, thus adding to the difficulty of predicting what the ultimate price of an imported article will be in China. In the round table on silver this point was brought out clearly by a member of a large foreign business concern in Shanghai who showed that, in addition to the uncertainty of making advance quotations in silver currency for goods which had to be paid for by the importing firm in gold, there was the new uncertainty of not knowing how much must be added to the silver-price quotation

[6] For detailed figures and the method of inquiry see E. Kann, " How Much Silver Is There in China? " *Chinese Economic Journal*, April, 1931. It is calculated that the equivalent of 2,200 million silver dollars is the minimum silver-money circulation of China, representing a total of 1,700 million troy ounces of fine silver. A total of 800 million troy ounces is estimated for silver in hoard and in the form of ornaments, etc., making a grand total of 2,500 million ounces.

in order to cover the amount of the import duty. He proceeded further to develop an interesting argument concerning the normal buying power of a given Chinese district or industry. It had been the experience of his firm that this buying power could be fixed fairly rigidly at so many million silver dollars, and that exchange fluctuations with resultant price changes for the Chinese consumer produce little variation in this total buying power. If silver prices are doubled, the ordinary consumption of that particular imported product will decrease by about one-half. By way of illustration, he referred to the oil business in China, stating that the greatest variation in the total amount of money spent by Chinese on kerosene oil in the past few years has been under 5 per cent. This remarkable elasticity of demand, to use the economist's jargon, is an indication of a fairly constant purchasing power and is partly attributable to the fact that the Chinese consumer is quick to avail himself of locally produced substitute commodities — vegetable oils for kerosene, in the present example — whenever price changes make it profitable to do so.

It therefore became clear to many members of this round table, as it had, indeed, to former groups, that a depreciated exchange was less to be feared than a depreciating exchange, and that wild fluctuations of rates rather than high or low rates were the prime obstacles to trade, just as changes in tariffs rather than high tariffs were the greatest bugbear of international commerce. Given some degree of stability, business can adjust itself to high or low exchange rates; without stability it stagnates or is paralyzed in an orgy of speculation. With silver at its present low level, it was shown in one discussion, China's export trade ought normally to have expanded rapidly when Chinese products could be purchased by gold-standard countries at abnormally cheap prices; yet, in large measure, because of the chance of further depreciation, dealers had hesitated to make contracts and had postponed placing orders, with the result that the prices and production had become further disorganized and exports had greatly decreased in 1930 and 1931. While it was admitted that the exchange risk was not the sole or even the chief factor in the situation, it had undoubtedly exercised a depressing influence.

Unification of currency. — A parallel if not identical consideration was brought to the attention of the round table by a Chinese banker who, in examining the possibilities of adopting a stabilized gold-exchange currency for China, pointed to the essential need for some internal stability and unification of currency as the prerequisite for the adoption of a gold standard.[7]

[7] The question was a matter of too common knowledge in the round table to be examined at length, but its fundamental importance was recognized. So long as the present chaos in the matter of note issues, inconvertible paper currency, and debased subsidiary coinage continues, and so long as two major units of currency — the tael and the dollar — are used side by side and one of them (the tael) varies in weight and value from city to city, there can be little real progress toward a solution of China's monetary problems and, moreover, the adoption of some form of gold standard will be shorn of many of its benefits. For further comment on the subject see Araki, *op. cit.*, pp. 3–23;

Not the least of the economies which might be effected by some such plan of unification would be the welding of the financial and banking system of China into a more efficient and sensitive working unit than it now is and the elimination of at least part of the expensive system of local exchange rates between one city and another. The complete removal of these internal exchange variations, however, would depend on the improvement of railways and telegraphic communications as well as on the unification of the coinage and note issues. In this connection, an American member alluded to the analogous problem of local " cross-rates " which had formerly existed in the United States but had been wiped out by the setting-up of the Federal Reserve System under which transference of funds from one part of the country to another could be effected promptly and cheaply by telegraph without necessity for the actual movement of bullion or notes. It was thereupon revealed that a beginning of the same system has already been made in China. The Central Bank of China has now made arrangements whereby its branches in certain other cities will, upon presentation of the Bank's notes, give telegraphic transfers on the head office in Shanghai, without the usual commission charges.

III. SILVER A WORLD PROBLEM

Although the discussions for the most part were confined to the special silver problems of China, some time in the round table, as well as in the earlier discussions on Pacific trade, was devoted to the more truly international problems of silver, with special reference to the conditions attending the production of silver in modern times and its ratio (both in production and value) to gold. A Canadian member gave a concise account of the trends in production and prices since 1873 when the great fluctuations began. The facts, however, are widely known today and were familiar to most members of the round table, so that no more than the baldest summary is called for here.[8] Despite the extraordinary fluctuations which have occurred in the gold price of silver in the last seventy years, it is well known that the physical ratio of production has remained remarkably constant at about 1 unit of gold to $14\frac{1}{2}$ of silver — a fact which is the basis of the opinion held by certain monetary authorities that this is the " true " or " natural " ratio between the two metals, and that their prices should accordingly bear approximately the same relationship — as indeed they did, on the average, for some three hundred and fifty years since the discovery of America. But with the world-wide adoption of the gold standard, beginning with Germany and the bimetallic countries in the last century and ending with India in 1926 and Indo-China in 1929, great quantities of demonetized silver have been thrown upon the

---

Second Report on Progress in Manchuria, to 1930, pp. 182–99; and Commission of Financial Experts (Kemmerer Commission), *Project of Law for the Gradual Introduction of a Gold Standard Currency System in China,* pp. 45–56.

   [8] See W. F. Spalding, " Memorandum on the Position of Silver in the Far East," above, pp. 198 ff.

world-markets and have tended to depress prices. The tendency has been aggravated in post-war years by the practice — initiated by Great Britain and followed by most other countries except the United States, Spain, and Canada — of reducing the silver content of their subsidiary silver coins and selling the metal thus obtained in the open market. Furthermore, the slump in prices has probably been unnaturally severe and more than conditions of immediate supply and demand would warrant because of the knowledge on the part of dealers that the Indian Government still possesses a fund, popularly estimated at some 300 million ounces, not yet placed on the market. The ever present threat of new sales from this source has dragged prices still lower.

If it is asked why, in the face of this glut of silver and the drastic fall in prices, the metal still continues to be produced in equally great volume, the answer is to be found, according to this member, in the fact that, as a result of technological progress, about two-thirds of all new silver is now produced not from silver mines, but as a by-product from other enterprises — such as gold, lead, zinc, and copper mines — and that the customary regulating effect of price on output is thus no longer fully operative. Silver, he stated, will continue to be produced as a by-product long after prices have dropped far below the level at which production in the best " straight " silver mines would be profitable.

These facts concerning silver as a commodity are not new or unique in the history of metal production. The reason for their importance and the reason why they were discussed in the round table were found to consist in their relation to the problem of gold production and the future monetary gold reserves of the world. The same Canadian member tersely summed up the problem thus:

" The situation with regard to gold is that production at the present moment is about twenty million ounces annually. It has been fairly steady at that level for the last few years and is expected to remain steady for, at any rate, another five years. The more optimistic of those who are familiar with conditions in South Africa — the largest producer — believe that no great decline in the annual output will occur until 1940 or thereabouts. But unless new and quite spectacular discoveries are made in the meanwhile — and the regions where there is any prospect of new discoveries are now very few — there will be a steady and appreciable reduction from that date. Consequently, there will be serious risk of a shortage in the supply of gold needed to maintain the financial structure of the world, in which case some other backing for the world's currencies, such as silver, will have to be found."

These views evoked support from several representatives of the Shanghai banking community. They admitted the possibilities of further gold discoveries in such regions as Australia, though it was felt that these could not be important enough seriously to impair the force of the argument. They also agreed in part with the suggestion made by American members that economies were possible in the use of gold, and still more that great improvements were possible, if not at present probable, in the distribution of gold reserves.

But they nevertheless felt strongly that there was still an important place for silver in the world's monetary basis. An official of one of the principal Chinese banks maintained that there would be a real risk of an acute gold shortage and danger of a collapse in the credit system unless some other metal, such as silver, were used to supplement gold. For that reason, and not for its effect on raising silver prices or stabilizing China's exchange, he was in favor of an international conference on the silver situation. As far as China was concerned, he agreed with a former Chinese speaker that China would do well to keep to her silver standard for the present, applying herself meanwhile to the task of internal currency unification. Silver, he felt confident, would recapture much of its former prestige with the increasing scarcity and uneconomical distribution of gold. With a number of members, he remained somewhat skeptical of the possibilities of future improvements in gold distribution by reason of the development of the Bank of International Settlements. This possibility was suggested with considerable conviction by two American members who argued that through this institution the benefits which arose from a unified system, such as the Federal Reserve in the United States, might be extended in time to the world's financial mechanism:

" If some day, instead of having nationalistic America and a nationalistic Federal Reserve System to manipulate the gold reserves as part of a national policy, we should concentrate the world's gold in a central reserve, we might obviate all the fluctuations which have characterized this depression. Scientifically, J. M. Keynes has long since pointed out, we could have an internationally managed currency without any backing at all, either of gold or of silver. But to have this would imply a restraint from the application of political pressure to banking agencies, in a degree which we cannot envisage today. Rather than look ahead to the establishment of an international bimetallism which leads to all the difficulties experienced in America and elsewhere, is it not possible, first, to effect economies in the use of gold and, second, to devise means of increasing the efficiency and prestige of the Bank of International Settlements and thus to avoid these great credit fluctuations generally or the occurrence of such catastrophes as the virtual collapse of the Reichsbank and the recent crisis in Great Britain? "

But to the Chinese member such a solution seemed very far from the bounds of possibility in the present lack of international confidence and understanding. " The peoples of the world," he said, " have no confidence in each other. The Great War has not taught us any lesson at all. And in the absence of that confidence, the concentration of gold reserves at Basle is a very remote possibility." The truth of this was readily admitted by the round table, as were the inevitable delays which modern democratic political conditions impose on real progress in international co-operation. But it was also acknowledged, as the chairman indicated in his summing-up, that changes in public opinion do occur — especially under the stimulus of some economic catastrophe — and the ready acceptance of the war-debt moratorium in America is but one example of the fact that governments and executives can easily underestimate the extent to which public opinion has advanced toward the solution of an international dilemma.

PART III

POLITICAL RELATIONS IN THE PACIFIC

CHAPTER VIII

THE DIPLOMATIC MACHINERY OF THE PACIFIC

DATA PAPERS

1. STEPHEN A. HEALD. *Draft Syllabus for the Study of Diplomatic Machinery in the Pacific* (mimeographed, British Group).
2. SIR WILLIAM HARRISON MOORE. *The Dominions of the British Commonwealth in the League of Nations* (Australian Council) (reprinted from *International Affairs*, X, No. 3 [May 1931]).
3. R. K. FINLAYSON. *The British Commonwealth and Its Relation to Pacific Problems* (Canadian Council).
4. HAROLD S. QUIGLEY. *An Introductory Syllabus on Far Eastern Diplomacy* (American Council).

REFERENCES

1. ARNOLD J. TOYNBEE. *Survey of International Affairs, 1930, Part IV: China* (British Group).
2. FREDERICK V. FIELD. *American Participation in the China Consortiums* (American Council).
3. GUY H. SCHOLEFIELD. "Japan and New Zealand," chap. xi of *New Zealand Affairs* (New Zealand Council). Christchurch, 1929.
4. F. W. EGGLESTON. "Disarmament and the Pacific," *Pacific Affairs*, December, 1930.
5. TRISTAN BUESST. *The Naval Base at Singapore* (mimeographed, Australian Council).
6. J. B. CONDLIFFE (ed.). *Problems of the Pacific, 1929* (Chicago, 1930), chap. viii, Doc. XV.
7. CHARLES P. HOWLAND. *Survey of American Foreign Relations.* New Haven, 1930.
8. H. B. MORSE and N. F. MACNAIR. *Far Eastern International Relations.* New York, 1931.
    (For further references see *Problems of the Pacific, 1929*, pp. 243–44.)

INTRODUCTORY NOTE

In the introduction of his chapter on "Diplomatic Relations" in *Problems of the Pacific, 1929*, the editor has pointed out that the Institute of Pacific Relations is concerned with the study of questions of international diplomacy, in so far as they relate to the Pacific area, but does not itself employ methods of diplomacy with a view to solving political problems. The same popular misunderstanding of the Institute's functioning which he then noted again made its appearance at the China Conference. It led to denunciations, particularly in the Chinese press, of the Institute's ineffectiveness in a critical political controversy between two of the nations represented. In contrast, the members of the Conference itself were well aware on this occasion that their round-table discussions did not serve the purposes of official diplomacy and could not use its characteristic processes. That in spite of this full understanding of the scope of their task practically the whole membership of the Conference devoted its time on two successive mornings to questions of the diplomatic machinery of the Pacific area is explained by their realization that one of the outstanding problems in the Far Eastern situation was the limitation of the political intercourse between two great nations to the established methods of diplomatic negotiation. It is easy for a private individual to submit for comment and criticism some idea he may have as to ways in which the diplomatic machinery may be improved; it is not easy to do so for an officer of a ministry of foreign affairs whose personal opinion is subject to interpretation as an expression of his government's views.

The usefulness of a discussion by private citizens of matters of state depends on the fulness of their information and their understanding of the issues involved. In this respect the round tables of the China Conference were probably as well equipped as any other international group of private citizens that has in recent years tackled these difficult problems; for among them were enough who had had inside experience of official diplomatic negotiation and more who, as teachers and publicists, had given to them close and studious attention for many years. Experience of the functioning of diplomatic intercourse in connection with specific causes (such as the suppression of the opium traffic, the regulation of international migration, public-health measures, the reduction of armaments, and the like) on the part of many of the lay members helped to give this discussion reality.

That acute questions of the day, especially those raised by the Manchurian dispute, took a disproportionate share of attention was inevitable. There was a genuine search for new guaranties of international peace and co-operation, not a display of scholarship or of forensic eloquence. By devoting themselves largely to the international structure in relation to a real threat of war, the Conference was soon led to realize the greatest if the least avoidable defect of the diplomatic machinery: its inability to do justice to the imponderable psychological factors in situations where the emotions are deeply stirred. Thus, it was found that the instruments employed to affect public opinion are inextricably bound up with the instruments of official diplomacy. And it is in the borderland between the areas of formulated national policy and formless ambitions and interests that such an agency as the Institute of Pacific Relations functions with particular effectiveness. Those who had expected the Conference to sit in judgment on the merits of a specific controversy were fortunately disappointed. The discussion of diplomatic machinery afforded an opportunity, rather, for applying to a crisis to which governments must attend with the recognized methods of diplomatic procedure the thinking of men and women less circumscribed by rules and precedents. It was permissible for them to search for possible motivations of which the diplomat can take no official cognizance. They could play with ideas, whether these were susceptible of immediate realization or not. And they were free tentatively to advance suggestions for possible solutions, later to modify them or to take them back again, without that danger to national prestige which attends such vacillations once a proposal has been launched by a government's official spokesman.

There was no such wealth of documents before the round tables on the present occasion as had been presented at the Kyoto Conference. The chief reason for this was that at that meeting of the Institute the Pact of Paris was yet an outstanding novelty in international relations, and the recent discussions of it were yet in everyone's mind. Moreover, that Conference had offered the first opportunity to review the activities of the League of Nations in relation to the Pacific area and to consider suggestions for supplementing it with regional machinery in that area. There had been no striking new developments of the diplomatic structure when the Program Committee of the Institute met in December, 1930; and the subject was not then scheduled on the tentative agenda for the China Conference. However, in the following months there were signs that once more difficult problems in international relations, and new situations casting doubt upon the adequacy of the present diplomatic machinery for handling them, would be brought prominently before the members of the 1931 Conference; and so, at the specific request of one of the national councils, the Program Committee added this subject to the proposed agenda. This late decision accounts for the fact that the China Conference did not have before it a syllabus on this topic prepared by the Institute Secretariat (an omission compensated by the subsequent contribution of an admirable outline of discussion by a member of the British group); and that none of the groups presented data papers relating to it in its entirety. The careful presentation of the whole subject and of its discussion at the Kyoto Conference, in *Problems of the Pacific, 1929,* should, therefore, be regarded as an essential introduction to what follows. In a sense, the round tables in 1931 were simply in continuation of a discussion, ranging over a wider area and more fully implemented, two years earlier.

One other difference in the treatment of this subject in 1929 and 1931 is worthy of mention. In the former Conference, questions concerning the diplomatic machinery came almost last on the agenda, after floodlights had played upon many of the troubles in the international relations of the Pacific. In the 1931 Conference, these questions preceded and led into the discussion of the more specific sources of friction. The earlier arrangement had the advantage that members had become realistically aware of the many involved and delicate relationships between peoples before dealing with the machinery of official communication between governments; the other was motivated by the belief that it was useful to see the problems of the political relations in a wider perspective before tackling such specific topics as the status of aliens, international migration, or foreign navigation on China's waterways, and particularly the acutely controversial topics surrounding her leases, concessions, and settlements. On the whole, this expectation of gain in perspective was realized; but, on the other hand, this introductory period produced an understandable impatience on the part of those who were eager to get on to a consideration of concrete situations of conflict. And the hope that this arrangement, by expanding the range of concern over the whole Pacific basin, would take the edge off too sharp a controversy over the Manchurian crisis was not altogether realized.

EXTRACT FROM THE DRAFT SYLLABUS FOR THE STUDY OF DIPLOMATIC MACHINERY IN THE PACIFIC

By Stephen A. Heald

I. LIMITATIONS OF THE BRIAND–KELLOGG PACT AND SUGGESTIONS FOR IMPLEMENTING IT [1]

i. WHAT IS THE SCOPE OF THE PACT? [2]

ARTICLE I. — The High Contracting Parties solemnly declare in the names of their respective peoples that they condemn recourse to war for the solution of international controversies, and renounce it as an instrument of national policy in their relations with one another.

ART. II. — The settlement or solution of all disputes or conflicts of whatever nature or whatever origin they may be, which may arise between them, shall never be sought except by pacific means.

ii. FROM WHAT LIMITATIONS DOES THE PACT SUFFER?

a) Five States are not bound by the Pact, viz.: Argentina, Bolivia, Salvador, Uruguay and Brazil. While the first four are bound by the League Covenant, the last (Brazil) is not.

b) The Pact provides no machinery for a consultation, the enforcement of Article I, or for carrying out the provisions of Article II — the settlement of disputes by pacific means.

Although 50 States are bound both by the League Covenant (which provides the necessary machinery) and the Pact, among those bound by both are not included the United States of America, the Union of Socialist Soviet Republics (or Afghanistan, Brazil, Costa Rica, Egypt, Mexico, Turkey, Danzig or Iceland).

c) Lack of confidence in a new experiment, uncertainty of the intentions of the U.S.S.R., and knowledge of the reluctance of the U.S.A. to accept sanctions.

d) Lack of agreement on the subject of neutrality and neutral rights.

iii. IN WHAT WAY COULD IT BE IMPLEMENTED?

It has been suggested that

a) The U.S.A. might classify in advance the action which it would take in an emergency.

b) The U.S.A. might enter into a Consultative Pact.

c) Agreement might be reached on the procedure for invoking the Pact. This might be in the form of consultation or conference, mediation and enquiry.

How should this be initiated? Should the U.S.A. as the depository of ratifications and adhesions take the first step (but the reluctance of the U.S.A.

---

[1] Refer to Raymond T. Rich and Dennis P. Myers, *Draft Syllabus for Study of the Implementation of the Pact of Paris*. World Peace Foundation, 1931.

[2] General Treaty for the Renunciation of War as an Instrument of National Policy, signed August 27, 1928.

to bind herself to a certain course of action is known), or the League under Articles 11, 12, 17?

Should the first great Powers between whom the final negotiations in the matter of the Pact were completed form a Consultative Committee or should it be enlarged to include the 15 original signatories or all the nations who are bound by the Pact? Would it be possible for non-member States to agree to use the organs of the League as provided for in Article 17 of the Covenant (or Articles 50–54 of the Draft Disarmament Convention)?

Should there be an independent Secretariat or independent diplomatic machinery? Could such machinery be regional? How would this work out in the Pacific?

iv. HOW COULD THE PACT BE ENFORCED?

It is important to realize that sanctions, while accepted in the League Covenant, are not favoured by the U.S.A. (cf. Reservation made on ratification of Four-Power Pacific Pact). Certain resolutions have, however, been introduced, in Congress, designed to provide some power behind the Pact and to clarify the attitude of the U.S.A. towards (*a*) a Pact-breaking State (Capper and Korrell Resolutions) (*b*) any State which is in armed conflict with another (Burton, Porter, Fish Resolutions).

Note on these resolutions:

Capper Resolution (1929):

1. When U.S. President determines and proclaims a country as having violated the Pact, it shall be unlawful — unless otherwise provided by Act of Congress or proclamation by President — to export arms, etc., to such country, until President proclaims that violation no longer exists.

2. U.S. nationals in such a case shall not be protected by their Government " in giving aid and comfort to a nation which has committed a breach of the Pact."

3. Other nations should be invited to agree to a similar attitude towards their nationals.

4. Only to apply in case of breach by war against a Government which has declared adherence to a similar policy.

Burton Resolution (1928):

When President recognizes existence of war by proclaiming neutrality of U.S.A., it shall be unlawful to export arms, etc., to any such belligerent.

Korrell Resolution (1929):

When President shall by proclamation recognise act of a co-signatory Party as constituting a violation of the Pact, it shall be unlawful except by consent of Congress to export arms, etc.

Porter Resolution (1929):

Whenever President finds existence in any country or countries of conditions of domestic violence or international conflict and makes proclamation to that effect, it shall be unlawful to export arms, etc., to such a country or countries, until otherwise ordered by President or Congress.

Fish Resolution (1929):

Whenever President recognizes existence of war between foreign nations by making proclamation of neutrality of U.S.A., it shall be unlawful, except by consent of Congress, to export arms, etc. (Nothing in resolution being construed to interfere with sale or shipment of foodstuffs, oil, coal, cotton, leather, copper, lead, zinc, iron, timber, wool, automobiles or other manufactured articles not commonly or commercially known as arms, etc.)

The invocation of the Pact of Paris by the United States in the case of the Soviet-Chinese dispute over the Chinese Eastern Railway in 1929 provides interesting evidence of the need of implementing the Pact. It showed particularly

i. The need for proper procedure — the rather cumbrous method of invoking the Pact involved delay and uncertainty.

ii. The need of defining aggression, and deciding " when is a war not a war? " The time element is very important. While discussion is proceeding as to whether a country is an aggressor or not, it is possible that the war may be vigorously prosecuted and the Powers may be confronted with a *fait accompli*.

iii. The need of machinery for carrying out Article II of the Pact.

2. SUGGESTIONS FOR EXTENDING THE INFLUENCE OF THE LEAGUE OF NATIONS IN THE PACIFIC

From examination of the League of Nations organization emerges the fact that of the States of the Pacific seaboard Japan and the British Dominions have been active in co-operation while the other member-states, Siam and China, and non-member States, U.S.A. and U.S.S.R., have participated in certain aspects of the League's work. Considerable encouragement is also to be gained from the interest in the work of the League evinced by China during the last two years, which has found practical expression in the invitations which have been extended by the Chinese Government to and accepted by certain League officials to visit China and to submit suggestions and recommendations on matters concerning reconstruction and finance, communications and transit, health, labour conditions and general questions. This fact demonstrates that China considers the assistance of the League of Nations valuable; and if China were to become an active and constructive member of the League of Nations, especially during the period when, as will happen shortly, she is once again elected a member of the Council, an important step will have been made towards strengthening the influence of the League in the Pacific.

At present certain obvious difficulties weaken the League's position in that area, namely:

1. The non-membership of the U.S.A. and the U.S.S.R. (the value of the League system depends on universality).

2. The geographical situation of the League Secretariat.

3. The natural preoccupation of the League with problems which appear to be chiefly European and Western. (This of course is partly due to the absence of the U.S.A. and U.S.S.R. and the somewhat obscure part played by China at Geneva, due to inevitable difficulties at home.)

4. A feeling that the League idea is a Western product and that some form of federal association would be more acceptable in the Pacific, where there is no relative equality of economic development or political status and no homogeneity of political outlook.

5. A suspicion that the League system is too much under the domination of the great European Powers.

6. Other difficulties include (*a*) the reluctance of other states to accept the strong voting power given to the British Commonwealth by the separate membership in the League of the Dominions, (*b*) the feeling in China that the League regards China in spite of her area and population as a minor State without a right to a permanent seat on the Council.

i. HOW COULD THESE DIFFICULTIES BE OVERCOME?

1. The first difficulty in the case of the U.S.A. and U.S.S.R. might be if not overcome at least lessened by further co-operation between these States with the League on the present lines.

2. The geographical difficulty might possibly be overcome by an extension of the idea of a Far Eastern Centre to include all aspects of the League's work, one of the chief duties of which would be to make the work of the League better known in the Pacific by the regular distribution of information. A reference to this was made by Sir Thomas Wilford in his speech at the Twelfth Assembly. (At present the centre at Singapore is concerned purely with health questions and the broadcasting of warnings of epidemics, etc.)

In this connection (as in the case of Singapore) more use might be made of the facilities offered by broadcasting.

3. There might perhaps be created eventually a Pacific Commission on the lines of the Committee of Enquiry for European Union to which (as the U.S.S.R., Turkey, etc., to the European Committee) Pacific States, non-members of the League (i.e., U.S.A. and U.S.S.R.), might be invited. The fact that those European States directly interested in the Pacific would also be members of the Commission would serve to consolidate the bond and would prevent the Commission from acting to the prejudice of the whole League idea by awakening interregional rivalry.

With the establishment of such an organization it might be possible to hold a meeting of the Council in the Far East (though on account of the time this would involve such meetings would have to be very occasional).

It seems possible, however, that if the link between China and the League were well forged, with Japan and the British Dominions already active in co-operation, Siam a member of the League, and the U.S.A., and the U.S.S.R. to a lesser degree, willing to participate in certain sections of the League's work, much might be hoped for in this all-important area.

A closer study of Far Eastern problems from a Pacific point of view together with frequent visits of League officials to the Pacific area might help to produce this result.

4. On the other hand, the criticism that the League system is unsuitable

politically, geographically and socially to the Pacific area may be valid; in which case some system will have to be devised which will combine the experience of the League and the valuable elements in League machinery with ideas of association more acceptable and suitable to the peculiar circumstances of that area.

3. OTHER SUGGESTIONS FOR IMPROVING, REVISING, AND SUPPLEMENTING THE EXISTING INTERNATIONAL MACHINERY IN THE PACIFIC

The case of the Pact of Paris has already been discussed in a previous section, as, owing to the fact that it provides no machinery, it does not properly fit under this heading. In this case some indication has been given of the general lines on which the Pact might be implemented and enforced both generally and in the Pacific — the principal difficulties being the suspicion of the U.S.S.R. for forms of pacific settlement devised by so-called " Capitalist " States and the reluctance of the U.S.A. to bind herself in advance to taking any fixed course of action.

Similarly in the matter of the League Organization suggestions have already been made of the lines on which the influence of the League might be increased in the Pacific.

Mention should be made here also of the importance of the accession of the United States to the Permanent Court of International Justice. The signature of the Protocol by the U.S. representative has not yet been ratified.

Further, from the League point of view (without entering into the arguments for or against these instruments) a general acceptance by Pacific States of the General Act for the Pacific Settlement of International Disputes would contribute towards the provision of " all-in " machinery.

i. WHAT OTHER MACHINERY COULD BE DEVISED?

It will be convenient when discussing this to have before one's eyes a summary of the existing instruments with their principal defects:

1. *The Pact of Paris.* — *All Pacific States* signatories. But purely moral undertaking lacking machinery for implementation or enforcement.

2. *The Washington treaties: Not signed by U.S.S.R.* (*a*) *Pacific Four-Power Pact.* — Signed by Great Britain, U.S.A., France and Japan. Respect for rights — consultation " for adjustment and consideration " — concerted action in the event of aggression by another State. *But,* limited to insular possessions and insular Dominions only. Thus a dispute on the mainland involving Japan with China or the U.S.S.R. would not come within the scope of the Treaty. Vague machinery. Reservation regarding domestic jurisdiction. Statement by U.S.A. on ratification that treaty contains " no commitment to armed force, no alliance, no obligation to join in defence." China and the U.S.S.R. are not signatories. (*b*) *Nine-Power Treaty regarding China.* — Signed by Great Britain, U.S.A., France, Italy, Japan, China, Belgium, Netherlands, Portugal. Non-aggression against China — no discrimination by China or in China against any States. The Open-Door policy.

In both these treaties the provision for consultation is very vague, and there is little or no machinery.

3. *The League of Nations.* — Covenant not signed by U.S.A. or U.S.S.R. Headquarters in Europe — China until recently not an active Member.

4. *Bilateral treaties for the Pacific settlement of disputes.* — Between States of the Pacific seaboard as distinct from European States directly interested in the Pacific Area there are disappointingly few bilateral treaties for the pacific settlement of disputes. With the exception of the U.S.A., with 5 Arbitration and 6 Conciliation Treaties, Siam with 2 Arbitration Treaties and China with one Arbitration Treaty and one Conciliation Treaty, the other treaties of Arbitration and Conciliation which concern the Pacific Area are between European States. There are also a number of commercial treaties which contain a clause or clauses providing for the settlement of disputes by pacific means.

(Signature of the Optional Clause and the General Act is equivalent to a number of bilateral treaties; but Japan and China [and naturally the U.S.A. and U.S.S.R.] are not bound by the Clause or the Act, although they have signed the Statute of the Permanent Court of International Justice.)

ii. SUCH BEING THE POSITION WHAT NEW MACHINERY COULD BE DEVISED?

1. *A Pacific Locarno* has been suggested; but an instrument of this nature, i.e., pledges with guarantees, does not appear applicable to the Pacific.

2. *A Pan-Pacific Union of Governments* on the lines of the Pan-American Union and provided with similar machinery, e.g.:

i. Resolution condemning war.

ii. Inter-Pacific Treaties of Arbitration and Conciliation (with Protocol of Progressive Arbitration).

iii. Pan-Pacific Courts and procedure for the use of good offices.

While such an arrangement might be accepted by other States, what would be the attitude of (*a*) the U.S.S.R., and (*b*) the League of Nations?

3. *A Pan-Pacific Pact of Friendship and Non-aggression* on the Soviet model, supplemented by agreements for the submission of disputes to Conciliation.

What would be the attitude of various States to the Neutrality clause in such treaties?

4. *A Pacific Collective Treaty of Non-aggression* on the lines of *League Model Treaty " E."*

5. *Combination of elements in various treaties.*

6. *A regional agreement for the implementation of the Pact of Paris* — providing procedure for calling Pact into operation — the exercise of good offices — mediation — inquiry — conciliation (and possibly for its enforcement by arms embargoes, and economic and financial sanctions?).

The main question raised in this section is as to whether it is better to improve the existing machinery or to create new machinery.

In favour of the first alternative it is agreed that the multiplication of instruments tends to weaken their general effect, and that the existing machinery is adequate provided that steps are taken to adapt or implement such instruments as are already provided.

On the other hand it is stated that the League organization is viewed with some suspicion in China and that the U.S.A. and the U.S.S.R. are opposed to membership in it. The Washington treaties do not include either China or the U.S.S.R., and the procedure provided by them is both vague and limited. While the Pact of Paris might be implemented, it would be better, it is suggested, to devise some form of Pacific pact which would take into account the different political outlook of, for example, China and the U.S.S.R. and would be acceptable to ideas of foreign policy in the United States.

ADDRESSES

MANCHURIA — A CASE PROBLEM

I. THE APPLICATION OF EXISTING INSTRUMENTS OF POLICY

By Kenzo Takayanagi
Professor of Law at the Imperial University of Tokyo

The present peace machinery — not only in the Pacific but throughout the whole world, including the League of Nations and the Pact of Paris — is held in contempt by two groups of thinkers. The first group consists of the imperialists and the ultra-nationalists who regard peace machinery in general as helpless ships sailing against the current of everlasting struggles of nations for existence and aggrandizement. They consider themselves realists and look upon all of these " idealistic plans " as vain attempts of the Utopians. There is another group, the communists, who hold that peace machinery as it stands is, after all, a clever device for the great capitalistic nations to maintain their *status quo*, or sometimes that it is a league to fight against Communist Russia. Now, these arguments, coming from these two groups of thinkers, are not convincing to us liberals. We still believe that human relationships can be bettered by our faculty of reasoning, by study of facts, and by reasonable adjustments. We must, however, recognize that the criticisms of the imperialists and the communists have some element of truth. We must be on our guard not to be too idealistic in our planning on one hand, and not to act the part of the conservators of the *status quo* alone.

The Institute of Pacific Relations consists of liberals, in the large sense of the word. This group consists mainly of the liberal element of the Pacific countries. And the question of peace machinery in the Pacific has naturally attracted the attention of members of the Institute from the very beginning. In the First Conference the discussion was rather of an elementary nature. In the Second Conference, Professor Shotwell came with a definite plan, drafted by himself in collaboration with Professor Chamberlain; and although that plan was intended to form the basis of a treaty between the United States and France, he sounded the opinion of the Japanese members as to whether that kind of plan would be acceptable to the Japanese. That plan itself has not come to take the form of a treaty. It has been fundamentally modified in the course of official discussion. It was more definite in many respects than the Pact of Paris. It had its machinery and its methods for the settlement of disputes carefully worked out. But the Pact of Paris, the Kellogg-Briand Treaty, is in a sense the outcome of our discussions at the 1927 Honolulu Conference. It came out in a different form; but still our discussions had something to do with the coming into effect of the Pact of Paris. The Pact, in my opinion, constitutes a great advance in peace machinery. As you know, the Covenant of the League of Nations did not abolish war. There was room left for war being resorted to. But the Pact renounced war as an instrument of national policy, and the contracting parties agreed that they would not attempt to solve international disputes except by pacific means. It is true that war cannot be abolished by treaties alone. Certain social, economic, and political conditions are necessary for the abolition of war. But still I think this Pact made a great contribution in supplementing defects of the Covenant of the League, and in securing the support of America and Russia for the movement for peace, which is, after all, the aim and object of the League machinery. America and Russia participated in this peace arrangement, and that is really a big factor in international relations.

Hugo Grotius is my favorite author, and one of the great topics he discusses in his *De jure belli ac pacis* is whether there can be such a thing as a just war, and, if so, on what conditions. He takes the position that there is such a thing as a just war in view of the texts of the Bible, the old philosophers, and the Church Fathers. He cites all the classical passages bearing on this subject and tries to explain that his position is not in conflict with the teachings of Christ or of the prophets, or of the Greek philosophers. Since Grotius, all treatises on international law have adopted the distinction between a just and an unjust war.

The remarkable thing about the Pact of Paris is that the distinction between a just and an unjust war has practically been discarded. Instead, a distinction is now to be made, in view of the provisions of the Pact of Paris, between war as an instrument of national policy and defensive war or self-defense, which is recognized not in the text itself, but by the understanding of the signatories. Now some international jurists, just after this Pact came into effect, said that there was little to choose between the old and the new distinction, and that there was little progress in substituting a new classification for an old one. But I am of the opinion that the new distinction marks progress on the path of peaceable ordering of international society in that it has a tendency to narrow the sphere in which justification for warlike operations may be allowed.

Of course, defensive war is a term of rather vague connotation. In municipal law in civilized countries, the conception of self-defense is strictly defined. Self-defense is a privilege which is recognized as legitimate in all civilized countries. However, if you trace the history of self-redress, of which self-defense is a type, you will find that its sphere has been flexible according to the conditions in which the principle of self-redress had to operate. The philosophy involved is that if the social order is such that legal methods can easily be resorted to, then self-redress is confined to a very narrow area. But if such conditions do not obtain, then the sphere of self-redress is naturally widened.

That seems to be a generalization which can be evidenced by the history of self-redress. And similar considerations should govern in defining defensive war under the Pact of Paris. Of course, if defensive war is allowed within an extended sphere there will be the same abuses as under the old classification of just and unjust wars. But if you identify the concept of defensive war in international law with the concept of self-defense under municipal law, the rule would not function.

Be that as it may, it is certainly great progress in the way of peace that nowadays a state cannot do something which would have been perfectly justified before the Pact of Paris. I think in this respect alone the Pact has done a great deal for the betterment of the peaceable ordering of nations.

There is now much talk about Japan and the League. From the reports of the newspapers, Japan seems to stand in a rather unfavorable position, and there seems to be a general impression that Japan had defied the League of Nations. As I understand the situation, Japan has not defied the rules of the Covenant at all. What Japan did was to express in no uncertain terms the view that the Manchurian situation was one which could not adequately be dealt with by the Council which was not in a position to know this complex situation, and that the question might be better dealt with by direct diplomatic negotiations between the Government of Japan and the Government of China. That seems to be the view that Japan takes of the Manchurian controversy. Now what she is doing at Geneva is to convince the Council that her view is the correct one. She has resorted to all sorts of legal devices within the bounds of the Covenant; she is acting within the rights accorded to her by the Covenant. If the League of Nations makes a decision which Japan considers to be destructive of her vital interests, what will Japan do? That is a question for the future. We do not know. But if I understand the situation correctly, I do not think that Japan will go to the length of receding from the League of Nations or take any such extreme step. I just mention this to show that the general impression at the present moment that Japan has defied the League is, in my opinion, an erroneous one.

The question has been sufficiently discussed in some of the round tables whether the League of Nations, so far away from the Oriental stage, is in a position to appreciate all the facts and factors in the situation in order to solve justly the problems arising in the Pacific. In other words, the question came up whether it was expedient to stick to the old idea of universalism or whether it was better to recognize, in some form or other, the exigencies of regionalism. This question was also discussed in our last Conference, and in that Conference our Chinese friends considered that the League was too far away, that the League could not know the actual situation in China, and that China was therefore rather indifferent to the League. That was the general sentiment of China *vis-à-vis* the League of Nations at the time of the last Conference. And probably some of the members expressed the view that a branch of the League, or some similar arrangement, might better serve the Pacific area. Now since that time Japan is experiencing that kind of situation in a practical way, and I think this is one of the most important questions which the League of Nations has to solve in the future.

It seems to me that the conception of universalism — the League as a universal organ, to deal with all disputes arising throughout the world — is a very valuable one. There should not be too many competing organs. There is much justification for that argument. But that conception may well be reconciled with an attempt to set up here in the Pacific an organ to investigate in a realistic way the conditions in China and Japan, and ultimately to solve the international difficulties in the Pacific area. Arrangements may be made in such a way that such an organ will not do away with the idea of the universality of the League. And in such arrangements the United States and Soviet Russia should be invited to take part in some capacity or other.

The Manchurian question, for instance, cannot be properly discussed and studied in all its bearings without the presence of all important countries interested. The Manchurian trouble is very complex. If my understanding of the situation is correct, the trouble there and the problems that constantly arise in that area come from two important factors which must be considered.

First, Chinese nationalism. China is endeavoring to become a modern state in the full sense of the word. Of course, even in the West, the concept of the sovereign state did not come into political thinking until the beginning of modern times. However, in all the arguments for the solution of the various problems relating to China, the Chinese advocates in the last analysis go back upon the concept of sovereignty. I think that the realization to its fullest extent of this idea of a sovereign and autonomous state is the goal of New China. Well, is China a sovereign state?

One of the most interesting questions in jurisprudence is whether the essence of corporate personality is a reality or whether it is a mere fiction. The controversy on this question seems to be the continuation of the medieval philosophical discussion as to realism and nominalism in a new guise in the field of jurisprudence. Now, a friend of mine — not a Japanese — who is a very well-known international jurist, and who is also interested in legal philosophy, is a strong advocate of the so-called entity theory of corporate personality, the theory that a corporate personality is based on reality. That theory asserts that corporate personality comes into existence not because some other persons recognize that the corporate personality exists, but because it actually exists. He applied the implications of this theory to China. He is of the opinion that there is no such thing as a Chinese state because state personality must be based on the existence of government. This is a logical conclusion from the theory of corporate entity. According to his theory, where there is no government there is no state. I was rather inclined to attach some importance to the nominalist view of the matter. I said that the Powers have treaty commitments which recognize that China is a sovereign state. He said that where there is nothing existing, then you can not have it exist by saying that it exists. I do not believe in that thesis myself, nor do any of the Japanese jurists believe in that thesis. Still it must be admitted that the facts on which this jurist bases his theory have some ground.

The situation in China shows that the sovereign state in the Occidental sense with its concomitant governmental appurtenances exists rather as an aspiration than as a reality, and we must recognize this. There is no central government that really and effectively governs the whole area. There are several governments within that area, and actually this situation forms one of the great difficulties that the Powers encounter in their dealings with China. Even in those circumstances, it still may be considered that China is a sovereign state, in case other states recognize that China exists as a sovereign state. That is my view.

It is my firm conviction that the rising Chinese nationalism will grow. This growing nationalism for which we have great admiration and with which we have much sympathy sometimes manifests itself in a way rather embarrassing to the Japanese as well as to other nationals. The anti-Japanese and anti-foreign textbooks which are very widely used in the schools and the boycotts of Japanese or other foreign goods are notorious examples. Those movements are sometimes carried on with tactics which look very much like the communistic tactics, probably under Russian influence. Those and similar hostile manifestations of nationalism are naturally very irritating to the Japanese people, and that is especially true when they appear in Manchuria.

I traveled through Manchuria last summer to study the situation there. I found that it was very bad. The contacts between the Chinese and Japanese, either official or unofficial, either military or civilian, left a great deal to be desired; and there seemed to be definite attempts on the part of the local authorities to oust Japanese interests from Manchuria. There was a general impression on the Chinese side that these Japanese interests are really outposts of Japanese imperialism, and they were trying to drive away all these manifestations of Japanese economic imperialism. That sort of spirit was very strong, which naturally irritated resident Japanese. The situation bristled with the danger of explosion. That same condition apparently also existed at the time of the last Conference of the Institute of Pacific Relations, when many proposals were put forward to avoid an explosion in Manchuria, none of which, however, came into fruition.

The rising nationalism of China manifests itself in various concrete forms in Manchuria, and if that desire on the part of China has to be recognized to its fullest extent, the only way is for Japan to pack up her baggage and get out of Manchuria.

Now I come to the Japanese interests in Manchuria. The Japanese interests in China proper are similar to the interests of the other Powers, and are capitalistic interests, if I may use the expression. They do not differ from the interests that Great Britain, France, or the United States have in China. Japan naturally wants to have her investments well guarded by law, and to carry on business under the protection of a good government. The interests are chiefly capitalistic, and the same is true of certain interests which Japan has in Manchuria, but there are other factors which make the Manchurian situation somewhat different from the situation in this part of China.

Apart from the sentimental factor that Manchuria has been obtained for China by the sacrifice of the precious blood of our soldiers and an immense amount of money and property, there are three types of Japanese interests in Manchuria. First, the capitalistic interests; second, if I may say so, the proletarian interests — I refer to the big Korean population in Manchuria; and third, what may be called the strategic interests. The second factor to a certain extent, and the third factor especially, result from the geographic propinquity of Manchurian and Japanese territory. Japan feels that she has a vital interest in the economic development of Manchuria. The world-situation in which Japanese emigration finds every door closed and high tariff walls have been built up — I do not mean to blame the countries which adopt those measures, inasmuch as these are sometimes necessary under present conditions — makes Japan feel that in Manchuria she must have her existing economic interests well protected, and also an opportunity to develop her economic interests.

The second point is a strategic one. We are still in the dark as to the future of Soviet Russia. We do not know what will be the outcome of that interesting experiment. We are very much interested, and we admire some parts of her system. The foreign policy of Russia has, in the short space of fifteen years, gone through three stages of development. In the first stage, the revolutionary leaders were rather indifferent to the foreign policy — the foreign office was an unimportant bureau of the Russian administration. In the second stage, Russia seems to have considered that propaganda for the world revolution was necessary for her own protection, and created much apprehension on the part of neighboring countries. But in the third stage, at present, Russia has started on the Five-Year Plan, and because of the requirements of capital and trade, seems to be trying to come into friendly contact with capitalist states. Now, whether that policy is compatible with the tenets of communism is primarily for the Russians to answer. But we are particularly interested in the answer, because Soviet Russia is probably of the opinion that communism is the best system not only for Russia but for all humanity, and that capitalism should be destroyed all over the world. When her house is set in order, and she becomes a strong power, with her abundant natural resources, and with the introduction of American technology, what will happen next? Will Russia adopt the precept of Mohammed and say " The Koran or the sword," or will Russia continue to co-operate with capitalistic countries? This question is highly interesting to students of Russian politics. There is a fear, rightly or wrongly — I am not a prophet, and I do not know whether such fear is justified or not — that when Russia has set her house in order she will revert to the old policy of propaganda. Of course, Outer Mongolia is already under her sway, and she may determine that Manchuria shall also come under her communist régime, if necessary by an appeal to arms. That factor is important to Japan from her strategic standpoint.

The whole question of Manchuria resolves itself into three parts: What will Russia do? What will Japan do? What will China do?

To sum up, I am convinced that the League machinery and the Pact of Paris should be maintained and further developed. If the machinery of the League is modified to suit the conditions in the Pacific area, I believe that the friction arising from those complex conditions might well be dealt with. I have taken up Manchuria by way of illustration. My main thesis tonight is that Geneva is too far away to appreciate the complex conditions obtaining in the Far East. Members of the League Council may fall into the error of judging things by superficial observation of events and the mere study of the provisions of the treaties contained in MacMurray. A permanent body, either a part of the League or an independent unit affiliated with the League, and with America and Russia co-operating, is highly desirable for dealing, not only with the Manchurian question, but with questions relating to the whole international situation in the Orient.

II. THE PENDING CASES AND THEIR ADJUSTMENT

By SHUHSI HSU

Professor of Political Science, Yenching University, Peiping

Yesterday I listened with interest to the speech on the Manchurian question which Professor Takayanagi made at the general session on Diplomatic Machinery for the Pacific Region. I felt with particular satisfaction that the professor had come to share with some of his Chinese colleagues the view that the League of Nations might be supplemented by some machinery in dealing with the daily problems of the Pacific, especially the Far East. I still recall vividly how in the discussion at the Kyoto Conference he disapproved of the suggestion made by members of the Chinese delegation along this line.

One is disappointed, however, by the fact that Professor Takayanagi has gone to the extreme of denying that the League is a useful agency for dealing with matters of world-concern like that which it is now handling. Perhaps he has only failed to see the issue involved in the actions of the

League Council with reference to the recent [Manchurian] incident.   In adopting the resolution of October 24, calling upon Japan to withdraw her troops within the railway areas before beginning negotiations with China on pending cases, the League Council did not pass upon those cases, but upon the measures employed to settle them.   The question at stake is whether a signatory of the League Covenant and the Anti-war Pact has a right to resort to forceful measures to settle her differences with another signatory.   The question is not whether Japan is right or wrong in her differences with China.

With a Council formed of the most responsible of the world's leaders, devolution of its function in the settlement of international differences is necessary.   Chronic problems occurring in a region far removed from the seat of the League can be better handled by machinery other than, though still subsidiary to, the League.   It is partly for these reasons that the present speaker has submitted a memorandum to this Conference suggesting that China and Japan enter into an agreement to set up some form of a permanent conciliation commission for Manchuria.[3]   But this is different from saying that the League Council is not competent to handle questions relating to that region when submitted to it.   As was well said by the Chairman of the Conference yesterday, if Mr. Yoshizawa could efficiently handle minority problems in Europe, why should we suspect that the foremost statesmen of the world would fail to understand Far Eastern situations? . . . . So far as broad questions like the one that has just been passed upon by the Council are concerned, locality is of no consequence, and so far as specific questions like those pending between China and Japan are concerned, they would be handled by commissions anyway.   There is no justification for suspecting the competency of the Council in the matter.

The Manchurian situation is after all not difficult to understand.   The majority of the several hundred cases that are pending between China and Japan, with the exception of a few relating to railways, are either Japanese cases against China arising from the question of lease by negotiation, or Chinese cases against Japan arising from the question of Japanese armed forces in Manchuria.   The question of lease by negotiation hinges upon the question of whether the treaties concluded under the terms of the Twenty-one Demands are valid in view of their repudiation by China on the ground of the peculiar circumstances under which they were concluded, and of the fundamental question of equity and justice.   The question of Japanese armed forces in Manchuria hinges upon: first, the question whether there is any treaty basis upon which Japan has maintained them; and, second, the question whether they have any right to interfere with the internal political development and the daily life of the Chinese people.   Both classes of pending cases are evidently quite simple.   The cases relating to railways, to which Japan, we understand, has attached the largest share of importance, are no exception to the rule.   The question of the Tahushan-Tungliao Railway is the question,

[3] *The Manchurian Dilemma — Force or Pacific Settlement* (data paper, China Council).

first, whether there is such an agreement between China and Japan, as is often alleged, barring the former from constructing lines parallel to the South Manchuria Railway; and, second, whether that line could be considered as a parallel line in view not only of its distance from the Japanese line, but also of the fact that Japan made no protest on the same ground when the Chinchow-Aigun Railway scheme, of which the present railway is but the southern section, was mooted, or against the Mukden-Hailung Railway, although the latter runs closer to the Japanese line. As to the completion of the projected Kirin-Hueining Railway, it depends upon whether Japan has any moral right to compel the Chinese people to complete a project which she had induced the Anfu Government to launch at a time when the latter was fighting against the people, even though she paid into the war chest of the rebel government the hard cash of ten million gold yen.

Professor Takayanagi claims that the complexity of the Manchurian question lies in two factors: (1) Chinese nationalistic aspirations; and (2) Japanese special interests, economic, strategic, and historical.

Concerning Japanese special interests little needs to be said, as the vagueness of the term which once used to bring havoc upon international relations has ceased to possess any more magic power since its public repudiation by the Powers assembled at the Washington Conference. Japanese economic interests in Manchuria are all creatures of treaties. They are no more special than any other foreign economic interests in China. Any economic interest must be owned by someone. Every individual economic interest must be located somewhere. As to the so-called special strategic and historical interests, there is not even a legitimate basis for the interests themselves. Still less can anything be said for their being special. Professor Takayanagi admitted that the fear of Russia was not necessarily substantial. Even if we should grant the presence of a Russian menace, Japan could have a right to set up a system of defense only within her own boundary. By historical interest the learned professor must have meant principally the Russo-Japanese War. If so, he may be reminded that, if that war did give rise to any claims at all, they are all liquidated in treaties. What is left over to merit consideration cannot therefore be more than a pride for the achievement as well as a remorse for the losses in life and property entailed upon the poor innocent Chinese peasants of South Manchuria through a devastating war not of the creation of themselves or of their nation.

In speaking of special interests, Professor Takayanagi may be just repeating what many of his countrymen used to say. Yet we cannot but be surprised to hear him question the sovereignty of the Chinese state, although he takes care to shelter himself under the authority of another jurist in broaching the subject.[4] Apart from the question of formal recognition, China has been exercising effective control over her territory and people from time im-

---

[4] At a subsequent round-table meeting, Professor Takayanagi reiterated the statement that both he personally and, so far as he knew, the Japanese Government took the nominalist view of Chinese sovereignty over Manchuria.

memorial. This fact is not altered by her granting exemption from juris-diction to aliens or temporarily suffering from dissension through civil wars.

Perhaps in speaking of Chinese aspiration to sovereignty Professor Takayanagi has in mind Chinese aspiration to the recovery of lost rights. But this is a normal, healthy, and legitimate phenomenon, and we fail to see why it should so complicate the situation as to make it not suitable for the League Council to deal with. The learned professor has spoken of boycott as a phase of that aspiration. It must be said that, if it is a phase at all, it must be quite accidental. Boycott has been employed thus far only as a means to show resentment against Japanese aggression. If Japan continues in her policy of coercing China whenever she wants her to part with her rights, there will always be boycotts, no matter whether there be an aspiration to the re-covery of lost rights or not.

It is clear that the Japanese assertion that this situation is too com-plicated for the League Council to handle has no substantial basis. One is, therefore, forced to the conclusion that, in refusing to comply with the Council decision of October 24, Japan must either have possessed a psy-chology that is not entirely normal, or merely been unwilling to terminate her act of aggression. . . .

There is perhaps no other time in the history of international relations since the last European War as critical as the coming few weeks. It would be in the interest not only of Japan and China but also of the world at large for liberal-minded people of both countries to unite in their efforts to in-fluence their respective governments and peoples in favor of moderation instead of defending their acts indiscriminately. As a student of the Man-churian question, I can assure my colleagues from the island empire that there is no indication to my knowledge that China has any intention of ex-cluding her neighbor from a share in the plentifulness of the Manchurian provinces. On the contrary, she would welcome her co-operation in their development if she could be assured that it would be carried out with full respect for her sovereign rights. As to the pending cases, it seems that the Chinese Government is just as anxious to seek their solution as the Japanese and, in fact, would have approached the Japanese Government on the subject if it had been confident that the latter would treat with China on the basis of equity and justice. How to restore confidence and promote co-operation is the question. At least we know it cannot be attained through the resort to force or the refusal to remove force after its hasty application.

QUESTIONS FOR ROUND–TABLE DISCUSSION

The following questions were recommended by the Program Committee as an outline for discussion:

1. What problems or reasons require the provision of international diplomatic machinery in the Pacific? How far could international questions, e.g., disarmament, be dealt with regionally in the Pacific area?
2. What international machinery is in existence in the Pacific area? What is the application of
   a) The League organization (Covenant, General Act, Optional Clause, Conventional Financial Assistance) and the Permanent Court of International Justice?
   b) The Briand-Kellogg Pact?
   c) The Washington Treaties (Four-Power Pacific Pact, Five-Power Naval Treaty, Nine-Power Treaty)?
   d) Bilateral treaties between countries directly interested in the Pacific area?
   e) Such machinery as exists within the British Commonwealth for the settlement of disputes between its Pacific members?
3. To what extent are Pacific countries co-operating with existing machinery?
4. What steps could be taken to extend the influence of the League of Nations in the Pacific?
5. From what limitations does the Briand-Kellogg Pact suffer? In what way could it be implemented?
6. In what way could the existing international diplomatic machinery such as the Washington and other conventions in the Pacific be improved, revised, or supplemented?
7. What other machinery could be devised?

SUMMARY OF ROUND–TABLE DISCUSSIONS

After the address by Professor Takayanagi, reproduced in the preceding pages, it was natural that in all of the four round tables which simultaneously discussed the diplomatic machinery of the Pacific, the Manchurian situation was taken as the chief " case " before the Conference, in reference to which the adequacy of existing organs and instruments of international dealing was to be considered. Attempts by several of the chairmen to place the discussion upon a broader basis of experience in the Pacific area failed; not even extraterritoriality, which was brought up in one group as a suitable subject for analysis as part of the diplomatic history of the Far East, long held the attention, since the latest developments in Manchuria and in Geneva at the time made some members feel that the existence of the League itself, and at the same time the reality of the more recent Paris Peace Pact, were at stake.

Of course, not all of the group discussions followed the same order; and some were more successful than others in covering the ground laid out in the agenda recommended by the Program Committee. But there were many points of agreement in their reports, as later summarized by the chairmen before the Conference as a whole — both as regards the importance attached to different phases of the subject and as regards specific interpretations and recommendations. It is possible, therefore, without doing too much violence to the actual thought process of the Conference, to give a composite picture of its discussions of the present subject, and so to present the reader with a slightly more orderly record of what was said than a literal transcription of the give and take of group discussion would permit.

I. THE CASE OF MANCHURIA

The extraordinary divergence of opinion in China and Japan as to the proper functioning of the League in the Manchurian crisis was in everyone's mind. To many members of the Conference it seemed inconceivable that a member-state of the League that had also signed the Briand-Kellogg Pact should wish to oppose strenuously a League inquiry into its military operations on foreign territory and yet declare itself entirely loyal to both. Others sympathized with Japan in her stand that an appeal to a third party for intervention is justified only when direct negotiation between two states has failed; and that in the present case, owing to special difficulties and misunderstandings, the diplomatic machinery had not yet been adequately tested. (It should be remembered that these discussions took place on October 27 and 28, 1931.) There was the further difficulty exemplified in the Manchurian case, that one side to the dispute desired primarily to negotiate concerning the most recent, acute issue of controversy, while the other insisted that this must be considered in connection with other pending questions. These pending questions, still further to complicate the matter, arose from a treaty by which the first party, owing to the circumstances under which it had been signed by a preceding government, did not consider itself bound, while to the second party it was an international commitment that could be changed only by treaty and which it did not wish to change. In other words, it would have been difficult to choose a more complicated example from recent history with which to test the working of the present diplomatic system. That not even the most elementary facts concerning the Japanese occupation of Manchuria could be accepted as agreed upon perhaps made the case more typical than it would have been had the discussion moved on a basis of agreement as to the facts in the case. But it was a little bewildering for those less familiar with the facts to find the Far Eastern members often contradict each other on matters of information and charge each other with uncritically accepting statements given out by the propaganda machines of their respective countries. Equally unconvincing were efforts, as honestly made, to reconcile conflicting interpretations of the League Covenant and of the Kellogg-Briand Pact. Chinese members justified the appeal to the League with reference to paragraph 2, section 1, of article 11 of the former which declares it " the friendly right " of member states to bring to the League's attention " any circumstances whatever . . . . which threatens to disturb international peace or the good understanding between nations upon which peace depends," and article 12 under which such a state pledges itself to " submit . . . . any dispute likely to lead to a rupture " and " in no case to resort to war . . . . until three months after " such submission. Japanese members, on the other hand, stated the case for their Government by asserting that there was no threat of war in Manchuria, and that the movement of troops complained of represented no more than local action on the part of small military units guarding the South Manchurian Railway under acknowledged treaty rights, to defend themselves and the lives and property of other Japanese under their care. They gave it as their view that by appealing to the League on the grounds of an alleged military aggression, the Chinese Government merely desired to escape the necessity of settling promptly a large number of outstanding issues. And they further explained this appeal to the League as a Chinese custom of old standing to divert a forceful demand upon themselves by dragging in a third party, to " fight fire with fire."

The presentation of the Manchurian " case," then, while it did not take the form of unbiased factual statements that all might accept as a basis for discussion, had the vitality of a real issue and gave the members of the Conference an opportunity to view the illustrative situation precisely as it would come before any organ of international negotiation, an inchoate mass of assertions and charges, interpretations and innuendoes, appeals to history and to world-needs, explanations with economic interests and suggestions of underlying national sentiments. Thus viewed, the case might have appeared hopeless but for the practical nature of the inquiry immediately brought to bear upon it. The question before the Conference was not which side is right, nor even what precisely are the facts in this case — but, what use has been made of existing diplomatic machinery, and with what results? Thus limited, the relevant experience, even in so complicated a case as this, was not difficult to ascertain, since outwardly at least it is on record.

The Conference thus, starting from an " incident " (the occupation of Mukden on September 18, 1931), that seemed to call for immediate diplomatic action, was led to see all the preceding and surrounding circumstances also in relation to the international machinery of the Pacific and so learned, within the developing picture of a single situation, to discern the reasons for failures and inadequacies in the existing structure.

II. LIMITATIONS OF PRESENT MACHINERY

DIRECT DIPLOMATIC NEGOTIATION

Japanese members and others had no difficulty in convincing the round tables that, after all, direct diplomatic negotiation between two countries is the oldest and, on the whole, still the most effective method of dealing with a dispute between them. It avoids long delays, makes for an understanding of secondary as well as primary issues, and takes place within a pattern of agreements and commitments uncomplicated by the less well-known interests and plans of third parties.

But diplomacy of this kind, the Conference did not need to be reminded at length, had largely become discredited because it tends to oversimplify an issue and lay up trouble for the future. In such a situation, it has often happened that a state in direct negotiation with another, and without appeal to an outside force, found itself obliged to promise more than it could fulfil. The channels of direct diplomatic negotiation may, as they actually did in the Manchurian case, become choked with unsettled minor cases simply because, where a fundamental treaty does not rest upon sound foundations of equity, they accumulate too quickly. And as the unsettled issues mount, they coagulate and form a conflict that enters deeply into the emotional life of the nations concerned.

But the chief reason why bilateral negotiation has so largely given way in world-affairs to more inclusive forms of international dealing is the growing community of interests among many nations. Rarely does a conflict occur today that is charged with danger only for the immediate disputants. When vital interests are at stake, as in Manchuria, destructive forces may be released which neither of them may be able to control. It was pointed out by a British member that the advantage of League participation in such an international controversy lies precisely in the fact that it is not simply a third party or bound by traditional diplomatic procedures but can, in the larger international interest, apply any one of a variety of methods.

Japanese members of the Conference were ready to admit that, in the instance of Manchuria, the conflict had outgrown the dimensions of an issue susceptible to the ordinary processes of diplomacy. They did hope, however, that through direct negotiation between China and Japan the greater number of the unsettled differences under existing treaties might be solved, realizing that underneath these there were more fundamental problems which it would not be wise to try to solve without the fullest participation of other powers interested in the Far East, and preferably that of the League as the most fully grown instrument of truly international action.

The principal reason, it appeared, why direct negotiation alone cannot be relied upon to produce harmony among the nations of the Far East is that they are neither equals nor combined in balanced groups.

China and Japan are both recognizing each other as sovereign states, and as such have entered into mutual treaty relations. Thus, much discussion was occasioned by a passage in Professor Takayanagi's introductory address [6] where, in the minds of some of his audience, he seemed to throw doubt upon the reality of Chinese sovereignty over that large part of her territory in which the power of her central Government is extremely diluted.[7]

It appeared to some who listened to the careful expositions of the Japanese difficulties in Manchuria that two contradictory claims were being made:

[6] See pp. 233 ff.

[7] The same doubt was later expressed more positively by the Japanese delegate, Mr. Yoshizawa, in his statement before the meeting of the League Council in Paris on November 17, 1931.

a claim to recognition by the National Government of China of all the obligations imposed upon her by previous treaties; but a claim also that, because of the impotence of the central Government, Japan had a right to negotiate directly with provincial authorities and even with claimants for authority unrecognized by the Nanking Government. This peculiar diplomatic situation is not one sought by the Japanese Government, it was said, but one that gradually arose from the practical necessities of situations in which Japan had to protect her vested interests and those of her citizens as best she could.

Misunderstandings arising from this complicated form of diplomatic communication and action had been increased, it seemed, by Chinese unfamiliarity with the exact nature and working of the diplomatic machinery of Japan. China has always been very sensitive of her national honor and so has found cause of offense in often finding herself confronted, not with the formally appointed minister of the Emperor, but with some consular officer. But it so happens that consular officers hold a much higher rank in the Japanese service than is usually the case and are charged with a corresponding degree of responsibility; so that Japan obtains her contacts with other countries and deals with them through a greater variety of channels. Such differences in the organization of the foreign offices themselves and their subordinate organs thus proved another reason why direct diplomacy often does not function well.

But the success of a bilateral diplomatic relationship is necessarily influenced by the nature and volume of treaty relations which each of the countries has with other countries. It so happens that China has found much value in bilateral treaties and has concluded many of them in the last few years, particularly to modernize her trade relations with other countries. Japan, on the other hand, has entered into few such engagements and particularly has refrained from concluding bilateral treaties of arbitration.[8]

A rather full discussion, at one of the round tables, led to the conclusion that bilateral arbitration treaties, though limited in their function as guaranties of world-peace, are not inimical to the larger international pacts and, indeed, are encouraged by the League because they free its machinery from much cumbersome controversial problem material that only indirectly affects other countries than those in a direct bargaining relationship. They have the advantage, it was felt, that the two interested parties are usually far more familiar with the relevant facts than any others can be expected to be. On the other hand, the point was made in one round table that bilateral treaties of arbitration have the disadvantage, at least for the weaker countries, of tending to stabilize the *status quo*. For, in the conclusion of such a treaty one power will tend to take the existing state of affairs as its basis for nego-

---

[8] It was pointed out in one round table that this attitude was due in part to Japan's experience in the " House Tax " case of 1904 when the Hague Court gave judgment against her in a dispute arising out of treaty rights with foreign powers involving the taxation of real estate owned by foreigners in Kobe and Yokohama.

tiation and to impose a legal sanction on the maintenance of the existing conditions which may not, in the long run, be satisfactory to the other power. If kept open for political negotiation instead of being bound to the letter of the treaty, such conditions could later more easily be modified. Furthermore, in many individual cases similar to the present one in Manchuria, agreement to submit differences to arbitration or conciliation had in practice failed because one of the parties to the agreement would not admit that the provisions of the treaty were applicable.

For these and other reasons, the existence of an arbitration treaty between China and Japan would probably not have greatly ameliorated the present situation. The general tendency, it seemed, was for certain types of treaty agreement, especially those demanding recourse to arbitration and conciliation, to find expression in inclusive rather than in bilateral treaties. With the increasing complexity of trade and political relations, the specific interests of two states rarely can be isolated from those of other states; hence the likelihood that in the future there will be more treaties to which numbers of powers are signatories and further implementation of such treaties existing today.

FUNCTIONING OF THE LEAGUE

The Conference did not attempt to pass judgment on the League of Nation's action in the specific case under consideration, which was yet to be completed in the days to come. But the various round tables endeavored to find reasons why so acute a situation could have arisen between two states both of which were members of the League and co-operators with it in many of its activities. Only through discovering whatever flaws there might be in the existing League machinery, it was thought, was it possible to arrive at practical suggestions for its improvement or supplementation.

Perhaps the major outcome of this part of the discussion was recognition of the fact that the League, like any sovereign state, is concerned for its own continued existence. It cannot afford to take action, or to permit action on the part of member-states, that might endanger its authority within the limits of its recognized functioning. " The present crisis is the greatest test of the League," was a phrase repeatedly heard. Or again, " If it fails in settling this issue in co-operation with both China and Japan, the moral power of the League will be seriously weakened." There was divided opinion as to whether the League Council had not, by its action on the Manchurian issue, itself created a situation in which, whatever the outcome, its influence in the Far East was threatened. But no concrete suggestions were made as to possible ways in which it might have avoided, without even worse consequences, to act upon the appeal of China. The fact that, to maintain its position, the League was practically forced thus to respond, at the risk of alienating the most powerful nation in the Far East, was recognized as a weakness, inevitable in this phase of the League's development.

More often repeated than any other statement was the expression of the opinion that the absence from the League of two great powers, the United States and the Union of Soviet Socialist Republics, was a source of considerable weakness. It was due to the circumstances of the League's inception, an official of the League who attended the Conference as an observer reminded it:

"The League began to work under the pressure of the European war and grew out of European problems which it left behind it. The first great event in its history was the refusal of the United States to take up its membership; and that refusal was based mainly on the idea that the League was a European organization. This contributed greatly to the difficulties of the League in those early years in learning to be something more than a European organization.

"At first, I think, its non-European members felt that they were in Geneva listening to discussions in which they took little interest and less active part. Gradually they have come to be more a part of the League; and the members of the League have learned that they must take as much part in problems of distant countries as in their labors in Europe."

He proceeded to give instances to show that in this gradual shift from a mainly regional to an altogether international concern the League had already made considerable progress. But the old difficulty had not yet entirely been overcome.

"Geographical distance makes the completion of the process a matter of difficulty. The League method usually involves setting up technical commissions to study questions before any action is taken. This is clearly difficult in the case of distant countries. It is expensive and difficult also for distant countries to send their best people to Europe; they may have to spend months in travel for a fortnight's meeting. It has also happened that non-European countries were not well represented by specialists or not represented at all. So they have not been able to take part in the expert committees as they should." [9]

In this matter also he reported progress. The question of cost, another item on the debit side of the League's functioning, was referred to also by other speakers. The New Zealand delegates, it was reported, had opposed an increase in the League's budget at the last meeting. Some member countries were now maintaining offices in Geneva in order to keep in touch with the different aspects of the League's work without having constantly to send expensive delegations.

Then there was the time element as another factor. Some important problems, even European ones, had been dragging on for years, it was said, without the League being able, apparently, to produce satisfactory solutions. On the other hand, the very slowness of the League's functioning on some of these issues was claimed as an advantage: it had helped to subdue the acute phases in a more general consideration of the difficulties encountered and thus engineered situations in which reasonably satisfactory solutions had become more possible and had, in fact, been reached.

[9] For an interesting statement of the difficulties that arise from the geographical remoteness of some of the member countries, see Sir William Harrison Moore, *The Dominions of the British Commonwealth in the League of Nations* (reprinted from *International Affairs*, X, No. 3 [May, 1931]).

III. THE PROS AND CONS OF REGIONALISM

There was divided opinion on the question whether the distance of Geneva from the present place of difficulty in international relations was a serious hindrance to the League's efficient functioning. Can any international body or instrument, no matter how constructed and how implemented, ever function successfully on a regional issue, far from the center of international activity? The answer given by most of those who addressed themselves to this question was to the effect that such success probably would be proportionate to the extent of devolution or decentralization; but that at some point in this process the weakening influence of divided authority and counsel would begin to outbalance the advantage gained from greater directness in dealing with complex situations.

It was felt that the possibility of regional disarmament presents problems somewhat different from those of regional machinery for international diplomacy. Although several of the great Powers have naval bases in the Pacific area, these tend to be so far removed from the home base as practically to constitute their Pacific fleets separate units that can be reduced by regional agreement.[10] But a real difficulty lies in the fact that the relative military strength of different countries becomes more disproportionate when a regional political configuration takes the place of the world political configuration. It would be difficult to secure agreements under which the stronger nations would dissociate their regional strategy from the strategic implications of their world-policy. A spokesman for one of the Pacific countries pointed out that unless such agreement could be reached, it would be impossible for Powers on the Pacific to reduce their armament under regional agreements. It was felt, in short, that, regionally considered, disarmament must follow rather than precede a political rearrangement under which a larger dependence upon peaceful means of settling disputes might make a limitation of the use of force more practicable.[11]

In the political relations of the Pacific countries the choice does not lie, the Conference was reminded, simply between direct diplomacy and appeal to a single world-organization, the League. There is another kind of regionalism, exemplified by the Nine-Power Treaty, in which a number of states agree upon a joint policy in relation to a given region or country. The question, therefore, is whether in dealing with a specific disturbance of peaceful relations between two countries an appeal to the more inclusive organism, the League, is more advantageous than an appeal to the signatories of such a regional agreement. In the Manchurian case, China has seen fit to appeal to the League. Some members of the Conference thought that recourse to the Nine-Power Treaty would have been preferable, as it would have kept the discussion within the groups most vitally interested and consequently

10 See F. W. Eggleston, *Pacific Affairs*, December, 1930; and Tristan Buesst, *The Naval Base at Singapore.*

11 On this subject some of the references given by Professor Quigley's *Introductory Syllabus on Far Eastern Diplomacy*, pp. 26–27, proved helpful.

most capable of applying to it knowledge and power. On the other hand, China's choice of the League was clearly motivated, as several speakers pointed out, by her fear of being confronted with a solid group of foreign interests — the result of past experience. A Chinese member explained why this attitude did not also make for distrust of the League.

" China for long has hesitated to avail herself of the good offices of the League, for two reasons: Her experience in the past has been that in international dealings she has had to fight a combination of foreign powers. The League itself, in the earlier years of its existence, made little effort to establish contacts in China and to get its purposes understood. But in recent years, the League has done just this. By rendering concrete services to the Chinese people it created a closer relationship and gave evidence of its humanitarian concern; so much so that China has invited the League to co-operate in various special branches of her domestic administrative problems. It was natural for us to appeal to the League, not as a third party, but as children would appeal to their elders when they quarrel."

The question, then, was why did Japan seemingly take a very different attitude toward the League? What, precisely, was the political philosophy that directed her to reject a disinterested inquiry into the causes of the immediate crisis in her relations with China? The reason was, it appeared, that to Japanese thinking there was no such crisis, no particular point at which her difficult relations with China reached an acute stage when it became a matter of world-concern rather than regional concern.

But the concept of regionalism itself required further analysis: To some of the round tables the Pacific area as such seemed to suffer from the same disadvantages as the universal scope of the League when it came to a concentrated attention of interested powers upon the problems of a specific, limited area, Manchuria. On many questions of international policy, they felt, it was desirable to think in terms of a Pacific region; but in the case of the Manchurian difficulty only two, or at most three, powers were so intimately concerned that the interest of other Pacific countries in that situation did not materially differ from that of the more distant non-Pacific countries. To this contention the answer was made that, with the practical aims of diplomatic machinery in view, the concept of a Pacific area seemed to have advantages over the narrower concept of a politically self-contained region — the Far East, or the Northwestern Pacific. It would insure that questions of both a permanent and a transitory kind, in so far as they not only involved the countries of the Far East immediately concerned but assumed a world-character would be dealt with by interested countries, not too distant to lack knowledge, and yet sufficiently varied in their economic and political relations with the Far East to provide a background of neutrality and world-opinion.

It was in the assumption of need for such a larger regional structure rather than that of new machinery for dealing with the affairs of more limited geographical areas that the subsequent discussions of possible improvements in the existing implements of international relations took place. The general feeling seemed to be that, though theoretically — and increasingly in fact also — the League of Nations is an organization with universal concern in every part of the world, it is nevertheless still too close to its European origins to serve in its present form all the particular needs for new methods of international transaction in the Pacific area. It was for this reason, rather than with the thought of the present Manchurian crisis, admittedly in part at least of much narrower regional scope, that this phase of the discussion closed with the practically unanimous agreement that *some* regional, in the sense of Pacific, addition to the world diplomatic machinery is needed.

IV. SOME SPECIAL DIFFICULTIES

Before coming to the suggestions for such additions to the diplomatic machinery of the Pacific area, it may be well here to group together those comments, interspersed with other round-table discussions, that bear upon a variety of difficulties in the way of a smooth working of international relations. Passing reference has already been made to some of them.

THE UNITED STATES AND RUSSIA

Not only their absence from the League (see p. 246) but also the uncertainty of their international policies makes these two great powers factors of perplexity in any Pacific situation. Traditionally, the policy of the United States, it was said, is to deal directly with international issues and to " fight shy " of far-off action. Nevertheless, for more than thirty years there has been an increasing tendency to co-operate with other foreign powers in the Far East. The question is whether this development has gone far enough to assure the countries of the Far East, and those having direct interest in that area, that the United States would not, in any eventuality, resort to independent action if important interests were at stake. On the one hand, with the increase of her relative strength in the Pacific, she may be more disposed than she was on previous occasions [12] to defend the " open door " in China against any aggressor; on the other hand, public opinion in America, as in the rest of the world, is becoming more disposed to rely upon co-operative processes of international action for the protection of national interests. It was thought probable, therefore, that any new international machinery for the purpose of guarding the peace and the *status quo* in the Pacific region would have the active co-operation of the United States, but that possibly there might be difficulties in the way of securing her membership in any permanent organization if that were to involve a sacrifice of the freedom now enjoyed by that country in the pursuit of her foreign policies. American members of the Conference themselves disagreed in their forecasts: some saw no prospect of their country joining any organization in the Pacific, whether part of the League or outside of it, if it were at all similar to the League in aims and methods; others saw in the recent actions of the United

[12] See Frederick V. Field, *American Participation in the China Consortiums*, pp. 12 ff.

States Government a change of attitude which promised well for an even more intimate and direct association with the League in its representation of world-interests in the Far East.

The case of Russia is different. Here the uncertainty arises only in part from a possibility of change in the present Russian attitude toward Far Eastern problems, and in part from a possibility of changes in the attitudes of other powers toward her. The fear was expressed that, upon the conclusion of her present " five-year plan," Russia would revert to an imperialistic policy in Eastern Asia. Others feared even more a return of Russia to an active policy of international communist propaganda, especially in China and Japan. Indeed, this eventuality colored the whole attitude of the Japanese toward the Manchurian situation. With special regard to the diplomatic machinery of the Pacific, the question was raised whether there was any possibility of creating an organization that would not simply be a defense of the capitalist countries against communist aggression but flexible enough to permit of co-operation between countries with different political philosophies in a joint concern for world-peace. As if in answer to this question, the Pacific Council of the Institute subsequently, by inviting an interested organization in the U.S.S.R. to form a national council of this body, declared its faith in a democratic process of joint effort without regard to the dominant political and economic principles of the participant national groups.

UNFORMED INTERNATIONAL LAW

One of the difficulties that went through the whole discussion of diplomatic machinery was the variety of interpretations placed upon international commitments. Another was the lack of distinction between legal and political functions. On some of the questions most eagerly debated there was no clearly established international law; yet a tendency was apparent to assign to long-established traditions and modes of action the validity of law. There was criticism, on the other hand, of the tendency to assign a sort of sanctity to the *status quo* in international relations, no matter how it had arisen historically or whatever its political and economic consequences. Political and legal questions thus were entangled in a way that was likely to lead to misunderstanding.

It is necessary, a British member pointed out, to know the political problems of a country, its problems of strategy, and its legal traditions and attitudes before it is possible fruitfully to discuss any general scheme of disarmament or settlement of outstanding controversies in which it may have a part. Again the Manchurian situation served as an example of the difficulties in the way of a satisfactory solution when the two countries opposing each other differ so greatly as they do in these various respects. Thus a Chinese speaker who had recently been in Manchuria considered it a " legal somersault " to speak of the conditions there as anything but war. Japanese speakers, on the other hand, were able to convince many of the members of the absolute sincerity of their Government when it insisted that the occupation of towns and areas outside the railway zone and other military operations were strictly within the compass of police functions authorized under the treaty that governs the administration of the railway zone leased to Japan. The Japanese, on their part, with the background of their own political situation and effective power of government, accused the Chinese Government of complicity in the excesses that had attended the boycott against Japanese goods in Shanghai and other cities; while to the Chinese mind, accustomed to a less rigid functioning of the central Government, such charges seemed preposterous.[13]

But the most tragic diversity of attitude toward international law, as seen in its consequences, was the difference shown to exist in the interpretation of the very instruments that had been created to avert the sharpening of conflict to the point of violence. At the time this round table met, Japanese members considered as contrary to the spirit of the Paris Treaty the League of Nations' response to China's appeal under article 15, while they considered the actions of their own Government entirely in the spirit of the League Covenant, particularly article 10. Others considered Japan in error when she interpreted the proposal of the League to appoint a commission of inquiry as a setting-up of a court of inquiry with quasi-judicial functions. The Institute's own practices had shown that there were other ways in which the results of such factual inquiries might be used in dealing with an international difficulty. To this a Japanese rejoinder was that such a special commission, sent at a time of acute controversy, was necessarily more in the nature of a temporary high court than in that of a scientific study of fundamental problems, such as only a permanent organization conversant with conditions in the Far East could be expected to make.

An official of the League, in a brief address before the Conference as a whole, referred to the difficulty of clearly distinguishing in its operations between administrative and political functions. The distinction, he said, is not an absolute one. Often an administrative approach to social and economic questions makes it easier to deal with political differences. But he also intimated that in practice the League has sometimes branched out from political consideration into the rendering of administrative services, notably so in Latin America and in China. Given the accepted aim of the League to contribute toward the settlement of complex international difficulties, Chinese members could see no essential difference between these forms of approach and the one it had requested, the appointment of a commission of factual inquiry. Why should not any method be permissible that promised to ease the path toward a solution?

But it was not only the functioning of the League that provoked questions of international law and comity. The Briand-Kellogg Pact and its interpretations likewise contributed to a seeming confusion, more especially among those who had not previously given much study to its scope and purpose. To what extent and in what ways could a treaty be considered binding

[13] See further below, p. 302.

upon the conduct of nations if it provided so little guidance for common understanding of its implications? War itself remained so undefined that it was impossible to tell, for example, whether the present situation in Manchuria came under that category or not. What precisely were the " pacific means " by which, under article 2, all disputes between the signatory nations were to be settled? The Pact provides no machinery for consultation, much less for settlement of disputes. What is the situation when one of the signatory powers is also bound by the League Covenant and the other is not? Questions such as these were raised, but no one attempted to answer them. The general feeling seemed to be that, since the United States itself had promised co-operation with the League in the proposed inquiry in Manchuria, it was not likely to proceed at an early date with efforts to implement its later creation, the Kellogg Pact. This view was strengthened by a realization that none of the plans to that effect which have been submitted to the Congress of the United States (see p. 225) have matured or even received much popular commendation. Although the United States had drawn the attention of China and Japan to the provisions of the Pact, of which both are signatories, this instrument seemed destined to remain a gesture — albeit an important and influential one.

Regret was expressed in passing to the fact that no effort had been made in the present emergency to use the Washington treaties. Unlike the Pact of Paris, the Nine-Power Treaty does contain in embryo recognition of the need for special machinery in the Far East. Indeed, it had been agreed to set up a board of reference, to be established in China, to which any question arising under other provisions of the treaty might be referred for investigation and report. It was due to a political accident that this proposal to which all the nine Powers, including China, had agreed was not carried out at the time.[14] It was, therefore, quite possible if the Powers so desired now to formulate the detailed plan for the constitution of such a board and set it to work. But here again the Conference felt that, appointed at such a time as this in the midst of a crisis, a board of reference would share those features to which Japan objected in a special League commission of inquiry, while the Chinese Government probably would have less confidence in such

[14] The Nine Powers represented at the Washington Conference on the Limitation of Armaments, on February 4, 1922, passed a resolution to implement the general policy previously agreed upon, " to stabilize conditions in the Far East, to safeguard the rights and interests of China, and to promote intercourse between China and the other Powers upon the basis of equality of opportunity." It was resolved " that there shall be established in China a Board of Reference to which any question of the aforesaid Articles may be referred for investigation and report," and furthermore that a special committee previously proposed with reference to the Chinese tariff " shall formulate for the approval of the Powers concerned a detailed plan for the constitution of the Board." A number of difficulties in the way of a smooth functioning of such a board within reasonable limits of authority had been mentioned in the course of discussion before the resolution was adopted. Subsequently, the whole scheme fell through, owing to the fact that the tariff conference subsequently held, in 1925, ended in a deadlock, so that no board of reference was set up.

newly established board (too similar to the objectionable diplomatic body
vis-à-vis China) than it has in the League. If such a board of reference had
been set up by the nine Powers at the time of the Washington Treaty, and thus
had had time to establish confidence in its methods, it was felt, the case would
have been quite different — and, in fact, the board probably would have
functioned long before the situation became acute.

Another element of uncertainty as regards the exact status of all previous
commitments was the emergence, at the time of the Conference and in the
months preceding it, of a theory which, though discussed in the past, notably
in connection with the Kellogg Pact negotiations, now seemed on the verge
of becoming an accepted part of Japanese policy. This is the theory of a
so-called Far Eastern Monroe Doctrine. The question was asked whether
Japan was construing article 21 of the League Covenant [15] as recognizing
that she held in Manchuria a special position analogous to that of the United
States in Central and South America. The answer was that this still was a
theory held by only one school in Japan which considered it quite logical, in
view of the recognition of one regional sphere of influence with special rights
and responsibilities, to recognize a similar sphere in the Far East. More
moderate thinkers in Japan, it was said, did not insist upon such logic.
Nevertheless, foreign observers of Far Eastern affairs construed some of the
more recent actions of Japan, and especially its objection to a League commission of inquiry, as evidence that there was growing up a " Monroe Doctrine
attitude " in Japan; indeed, that the assumption of such a policy was necessary for an understanding of many features of the Manchurian situation.[16]

The greatest difficulty, illustrated anew by the Manchurian incident,
was the magic formula " vital interest " which had played so damaging a
part in nearly every effort to set up a practicable instrument of peaceful
settlement of international disputes. As the relative advantages and defects
of the various treaty provisions were rehearsed, members of the round tables
could not but be impressed with the apparent inadequacy of all of them in
the face of a situation of conflict in which one party considered its vital interests at stake. A Chinese student of international affairs crystallized this
sentiment when he said:

" The larger political questions are beyond the possibility of solution by legal
minds. That is the reason why the existing diplomatic machinery is not effective.
There is enough machinery for ordinary purposes; but if the parties concerned think

[15] Article 21 reads: " Nothing in this Covenant shall be deemed to affect the validity
of international engagements, such as treaties of arbitration or regional understandings
like the Monroe Doctrine, for securing the maintenance of peace."

[16] A current Japanese point of view on this matter would seem to be, rather, that
in some recent developments in the Western Hemisphere the original implications of the
Monroe Doctrine have become widened; the analogy between Japanese claims as to special
interests in Manchuria is not with such claims as an American nation might make under
the Monroe Doctrine as historically recognized, but with recent claims of the United States
in the Caribbean and in Central America. For a discussion of this subject see C. Walter
Young, *Japan's Special Position in Manchuria* (Baltimore, 1931), pp. 340 ff.

that an issue is vital, the machinery will not work. If Japan thinks that the Manchurian problem is not a matter that diplomacy can settle, then there is an end to the usefulness of diplomatic machinery."

On another occasion, a Japanese member said:

" There is a fable of two brothers: the older one rich, wise, and experienced, the younger one rash and ambitious. This younger brother has made a good job of his lesser estate and comes to his elder brother to beg some raw material from his vast estate upon which to work. He is refused, and a quarrel ensues. A third person is called in to settle their quarrel and robs them both. Manchuria is that portion of China's vast estate upon which Japan, overpopulated and in need of raw materials, has begun to work, for the benefit of both. There is a quarrel now, and a danger that the big neighbor to the north will come in and deprive both China and Japan of the fruit of their work in Manchuria. China might be able to spare a province and never miss it. But Japan cannot spare a foot. To her it is a question of life and death."

In contrast, other members pointed out that wherever there is a recognition of the value of orderly procedure and respect for law it must be possible to devise a machinery capable of dealing even with the most threatening situations in accordance with the wording and the spirit of the treaties. To the minds of many of the Oriental members of the Conference, the events of recent weeks had already produced a tension that could not be removed or affected by the necessarily slow process of working out, through the existing diplomatic machinery, new implements of negotiation.

Vital interests, it appeared, at least to some of the Conference members, are everyday interests melted in the furnace of passion into a single glowing emotion. Thus, at many points the round tables were led to occupy themselves with those atmospheric conditions that determine the relative heat of controversies between nations, conditions that may be conducive to a smooth working of diplomatic machinery or again to its inefficacy and destruction, conditions which, however, are themselves likely to change under the impact of new influences.

PUBLIC OPINION

In one of the round tables a Japanese member gave three reasons for his country's deep concern in the maintenance of its rights in Manchuria; each of the reasons was related to a state of public opinion that had assumed emotional intensity. They were, first, a sentimental historical attachment growing out of Japan's sacrifices in the Russo-Japanese War; second, vital economic interest; and third, fear of Communist Russia. These reasons correspond to three common human motives which, in this case, have been intensified by two factors, remembrance of past experience and national education: love of national glory, as exemplified by past acts of heroism; desire for economic security; fear of social instability and disorder. A Chinese member of the round table immediately expressed the appreciation which all liberally minded persons must have for the reality of such sentiments as these and went on to point out that Chinese interests in Manchuria likewise rested upon a solid public opinion fortified by sentiment. Historically, of course, the Chinese stake in Manchuria is both older and more closely interwoven with her fortunes. Economically, both migration and commerce have made Manchuria essentially a part of the Chinese commonwealth. Strategically, it is popularly considered a bulwark against attacks upon the heart of the republic.

The extent to which government policy follows public opinion was brought out in another round table when a Japanese member stated that his Government, in rejecting the decision of the League concerning a commission of inquiry in Manchuria, was necessarily acting according to the will of the people. Others questioned the implied lack of freedom on the part of a government with respect to its foreign policy. For example, when the Portsmouth Treaty was concluded in 1905, said one member, the majority of the Japanese people were dissatisfied with the treaty, and mobs fired the Shimbashi station. But the Japanese statesmen at that time wisely did not follow the people's demands.

There was too much tendency to accept public opinion as though it were static and incapable of change, according to an American opinion.

" Public sentiment should always be taken as something that can be molded. During the early days of the war public sentiment in the United States toward Great Britain was such that it would have been easy to inflame it in support of a war upon that country. . . . . Public opinion is an amorphous mass. But it is not an irremovable fact. It must be considered in any current situation; but it can be changed by a program of education. We have our propagandas of mutual antagonism; we are learning that propaganda can also be used for purposes of peace. The Japanese sentimental attachment to Manchuria could be educated away if that were part of Japanese policy. The Chinese could teach their people to respect the present treaties irrespective of their background, if they so desired. Korea might have served the purpose of cementing relations between Japan and China; just as Canada, through a century of frequent difficulties between the United States and Great Britain, has served the purpose of cementing the relations between those two countries. In the present Manchurian situation no machinery will in itself be adequate to produce lasting stability and peace. An educational program is needed, not simply to make acceptable to public opinion any decision which a League commission or any other body might make, but to prepare two peoples for systematic peaceful co-operation twenty years ahead."

The idea that diplomatic machinery in itself is insufficient so long as there exists a strong sense of fear was expressed by both Japanese and Chinese members. "With the increasing fear of foreign aggression, China is rapidly being forced to think in military terms," said one of the latter. " In consequence of this fear the country will perhaps before long adopt a more militant policy."

Was there, then, in this seeming vicious circle between aggressive national policy and emotional control of public opinion no opening for helpful agencies of education? Such an opening, further analysis suggested, does exist if one distinguishes the more permanent influences upon feelings and attitudes from those that surround specific objectives of national policy. Thus, for example, it was denied that there is anything in the racial psychology of the Orient that makes for exaggerated antagonisms and against an effective popular support of peaceful diplomatic negotiation. Indeed, such a suggestion was resented by some members who felt that it was a typical assumption of Occidental superiority. The mutual attitudes of contempt, derision, or fear to be found between Oriental peoples, it was stated, were very much the same as are to be found in other parts of the world. Both China and Japan consider themselves superior to each other — the one on the ground of its more ancient civilization, the other on that of its more efficient present civilization.

These prejudices, as in Europe and America, it was found, are imbedded in the educational systems of these countries; and there was much discussion of the part played in their stimulation especially by two agencies, the school and the press. An American member gave it as his opinion that the effect of these agencies is difficult to eradicate: " The American Congress is legislating today on the basis of ideas taught forty years ago when the present Congressmen went to school." A Canadian member observed that American school textbooks still contained materials written from the anti-British point of view of a century and a half ago. Chinese textbooks had recently been the object of attack by both Japanese and Chinese writers.[17] A Chinese member drew attention to the serious effect of such prejudiced textbooks. In their teaching the rising generation often is led to look upon the current problems of their nation as entirely due to foreigners with little effort to secure awareness of their own national deficiencies. While Japanese textbooks were not criticized for any distinctly antiforeign propaganda, fault was found with them as furthering an aggressive policy of penetration in Manchuria, and as being made the tools, generally, of Japan's foreign policy. A Japanese member praised the effective action of educational officials in Hawaii in eradicating from the schoolbooks all anti-Japanese references and increasing materials that produce international good will — action which, he believed, had been largely instrumental in creating that mutual understanding and appreciation that distinguishes the Hawaiian popular attitude.

Nationalism, it was conceded, is taught in the schools of all countries; a distinction must be made between three elements: the teaching of patriotism which is wholesome and essential, that of an exaggerated nationalism which intensifies the emotional approach to all questions of foreign relations, and deliberate misstatement and misinterpretation in furtherance of an immediate object of national policy. As regards the last named, attention was drawn to a proposal by a subcommittee of the League of Nations' Committee on Intellectual Co-operation for an interchange of objections from any one nation to hostile and misleading information concerning it contained in the public-school textbooks of another nation.[18]

One difficulty, it was stated, was that current crises in national affairs

[17] " Anti-foreign Teachings in New Text-Books of China," the *Sokokusha,* 1929; *North-China Daily News,* October 24, 1931.
[18] This subject is further discussed below, pp. 490 ff.

and the attitudes engendered by fear are inevitably reflected in the classroom. Thus, in China today the teaching of the textbooks may be less influential than the nationalistic feeling aroused, on the one hand, by foreign occupation of Chinese territory and, on the other, by the anti-Japanese boycott. A teacher testified to the difficulties experienced in such an exceptional situation — when students are actually organizing themselves in antiforeign agitation — to preserve a spirit of objective study. In this connection the strikes of students against educational authorities that seemed to them insufficiently sympathetic with their ardent patriotism were also mentioned.

" Intellectual disarmament," in the opinion of most members, must at least accompany the setting-up of an effective machinery of diplomacy, if not precede it. President Hoover was quoted as saying that in the last instance public opinion settles every international issue. The Manchurian episode again illustrated, many thought, the acute danger of this determining influence when public opinion itself is ill informed or actually misled by propaganda.

Few concrete suggestions were made as to ways in which, more specifically, educational means might be used to produce public support for peaceful negotiation and its instruments. Japanese members in this connection instanced the excellent work of their national League of Nations Association in which several of them were taking an active part. They believed that this work had contributed to a continuing faith in the essential worth of the League in spite of much popular criticism of the League's action on the Manchurian issue. An Australian member recommended the organization of a permanent " propaganda for peace," in the charge of competent educational specialists, not as part of the official diplomatic machinery but quite independently of it, in the control of an impartial voluntary organization.[19]

V. REGIONAL AIDS TO EXISTING MACHINERY

VOLUNTARY INQUIRY

Suggestions for voluntary action were not limited to educational functions. In all the round tables voluntary participation in the processes of international political relations was advocated in one form or another. Perhaps the most important of these suggestions was a reference to the commission appointed in 1913 by the Carnegie Endowment to investigate, with the consent of the governments concerned, the " causes and conduct of the Balkan Wars." It was believed that such an inquiry if undertaken by an unprejudiced organization without a political stake of its own in the Far East might, because of its unofficial character, have the consent of the Governments of China and Japan. The co-operation of influential groups of citizens from these countries in the activities of the Institute of Pacific Relations, and in the present Conference at a time of extreme tension between the two nations, would

[19] Such organizations, with the sole aim of creating better understanding of international issues and of available methods and procedures for dealing with them, of course, already exist in most of the Pacific countries.

seem to indicate, it was said, that the reasons of the respective governments for objecting to some proposed diplomatic method of inquiry (Japan to a League commission of inquiry; China to a board of reference under the Washington Treaty) did not necessarily extend to a friendly and competent investigation of all the factors in the Manchurian trouble on the part of a voluntary organization in which citizens of both these countries were represented. The objection to other proposals, in either case, had not been to the fullest exposition of the facts in the case but to a possible association of such fact-finding activity with a quasi-judicial procedure or the formulation of international policies. This suggestion was taken up by a Japanese member who strongly favored such a self-appointed committee as a body that could immediately get to work, secure an unprejudiced statement of the fundamental facts as well as the more recent allegations of hostile action (Japanese occupation of Chinese territory in Manchuria; boycott and agitation against Japanese in Chinese cities), and so pave the way for a permanent and official board of inquiry and conciliation.[20]

At a later meeting a round table on "International Co-operation in Research and Discussion," a representative of the League of Nations drew attention to the recently formed Balkan Conference, an organization modeled somewhat after the Institute of Pacific Relations but more definitely motivated with a desire to conciliate outstanding differences between states.

"Its first meeting was held at Athens last year. Representatives were present from all the Balkan countries. The Conference began under conditions of great difficulty. Bulgarian delegates had sent word a week before that they could not take part unless the question of national minorities were fully discussed. During the first two days there was evident much antagonism. From then on through the eighth day there was the finest spirit.

"The Conference is composed of six national councils, representing each one of the Balkan States. It holds annual sessions. It differs from the I.P.R. in that it passes resolutions. Since the Balkans have long been a very troubled area, it is significant that this is the first area in Europe to have such an organization. It has a permanent secretariat which moves around in these countries. It is unofficial and not part of the League. Once the Conference was under way, any semblance of an official atmosphere disappeared, although the delegates were appointed with the knowledge and approval of the respective governments."

Asked whether he thought that the work of the Balkan Conference might be more effective if it did not pass resolutions, the League representative replied that it probably was desirable, in any case, to have resolutions passed on practical, administrative questions. As to political problems, it

[20] At a later round table a Japanese member suggested that, apart from a conciliation commission which can deal effectively only with current cases, there might be appointed a " clearance commission " to examine all outstanding cases of difference between the Chinese and Japanese in Manchuria, from a legal point of view and without regard to policy. Such activity might result in the establishment of a " balance sheet " of debit and credit for each country, to be submitted to the two governments for negotiation. He suggested that such a commission might be made up of an equal number of Chinese and Japanese jurists with a neutral observer.

was probably correct to say that European assemblies of this kind are accustomed to speak to resolutions and would not take kindly to any other form of procedure. Also, the work of the Balkan Conference centers more on conference and less on research than the Institute of Pacific Relations; and the respective delegations try to secure governmental action upon the resolutions passed in conference. The relative nearness of the Balkan States to each other, he added in reply to a question, naturally leads to greater emphasis on conference. It also makes possible a more complete committee organization but, on the other hand, involves a danger that too many subjects are opened up for discussion.

LEAGUE OF NATIONS COMMISSION OF INQUIRY

It has already been shown in a previous section (p. 243) why the present diplomatic machinery of the Pacific was considered inadequate and, specifically, why Japan considered the existing provision for inquiry under the League Covenant inapplicable to the Manchurian situation. But the appointment of such a commission of inquiry was considered not only with a view to the immediate emergency; to many members it seemed a suitable initial step toward a more permanent increase of League activities in the Far East and in the Pacific area. That *some* new machinery was desirable seemed, as has already been said, the unanimous opinion of the Conference. A Chinese member reminded one of the round tables that, even before the incident of September 18, China had appealed to the League to send a commission to Manchuria to study the whole situation. China was convinced that the ordinary diplomatic machinery did not suffice to settle the many outstanding disputes between her and Japan; this view evidently had not been wholly appreciated in Japan, or even by all Chinese commentators. It was not an appeal to a superior police force, or to a third party to help China out in a difficulty, but a genuine desire for peaceful settlement of the outstanding questions in the spirit and with the methods of the League Covenant. This gave Japanese members an opportunity to voice an objection against the proposed procedure that was more general than merely the fear that the specific inquiry would take on the character of a court: a commission appointed *ad hoc* could not fulfil the function of an extended activity of the League in the Pacific area which they also desired. At Kyoto, they had approved the idea of a joint commission with League participation, and they were ready now to give careful consideration to any plan that would effectively lead from unbiased inquiry to conciliation and the working-out of solutions for the more fundamental problems in the relationship between China and Japan. While it was true that a Japanese member of the League had functioned successfully as chairman of a committee dealing with problems of national minorities in Europe, probably no one on that continent would have considered a Far Eastern committee appointed *ad hoc* competent to adjudicate the dispute between France and Germany over Alsace-Lorraine. Such deep-seated controversies could not be clarified, much less settled, in that way.

Chinese members again emphasized the fact that on their part the proposed inquiry had been intended only as a first step, in line with the Japanese proposals made at Kyoto.[21]

As a result of this exchange of opinions, the difference became clearer between an *inquiry*, resulting in a report of findings, and *observation*, which may be carried on continuously. It would be exceedingly difficult in the Manchurian controversy for any body of persons, however competent, to reconstruct from evidence long obscured and overlaid by more recent happenings the gradual accumulation of grievances on both sides and the emergence of major issues; but a permanent body, watching the course of events, making detailed studies on the ground whenever a specific incident warranted such particular inquiry, might well after some time be extremely well informed about every issue: its origin, its course of development, and the exact nature of the difficulties to be met. It was natural, therefore, for the discussion to shift to a quest for a form of permanent organization that would have the confidence of the contending parties.

One of the suggestions was that the League Council, instead of sending a commission of inquiry from Geneva, appoint a number of foreign ministers, already in the Far East and presumably somewhat acquainted with the history of the Manchurian dispute, to act in that capacity. Such an appointment would have the advantage of co-operation from the United States which already had dispatched diplomatic representatives to Manchuria to report on the situation. Possibly the Union of Soviet Socialist Republics also might be represented; and of course the Governments of China and Japan would appoint their representatives to serve on such a commission. There were several objections to this: China is suspicious of any body composed of foreign diplomats, simply as a result of her long experience of adverse decisions on the part of such a diplomatic body. More important, such a commission would again be merely a temporary expedient and could not fulfil the function of a continuing liaison between the League and its Far Eastern members.

FAR EASTERN COMMITTEE OF THE LEAGUE

Next, therefore, the possibilities of a standing committee of the League for Far Eastern affairs, with its seat in the Far East, were explored. Such arrangement might take several forms:

The League already had adopted the practice, it was pointed out, of appointing particular agencies of the secretariat to deal with the problems of particular areas. Hitherto such special committees had had their seat at Geneva, since the distances from the regions studied were not great. But there was no reason why such branch committees might not be established in other parts of the world. A branch secretariat in the Far East would have the advantage not only of keeping the League in touch with Far Eastern affairs, but of creating in Geneva itself a gradually increasing personnel of informed officers if staff members were given the opportunity of being de-

[21] See *Problems of the Pacific, 1929*, p. 207.

tailed to the Far Eastern post for two or three years. Such an arrangement would go far to offset the remoteness of the League center from the Far East.

One question was: " Would such a special committee be needed for Manchuria alone or should it extend its operations to the whole of the Pacific area? " Another question was: " Would a mere branch office of the League secretariat suffice to meet the cases? " Some members thought that if the machinery were too subordinate, it would not lessen the problem of geographical distance from the League center at Geneva. It was felt also that such an organ of the League would have to be invested with sufficient authority to carry weight: " In dealing with human disputes we are still unable to do without the personal factor." Somewhat to the same effect, a Japanese speaker considered it important that this should not be just a routine office, to pass on to Europe current information, but a branch staffed with men qualified to make studies of some profundity:

" We have here three types of civilization in conflict: that of Japan might be called capitalistic, that of Russia communistic, and that of China rather old-fashioned, belonging to the pre-capitalistic era, and with a future yet uncertain. The mutual impact of these civilizations requires careful study and working-out of new formulas. The need is urgent, especially in view of the uncertainty of Russia's policy — whether she believes in the tactics of violence or not."

As to the scope of such an organization, it was felt that probably it would not be wise to limit it to a single, particular area of present acute difficulty — though some members thought in those terms — but that it might be better to co-ordinate in such an office all the varied activities carried on by the League in the western part of the Pacific, including the advisory functions in China, control of the health center in Singapore, and any other administrative bureaus that might yet be established. Instead of a single committee or commission, it was preferable to have a co-ordinating office for a variety of activities, with joint services of information, library, and the like. A Japanese speaker pointed out that if such a standing committee had been in existence during the last two years, it might have rendered valuable educational service in regard to the Manchurian difficulty which during that period was assuming threatening proportions; the public mind might have been educated to the need for a speedy solution of the main issues. Apart from the direct influence on the Far Eastern countries, the dissemination of unbiased information from such an office would be very helpful also in educating the rest of the world, so that the passing events would be judged more correctly. A British member drew attention to the great advantage which such a permanent office would have in aiding those League officials and others who are from time to time coming to the Far East to study specific questions in the fields of economics, education, public health, and the like.

At this point many members were surprised to hear that, as a matter of fact, the League already has a Far Eastern Committee, recently established by resolution of the Council as a permanent part of the secretarial organization. The proposal now made simply amounted to a transference of that committee to the Far East, possibly with additional functions and with changes in personnel.

The best location for such a bureau in the Far East was considered only in passing. One member expressed the view that it should have no permanent habitat but travel through the whole area, wherever its services were most needed at any one time. This suggestion, however, did not seem particularly practical. Another question raised was: Why should the Far East or the Pacific area be singled out for such special attention on the part of the League; were not other parts of the world in equal need of it? The reply to this was that it might be well to follow an opportunist policy. If this branch office proved useful, the League probably would eventually establish similar centers elsewhere.

FAR EASTERN COUNCIL OF THE LEAGUE

Chiefly, it seemed, from considerations of prestige and influence on world-opinion, many members remained unconvinced that a secretarial branch office of the League would best answer the purpose in mind. Why should not the Council of the League itself be subdivided, so as to have a permanent international body in the Pacific area, directly appointed by the member-states, to balance the Europe-centered League Council in Geneva? A Chinese member who for many years has worked in behalf of the League said:

" Ever since its establishment the League has been the League of Western Europe. Japanese and Chinese members were practically sitting as ' observers.' But the League in the last four weeks has taken up a tremendous question. There are many problems awaiting the League's study in the Orient. It is most desirable that a regional council or standing committee of the Council be established in the Far East — with the United States and the Union of Soviet Socialist Republics as members."

It does not suffice, said others, for the League to have only an administrative office in the Far East, with advisory functions. There are decisions to be made in this area, often on issues that arise suddenly. " But," replied a British member, " such burning questions are likely to arise in any part of the world; additional Councils, as suggested for this area, would add too great a burden to the League which some of the member-states now have difficulty in helping to support. Such a proposal expresses no more than a pious hope." With this view many members seemed to agree.

FAR EASTERN MEETINGS OF THE LEAGUE COUNCIL

As a possible alternative, the round tables considered the relative advantages of occasional Far Eastern meetings of the League Council as a whole. A Chinese member stated that the National Government of China had in the earlier stages of its existence held political council meetings in Peking, Wuhan, and other cities; and that these councils were only later united in a central government. Why could not the League once every few years meet in some other place than Geneva? [22] Tokyo, Nanking, and Mukden were mentioned by various speakers as suitable localities for an early Far Eastern meeting of the League Council to consider the Manchurian conflict. South America, it was said, probably was the only other large region that might have a similar claim to special attention on the part of the League.

The chief difficulty anticipated was that the League at all times has many problems to consider, large and small, which require continuous attention. If Council meetings were held at a great distance from Geneva, probably those most concerned in these matters could not attend; or important decisions would be held up simply because the time of the Council was absorbed by regional affairs. This difficulty might partly be overcome, one member suggested, by the designation of substitutes for members who could not spare the time for long-distance travel. Another way out might be the appointment of a subsidiary Council. This method would have the additional advantage that it might make it possible for the United States and Russia to take part without bringing up the question of their full membership in the League.

This suggestion subsequently took on a somewhat different form, as proposing the organization of regional conferences by the League, possibly of a permanent nature, to meet either at regular intervals or from time to time as occasion arose, to act for the Council in the Pacific area without actually being part of the League Council.

PERMANENT ORGANIZATION INDEPENDENT OF THE LEAGUE

With a view to practical possibilities, this last-named suggestion narrowed down again to a proposal for a regular conference of foreign secretaries and Far Eastern ambassadors and ministers — a type of organization which would be almost independent of the League and might, for the Far Eastern countries, that is, especially for China, have the same objections as the committee of diplomatic representatives earlier considered.

There were, however, many who saw an advantage in a form of organization quite independent of the League. One suggestion was that the relation of such an organization to the League might be similar to that of the International Labour Office — allied to but not part of the parent-institution. This proposal had the support of Japanese members who thought that such a body, set up to deal with Pacific questions, would not be in conflict with the League. But since the aim evidently was to secure intimate attention to the affairs of the Far East, the suggestion came back to a bilateral arrangement between China and Japan, a permanent commission to study all the outstanding issues between them and to report back to their respective governments.

[22] The proposed meeting of the Council in Paris, to suit the convenience of its President, was mentioned as setting a precedent, though a relatively local one, in this respect. There have also been previous meetings of the Council away from Geneva.

This proposal did not appeal to many of the Chinese members who insisted that an international point of view must be brought to bear upon those issues through the participation of disinterested neutrals. But in the course of the discussion judgments were somewhat modified by a more thorough consideration of the way in which such a bilateral board of conciliation would actually work. Particularly impressive in this connection was an account given by a Canadian member of the constitution and working of the International Joint Commission between the United States and Canada, which for more than twenty years has peacefully adjusted all boundary disputes between these two countries.[23] It was felt that if such a commission had been in existence between China and Japan, even in the last two years, most of the many mutual grievances, and especially many of the outstanding claims of Japan, could have been settled or at least sufficiently advanced toward settlement to prevent the growth of a dangerous belief in the necessity of force. That this feeling of an impending crisis as inevitable was not limited to Japan may be illustrated by the remarks of a Chinese speaker when the chairman inquired whether there were reasons why the system that was working so well in North America might not be applied with similar success to Manchuria. He said:

" This example of a working international machinery is useful for reference and study. But, after all, it is limited to machinery. The question is whether when such instrumentalities are set up one must not presuppose that those who do so are committed to a policy of peace. If that premise is not there, it will be in vain to set up any kind of machinery — it will meet no practical purpose."

This fatalism, this readiness to believe that the other side is not disposed to use new and better tools of international dealing for the purposes for which they are meant, is characteristic, it was pointed out on another occasion, of a situation that has gone too far to be dealt with by the two parties involved alone. It is just at such a point that participation of neutral outsiders is essential to bring the controversy back to a point at which the situation can again be seen as a complex of detailed, manageable issues. The Conference was reminded that the Council of the League of Nations, in its famous resolution of October 24, had actually recommended the establishment of such a commission of conciliation in the Far East, with League participation to provide the needed background of neutral yet concerned interest.

FUNCTIONING OF THE INSTITUTE OF PACIFIC RELATIONS

The tragedy of the situation, then, seemed to be that at the very time when prompt action was needed to prevent an international catastrophe, the very instrumentalities that might have served to substitute an orderly process of inquiry and conciliation for violence were not available. The situation needed prompt and direct approach, with as much assistance from disinterested friends of the two parties in dispute as could be brought to bear upon it without the need of setting up cumbrous machinery. It is not surprising

[23] See *Problems of the Pacific, 1929*, p. 221.

that in these circumstances many members of the Conference were seeking for some way in which their own organization, unofficial, inexperienced, and feeble though it was in dealing with such great issues, might be of some help.

Reference has already been made (p. 257) to the somewhat analogous circumstances in which the Carnegie Endowment, in 1913, attacked a similar problem in Macedonia. The question was asked whether in this emergency the Institute of Pacific Relations might not depart somewhat from the intentionally limited scope of its functioning to initiate a task which later on, in more propitious times, might be continued, perhaps, more suitably under other auspices. There was obvious need for inquiry and for an attempt at conciliation. There was need, further, for a temporary liaison between such direct negotiations as might be possible in the Far East and the League of Nations until such time as either the League itself or the Governments could provide more permanent machinery.

The discussion had shown the close relation between diplomacy and public opinion; it was precisely in this borderland between the official methods of international negotiation, on the one hand, and the education of public opinion on the other, that the Institute was functioning. In the Institute, prominent citizens of the Far Eastern countries had learned frankly to discuss their difficulties with colleagues from other Pacific lands, among them now not only Americans but henceforth also Russians.[24] While it was useful to have such discussions as those of the present Conference biennially, could not a smaller group, representative of these countries, meet more continuously in the intervening period, and especially in the immediate future, for the specific purpose of examining all the known facts in the Manchurian situation and interpreting the issues in a way conducive to a constructive formulation of possibilities of conciliation? Since no resolutions are passed at Institute conferences, it is not possible to state to what extent this proposal met the approval of the members. But to the recorders it seemed that there was a consensus of opinion to the effect, at least, that the Institute should further explore, with the Japan and China councils, the possibility of undertaking in the near future some activity in the general area of the suggestion made. Briefly, that area in the minds of the round-table members would seem to include: factual inquiry, especially of the immediate points at issue between China and Japan in Manchuria; study of the more fundamental differences in interest and policy affecting the relation of both countries to this territory; inquiry into possible methods of conciliating these differences; further study of various proposed methods and technical devices for supplementing the diplomatic machinery of the Pacific, with special reference to Manchuria and other outstanding problems in the Far East; education of public opinion throughout the world in regard to both the acute situation in Manchuria and the more basic factors that have produced it.

[24] A Soviet Union Council of the Institute had just been formed (see p. 250).

PART IV

CHINA'S INTERNATIONAL RELATIONS

CHAPTER IX

EXTRATERRITORIALITY

DATA PAPERS

1. MINGCHIEN JOSHUA BAU. *The Status of Aliens in China* (China Council).
2. RALPH ARNOLD. *The Status of Aliens in China* (British Group).
3. W. H. MALLORY. *Extraterritoriality in China* (mimeographed, American Council).

REFERENCES

1. *Syllabus on China's Foreign Relations.*
2. J. B. CONDLIFFE (ed.). *Problems of the Pacific, 1929*, chap. iv, Docs. V and VI.
3. SHUHSI HSU. *Questions Relating to Manchuria* (China Council).
4. MAJOR GENERAL YASUNOSUKE SATO (retired). *Sino-Japanese Problems* (Japan Council).
5. SABURO YAMADA. *Legal Status of Aliens in Japan* (Japan Council).
6. GORDON LINDSAY and D. R. MICHENER, *Legal Status of Aliens Resident in Canada;* H. F. ANGUS, *The Legal Status in British Columbia of Residents of Oriental Race and Their Descendants* (Canadian Council).
7. RALPH ARNOLD. *The Status of Aliens in Great Britain* (mimeographed, British Group).
8. JOSEPH P. CHAMBERLAIN. *Aliens in the United States* (mimeographed, American Council).
9. T. D. H. HALL. *Status of Aliens in New Zealand* (New Zealand Council).
10. K. H. BAILEY. *The Legal Position of Foreigners in Australia* (Australian Council).
11. HAROLD S. QUIGLEY. *An Introductory Syllabus on Far Eastern Diplomacy* (American Council).
12. CARL F. REMER. *Foreign Investments in China* (mimeographed, International Research report), pp. 45 ff.
13. THOMAS F. MILLARD. *The End of Extraterritoriality in China.* Shanghai, 1931.
14. CHARLES P. HOWLAND. *Survey of American Foreign Relations* (New Haven, 1930), chap. iii.
    (See also references in chapters on " The Future of Shanghai " and " China's Inland Navigation.")

EXTRACTS FROM DATA PAPERS

I. THE STATUS OF ALIENS IN CHINA [1]

By MINGCHIEN JOSHUA BAU

The origin of extraterritoriality dates back to the days of the Opium War (1839–42), when in the Supplementary Treaty Respecting General Regulations of Trade concluded with Great Britain on October 8, 1843,[2] governing the British trade at the first five treaty ports and supplementary to the Treaty of Nanking of 1842, extraterritoriality of a unilateral kind was granted for the first time. Today there are yet sixteen states enjoying the rights of extraterritoriality; the United States of America, Belgium, Brazil, British Empire, Denmark, France, Italy, Japan, Mexico, The Netherlands, Peru, Portugal, Norway, Spain, Sweden, and Switzerland.

The practice of extraterritoriality is so well known that it almost needs no reiteration. As a rule, it follows the personality of the defendant or accused. It exempts foreign nationals enjoying the privilege from the judicial process of territorial tribunals as well as from the violability of premises. With the exception of special courts established by Great Britain and the United States of America, and by France and Italy which have each a special judge for China, and by Japan which has assigned consular judges to the consulates general at Mukden, Tientsin, Shanghai, and Tsingtao, and by Norway which has a consular judge at Shanghai, the consuls of all the Powers concerned, in general, are authorized to exercise extraterritorial jurisdiction in courts known as consular courts. The laws applied in these extraterritorial courts are the laws of the states exercising extraterritorial jurisdiction, save rights of realty which are determined according to *lex situs* and also probably in cases involving local customs and municipal ordinances. The tribunals that have jurisdiction over mixed cases between a Chinese defendant and a foreign plaintiff have been commonly known as mixed courts, and a foreign assessor is usually permitted to attend trials in such courts. In the agreement, however, relating to the Chinese Court at the International Settlement of Shanghai, February 17, 1930,[3] the practice of foreign assessors is relinquished.

As a corollary of this practice of extraterritoriality, until and unless it is abolished, extraterritorial aliens, excepting missionaries and those engaged in philanthropic work, are not entitled to unrestricted travel, trade, and residence in all parts of China — known as the interior of China — save for excursions from the ports open to trade and to a distance not exceeding 100 *li* and for a period not exceeding five days; and their activities are generally confined to the treaty and open ports and, in most instances, to special areas in these ports.

The Koreans in Chientao constitute a unique exception. Unlike other

---

[1] From data paper of the same title (China Council), pp. 3–25.

[2] *State Papers*, XXX, 398 ff.

[3] *Laws, Regulations and Legal Documents of the National Government* (Judicial Yuan, 1930), p. 1831, art. 3.

aliens, they are subject to Chinese laws and courts, in civil and criminal cases, on equal footing with the Chinese. Japan reserves only the right to delegate an assessor to attend trials with the right to protest and to demand a new trial by officials specially selected, and in important cases involving lives of persons, to be given previous notice of trial.[4]

Repeated attempts have been made to secure the relinquishment of extraterritoriality. As early as 1902, China made a move in this direction and obtained the consent to abrogate this special privilege, upon the successful introduction of judicial reforms to be undertaken by China, from Great Britain in the Treaty of September 5, 1902; [5] from the United States of America in the treaty of October 8, 1903; [6] from Japan in the Treaty of the same date; [7] from Portugal in the treaty (unratified) of November 11, 1904; [8] and subsequently from Sweden in the treaty of July 2, 1908 [9] and from Switzerland in the Treaty of June 13, 1908.[10] At the Paris Peace Conference, 1919, China submitted a request *inter alia* for the abrogation of extraterritoriality, which was not given favorable consideration; but in consequence of the allied victory in the Great War, 1914–18, she succeeded in recovering extraterritoriality from Germany, Austria, and Hungary and subsequently from Russia.

At the Washington Conference, 1921–22, China again submitted her claim.[11] In response the Powers represented at the Washington Conference, other than China, willing to relinquish extraterritorial jurisdiction as soon as judicial reforms of China should warrant so doing, authorized the establishment of an International Commission consisting of one representative from each of the Powers, signatory or acceding, to make necessary inquiries relating thereto and asked that China should appoint a representative to sit as a member of the Commission and afford facility for the successful accomplishment of its task.[12]

In pursuance of this decision of the Washington Conference, the International Commission on Extraterritoriality in China met in Peking, on January 12, 1926. The representatives of the thirteen Powers were present, to wit: The United States of America, Belgium, British Empire, China, Denmark, France, Italy, Japan, The Netherlands, Norway, Portugal, Spain, and Sweden; of which Denmark, Norway, Spain, and Sweden were the Powers that acceded to the Washington Resolution. On September 16, 1926, the Commission rendered a joint report.[13]

[4] Agreement Relating to the Chientao Region, September 4, 1909 (MacMurray, *Treaties and Agreements with and concerning China* [1909/10]).

[5] Hertslet, I, No. 28, 182, Art. XII.

[6] Hertslet, I, No. 100, 575, Art. XV.   [7] Hertslet, I, No. 66, 386–87, Art. XI.

[8] MacMurray, 1902–9, Art. XVI.   [9] MacMurray, 1908/11, Art. 10.

[10] MacMurray, 1918/8, in the attached Declaration of the same date.

[11] Senate Document 126, 67–2, pp. 475, 499, 504, 528, 503, 601, 505, 519, 548, 732, 480, 502, 572, etc.

[12] *Ibid.*, p. 98, 4th Plenary Session, December 10, 1921.

[13] The Chinese delegate, Dr. Wang Chung-hui, in signing the report, made the statement: " By signing this report, my approval of all the statements contained in Parts I, II, and III is not to be implied."

RECOMMENDATIONS OF THE REPORT

In general, the Report was unfavorable to China's claim for the abolition of extraterritoriality. It virtually stated that, as far as her claim for the relinquishment of extraterritorial jurisdiction was concerned, China was as yet found wanting. To put it in a more courteous way, as the Commission did, it rendered the opinion that when the recommendations of the Commission should have been reasonably complied with, the several Powers would be warranted in relinquishing their respective rights of extraterritoriality.

The essential features of these recommendations should be carefully noticed. Respecting the reforms she should undertake prior to the abolition of extraterritoriality, it is insisted that China should forthwith achieve the independence of the judiciary, the elimination of the magistrates' courts and other unsatisfactory features of her old police and prison systems, the extension of modern courts, modern prisons, and modern detention-houses, the definite and regular adoption of legislation, the completion and enforcement of criminal, civil, and commercial codes, and the making of adequate financial provision for her judicial system. Relating to modifications in the existing systems and practice of extraterritoriality, it is urged that the extraterritorial powers should undertake the application of Chinese laws and regulations, the elimination of foreign assessors in mixed cases, the bringing of mixed courts in settlements and concessions more in accord with the organization and procedure of the modern Chinese judicial system, including permission of foreign lawyers to practice in all mixed cases, the correction of abuses in the extension of foreign protection to the Chinese, the periodical compulsory registration of extraterritorial nationals, and the ordering of payment of taxation by exaterritorial nationals. With reference to mutual assistance in judicial administration, it is recommended that the authorities of China and those of the extraterritorial Powers on the one hand, and the extraterritorial Powers among themselves on the other, should make arrangements to recognize the validity of all agreements between foreigners and Chinese providing for the settlement of civil matters by arbitration, and to secure the prompt execution of judgments, summons and warrants of arrest or search reciprocally in their respective spheres of jurisdiction. As a last condition for the relinquishment of extraterritoriality, the understanding is specifically stated that, upon and after the abolition, the nationals of the Powers concerned are to enjoy in all parts of China freedom of residence and trade and civil rights.

After the publication of the report, there was a relaxation in the efforts of the Chinese Government for the abolition of extraterritoriality, the Nationalists being then too much absorbed in a northward expedition against the old militarists. With the capture of Peking in June, 1928, by the Nationalist forces, and the apparent unification of the country, the National Government at Nanking moved again in the direction of the abrogation of the unequal treaties. The attention was focused on tariff autonomy which was deemed of paramount importance, eclipsing the extraterritoriality issue.

In the process, however, of negotiating for tariff autonomy, the National Government at Nanking were able to conclude five treaties which provided not only for tariff autonomy but also for the conditional surrender of extraterritoriality.

THE FIRST FIVE TREATIES

The five treaties are the Sino-Belgian Treaty of November 22, Sino-Italian Treaty of November 27, Sino-Danish Treaty of December 12, Sino-Portuguese Treaty of December 19, and Sino-Spanish Treaty of December 27, 1928. In the annexes to these five treaties, it is definitely stated that these Powers concerned should relinquish their extraterritorial rights on January 1, 1930, but that before the said date the Chinese Government should make detailed arrangements for the assumption of jurisdiction over the nationals of the Powers concerned; but that, failing such arrangement on the said date, the nationals of the Powers concerned should thereafter be amenable to Chinese laws and jurisdiction, in the case of the Belgian Treaty, as soon as the majority of the Powers now possessing extraterritorial privileges in China, and in the case of the Italian and other Treaties, as soon as all the Powers other than China which directly participated in the discussion of Pacific and Far Eastern Questions at the Washington Conference,[14] shall have agreed to relinquish them. Meanwhile, in the same annexes the Chinese Government undertakes two important declarations: (1) on or before January 1, 1930, the civil code and the commercial code, in addition to other codes and laws now in force, will be duly promulgated; and (2) when the nationals of these Powers concerned in China cease to enjoy the privileges of consular jurisdiction and other special privileges, and when the relations between the two countries are on a footing of perfect equality, the Chinese Government, in view of the fact that the Chinese citizens, subject to the limitations prescribed in the laws and regulations of the Powers concerned, enjoy the right to live and trade and to acquire property in any part of the territory of these Powers concerned, will grant the same rights in China to the nationals of these Powers concerned, subject to the limitations to be prescribed in its laws and regulations.

It is thus seen that in the annexes of these five treaties a definite date was set for the abolition of extraterritoriality — namely, January 1, 1930 — and that the promulgation of the civil code and commercial code was made obligatory before the date set above. It is, however, to be regretfully pointed out that in exchange for the surrender of extraterritoriality, the Chinese Government was compelled to open up the interior of China not only to foreign travel, residence, and trade, but also to the acquisition of property including real estate. This condition is not found in previous Chinese treaties, nor is it conducive to the best preservation of Chinese soil.

[14] The United States of America, Belgium, the British Empire, France, Italy, Japan, the Netherlands, and Portugal.

CHINA'S BOLD DRIVE

With these five treaties as a starting point, the Chinese Government made a bold drive on the other Powers interested for an early settlement of the question of extraterritoriality. To this effect, it sent, on April 27, 1929, identical notes to the diplomatic representatives of the American, British, and French Governments; and on the same date three other notes of substantially the same nature were dispatched to the diplomatic representatives of the Dutch, Norwegian, and Brazilian Governments.[15]

They were simple notes asking for an early surrender of extraterritoriality with the general assurances of the promulgation of the civil code and the commercial code before January 1, 1930, the rapid extension of the modern courts and prisons throughout the country, and the adequate protection of the legitimate rights and interests of the foreign nationals concerned.

The replies of the Powers so approached deserve a closer study.

The American note of August 10, 1929,[16] in essence, pointed out two leading defects in the Chinese judicial system: first, the absence of an adequate body of known law, and, second, what is more important, the lack of an experienced and independent judiciary free from extraneous influence. It further took the stand that the recommendations as made by the International Commission on Extraterritoriality in China, particularly with reference to the independence of the judiciary, should be reasonably fulfilled, or, at least, in far greater measure than was the case then, before the American Government could feel safe to entrust the security of American life, liberty and property to the jurisdiction of the Chinese laws and courts. It ended, however, with a friendly expression of readiness to participate in negotiations which would lead to the gradual relinquishment of extraterritorial rights, whether geographical, or jurisdictional, or both.

The British reply, also of August 10, 1929, was just as unfavorable, or even less favorable than the American. After tracing the historical *raison d'être* of the extraterritorial system in China, it virtually set forth the opinion that, prior to, and, as a prerequisite for the relinquishment of extraterritorial jurisdiction, " the western legal principles should be understood and be found acceptable by the people at large no less than by their rulers, and the courts which administered these laws should be free from interference and dictation at the hands not only of military chiefs but of groups and associations who either set up arbitrary and illegal tribunals of their own or attempted to use legal courts for the furtherance of political objects rather than for the administration of equal justice between Chinese and Chinese and between Chinese and foreigners." [17] What is more, it positively declined to entertain any request for an immediate abolition of the extraterritorial jurisdiction, but expressed willingness only to examine in collabora-

---

[15] *Week in China,* May 11, 1929.

[16] *Ibid.,* August 31, 1929.

[17] " British Answer on Extraterritoriality, August 10, 1929," *Peking Leader,* September 5, 1929.

tion with the Chinese Government the modifications that might be made in the existing system and practice of extraterritoriality as already set forth in the British declaration of December 18, 1926, and the British proposals of January 26 and 27, 1927.[18]

The French reply of the same date succinctly expressed the opinion that the fulfillment of the recommendations made in the Report of the International Commission on Extraterritoriality, September 16, 1926, was a necessary prerequisite to the renunciation of the extraterritorial jurisdiction.[19] The Dutch reply of the same date virtually echoed the sentiments and opinions of the American. The Norwegian reply of August 14, 1929, simply stated that Norway would be prepared to abolish extraterritoriality when all the other Powers should do so.[20]

With these replies, the Chinese Government did not feel satisfied. It issued a rejoinder on September 5, 1929.[21] In essence, it appealed to American idealism and to the further enhancement of friendship and material interest through an early relinquishment of extraterritoriality. It pointed out the mistake of the Powers in judging the conditions of Chinese law and judicial administration in the light of the 1926 Report, as since then and under the new régime, the political and judicial systems of China had assumed a new aspect. It pleaded that inasmuch as she found it fit and proper to surrender the Capitulations in Turkey, and as the Chinese judicial system did not suffer in comparison with that of Turkey at the time of abolition, America should be as generous with China, as she was with Turkey. It further reminded her that inasmuch as the several Powers which had agreed to surrender extraterritoriality on January 1, 1930, felt it safe to intrust their nationals to the care of the Chinese jurisdiction, she could likewise feel assured of the same security.

The rejoinder to the French reply, dated September 7, 1929, conveyed approximately the same ideas as those expressed in the second note to the United States of America.

During the course of the negotiation, some appreciable progress was made. Mexico, in a note of November 12, 1929, declared her willingness to accede to the termination of extraterritoriality and not to demand in the future the same privileges.[22] Likewise, on January 27, 1930, Brazil, in reply to the Chinese note of April 27, 1929, declared that she would be prepared, with the collaboration of the other friendly and interested Powers, to enter into negotiations with the Chinese Government for the purpose of reaching a final agreement for the suppression of the privileges of extraterritoriality.[23]

---

[18] Bau, *China and World Peace*, pp. 57–67.
[19] *Week in China*, September 14, 1929.
[20] *Ibid.*
[21] *Ibid.*
[22] *Laws, Regulations and Legal Documents* (Judicial Yuan, 1930), II, 1457.
[23] *Week in China*, March 1, 1930.

THE ABOLITION OF COMMISSIONERS FOR FOREIGN AFFAIRS

Parallel with the attempt to accomplish the abolition of extraterritoriality by January 1, 1930, the Chinese Government made a move in the direction of the administration of matters relating to foreign nationals. Hitherto local authorities appointed commissioners for foreign affairs in the different localities for the management of foreign affairs, and foreign consuls located in the different localities assumed even diplomatic rôles in the negotiation for the settlement of the same. As a measure of centralizing the administration of such affairs and of eliminating the unusual practice of consular diplomacy, the Chinese Government ordered the gradual abolition of the posts of commissioners in the course of the year of 1929 and the centralization of the administration of diplomatic matters in the hands of the Central Government and the delegation of power to the local authorities for the handling of non-diplomatic affairs concerning foreign nationals. Accordingly, on August 12, 1929, it issued a set of regulations concerning foreigners in China, as follows.[24]

1. After the abolition of the posts of commissioners for foreign affairs, all diplomatic issues arising in any district shall be referred to the Central Government for action, and the local government shall not deal directly with the foreign authorities or operate any organ similar in nature to the office of commissioner for foreign affairs.
2. After the abolition of the posts of commissioners for foreign affairs, all affairs pertaining to foreign nationals shall be handled on the same basis as the cases pertaining to the Chinese, unless otherwise specified in mandates or ordinances of the Government.
3. After the abolition of the posts of commissioners for foreign affairs, all non-diplomatic affairs pertaining to foreign nationals — such as establishment of trade and commerce, leasing of land, issuing of deeds, travel permits, passports, naturalization, protection and arrest of foreigners — shall be handled by the special municipality where such a municipality is already in existence, or by the ordinary municipality, or, where the ordinary municipality is not in existence, by the district government. Every municipality, special or ordinary, and every district government, shall assign such affairs, according to their nature, to their respective departments or bureaus for administration.
4. After the abolition of the posts of commissioners for foreign affairs, the authorities in charge of the aforesaid affairs pertaining to foreign nationals, shall immediately turn them over to the Minister of Foreign Affairs, wherever a diplomatic issue arises.
5. Whenever it deems necessary, the Ministry of Foreign Affairs may take the direction of affairs relating to foreign nationals, and managed by the municipality, special or ordinary, or by the district government.
6. After the abolition of the posts of commissioners for foreign affairs, all appeal cases involving Chinese and foreign litigants shall be handed over to the special commissioner for foreign affairs for the province concerned; and, when the latter post is abolished, such cases shall be handed over to the proper courts concerned.
7. After the abolition of the posts of commissioners for foreign affairs, all passports for travelling abroad and passports for persons in the government's diplomatic

[24] *Laws, Regulations and Legal Documents of the National Government at Nanking* (Judicial Yuan, 1930), p. 1459.

service shall be issued by the Ministry of Foreign Affairs alone. Ordinary passports shall be forwarded by the Ministry of Foreign Affairs to the special and ordinary municipality or to the district government to be issued to applicants in accordance with government regulations.

8. After the abolition of the posts of commissioners for foreign affairs is effected, the Ministry of Foreign Affairs shall notify the Ministers of the various Powers to the effect that all diplomatic cases shall be dealt with by the Central Government, and that the foreign consuls stationed in the various cities in China be instructed to inform their respective nationals to approach the competent local authorities concerned in regard to all non-diplomatic affairs.

9. After the abolition of the posts of commissioners for foreign affairs, all competent persons heretofore in the employ of the said offices shall, whenever possible, be retained in government service.

THE MANDATE OF DECEMBER 28, 1929

As a measure to satisfy the Chinese clamor for the early abolition of extraterritoriality, and in pursuance of the date set in the aforesaid five treaties, the Chinese Government issued a mandate on December 28, 1929,[25] terminating extraterritoriality by January 1, 1930; and ordered the Executive Yuan and the Judicial Yuan to prepare as soon as possible a plan for the execution of the mandate to be passed by the Legislative Yuan with a view to promulgation and enforcement. The mandate follows:

In every full sovereign state foreigners as well as its nationals are equally amenable to its laws and to the jurisdiction of its tribunals. This is an essential attribute of state sovereignty and a well established principle of international law. In more than eighty years China has been so shackled by consular jurisdiction that the jurisdictional authority cannot touch foreigners.

Now in order to restore her inherent sovereign jurisdiction, it is hereby decided and declared that on and after the first day of the first month of the nineteenth year of the Republic (January 1, 1930), all foreign nationals in the territory of China now enjoying extraterritorial privileges shall be subject to the laws and ordinances duly promulgated by the central and local government of China.

It is unnecessary here to state the defects and disadvantages of such a system. So long as extraterritoriality is not abolished, so long will China be unable to exercise her full sovereignty.

The Executive Yuan and the Judicial Yuan are hereby ordered to instruct their responsible officers concerned soon to prepare a practicable plan for the execution of this mandate to be submitted to the Legislative Yuan with a view to its promulgation and enforcement.

A subsequent statement, however, issued by the Ministry of Foreign Affairs, December 30, 1929,[26] declared that the actual process of re-establishing Chinese sovereignty by the abolition of extraterritorial rights would begin on January 1, 1930, and that the Chinese Government was prepared to consider and discuss within a reasonable time any representations made with reference to the plan now under preparation in Nanking. It is thus evident that the real purport of the above Mandate is not to effect the termination of

[25] *Laws, Regulations and Legal Documents of the Chinese Government* (Judicial Yuan, 1930), p. 1458.

[26] *Chinese Social and Political Science Review,* April, 1930, Public Documents Suppl., pp. 1–2.

extraterritoriality by January 1, 1930, but to serve as an indication of the earnest desire of China to consummate its abrogation in the very near future and as a gesture for the interested Powers to reach a settlement immediately.

Negotiations were thereafter reopened. Unfortunately, a serious civil war intervened in 1930 between the Central Government and the provinces of the Northwest and the Southwest, which upset and interrupted diplomatic parley. It was not until toward the winter months of 1930 that the Central Government, in co-operation with the Northeastern forces, was able to defeat the opposition and enable the Ministry of Foreign Affairs to resume negotiations.

This time the negotiations were carried on in dead earnest. The Chinese Government was driven to this step, not only because of the apparent necessity of substantiating the Mandate of the previous year, but also because of the imperative urge to be able to present concrete results at the forthcoming convocation of the People's Convention on May 5, 1931. But the negotiations soon reached a deadlock. The leading Powers — the British Empire, the United States of America, France, and Japan — all showed a disinclination to give immediate assent and asked for special arrangements unacceptable to the Chinese Government. The only meager fruit of this strenuous endeavor was the conclusion of two more treaties, one with The Netherlands and the other with Norway, on April 23, 1931, the latter states agreeing to relinquish extraterritoriality as soon as the other Powers should do so.[27]

TERMINATION OF EXTRATERRITORIALITY BY JANUARY 1, 1932

On the eve of the convocation of the People's Convention, driven by the necessity of the occasion, and consistent with the Declaration of December 28, 1929, the Chinese Government, on May 4, 1931,[28] promulgated regulations governing aliens who still enjoyed extraterritorial privileges on December 31, 1929, and subjecting such foreigners to Chinese laws and courts. Two mandates were issued on the same date, one ordering the enforcement of these regulations by January 1, 1932, or, what is the same, the termination of all extraterritorial privileges by that date, and the other commanding all the subordinate organs and units of the Government to put them into effect by the same date.[29]

The Regulations, composed of 12 articles, follow:

1. The term Aliens mentioned in this set of regulations covers specially those who still enjoyed extraterritorial privileges on December 31, 1929.
2. Aliens shall be subject to the jurisdiction of the Chinese courts of the various grades.
3. Special benches for the trial of civil and criminal cases involving aliens as defendant or accused shall be established in the district courts and their related superior courts in the following localities:

[27] The text of these two treaties are yet unpublished (*Week in China*, May 2, 1931).
[28] *Government Bulletin: Chin Fu Kung Pao*, No. 764 (May 5, 1931).
[29] *Ibid.*

1. Special Area of the Northeastern Provinces   6. Hankow
2. Shenyang (Mukden)   7. Pahsien (Chunking)
3. Tientsin   8. Minghau (Foochow)
4. Tsingtao   9. Kuangchow (Canton)
5. Shanghai   10. Quanming (Yunnanfu)

4. The presiding judge of the court in question shall be concurrently the presiding judge of the special bench.

5. Aliens as defendant or accused may submit written petition to have their civil or criminal cases occurring under the jurisdiction of the courts situated outside of the localities mentioned in Article 3 to be subject to the jurisdiction of the courts situated outside of the localities mentioned in Article 3.

6. In these special benches there may be established legal counsellors appointed out of jurists of good moral character and adequate legal training upon the recommendation of the Minister of Justice. Legal counsellors are not restricted only to Chinese nationality. They may by writing present opinions to the respective courts, but shall not interfere in the trial.

7. The arrest and detention of aliens and search of their residences and premises shall be done in accordance with the law of criminal procedure. Aliens arrested on charge of criminal offense shall be handed to the court for inquiry not later than 24 hours after the arrest.

8. Agreements of arbitration entered between aliens or between aliens and other persons, upon the request of one or both parties of the litigation, shall be recognized as valid by court, and the stipulations therein duly enforced by the same; but the presence of one of the following conditions renders such null and void:

   a) Contrariness to public peace and order
   b) Contrariness to good morals and customs
   c) Invalidity as recognizable from the general principles of law

9. Aliens as litigants in civil and criminal cases may, in conformity with law, appoint Chinese or foreign lawyers to be their agents or attorneys. Regulations governing lawyers shall be applicable to foreign lawyers taking charge of such cases.

10. Aliens committing police offenses shall be tried by a court of justice or police tribunal. The police tribunal may impose a fine below 15 *yuan*, excepting in the case of a repeated offense. In case the aforesaid fine is not paid within 5 days after the rendition of judgment, it shall be commuted to detention at the rate of one dollar for one day, any fraction whereof shall be reckoned as one day.

11. The detention houses and prisons for aliens shall be designated by the Minister of Justice.

12. The commencement of the enforcement of these regulations and the duration of their enforcement shall be determined by a Mandate of the National Government.

The *modus vivendi* as set forth in the above regulations provides for special benches in the district courts and their related superior courts in the ten centers of foreign residence and trade. The jurisdiction of these special benches shall cover all civil and criminal cases involving aliens as defendant or accused. The judges shall be specially selected and appointed by the Ministry of Justice, the presiding judge of the court to be concurrently the presiding judge of the special bench. Legal counsellors are to be attached to these special benches whose appointment is not confined to the Chinese. Subject to the Chinese laws and regulations, foreign lawyers may practice in these special benches as agents or attorneys of foreign litigants. The Writ of

Habeas Corpus is provided, inasmuch as aliens arrested on charge of criminal offense shall be handed over to the court for inquiry within 24 hours after the arrest. The authority of the police tribunal is restricted to the imposition of fine not exceeding 15 *yuan,* or, in lieu of fine, detention at the rate of one *yuan* for one day. Agreements of arbitration, upon the request of one or both parties to the case, are to be recognized as valid and to be duly enforced.

Thus, all extraterritorial aliens are to be subject to the jurisdiction of Chinese laws and courts on and after January 1, 1932. And out of the sixteen Powers still enjoying extraterritoriality, seven powers, namely, Belgium, Italy, Denmark, Portugal, Spain, Norway, and The Netherlands, have already concluded treaties relinquishing extraterritoriality, and two Powers, e.g., Mexico and Brazil, have signified their approval of its abrogation; and there are yet left only seven Powers — the United States of America, the British Empire, France, Japan, Peru, Sweden, and Switzerland — that are to be brought into line with the Chinese movement for the abolition of extraterritoriality.

STATUS OF ALIENS UNDER TREATY STIPULATIONS

Now we shall turn to the status of aliens under the treaty stipulations other than those having bearing on extraterritoriality.

Extraterritorial aliens are confined to ports opened by treaties known as treaty ports and those voluntarily opened by China, called open ports. There are now altogether 71 treaty ports and 23 open ports.[30] In the treaty ports and their immediate vicinities, extraterritorial aliens enjoy the right of residence, trade, industry, manufacture, and pursuit of any lawful avocation, and, for these purposes may rent or buy houses, lease land, and construct buildings, warehouses, churches, hospitals, and cemeteries.[31] In the open ports, they enjoy practically the same aforesaid rights and privileges as in the treaty ports. In the interior of China, they can travel for pleasure or business only under passports issued by their consuls and countersigned by the Chinese local authorities.

In addition, they enjoy the protection of trade-marks against infringement or imitation.[32] In pursuance of the treaties for reciprocal protection of trade-marks, they shall, in accordance with Chinese law, enter application for exclusive use, accompanied by certificates of nationality.[33] The privilege of the exclusive use of trade-marks is to last for a period of 20 years from the date of registration, subject to renewal upon petition, and each grant to last only for 20 years.

[30] List of treaty and open ports furnished at the request of the American Legation in Peking by the Ministry of Foreign Affairs (MacMurray, II, 1507).

[31] Treaty of Tientsin between Great Britain and China, June 26, 1858 (Hertslet, No. 6, p. 23); Treaty of Peace between China and Japan, April 17, 1895 (MacMurray, 1895/3); Treaty of Commerce and Navigation, July 21, 1896 (MacMurray, 1896/4).

[32] Treaty between Great Britain and China, September 5, 1902 (Hertslet, No. 28, Art. VII); Treaty between China and the United States, October 8, 1903 (MacMurray, 1903/5); Treaty between Japan and China, October 8, 1903 (MacMurray, 1903/4).

[33] Article 21, Ordinances Governing the Application of Trade-Mark Law (*Trade-Mark Law promulgated,* May 5, 1930; published by the Bureau of Trade-Marks).

They also enjoy the protection of copyrights duly registered in conformity with Chinese regulations, on the books, pamphlets, maps, and charts, etc., specially prepared for use in the education of the Chinese people, or written in the Chinese language, or translations into Chinese of any book. In accordance with the Chinese Copyright Law, they shall apply for registration of copyright. This right shall be limited to the nationals of those states which extend protection of copyright to the Chinese living in their territory. The copyright so granted shall last for a period of 10 years from the date of registration.[34]

In South Manchuria, instead of being confined to the treaty and open ports, Japanese subjects possess the rights of travel, trade, and manufacture in all parts of that region.[35] They may also lease land, by negotiation, necessary for erecting suitable buildings for trade and manufacture and for prosecuting agricultural enterprises, for a period not more than 30 years, subject to the possibility of unconditional renewal.

STATUS OF MISSIONARIES

The missionaries of the extraterritorial Powers enjoy the same rights as the other extraterritorial aliens. In addition to religious toleration and peaceful proselytization,[36] they enjoy the added right denied to the other extraterritorial aliens: that is, they may reside and undertake missionary enterprise in the interior of China, rent or purchase land, and erect buildings thereon for use as residences, hospitals, schools, churches, etc. The said property, however, shall be held in trust by the Chinese members of the local church or mission, and the ground still remains Chinese soil.[37]

The provisional regulations, regulating foreign missions in renting or leasing land in the interior of China,[38] permit foreign missions, under the authority of the treaties made between China and these states, and subject to the Chinese laws and taxes now in force or to be made or levied in future, only to establish churches, hospitals or schools in the interior of China and to rent or purchase houses. They shall register their title deeds at the local government. Subject to the control and nullification of the local government, they shall not acquire premises or land beyond the necessity of their undertakings, nor utilize their property for commercial or profit-making enterprises. Purchases of land are forbidden, and those made before enforcement of these regulations shall be regarded as leases in perpetuity.

The lease contract shall contain the following four provisions:

[34] Ordinances regulating the application of Copyright Law, promulgated May 10, 1928 (*Laws, Regulations and Legal Documents of the National Government at Nanking* [Judicial Yuan], pp. 1179–80).

[35] Treaty respecting South Manchuria and Eastern Inner Mongolia, May 25, 1915, Art. 3 (MacMurray, 1915/8).

[36] The Sino-American Treaty, June 18, 1858, Art. XXIX (Hertslet, I, 551).

[37] The Sino-French Agreement, February, 1865 (Hertslet, I, 320).

[38] Promulgated June 1, 1928 (*Laws, Regulations and Legal Documents* [Judicial Yuan], p. 1460).

1. Period of the lease
2. Boundaries and size of the land, or dimensions and form of the house
3. Use of land or house within the sphere of missionary enterprises
4. The nationality of the mission [39]

STATUS OF NON-EXTRATERRITORIAL ALIENS

The non-extraterritorial aliens of the treaty Powers enjoy still greater rights and privileges. In respect of travel, residence, trade, industry, and manufacture, they are not confined to the treaty and open ports, but are permitted, subject to the laws and courts of China, to undertake these activities in all localities where the nationals of any other country shall be permitted, and in the same manner and under the same conditions as the nationals of any other country. They enjoy an additional right — the right of acquiring property, including ownership of land. It is definitely stated, as we have seen, in the five treaties, concluded between China on the one hand, and Belgium, Italy, Denmark, Portugal, and Spain, on the other, in November and December of 1928, that the aliens of these states, upon relinquishment of extraterritoriality and when the relationship between the two countries is on a footing of perfect equality, shall enjoy the right to live and trade and acquire property in any part of China, subject always to the limitations to be prescribed in her laws and regulations. Again, in the Treaty of Amity and Commerce between the Republic of China and the Czechoslovak Republic, February 12, 1930, which may be taken as sample or model for all the treaties concluded or to be concluded between China and the other non-treaty Powers, it is likewise stipulated:

The Nationals of each of the High Contracting Parties — shall have the right, subject to the laws and regulations of the country, to travel, reside, establish firms, acquire or lease property, work and engage in industry or commerce in all the localities where the nationals of any other country shall be permitted to do so and in the same manner and under the same conditions as the nationals of any other country.[40]

II. JAPANESE SUBJECTS IN MANCHURIA

a) A CHINESE VIEW [41]

By SHUHSI HSU

Along the Korean border large numbers of Koreans, especially in the *hsiens* of Yenchi, Holung, and Wanching on the Tumen River, have been found since long before the days of the Russo-Japanese War when Japan first secured a foothold in Manchuria. In 1909 by the agreement relating to the Tumen boundary signed on September 4th, so far as the Koreans in that region were concerned, their residence " on agricultural lands " was recog-

---

[39] *Statutes Compiled and Published by Legislative Yuan*, II, 173–74.

[40] Copy of the Text of the Treaty, published by the Chinese Ministry of Foreign Affairs, 1930.

[41] From *Questions Relating to Manchuria*, pp. 19–25.

nized by China. As to the country beyond the frontier belt, the residence of Koreans and, in this case, also of Japanese seems to have mainly begun only since 1915 when " Japanese subjects " were permitted by the treaty concluded under the terms of the Twenty-one Demands to travel and reside in South Manchuria with a right to lease land " by negotiation," and to engage in joint agricultural enterprise in Eastern Inner Mongolia with " Chinese subjects." As matters stand, inland Japanese subjects are found as in the regional distribution shown in Table I.

TABLE I

	Japanese	Koreans	Total
The Tumen region..........	392	361,294	361,686
South Manchuria...........	567	137,975	138,542
Eastern Inner Mongolia.....	501	3,894	4,395
North Manchuria...........	731	38,205	38,936
Total..................	2,191	541,368	543,559

In the table two points stand out very prominently, one being that of the Japanese subjects in the interior of Manchuria 99 3/5 per cent are Koreans, and the other, that, of these Koreans, more than two-thirds are found in the four-*hsien* Tumen region.

Japanese subjects found in the interior of Manchuria would not necessarily have constituted a problem, had it not been for the following complications:

A. INLAND CONSULAR JURISDICTION

As stipulated in the agreement of 1909, the Koreans, whose residence " on agricultural lands lying north of the River Tumen " China recognizes, are to be under Chinese jurisdiction, but Japan may have observers from her consulates there present in all court proceedings concerning them with power to apply for new trial.

According to the treaty of 1915 the Japanese subjects permitted by the same to be in the interior of South Manchuria and Eastern Inner Mongolia are subject to —

a) Local jurisdiction in matters of police and taxation;

b) Consular jurisdiction in mixed civil and criminal cases other than mixed civil cases relating to land; and

c) Joint jurisdiction in mixed civil cases relating to land.

Since 1915 Japan has extended against Chinese protest the kind of consular jurisdiction as provided for in the treaty relating to South Manchuria and Eastern Inner Mongolia, evidently by interpreting the term South Manchuria to include the Tumen region.

B. CONSULAR POLICE

In 1917, under the cover of the Chengchiatun Incident, police was first introduced by Japan against Chinese protest into the consulates along the

South Manchurian Railway. In 1920, under the cover of the Hungchun Incident, similar steps were taken with reference to the Tumen region. The ground that has been advanced to justify such a measure has been that consular police is but a " corollary of the right of extraterritoriality." In these cases, it may be added, Japan has gone beyond even the provisions relating to the matter in the treaty concluded under the terms of the Twenty-one Demands. As matters stand, there are —

a) Six police headquarters in the vicinity of the South Manchuria Railway, one at the consulate-general at Mukden and one each at the consulates of Yingkow, Liaoyang, Tiehling, Changchun and Antung, with thirty-eight stations and substations at various points and a total force of some 222 officers and men;

b) Five police headquarters in the Tumen region, one at the consulate-general at Lungchingtsun and one each at the subconsulates of Chutzuchia, Taotaokou, Paitsaokou, and Hungchun. with thirteen stations and substations at various points, and a total force of some 420 officers and men.

C. KOREAN ALLEGIANCE

In addition to the exercise of consular jurisdiction and the extension of police protection over Japanese subjects in the interior of Manchuria, Japan also maintains, so far as the Koreans are concerned, the principle of indelible allegiance, and refuses to recognize their naturalization as Chinese citizens. This later measure has made the question of inland Japanese subjects doubly serious, especially with reference to the Tumen region where the Koreans form the major part of the population.

Unlike Port Arthur and Talienwan and the South Manchuria Railway the question of Japanese subjects in the interior is one toward the solution of which local authorities could make their contribution, and ever since the problem became serious in recent years with the influx of Koreans for the cultivation of paddy fields, the governments of the provinces most affected have not failed to take the matter into their hands. The policies that have been adopted for " the interior " outside of the frontier zone and " the interior " of the frontier zone are different, evidently on account of a practical situation. While Koreans are permitted to reside in the latter region, they are required to become naturalized as Chinese citizens if they choose to remain in the former.

The Chinese people earnestly hope that Japan will cease (a) to claim the allegiance of Koreans naturalized as Chinese citizens in accordance with the laws of China, (b) to excercise consular jurisdiction over Japanese subjects, found in the interior, and (c) to maintain police at the consulates in Manchuria.

The importance of the question of Japanese subjects in Manchuria scarcely needs emphasis. In the interior of this group of Chinese provinces there are 543,559 aliens, of which 541,368 are presumably to remain permanently aliens, while these together with the remaining 2,191 are under an alien jurisdiction and are protected directly by an alien police force maintained in the consulates and indirectly by an alien army that has garrison points spreading from the coast to the heart of the country, which in time of emergency does not have even to cross a frontier to appear on the scene of activity; and these 543,559 aliens are yet to be reinforced by births as well as by newcomers who have such an easy access to the country as provided by hundreds of miles of a common Sino-Korean frontier and scores of points along the South Manchuria Railway. One needs but to imagine for oneself what the question may mean to China!

Yet is it necessary for Japan to keep the question alive? Japan, of course, does not claim jurisdiction over her emigrants to other countries, and still less sends police after them for their protection. As to their allegiance, Article XX of her nationality law of 1899, as revised in 1916 and 1924, says:

1. A person who acquires foreign nationality voluntarily loses Japanese nationality.
2. A Japanese who, by reason of having been born in a foreign country designated by Imperial Ordinance (i.e., any of the following: The United States of America, Argentina, Brazil, Canada, Chile, and Peru), has acquired the nationality of that country, and who does not as laid down by order express his intention of retaining Japanese nationality, loses his Japanese nationality retroactively from his birth.
Persons who have retained Japanese nationality in accordance with the provisions of the preceding paragraph, or Japanese subjects who, by reason of having been born in a designated foreign country before its designation in accordance with the provisions of the preceding paragraph, have acquired nationality of that country, may, when they are in possession of the nationality of the country concerned and in possession of a domicile in that country, renounce Japanese nationality if they desire to do so.
Persons who shall have renounced their nationality in accordance with the provisions of the preceding paragraph lose Japanese nationality.
3. Japanese subjects who, by reason of having been born in a foreign country other than the foreign countries indicated in paragraph 1 of the preceding article, have acquired the nationality of that country, may, when they possess a domicile in that country, effect renunciation of Japanese nationality by obtaining the sanction of the Minister of the Interior.
The provisions of paragraph 3 of the preceding article shall apply, *mutatis mutandis,* to persons who shall have renounced nationality in accordance with the provisions of the preceding paragraph.

The foregoing provisions are as liberal as can be. Now if Japan does not wish to create a problem for other countries with her emigrants, it is difficult to see why she should adopt a different attitude with reference to China.

If Japan were prepared to help solving the problem, it would cost her very little. In the first place, she needs only to give up the claim to the allegiance of her emigrated subjects, which claim is at best very shadowy by comparison with the conflicting claim of the country of their adoption. In the second place, she needs only not to insist upon the right she acquires under the terms of the Twenty-one Demands, nor to give an extended interpretation to the right of extraterritoriality. If it is admitted that the latter right should no more be maintained for aliens who sojourn in China for the purposes of trade and the propagation of Christianity, how much less should an extended interpretation of it be allowed to rule with reference to aliens who migrate to China to stay?   As to the right acquired under the terms of the Twenty-one Demands, it may be assumed that the Japanese people will insist upon it in this case no more than in the cases of Port Arthur and Talienwan and of the South Manchuria Railway.   Apart from the unfortunate circumstances under which the Demands were imposed, the terms with regard to Japanese subjects in the interior of Manchuria are so fundamentally in conflict with the independence of China that no people with some respect for a fellow nation ought to bear seeing them continued in force.

b) A JAPANESE VIEW [42]

By JUMPEI SHINOBU

One of the difficulties encountered by the Koreans in Manchuria is the divergence of the naturalization laws of China and Japan.   The Chinese Law of Nationality, promulgated on February 5, 1929, was drafted almost on the same lines as the nationality law of Japan, by adopting the principle of *jus sanguinis* instead of *jus soli* — that is to say, the principle by which the descent or blood is to be taken as the decisive factor in determining a person's nationality, without considering the soil on which his birth has taken place.   The conditions required for naturalization provided in the Chinese and Japanese laws of nationality are in the main the same, but with the exception, among others, that the Chinese law lacks the requirement provided for in the Japanese law, that one who acquires the new nationality should *de jure* lose his original nationality.   Under the Japanese law, a Japanese subject on acquiring by choice a foreign nationality loses his original nationality as a Japanese (Art. 20).   The Japanese law also provides that no permission of naturalization to Japan shall be given to a foreigner who, by acquiring Japanese nationality, would not *de jure* lose his original nationality.   The Chinese Law of Nationality lacks such a requirement.   Consequently, when a Korean naturalizes, legally in accordance with the Chinese law but unofficially in the light of the Japanese law — unofficially, because the Japanese Law of Nationality does not so far apply to Korea, and therefore a Korean is not permitted to become a Chinese citizen from the point of view of the Japanese law — he has a double nationality, both Chinese and Japanese. This fact of double nationality is unavoidable in so far as there exists a divergence between the laws of the two countries.

The question may be asked why the Japanese Law of Nationality is not applied to Korea.   I am not in a position to give an official explanation; but apparently there are at least three reasons: First, there are quite a number of insubordinate Koreans in the Chien-tao district.   If they were allowed

[42] Summary of a statement made in round-table discussion, corrected by the author.

to naturalize officially to China, or in other words if they were to lose Japanese nationality, supervision and control over them would be out of reach of the Japanese authorities. Second, there may be some anxiety on the part of the Japanese Government on the ground that Koreans naturalized to China might not enjoy the same protection of life and property on the part of the Chinese authorities that is afforded to Chinese citizens.

The Sino-Japanese Agreement of 1909, relating to the Chien-tao region, provides that such Korean subjects shall be accorded by the Chinese authorities equal treatment with Chinese subjects; and, similarly, that in the matter of taxation and all other administrative measures, they shall be placed on an equal footing with Chinese subjects. But experience since that time has shown that the Koreans have been treated most unequally. I am not going to cite cases though they are numerous. So there is doubt, seemingly, on the part of the Japanese Government whether it would be advisable, for the present, to permit the naturalization of Koreans to China.

And, as a third reason, there is uncertainty as to the policy of China in regard to the naturalization of Korean residents. Apparently, there was a time when China encouraged their naturalization in more or less degree, in order to develop the cultivation of paddy-fields in Manchuria — a rather weak point with the Chinese farmers in that region, while the Koreans have a high reputation for it. But recently the Chinese authorities seem to have changed their opinion and are no longer welcoming the naturalization of Koreans, alleging that these immigrants are forerunners of an aggressive policy on the part of Japan in Manchuria.

To illustrate this last point, let me cite here a few official ordinances issued by the Chinese authorities in Manchuria, taken from among numerous similar ordinances and instructions, secret as well as published:

Japan, by making the Koreans forerunners of their encroachment upon the Four Eastern Provinces, and by instigating them to seize every opportunity to come into collision with us, is trying to fish in troubled waters. The Wanpaoshan affair which has cost us a great loss of lives and property is one of the results. Though this incident and others took place at the instance of Koreans, their author in every case was the Japanese who took a leap in the dark. In order henceforth to root out such evils coming from Japan, nothing is more urgently needed than to begin with the expulsion of the Koreans. For the purpose of eradicating these evils, therefore, all contracts actually existing between Chinese and Koreans as to joint undertakings for the cultivation of paddy-fields, as to hiring Koreans or renting houses to them, shall be considered cancelled by the end of this year, so that the Koreans cannot but leave the province. Police authorities of every district are hereby instructed to bring this to the full knowledge to the chiefs of the police substations as well as to the inhabitants under their respective jurisdiction.[43]

A police ordinance reads:

1. All Koreans residing in the district under your jurisdiction shall be subjected to every possible pressure to cause them to leave immediately.

[43] Ordinance of the Mukden Government to the police authorities under its jurisdiction, July 11, 1931.

2. Any Koreans who go about the district under your jurisdiction shall be arrested as insubordinates.

3. Any Chinese who sells lands, paddy-fields, or other property to Koreans or allows them to engage in such enterprises shall be heavily punished.

4. Since the development of the recent disturbances in Korea, through which a large number of Chinese lost their lives, was the result of tacit permission on the part of the Japanese authorities, you are instructed to cause the local communities to make the utmost efforts in anti-Japanese agitation.[44]

An ordinance of the Kirin Government to the police authorities reads:

When men under your command meet a Japanese supposed detective, they are empowered to kill him under a pretext of self-defense.[45]

The fundamental difficulty of Manchurian problems rests on the complexity or interweaving of *de jure* treaty rights with *de facto* situations. It is an admitted fact that Japan has several special rights in Manchuria. A special right may be defined as a right enjoyed by a particular foreign nation under a particular treaty with a given country, in view of particular international relations, economic, strategic, or historical. It is in principle a *de jure* treaty right, but it is not infrequently a *de facto* right, not based on a specified treaty but on a so-called *fait accompli*. Thus a special right is an antithesis of a general or common right enjoyed not only by a particular nation but by all foreign nations, either directly under their treaties with a given country or indirectly by virtue of the Most Favored Nation Clause. Generally speaking, the purpose of creating a special right is that of preserving and consolidating the vital concern, or interest, which a country has in relation to a particular territory of another country wherein that right is to be created.

That Japan has vital concerns in her relations with Manchuria is beyond question. Those concerns were, a score of years ago, mainly strategic — in her defensive position against a possibly recurrent aggression on the part of Russia. They were rather negative in character. Since then, with an increasing economic necessity demanded by Japan's national livelihood, her interests have become of a more positive character. As Manchuria is a region in which Japan has vital concerns, she has created there various special rights, in order to preserve and consolidate her relations with that region. It should be noted that some of them are not special rights in the strict sense of that term, because other nations enjoying the Most Favored Nation treatment under their treaties with China are legally entitled to enjoy the same rights as Japan; but they may be considered special rights in the assumption that practically other nations are not likely to exercise these rights to the same extent as the Japanese. For instance, it is inconceivable that Americans or Europeans would want to come and engage in agriculture in Eastern Inner Mongolia; so practically such may be considered as Japan's special right.

[44] Police ordinance of Fuchon District (Liaoning Province), July 11, 1931.

[45] Ordinance of the Kirin Government to the police authorities under its jurisdiction, dated August 9, 1930.

I cannot here enumerate the details of Japan's special rights in Manchuria but would point out that at least one-half of them are today practically dead letters, owing to the non-fulfillment of treaty obligations on the part of China. Some Japanese rights lack any legal basis; but legal basis is not the only element in the creation of special rights. The necessity of having Japanese policemen in Manchuria is as yet beyond dispute. The Chinese police force in Manchuria has no discipline, and its standards lack the confidence of foreigners.

QUESTIONS FOR ROUND–TABLE DISCUSSION

The following questions were recommended by the Program Committee as an outline for discussion:

STATUS AND PROPERTY RIGHTS OF ALIENS IN CHINA

1. What are the obligations of a state under international law to protect resident aliens? By what means are these obligations usually fulfilled?
2. Is China's fulfilment of such obligations rendered more difficult by
   a) The dispersion of authority between regional governments?
   b) Treaty commitments exempting foreigners of certain treaty powers from Chinese jurisdiction?
3. What extraterritorial privileges are claimed by foreign powers in China?
4. If extraterritorial privileges are relinquished, to what judicial organization will foreign residents become subject? What progress has been made in the provision of modern courts and prisons? In the completion of legal codes? In establishing the independence of the judiciary? In extending the effective control of the regularly constituted law courts over all sections of the population, including the military forces, and in preventing the exercise of arbitrary authority by irresponsible or self-appointed bodies?
5. What has been the experience of foreigners not possessed of extraterritorial privileges as defendants in Chinese courts?
6. What bearing have recent missionary experiences upon
   a) The relinquishment of special missionary privileges?
   b) The question of extraterritoriality generally?
7. What in general are the property rights in which an alien may expect to be protected by a modern state?
8. In what main respects do the property rights held by foreigners in China go beyond those commonly granted by states, in
   a) Nature and extent?
   b) Manner of acquisition?
   c) Measures taken by foreign states for their protection?
9. Does China limit the rights usually given to foreigners?
10. What facilities does China possess for protecting the property rights of foreigners and how effectively are they being exercised?
11. What is the effect of the existence of foreign property rights, and of the measures taken by foreigners to protect them, upon:
    a) The economic development of China?
    b) The political development of China?
12. What solutions can be proposed of the problems arising from the foregoing questions?

LEASES, CONCESSIONS, AND SETTLEMENTS

1. What light does the recent working of the restored Chinese Court at Shanghai throw upon the general problem of extraterritoriality?

SUMMARY OF ROUND–TABLE DISCUSSIONS

Partly owing to the fact that questions dealing strictly with the subject of extraterritoriality had been placed by the Program Committee on the same agenda as questions dealing with other aspects of China's foreign relations, the round tables in some instances departed rather widely from the limited scope indicated by the announced subject. But the diversity of the ground covered by the four round tables is explained in part also by a conflict in definitions. Some members desired to discuss extraterritoriality in the precise, legal meaning of the term — the exemption of foreigners from the jurisdiction of the courts of the country where they are domiciled; others, less correctly but perhaps more realistically, regarded this particular form of privilege as inseparable, for practical purposes, from other forms of foreign privilege with which, in China, it has become closely bound. The *Syllabus on China's Foreign Relations* before the Conference contained no separate section on extraterritoriality but referred to phases of that subject under other headings.

In addition to one data paper summarizing the recent history of extraterritoriality from an American point of view, a series of data papers on " The Status of Aliens " — in Australia, Canada, China, Great Britain, Japan, New Zealand, and the United States — provided ample comparative material. One of them, that by Mr. Bau, deals in its entirety with the subject of this chapter and has here been reproduced in part (pp. 270–82). Materials provided at the preceding Conference [46] were utilized rather fully to provide a background of information and proposal. The round tables in 1931, therefore, were in the main continuations of those held in 1929 and largely confined themselves to the more recent developments of extraterritoriality in China and the case for and against its speedy abolition, taking into account the newer negotiations betweeen China and the foreign powers. The general principle of abolition could be taken as agreed; but it was desirable to review some of the difficulties in the way of its early consummation and to examine proffered suggestions for graduation of the process.

For purposes of discussion, the following definition given by Dr. Bau was adopted:

> By extraterritoriality is meant the special privilege of exemption from the operation of the territorial law and tribunal. While in international law it is a fundamental principle that the territorial sovereign exercises supreme power over all the people, nationals or aliens, living within the limits of the territory, the grant of this special privilege nevertheless limits or impairs the supreme power of the territorial sovereign to the extent that aliens enjoying the privilege are exempt from the jurisdiction of his law and tribunals; and it confers upon the privileged states the right to extend their jurisdiction over the realm of another state and to exercise, on behalf of the territorial sovereign, jurisdiction of their own law over their nationals through their own consular and diplomatic offices or through the establishment of consular and other extraterritorial courts.[47]

Under existing treaty provisions, the larger foreign communities in China are exempt, in the main, from Chinese jurisdiction in Chinese courts and can take their Chinese employees out of the jurisdiction of these courts. Civil cases between Chinese and nationals of treaty powers are determined by the tribunals and the laws of the defendant's country. Those between nationals of treaty powers and other foreigners when the former are the defendants are

---

[46] *Problems of the Pacific, 1929.*
[47] Mingchien Joshua Bau, *The Status of Aliens in China*, p. 2.

determined by the former's courts, and by Chinese courts when the latter are defendants.   In criminal cases the Chinese police may arrest a foreigner who is national of a treaty power but must promptly turn him over to a court (i.e., usually the consular court) of his own country for trial.

Mr. Bau's paper gives the main lines of recent negotiations for the abolition of these rights of aliens.   There is no longer any doubt in the minds of impartial students of the subject that in principle their continuation is in conflict with the dignity of a sovereign state that desires to enter into world-relations on a basis of equality and mutuality of obligations.   But in practice the abandonment of these rights is made difficult by the fact that institutions, vested interests, and attitudes have grown up under their influence.   Hence the conviction on the part of nationals who enjoy these privileges that such abandonment must be gradual and under special safeguards.   This view was taken in the present Conference, particularly by British and Japanese members with special knowledge of the business situations and personal relationships that would be affected by the relinquishment of these rights.   On the other hand, the need for their continuance was not admitted by many students of the matter who have observed the ill effects of extraterritoriality upon both the domestic problems and the foreign relations of the Chinese Government. These also were well represented in the round tables.   The discussion, then, hinged largely upon the actual conditions in China today that must affect judgments as to the desirability of an early abolition of extraterritoriality.

I. PRESENT CONDITIONS

PERSONAL SAFETY

Before giving up special protection of their nationals, the treaty powers are requiring evidence that their personal safety would be equally assured if they were subject to Chinese jurisdiction.   There was considerable discussion of the question whether these powers, in their negotiations with the Chinese Government, did not insist upon guaranties far in excess of those granted to aliens in other sovereign states.   A Japanese member gave the following brief account of the general legal situation in this respect:

" Under international law and usage, the obligation to protect resident aliens who are traveling in the country or engaging in lawful pursuits, and who are not preaching doctrines detrimental to national peace and order, is almost universally recognized.   The rights of resident aliens, and their corresponding obligation to respect the laws of the state in which they reside, are usually guaranteed in commercial treaties between the countries concerned.   Furthermore, the state in which aliens reside has the obligation of granting them a protection before the law as regards safety of person and of property, at least equal to that granted to nationals. Even where there is corrupt administration of the law against nationals, such condition is not accepted as an excuse for a similar administration of the law against aliens.   These obligations are fulfilled by means of municipal laws for that purpose, by instructions to the officials concerned, and in other ways.

" While aliens stand under the territorial jurisdiction of the state in which they reside — in other words, while that state has the right as well as the obligation to protect them — their home state also holds a right to protect them, and can exercise that right when any of its citizens abroad are injured by an organ of the state in which they reside or by its citizens. The exercise of this right is accentuated when aliens have extraterritorial privileges in the state where they reside. But even without them, this right can be exercised in various ways — such as diplomatic insistence that the wrongdoers be punished in accordance with the law of the land, or upon damages being paid to the injured persons; or it may take the form of reprisals to make the other state comply with the demands of the complainant state. The use of any of these means depends upon the merits of the particular case; and it is impossible to lay down hard-and-fast rules concerning it. The principle is that state responsibility arises when, contrary to the state's obligation of protecting resident aliens, an injury is committed against an alien, either maliciously or through culpable negligence. Which of the state organs should bear the responsibility and how far that responsibility goes also depend upon the nature of the particular case."

It was brought out at another round table that treaties for the protection of aliens are superior to the laws of states which frequently, in specific cases, had been declared invalid in international law. But with such general interpretations as these which seemed to invite uncertainty as to the actual nature of mutual international obligations in the protection of alien residents, there was considerable dissatisfaction.[48] They suggested as permissible, according to some members of the round tables, the exercise of undue pressure by powerful against weaker states, and the pursuit of political advantages in the form of claims for redress of individual grievances. They contended that the exercise of a state's right to protect its citizens when these reside or travel in a foreign country must necessarily be influenced by the relative safety of all residents in that country, that is by the relative strength of the government. Thus, a European power would be justified in expecting not only full compliance with her obligations but even generosity on the part of such a country as the United States in compensating for injuries suffered by a foreign resident at the hand of citizens of that country, even though it might not be possible to prove actual negligence of the authorities in their duty to protect him. (An actual incident of this kind was quoted in several round tables.) On the other hand, governments did not normally expect a country with unsettled conditions to provide more protection for its foreign residents than it was able to provide for its own citizens. For example, no such demands had been made by the foreign powers upon the Republican Government of Germany during the period of disorder and reorganization after the armistice. Against this contention, it was pointed out that China, not only in her older treaties but also in more recent declarations, had recognized the correlation between special protective rights of the treaty powers over their citizens resident in China

[48] The International Research Committee of the Institute, at a later meeting, decided to make the various national studies as to the legal status of aliens in Pacific countries the basis of a comparative study, taking account also of differences in legal traditions and in the actual social and political conditions that affect the status of aliens in the various countries (see p. 415). Since the material obtained toward such a comprehensive survey, in the form of data papers contributed to the present Conference, is thus likely to be used in the preparation of a separate publication, these papers (listed on p. 412) are not reproduced in this volume.

and the limitations imposed upon their status and freedom of movement under existing agreements.[49]   Implied recognition was also seen in the military protection often given foreign travelers by Chinese authorities in regions where the regular police force does not suffice to insure their safety.   Nevertheless, such special protection, it was admitted, might also be interpreted with practical and political motives apart from a theoretical acceptance of an international obligation to treat aliens better in this matter than citizens. Certain South American states, as well as China, it was said, had definitely rejected any obligation to accept an international standard in the measures adopted to protect foreigners.   Nevertheless, China had, through Article XVIII of the Treaty of Tientsin, accepted such obligation in regard to citizens of all countries to which the Most Favored Nation Clause applies.   Its case for a limitation of that responsibility, a Chinese jurist declared, rests upon the interference with the normal functioning of a state's protective organs by the extralegal measures which certain treaty powers were taking on behalf of their citizens resident in China.   This contention, also made by others, in one round table led to a spirited discussion of Japan's activities on behalf of its Korean subjects in Manchuria.

THE CASE OF JAPANESE SUBJECTS IN MANCHURIA

The chairman suggested that extraterritoriality has a different significance in Manchuria from that which it has in other parts of China because the legal right of foreigners to separate jurisdiction is complicated here by the exigencies of two great economic enterprises, the South Manchuria Railway and the development of a rich agricultural area with the aid of immigrants.   It was admitted that, lacking objective factual studies, neither Chinese nor Japanese understood all the problems in human relations and the functioning of law in this area.   After a Japanese member had broadly outlined the major phases of the legal situation in regard to the status and treatment of Koreans in Southern Manchuria,[50] the question was raised how the special provisions made by Japan for the protection of her nationals in Manchuria compared with those made either by Japan or by other powers in other parts of the Chinese territory where large numbers of their nationals reside.   It appeared that, consistent in her policy, Japan is maintaining a consular police force in Amoy, where there are some ten thousand Japanese — but with this difference that the arrangement for the protection of Japanese nationals there has the consent of the Chinese authorities, whereas the Japanese police force in Manchuria (outside the railway zone) does not have, and never has had, the consent of the Chinese.   The system in both places did not, it was stated, work in the same way: in Manchuria, the Japanese were employing, apart from the policing of the South Manchuria Railway, an extensive police force, subject to their consular court, nominally employed to deal with Japanese offenders but actually often assuming police functions over Chinese as well as

49 Charles P. Howland, *Survey of American Foreign Relations*, p. 183.
50 For Mr. Shinobu's statement see pp. 286–89.

foreign citizens.   Thus a case was cited in which a Chinese had been arrested by the Japanese police in his home, thirty li from the railway zone.   Such incidents, according to Japanese spokesmen, often arose, under an arrangement with Chinese officials, when a speedy arrest can best be secured through immediate apprehension by the Japanese police.   As a rule, such prisoners are at once handed over to the Chinese police.   But it was admitted that errors sometimes arise, usually through excessive zeal on the part of Japanese guards; and that there might have been even worse cases, as alleged, in which Japanese police officers mishandled Chinese prisoners instead of handing them over to the proper authority.   The number of unfortunate incidents and disputes, it was agreed, clearly showed that recourse to diplomatic negotiation could not insure speedy justice.

It was also stated that, even before the occupation of Mukden, on September 18, Japanese police were frequently stationed outside the railway zone which they had a right to protect.   There was a difference of opinion as to whether Japanese police stations located in consulates near the South Manchuria Railway [51] are strictly in accordance with treaty rights, particularly when, as is often the case, they have numerous substations outside a Japanese settlement or concession.   In this matter, Japanese assumption of *de facto* authority was unfavorably compared with the stricter observance of their extraterritorial rights on the part of other treaty powers in various parts of China.   An explanation for this was seen in the difference between the actual conditions within which protection must be provided for foreign residents.   But another explanation given was that Japan in its police measures in Manchuria was moved less by a desire to protect its Korean subjects than by a desire to prevent these from using Manchuria as a center of agitation against Japan.

There thus appeared to be a triangular situation, perhaps unique in the world: First, the Koreans, for the most part simple peasants with no other desire than to profit from opportunities of making a living better than those they could enjoy at home; but among them rebellious elements who hoped, by becoming Chinese citizens, to escape their subjection to Japanese authority but had failed in this because of Japan's refusal to accede that right to them.   Second, the Chinese inhabitants, also composed of two groups — the one a simple farmer class, resenting what seems to them an encroachment of immigrant farmers upon their land and markets; [52] the other, more politically motivated, opposing this immigration movement from the fear that it was part

[51] Hsu, *op. cit.*   See pp. 283–84 of this volume.

[52] Study of the Wanpaoshan incident from such information as is available shows a striking resemblance between Korean immigrant experiences and those of Japanese immigrants in California twenty years ago.   The development of popular opinion toward the new settlers, in both cases, followed the same line; and the form taken by the local residents' resentment of immigrant competition for land was almost identical.   In both cases, the fact that these immigrants could not be naturalized and thus become absorbed in the general population had the same effect of sharpening what otherwise would have remained an economic and social conflict into a political one.

of the strategy of Japanese aggression upon Chinese sovereignty. Third, the Japanese, exasperated by barriers to the establishment of an orderly development of their economic interests, and apprehensive of dangers to their treaty rights upon which rest, not only heavy financial and human investments, but also the country's larger policies — rights that have been disputed with increasing directness and vehemence by Chinese authorities.

While it was admitted by Chinese members that the lives of Koreans in Manchuria are less secure than they should be under the general provisions of the 1909 Treaty and under the common obligations that rest upon civilized communities, they stated that there were no complaints of lack of protection for Korean settlers in Manchuria prior to the annexation of Korea by Japan. Japanese members had no quarrel with this statement but added that twenty years ago any foreigner was safer in Manchuria than he is now, so that Sino-Japanese differences did not appear to be the only factor in the unfortunate change. Thus the discussion shifted to the question whether the general situation, and not only the condition of the Korean immigrants, had been worsened by a growing political instability and weakening of the forces of the Government, owing in large measure to the political differences between China and Japan. As one Chinese member remarked:

" When a foreign power imposes all kinds of extralegal measures to protect its subjects in another country, including the use of its own police and troops, how can the functions normally performed by a government to protect the lives of aliens be expected to work? "

As to the ordinances issued to local chiefs of police, asking them to assist in the discouragement of Korean residents (see pp. 287–88), Chinese members felt that, in an exaggerated form, they represent a natural reaction by Chinese officials in Manchuria to the insistence upon the part of the Japanese to enforce treaty rights which the Chinese Government does not recognize. There is no inconsistence, they held, between such orders and the earlier disposition of the Manchurian authorities to encourage Korean immigration. Rice culture was new to the native inhabitants, and the Koreans were welcomed during the earlier efforts to introduce this crop. But the experiment had failed because the Chinese and Japanese Governments had not come to an agreement as regards the legal status of these immigrants. Even then, no aggressive steps had been taken to get rid of them until recently when the Japanese had begun to force their concept of the Koreans' legal rights in Manchuria upon the authorities.

Thus the complication introduced into the problems of extraterritoriality by dual citizenship absorbed some attention. While there is some doubt as to the existence of a binding international legal decision, it was pointed out that in a recent decision a distinction was drawn between the jurisdiction over a naturalized alien from a country that does not recognize his alienation of citizenship when the case arises in his country of origin and such jurisdiction when the case arises in his adopted country; in that decision the Hague tribunal had held that the country of origin cannot claim control over the naturalized citizen in the country where he is naturalized and where he lives. It is doubtful, however, whether this view would affect the case of the Koreans in Manchuria because, on the one hand, Japan has not granted its Korean subjects full rights of citizenship and, on the other, it has special extraterritorial treaty rights of jurisdiction over all its subjects living in Chinese territory.

Consideration of the problem of Korean safety in Manchuria also invited further discussion of the effect of abnormal conditions of public life upon the protection of aliens in China generally. Two phases of such special difficulty, it was felt, had to be distinguished: one is the prevalence, in some parts of China, of temporary disorder, or inadequate control of insubordination; the other, a more continuous decentralization of government. One is a disruption of the normal functioning of government; the other, a dispersion of authority.

LAWLESSNESS AND THE PROTECTION OF ALIEN RESIDENTS

The Japanese case for extralegal measures of protection for its subjects is based largely upon the prevalence of banditry in Manchuria. The question was repeatedly discussed with some heat whether the very measures which Japanese officials were taking outside the South Manchuria Railway Zone and the Leased Territory of Liaotung had not in fact increased the insecurity of life and the formation of criminal gangs. It was also said that similarly the concessions and settlements throughout China, by harboring revolutionary elements, had increased instability. Rebel leaders were able here to recruit bands which later preyed upon the countryside. More serious still were the facilities here enjoyed by rival military leaders to form separatist movements and to engage, sometimes successfully, in expeditions against the established Government, local and national. The resulting state of uncertainty made for lawlessness in which naturally the lives of foreigners were less secure than they would be in a normal state of affairs.

The tendency of extraterritoriality to react againt the safety of nationals who enjoy that right was a point brought out in several round tables. When the established authorities are not normally looked to for their protection, they can hardly be expected in abnormal times to be able to carry out that function, Chinese members said. The example of other countries was mentioned where foreign residents not enjoying extraterritorial privileges were not exposed to unusual risks in times of revolution or social disturbance. A Japanese member testified to the fact that, before there were extraterritorial rights, Japanese travelers in chairs and on donkeys in the interior of Manchuria were safer than they are now. A foreigner who has long resided in China said:

" We are safe only in so far as public opinion protects us, since the Government in Nanking cannot protect us. Foreigners have no right in China if they are not willing to take the risks the Chinese people themselves take in what we may characterize as an intermittent state of war within the country."

If extraterritoriality were voluntarily given up by the foreign powers, he thought, the Chinese people could easily be persuaded to afford special protection to the foreigners living in their midst. A Chinese member said:

" The creation of special privileges for foreigners in China was warranted by some facts that have been pointed out. But now their continuance is creating a state of mind that makes them a source of insecurity. The abolition of these rights may cause inconvenience; but their existence today arouses antiforeign feeling, and also hinders internal development. Many Chinese understand only the negative side of the nationalist movement — the ' down with ' side."

But particularly was the use of troops for the protection of aliens singled out for criticism on the ground that it makes matters worse. A case was cited in which the sending of troops from a Japanese garrison to protect Japanese subjects during an expected clash between southern and northern Chinese armies produced unfortunate incidents by drawing attention to the alien group and visiting the popular wrath upon them. " Are Japanese lives in Manchuria safer since the eighteenth of September? " a Chinese asked pointedly. A foreign police or military guard set up outside a concession or settlement to protect the nationals of a foreign power will almost invariably interfere with the performance of their duties by the regular Chinese police authorities, others testified. There have been hundreds of grievances from Japanese subjects before such special guards were set up, was a Japanese retort. A Japanese member said in another round table:

" There are about two hundred thousand bandits in China, and twenty or thirty thousand of these are in Manchuria. Kidnapping of foreigners there is common. Most of the people, as well as the most valuable property, are concentrated along the railway lines, but not necessarily within the narrow zone under Japanese control. It is for this reason that the Japanese troops guarding the South Manchuria Railway frequently are called upon to protect Japanese subjects against bandits."

The presence of foreign gunboats in Chinese waters also was held responsible by some speakers for increased insecurity.

" During the Taiping Rebellion foreign warships helped to protect foreigners. Now they come in so freely that they cause trouble and inconvenience for the nationals they are supposed to protect. They make for bad feeling."

Another Chinese member said:

" Gunboats excite the uneducated people. Tension in the streets of Shanghai has lately been increased by the parading of Japanese marines. They produced popular resentment against the very people they were intended to protect."

DISPERSION OF AUTHORITY

This term, taken from the suggested agenda (question 2a), produced a certain amount of confusion, since evidently a distinction must be drawn between a disruption of authority due to the weakness of the central Government and an orderly decentralization of authority as between the national and the provincial Governments. Both forms of dispersion, it was agreed, obtain in China and militate against the safety of foreigners. While there are many parts of China where the provincial authorities are entirely capable of maintaining order and have shown their willingness to protect foreign residents effectively, nevertheless the somewhat loose co-ordination of their police and military functions with those of the central Government is a source of difficulty.

Exceptional in this respect, many residents in China felt, is the so-called " Communist bloc " in South Central China, an area in Hunan and Kiangsi practically independent of both Nanking and Canton, where, owing to organized depredations upon property, neither Chinese nor foreign residents are said to be safe. Here, and at previous times in parts of China that have since been subdued, foreigners have often been held responsible for the large and irresponsible distribution of arms and ammunition. To this charge one foreign resident replied that it is practically impossible for a foreign government to control a shipment of arms after it has left the country of origin. Nevertheless, it was felt that foreign firms are, or have been, implicated in the delivery of quite considerable armaments to the very groups that endanger life in the unstable provinces.

Another complaint, frequently reiterated, was that certain foreign powers, particularly Japan, deliberately weaken the central Government by dealing directly with provincial and local authorities instead of using the regular channels of diplomatic negotiation. Japanese liberal opinion regrets this state of things but considers it inevitable; in Japan, likewise, there was a time, sixty years ago, when foreign governments were obliged, as a matter of practical necessity, to deal with local *daimyos* because the national Government did not, in fact, exercise control over the whole national territory. The validity of this comparison was not recognized by all Chinese members: so long as foreign governments recognize the Nanking Government, they said, they should carry on all their negotiations concerning their nationals with the foreign office of that Government. Even though that Government at times refers a foreign government to a provincial authority, such decentralization of power for the purpose of expediting matters does not justify such complete disregard for the existence of the National Government as the Japanese had shown in their dealings with Manchurian problems during the last year or so. This preference for negotiation with the local authorities had obviously increased their actual independence and so counteracted all efforts to strengthen the hold of the National Government over its provincial organs. In one round table, at least, this discussion led to the recognition of a real problem, owing not to the machinations of a foreign government hostile to the central authority in China but to the difficulty experienced in getting any kind of satisfaction from a presentation of grievances in the national capital. That difficulty can readily be explained, it was thought, with circumstances for which no one is to blame; but while it is to the interest of the foreign powers to strengthen the National Government of China, their extraterritorial right to protect their citizens would seem to imply also the responsibility of doing this effectively; and that in many cases means getting such satisfaction as it is possible to obtain through direct negotiation with local authorities. A Chinese member said:

" Much of the trouble is due to the radical changes that have taken place in our Government and have placed untrained officials in positions of authority. Two views are current in China as to the kind of policy required in this situation. One is that this disintegration which has been going on for thirty years must be permitted to continue until we have a federal government with self-governing provinces. The other is that the disintegration of national authority must be checked until we have all power concentrated in the National Government. This, naturally, is the view of the Nanking Government. The first policy may practically be forced upon us as a result of the developing condition. But the other policy has been greatly strengthened of late by the unification of Chinese national sentiment in the face of foreign military aggression upon Chinese sovereignty in Manchuria. There has been a considerable change of feeling in this respect. Manchuria itself has, during the last two years, associated itself more closely with the Central Government — to the evident displeasure of Japan. Not long ago, the Nanking Government was able to mobilize Manchurian troops to suppress insurrection in the North; and the new difficulties with Japan have produced the *rapprochement* between Nanking and Canton. Time and patience are needed to make a strong national government a reality. A change of attitude toward this problem on the part of most of the foreign powers comes to our aid."

A British member indorsed this view but emphasized the necessity that the National Government itself contribute more toward the centralization of its functions. Too many important government offices are distant from the seat of the Central Government. A strengthening of the Central Government, he suggested, could well go hand in hand with purposeful decentralization. The country was too large to be administered from one center. At present too many essential government functions were scattered while many activities were directed from Nanking that could better be carried on in accordance with the judgment of local officials. The foreign powers, he held, might make one essential contribution to the strengthening of the National Government of China by removing their legations to the capital. Many difficulties that arose in the joint responsibility for the protection of foreign residents could be smoothed out if the accredited representatives of foreign powers were in more personal contact with the Chinese leaders, instead of remaining isolated in a city six hundred miles distant.

PROPERTY RIGHTS

The Chinese Government's ability to provide adequate legal protection for foreign residents, as apart from police protection, was questioned repeatedly during the round-table discussion. One phase of it, the functioning of the courts, was brought up more specifically in connection with the protection of property rights. The right of a nation to limit the privilege of foreigners as to places of residence and ownership of real estate is recognized internationally. In China this was from the start associated with the treaty provision for extraterritoriality. With the limitation of the right of residence to the treaty ports, China sought to limit the penetration of foreign influence. But this has never stopped nationals of the treaty powers from carrying on business in the interior of China. There is an impression that nationals of treaty powers in fact do hold property in China outside the concessions and settlements, and that the authorities are aware of this. But at the round table where this statement was made, the actual situation was fully explained. Since they throw light on the probable consequences of the abolition of extraterritoriality for foreign business, the scattered remarks on this subject of a British member with large business experience throughout China are here given in full:

" A considerable amount of property is used by firms of the treaty powers in the conduct of their business both inside and outside of the treaty ports. In the settlements and concessions, there is, of course, no difficulty about the foreign ownership of property. In the interior, the land on which such property stands is always owned or purchased for this purpose by a Chinese, usually an agent of the company. Land is not dear, and the financing of such land purchases not difficult. The foreign firms that do business in the interior lease the warehouse, the packing plant, the oil installation, or whatever premises they require. If the agent has not enough capital to build these premises, the money is lent him on mortgage. Interest on the mortgage is charged against the rent. There are no separate secret agreements. Great tribute is due to the honesty of both the Chinese and the foreigners engaged in these business transactions. I cannot remember a single case in ten years in which either side has defaulted in these undertakings. Usually a lease is signed, terminable in thirty years. Since practically any foreign business conducted in an orderly way in China pays, difficulty as to payment is rarely encountered. Usually the agent pays off interest and principal in a few years.

" In this connection it should be said that the credit situation in China is unusually good. It compares favorably with that in any other country in which our company does business. The Chinese business man is determined to pay his debts and very rarely needs to be taken into court. There are, perhaps, special reasons for this favorable situation: the sub-judicial machinery, that is, the non-legal tradition that surrounds business in China, takes care of most cases of dispute. There may be guaranty bonds. There is enforcement of contracts by guilds and chambers of commerce. Above all, there is the sharing of an individual's responsibility by his whole family; this is an indirect but essential part of the system. There is, thus, not the same necessity to rely on court judgments as there is in other parts of the world.

" But this does not mean that we are obliged to avoid recourse to the courts. I can state without hesitation that in the more normal parts of China the courts, when appealed to in civil cases, operate with a fair degree of speed and justice. They are satisfactory to the foreign firms. There is reasonable security for property as well as for persons in places far more numerous than those in which conditions are abnormal. By these I mean districts that have suffered outbursts of disorder during which an army may sweep over the place and interfere with the normal functioning of the courts. Such conditions have become quite exceptional; and they are the only reason why the question whether extraterritoriality may safely be abolished cannot be answered with a simple yes.

" In the cases in which we have had to resort to court procedure during the last few years, the courts have usually given what we recognize as justice and have enforced their decisions. Our lawyers, Chinese, succeed in these cases through use of the normal procedure, as in any other country.

" We have had little or no experience of the functioning of the courts in respect to safety of person, although our travelers, young Englishmen and Americans, constantly travel over all the provinces. We rarely have complaints from them; the Chinese courts place no unnecessary handicaps in their way. In fact, these young men are practically unaware of the existence of their extraterritorial rights, since they have no occasion to make use of them."

A very different account of the situation was given by a Japanese member of the same round table. He said:

"In case extraterritoriality is relinquished, the judicial organization to which foreigners will become subject naturally is the Chinese court system. The structure of these courts and the jurisdiction of their various classes are entirely within the competence of Chinese law. Modern Chinese courts and prisons, codification of the laws, the degree of independence of the judiciary, and the interference with it by irresponsible outsiders — these are subjects fully discussed at the Kyoto Conference.[53] But so far there has been no progress in the reform of the evils then disclosed, except in outward form.

"The first and primary requirement for the reform of the Chinese judicial system must be, I think, the independence of the judiciary from outside influence. The actual conditions in this matter are apparently far from ideal. There may be many causes. One is that the judges are usually very poorly paid. They have no security in their official position. They cannot summon before the court any accused man if he is of high standing. In civil cases, they cannot carry out distraint or execution upon high officials, for example, even after judgment. If they take an independent attitude they are at once ousted from office by the pressure of outside influence. How can one expect independence of the judiciary under such circumstances?

"An extension of modern courts to the interior of China is apparently intended, in accordance with a plan extending over five or seven years, beginning from last year if I am rightly informed. But the execution of this plan involves a heavy burden of expense; and I am not aware of the extent to which the fiscal condition of the Chinese Government actually answers this requirement.

"On the other hand, there is evidently ample ground for distrust as regards the effective control of the law courts over the populace in general and the military force in particular. Prevention of the exercise of arbitrary authority by irresponsible, self-appointed bodies is very ineffective. To prove this, an illustration from the recent boycott movement against Japanese goods may suffice: The Anti-Japanese National Salvation Association is daily arresting and detaining Chinese merchants who are alleged to have dealt in Japanese goods; and their shops and godowns are searched. Such actions are evidently offenses against the law, since Article 44 of the Chinese procedure expressly provides that 'arrests must be made on warrant for arrest issued by a competent court'; Article 67 of the same law provides that 'detention must be effected on detention warrants'; and Article 142 provides that 'search must be made on search warrant issued by a competent court.' If, as Chinese authorities often declare when this charge is made by Japanese, the association named has no official connection with the Government, it is clear that the prevention of the exercise of arbitrary actions by self-appointed bodies is absolutely nonexistent.

"Such being the general situation, we are bound to come to the conclusion that the question of the relinquishment of extraterritoriality must be dealt with most cautiously by the foreign powers, even though they have full sympathy with China's aspiration in this respect."

A Chinese member argued that, as a membership organization, the League for National Salvation had a right to inflict upon its members such

[53] *Problems of the Pacific, 1929*, pp. 99 ff.

punishments as it saw fit for infringement of the articles of association. But it was generally felt that its operations had come dangerously close to, and in some instances exceeded, the limits to such activities expressly set by law. The inactivity of the Government on the complaint of Japanese, reinforced by official representations from the Japanese Government, was to be explained with inability to go counter to so strong and universal an expression of public sentiment as was evidenced in this case. It was compared with similar inability of other governments, in times of general emotional disturbance, to check the excesses of inflamed public opinion. The circumstances could not, it was argued, be considered as sufficiently typical of the state of law in China to warrant any conclusive deduction from them as to whether it was safe to relinquish extraterritoriality. But they did forecast serious difficulties if such relinquishment were to take place immediately without adequate safeguards to cover situations of abnormal tension. Similarly, many cases cited to illustrate an insufficient functioning of the Chinese courts in Manchuria were considered, not so much as arguments against a speedy relinquishment of extraterritoriality, but as arguments in favor of a demand for carefully considered safeguards during a period of transition.

In this connection a Chinese member admitted that the judiciary had not, in the last few years, functioned so well as it did during the early years of the Republic, in spite of a serious attempt to reform the courts. Domination by militarists has become a more serious factor with the recurrence of revolution and civil war. Others saw an explanation for this phenomenon in an increasing tendency of the Chinese lawyers to resort to litigation, in imitation of Western examples of procedure which had been eagerly studied. In the earlier years there was more reliance upon the sub-judicial forms of procedure mentioned above. The Japanese contention that judges are inadequately paid and do not have the customary security of tenure in office was confirmed by other foreign residents in China. But there was evidence of considerable concern in this matter on the part of the Chinese Government and promise of early reforms. There was a tentative plan, it was reported, to pay adequate salaries to the judges of the first, second, and third class — with the distinct object of increasing their independence.

The particular charge frequently made that Chinese courts are subjected to undue influence by military authorities was, on examination, found to be unsubstantiated. In all parts of China, except those undergoing a violent political disturbance, as now in Manchuria, such interference is quite exceptional. One such exception, it was admitted by Chinese members, was a recent case in Shantung where the military authorities, accepting the verdict of popular opinion, had intervened in a manner contrary to the finding of the local court. Chinese members contended that cases of interference on the part of Japanese military authorities with Chinese courts in Manchuria were both more frequent and more serious.

Apart from the independence of the courts, two questions engaged the attention of the round tables: Were the laws administered by the Chinese courts satisfactory, as viewed from the standpoint of common practice in civilized countries? Could the decrees of the courts be expected to be adequately enforced?

On the former question, such testimony as was available seemed favorable. A committee of foreign jurists, appointed under the provisions of the Nine-Power Treaty and presided over by Silas H. Strawn, had in 1926 issued a report containing definite recommendations as to legal enactments necessary to overcome weak points in China's civil and criminal laws. [54] The Chinese Government, it was generally admitted, had made great efforts to bring the laws of the country in line with these recommendations and between 1927 and 1929 had codified the whole body of civil and criminal laws. The civil code, proclaimed in 1930 and largely based upon the models of the German and Japanese, was particularly singled out for praise. If properly enforced, this code, it was said, would certainly make it possible for foreigners to do business in China. The question was asked whether these codes had not been enacted mainly to satisfy the foreign powers that extraterritoriality could now be relinquished, and might thereafter be modified in important points. This eventuality was declared by a competent Chinese jurist to be highly improbable. Chinese as well as foreign enterprises were now basing their future development upon such enactments as those regulating banking, shipping, and factory management, which, therefore, could not be radically changed. Indeed, the civil code, according to one Chinese spokesman, was planned for the future rather than to meet an immediate situation:

" It was thought necessary to frame a code in accordance with the best codes in the world, although it was realized that some of its provisions would probably have to be ignored for the time being. For example, in our new code the daughters of a family have a right to an equal share of the division of the property. A court has ruled that this provision is applicable and is retroactive. This immediately started a series of litigations, especially in our modern cities, on the part of daughters who previously had had no claim on the family estate. But after a while the litigations died away because the great majority of the people would not go to the trouble of claiming a few dollars. The code stands, and if a daughter wishes to present a claim she can expect a fair judgment. But in this respect the code is ahead of public opinion and the common law. Local usage in China usually takes precedence over provincial, and provincial over national usage. So, in such matters as interest rates on loans, the national code will probably not be effective for a long time to come."

There was considerable discussion of the question whether this admitted lag between enactment and enforcement would be a serious danger to the safety of foreign business interests if these came under Chinese jurisdiction. As one member phrased it:

" Foreigners are not so much concerned with what is in the laws or the codes as with the justice, certainty, and uniformity of their administration. They want to be sure what sort of treatment they have to expect from the courts."

[54] Howland, *op. cit.*, pp. 179 ff.

Another said:

" If the present factory law were enforced, every foreign factory in China might have to be closed. The regulations promulgated concerning mining presuppose a system of management as highly developed as anywhere in the world. Foreign concerns are frequently brought into court now for infringements of the factory and mining laws, with no possibility of appeal, except through diplomatic intervention, even though these laws are not enforced in the case of Chinese companies."

Recourse to diplomatic action in such cases of seeming discrimination, another foreign member stated, was unrewarding for the reason already mentioned, namely, that the Chinese Government is not strongly centralized. This explanation seemed somewhat to conflict with frequent references by other foreign round-table members having business interests in China to the effect that the courts are too much under the influence of the Kuomintang and swayed by the policies of the central party organization. A more convincing explanation of the situation was one already referred to, the unsatisfactory status of the judiciary:

" When a Chinese mine has been found guilty of infringing upon the provisions of the law, it closes for a while and then opens again under the same conditions — except for the fact that some official has $50,000 in his pocket."

PRISON REFORM

Closely connected with the subject of law enforcement is the question whether the penal system administered by the Chinese courts is at all comparable with that of other countries. On this matter there was considerable diversity of opinion. The present disposition of the Chinese Government seemed to be to provide model prisons, especially in those regions where foreigners not enjoying extraterritoriality rights are liable to become " the state's guests." As one Chinese member observed, " We wish to treat our guests to a sort of special first-class accommodation." A case was cited in which a considerable number of Russians were incarcerated in the Peiping model prison. According to an impartial neutral observer, their treatment was far better than that accorded to native prisoners; they had better food, baths, and other privileges not commonly in use. Remembering their earlier hardships, some of these prisoners later refused to take advantage of a release before their term of sentence was completed. Another model prison, in Manchuria, was declared by a Japanese speaker to be in accordance with modern ideas but so badly overcrowded as to nullify all the good intentions:

" There is yet plenty of room for reform. Some months ago I had the privilege of seeing a prison, a so-called model prison, in a certain part of Manchuria. The outward appearance of the entire building was perfect, but the substance did not correspond to that appearance. I was told by an official in charge that the official capacity of that prison was one thousand; but there were thirteen hundred. More than half-a-dozen prisoners had been thrown into a cell for solitary confinement. The sanitary conditions, with such overcrowding, must be very bad. For these thirteen hundred prisoners there were only two physicians, one a surgeon with

European medical education, the other a physician of the traditional Chinese school. I was permitted to see the gallows room. In a corner of that room I saw the body of a prisoner who, I was told, had died from some disease. It had been thrown there two days ago. This may suffice for inferring the conditions of Chinese prisons as a whole."

Many foreign members felt that this condemnation did not differ greatly from that of outdated prison systems in process of reform with which they were thoroughly familiar at home. It was frankly admitted by several Chinese speakers that conditions as to prison accommodations and administration vary widely in the different parts of the national territory and that, with the great diversity of Eastern and Western penal traditions, and of standards of living, it was not practicable to subject Chinese and foreign prisoners to identical conditions. Evidently, their Government was not merely endeavoring to set up here and there a demonstration of its ability to apply modern methods but, while gradually reforming the prison system as a whole, would be willing to grant exceptional treatment to foreign offenders if extraterritoriality were relinquished.

GERMAN AND RUSSIAN EXPERIENCES

There was difference of opinion also on the question how German and Russian nationals, who no longer enjoy extraterritorial rights, are faring in relation to the Chinese courts. The general testimony was to the effect that both apparently had found their subjection to Chinese jurisdiction quite tolerable. Their lives and property seemed no less secure than those of other foreigners outside the settlements and concessions. In one round table it was stated that German business in China had developed rapidly in recent years. In another, reference was made to the seemingly flourishing condition of Russians — many of them penniless refugees a decade ago — in Harbin. A Japanese member said:

" Reports vary and no reliable and decisive information has as yet come to my knowledge. Last April, when I was in Harbin, I heard many grievances from the Russians. In Mr. Woodhead's brief work on China's extraterritoriality [55] many illustrations are quoted of complaints by foreigners whose right of extraterritoriality was already relinquished. At Harbin I heard few complaints from the Germans. It was explained that the Germans are taking great pains not to be trapped in criminal accusations, and that, in civil cases, they try to settle disputes as much as possible through compromise, believing that a lawsuit would bring them a great loss even if they won it."

Another explanation was that, in the case of German nationals, objections to the verdicts of Chinese courts were handled through diplomatic channels, so that in practice the relinquishment of extraterritoriality did not greatly hamper them. Most German residents and their more important firms are, of course, in the treaty ports where the attitudes of the Chinese

[55] H. A. W. Woodhead, *Extraterritoriality in China* (reprint from *Peking and Tientsin Times,* September–October, 1929).

courts conform more to Western practices than they do in the interior. But it was also stated that German business men have capitalized their exceptional political position to some extent in creating for themselves relations of special mutual trust and confidence with Chinese business men. Russians do not seem to have fared quite so well, possibly because their business is largely in Manchuria where the influence of the large settlements, with their modern methods of doing business, has not completely penetrated.

On the whole, the judgment of the round tables was that the experience of these two nationalities without extraterritorial rights could not be accepted as conclusive, though it seemed to disprove some of the worst apprehensions of what abolition of that right would mean.

THE EXPERIENCE OF CHRISTIAN MISSIONS

Missionaries in China are in an especially favorable position to judge the probable consequences of relinquishment of extraterritoriality. They have often expressed that judgment in no uncertain terms.[56] Spokesmen for Christian institutions from different parts of China in the present Conference reiterated the opinion that all special privileges enjoyed by them as nationals of foreign powers were handicaps rather than helps to their enterprise. The Chinese Government, in fact, had intimated that with the relinquishment of extraterritoriality these institutions would be given wider powers than they now enjoy as to ownership of property. At present such property may be acquired for educational purposes only, and in the name of particular missions only. Property cannot be held by missions for purposes of investment. Local authorities, at present, sometimes insist on making this latter provision of the law retroactive and thus inflict hardship. In some cases, foreign missions have voluntarily relinquished property rights where they constituted a cause of friction. The gradual transference of administrative functions to competent Chinese hands also had materially contributed toward a better feeling. Generally speaking, missionaries are more likely to suffer from the opposition of local public opinion than from that of the Central Government; this, it was explained, was particularly due to the jealousy of Chinese doctors and, in the more remote districts, a latent popular suspicion of Western medical practices.

Missionaries in China from different parts of the British Empire seemed to agree with the following statement of an American missionary at a general session of the Conference:

" Speaking as an individual, I have hoped for years that my Government and also others concerned would before this have indicated their desire to abolish extraterritoriality. For us, living in the interior, it has not, I think, been of any practical value; and it does a great deal of harm. If we think of China not as it ought to be but as it is, the removal of this irritation will help not a little toward attaining the very things that all foreigners having to do with China desire.

" One difficulty is that many things not originally intended in the arrangement are involved in extraterritoriality. . . . For us in the interior, the only thing that

[56] *Problems of the Pacific, 1929*, pp. 103–4; Howland, *op. cit.*, p. 81.

is of concern as regards extraterritoriality is that foreigners have occasionally to go to law with Chinese. I am told, the Chinese Government is planning a series of law courts for foreigners who have legal cases against Chinese, with special judges, interpreters, and publicity. China will be on her mettle to deal with these cases as they should be dealt with. That provision, with all that is involved in China's desire to satisfy the world in instituting a new judiciary, will help to simplify those very few legal cases that concern foreigners living in China — a very small proportion indeed. I have noticed that the three greatest American economic interests in China are all preferring to work through and with the Chinese people.

"Have we foreigners any right to be in China under present conditions, in this time of stress, unless we make it something of an adventure? It is an adventure even for the Chinese themselves. If we are going into the interior of China we should accept the conditions as they are. We can carry on far better without this practically valueless treaty relationship. The Chinese people are not and have not been, so far as we have known, anti-foreign. They are anti-foreign-aggression."

PUBLIC OPINION AND THE LAW

The popular attitudes toward the law in different parts of China thus emerged in the discussion of almost every phase of the general topic of extraterritoriality as an important factor that must be reckoned with in the formulation of safeguards in the event of its relinquishment. It has already been seen in another connection (p. 164) that the Chinese conception of legislation differs materially in one essential point from that of most countries. One member said at one of the round tables:

"It is not a matter of accident that the two great continental countries, China and the United States, seem to legislate on the basis of a different assumption than that which underlies the lawmaking of island countries like Japan and Great Britain. When the Chinese Government places a factory code on the statute book, or the American Government a constitutional amendment prohibiting the manufacture and sale of alcoholic liquor, they know that vast differences of custom and attitude in different parts of their territory will make full enforcement a matter of gradual achievement. When small countries, with a more unified territory, pass laws, they expect to see them observed immediately and are able at once to provide adequate machinery for their enforcement. It is not fair to compare the relative fulness with which, especially, social legislation becomes effective immediately after enactment when the terms of that legislation themselves have been influenced in the larger countries by the realization that, for some time, it must represent an aspiration gradually to be transformed into reality. In China, as in the United States, the passage of a law that is not at once wholly enforcible may serve the very useful purpose of a declaration of national policy. If only laws were passed that can at once be administered in every detail, there would be no education of public opinion, and progress would be much slower. To prevent such laws from being entirely futile, there must, of course, be centers of demonstration that they can be enforced with the desired results; and there must not be too much delay in widening both the area and the scope of their application. Just at present, China seems to be engaged in such a gradually enlarging demonstration of modern legislation. It remains to be seen whether every opportunity will be utilized to speed its application in its entirety and over the whole national territory."

Chinese members stated that such laws as the Factory Act were not intended as declarations of policy only, but that there was an actual plan of putting them into operation over a given number of years. In answer to the criticism that foreign residents did not know what part of a given law they were expected to obey, it was said that temporary suspensions were as clearly and definitely published by the Government as the promulgation of new laws and regulations.

But apart from this difference it appeared that the whole relationship between the popular sense of justice and the administration of law is different in China from what it is in Western countries. " Modern economic development," a British member very sympathetic toward Chinese aspirations said, " will be simply impossible unless the people have more regard for the law, and the Government itself is held accountable for its actions under the law." " But why should all the essentials of Chinese life be revolutionized to meet the exigencies of an industrial development of very doubtful possibilities? " a Chinese member asked.

" There are certain deep-rooted customs in China that must be respected. You have to get into new customs gradually rather than jump into them. When there is a conflict between custom and law in a matter affecting the social traditions, you have to pay a certain respect to the feeling of the people. When a foreigner is involved we want to treat him fairly, without reference to our own customs. For this reason our new courts will have special interpreters and foreign expert advisers; but their especial advantage will be publicity."

Another Chinese member said:

" In the legal code there is an unwritten understanding that local customs take precedence over the provincial, and the provincial over the national. The various districts of China are so different one from another that this rule has quite naturally been applied by judges during the present period of transition. The code itself does not make any exceptions, and the principle of adaptation is not specifically mentioned. But our most distinguished jurists recognize the need for a transition from the old to the new legal system.

" China has attempted to adapt to her needs the Continental codes most capable of being transplanted to a foreign land; but the common law is preserved in the respect for traditions and local usages, except where these are in violent contrast with the new legal requirements.

" The old courts never have been a branch of the Government, and the magistrate was supposed to function often as judge, detective, and policeman in one. There was no system of detection of crime, no public defense, no lawyer or attorney, and no police. That is the reason why we have acquired this age-long fear of going to the courts; and it will take some time to improve this condition. This new system of training lawyers and judges, of public defense in the courts, is strange to the people. Where cases have been tried in such courts, the results have been quite fair, so far as I know. But the replacement of the old system cannot be made very quickly." [57]

Another Chinese member reminded the Conference:

" Our situation differs from that of other countries in one condition that makes such gradual adaptation possible: What would be legal cases elsewhere are largely

[57] For a brief description of this older system see H. B. Morse, *The Trade and Administration of China*, pp. 59 ff.; also A. D. A. de Kat Angelino, *Colonial Policy* (data paper, American Council), I, 329 ff.

handled by members of the family, the elders. When people take matters to the courts, it is a very serious affair."

These and other explanations sufficed to give the Conference a sense of the great difficulties that inhere in any plan which the Government of China might adopt under pressure to apply national safeguards to the protection of foreign residents that would be effective in the near future, when judged by the standards of state protection afforded to citizens and aliens alike in other countries.[58] But they also gave plausibility to the claim of many missionaries and others living in the interior sections of China that a friendly esteem of their neighbors is far more important for their personal safety than any protection that either their own or the Chinese Government could afford them.

The crucial problem in regard to this whole matter, from the point of view of relinquishment of extraterritoriality, was expressed by a British member when he said:

" The Chinese concept of law evidently belongs to a civilization totally different from that of the West. But treaties cannot be based upon *both* Eastern and Western concepts of law." [59]

In some way, it was felt, this hiatus must be bridged before the powers now enjoying extraterritorial rights can safely relinquish them. The tacit agreement on that point might, therefore, serve here as the connecting link with the next section:

II. STEPS TOWARD THE ABOLITION OF EXTRATERRITORIALITY

During the autumn of 1930, negotiations started between the Governments of China, Great Britain, and the United States looking toward an agreement concerning the conditions that must surround relinquishment to make it acceptable to all three of these powers. These negotiations, which were to lay the basis also for negotiation with the other treaty powers concerned, have not yet been completed. The American Government has demanded, among other conditions, that the procedure of relinquishment be graded in consecutive steps paralleling a series of advances in the improvement of China's administration of justice. The Chinese Government has felt so sure that it could meet the larger demand implied in this condition, and

[58] Incidentally this comparison of legal philosophies also corrected a false impression which some Japanese members had had of the authority behind the activities of the anti-Japanese National Salvation Association. In their own country such an organization, they said, could not function without the authority of the Government; and for this reason they had taken it for granted that the activities of this Association represented a government policy, the existence of which this explanation made more doubtful.

[59] A subcommittee of the Program Committee, on cultural relations, had previously given sympathetic consideration to a proposal for a joint study by the national councils most concerned of the essential differences between Occidental and Oriental concepts of justice. See below, p. 468.

also the conditions made by the British Government, that it issued a mandate on December 28, 1929, declaring extraterritorial privileges at an end, as from January 1, 1930. But this did not mean that the mandate actually went into effect on that day. On May 4, 1931, the Chinese Government issued a new mandate, promulgating the regulations which should govern Chinese jurisdiction over the nationals in enjoyment of extraterritorial rights prior to December 31, 1929, to become effective on January 1, 1932. These regulations, again, which have never been published, are intended not as absolute, unilateral decrees but as a basis for further negotiation.[60]

Nevertheless, Chinese statesmen agree with those of Great Britain and the United States, it was reported, that so difficult and important a change in the status of nationals of these countries in China must proceed in stages and with adequate safeguards. In the round tables on extraterritoriality it was taken for granted that this must be the case. The only difference as between Chinese and foreign members was that the former were insistent upon the need for a definite date and definite agreement upon reasonable conditions of further steps toward an ultimately complete relinquishment. They reminded others that these negotiations had been going on for nearly thirty years.

As a first step it seemed agreed that in given localities a substitution of Chinese for foreign courts, but with a specially trained judiciary and the aid of foreign counselors, would be advisable. A Chinese member said:

" The Chinese Government wants to bring all courts up to a certain level. This naturally takes time. A transition period has to be passed through. We do not want to inconvenience foreigners; so we propose special courts for them, each of them to have jurisdiction over a certain area, not only in the port cities. The cases arising inland would be taken to these centers; this would be no more inconvenient for foreigners living in the interior than the present arrangement under which they are obliged to take their case before a consular court, often at a considerable distance."

Such special courts, a foreign jurist declared, would be particularly valuable in accustoming foreign residents to Chinese law and jurisdiction if they were to make it a special function to publish their decisions and the grounds upon which these have been arrived at. The question was asked whether it would not lead to confusion if the laws of the country were to be interpreted differently for natives and for foreigners. To this Chinese members replied that there was no such intention. The special courts would administer the same law; but in so far as there might be differences in the customs as to personal or trade relations between foreigners and Chinese against those current in the relations between Chinese citizens, similar adjustments to custom would be made in these courts as the Chinese courts are always in the habit of making when dealing with local differences in customary law. This, of course, applied primarily to the civil code; applica-

---

[60] A proclamation of December 31, 1931, further postponed enforcement of the regulations, owing to the disturbed condition of China's foreign relations.

tion of the criminal code must be universal in the interest of justice. The new courts, it was anticipated, would be administered by jurists who have had training in Western law schools. Moreover, there would be no uncertainty on the part of litigants as to whether their case would be tried in a modern court or one of the old-established Chinese courts, because these courts would deal with all cases in which foreign residents were concerned.

It was not known at the time whether the British Government had not already gone so far as to express its assent to a total abolition of all privileges as to separate courts and judicial arrangements for its nationals, except for the four treaty ports of Shanghai, Canton, Tientsin, and Hankow, where the present consular courts were to be retained. Foreign residents in the International Settlement of Shanghai seemed to be willing to accept such a compromise, in the belief apparently that all important civil suits would be tried in one of the settlements anyhow. But there was some doubt among foreign members of the round table whether it would be possible under present conditions to give up the right to consular jurisdiction in criminal cases, even in the interior. Chinese objection to a suggested separate treatment of civil and criminal jurisdiction was that such a process — that is, the continuation of the present system unchanged in criminal jurisdiction — would again indefinitely postpone the complete embodiment in actual institutions of the principle of relinquishment. They were faced, however, with the reminder that a legal situation created eighty years ago, at that time with the consent of the Chinese Government which did not then wish to be bothered with jurisdiction over foreigners, had become so fundamental a condition for the existence of foreign enterprise and residence on Chinese soil that it could not be expected to yield easily to a change in policy. On their part, representatives of foreign enterprise in China recognized the soundness of the Chinese demand for definiteness in both the terms of new agreements for relinquishment and the nature of the conditions imposed. With the early expiration of the British and French commercial treaties with China — in 1933 and 1935 respectively — it seemed particularly desirable to have this whole matter cleared up at an early date.

Again, as at Kyoto, some curiosity was displayed as to the ways in which relinquishment of extraterritoriality formerly enjoyed by foreign residents had been carried out in other countries, and with what results.

Several Japanese speakers referred to the difficulties which their own country had experienced in persuading the foreign powers to relinquish extraterritoriality. Looking backward, it was not difficult for them to see, they said, that the Western legal system was superior to that which had obtained in Japan, and that extraterritoriality, though long resented by the Japanese, could not safely have been abolished until after Japanese laws and their administration had been brought into line with the best Occidental standards. The process took thirty or forty years, during which there were constant complaints that foreigners were abusing their privileges.[61] A Japanese speaker said:

"We never felt that we were beneficiaries of the system of extraterritoriality. But we did not simply declaim against it. We attempted to attain abolition through education of the judiciary, and through the revision and reform of our judiciary system, until we succeeded."

In a less controversial spirit, another Japanese member endeavored to give historical reasons why Chinese experience in this matter could not have paralleled Japanese experience:

"The whole situation comes out of the contact between the Occidental type of culture on the one hand and the Oriental type of culture on the other. China had a legal order, just as Occidental countries had a legal order. But it was of a different type. We understand that point very well because it is only fifty or sixty years since we had that same type of legal order. The law was mostly customary — not based on legislation or judicial precedent but on the custom of popular action; and disputes were decided mostly by conciliation, not by judicial settlement. But Japan had developed a kind of judiciary law; and this is a distinguishing point between China and Japan of the Tokugawa period.

"The distinguishing characteristic of Western law is the development of a legal profession. Occidental civilization has the tradition of Greek and Roman orators, and thus the growth of a modern legal profession. If you examine the Oriental systems from Babylon and Egypt to modern China and Japan, you will find a very slight development of this profession. So we naturally have a conflict between their type of legal order and the European type. Modern commerce could not be carried on by Europeans with the Oriental type of legal order. Hence extraterritoriality was a *modus vivendi*.

"China has largely retained her old type of civilization: you see it when you go to the countryside, while the new China is largely in the big cities. This new China has developed nationalism. So you have the transition from the old type of society to the new, and therewith a conflict. Readjustment is necessary, but the difficulty is great because there is conflict such as we did not experience in Japan to the same extent. There is this sharp conflict between the Chinese aspiration to become a modern state and the masses of Chinese people who would rather stick to the traditional culture. In other words, China cannot become a modern state in a day.

"Of course, China's nationalism will win. It was Japan's experience, and China will follow. But in the meantime there will be many difficulties. Here Japan and the Western powers have similar problems to face: their interests cannot be protected under the old type of legal culture, and adjustments are being made adequately to protect these interests according to the Western method.

"The problem of extraterritoriality can be solved only by two factors: one is for the foreign powers, including Japan, to understand the real aspirations of the Chinese people to become a modern state, and the psychological elements involved; the other is for China to understand — and not only superficially — the situations in which the nationals of other countries are placed in China and to seek after their welfare."

A British member reminded this round table that in Japan, as in China, extraterritoriality was but one phase of the treaties providing for other relationships with Occidental countries that had proved of distinct benefit to the peoples of the Far East. While Japanese members entirely associated

[61] See F. C. Jones, *Extraterritoriality in Japan*. New Haven, 1931.

themselves with this view, the Chinese were not convinced. They seemed to look at each other and at their foreign guests as though asking themselves, what exactly is it that these people have brought us that is so much to be preferred to our own civilization? And some of them said it.

One foreign member doubted whether the reform of the Japanese courts and legal practices in the direction of Westernization had really gone farther at the time extraterritoriality was abolished in Japan (1899) than it had now gone in China. Others gave it as their view that the progress in Japan in this respect in the quarter century preceding abolition really had been re-markable — not on account of any superiority of the Japanese over the Chinese, but simply because the national Government of Japan, with its much smaller territory, had none of the principal difficulties in the way of reform that are confronting the national Government of China. An American who had closely followed this development in Japan gave it as his opinion that, though the Chinese Government has not the same power to enforce its decisions, nevertheless its moral influence on the whole nation would prob-ably suffice to make a system of special courts for foreigners, such as had been proposed, work even now without giving cause for criticism.

The methods adopted in the abolition of extraterritoriality in Siam, and the conditions surrounding it, were discussed at greater length, since they pre-sented actual suggestions for possible safeguards to foreign interests in China during a period of transition from the old system to the new.[62] As at Kyoto,[63] Chinese members again objected to the Siamese model because it would further postpone the eradication of one element that most offends China in the present arrangement: the interference with Chinese sovereignty. They were more hospitable to various suggestions of modifying the functioning of Chinese courts than to any suggestion of continued jurisdiction by consular courts, no matter how far these might go in their recognition of Chinese law. Siamese public opinion, they said, did resent the present arrangement with its possible interference by foreign judges, even though actually there had been no frequent use of the right of evocation, when it did not at all resent the assistance of foreign advisers in Siamese courts.

" There will be little objection in China to foreign advisers during a period of transition; but Chinese will resent foreign judges sitting as assessors. Most of us think even foreign advisers unnecessary; for if they should consider themselves un-justly treated foreigners can always have their case taken up by diplomacy."

CONCLUSION

There was agreement that the larger foreign business concerns in China already were experienced in the use of the diplomatic channels to further their legal interests, in spite of extraterritoriality. In fact, Chinese members considered the prevalence of diplomatic usages in legal dealings between

[62] G. W. Keeton, *The Development of Extraterritoriality in China* (London and New York, 1928), II, 271.

[63] *Problems of the Pacific, 1929*, p. 112. See also Howland, *op. cit.* pp. 194–96.

Chinese and foreign residents a particular weakness of the present system. Many cases are decided, they said, not on a firm legal basis but on agreements between foreign consuls and Chinese officials, constituting a body of accepted customs and usages. Big firms have political as well as legal advisers. While it is customary in some Occidental countries, such as the United States of America, for public utility companies to have officers whose duty it is to deal with the legislatures and with public opinion, in China such staff members too often engage in direct legal activities, through the consular courts, to have essentially legal cases taken care of through diplomatic negotiation. The main object of any new system, they thought, should be to lessen rather than to enlarge this form of jurisdiction by making all special safeguards that may possibly be needed to protect foreigners subject to what essentially would be a Chinese legal procedure and not a political transaction.

There was, then, agreement that to secure a working basis for a temporary arrangement to aid transition from extraterritoriality to its complete relinquishment there must be adjustment from both sides. The Government of China must provide more fully and more rapidly for reforms that are already under way, especially greater security and independence for the judiciary and better training for all court officials. The foreign Governments must show greater willingness than they have shown so far to recognize Chinese sovereignty, by reserving for themselves rights to protect their nationals only in those localities and circumstances in which really important vested foreign interests, grown out of extraterritoriality, are involved. Chinese justice must, in practice as well as in theory, still further adapt itself to Western codes of law, now accepted throughout the greater part of the world. Foreign residents in China must become more tolerant of the Chinese attitude toward law, and especially the customary law in which it is rooted and which in turn is the outcome of a historical experience different from that of other regions of the world.

A Chinese member summarized the situation in a general session of the Conference when he said:

"One thing, it seems to me, is very clear as regards China's relations with other powers, and that is, we are in a process of readjustment. The Chinese seem to feel hopeful that of all the outstanding questions this very knotty one of extraterritoriality, more especially, will soon be satisfactorily settled. From the time that Sir Austen Chamberlain made his declaration,[64] a new era has opened up in the relationship between China and the foreign powers. We believe that the enlightened policy of the British Government and enlightened opinion in America will be sufficient to guide us through the constructive period of readjustment. Even as late as last May, Sir Miles Lampson [the British minister to the Chinese Government] was reported as saying that the framework and principles of policy had been decided upon. It is now only a question of filling in details. So, I sense a general spirit of optimism as regards this aspect of China's foreign relations."

[64] The famous "Christmas Memorandum" of December, 1926, in which the British Secretary of State for Foreign Affairs intimated his Government's willingness to make far-reaching concessions in the modification of its treaty rights with China.

The spirit of the general outcome of the discussion was well summarized by one of the round-table chairmen, a foreign business man who has long resided in China:

" Extraterritoriality is the subject on which China's foreign relations have largely been turning in recent years. But for all practical purposes, it has already vanished from a large area of China. It is there in principle and in treaties and law, but in practice it does not exist. And the reason it does not exist is that a large number of foreigners of all nationalities are moving about and trading there, in accordance with the treaties, but also in accordance with Chinese law. You hear little about these foreigners because they are normal human beings engaged in normal jobs; and both they and the Chinese among whom they live are reasonable people and so manage to get on together.

" The only acute points exist where you have concentrations of modern interests and modern living communities — places like the big treaty ports, like parts of Manchuria. There problems arise not because the Chinese are bumping into the foreigners, not because of an inherent naughtiness in Chinese or in foreigners, but because in those places there is a new kind of life. Modern industries, modern commerce, modern mining, modern railways, enterprises that have, in the last half-century, introduced new methods of doing things, have brought about a need for new kinds of contracts, of relationships, between man and man, between company and company, and sometimes between government and government.

" We have tried to see in what ways we can help to lift these inevitable problems to a higher level. They are problems that affect not only big business, but they affect us all. We want to find out how we may be able to live here and get on with the Chinese without constantly annoying them, and at the same time help them get into the swing of the modern world."

CHAPTER X

THE FUTURE OF SHANGHAI

DATA PAPERS

1. *Syllabus on China's Foreign Relations,* pp. 46–48.
2. A MEMBER OF THE BRITISH GROUP. *The Status of Aliens in China.*
3. AKIRA NAGANO. *Development of Capitalism in China,* pp. 10–12.

REFERENCES

1. *Report of the Hon. Mr. Justice Feetham, C.M.G., to the Shanghai Municipal Council, 1931,* Vols. I–III.
2. " Digest of the *Feetham Report," Pacific Affairs,* IV, No. 7 (July, 1931), 586–614 and 626–33; No. 9 (September, 1931), 806–24.
3. " Shanghai," *The Round Table,* MCMXXXI, No. 84 (September, 1931), 738–68.
4. J. P. CHAMBERLAIN. *The Feetham Report on Shanghai* (reprinted from *Foreign Affairs,* October, 1931).
5. J. B. CONDLIFFE (ed.). *Problems of the Pacific, 1929,* pp. 129–41, 356–67.
6. THOMAS F. MILLARD. *The End of Extraterritoriality in China* (Shanghai, 1931), pp. 127–52.

INTRODUCTORY NOTE

The foreign settlements in China have for some time been the center of the discussion of extraterritoriality. The thought has frequently been expressed that the rendition of extraterritorial rights might have been accomplished long ago, were it not for the large vested interests that have grown up in the settlements and the need for their protection.[1] At the Kyoto Conference of the Institute, the discussion of extraterritoriality was immediately followed by a round table on the concessions and settlements; and the part played by these in China's foreign relations was considered with an emphasis on legal technicalities that must needs arise from a situation in which trade and investments rather than the complexity of normal community interests color the entire attitude of at least one party to the controversy.

The International Settlement at Shanghai has long been the chief bone of contention between China and the foreign powers, and as such it deserves the special attention that was given it at Kyoto and again at the Institute's fourth conference, held in the International Settlement itself. Almost every one of the outstanding issues here finds, not only a telling illustration, but its fullest embodiment. What is characteristic of the controversy over Shanghai is also characteristic of the whole relationship between the foreign powers and China. In each case, one main interest, that of the legal status, has overshadowed, and naturally so, many other important aspects of both the shared and the divergent interests of China and the foreign powers. In the International Settlements, the question of status, since it involves the jurisdiction of both the municipal government and of the courts, is essential to the safety of life and property. But there are many aspects of the economic and so-

---

[1] *Problems of the Pacific, 1929,* p. 196.

cial life that are not directly affected by it and could profitably be discussed in others of their many aspects. The communities that have formed under the protection of foreign flags might have formed anyhow as a result of many factors; [2] but in most of the recent reports and discussions they are treated as essentially the products of a political process. Nevertheless, it is admitted that no matter how they have come into being, these communities and their welfare now are, or ought to be, a major object of concern, and not simply their functioning as contact points in international relations. For, they have become permanent and are composed of groups and individuals with normal local interests and desires, both economic and non-economic.

Thus the International Settlement of Shanghai may be envisaged as a center of conflicting economic interests, native and foreign; but it will be more realistic to think of it as a community made up of a million or so human beings, nine-tenths of them Chinese,[3] who are concerned not only with the safety of life and property but adventurous as the rest of us. No matter why they or their forefathers have come to live in the International Settlement, its present inhabitants are motivated very much like other people.

It has seemed necessary to preface the account which follows with this reference to the concrete, human aspect of the Shanghai situation because, as at Kyoto, it was discussed from a political and legal rather than sociological or economic point of view. While, for example, the objective of good city government was assumed, no attempt was made in the round-table session to analyze this term as to the various shades of meaning it might have for Chinese and for foreign residents. As yet the functioning of the municipality and of the court — the legal framework of the community's life — provides too many unsettled questions for discussion to permit of more concentrated attention by an international conference upon the future of Shanghai in terms of health and labor conditions, the education and protection of its children, recreational and cultural opportunities, the mutual co-operation of groups and classes — in terms, that is, of the concrete conditions of a satisfactory civic life.

[2] See Joseph P. Chamberlain, *The Feetham Report on Shanghai* (reprint from *Foreign Affairs*, October, 1931), p. 9.

[3] The population of the Settlement proper, in round numbers, is 27,000 foreigners and 970,0000 Chinese; that of the French Concession 12,000 foreigners and 422,000 Chinese; that of the Chinese city of Shanghai 9,800 foreigners and 1,680,000 Chinese.

EXTRACTS FROM ADDRESS

Since a full exposition of the problems surrounding the International Settlement at Shanghai had been given in the report of the previous Conference,[4] and since the members of the China Conference had received a fairly comprehensive summary of the Feetham report,[5] it was felt unnecessary to review the facts and the recommendations. It had become obvious in the preliminary meetings of the Program Committee, however, that members of the China Council were far from satisfied, either with Justice Feetham's report or with its implications. For this reason, Dr. C. L. Hsia, president of Medhurst College, Shanghai, who has since taken up the post of first secretary to the Chinese Legation in London, was asked to present a critical comment on the Feetham report before the whole Conference at one of its evening meetings. This comment, edited to serve as a data paper for the subsequent round-table discussion, is given below in slightly abbreviated form.

THE REPORT OF MR. JUSTICE FEETHAM AND THE FUTURE OF SHANGHAI

By Dr. C. L. Hsia

Mr. Justice Feetham had an exceedingly warm and friendly reception from all classes of Chinese. The Chinese did not prejudge him; in fact, he was highly respected, and great hopes were entertained all around of his important inquiry and eventual recommendations bringing a satisfactory solution to the intricate situation. After the publication of his report, the Chinese were greatly disappointed. There has been no bitterness or ill-feeling of any kind but just genuine and universal disappointment. It is not very easy to give an accurate analysis of the factors that have brought about this general feeling of disappointment. I venture to mention two causes for the purpose of discussion.

In the first place, his way of presentation is somewhat unfortunate in many places. In his anxiety to maintain the *status quo* for some years to come and to preserve the essential elements of the existing régime as the basis of the future government of Shanghai, he has placed too great an emphasis on the benefits of the International Settlement, and thus gives rise to the impression that he has been partial to and become a defender of the Shanghai Municipal Council. This may be quite unintentional on his part, but there are substantial grounds for a certain feeling of resentment, justified or not. For instance, there is his elaboration of the *Theory and Practice as to Defence and Neutrality of the Settlement* (I, 38–43) and his emphatic support of the view on the Land Regulations as presented by an official of the Council, without allowing space for other points of view on the subject (I, 61). If he had

[4] *Problems of the Pacific, 1929*, pp. 129–41, 356–67.
[5] *Pacific Affairs*, July and September, 1931; see above. Copies of the report itself had been distributed in advance to the more interested members.

given a chapter on the anomalies of the Shanghai International Settlement instead of making repeated efforts to uphold the Anglo-Saxon standards and methods of government as the model to which China must conform, he would have removed some of the unnecessary resentment on the part of the average Chinese reader, and infinitely strengthened his position when it came to his actual proposals later. Hence, after the publication of Volume I of the Report, the Chinese lost much of the enthusiasm of the earlier days. They were still eager to read Volume II, but they will read it in disillusionment.

In the second place, his actual proposals do not come up to the expectation of the Chinese. It is true that some hopes were not justified, if anyone had expected that Mr. Justice Feetham could propose a scheme to satisfy all parties. That would indeed have been a miracle, and of course Mr. Justice Feetham is no miracle worker. He is too anxious about the great commercial and business interests in Shanghai. He proposes so many safeguards and conditions, with the result that the rendition will be an exceedingly slow and far-distant affair — so far-distant that he declines to give us even a probable picture of the state of affairs when rendition is ready to take place, or the state of affairs after rendition has taken place. Frankly, he is not interested in the final drama; he only sees the great difficulties now. He seems to say that, since rendition is out of the question, let us see what we can do to make the Settlement life run smoothly. His proposals are generally of that nature, and one does not see how they are related to the question of ultimate rendition. That picture is not shown at all.

The Chinese are naturally taking Mr. Justice Feetham's opinion seriously when he says that the minimum period of transition required will be "a question of the number, not of years, but of decades" (II, 139). Any diehard might have said that, and unfortunately the report has strengthened the hands and arguments of the diehards and alienated the support of the moderate Chinese. To put it very bluntly, Mr. Justice Feetham thinks that the present régime is not permanent and that the time will come for rendition of the Settlement (II, 133), but that certain conditions (four, II, 140) must be adequately fulfilled before rendition can become a practical policy. These conditions will certainly take decades and perhaps centuries. Meantime the Chinese must be satisfied with " increasing co-operation " between the foreign and Chinese communities and increasing participation in the work of local government under some modification of the present system, thus paving the way to the eventual establishment of a new system, based on a Charter granted by the National Government, without any indication as to when that will be and who will be the judge as to the fulfilment of these conditions. It seems no wonder that the Chinese should feel disappointed. If Mr. Justice Feetham had not visited Shanghai, no foreign diehard could have said more.

In short, from the Chinese point of view, Mr. Justice Feetham does not give any satisfactory answer to two important questions: What is the status of Shanghai? and What is a plan of rendition?

One can only express profound regret that through its manner of presentation and the lack of anything concrete in his proposals, the report is not receiving the attention it deserves and is losing the Chinese support imperatively needed for its eventual success.

A FEW CRITICISMS

The terms of reference. — On December 6, 1929, the Shanghai Municipal Council issued an announcement to the Press on the subject of Mr. Justice Feetham's impending visit to Shanghai, which included one long paragraph in explanation of the Council's action, and this constituted the terms of reference for his inquiry. The paragraph reads as follows:

Ever since the publicly announced policy of the Foreign Powers, and particularly America and Great Britain, with regard to the gradual relinquishment of extraterritorial privileges in China . . . . during the transitional period which must necessarily ensue before such a policy can become fully effective, as well as the necessity of devising some constructive plan or scheme which, while giving full consideration to the aspiration of the Chinese people, will at the same time afford reasonably adequate protection during this transition period to the great foreign commercial and business interests which have been developed in Shanghai [I, 1].

When the Shanghai Municipal Council mentions the publicly announced policy of Great Britain, one naturally thinks of the " Christmas Memorandum " and Sir Austen Chamberlain's speeches and such passages as these: " We are willing to meet the Chinese more than halfway," " We realise all the present inconveniences, but we are thinking of the next century." I do not know whether it is unfair to ask whether the spirit in which Mr. Justice Feetham penned his final recommendations was quite in accord with the spirit of Sir Austen Chamberlain's speeches and the British Christmas Note.

In devising some constructive plan or scheme, Mr. Justice Feetham was requested to give full consideration to the aspirations of the Chinese people, while at the same time affording reasonably adequate protection to the great commercial and business interests in Shanghai. Any fair-minded reader will agree that Mr. Justice Feetham has not given full consideration to the aspirations of the Chinese people, but at the same time has afforded more than reasonably adequate protection to the foreign commercial and business interests in Shanghai.

Theory and practice as to defence and neutrality of the Settlement. — Mr. Justice Feetham has written an excellent and masterly chapter on the origin and development of the Settlement, but most curiously he devotes the very last section — five pages of it — to an exposition of the development of a special doctrine as to rights which, by virtue of its peculiar position, the Settlement community should be deemed to possess. These are rights of " Defence, Armed Neutrality, and Exclusion of Chinese Armed Forces " (I, 40). Any student of international relations can see that these are anomalies, pure and simple, created by a series of special circumstances and peculiar conditions in Shanghai, claimed under the general and universal right of self-preservation and unwillingly acquiesced in by the Chinese Government because of its military weakness. No such legal right exists under international law, under the treaties or even the Land Regulations.

Land Regulations. — Personally I always think that discussion as to the validity of the Land Regulations will never lead anywhere at the present stage of Shanghai's development. It is not a profitable discussion, nor do I think it is necessary, for, though the Chinese Government has never formally sanctioned them, the local authorities have never repudiated the main provisions of the Land Regulations, as far as I know.

Mr. Justice Feetham accepts the memorandum of an important official of the Shanghai Municipal Council with the following comment:

The effect of this memorandum is to show that whatever doubts may have existed prior to 1899 as to the validity of the 1869 Regulations, owing to their lack of sanction by officials of the Chinese Government, no room for such doubts remained after the steps taken in 1898 with regard to the approval of the new Regulations then put forward, and the acceptance by the Taotai in 1899 of all existing Regulations as applying to the extended area of the Settlement [I, 61].

He does not seem to realize that there are other views that may also deserve consideration. For instance, Professor Manly O. Hudson, of Harvard University and the Secretariat of the League of Nations, a jurist of international reputation, made a careful study of the subject during his visit in Shanghai. He had all the facts and documents before him. His considered judgment is:

The present Land Regulations must, therefore, be taken to have been agreed to by a local and somewhat subordinate Chinese official; it is only by acquiescence that the more responsible Chinese authorities are committed by them [" International Problems at Shanghai, " *The Round Table*, VI, No. 1 (October, 1927), p. 79].

One cannot help being surprised when the Justice quotes Mr. S. Fessenden's speech of April 13, 1927, with apparent approval. Mr. Justice Feetham says:

The Council's case as to the origin of the Settlement was succinctly stated by the Chairman of the Council in his speech at the Annual Meeting of Ratepayers held on April 13, 1927, as follows:
" Shanghai as a municipality was not created by and does not derive its powers of government from the legislative assembly of any single state or country, nor from the mandate of any single sovereign power. It was created by and derives its powers from an agreement made between the so-called Foreign Powers on the one part and the Chinese Government on the other part.
" This agreement, which for the want of a better name is known as the Land Regulations, has all the sanctity of a treaty, being as it is a solemn and inviolable compact between sovereign nations.
" In substance and effect, although not in form, it is a treaty of the highest class, being as it is not merely a bilateral agreement between two sovereign powers, but an agreement to which many sovereign powers are parties " [II, 118].

My astonishment is complete that Mr. Justice Feetham is so naïve as to accept such a definition of the Land Regulations with apparent approval. This, to my mind, is only semi-academic discussion. The future of Shanghai does not depend upon the validity of Land Regulations. I have gone into it just to show the general attitude taken by Mr. Justice Feetham and the way he loses the support of some thinking Chinese.

In connection with Land Regulations, the general grievance of the Chinese authorities and people is often not so much the Land Regulations themselves but rather the interpretation and application of them. Any honest and careful observer will admit that the Land Regulations do not give a true picture of the wide powers actually exercised by the Shanghai Municipal Council, e.g., the police force, the Shanghai Volunteer Corps, etc. Here Mr. Justice Feetham volunteers the following defence:

> In particular instances the Council's view of the facts, or its contention as to the interpretation of treaties, may have been right or wrong, but there is no mistaking the reality and importance of the difficulties with which it was confronted. The Council was in fact striving to build up a serviceable structure of government, partly on a basis of usages which went beyond the letter of treaties; but the strength of its case lay in the fact that the conditions under which the treaties (including under that term the Land Regulations) had to be applied, were such that unless their provisions were in some way supplemented by usage, they would have been unworkable, and the authority which they purported to confer in regard to the government of the Settlement would have proved valueless [I, 110].

This opinion, to many Chinese, is very similar, only couched in more refined and restrained language, to that of Mr. Kotenev (the author of *Shanghai: Its Municipality and Mixed Court*), as a " logical result of the law of necessity," or " the lawful needs of foreigners." Of course, " necessity knows no law."

The situation shows the aggressive attitude of the Shanghai Municipal Council and is aptly summed up in a paradoxical statement by a Shanghai Municipal Council historian, Mr. Couling: " They [the Land Regulations] became more clearly binding on the foreigner through being contested, they became binding on the Chinese through not being contested " [Couling, *History of Shanghai,* p. 76]. Contest by Chinese could only mean official protests, popular agitation and strikes.

Uncalled-for comments. — There are also certain remarks made by Mr. Justice Feetham, perhaps quite unconscious of their offence, but nevertheless uncalled-for because they are not so universally true as he may think:

1. Local administrators, even those occupying comparatively subordinate positions in the official hierarchy, seem to have been left a fairly free hand to manage things in their own way, and to make what they could for themselves out of the inhabitants of the area under their charge [I, 98].

2. In a country where it was for many generations the recognised practice to purchase official posts, and where officials expected, as a matter of course, to make money out of their positions by exacting or accepting contributions from those with whom they were brought into contact in the performance of their official

duties, the making of private payments to public officials for their services is to be regarded by members of the public as a natural and proper method of procedure; where such a tradition has been established it is extremely difficult to prevent bribery, and to educate subordinate officers to recognise and to conform to standards different to, and higher than, those of the community to which they belong and in which their work lies [II, 81].

Such a generalization, if I may say so, is not worthy of a serious report of this nature. This sort of thing might occur in any country, though it may be that such things are more frequently left unpunished in China than they are in some other countries.

I mention these points and quote these passages not so much with a view to criticize Mr. Justice Feetham, but rather to account for the poor reception the report has had from Chinese in general.

RENDITION

I must now come to the most important part of the report — Part V on " Rendition." Mr. Justice Feetham defines rendition as follows: " I understand the term ' rendition ' as meaning the termination of the existing Settlement régime, and handing over of the actual administration of the Settlement to Chinese control."

As you may remember, Mr. Justice Feetham outlined his discussion with four questions:

1. What is the case for and against rendition? Are the arguments in favour of rendition, whether as a policy for immediate or ultimate adoption, such as should command assent?
2. In the event of rendition, what is to be the new régime which would be substituted for the old?
3. Is rendition, if accepted in principle, to be regarded as the immediate or ultimate goal? That is, is the change to be carried out immediately, or only after the lapse of a transition period?
4. If there is to be a transition period, what is to be the length of that period, or what are the governing considerations in accordance with which the length of that period should be determined?

To the first two questions, Mr. Feetham's answers are negative. On the first he says:

The case against rendition, therefore, does not go the length of asserting that there is no case, on theoretical ground, in favour of rendition. It really depends on the contention that even though rendition may ultimately be desirable for the purpose of satisfying the national aspirations of the Chinese people, under present circumstances it is practically impossible owing to the disastrous results that would inevitably ensue [II, 122].

To the second he answers:

It will, however, be recognised that the conclusion which I have reached — that under present conditions immediate rendition is wholly impracticable — is in accordance with foreign and Chinese opinion in the Settlement [II, 132], ... for rendition under present conditions would be inconsistent with security [II, 133].

To the third question he says that there is substantial agreement on four important points:

1. That the present régime under the Land Regulations is not to be regarded as permanent, and that the time will come for rendition of the Settlement when certain *conditions* have been fulfilled.
2. That when the time has come for rendition, there should be substituted for the present régime under the Land Regulations a new régime, to be established under Charter granted by the National Government, conferring full rights of local self-government on the Settlement, on the basis of continued co-operation between foreigners and Chinese, either as a separate unit or as a part of the City of Shanghai.
3. That a transition period is necessary before rendition, followed by the establishment of a Charter régime, can be regarded as a practical policy.
4. That during this period the affairs of the Settlement should be conducted on the basis of close co-operation between the foreign and Chinese communities in the Settlement.
   There is thus agreement as to the ultimate goal of future policy; as to the necessity of a transition period before that goal is reached; and as to the basis on which the affairs of the Settlement must be conducted during that transition period [II, 133].

To the fourth question he lays down five conditions, only upon the fulfilment of which will rendition become a practical policy. These conditions are such that probably not decades but centuries must elapse before they are fulfilled. As conditions to rendition they constitute an impossible barrier.

At first sight, Mr. Justice Feetham's argument is cogent and unassailable; but to many Chinese it is not at all convincing. Really, there are serious weaknesses. In the first place, he has not taken all factors into consideration. Hence his conclusion is based upon incomplete premises.

1. Take for example his " four points of agreement between foreign and Chinese communities " (II, 133). He assumes that there is substantial agreement between his so-called " responsible " members of both communities in the Settlement, foreign and Chinese. But he forgets that Shanghai is a part of China, and that Shanghai is not an isolated area belonging to the handful of business men in the Settlement. It is true that constructive reform must be carried out by the people living in Shanghai, but the governments of these nations that have trading relations with China have a great deal to say on the subject, and still more the Chinese Government, and the rest of China will not leave the fate of Shanghai to the Shanghai Chamber of Commerce or the Bankers' Association. Great national upheavals may sweep over and carry away the Chinese in Shanghai; and, not the less unlikely, foreign governments, for the sake of wider issues of trade and other world considerations, may be compelled to overlook the handful of local foreign business interests in Shanghai. I wish Mr. Justice Feetham had been here in 1925 or 1927 to see for himself that Shanghai is after all not such an island of security as he imagines it to be, having seen it under peaceful conditions.

2. It is true that many Chinese will agree that " certain conditions " are necessary or even reasonable for rendition. But Mr. Justice Feetham is quite

misled if he thinks any responsible Chinese will agree that all those five conditions are necessary or even practicable. No, not even the most moderate of them.

3. Again, during the transition period there is to be *close co-operation* between foreign and Chinese communities in the Settlement. I think Mr. Justice Feetham is quite mistaken if he thinks under the term *close co-operation* the Chinese will be contented with a minority on the Council and the power of Chinese always checked and circumscribed.

4. All Mr. Justice Feetham's careful calculation may be upset at any time by the sudden outburst of national feeling when it comes to the end of its patience and is highly irritated.

5. Mr. Justice Feetham does not allow in his calculation the fact that every right-minded Chinese business man is a patriot at heart. His action is not always dictated by his balance sheet and investments.

Another serious drawback is that he has assumed quite unconsciously a " superiority complex " which has greatly prejudiced the ultimate success of his scheme. For example, in more than one place he says, substantially, " Rendition will, however, ultimately be justifiable and necessary in order to satisfy the national aspirations of the Chinese people, and to enable the National Government of China, by the exercise of its own authority, to provide for the future municipal government of the Settlement " (II, 139). In a discussion of this kind, we could get Mr. Justice Feetham highly irritated by asking a few Socratic questions: When will the rendition be? (He has answered that it will take decades.) Who is to be the judge that these conditions have been fulfilled? Why should Great Britain, or Norway, or any other foreign government, be the judge? What if China does not agree to it? What happens if China adopts a different political structure? Will it mean then that rendition shall never take place? What happens if China never comes up to the standard required by Mr. Justice Feetham?

In short, at the back of all this, Mr. Justice Feetham unconsciously assumes that Foreign Powers will always be prepared to maintain the *status quo,* by force if necessary. Apart from the justifiability or not of this assumption, the Chinese naturally resent this attitude. This is what I mean by his " superiority complex." Most sons nowadays, and for that matter daughters, would resent it if their fathers attempted to map out their careers for them in that dictatorial manner, though even with the best of intentions, laying down laws and conditions for their children's growth.

In my opinion, Mr. Justice Feetham has not fully understood the psychology of the Chinese people, especially the political psychology; he has unconsciously taken up an attitude which lessens his effective presentation to the Chinese; and finally, he has left out several important considerations and thus based his reasoning on insufficient and incomplete premises, with the result that his recommendations, plan or scheme will suffer accordingly.

I do not say, for a moment, that all his recommendations are impracticable. Some of his recommendations, I think, deserve close study and careful attention. But the scheme as a whole must be recast in order to make it acceptable to the Chinese.

CONCLUSION

Roughly, the situation of Shanghai can be stated in this way: There are three possible alternatives for the future of Shanghai: (1) the policy of the *status quo,* (2) the policy of immediate rendition, (3) *via media,* the policy of gradual rendition, through a transition period. I think Mr. Justice Feetham is right when he says the third is the only practical policy. But it is all-important to devise what kind of *via media.* I think there are three ways to carry out the policy of gradual rendition:

1. Rendition, depending upon the fulfillment of many and difficult conditions, which serve as perfect safeguards and allow no risks.
2. Rendition depending upon the strict working out of a complete program leading to the ultimate rendition. This is only feasible when there is perfect understanding between all parties concerned and there are men responsible for the working out of the agreed program.
3. Steps for rendition to be taken immediately — the transfer of important powers depending upon a few (one or two) liberal and reasonable conditions being fulfilled and observed.

To my mind the last way is preferable to the other two for the following reasons:

1. Political institutions are most flexible and cannot be foreseen or anticipated with any degree of certainty.
2. There is no such thing as perfect safeguards in this world, especially in the development of political institutions. The best safeguarded political experiments have often proved to be utter failures.
3. Real statesmanship does not consist in making safety devices, but rather it must be a venture in faith, faith in the sanity and good sense of man, whether he is English, American, Japanese or Chinese, and the ultimate triumph of reason. Is not in our own times the League of Nations but a venture of faith? I may say the Institute of Pacific Relations is built on the faith of men and women who believe human effort and reason will succeed in the end, although we know not whither we are going and how we may get there. This, to my mind, is the greatest failing in Mr. Justice Feetham. He does not possess in sufficient measure that spirit of venture and of faith in the Chinese people which should light up every scheme for the ultimate solution of the problems of Shanghai.

I may speak like an idealist, but I believe that without idealism there is not much hope for the future of Shanghai. Again I may appear specially to plead China's cause and to champion the aspirations of the Chinese people. But that is not so. I speak as a man who is intensely interested in the welfare of Shanghai and as its sincere well-wisher. If I were to speak here as a Chinese nationalist, I am afraid Mr. Feetham's report would have received a much rougher handling.

My earnest desire is not to destroy whatever good work Mr. Feetham has done — and I think Mr. Feetham has done a great and lasting work in that he has brought out very clearly and in an unmistakable manner some of the important issues. My earnest desire is to build on what foundation he has laid and try to correct some of the wrong biases. Through the efforts of this body, officially and unofficially, Chinese, Americans, and Frenchmen of the same standing as Mr. Justice Feetham should be invited to continue the work which Mr. Feetham has so well begun, and to explore further. Mr. Feetham speaks of a double process, but I am sure every one will agree with me when I voice the hope that there should be a triple process. We cannot solve the Shanghai problem without the hearty co-operation of the French people and Government.

Through continuous study and effort and the creation of a sufficiently strong public opinion, I like to dream that in no distant future the Chinese and other governments concerned may be persuaded to invite and accept and abide by reports submitted by an international commission consisting of Chinese and foreign experts of the highest reputation, and thus settle once for all the thorny problems of Shanghai, so that within a generation the people of this great city may be so happy and prosperous that they will forget that there was ever such a thing as the necessity for a Feetham report, or any discussion of the " Status of Shanghai " and " The Shanghai Question."

SUMMARY OF DISCUSSION ON DR. HSIA'S ADDRESS

A member of the British group opened the discussion by pointing out that progress in solving the problem of the future of Shanghai could best be made if such criticism as that just heard were carefully considered. In judging the Feetham report and its insufficiencies it was necessary to keep in mind that the only criterion which justified a conference largely composed of foreigners to concern themselves with this matter was the welfare of China. If outside interests were endangered by proposed changes in the status of Shanghai, then Chinese interests also were endangered. If such changes were felt to be contrary to the requirements of China's political stability and economic development, then they would be equally hurtful to the foreign residents and the foreign powers. In general, it was possible to accept the political principles taught by Dr. Sun Yat-sen as providing the goal that must be worked toward. The founder of the Republic had realized that democracy can flourish only by the rule of law. The Feetham report was valuable, if for no other reason, because it again emphasized that principle.[6]

A former officer of the Chinese city of Shanghai humorously defended himself and his former colleagues against the charge seemingly implied in the Feetham report that Chinese municipal officers habitually enrich themselves by graft. One of the chief defects he found in the report was that it seemed to identify Chinese national interests with those of the relatively small group

---

[6] " That the Settlement has been able to exist and to grow under the peculiar constitutional difficulties which faced it is a great tribute to the political sense of the community " (Chamberlain, *op. cit.*, p. 4).

of Chinese business men and investors who are influential in the affairs of the International Settlement.

Justice Feetham had not shown at what point the claims of the foreign community to extensions of their rights beyond the boundaries of the Settlement ceased to be justified. If the Council were to be permitted to control the roads around the Settlement, because these were built by them for the convenience of foreign residents, what logically prevented these foreigners from exercising the same right over a road from Shanghai to Peiping?

As had been pointed out by others,[7] the International Settlement provided security for Chinese lives and property in times of danger. But the general effect of this place of refuge on the national life was by no means beneficial. Its very existence tempted citizens of wealth and influence to seek shelter for themselves in times of stress instead of sharing and even leading in the task of national reformation. Its existence — as a foreign occupation of national territory anywhere — provided a ready excuse for national inadequacies and a lightning conductor for popular dissatisfaction. " Everything is due to foreign aggression. We cannot tax them, and we cannot make them obey our laws." Movements against the Government were hatched within the walls of such a shelter, and dissenting political minorities attacked governmental policies in the guise of attacking the foreigners intrenched on the national soil. These influences, in their totality, were even more damaging, he thought, than the notorious fact that the settlement was harboring many criminals and, indeed, by providing them with a ready refuge from the national courts of justice, encouraged crime.

Without the International Settlement of Shanghai, there would have been no revolution in 1911. To this day it was the place where revolutions were planned and carried into effect. The revolutionary runs no risk so long as he can readily retreat for comfortable retirement into a community where the national government cannot apprehend him.

It seemed to him that Justice Feetham had not learned of such realities, nor had informed himself about the actual functioning of the Settlement's municipal administration. After all, what was good government? It was admitted, for example, that the communists had produced beneficial changes in the government of the Province of Kwangtung — did that justify the communist régime? Fine roads and fine buildings alone did not make good government.

Justice Feetham had been unfair in contrasting the administration of the International Settlement with that of the Chinese city of Shanghai. With wharves and warehouses, large commercial enterprises and attractions for wealthy residents, the Settlement of course disposed over a vastly greater tax capacity than the old town. Let the officers of the Shanghai Municipal Council for a while take over the various departments of the Shanghai municipality and carry on with its much smaller sources of revenue — only so could there be a fair basis of comparison!

[7] E.g., *The Round Table*, MCXXXI, No. 84, 750 ff.

Justice Feetham had idealized the municipal government of the Settlement, without, apparently, realizing that its repression of crime compares unfavorably with that of other large Chinese cities. Armed bands abound in the Settlement, and kidnapping is a frequent event. The blame for this condition did not, of course, rest upon the police authorities; rather, it was the result of divided jurisdiction. Shanghai was notorious for its commerce in opium and for its gambling. Without unification of control, evils such as these could not be removed. And unwilling to recommend such unification, Justice Feetham had not, apparently, been willing to discuss them.

No more than Dr. Hsia did he advocate rendition without preliminary safeguards. " Shanghai, the largest center of Chinese foreign trade and industry, holds a key position in the economic life of the whole nation. Until the National Government is able to defend it against any foreign power motivated by aggression, a friendly partnership in the city between China and the foreign powers is the only possible *modus vivendi*."

QUESTIONS FOR ROUND–TABLE DISCUSSION

The following questions were recommended by the Program Committee as part of a general outline for the discussion of " China's Foreign Relations."

LEASES, CONCESSIONS, AND SETTLEMENTS

1. What has been the effect, in such areas as the British concession at Tientsin and the International Settlement at Shanghai, of the admission of Chinese residents to a greater share in the government of the areas?
2. What has been the effect of rendition, in the areas that have been handed back to Chinese control, in such matters as efficiency in government, taxation, trade, public works, and improvements? To what degree have abnormal conditions in certain regions at certain times complicated the administration of restored areas?
3. What is the nature and working of municipal administration in such Chinese cities as Canton, Greater Shanghai, Peiping, and Hankow?
4. Does the report of Mr. Justice Feetham give a complete and satisfactory analysis of the situation in Shanghai?
5. What light does the Feetham report throw upon the problem of the future municipal government of Shanghai? What is the value of Mr. Justice Feetham's proposals in regard to the problem? What practical steps toward its solution can be taken in the immediate future?
6. Are similar steps applicable also to the remaining foreign concessions and settlements which have not yet returned to China?
7. What light does the recent working of the restored Chinese Court at Shanghai throw upon:
   a) The policy of rendition?
   b) The general problem of extraterritoriality?
8. What is the present situation with respect to the leases still held by foreign powers?

SUMMARY OF ROUND–TABLE DISCUSSION

True to the purposes and methods of the Institute, the round table on " The Future of Shanghai " did not attempt to sit in judgment upon Justice Feetham's report but turned to a study of constructive suggestions for ways leading toward the agreed goal of rendition. But because Dr. Hsia's address, a few evenings before, might have given the impression that foreign opinion on this subject was solidly lined up against Chinese nationalist opinion, the fact was first established that this was not the case, and more specifically that the then ruling party in Great Britain, the Labour party, unfortunately without a spokesman at this Conference, was not identified with the opinions and policies of the British interests in Shanghai represented at the round table. As to Chinese opinion, the fact most commented upon by foreign members was the apparent indifference expressed by the small Chinese attendance at this round table, and the lack of interest shown by Chinese members in the detailed discussion of this subject. Even the tentative proposal made in its course for setting up a new type of municipal government for the external roads area of Shanghai (see below, pp. 334 ff.) elicited but little interest among Chinese members during the conference.

The first question presented at once led into the heart of the practical issues: Seeing that the foreign authorities in the International Settlement have already recognized the new Criminal Code of the Nationalist Government, asked one of the members, would it not be equally possible for them to recognize the Government's new Civil Code? Even Chinese legal practitioners in Shanghai were unable to answer this question with an unqualified " yes." The Chinese Civil Code, they stated, has been drawn up on the models of the Japanese and German codes and thus may be regarded as essentially in conformity with the highest standards of Western jurisprudence. Nevertheless, in such matters as laws of inheritance it necessarily deviates from these models since it must conform somewhat to old-established social and economic practices. In interpreting such laws that touch the intimate traditions of a people, even the courts of Western countries would be likely to differ.

While the only really satisfactory court for Chinese litigants would be a Chinese court, and for British litigants a British court, nevertheless, a Chinese member suggested, it might not be impossible to have the Chinese Civil Code administered in the International Settlement by a single Chinese court. The question was then asked whether a court with composite membership, even though it might lead to diversity of interpretation, was not preferable to having different courts administer different legal systems in the same community. To this the Chinese spokesman readily agreed, but he thought that it might be possible to take a larger step in the direction of uniformity: Chinese lawyers do not recognize the necessity for maintaining the foreign courts, even during what might be called a " transition period." They feel that, as in other countries, one system of laws, administered by one court, both for nationals and for foreigners, is far preferable to any other kind of arrangement. But there is this fear of injustice through the misinterpretation by foreigners of what the law means. This, one of the Chinese members thought, might be sufficiently guarded against by inviting to the International Settlement a commission of foreign jurists to assist the court.

Others, while sympathetic with this suggestion, did not believe that such a commission would be accepted by the foreign community as a sufficient safeguard; some additional form of protection seemed to be needed to facilitate its adjustment to a new code during a period of transition. A model for such protection might possibly be found in the right of appeal to the diplomatic body, as granted to foreigners in Siam. This right of evocation, it was explained, was granted during ten years before there was complete abolition of extraterritoriality, to enable a foreign litigant to take his case out of the Siamese court into the diplomatic courts if he thought that the former's decision had done him a gross injustice. In fact, however, this right was exercised only once in the whole period of ten years. No optimism was expressed that such a provision would, in practice, work out the same way in China. The contrast of opinions and interests was so great that a frequent use of the right of evocation would have to be expected — with the result of undermining confidence in the Chinese court and of increasing international friction.

The round table was reminded at this point of a suggestion made in a paper prepared for the Kyoto Conference of the Institute, two years before, by Professor James T. Shotwell, of Columbia University. He had suggested that there should be established in Shanghai, and in four or five other places, special courts for applying the new legal code to cases growing out of industrial and commercial situations, with a personnel especially familiar with such situations and the law concerning them. In addition to such courts of first instance, there might be at least one court of appeal.

These should be courts in which the foreign as well as the Chinese litigants would have recourse to principles already familiar to them and so enable the Chinese code of laws to be widened out " from precedent to precedent " to cover that field of conflicting national usages which by its very nature contains so much of the elements of possible international misunderstanding.[8]

Such courts would, of course, have to be equipped with adequate machinery for law enforcement and satisfactory adjustment with the political authorities, both local and national. Professor Shotwell had indicated in some detail how such courts, so far from perpetuating the existence of foreign legal systems on Chinese soil, might in a relatively short time create foreign as well as Chinese confidence in a purely Chinese system and its actual administration.

Why should not the International Settlement of Shanghai be the first community, it was asked, to make such an experiment without, at first, giving up the consular courts, so long as foreign interests considered themselves in need of them? In practice, it would mean the establishment of a special court where Chinese judges would administer Chinese law — but with this safeguard that the president of the court and the judges were appointed on the recommendation of the consular body — that is, were men in whom the foreign residents have confidence. When foreigners wanted to sue Chinese, they would bring their case before this court. If it functioned satisfactorily, it would meet one of Justice Feetham's most important conditions for the future rendition of the Settlement — competency and independence of the judiciary.

Since none of the proposals so far made seemed altogether acceptable, a Chinese member suggested that perhaps the last one might be modified by having all cases now presented to the foreign courts in the French Concession and in the International Settlement go to one special high court with foreign advisers. Such innovation should be accompanied by the creation of a joint police force, Chinese, under highly qualified police officers, strong enough to supplant the Chinese and foreign troops now employed to guard the three separate administrative areas. He believed that the removal of the troops, Chinese and foreign, would have a most wholesome and beneficial influence

[8] *Problems of the Pacific, 1929,* p. 353.

upon the civic life of Shanghai; it would help to transfer the final power of government from the military or semi-military to the civil authorities and thus pave the way for increasing self-government in all three areas. The enforcement of law and order would become a wholly civil affair instead of being subjected to military authority.

Thus the discussion swung back from a consideration of the administration of law to the more inclusive problems of municipal government and of its present division under separate authorities. One member thought that a far-reaching experiment in the direction of unification — incidentally removing many of the features of the International Settlement that are most obnoxious to the Chinese — might be best carried on, first, in the outside area of Greater Shanghai where vested foreign interests are less strongly intrenched and less in need of protection but which already contained a considerable foreign population. He advocated that a Joint Council in this area be created to take the place of the present uncertain and undefined responsibility between the International Settlement and the Chinese Government, and of any contemplated further extension of foreign authority. The police force would be Chinese, likewise the personnel of the health department and that employed in maintenance of roads and in other public works. Chinese heads of municipal departments would function with foreign advisers. The Shanghai Municipal Council, the governing body of the International Settlement, might for some years meet the deficit on the budget during the growth of the revenues to be obtained through taxes on land values created by municipal improvements.

In this way, a fully qualified municipal personnel would be trained up, later to take over the present International Settlement when rendition eventuates. Such a council might, in the first instance, be appointed jointly by the present municipality of Greater Shanghai and by the Shanghai Municipal Council. As one member paraphrased the idea: the new system would be inaugurated by a bureaucracy, eventually to launch a democracy.

The proposal raised the further and more fundamental question: How do the Chinese envisage the future of Shanghai under Chinese authority? Have they in mind a form of self-government along the general lines of that now obtaining in the International Settlement, or continuance of a bureaucratic government, with the appointment of the highest officers by the National Government, as now obtaining in Greater Shanghai?

The ideal toward which interested Chinese were working, it was emphatically declared, was self-government. They felt justified in recommending a democratic experiment in the city of Shanghai because that city already contains more educated Chinese who have been trained in the rudiments of self-government than any other place. It was quite true, on the other hand, and this seemed implied in the question raised, that the present Kuomintang régime is not pushing toward the ideal of self-government sincerely advocated by the founder.

The present mayor of Greater Shanghai should at once appoint an advisory council to devise means of increasing representative government without lowering the standards of good administration. On this point, which is closely related to the constantly recurring arguments against any changes in the administration of the International Settlement itself that might interfere with municipal efficiency, a member of the British group made an interesting contribution:

" During the South African War, before it was half over, Lord Milner wished to initiate municipal institutions in Johannesburg. Here was a great mining town; to hold elections at that time was impossible. He therefore picked out about sixteen of the ablest men in the community and appointed them to form a municipal administration. In addition, it was their duty to set up self-government as soon as peace came.

" Never did a set of men work better or with more public spirit than these sixteen. They carried out their mandate. In the shortest possible time after the peace had been signed, they framed an electoral system and held elections. An elected city government was set up.

" Johannesburg has never had as good a governmental body as that which Lord Milner appointed. But their mandate was so precise and public opinion was so strong that there never could be any question that, the moment peace came, representative institutions would follow. If it had not been for the preciseness of that mandate, things might have drifted on for a very long time before the second part of their mission was carried out. The feeling had become so strong that they could administer Johannesburg better than anyone else.

" That is a universal experience in situations of this sort. I have watched Cabinets in England which, after a considerable period in office, could not help developing the feeling that they knew so much more about the affairs of state than anyone else could know that they should continue in office.

" In the long run, when you allow such a system to go on, that body of rulers, however great their merit and knowledge, will degenerate. It is for that reason that you have to come back to some representative system even if, for the time being, it puts into power a set of men who are less experienced, and sometimes less public-spirited, than the body selected by one man.

" I should view with great distrust any proposal to start such a system as the setting up of a joint bureaucratic government for Greater Shanghai unless the task of that appointed body were definitely limited in time. It should be part of their task to frame, after the administration has been set on foot, a system of popular representation which would be implemented by the sovereign power of the country, the Chinese Government.

" The need for a defined period after which such a body, appointed by the Mayor of Shanghai and the Municipal Council of Shanghai, should give way to representation is illustrated by the history of the Kuomintang itself. No one can read the works of Dr. Sun Yat-sen without recognizing the sincerity with which he looked forward to self-government as the only possible alternative to dynastic government. But the party still finds it difficult to say that the moment has arrived when any section of the people of China can be asked to exercise their choice in the selection of representatives."

There remained the question how such a charter, embodying both a temporary joint council and a mandate to prepare for a system of representative local government, might be brought about. The area in question is wholly Chinese, so that direct action by the Chinese Government rather than negotiation between it and the foreign powers would seem to be re-

quired. But, on the other hand, this is precisely the area concerning which
there has been a good deal of debate between the Government and the International Settlement of Shanghai as regards the latter's extension of authority.
Indeed, the whole of the third volume of Justice Feetham's report is devoted
to this subject. Questions of road making, of policing, of public health, and of
taxation are involved. Chinese opinion concerning the exercise of administrative and governmental functions by the International Settlement over this
suburban area are divided: landowners and residents have naturally benefited from it; but political influences have made it difficult to arrive at
a *modus vivendi*. To avoid conflict, the Municipal Council of the Settlement
has for a long time found it necessary to postpone needed improvements; and
although some outstanding controversies have been settled, there is always
a danger of clashes between two bodies of armed police, owing allegiance to
two separate authorities with competing claims for jurisdiction and maintenance of order in the same area and often on the same roads.

But is the scheme practical? To a Chinese participant of the round
table it did not seem so. For one thing, there were no present revenues from
which to support such a system of municipal government; for another, since
it applied to an outlying area with few important industrial or other economic
developments, the administrative positions which the scheme had to offer
would not be likely to attract the best minds. Furthermore, among the residents in this suburban area there were relatively few educated Chinese who
might be expected to take a leading part in such a scheme, compared with the
large number of such persons in the International Settlement. Others thought
that such a scheme would sidetrack the essential task of bringing the control
of the International Settlement more into harmony with the just claims of
the Chinese people.

The round table, therefore, once more directed its attention to the central
problem of jurisdiction. One service rendered by the Feetham report, it was
felt, was that it had convincingly shown where the kernel of the whole difficulty lay: it was the working of extraterritoriality in a particularly complex
setting. The question was: In whose hands are the sanctions for the security
of the Settlement to lie? Dr. Hsia's address [9] had given a Chinese view of
the Feetham report as a whole; but he had not attempted specifically to
assess the value of Justice Feetham's recommendations. One foreign member essayed the following synopsis of these recommendations:

" In the first place, the report is based entirely on the assumption of ultimate
rendition. I am not sure that Dr. Hsia did justice to it in that respect. He seemed
to think that Justice Feetham had put rendition out of his mind. With this I do not
agree. The following sentence from the report, for example, seems to me to justify
my interpretation:

" ' Rendition will . . . ultimately be justifiable and necessary in order to
satisfy the national aspirations of the Chinese people, and to enable the National
Government of China, by the exercise of its own authority, to provide for the future
municipal government of the Settlement.' [10]

[9] See pp. 319 ff.   [10] II, 139.

"He decides that immediate rendition is not possible, that it would involve too many risks — among them, insecurity in time of civil war; insufficient protection of life and property; arbitrary taxation; arbitrary exercise of governing power; destruction of the representative system. It is not a question of incurring minor risks, such as that of temporary diminution of municipal efficiency, but a question of imperiling, possibly destroying, foundations.

"Of course, the Chinese and the foreigners stand in different camps on that point. Even among the foreign residents in China there may be disagreement.

"From his unconditional support of the principle of rendition, Justice Feetham goes on to the question of a transitional régime. He considers such a change in régime essential because the present administration of the International Settlement needs reforms in many directions. Some of these, already overdue, he says, should be taken in hand at once. A change in control can take place satisfactorily and without serious risks only if a bridge has first been built between the old and the new régime — particularly through admitting more Chinese to participation in municipal government than at present.

"We may pass over Justice Feetham's views as to the procedure of that change, except for his statement that it must be by consent of both the Chinese Government and the foreign Governments.[11]

"The report discusses what has to be changed: Constitutional reforms are needed, we are told, in five departments:

"First, as to the composition and functions of the ratepayers' meetings — the organization through which representative views of the ratepayers are expressed. They elect the Municipal Council and have certain legislative powers. Justice Feetham's principal recommendation is that there be created a representative body, consisting of both foreigners and Chinese, on some agreed basis as to the respective shares or representation to be accorded to each community, and that the functions of the present Ratepayers' Meetings be transferred to this representative body.[12]

"Second, as to the composition of the Municipal Council itself and the scope of its powers. Briefly, the recommendation is that the number of councillors be increased so as to make the Council more fully representative of the Settlement community as a whole, both foreign and Chinese; and that the power to make by-laws be vested in future in the Council instead of being vested, as at present, in a Special Meeting of Ratepayers with special quorum requirements.[13]

"Third, that a court be established of representatives of the foreign consuls, but including Chinese members, to confirm the by-laws made by the Council, with power of final decision, that is without any further reference to Ministers of Foreign Powers or to Chinese Government authorities.[14]

"Fourth, that the Chinese courts be given jurisdiction in all cases, civil or criminal, arising in the Settlement, in which persons subject to their jurisdiction are concerned as defendants; and that any obscurity existing on this point in the provisions of the present agreement be cleared up.[15]

"Fifth, that provision be made for the payment of more adequate salaries to the judges of the courts, and for greater security of their tenure of office."[16]

A Chinese member of the round table expressed entire agreement that Justice Feetham's recommendations on these points and others signify substantial advances over the present government and administration of the Settlement; also that he had expressly given it as his opinion that extraterritoriality must eventually be abolished. But his general indorsement of the

---

[11] II, 151.
[12] II, 160.
[13] II, 184.

[14] II, 228.
[15] II, 236.
[16] II, 236–37.

policy of rendition did not satisfy the Chinese. The report did not indicate how it was to be accomplished. In the proposed changes for a " transition period," the status of the International Settlement would remain fundamentally as it was — specifically, there was no proposal to abolish the permanent foreign majority in its Council. He did not believe that it was necessary for the foreign settlement in this way to fortify itself against the possibility of civil war. The landing of foreign troops remained as much as ever a possible expedient of last resort; and other safeguards in such an eventuality could be provided for by treaty between the governments.

With this other speakers did not agree. If a wave of communism were to sweep over China, for example, no treaties with the present Government would avail. As distinct from civil war there was civil disorder. When there is no longer a semblance of government, conducting military operations on a fairly large scale, reliance upon a city government with a Chinese majority does not suffice for protection, even though for ordinary purposes it is strong enough. Again, however, Chinese speakers felt that a well-organized local police force is all that any community can be justified in expecting from its city government as a protection against such sporadic outbursts.

The question was raised whether the Feetham report would be substantially acceptable to the Chinese people if the Shanghai Municipal Council were to adopt a policy similar to that of the Chinese Maritime Customs, of gradually increasing the Chinese personnel, eventually promoting Chinese officers also to the most responsible and most highly technical positions which at first must be reserved for foreigners. To this the answer was that three areas of participation must be clearly distinguished: the structural, the administrative, and the political. The Chinese could not be satisfied with advances only in administrative appointments if they were to be excluded permanently from actual power. Under Justice Feetham's proposals, the Chinese members in the Municipal Council would still number only nine out of twenty-two. That arrangement, presumably, would last as long as the " transition period "; at least there was no indication how it might be changed. The Chinese would like to see, not an immediate equality with the foreign councilors in voting strength, but a gradually increasing participation.

But even this discussion of ways to increase Chinese participation and to democratize the functioning of the Municipal Council did not go deep enough for some of the round-table members. Essentially the criticism of the Chinese, as interpreted for them by a foreign member, was that the International Settlement was and, under Justice Feetham's proposals, would remain a state within the state, operating with a charter from their own government. Their questions were directed not only toward the foreign powers but toward their own government as well: What was the attitude of the Chinese Government — not to this or that proposal for correcting the inequalities of the present Settlement constitution, but to the political status of the Settlement itself? There could, of course, be no authoritative answer. After all, it was felt, there was no need to deal with absolutes; it was better to deal with the larger question as one concerning a situation in flux. Justice Feetham, it was pointed out, had rejected an immediate Chinese majority on the Council for the same reason for which he had rejected immediate rendition. But his recommendations did provide, for the time being, for a larger Chinese representation than for any of the foreign communities.

China is not simply confronted, others commented, with one foreign power in dealing with the problems of the Settlement, but with all the more important powers. Did not the Feetham report indicate some of the ways, at least, in which the approach toward rendition might be eased and rendition itself be accelerated? Those who insisted that there must be a Chinese majority in the Council first seemed to overlook other possibilities of hastening the process. Obviously, if the political status of the Settlement is to be revised, there must be revision of the treaties on which it is based. How might such revision best be carried through? Justice Feetham had indicated his own ideas as to this process, though not in any detail. He had suggested negotiation between the diplomatic body and the Chinese Government. But here a question of initiative arose. The Chinese Government, it was suggested, could hardly be expected to negotiate with foreign powers a treaty that would perpetuate, in the form of a new charter, what was essentially an acknowledgement of foreign control over a piece of Chinese territory. It was for this reason that Chinese spokesmen had considered so important the early achievement of a Chinese majority on the Municipal Council. Any proposal for a new charter not based upon such majority participation by the Chinese would clearly have to come from the foreign community and be submitted by the diplomatic representatives of the foreign powers. Even for a committee of inquiry, like that appointed under the Nine-Power Treaty to work out a scheme for the rendition of Weihaiwei, the initiative must come, in the first instance, from the foreign governments concerned.

So much for the process of having negotiations started. As to the substance of a proposal that might thus be made to the Chinese Government, it was felt that the Feetham report might provide a basis in that it gave the fullest argument for the necessity of a period of transition, with the ultimate aim of complete rendition. It might thus be possible for representatives of the foreign powers to negotiate with the Chinese Government an agreement for a charter conferring upon the International Settlement of Shanghai a special status over a given period, say twenty years. It would be understood that at the end of that time new negotiations would lay the basis for an agreement more satisfactory to the Chinese people and Government. Eventually the future of Shanghai must rest on the permanent foundation of international good will and real partnership.

CHAPTER XI

INLAND AND COASTAL NAVIGATION

DATA PAPERS

1. MINGCHIEN JOSHUA BAU. *Foreign Navigation in Chinese Waters* (China Council).
2. G. WARREN SWIRE. *The Coast and River Trade of China* (mimeographed, British Group).
3. J. P. CHAMBERLAIN. *Foreign Flags in China's Internal Navigation* (American Council).
4. A MEMBER OF THE BRITISH GROUP. *Entrance and Clearance of Steamers Trading on the China Coast and Chinese Inland Waters.*

REFERENCES

1. *Syllabus on China's Foreign Relations*, pp. 17–18, 26–29.
2. M. JOSHUA BAU. *The Status of Aliens in China*, p. 34.
3. A MEMBER OF THE BRITISH GROUP. *The Status of Aliens in China*, p. 16.
4. AKIRA NAGANO. *Development of Capitalism in China*, pp. 4–6.
5. F. F. A. "Foreign Shipping in Chinese Waters," *Chinese Economic Journal*, March 1931, pp. 249–58.

EXTRACTS FROM DATA PAPERS

I. A HISTORICAL SURVEY [1]

By Mingchien Joshua Bau

It is a generally recognized principle and practice in international law that inland navigation and coasting trade are usually reserved for vessels of nationals. By inland navigation is meant navigation in inland territorial waters, particularly national rivers. Foreign vessels are generally excluded from navigation in such waters, save by treaty grant or as part of international trade. Coasting trade, or cabotage, is navigation and trade between two or more ports, situated on a maritime coast of the same state. Foreign vessels are likewise commonly excluded from such trade, save by treaty stipulation or as part of international trade, and save in the case of innocent passage in time of peace. China, however, constitutes a leading exception to this rule and practice of international law. Her inland waters and maritime coast are open to foreign navigation and trade. What is worse, the greater share of such navigation and trade is taken by foreign vessels.

The right of coasting trade between the first five treaty ports — Canton, Amoy, Foochow, Ningpo, and Shanghai — was first granted to American vessels in 1844.[2]

"The citizens of the United States are permitted to frequent the five ports of Quangchow, Amoy, Fuchow, Ningpo, and Shanghai, and to reside with their families and trade there, and to proceed at pleasure with their vessels and merchandise to or from any foreign port and either of the said five ports, and from either of the said five ports to any other of them; but said vessels shall not unlawfully enter into the other ports of China, nor carry on a clandestine and fraudulent trade along the coasts thereof; and any vessel belonging to a citizen of the United States which violates this provision shall, with her cargo, be subject to confiscation by the Chinese Government" [Art. III].

By the operation of the most favored nation clause, the other Powers having treaty relations with China and enjoying the most favored nation treatment *ipso facto* received the same privilege. Thus, the coasting trade, first granted in 1844, was confined to the inter-port trade between the first five open ports, and clandestine or fraudulent trade with ports not open to foreign trade was forbidden. The right of foreign ships of war to visit the ports of China was likewise first granted to the United States of America in 1844.[3]

"Whenever ships of war of the United States, in cruising for the protection of the commerce of their country, shall arrive at any of the ports of China, the commanders of said ships and the superior local authorities of government shall hold intercourse together in terms of equality and courtesy, in token of the friendly

---

[1] Extract from data paper, *Foreign Navigation in Chinese Waters* (China Council), pp. 1–14.

[2] Treaty of Wanghia, July 3, 1844, *Treaties between China and Foreign States* (Maritime Customs of China), I, 677 ff.

[3] *Ibid.*, Art. 32, p. 689.

relation of their respective nations; and the said ships of war shall enjoy all suitable facilities on the part of the Chinese Government in the purchase of provisions, procuring water, and making repairs, if occasion requires."

It is interesting to note that the right of visit accorded to the American ships of war was not restricted to the first five treaty ports but extended to all the ports of China.

The opening of the Yangtze River to foreign trade and navigation was first made by Great Britain in 1858,[4] as a result of the second war between China, on the one hand, and Great Britain and France, on the other:

" British merchant ships shall have authority to trade upon the Great River (Yangtze)" [Art. X].

Three other ports on the Yangtze were opened by the same Power, Chinkiang in 1859, and Hankow and Kiugiang in 1860. Meanwhile, the scope of the coasting trade was extended to five other ports — Newchang, Chefoo, Taiwan (Formosa), Swatow, and Kiungchow (Hainan).

THE OPENING OF THE AMUR, SUNGARI, AND USSURI

The Amur, Sungari, and Ussuri rivers were opened to Russian trade and navigation in 1858: [5]

" Dans l'intérêt de la bonne intelligence mutuelle des subjets respectifs, il est permis aux habitants riverains de l'Oussouri, de l'Amour et du Soungari, subjets de l'un et de l'autre Empire, de trafiquer entre eux, et les autorités doivent réciproquement protéger les commerçants sur les deux rives " [Art. II].

This right, however, was annulled by the agreement between China and Soviet Russia, May 31, 1924.[6]

" The Governments of the Two Contracting Parties agree to annul at the conference as provided in the preceding article all conventions, treaties, agreements, protocols, contracts, etc. concluded between the Government of China and the Tsarist Government and to replace them with new treaties, agreements, etc., on the basis of equality, reciprocity, and justice, as well as the spirit of the declarations of the Soviet Government of the years of 1919 and 1920."

The scope of the coasting trade was further widened in 1860, when Tientsin was opened as a treaty port,[7] and in 1869 when Wenchow (Chekiang) and Wuhu (Anhui) were added to the list of treaty ports; but Kiungchow (Hainan) was eliminated from the same.[8]

---

[4] The Treaty of Tientsin, June 26, 1858 (Hertslet's *China Treaties*, No. 6, pp. 18 ff.).

[5] The Treaty of Aighoun between China and Russia, May 16, 1858 (Hertslet, No. 80, pp. 454 ff.).

[6] *Treaties and Agreements with and concerning China, 1919–1929* (Division of International Law, Carnegie Endowment for International Peace), pp. 133 ff. [Art. III].

[7] Art. IV, Treaty of Tientsin between Great Britain and China, October 24, 1860 (Hertslet, No. 8, p. 48); the Supplementary Convention to the Treaty of Commerce and Navigation of June 26, 1858, between Great Britain and China, signed at Peking, October 23, 1869 (Hertslet, No. 11, pp. 61 ff.).

[8] *Ibid.*, Arts. VI and VIII.

THE BEGINNING OF INLAND NAVIGATION

Heretofore, the coasting trade and inland navigation were limited only to treaty ports on the Yangtze or along the seacoast, and trade and navigation in the interior was forbidden. But in 1869 [9] trade and navigation in the interior of China of a limited character was for the first time granted. British merchants might go to the non-treaty ports or places in the interior with their own vessels of Chinese type, or propelled by sail or oar, duly provided with passports and certificates of registration issued by the Chinese Commissioner of Customs, to sell foreign goods, purchase native produce, or carry native produce into the interior for sale. In 1876,[10] the words " *nei-ti* " — " inland " — regarding carriage of imports inland, and of native produce purchased inland, were defined to apply as much to places on the seacoasts and river shores as to places in the interior not open to trade. Thus, the scope of inland navigation and coasting trade was extended to all non-treaty ports or places in the interior of China, subject only to the limitations of the use of vessels of Chinese type or propelled by sail or oar and the provision of passports and certificates of registration.

The extent of coasting trade and inland navigation was again broadened in 1876,[11] by the addition to the list of treaty ports of Ichang (Hupeh) and Pakhoi (Kwangtung), and by the opening on the Yangtze River as ports of call of Tatung, Anking, Huk'ou, Wusueh, Luchik'ou, and Shashih; and in 1890,[12] by the opening of Chunking as a treaty port and by granting to the British subjects the right to charter Chinese vessels or to provide vessels of the Chinese type for the traffic between Ichang and Chunking.

The opening of Long-Ki-Kong and the rivers of the Cao-Bang to trade and navigation from Lang-San to Cao-Bang was procured by France in 1887,[13] when the right of navigation and trade therein was granted to French and Annamite merchant vessels.

THE OPENING OF THE UPPER YANGTZE

The opening to steam navigation of the Upper Yantze River, the Woosung River, and the Canal from Shanghai to Soochow and Hangchow was obtained by Japan in 1895.[14] In the same year, the list of treaty ports was further enhanced by the addition of Shashih (Hupeh), Chunking (Szechuan),

---

[9] The Supplementary Rules and Tariff drawn up in connection with the aforesaid British Convention of October 23, 1869 (Hertslet, No. 11, pp. 67 ff.).

[10] The Agreement of Chefoo between Great Britain and China, September 13, 1876 (Hertslet, No. 12, pp. 73 ff.).

[11] The aforesaid Chefoo Agreement.

[12] The Additional Article to the aforesaid Chefoo Agreement, signed at Peking, March 31, 1890 (Hertslet, No. 18, p. 94).

[13] The Additional Convention of Commerce between France and China, June 26, 1887 (Hertslet, No. 48, pp. 311 ff.) [Art. VI].

[14] The Treaty of Shimonoseki, April 17, 1895 (Hertslet, No. 62, pp. 362 ff.) [Art. VI].

Soochow (Kiangsu), and Hangchow (Chekiang); and in 1896 the list of the ports of call by the accession of Woosung.[15]

The list of ports of call on the Yangtze was once more increased in 1897 by the opening of Kongmoon, Komchuk, Shiuhing, and Takhing.[16]

THE OPENING OF THE WEST RIVER

The opening of the West River was secured by Great Britain in 1897,[17] when there were opened those ports on the said river — Wuchoufu (Kwangsi), Samshui City and Kou Kun Market (Kwangtung), with the freedom of navigation for steamers between Samshui and Wuchow, and Hongkong and Canton.

THE INLAND STEAM NAVIGATION REGULATIONS OF 1898

In the memorable year of the international battle for concessions — 1898 — as a consequence of one of the British demands for the opening of all the inland waters of China to foreign navigation and trade, the Chinese Government issued three sets of regulations governing inland steam navigation.

The first set, issued by the Tsung-li Yamen, on July 28, 1898,[18] embodied those rules.

The inland waters of China are hereby opened to all such steamers, native or foreign, as are registered for that trade at the treaty ports. They shall confine their trade to the inland waters — that is, waters in all parts of the interior of China — and must not proceed to places outside of Chinese territory.

Such steamers are to be registered at the Customs House and there take out customs papers renewable annually at the payment of taels 10 on first issue and of taels 2 for each annual renewal, and subject to the rules in force at the Customs House.

The second set was the regulations governing trade on the Yangtze River, Peking, August, 1898.[19]

The merchant vessels of the treaty Powers are authorized to trade on the Yangtze River at the following treaty ports, Chinkiang, Nanking, Wuhu, Kiukiang, Hankow, Shasi, Ichang, and Chunking; and to land and ship goods in accordance with special regulations at the non-treaty ports, Tatung, Anging, Hukow, Luchikou, and Wusueh. Shipment or discharge of cargo at any other port on the river is prohibited, but passengers and their baggage may be landed and shipped at Kiangyin, Ichang, Hwangtsekang, and Hwangchow.

Merchant vessels are divided into three classes:

[15] The Sino-Japanese Treaty of Commerce and Navigation, July 21, 1896 (Hertslet, No. 64, p. 375) [Art. V].

[16] Also see West River Regulations, July 30, 1904 (MacMurray, *Treaties and Agreements with and concerning China* [1904/3], pp. 484 ff.).

[17] The Special Article attached to the Sino-British agreement relative to Burmah and China, signed at Peking, February 4, 1897 (Hertslet, No. 22, pp. 113 ff.).

[18] Hertslet, II, No. 138, 721 ff.

[19] *Ibid.*, No. 139, 723 ff.

1. Sea-going vessels trading for the voyage up river beyond Chinkiang;

2. River steamers running regularly between any of the river ports or Shanghai and any river port;

3. Small craft (lorchas, papicos, junks, etc.).

Sea-going vessels must deposit their registers with the consul, or, if consularly unrepresented, with the Customs at Shanghai, Woosung, or Chinkiang, where the Customs will issue a " special river pass " for sailing and trading up the river beyond Chinkiang, such special river pass to be surrendered upon return.

River steamers may deposit their registers at the Consulate at Shanghai, or, if consularly unrepresented, at the Customs House, which will issue a river pass valid during the current year; such river pass to be renewed every year at Shanghai, or, in the case of river steamers trading above these places and not returning to Shanghai, at Hankow or Ichang.

The small craft, lorchas, etc., owned by foreigners, if provided with registers and entitled to fly national flags, are required to take out a special river pass either through the Consulate or from the Customs direct at Chinkiang if proceeding farther up the river; papicos, etc., owned by foreigners, but not provided with registers or entitled to fly national flags, are to take out Customs papers at the port to which they belong, and the Chinese junks chartered by foreigners are only available for conveying foreign-owned cargo from treaty port to treaty port, and must take out special junk papers at the Customs.

The third set was the supplementary rules under Inland Steam Navigation Regulations issued at Peking in September, 1898,[20] which stipulate that all inland going steamers are to pay tonnage dues once in four months at the treaty tariff rates, at the port where registered.

A revision of the 1898 regulations [21] was made after the signing of the Mackay Treaty in 1902.

British ship owners are to have the right to lease warehouses and jetties on the banks of waterways for terms not exceeding 25 years, with options of renewal on terms to be mutually agreed upon.

Foreign merchants are to pay taxes and contributions on these warehouses and jetties on the same footing as Chinese owners of similar properties.

The main object of the British Government in desiring to see the inland waterways of China opened to steam navigation being to afford facilities for the rapid transport of both foreign and native merchandise, they undertake no impediment to the transfer to a Chinese company and the Chinese flag of any British steamer which may now or hereafter be employed on the inland waters of China, should the owner be willing to make the transfer.

Thus, inland waters whose navigation was originally limited to foreign-owned vessels of Chinese types or propelled by sails or oars are now thrown open to foreign and native steam navigation. . . .

What was originally a voluntary concession on the part of the Chinese

[20] *Ibid.*, No. 140, 726 ff.
[21] Hertslet, No. 28, Annex C, pp. 187–88.

Government is now secured by treaty stipulation and made unchangeable save by mutual consent. These regulations are still in force today.

Meanwhile, the extent of foreign trade and navigation was again broadened by addition to the list of treaty ports Changsha (Hunan), Wanhsien (Szechuan), Nganking (Anhui), Waichow (Kwangtung), Kongmoon (Kwangtung),[22] Mukden, Tatungkow (Fengtien),[23] and Antung (Fengtien),[24] and by the appendage to the list of ports of call Pak Tau Hau, Lo Ting Hau and Do-Sing, and by the opening of the ten passenger landing stations on the West River, Yung Ki, Mah Ning, Kau Kong, Kulow, Wing On, How Lik, Luk Pu, Yuet Sing, Luk To, and Fung Chuen.[25]

The opening of the Inland Waters of Manchuria to steam navigation, besides the Russian navigation on the Amur, Sungari, and Ussuri rivers which we have already seen, was accomplished by Japan in 1903.[26]

THE OPENING OF THE INLAND WATERS OF MANCHURIA

The Chinese Government agree that any Japanese steamer capable of navigating the inland waterways, upon reporting at the Maritime Customs, may proceed for the purpose of trade from a treaty port to places inland so reported, on complying with the original and supplementary regulations for steam navigation inland [Art. III].

. . . In accordance with the provisions of Art. III of the present treaty, all classes of Japanese steamers, whatever their size, provided they are capable of navigating the inland waterways, may, on complying with the regulations, receive an inland water certificate and ply to and from inland places, and that the Chinese Government will in no case raise difficulties and stop them.

During the negotiation of this article, we received a list from your excellencies of the Japanese steamers, . . . plying from Chefoo to inland places in Manchuria, under inland waters certificate and in accordance with the regulations for steam navigation inland, which vessels have not been prevented from doing so on account of their class.[27]

Meanwhile, the following places in Manchuria were added to the list of treaty ports: [28] Fenghuangcheng, Liaoyang, Hsinmintun, Tiehling, Tungkiangtsu, and Fakumen in the Province of Shingking; Changchun, Kirin, Harbin, Ninguta, Hunchun, Sanhsing in the Province of Kirin; Tsitsihar, Hailar, Aigun and Manchuli in the Province of Heilungkiang.

[22] Art. VIII, Sec. 12, Mackay Treaty of September 5, 1920.
[23] Art. X, Sino-Japanese Treaty of October 8, 1903.
[24] Art. XII, Sino-American Treaty of October 8, 1930.
[25] Art. X, Mackay Treaty of September 5, 1902.
[26] Sino-Japanese Treaty of October 8, 1903 (Hertslet, No. 66, pp. 383 ff.).
[27] Annex III, Imperial Chinese Commissioner for Treaty Revision to Imperial Japanese Commissioner for Treaty Revision, October 8, 1903 (Hertslet, p. 389).
[28] Treaty and Additional Agreement between China and Japan Respecting Manchuria, signed at Peking, December 22, 1905 (Hertslet No. 67, pp. 391 ff.).

The Treaty Powers enjoying inland navigation and coasting rights are herewith tabulated with their relevant treaties.

1. Great Britain:

   a) General Regulations for the British Trade at the Five Ports, July, 1843, which formed part of the Supplementary Treaty between Great Britain and China, October 8, 1843.
   b) The Treaty of Tientsin, June 26, 1858.
   c) The Treaty of Tientsin, October 24, 1860.
   d) The Supplementary Convention of Peking, October 23, 1869.
   e) The Agreement of Chefoo, September 13, 1876.
   f) The Additional Article to the Chefoo Agreement, March 31, 1890.
   g) The Special Article attached to the Agreement Relative to Burmah and China, signed at Peking, February 4, 1897.
   h) The Mackay Treaty, September 5, 1902.

2. The United States of America:

   a) The Treaty of Wanghia, July 3, 1844.
   b) The Treaty of Tientsin, June 18, 1858.
   c) The Treaty Respecting Commercial Relations signed at Shanghai, October 8, 1903.

3. Belgium:

   a) The Treaty of Friendship, Commerce and Navigation, signed at Peking, November 2, 1865.

4. Brazil:

   a) The Treaty of Friendship, Commerce and Navigation, signed at Tientsin, October 3, 1881.

5. Denmark.

   a) The Treaty of Friendship, Commerce and Navigation, signed at Tientsin, July 13, 1863.

6. France:

   a) The Treaty of Whampoa, October 24, 1844.
   b) The Treaty of Tientsin, June 27, 1858.
   c) The Additional Convention of Commerce signed at Peking, June 26, 1887.

7. Italy:

   a) The Treaty of Friendship, Commerce and Navigation, signed at Tientsin, July 13, 1863.

8. Japan:

   a) The Treaty of Shimonoseki, April 17, 1895.

   b) The Treaty of Commerce and Navigation, July 21, 1896.

   c) Protocol Respecting Japanese Settlement and Other Matters, signed at Peking, October 19, 1896.

   d) The Supplementary Treaty of Commerce and Navigation, signed at Shanghai, October 8, 1903.

9. Mexico:

   a) The Treaty of Friendship, Commerce and Navigation, signed at Washington, December 14, 1899.

10. The Netherlands:

   a) The Treaty of Friendship and Commerce, signed at Tientsin, October 6, 1863.

11. Norway:

   a) The Treaty of Peace, Amity and Commerce, signed at Canton, March 30, 1847.

12. Peru:

   a) The Treaty of Friendship, Commerce and Navigation, signed at Tientsin, June 26, 1874.

13. Portugal:

   a) The Treaty of Friendship and Commerce, signed at Peking, December 1, 1887.

14. Spain:

   a) The Treaty of Tientsin, October 10, 1864.

15. Sweden:

   a) The Treaty of Friendship, Commerce and Navigation, July 2, 1908.

Thus, there are yet 15 Treaty Powers still enjoying this special privilege of inland navigation and coasting trade, namely, Great Britain, the United States of America, Belgium, Brazil, Denmark, France, Japan, Italy, Mexico, The Netherlands, Norway, Peru, Portugal, Spain, and Sweden. Germany, Austria, and Hungary, which once enjoyed this privilege, have now lost it in consequence of the World War.[29] Soviet Russia voluntarily surrendered it in 1924.[30]

[29] Sino-German Treaty, May 20, 1921; Sino-Austrian Treaty, October 19, 1925; Sino-Hungarian Treaty, June 4, 1920. *Treaties and Agreements with and concerning China, 1919–1929* (Carnegie Endowment).

[30] Sino-Russian Treaty, May 31, 1924.

II. THE HISTORY OF FOREIGN SHIPPING IN CHINESE WATERS [31]

By G. WARREN SWIRE

As some evidence of the ever-increasing part played by foreign-style tonnage on the coast and rivers of China, the following dates of the inception of the principal concerns now running may be of interest. In 1867 the Boston firm of Russell & Company started to run vessels built on the model of the Mississippi river-steamers on the Yangtze, under the ownership of the Shanghai S. N. Company. In 1865 the English Hong Kong, Canton & Macao Steamboat Company ran vessels from Hong Kong to Canton and Macao. In 1873 the English China Navigation Company first ran ships both on river and coast. In 1877 Russell's vessels were taken over by the first big Chinese company, the China Merchants S. N. Company, which was started by Tong King Sing under semi-Government auspices. In 1881 the English Indo-China S. N. Company took over a number of vessels, which had been run in a rather desultory way for a number of years by Jardine, Matheson & Company, and started regular services on river and coast, in addition to their original service between India and China. In the eighties also the English-Scottish Oriental Company started its services between China and Siam and the Straits and was eventually in 1900 bought out by the Norddeutsche Lloyd, which continued to run until 1914. In 1898 the Osaka Shosen Kaisha started a service on the Yangtze, followed later by the Nippon Yusen Kaisha, who eventually took over a small concern running under the British flag, and in 1907 these two companies amalgamated their river services into a new company, the Nissen Kisen Kaisha. Between 1900 and 1914 the Norddeutsche Lloyd ran a service on the river, and between 1898 and 1914 Diederichsen Jebsen & Company, followed by the Hamburg-Amerika Linie, ran another on the coast.

In 1909 the Ningshao S. N. Company first ran a vessel to Ningpo; and from this beginning has been built up the present Sanpeh-Ningshao combine, which runs regular services on the river and irregular trips on the coast. The only other notable Chinese concerns are the Ching Kee S. N. Company, Limited, which from a start about 1909 between the ports north of Shanghai has now extended its sphere to include a share in the trade to Hong Kong and Canton, and the Ho Hong S. S. Company, Limited, which runs between South China ports, the Straits, and Rangoon.

In addition to the above regular lines there are a considerable number of Norwegian vessels usually on charter to Chinese and small Chinese one-ship companies, which buy or charter old tonnage and appear and disappear in accordance with the state of the freight market.

The general run of the China Coast trade is, with the exception of a few commodities, from north to south and is, as the next few lines will show, largely of a seasonal nature. The main lines of produce are:

[31] From *The Coast and River Trade of China* (mimeographed, British Council), pp. 1–3.

Beans and beancake.... From Manchurian ports to South China. (The latter is
                      used as manure.)
Ground nuts.......... From Tsingtao or Pukow to the south.
Rice .... From various river ports both to the north and to Canton.
Rice .... From Bangkok and Saigon generally to South China ports.
Cotton .... From middle Yangtze ports.
Wood oil .... From the upper Yangtze and Tungting Lake. (A big
                      article of export.)

Besides all this there is of course the ordinary general trade.

III. ANALYSIS OF THE PROBLEM [32]

By J. P. CHAMBERLAIN

Without the use of vessels of the foreign type, the enormous increase in
the internal trade of China would not have been possible. In 1874, the total
tonnage of coast trade entered and cleared at offices under the Inspector
General of Customs amounted to 7,562,824 tons. Only cargoes of foreign-
type ships, either Chinese or foreign-owned, are included in these statistics.
By 1912 this figure had risen to 60,135,015 tons, in 1927 it was reported as
71,695,212 tons,[33] and in 1929 it had passed the hundred million ton mark
to 103,583,855 tons.[34] The greatest share of this trade is carried under foreign flags. In 1929 only 30.35 per cent of the coast trade was carried in
Chinese ships. British ships took 44.21 per cent and Japanese 18.46 per cent;
Americans accounted only for 2.84 per cent. [35]

The reasons for the continued preponderance of the foreign flag are
both economic and political. Foreign vessels have the advantages of extraterritoriality. They are free from seizure by officers of the Government, they
can be searched only by the Chinese Maritime Customs, not by any Chinese
military or civil official; they are not subject to arbitrary taxes or imposts
without the approval of their consul. They can be sued only in the consular
courts of the flag, and their owners, individuals or companies, only before
their national consuls, so that in the case of collision or claims in respect to
cargo they are not under Chinese courts or Chinese law. On the other hand,
if they wish to sue Chinese for any cause, such as breach of contract, or tort,
they must proceed in the appropriate Chinese court. In practice, suits are
rare since differences are compromised or disposed of under a contract provision, in accordance with the age-old Chinese custom of settling controversies
by private means instead of going to the courts for redress.

Extraterritoriality extends to the foreign officers and members of the
crew; they can only be tried before their own national consul who is not

[32] Extract from a revised edition of *Foreign Flags in China's Internal Navigation*
(American Council).

[33] Morse, *International Relations of the Chinese Empire*, II, 395; *China Year Book*
(1929–30), pp. 174–75.

[34] Bau, *Foreign Navigation in Chinese Waters*, p. 17.

[35] *Ibid.*, p. 18.

necessarily the same before whom the ship is justiciable. Furthermore, even Chinese members of the crew cannot be arrested on board the ship and taken off without the consent of the consul of the nationality of the flag. They are amenable to Chinese law and Chinese courts, but owing to the right of the ship to freedom from the action of Chinese police on board, they have a degree of protection through the consul against arbitrary action. This protection, of course, will not be abused by the consul to protect criminals, or Chinese wanted for good reason by the Government. Foreign officers on Chinese ships enjoy the same rights of jurisdiction by their consuls. They also cannot be tried, even for faults of navigation, except before a consular tribunal.

Freedom from Chinese jurisdiction, which extraterritoriality affords, is modified by the power of the Chinese Maritime Customs. Customs officers board and search ships for customs purposes at whatever port they may happen to be and, of course, in their search include opium as a forbidden article. Whether coming down or going up river, or entering from the sea, the Customs officers may search a ship, seize and remove contraband goods, and assess duties. If fines are imposed on the ship for violation of the law, the Customs has an efficacious means of compelling settlement without recourse to the consular jurisdiction. A ship cannot clear from a port without their consent. When a ship from abroad enters, her papers are lodged with the consul who gives her a notice which, with her manifest of cargo, is handed to the Customs. She cannot clear and receive back her papers from the consul until the Customs have issued a " No Objection " paper, on being satisfied that all dues and charges against her have been satisfied. If she desires to enter the river trade with treaty ports she must have a " River Pass " issued by the Customs; and if she wants to stop at other than treaty ports she must have an " Inland Waters Certificate," also issued through the Customs, after her hull and boiler survey certificate has been approved by the Harbor Master. By their control over the ships coming and going, the Customs are able to enforce directly obedience to harbor rules and navigation regulations over foreign as well as Chinese ships. This is, in fact, the recognized way of controlling vessels. The high standard of the Customs service, under an English chief, with both foreign and Chinese officers, has made it a very effective and readily accepted organ of control.

The long period of civil war in China has been very harmful to the development of the Chinese mercantile fleet owing to the frequently exercised power of the Government to take over vessels for military purposes. The China Merchants Steam Navigation Company, the principal company, suffered seriously from this cause. Many of its ships have been requisitioned by the military and in some cases actually destroyed.[36] This action by the Government has often taken a great proportion of the shipping on a particular run. According to the *United States Commerce Report* for 1929, so many Chinese boats had been commandeered for the troops that few were

[36] *China Year Book* (1929), p. 790.

left in the service;[37] and during the fighting in the Yangtze Valley in 1924–25, most of the Chinese-operated river boats remained tied up at Shanghai, due to their liability to seizure. In 1928, the Customs report for Hankow notes that the year 1928 opened with only foreign tonnage running on the river, the Chinese lines not resuming operations till April, when " their reappearance caused a drop in freight rates," an evidence of the importance of their place on the river.[38] Even as late as 1931, the service of the Chinese lines on the Yangtze was crippled by the taking over of ships by the Military Department in the spring. The boats were released in the fall at the request of the merchants who wanted the service.[39]

Even though the Government now takes over the ships under contract providing for payment, the interference with the regular services of the lines and therefore their standing with merchants and their efficient operation in a long term must be hampered by the resultant interference with their regular service. The Chinese shipowners have lessened the inconvenience by forming a pool and supplying the tonnage requested by the Government in a fixed proportion among them so that no one line is crippled.

The disorders in the interior, resulting in an increase of brigandage and semi-independent generals, have brought out the advantage which foreigners enjoy from the protection of their gunboats. In 1929, the conditions on the Yangtze caused an increase in the patrol of foreign gunboats, and on the upper river even foreign ships could not safely navigate without gunboat protection.[40] The use of a warship against a general is illustrated by a recent case.

" On a recent trip from Ichang to Chungking, three ships of the Yangtze Rapids Steamship Co., escorted by the U.S.S. Guam, proceeded as far as Wanshien, where they anchored for the night, when they were boarded by a representative of General Yang Sen, who informed the ships' officers that the ships were required to transport troops to Fowchow. The vessels were not available for military service, and only the presence of the gunboat and the firm attitude of her commander prevented them from being commandeered."

However, the political advantage which foreigners enjoy is not the only reason for their predominant position in Chinese cabotage. Shipping is a business like any other which requires experienced management, on the alert not only to supply the shipper and passenger with the service he requires, but to foresee his future wants and to provide for them. Floating equipment is only a part of a shipping business. There must be wharf and warehouse facilities where goods can be assembled and held to await the call of the steamer, and this amounts in value at least to the equal of the vessels. There must be auxiliary services in rivers and canals to collect goods for the ports of call of the line vessels; shippers must be kept in touch with to hold their

[37] *North China Herald,* CLXXIII (1928), 172; *U.S. Commerce Reports* (1929), p. 816.

[38] *Annual Trade Report* (Imperial Maritime Customs, 1928).

[39] Shanghai newspapers, October, 1931.

[40] *China Year Book* (1929–30), p. 779.

old business and to develop new; there must be constant supervision from the head office and planning for vessels and lines to meet present and coming requirements of the trade. A vessel operator is a servant of shippers; his function is not primary but secondary, and he can fulfil it only by careful upkeep of his equipment, by watching the trade in his territory, and by being ready to supply its requirements. This implies a large capital investment and a constant addition to it to meet new needs. Vessel equipment, furthermore, is subject to deterioration and superannuation; allowance must be made for this important factor in cost as well as expense for repairs, before profits can be figured. The foreign lines have been able to provide such service to shippers under the difficult conditions existing during the troubles in China. Their ships have carried goods and thus created the steady flow of trade, at times when Chinese steamers found operation difficult, because of military measures or disorder; their equipment has been kept in condition to serve their trade. In the case of the Japanese river line, there is the further advantage of a direct subsidy on condition that regular trips be made to assure Japanese shippers of service.

In spite of the service foreign lines have given and give, there is a movement to exclude foreign flags from Chinese internal navigation and to preserve that branch of business for nationals. The objection of China to unequal treatment, the wish to regain full freedom to deal with internal Chinese matters as she will, is one of the causes for the movement. The treaty provisions, giving foreigners the right to navigate Chinese waters without reciprocity, are denounced by the public opinion which is most freely expressed in the country, and the withdrawal of extraterritorial privileges will, when it comes, affect the position of the foreigner. Extraterritoriality and the rights to navigate Chinese waters derive from different treaty provisions, but the importance of the former to the latter are evident. The movement finds frequent expression. In the *Chinese Economic Journal* of 1930, it is said that the Chinese Government intends to abrogate the right of foreign vessels to ply between inland ports. Chinese chambers of commerce, according to the same authority, are active in urging the Government to abolish inland navigation for foreigners. The Shanghai Navigation Association in 1929 requested the Government and the Central Executive Committee of the Kuomintang to take steps to abolish the privilege of inland navigation enjoyed by foreigners as a unilateral privilege and an obstruction to the development of native shipping.[41] In March, 1929, the Vice-Minister of Foreign Affairs announced that the Government intended to abolish navigation on inland coastal waters by foreign-owned vessels, and the representatives of the different ministries concerned met to formulate measures for the restoration of inland navigation to Chinese.[42] The progress of the idea appears in the recent declaration of the Kuomintang Congress that this one-sided privilege of foreigners be abolished, and in a speech by President Chiang Kai Shek

[41] *Chinese Economic Bulletin,* 1929, pp. 166, 244.
[42] *New York Times,* March 10, 1929.

in the Convention in which he advocated the same object, but said that two or three hundred thousand tons of shipping must be built in the next six years, thus emphasizing the need for more ships if the Chinese flag is to supplant foreign flags in Chinese waters.[43]

Chinese shippers say that it is hard to persuade Chinese capital to invest in shipping while the foreign interests are so strongly intrenched. Consequently, the development of the Chinese Mercantile Marine is retarded. This does not mean that Chinese ships are nonexistent. On the contrary, there are both regular lines, led by the China Steam Navigation Co., and tramps, which hold second place to the British in the Chinese coast trade from Shanghai. In 1873, the British owned 213 vessels doing coast trade between Shanghai and other open ports, the Americans 81, and the Chinese 11, out of a total of 361.[44] These figures do not include junks. In 1881, out of a total of 290 vessels carrying coast trade outwards from Shanghai, 161 were British, 22 American, 40 German, and 47 Chinese. In 1928, the Shanghai figures for coast and river shipping tonnage show the British Empire first with 36.99 per cent, China second with 34.9 per cent, Japan 19.85 per cent, America only 0.9 per cent.[45] In 1929, British tonnage had risen to 44.21 per cent, while Chinese had fallen to 30.35 per cent.[46]

The delay involved, and the heavy cost of supplying new vessels and land equipment, or of paying for the equipments of the existing companies, stand in the way of early transfer to Chinese owners of the complete control of coast and inland shipping. Even if the foreigners would consent to joint ownership, with 51 per cent of the stock in Chinese hands, that is, the control, it would nevertheless mean raising a very large sum of money to pay for the 51 per cent. Foreign owners, furthermore, reject the proposal of sharing ownership on the basis of Chinese control of the business, and probable Chinese management. Yet, the Chinese claim is reasonable, that, like other countries, they control their own cabotage, and decide for themselves whether and on what terms foreigners shall be allowed to share in it. The problem is, therefore, one of adjustment, to secure Chinese control as soon as possible, without hampering the management of the foreign lines too greatly in the period of transition. For, after all, the interest of the shipper and the merchant must not be overlooked. A sudden change resulting in the dislocation of a service to which they are accustomed would have serious effects on trade and on the prosperity of large groups in the population, at a time when stability is so much to be sought.

A process of development of Chinese management through co-operation with foreigners will profit all sides if the foreigners do not stand stubbornly for the *status quo* but acknowledge the inevitable Chinese supremacy in their own country.

[43] *Shun Pao (Shanghai Times)*, May 9, 1931.
[44] *Accounts and Papers*, XXVIII (1873), 145.
[45] *China Year Book* (1929–30), p. 287.
[46] Bau, *Foreign Navigation in Chinese Waters*, p. 18.

In personnel, too, foreign officers and engineers will, for a considerable period, be needed to man Chinese vessels in spite of the policy to reserve these places for Chinese. The Government has established schools for deck officers; but land instruction alone, useful as it is, cannot make navigators. Experience on the water alone can give the feeling of the sea and the recognition of discipline so essential to the commander and officers of a ship, and this experience must be gained by sailing as a minor officer under a skilful captain. While there are Chinese captains now in command of river and coast vessels, their number is limited, and it is fully recognized that there will, for many years to come, be a place for foreigners on the decks and in the engine rooms of Chinese ships. Confidence in some Chinese captains is evidenced by the fact that insurance companies on the Yangtze are willing to insure vessels with native captains when they have confidence in the particular individual in command. Chinese pilots have proved their skill and reliability; they are giving good service on the rivers and coasts on both Chinese and foreign vessels.

The transfer to the Chinese flag will, in some minor services at least, be made easy by the fact that the ownership is already Chinese. The ships are put under a foreign flag for the protection it gives, and if extraterritoriality and gunboats are withdrawn the owners will promptly register their boats as Chinese. There will be no difficulty in such cases over purchase of property. How far this ownership, in part or in whole, extends it is impossible to say. It does not apply to the more important companies, but it will affect the problem. For example, when the Italian Consul at Hankow in 1928 ordered the Italian flag removed from Chinese-owned vessels, it entirely disappeared from the upper river.[47] It is said that the British flag will be taken off most of the boats flying it on the West river when the advantage of foreign shipping disappears. The evil of using the foreign flag to cover Chinese property has been real in the past. Morse says that there are cases " where a foreigner with no capital — not a penny — opened branch firms in several places and ran steamers in his name and under his flag, but had no share in the working of the business and was never heard of, except when it became necessary to call a case out of the Chinese magistrate's *yamen* to the foreign Consular court." [48] At present, however, there is a reaction against this practice, and regulations governing foreign registration and flying foreign flags have been more carefully enforced.[49]

China is making preparation for the assumption of control over her navigation. Until recently there was little law and little administrative organization to provide for the needs of a mercantile marine. What regulations and supervision existed were under the control of the efficient Maritime Customs; but with the extension of legislation to provide for nationality, inspection and surveying of hulls and boilers, registration of ship's

[47] *China Year Book* (1931), p. 97; *Annual Trade Report* (Chinese Maritime Customs, Ichang), p. 2.
[48] *The Trade and Administration of China*, p. 211.
[49] *China Year Book* (1929–30).

masters and crews, new bureaus have been created under the Ministry of Communication, indicating a tendency to take over non-revenue functions from the Customs.[50]   The lack of a general maritime law has been filled by an Act promulgated December 30, 1929, which will apply in Chinese courts and may, if found satisfactory, be adopted as law in foreign consular jurisdiction, thus substituting a definite single rule for maritime affairs in Chinese waters.   Ordinances governing the application of the law were promulgated on January 1, 1930.

There is much fear expressed of Government oppression of the shipping industry, which will affect foreigners as well as Chinese subjects if extraterritoriality be removed.   That such has been the case in the past is clear from the record of commandeered vessels, but the usual Chinese method of resistance to arbitrary government action, and of co-operation between the government and classes of people, has begun to take effect, now that more peaceful conditions exist.   The shipowners' association has already been able to arrange for better conditions in respect to commandeering ships and will, no doubt, be able to restrain other unjust action.   The merchants' and shippers' organizations will, it is probable, add their voices to that of the shipping association if regulations or taxes menace the service materially. The Government has already promulgated, on April 17, 1931, rules governing the organization of the Navigation Association, a move which may rather hamper than help the operation of the association.   It is important in the present-day political organization of China that such groups have wide liberty of action, as they form an indispensable means of popular control over the Government.

IV. REASONS AND PLAN FOR RECOVERY [51]

By MINGCHIEN JOSHUA BAU

Such being the general shipping conditions in Chinese waters, let us now observe the reasons why this right of inland navigation and coasting trade should as soon as possible be recovered.

First, the present condition of foreign navigation in Chinese waters is in contravention with the general principle and practice of international law which postulates the reservation of inland and territorial waters to nationals, save as part of international trade.

Second, it impairs the territorial sovereignty of China.   Inland waters and maritime coast being parts of Chinese territory and therefore subject to Chinese jurisdiction, the territorial sovereignty of China is impaired to the extent that it cannot reserve the right of trade and navigation in these waters to its nationals.

[50] Bau, *Foreign Navigation in Chinese Waters*, p. 29.
[51] Extract from data paper, *Foreign Navigation in Chinese Waters* (China Council), pp. 20–29.

Third, it affects the national defense of China. Inland waters and particularly maritime coast often constitute strategic centers of a state. To permit foreign navigation in these waters is to expose strategic defense to foreign observation.

Fourth, means of communication constituting the vital arteries of national life, it should not be controlled or dominated by foreign elements. It should be strictly regulated, controlled, and dominated by nationals.

Fifth, the economic loss every year through foreign shipping, inland and coastwise, is enormous. The development of Chinese trade, domestic and foreign, requires that such shipping should be undertaken by national vessels.

Sixth, the treaty grants being originally made either in consequence of ignorance or application of force, in this new era of the renunciation of war and the application of the principle of international co-operation, such grants become incongruous and inconsistent with the new order of the world, and should be corrected so as to fall in line with the modern enlightened practice among the community of nations.

TREATY POWERS DENIED THE RIGHT

In view of these reasons, China has definitely adopted the policy of recovering this lost right. The last grant of this right was made by the Manchu Government to Sweden in 1908.[52] The Chinese revolution having overthrown the Manchu Dynasty and established the Republic in 1911, the new régime, as an initial measure, has consistently refused to grant the said right to any Power that sought treaty relations with China. Consequently, the following states which have come into treaty relations with China have all been denied the enjoyment of this right:

1. Chile — Treaty of February 18, 1915
2. Switzerland — Treaty of June 13, 1918
3. Bolivia — Treaty of December 3, 1919
4. Persia — Treaty of June 1, 1920
5. Germany — Treaty of May 20, 1921
6. Russia — Treaty of May 31, 1924
7. Austria — Treaty of October 19, 1925
8. Finland — Treaty of October 29, 1926
9. Greece — Treaty of May 26, 1928
   Treaty of September 30, 1929
10. Poland — Treaty of September 18, 1929
11. Czechoslovakia — Treaty of February 12, 1930

PLAN FOR THE RECOVERY OF THE RIGHT

The detailed plan for the recovery of this right of inland navigation and coasting trade was made at a conference of the representatives of the Ministry of Foreign Affairs, the Ministry of Labor and Commerce, the Ministry of Finance, the Ministry of Communications, and the Law Codification Com-

[52] MacMurray (1908/11) pp. 740 ff.

mission, October–November, 1929. Five principles were adopted respecting the scope of the right to be recovered:

I. *Inland navigation.* — Foreign navigation in Chinese inland waters should be completely abrogated and hereafter prohibited. The regulations of 1898 governing steam navigation in Chinese waters, made part of the commercial treaties of 1902 and 1903 with Great Britain, the United States of America, and Japan, should be rescinded at the time of the conclusion of the new commercial treaties with the said Powers.

II. *Navigation on the Yangtze River.* — (*a*) Trade and navigation between two or more ports on the Yangtze River should be completely reserved to nationals and their vessels. (*b*) The entry, anchorage, loading, and discharge of foreign vessels on the Yangtze River should be permitted only as part of international trade and not in contravention with the principle set forth above, and should be limited only to certain ports having direct relation with foreign trade and designated by the Chinese Government, and this in exchange for reciprocal or equivalent concessions, and subject to unilateral termination on the part of China.

III. *Coasting trade.* — Coasting trade between two or more ports, save as part of international trade, should be wholly reserved for the establishment of wharves, office buildings, equipment, preparations for foreign trade, etc.

IV. *Leased territories.* — Coasting trade between and with leased territories should be regulated by the same principles which govern coasting trade between two or more ports. That is, leased territories should be regarded as Chinese ports with a view to their eventual retrocession.

V. *Boundary rivers.* — Navigation on boundary rivers should be arranged separately with the states concerned.

METHODS FOR NATIONAL INLAND NAVIGATION

Four methods were decided upon with reference to the carrying on of inland navigation and coasting trade after the recovery of the right.

I. A national navigation company should be organized. At the initial stage, the company should have twelve new-type river steamers of 2,000–4,400 tons and twenty sea-going vessels of 3,000–6,000 tons, with a total tonnage of approximately 140,000 tons. The initial capital of the company should be 50,000,000 *yuan,* 28,000,000 for the purchase of the 32 vessels at an average price of 700,000 *yuan* for a river steamer and 1,000,000 for a sea-going vessel, and the remainder for the establishment of wharves, office buildings, equipment, preparations for foreign trade, etc. The said initial capital shall be included in the national budget, to be paid out in instalments; and if the National Treasury should be unable to meet the obligations, it should be raised by a public loan, or appropriated out of the remitted portions of the Boxer Indemnity Fund.

In addition, for the encouragement of shipping business, government subsidies should be granted at the discretion of the National Government to the Chinese navigation companies by means of

a) Guarantee of interest
b) Judicious grant of subsidies
c) Promotion of co-operation or combination of navigation interests

II. The vessels, buildings, and accessories of the present foreign navigation companies should be bought, after due evaluation and discriminatory choice of vessels in respect of age and speed, outright with cash payment, and should thereafter be operated as Chinese lines. Deducting what the National Government may buy, private capital may take over the remainder.

III. In case outright cash payment is found impossible, arrangement may be made, with the consent of the foreign shipping interests concerned, to deliver the payments in instalments to be spread over a period of years, after the precedent set in the redemption of the Tsingtao-Tsinan Railway.

IV. The present foreign navigation companies should be reorganized into Chinese corporations with both foreign and Chinese capital. A definite period for the joint undertaking should be fixed after which the foreign interests therein should be redeemed. The following conditions should govern this arrangement of joint enterprise:

a) Limitation of foreign shipping business to the existing number of vessels and tonnage, with no right of expansion
b) Complete compliance with Chinese laws
c) Possession by Chinese of at least 51 per cent of the stocks or shares
d) Complete redemption of foreign interests at the termination of the period allowed.[53]

STEPS OF PREPARATION TAKEN

Meanwhile, definite steps of preparation are being taken by the National Government at Nanking to pave the way for the eventual recovery of the right and assumption of control over inland navigation and coasting trade.

I. Heretofore the administration of navigation and port affairs was entrusted to the Chinese Maritime Customs Service, directed by foreign administrators. The Ministry of Communications has taken definite steps to take over the said functions from the hands of the Chinese Maritime Customs. To this effect, under the control and direction of its Department of Navigation, the Ministry of Communications has established bureaus for the administration of navigation and port affairs at the leading centers of navigation and trade, that is, Shanghai, Tientsin, Hankow, Harbin, and Canton.[54] They are to exercise jurisdiction in their several localities in regard to vessels, sailors, port affairs, navigation, etc.

II. The enactment of laws relating to navigation has been well under way. The following laws have already been promulgated:

[53] It is interesting here to note that the competent authorities of the Chinese Government at Nanking are opposed to the method of joint enterprise and in favor of the establishment of a national navigation company (*Peiping Morning Post*, February 8, 1931).

[54] *Ibid.*, March 19, 1931. The establishment of such a bureau at Canton has been temporarily delayed by civil war.

a) Maritime Law — promulgated Dec. 30, 1929 [55]
b) Law Governing Vessels — promulgated Dec. 4, 1930 [56]
c) Law Governing the Registration of Vessels — promulgated Dec. 5, 1930 [57]
d) Ordinances Governing the Application of Maritime Law — promulgated Nov. 25, 1930 [58]
e) Law Regulating the Organization of the Bureaus for the Administration of Navigation and Port Affairs, established by the Ministry of Communications [59]
f) Regulations governing the Examination of Pilots — promulgated March 5, 1931 [60]
g) Regulations Governing the Examination of Navigation Offices on Rivers and Seas — promulgated March 7, 1931[61]
h) Regulations Governing the Registration of Steamers and the Issuance of Certificates thereto — promulgated May 2, 1931 [62] [63]

III. The training of officers and engineers for the navigation of Chinese vessels has also received special attention. Toward the close of the Manchu régime, a college of commercial navigation was established at Woosung, but, because of shortage of funds, it was soon closed down in the early years of the Chinese Republic. As a consequence, the officers of Chinese vessels were largely foreigners. In view of the decision of the Chinese Government at Nanking to recover the right of inland navigation and coasting trade, and to meet the needs arising out of the said recovery, the college was reopened in October, 1929, by the Ministry of Communications. There are now two departments established in the college, one in navigation, and the other in engine operation. There is also a similar college in Harbin.

IV. The policy has been definitely adopted to exclude foreigners from being pilots and navigation officers on Chinese rivers and seas, and to reserve the positions of the same for Chinese nationals. Laws to this effect have been duly promulgated in March, 1931.[64]

[55] *Statutes of the Chinese Government*, IV, 307 ff.
[56] *Public Gazette of the Ministry of Communications*, No. 207 (December 27, 1830), pp. 55 ff.
[57] *Ibid.*, pp. 65 ff.
[58] *Monthly Gazette of the Legislative Yuan*, No. 24 (December, 1930), p. 17.
[59] Passed by Legislative Yuan, November 29, 1930 (*Laws Passed by the Legislative Yuan*, IV, 206).
[60] *Public Gazette of the Ministry of Communications*, No. 231 (March 25, 1931), pp. 19 ff.
[61] *Ibid.*, No. 234 (April 13, 1931), pp. 7 ff.
[62] *Ibid.*, No. 245 (May 4, 1931) pp. 15 ff.
[63] Other laws have also been drafted and are now under consideration, such as Law Governing Government Subsidy to Shipping Business, Law Governing Government Subsidy to Shipbuilding Industry, Regulations Governing Commercial Ports, Regulations Governing Buoys, Beacons, Lighthouses, etc., for the Navigation Routes, etc.
[64] Regulations Governing the Examination of Pilots, promulgated March 5, 1931 (*Public Gazette of the Ministry of Communications*, No. 231 [March 25, 1931], pp. 19 ff.); Regulations Governing the Examination of River and Sea Navigators, promulgated March 7, 1931 (*ibid.*, No. 234 [April 4, 1931], pp. 15 ff.).

QUESTIONS FOR ROUND–TABLE DISCUSSION

The following questions were recommended by the Program Committee as an outline for discussion:

1. What are the specific privileges granted in various treaties in regard to coastal and inland navigation?
2. Does present practice exceed treaty privileges?
3. What have been the economic and political effects of foreign participation in the coastal and inland carrying trade of China, and what is the present position?
4. To what extent and by what methods does China at present discharge her responsibilities in such matters as
   a) Surveys of ports, pilotage, coastal lighting, harbor improvements, and landing facilities?
   b) Regulations of navigation, police measures, examination of ships, maritime law?
5. How far does extraterritoriality affect coastal and inland navigation
   a) In respect to ships and cargoes?
   b) In respect to personnel?
6. What would be the effect of the withdrawal of foreign ships?
7. What solutions can be proposed of the problems arising from the foregoing questions?

SUMMARY OF ROUND–TABLE DISCUSSIONS

The round table on " China's Coastal and Inland Navigation," included in the program of the Conference under the general heading of " China's Foreign Relations," concerned itself with the rights enjoyed by foreign shipping in coastal and inland navigation in China rather than with general economic or technical questions affecting this form of transportation and travel. Its two sessions had the advantage of participation on the part of several outstanding Chinese and foreign specialists on the subject; and the major data papers prepared for this discussion were frequently referred to.

It was pointed out at the opening that the figures presented by the various authorities on the proportion of Chinese and foreign shipping in Chinese waters did not entirely agree. This is due, the chairman explained, to different methods of computation, and to the use of different sources compiled for different purposes. Mr. Bau, using the Customs report on foreign trade of China, 1929, finds that in that year about one-third of the tonnage of vessels engaged in the coastal trade of China (30.35 per cent), and about one-quarter of the total tonnage of clearances between the open ports of China, was Chinese.

Mr. Swire finds, for the same year, a preponderance of Chinese registered tonnage in the coastal trade of the principal companies (about 60 per cent), and a preponderance of foreign registered tonnage in their river trade (about 70 per cent).

Other discrepancies appear when one set of figures is limited to tonnage actually engaged in trade during the year and another to tonnage registered, a considerable part of which may be laid up, owing to boycotts and other causes.

Taking the value of cargo carried, Mr. Bau arrives at about 37.5 per cent as the Chinese contribution to the coastal trade between the open ports in 1929; and Mr. Swire at about 30 per cent. Mr. Swire's figures do not include junks and other small shipping, which, apparently, is included in Mr. Bau's figures.

After considering other available sources of information, the round table agreed on a general statement to the effect that in the total tonnage of vessels actually engaged in the river and coastal trade of China foreign shipping predominates at the ratio of about three to two, but that if the value of cargoes carried is considered the preponderance of foreign shipping is at the ratio, more nearly, of three to one. This was accepted as a rough estimate rather than a conclusion from any one specific set of figures.[65]

It was agreed further that, for purposes of future policy, these inclusive figures are not very significant, anyhow, since they comprise both line services and chartered or seasonal tonnage. The regular services are carried on, usually, by companies of some standing, with a more or less regular merchant clientèle and with specialized ships, generally in advance of the requirements of the trade; the company is less concerned with the profits from a particular voyage than with average profits over a period of time. Owners of irregular ships, or tramps, on the other hand, will use them wherever they see an immediate profit. Often such boats are chartered to supplement regular lines when trade is good. At present, owing to the world-depression, the total tonnage in Chinese waters is less than it has been for many years; and in consequence the demand for such additions to the regular services is insignificant.

I. THE GROWTH OF CHINESE SHIPPING AND ITS IMPEDIMENTS

Since the specific privileges granted in various treaties to foreigners in regard to coastal and inland navigation in China are fully set forth in the data papers, the round table spent little time in enumerating or describing them. There was, however, keen discussion of the question whether these privileges in fact impede the growth of Chinese shipping.

Chinese spokesmen held emphatically that they do. Chinese navigation already has made progress in the last three years, they stated. If given the chance of fair competition it would be able to carry all the cargoes in Chinese waters now carried in foreign vessels. The special advantages enjoyed by foreign companies under the treaty provisions for extraterritoriality were merely mentioned, to be taken up later (see below, p. 364). The particular difficulty emphasized at this point was the government subsidy enjoyed by Japanese companies operating in Chinese waters, which was

[65] See Bau, *Foreign Navigation in Chinese Waters*, pp. 15 ff.; Swire, *op. cit.*, pp. 16 ff.

held in part responsible for the large share taken by Japanese shipping in this trade (about one-fourth, according to one estimate). The Chinese Government, it was stated, has not been in a position during the last ten or fifteen years to match this advantage of the Japanese companies with subsidies of its own to Chinese owners. With the low rates made possible by the Japanese Government subsidies, and the advantages of direct shipping to Japanese ports, Chinese companies cannot compete at a profit; much less can they build up their fleets and replace outworn vessels with newer ones.

In illustration of this situation, it was pointed out that from 1927 to 1930 Chinese owners have chartered vessels with a total tonnage of from 50,000 to 100,000 for seasonal trade on the Russian coast, while at the same time they supplied only a minor part of the shipping services on their own national coastal and river waterways.

The causes of relative failure of Chinese shipping on Chinese waters in competition with foreign shipping, as seen from a foreign shipowner's point of view, are set forth at length in the memorandum by G. Warren Swire. Briefly, they are:

1. Lack of hereditary skill in management, design, and construction
2. Lack of a developed company system
3. The family system of running business in China
4. Lack of government requirements that insure seaworthiness and low insurance charges
5. Lack of experience and efficiency in providing wharf and warehouse facilities
6. Low standards of professional ability required by Chinese law for navigators and engineers
7. Government interference with management
8. Commandeering for trooping in civil wars
9. In the lower grades of Chinese personnel: corruption, slackness, and overstaffing
10. Insufficient depreciation and allocation of reserves
11. Purchase of unsuitable and uneconomical tonnage
12. Insufficient attention to repairs and overhauls
13. Excessive attention to the merchant's wish for low rates, at the expense of an adequate return on the capital invested in shipping

A Japanese member, on the basis of statistics collected from Japanese and other foreign shipping companies, expressed the belief that the proportion of Chinese participation in the inland and coastal navigation of China is even smaller than might be deduced from the official figures. He very much doubted the possibility that in the near future Chinese shipping could be sufficiently developed to meet the demands of this trade.

" The Japanese Government subsidies have been made necessary, as a matter of national policy in no way inimical to Chinese business interests, to render an essential carrier service to Japanese merchants in China. In fact, the navigation company in charge of this work is not making money. The average annual dividend of this company during the last twenty-three years was 769,000 yen, and the average annual subsidy amounted to 680,000 yen, leaving an annual surplus of 89,000 yen, or, I am told, only 0.8 per cent when the subsidy is deducted. In short, the company is subsidized largely to enable the line to provide regular passenger services in compliance with the rules laid down by the Japanese Bureau of Navigation."

However, it was pointed out, British and other foreign concerns manage to exist in this trade without government subsidies; and in competition with them, Chinese shipping is not handicapped in this respect, at least. Furthermore, until some fifteen years ago, a Chinese company, China Merchants, actually did compete successfully with foreign shipping. Its eclipse, foreign members of the round table held, was due less to the enjoyment of special privileges by the foreign companies than to the internal situation in China. In the given case, frequent requisitions of vessels for the transportation of troops and supplies, and other interferences by national and local government officials and army commanders with the efficient management of the company made impossible that initiative and careful planning by trained and experienced executives which is so essential to success in shipping enterprise.

It was recognized, on the other hand, that this cause of failure, important though it is, does not at present represent the chief handicap to a rapid development of Chinese navigation in Chinese waters, since the Chinese Government itself is exceedingly anxious to further it in every possible way.

In this connection, attention was drawn to the existence of the Chinese Navigation Bureau, which is endeavoring to secure both better Chinese shipping services and to establish efficient Chinese ship registry and certificates. At present, Chinese vessels have to secure Lloyd, B.C., or B.T. load-line certificates and also foreign passenger certificates before they can operate outside Chinese waters. The Chinese Navigation Bureau now carries on the inspection and registration for the China coastal trade which in the past was under the jurisdiction of the harbor authorities in the various treaty ports. The Government, further, is providing facilities for the training of navigation officers, engineers, and shore personnel, in order to fill more rapidly with well-qualified Chinese men positions which, it is conceded, will for some time largely have to be held by foreigners.

Before proceeding to a discussion of ways in which Chinese inland and coastal shipping might be improved, some data were presented to show that foreign shipping has not been to the detriment of Chinese trade but, on the contrary, has played a beneficent part in China's economic development. With this interpretation, Chinese members of the round table expressed themselves as in full agreement. Nor did they, in answer to the second question of the agenda, charge that in their practices the concerns under foreign flags were assuming privileges exceeding those granted in the various treaties. One of them said:

"There are no specific complaints in this respect, but the Government and people of China take the position that the treaties themselves require modification. At the time they were made, China had no conception of what they would mean in practice. For example, take the first grant, in 1844, to American vessels of the right to trade between the first five treaty ports [see Bau, pp. 1-2]. The people of China could not have been expected to foresee what this would mean in the years to come. It is only now possible to realize the important part which shipping was destined to play in the economic and political life of China. The time has come to curtail the privileges unwittingly granted to foreigners. They enormously exceed those enjoyed by foreigners in the inland and coastal waters of any other country."

With this statement there was sympathetic agreement, though the subsequent course of the discussion showed that the growth of important interests vested on special treaty rights has introduced a factor of extreme difficulty into any practical proposal for the realization of China's ambition.

The first of these difficulties is that, in the interest of trade itself, shipping must not be exposed to the risk of arbitrary interferences by government authorities, national or local. This risk, according to both Chinese and foreign spokesmen, has already been somewhat reduced by the more reasonable attitude which the National Government has shown in recent years toward the Chinese shipping concerns that are subject to its authority. There has been no commandeering in the last three years, though there has been extensive requisitioning. The Government when in need of transports is chartering boats through the Chinese shipowners' association and returning them as soon as the service for which they are engaged has been performed. Although this is an interference with the regular business of these companies, and although the payments made — usually in national bonds that are at a considerable discount — are not satisfactory to them, they have found it possible to minimize the inconvenience by distributing the burden among themselves, so that none of them is unduly crippled at any one time. The owners, in fact, prefer this arrangement to a chartering of foreign tonnage by the Government; and in some cases it has been a source of profit.

Nevertheless, looking toward the future, Chinese owners feel that ships now sailing on inland waters under foreign flags should share in the risk of requisition. It was admitted by representatives of foreign shipping that in times of civil war this liability might prove a real handicap, as it has in the past, to the competitive ability of Chinese shipping. But it was a handicap, they said, to which nationals are subjected in every country with unstable political conditions, in competition with foreign concerns. On the other hand, the fact was brought out again that this handicap to the development of Chinese shipping was not, in the long run, as serious as it might appear; for the availability of vessels immune from requisition made possible a continued functioning of commerce in times of civil war, which otherwise might have been completely disrupted, with the consequence that trade itself would have been permanently set back.

While Chinese members of the round table agreed with this interpretation, they felt that foreigners were not, perhaps, sufficiently aware of the strength of China's awakening national consciousness, which, quite apart from economic arguments, made it a matter of humiliation to see the country's internal navigation so largely in the hands of foreigners.

" We must appreciate this psychological factor. The Chinese resent that their national shipping is not on the same basis as that of other countries. It may be that the Chinese people and Government are to blame for those political disturbances that have placed Chinese shipping under special handicaps. But we must understand the general desire of the people to be on an equal basis with foreigners. They ask foreigners, in this as in other matters, to share their risks. They feel that they are wronged in all their relations with foreigners so long as these occupy a privileged position under the law."

Before considering possible ways in which this situation might be changed, the round table further discussed possible means of improving the chances of successful competition by Chinese vessels within the present legal circumstances. It was pointed out that other countries, not subject to unilateral treaty provisions, as is China, also have shown increasing resentment over the prevalence of foreign vessels in their coastal and inland navigation. The larger foreign companies are necessarily better financed and more economically managed than the local companies in industrially less developed countries. The merchants and travelers would naturally patronize the boats under their own nation's flag if they offered the same advantages as those under foreign flags. Nevertheless, encroachments upon native shipping, or obstacles in the way of its growth, are looked upon, wherever they obtain, as a danger to the development of the country's trade in line with national policies.

II. SUGGESTED SOLUTIONS

At the opening of the second session of the round table, a Japanese member suggested five possible methods of securing Chinese preponderance in the navigation of Chinese waters. These may briefly be stated as follows:

1. Purchase by China of the foreign vessels
2. Joint undertakings between Chinese and foreign companies
3. Transference of foreign enterprises to the Chinese flag
4. Payment of special taxes by foreign vessels to the Chinese Government
5. Continuation of foreign rights in Chinese waters on a reciprocal basis

A plan for the creation of a national navigation company to buy out the foreign shipping companies was first worked out by a conference of representatives of various Chinese ministries held in October–November, 1929 (usually referred to as the Economic Conference), and is reproduced in the Bau paper (*Foreign Navigation in Chinese Waters*, pp. 25 ff.).

A Chinese member, familiar with the shipping trade, thought that a gradual expropriation of foreign shipping was feasible. It was, in fact, the only way in which a Chinese mercantile marine could get a start. At the present time, the Chinese tonnage may be only about one-fourth, as was stated earlier, of that required to serve the river and coastal trades. But with the existing slump, owners would be " reasonable " — the more so since many of their ships had been built for the coastal and river runs and could only at a loss be transferred to other services.

Others were more skeptical. Where was China to find the capital for such an enterprise? To build the required new tonnage would cost over 100 million dollars (Mex.); to buy old tonnage, even if it should cost only a fraction of that amount, also would overtax the Government's resources. In any case, ships alone, without the ancillary services, such as shore properties, harbor tugs and lighters, launches, etc., would be useless; and these services, according to one estimate, would at least double the cost of the deal.[66]

[66] See Chamberlain, *op. cit.*

The question was next raised whether a more gradual purchase would not be possible, without at the start demanding the relinquishment of the special foreign privileges, so that foreign companies could still continue. To this the objection is that it is precisely the existence of these privileges that makes it difficult for Chinese vessels to compete, and that under the circumstances it would not be feasible to add substantially to the existing fleet under the Chinese flag. If, on the other hand, extraterritoriality in inland navigation were abolished as a matter of principle, it might be possible temporarily to permit foreign companies to function largely as they have done in the past while gradually buying them out.

The suggestion was then made that it might be useful to distinguish between regular liners and tramp steamers in discussing the possibilities of an early relinquishment of these special rights granted by treaty. Chinese and foreign shipowners interested in regular runs are agreed in looking upon the tramp steamer as a dangerous competitor in times when there is not enough cargo to keep the regular liners busy. Would it be possible, the chairman asked, to start by modifying the treaty agreements so as to exclude tramps from the coastal and river navigation of China except when sailing under the Chinese flag or under a Chinese charter?

There was division of opinion on this question. A Chinese thought that such prohibition of foreign tramp steamers would sacrifice no important vested interest. They can always go elsewhere to pick up cargo and are thrown on the Chinese market only, anyhow, when business is not to be had at more profitable rates elsewhere, and often at times when the irregular vessels under the Chinese flag also suffer from lack of cargoes, to depress the rates. Others doubted the capacity of the existing Chinese fleet and of regular liners under foreign flags to take care of the total demand for tonnage in Chinese waters in times of good trade. Would the Government, they asked, take over enough of these tramp vessels to insure the permanent lines of a sufficient available tonnage when in need of such supplementations?

The answer was that the foreign tramps, with a modification of the proposed arrangement, might still be hired by the foreign companies, but that they would have to compete with the Chinese boats on an equal basis, without the enjoyment of special privileges and immunities. The chief object of such an arrangement, however, would be to prevent irregular vessels that carry on a good trade elsewhere from coming into Chinese waters during the winter months, just to cover their expenses, and thus by cutting rates to deprive the Chinese boats of cargoes necessary for their existence. If foreign companies felt they needed a reserve, they could buy old tonnage cheaply all over the world and charter it out elsewhere during slack seasons in Chinese waters.

An effort to secure examples of ways in which a similar difficulty of fluctuating demand is met in other parts of the world met with failure, since the conditions obtaining on the China coast are unique.

A foreign member of the group inquired whether, if the foreign companies added to their tonnage, and outside tramps were excluded from Chinese inland navigation, the Chinese owners would not still have to meet the same competition they found it so difficult to meet now. Would not there still be a surplus of tonnage that could be used to lower rates below the point at which Chinese shipping could be profitable? Others seemed to think that even now the existing tonnage, if properly distributed to meet both regular and unforeseen needs, probably would suffice in all but quite exceptional emergencies. Already there had been better planning in past months; and further improvements in this respect were quite feasible. This optimistic view was not shared by representatives of foreign shipping who still held that, with the difficulty frequently experienced, to find enough tonnage with which to move the northern crops to the great centers of the south, some arrangement would be necessary for permitting additional foreign vessels to be chartered in times of rush.

While this need might be taken care of by a fairly rapid increase of vessels under the Chinese flag, another problem had yet to be faced: How would Chinese owners or the proposed new Chinese company run the additional ships if they got them? While there are some very capable Chinese shipping managers, officers, and engineers, their number cannot rapidly be increased; China has not enough trained personnel now to run all of her shipping.

The Government and the interested Chinese groups, it was stated, fully realize this difficulty and already have made provision for better training facilities. The college of commercial navigation at Woosung, closed down in the early years of the Chinese Republic because of lack of funds, has been reopened in 1929, and another college has been established at Harbin. Moreover, there is no objection, it was said, on the part of the Government to the continued employment of foreign personnel until such time as it could be safely replaced. The Government has not been persuaded that, with the present precarious situation of Chinese shipping, it is worth while to enlarge the existing facilities for training personnel; but as soon as it saw a possibility of successful competition with foreign shipping, through the abrogation of special rights, it would do so.

Next the question of valuation was taken up. Supposing the Chinese Government, or the proposed new navigation company, were in a position to buy out foreign companies, could the two sides easily come to an agreement on the terms of purchase?

A Chinese member thought that this difficulty might easily be exaggerated. After all, it was quite common for vessels to change hands between foreign companies, without undue friction. The original cost of the ship was known; and the amount of depreciation could be estimated by an expert almost exactly. Moreover, according to Japanese experts, about one-half of the capital invested by the foreign companies in China's inland navigation is in land and equipment on shore. For this part of the purchase there could be a fairly exact valuation. Others agreed that if owner and purchaser could not agree on the price, both would probably be willing to abide by arbitration.

There remained, then, the all-important question of payment. The suggestion that the Government would provide bonds with which to pay the foreign owners was at once declared to be unacceptable. Japanese business men, for example, it was stated, had to remember an outstanding loan debt of some 673 million dollars (gold) and probably would insist that any purchase of Japanese property must be paid for in cash. A Chinese member admitted that the Government itself probably regarded the financing of railroads and certain other projects as more urgent at this time than immediate consummation of its desire to create its own mercantile marine.

The same financial obstacle presented itself when the second suggestion, the possibility of joint ownership, was considered. The necessary capital would still have to be found.

The Economic Conference of 1929, in addition to its plan for outright purchase and the establishment of a new national navigation company, had proposed, as a temporary expedient, the reorganization of existing foreign companies in the form of Chinese corporations with both foreign and Chinese capital (see Bau, p. 26, IV). Such an arrangement, it was said on the Chinese side, would be entertained only if so drawn up as to insure real participation, even though admittedly for some time there would be need for foreign technical experts.

Experience with joint ownership has not been favorable, according to a Japanese view. If one side to the agreement has control by virtue of owning more than 50 per cent of the share capital, it is likely to manage the concern in the interest of its own nationals alone. Business men are usually unfavorable to such arrangements. Others, likewise, declare that the foreign navigation companies would not be likely to agree to a minority share in the joint enterprise, "to let someone else run their business." The proposition is very different when it is a question of setting up a new form of enterprise. But the foreign owners would not wish to see their existing personnel replaced by the relatives of Chinese managers. The possibility that the agreement might provide for a management approved by both parties over a term of years until mutual confidence might be established was only briefly suggested.

A further suggestion that for some time foreign companies might be permitted to continue in this trade of inland and coastal navigation while being prohibited from adding to their tonnage except with express approval of the Chinese Government in an emergency likewise remained undiscussed.

A practical example was seen, however, in the Canadian provision in the law excluding foreign shipping from that country's inland and coastal navigation to the effect that any vessel built for the purpose of such navigation and in foreign ownership was permitted to continue in that operation.

Spokesmen for foreign navigation in Chinese waters naturally disliked this suggestion for the same reasons that had earlier led them to reject other proposals for limiting the actual or possible tonnage engaged in their business:

" The important thing, after all, is the trade itself. Any company limited in its tonnage can no longer cater to the trade and adapt itself to changes in the trade. Its system will sooner or later break down. The Chinese themselves should not want to run the risk of interfering with the development of their commerce. It is the duty of shipowners to provide not only for the actual demands but also for the development of trade. They cannot afford to do that if they are not allowed to plan ahead. Until there are enough Chinese ships to cater for the prospective trade when business improves, foreign catering should not be discouraged."

Others thought that this task might be further analyzed: It would be possible, for example, to allow foreign navigation companies to replace their tonnage and thus provide for changes in the character of the trade, but to put a stop to the increase of their tonnage, thus enabling Chinese navigation to take care of the gradual increase in trade. Without some limitation of the further growth of foreign enterprise, it was obviously impossible for Chinese navigation to get that new start which the people and the Government desire.

The third suggestion was next considered: May not the Chinese Government, without expropriating or buying out foreign tonnage, require that all vessels navigating the coastal and inland waters register under the Chinese flag? The question, for the purpose of this suggestion, is seen as a political rather than an economic one, as one of sovereignty rights rather than of ownership.

The principal objection of the Chinese to the present situation, said the chairman, seemed to be one of national sentiment: they do not wish to see ships flying the flags of foreign countries sail their inland waterways in such preponderating numbers. Would it be absurd to demand, in connection with the rendition of extraterritoriality, that henceforth these ships shall sail under the Chinese flag, with whatever abrogation of other rights this may entail?

Under the existing law, it was pointed out, such a thing would be impossible, since no companies can be registered as Chinese when more than 49 per cent of the capital is in foreign hands. But it might be possible to provide the existing foreign navigation companies with special charters, imposing new conditions, under a new law. The control would remain vested where it now is; the management of the companies would remain foreign; but they would be transferred to Chinese nationality.

Such an arrangement, Chinese members thought, would be acceptable at most as a temporary expedient; for it would leave unsolved the problem of developing Chinese shipping. On the other hand, it was stated that the foreign navigation companies would certainly not want to keep up their ships and their shore properties under an arrangement regarded as temporary unless from the start they were assured of proper compensation in an eventual act of expropriation.

One advantage of registration under the Chinese flag would be, according to one representative of foreign interests, that with the assurance of

Chinese jurisdiction, Chinese capital would be attracted to the navigation companies now operating under foreign flags. Foreign interests can organize navigation companies in Canada and elsewhere. Why should not the Chinese Government make possible the same arrangement here?

To the suggested transference of sovereignty there remained still to be made the objections voiced earlier to any change that would make the navigation services now in foreign ownership and under foreign flags subject to the risks of arbitrary taxation by the Chinese Government, even to special levies.

The present Chinese Government, it was agreed, would probably adhere to its policy of fair dealing and adequate compensation for services rendered. But there was always the danger of civil war and of requisition by local and national military leaders. That risk had not yet disappeared from the Chinese horizon.

The remaining two of the original five suggestions for solutions were only very briefly discussed. The imposition of a special tax on foreign ships engaged in inland and coastal navigation might be regarded either as a contribution to the national exchequer, or it might be regarded as a means to provide a fund for the development of Chinese shipping.

Treaties of reciprocity in the matter of inland navigation rights with other countries would be of no practical advantage to China, though they might assuage wounded national pride.[67] Nor would individual treaties overcome the obstacle to the application of the principle under the " Favored Nation Clause." Yet such treaties, it was thought, might point the way to new international understanding as a better safeguard for the future of navigation and trade than the endeavor to curtail foreign rights. Such curtailment has, with higher tariffs and other attempted defenses, been characteristic of the developing national policies in recent years. The restrictive barriers that have been raised by nations against the shipping of other nations have repeatedly occupied the attention of the League of Nations; and on the present occasion one of the speakers drew attention especially to the following resolution passed at the Second General Conference on Communications and Transit, held at Geneva in 1923:

With a view to ensuring the widest possible extension of the principles of freedom of communication, of equality of treatment, and of reciprocity, which are the basis of the Convention and Statute relating to the International Régime on Maritime Ports, adopted by the Conference held at Geneva on December 9th, 1923, and which govern, in accordance with the principles of the Covenant and also in conformity with the resolution of the Economic Conference held at Geneva in 1922, the rights laid down in the above-mentioned Statute,

Considering that the critical conditions in all countries are mainly due to the

[67] It was facetiously observed in the lobby that in a recent reciprocal treaty with Czechoslovakia (see Bau, p. 22), China had evidently endeavored to vindicate the reputation of Shakespeare as a scholar, endangered by his reference, in *The Tempest,* to the coast of Bohemia.

restrictions which have been set up and have become recently accentuated in regard to passenger and goods traffic,

The Conference recommends that all States, including those which are not members of the League of Nations, should accept the fundamental principles of the above-mentioned Statute, and should refrain from inequitable economic measures, such as, in particular, an abusive extension of the scope of the maritime coasting trade.

A general acceptance of this principle, one member suggested, would be a solution for China's trouble and a wholesome stimulant to shipping here as elsewhere.

All agreed to a recommendation that the Program Committee of the Institute place the general topic of " Restrictions of Shipping on the Pacific " on the tentative agenda for the next biennial conference.

PART V

CULTURAL RELATIONS IN THE PACIFIC

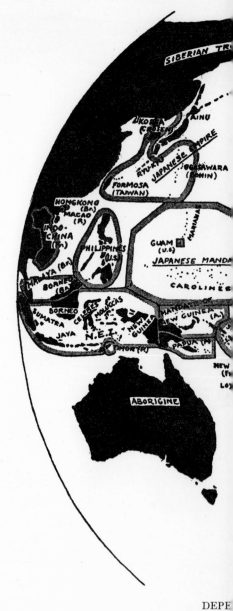

SIBERIAN TR

KOREA
(CHOSEN) AINU

RYUKYU JAPANESE EMPIRE

FORMOSA
(TAIWAN) OGASAWARA
(BONIN)

HONGKONG
(Br.)
MACAO
(P.)

INDO-
CHINA
(Fr.) PHILIPPINES
(U.S.) GUAM
(U.S.) MARIANA

JAPANESE MANDA

MALAYA (Br.) CAROLINES
BORNEO
(Br.)

BORNEO CELEBES MOLUCCAS MANDATE OF
SUMATRA NEW GUINEA (A.)

JAVA N.E.I. NEW
GUINEA PAPUA (A.)

TIMOR (P.)

NEW
(Fr
LO)

ABORIGINE

DEPE

(The bounda:

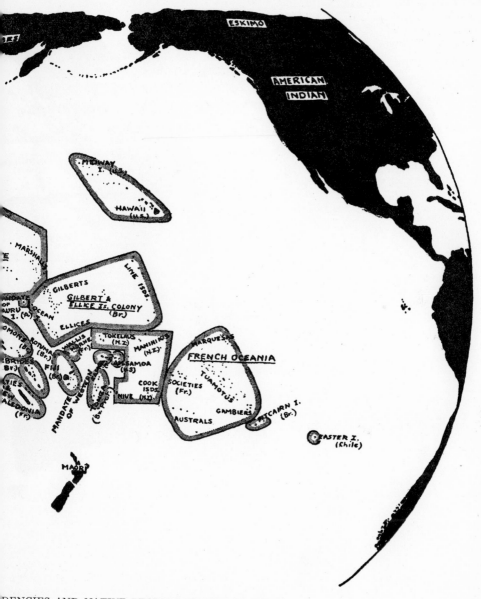

ESKIMO

AMERICAN
INDIAN

MIDWAY
I. (U.S.)

HAWAII
(U.S.)

MARSHALLS

LINE ISDS

GILBERTS

GILBERT &
ELLICE Is. COLONY
(Br)

ELLICES

OCEAN

OF
NAURU
I. (A)

SOLOMON
(Br.)

WALLIS
(Fr.)

TOKELAUS
(N.Z.)

MANIHIKIS
(N.Z.)

MARQUESAS

FRENCH OCEANIA

SAMOA
(U.S.)

MANDATE OF WESTERN

COOK
ISDS
(N.Z.)

SOCIETIES
(Fr.)

TUAMOTUS

FIJI
(Br.)

NIVE
(N.Z.)

NEW
CALEDONIA
(Fr.)

GAMBIERS

PITCAIRN I.
(Br.)

AUSTRALS

EASTER I.
(Chile)

MAORI

DENCIES AND NATIVE PEOPLES OF THE PACIFIC

s shown are not intended to indicate political spheres of influence)

CHAPTER XII

DEPENDENCIES AND NATIVE PEOPLES

DATA PAPERS

1. A. D. A. DE KAT ANGELINO. *Colonial Policy* (American Council). 2 vols.
2. *Some Labour Problems in Pacific Dependencies* (International Labour Office).
3. F. M. KEESING. *A Memorandum on Western Samoa and American Samoa* (International Research Committee, I. P. R.).
4. R. O. WINSTEDT. *The Constitution of the Colony of the Straits Settlements and of the Federated Malay States* (British Group).
5. D. CAMPBELL SCOTT. *The Administration of Indian Affairs in Canada* (Canadian Council).
6. F. BENITEZ. *Educational Progress in the Philippines* (Philippines Council).
7. P. MENDOZA GUAZON. *The Status of Philippine Women* (Philippines Council).
8. CECILIO LOPEZ. *The Language Situation in the Philippines* (Philippines Council).
9. MARIANO SANO. *Social Legislation in the Philippines* (Philippines Council).
10. MAXIM KALAW. *The Philippine Question* (Philippines Council).
11. SIR APRIANA T. NGATA. " Anthropology and the Government of Native Races "; W. H. COCKER, " The Mandate for Samoa " (chaps. ii and x of *New Zealand Affairs* [New Zealand Council]).
12. F. V. FIELD and E. B. FIELD. " Philippine Inter-island Migration "; " Social and Economic Backgrounds of Filipino Emigrants " (Appendixes J and K, *Filipino Immigration* [American Council]).
13. A. GOLDENWEISER. *Race and Race Relations* (American Council).
14. E. S. C. HANDY. *Cultural Revolution in Hawaii* (American Council).
15. ROBERT E. PARK. *The Problem of Cultural Differences* (American Council).
16. H. L. SHAPIRO. *Chinese Population in Hawaii* (American Council).
17. F. M. KEESING and MARIE KEESING. *Syllabus on Dependencies and Native Peoples in the Pacific* (International Research Committee).
18. JOSÉ G. SANVICTORES. *The Administration of Minority Groups* (Philippines Council).

REFERENCES

1. " Studies in Comparative Colonial Government." London: Royal Institute of International Affairs, 1930–31.

   i. W. ORMSBY-GORE. *The General Problem of Colonial Administration.*
   ii. A. D. A. DE KAT ANGELINO. *The Dutch East Indies.*
   iii. M. CHATEL. *Indo-China.*
   iv. IFOR B. POWELL. *Colonial Administration in the Philippine Islands.*
   v. PAUL MONROE. *Education in the Philippines.*
   vi. SIR EYRE HUTSON. *The Colony of Fiji and Territories under the Administration of the High Commissioner of the Western Pacific.*

2. SIR MAYNARD HEDSTROM. " Fiji: Its Position and Problems," *Pacific Affairs*, October, 1930.
3. K. YAMASAKI. " Japan's Pacific Mandate," *ibid.*, February, 1931.
4. A. VANDENBOSCH. " Colonial Labor Problems," *ibid.*, April, 1931.
5. F. M. KEESING. " The Government of Pacific Dependencies," *ibid.*, May, 1930.
6. F. M. KEESING. " Maori Progress on the East Coast of New Zealand," *Journal of the Board of Maori Ethnological Research*, I, Nos. 1 and 2 (1930).
7. CHARLES P. HOWLAND. *American Foreign Relations*, 1930, chaps. v–vii.

8. J. B. CONDLIFFE (ed.). *Problems of the Pacific, 1929,* chaps. i and ii.
9. J. B. CONDLIFFE. *New Zealand in the Making* (London, 1930), chaps. ii and xiii.

INTRODUCTORY NOTE

At the Kyoto Conference in 1929, the Institute initiated a study of the government of dependencies and native peoples in the Pacific area.[1] The resulting project was commenced early in 1930 under the direction of the International Research Committee with the co-operation of national groups and also of outside institutions, such as the International Labour Office, the University of Hawaii, the Bernice P. Bishop Museum, Honolulu, and the Board of Maori Ethnological Research, New Zealand. As a result, reports on a number of studies could be presented at the 1931 Conference, while others are still in course of preparation. The scope of these studies is indicated in the *Report* named, as follows:

To provide for adequate understanding of the international problems presented by the existence of these dependencies and mandates, an endeavor should be made to have presented to the 1931 Conference and subsequent conferences, statements of the present position and recent developments in each of these territories with reference to:

A. *Administration*

　　The method of government of the native population:
　　i. To what extent the indigenous systems of government has been preserved intact;
　　ii. To what extent a European system of government has been built upon the native organization;
　　iii. To what extent the native systems of government have in fact been Europeanized while retaining the forms of native life;
　　iv. To what extent the native system of government is being destroyed.

B. *Social Organization*

　　The present state of government and social organization with reference to:
　　i. Native education;
　　ii. Social systems;
　　iii. Land ownership;
　　iv. Administration of justice.

C. *Economic Development*

　　The present degree of economic development with reference to:
　　i. The chief economic resources;
　　ii. The utilization of native and imported labor;
　　iii. The sources of capital for economic development.

The point of view of this research project is indicated as follows:

Throughout Malaysia and the Pacific islands a demand for autonomy is emerging. Those charged with the administration of areas still dependent or of indigenous

[1] *Problems of the Pacific, 1929,* p. 655; *Report of International Research Committee to the Pacific Council at the Kyoto Conference,* Appendix A.

groups that maintain their identity alongside alien immigrant groups are increasingly taking account of the rights and needs of the " weaker " peoples and are seeking to fashion policies on a basis of intelligent understanding . . .

The task of utilizing native leaders and institutions for purposes of government is far more complex than that of controlling through absolute authority; increased contact between peoples is making for the disruption of indigenous cultures; the re-fashioning of native economies to conform more to modern commercial ideas is not easy; education is producing, in addition to expected results, at least a temporary disorganisation; and race mixture is bringing into existence new human groups for whom a place must be found. Though as human processes these are by no means unique, to dependent areas they offer special problems when the responsibility for their control is in the hands of an outside authority. Parallel to this difficulty, however, and no doubt largely in response to it, there is also an increasing application of knowledge to such problems. We hear today of the " art of colonial government," even of the " science of applied anthropology "; we see institutions being created to train administrators and to study indigenous cultures. Again a strong feeling has emerged, though hardly translated as yet into action, that international cooperation and exchange of experience on such problems would be invaluable.[2]

The geographical and political limitations of the subject, for purposes of inquiry by the Institute of Pacific Relations, are indicated by the following full list of Pacific dependencies, given in alphabetical order: [3]

Australia — Papua; Mandated Territory of New Guinea.
Chile — Easter Island.
France — Indo-China; New Caledonia and Loyalty islands; Wallis and Horne islands; Society, Marquesas, Tuamotu, Gambler, and Austral islands.
France and Great Britain — New Hebrides Condominium.
Great Britain — British Malaya; British Borneo; Hongkong; Solomon Islands; Fiji; Gilbert and Ellice islands; Tonga; Phoenix, Line, and other scattered islands; Pitcairn.
Great Britain, Australia, and New Zealand — Mandate of Nauru.
Japan — Formosa and Pescadores; south Saghalien; Ryukyu and other outlying islands; Mandated Territory (Mariana, Caroline, and Marshall islands).
Netherlands — Dutch East Indies (Java and Madura, Sumatra, Dutch Borneo, Celebes, Moluccas, Dutch Timor, Dutch New Guinea, and outlying islands).
New Zealand — Cook, Manihiki, Tokelau, and Niue islands; Mandate of Western Samoa.
Portugal — Portuguese Timor; Macao.
United States — Philippine Islands; Territory of Hawaii; Territory of Alaska; Guam; American Samoa.

No mention has been made in this list of numerous uninhabited islands and reefs which belong to the various nations. In addition to the foregoing dependencies we may list the following " native " or indigenous peoples in Pacific countries: the Australian aborigine; the Indian and Eskimo in Canada; the Koreans and the Ainu in Japan; the Maori in New Zealand; the Indian

[2] F. M. Keesing, *The Mandated Territory of Western Samoa and American Samoa,* pp. 1–2.

[3] For the present purpose, it is not necessary to indicate the exact category of political relationship for each of these dependent areas, particularly since in several instances it is in dispute. A detailed description of the political affiliations of the islands of the Pacific is given by Charles P. Howland in *American Foreign Relations* (1930), chap. vi.

in the United States; and various tribespeople in Siberia and Mongolia under control of the U.S.S.R. Even this is not an exhaustive enumeration, for no doubt numbers of similar peoples could be named as existing within China or in Central and South America.

The magnitude of the problems may briefly be indicated by the following quotation from the conference *Syllabus* on this subject:

There are today nearly 118 million people in Pacific dependencies, or approximately seven per cent of the total population of the world. The areas they occupy, scattered over the length and breadth of the Pacific, when added together total well over two million square miles, in fact an area almost three-fourths the size of the United States or Australia.

Of this great population the Netherlands control more than 52 millions, Japan about 24 millions, France 21 millions, the United States 13 millions, Great Britain together with Australia and New Zealand nearly 7 millions, and Portugal half a million. Over 108 millions of the total number constitute peoples native to these dependent areas; in addition there are at least six hundred thousand "natives" retaining their identity outside of dependencies proper, as the Indians of North America and the New Zealand Maori. Of the non-native populations in the dependencies more than seven and a half million are Chinese immigrants, approximately three-quarters of a million are Japanese, six hundred thousand are from India, and three hundred and seventy thousand are whites.[4]

The project, involving so scattered a localization and so many aspects, was necessarily conceived as involving long-time research and repeated conference:

The phrase "Pacific Dependencies" covers territories which range in size from hundreds of thousands of square miles down to a few hundred acres. They are scattered over millions of square miles of ocean, and they are populated, in some cases very densely and other cases very sparsely, by peoples varying from those of the old and highly developed civilisations of Java and Indo-China to the primitive headhunting tribes of Borneo and New Guinea.[5]

The 1931 Conference, then, offered the first opportunity to review the work already accomplished under this co-operative, international research project, and to consider with the advice of competent counselors how best to proceed. For this reason, the round table on " Dependencies and Native Peoples " was conceived of by the Program Committee as a " technical " round table; and, although many attended its sessions who could not be classed as authorities on the subject, nevertheless the nature of these discussions was distinctly influenced by the desire to formulate and recommend a worth-while and practicable program of further research.

    [4] P. 11. For the detailed statistical analysis on which this statement is based, see *ibid.*, Appendix.
    [5] *Some Labour Problems in Pacific Dependencies*, p. 2.

EXTRACTS FROM DATA PAPERS AND ADDRESSES

I. INTRODUCTION

From an Address by E. S. Craighill Handy

Some members of this Conference may consider it a waste of time to interject the subject of " Pacific Dependencies " into a meeting concerned with what they regard as more immediate questions. But from the round-table discussions already held it has become clear to me that some of the fundamental problems are essentially the same for a small atoll in Polynesia and for the vast country of China.

The fact is that in Oceania there are manifest in accentuated form certain processes which are to be seen also in the Far East: intensified contacts with modern Western civilization and disintegration of cultures. The effects are so evident in miniature that the islands may almost serve as experimental laboratories producing significant lessons for the great civilizations of the Far East, and indeed also for Europe and America.

We have been discussing in several round tables problems of trade and industry, migration and race. In relation to the former, the Pacific island region must be considered as of importance, for from it come such tropical products as sugar, copra and rubber. Not only is the region important, but also its people, since all through it are native peoples of varying types who are capable of becoming the future peasant population which will furnish the labor for the development of these industries so essential to world needs. Again, there is the factor of migration. Certain regions like Java are a potential source of labor supply for other parts of the world. Here come in such questions as the effect of immigration or exclusion laws, or the likelihood of the assimilation of native peoples, all very intimately related to labor and migration in the Pacific countries.

Furthermore, there are problems intimately relating to China, in that Chinese people have migrated and are migrating to islands throughout the Pacific. They are at once taking an important share in the development of the resources of the tropical Pacific, and mingling both culturally and physically with the indigenous peoples. Out of such mixture, together with Caucasoid mixture, new hybrid types are emerging that are more likely than pure native types to prove the source of the future peasant populations of the Pacific; that is, the new Oceanic peasantry will be descended from the union of Caucasian and Mongolian with the autochthonous people who for centuries have been adapting themselves to the physical environment of their island homes.

Finally, a significant point should be made with regard to the changes in culture that are taking place. In some of the smaller Pacific islands processes of revolution and disintegration of native cultures and the substitution of alien customs have proceeded with great rapidity, even to a point far beyond that of the larger and more civilized Asiatic nations. In their experience, I feel, lie some warnings and serious lessons, evidence of the dangers inherent in too sudden transformations, in the uprooting of peasant folk and leaving them, so to speak, dangling in mid-air without a culture mentally or physically satisfactory. The simple mind of peasant people is slow to change and is not capable of a sudden reflection of new kinds of objects. Hence there has been, in many parts of Polynesia, a mental and moral disintegration of high physical types, due to a sudden wrenching of their minds from the ideas to which they were accustomed.

II. THE HISTORICAL PERSPECTIVE

a) ANCIENT [6]

In the glacial period there appears to have been continuous land extending out from the Malay Peninsula and Southeast Asia. The large islands of Borneo, the Philippines, and others were at that time probably solid lands, with great river systems corresponding to the present straits. This area had a very primitive population, remnants of which still exist, as the pigmy peoples.

Two stocks appeared at a later period. The first of these was the Negroid type, found now in Melanesia; it is to be presumed that at some early period this Negroid stock existed throughout North Africa and Malaysia. The second was predominantly Caucasian in type; they were a people capable of moving about in boats and, spreading to the eastern limits of the Pacific, settled the vast region of Micronesia and Polynesia.

After them came the Malayoid people, related to the Mongolian, and this group flooded the same region, reaching even to the limits of Polynesia.

As a result of these migrations throughout the Pacific, there were in existence many primitive, isolated, and barbaric cultures. But from the time of the Christian era on, the whole region, even including Polynesia, came under the influence of the Chinese and Hindu civilizations. The consequence was that many of these Caucasoid and Mongoloid peoples and even some of the Negroids accepted elements of the higher Asiatic cultures. Hence many types of culture were developed, from the most barbarous to some which approach the highest standards of the ancient eastern civilizations.

b) MODERN [7]

In 1520 the first European vessel rounded South America. Until that time, it seems, mankind had approached the Pacific from the Asiatic side: Wave after wave of peoples and of cultural influences had moved eastward, to be spent near or far. As a result of different backgrounds, a diversity of environmental conditions, and long isolation, all these groups had tended to

[6] From the address by Dr. E. S. C. Handy.

[7] F. M. Keesing and Marie Keesing, *Syllabus on Dependencies and Native Peoples of the Pacific,* pp. 11–14.

become culturally and, at least in some instances, physically specialized. The Whites came into the region — not so long before themselves isolated " barbarians " of north and west Europe who had come under the influence of the great Mediterranean civilizations. During some four centuries they have ranged the Pacific, breaking down the barriers of distance and especially in the recent decades spreading a network of communications that bids fair to catch even the most remote peoples into the world life. In the course of this new phase of Pacific history there have emerged important problems of interaction and of cultural adjustment; particularly has this been so in the areas where, as a result of the imperialism of the last century and an inability on the part of the native peoples to resist encroachment, an alien authority and a strange culture have been imposed.

We may here distinguish two rather different lines of development in areas so dominated, based mainly on climate and resources. The temperate zones were " White man's country," but not the tropic, desert, or arctic zones. In the modern decades, therefore, those areas north and south of the equator which suited the Whites and in which they could get a foothold have been colonized — the greater part of North America and of Australia, New Zealand, and to some extent such subtropical places as Hawaii and New Caledonia. There the indigenous peoples have become outnumbered, so that under pressure of necessity they have had to adjust themselves drastically to the dominant culture. In contrast with this, the tropical and arctic areas, together with such places as deserts and unproductive islands, have been occupied merely by special types of Whites, chiefly administrators, missionaries, and those interested in economic development, bringing with them a limited amount of their home culture. There the native peoples are still in the majority, except in a few areas where Asiatic peoples, brought in usually as laborers, have come to outnumber them. We may note that, while up to the present the Whites have on the whole failed to colonize the tropics, there has been proceeding in the last few years a rapid eastward spread of Chinese and East Indian peoples, apparently well able to adjust themselves to the new conditions wherever they have been allowed entrance. This latest movement from Asia into the Pacific is one of the most significant phases of the modern period.

The interaction of the native peoples with the newcomers has been of two general types which we may call uncontrolled and controlled. The first of these, which included most early contacts, has had as its main basis a mutual exploitation and convenience: " Discoverers," sailors, traders, convicts, and in time settlers and tourists have brought their diverse influences on the native life, but without much idea of wanting to change and ameliorate. On the other hand, missionaries and especially the official representatives of the governing powers have sought in varying degree to control the natives, to direct or manipulate their cultures, or at least to protect them from the worst consequences of uncontrolled interaction. Particularly has this been so in the last few years, as philosophies and systems of government have increasingly been modified under pressure of public sentiment to take into

account the native and his problems.   Today as never before we hear of
" native rights," " trusteeship " and " tutelage."

III. PROBLEMS OF RACE MIXTURE [8]

From earliest days of contact there has been crossing between the
native peoples and the newcomers.   The invasion of the Pacific by Whites
and the introduction by them later of Asiatic laboring groups has been predominantly a masculine affair, hence this intermixture has taken the form
almost entirely of immigrant males, more or less transient, linking with native
women and leaving the great number of their children to participate in the
life of the native group.   While it would seem that wherever a settled White
society is nowadays in occupation such miscegenation is tending to lessen,
already in some places it has proceeded to the point where the " pure " native
stock is rapidly disappearing, or else where, even though the native group
is still numerically strong, the mixed bloods have become sufficiently numerous to develop a group life of their own.

There are some who mourn the passing of the pure native stock as also
of the native cultures, believing that racial integrity should as far as possible be preserved.[9]   They often speak of intermixture as having a degenerating
effect, even of the mixed bloods as inheriting only the bad characteristics of
both races; especially as it is feared that the island peoples will be absorbed
by Asiatic migrants.   Others, however, say that mixing is not only inevitable
over much of the Pacific but is also normal: that the so-called pure native is
really of mixed stock, that wherever in pre-White times native groups were
not isolated the process had been going on, and that in a modern age of communications it must continue on a greater scale than ever.   It is considered
that, far from being degenerating, such miscegenation will benefit the native
people both physically and socially.

Unfortunately, there is little scientific material available as yet concerning the results of intermixture, but the indications are such that for the
present it seems fair to assume that the mixed blood in most areas is on the
whole under no necessary biological handicap; whether this, however, could
hold true of such extreme crosses as the White and Aboriginal in Australia
or the Asiatic and Negrito is hard to say.   Yet there is no doubt that serious
problems exist in regard to the political and social status of mixed blood.
In some parts where miscegenation between groups has not proceeded far,
the mixed blood receives hostile treatment from both the native and the
non-native groups: his lot is then difficult, particularly where he is isolated
from fellow mixed bloods.   Elsewhere the mixed blood is accepted by the
native group but meets with discrimination from the dominant group, in

[8] *Syllabus*, pp. 39–42.
[9] That many of the changes popularly attributed to miscegenation are really due to
social changes was brought out in several of the data papers and was also the view taken
in the Conference discussion. See below, pp. 393 ff.

which case he is often found as the leader and sometimes the exploiter of the native. The issue arises as to whether this is good or bad, whether the mixed blood should be regarded as the natural leader in a transition from the old culture to the modern conditions or as a potent cause of disorganization and trouble in the native system. There are other areas where the mixed bloods have been prohibited or discouraged by the governing authority from participating in the life and benefits of the native group in the ways they might normally be permitted by native custom, as in holding land or positions of leadership; in that case they are given a status equivalent to that of the governing group. But sometimes formal citizenship or political rights are accompanied by an actual social discrimination, and such a situation is fraught with trouble. Even in those areas where the mixed blood community has become large enough to engage in a fairly normal group life of its own the fact of a limited sphere of economic opportunity may be productive of strain, especially in these days when the mixed blood is likely to meet competition from an increasing group of educated full bloods.

In view of these problems that have emerged as a result of miscegenation, the important question may be raised as to whether it is possible or desirable for the governing authority to endeavor to control the process. This has been attempted in some areas, as for instance by forbidding marriage between Asiatic laborers and native women. It is often the case, however, that a native woman will link up with an immigrant if it betters her economic status in spite of strong protests from native leaders and even in the face of such prohibition by the governing authority. One most significant issue involved here concerns the right of the governing authority to station groups of adult males without womenfolk in native areas: laborers White or Asiatic, official employees, soldiers and sailors, especially where such groups are transient. Without doubt, this has been an important factor in the social disorganization of past and present, and in the interests of the mixed offspring of such alliances it needs full investigation.

In concluding this discussion of intermixture, it may be well to remark that race mixture does not necessarily mean the disappearance or quick assimilation of the native. There may perhaps be found communities where mixing has proceeded so far, and discrimination on the basis of color is so marked, that those of fullest native blood are under a stigma, and hence it is socially advantageous to be as non-native as possible. In almost all areas, however, the native group will be a physical and probably a cultural entity for long after the last pure blood family may have been touched by the spreading alien strain. In some areas the mixed bloods are marrying back strongly into the mixed blood or else the native groups, and hence there seems a tendency toward the stabilization of a mixed blood type.

Perhaps the most instructive examples in these matters may be found in the Philippines, Netherlands East Indies, Hawaii, also in Central and South America, though the last do not come directly in the scope of this study.

IV. ECONOMIC DEVELOPMENT IN " BACKWARD " AREAS

a) A Triangle of International Interests [10]

Economic considerations must be regarded as a major cause, usually *the* major reason, for the control of dependencies by the great Powers; and the regulation of commercial development constitutes a principal task of the governing authority. Already many Pacific dependencies have become important producers of raw material necessary to maintain the economic life of the world: rubber, sugar, minerals, fertilizer, fruit, fish, oils. It is customary to measure, at least in large degree, the success of an administration from year to year by the statistics of trade and commerce.

In some areas there has been established a doctrine of economic custodianship, of regarding the governing group as " trustees of civilization for the commerce of the world "; elsewhere there has been " monopolistic exploitation " by which it has been considered right to develop dependencies primarily in the interests of the governing Power; nowadays, however, there has grown up a further doctrine of native trusteeship which would limit such exploitation of resources in the light of the present and future welfare of the native peoples. It may be said that the different areas show today various configurations of an economic triangle the sides of which are international interests, national interests and native interests.

In earlier days the white man tacitly assumed a right to force native peoples either to develop their own resources according to the western commercial economy, or else to stand aside and let others do it for them. But as experience has shown that the native could not become adjusted suddenly to a foreign system, and as the new development in some areas was marked by a decline and disappearance of native groups, a growing sentiment has brought about, first, the creation of various types of protection for the native and his resources, and, more recently, various experiments in educating the native to utilize such resources himself. By the time these movements had started, however, non-native interests were already strongly intrenched in most places. Hence the governing authority, even where most enthusiastic for native welfare, has had to take these into account. However, it has become usual in many areas for private enterprise to be controlled in various ways, especially in matters relating to land and labor.

Without doubt, the economic system built up in western society is today one of the most complex and highly specialized aspects of civilization. The administrator who seeks to lead a native people from a relatively simple subsistence economy to appreciate the western intensive division of labor, its competitive individualism, its devotion to the rhythms of clock and calendar, its philosophies of possession, thrift, ambition and the like is facing a problem, more so since native peoples are usually isolated from the pressures of necessity and urgent wants. The coming of the trader with goods that made un-

---

[10] *Syllabus on Dependencies and Native Peoples of the Pacific*, pp. 26-31.

necessary many laborious crafts, the cessation of warfare and of the economic isolation resulting from it, and similar factors have tended to produce in some areas a serious disorganization of the native economy: relaxation of earlier work rhythms, an alteration in the balance of labor between sexes, and other changes have slackened the earlier tension of native life. There has not been sufficient stimulus to bring about adjustment to the new economy, with the result that such communities are marked by " laziness," " instability " and " economic incompetence." Sometimes a condition of this kind has been countered by pressure of necessity, as where native groups have parted with their lands and so have had to engage in new types of work to make a living; elsewhere they have been forced or enticed into labor contracts, or the governing authority has compelled the native to work. But in other regions the very systems that have been reared to prohibit such " abuses " and to protect native communities from exploitation have sometimes tended to shelter them from the stress which, if the ideal is to make them competent in a wider sphere than that of their own group life, seems to be an essential of change; hence conditions of disorganization are in danger of being there perpetuated. It may be said that there are certain regions where such questions do not arise to any great extent, especially on the Asiatic mainland; and there are others where more or less successful adjustments have already been worked out, as in the case of " peasant proprietorship " in Java, the co-operative tribal enterprises among the Maori, and the leasing system in Tonga. In many situations, however, the economic position of the native involves problems for the administrator that will not be easily solved.

The first immigrants usually sought immediately to acquire tracts of land from the natives. It has been customary for the governing authority, on assuming responsibility for an area, to settle all claims of ownership by non-natives, then to institute some system of regulating further alienation of native lands or else to prohibit this altogether. Apart from this control over the exchange of land, many administrations have been faced with an extremely difficult task in determining the ownership in individualizing land titles among such owners where this has been thought desirable. In many regions the problems arising from the conflict between native customs of land holding and those of the modern economy have proved, and are proving, most acute.

Still another fundamental economic problem is that of labor supply. The native usually has little need to work in the white man's way, yet climatic factors in most dependencies make it impossible for the white man himself to do the type of manual labor that is required for tropical agriculture. In some areas the local natives were compelled to work, or else natives were brought willingly or unwillingly from other areas under various forms of contract. The " labor traffic " looms large in Pacific history, and appears to be still carried on in some of its less desirable forms in a few regions; for the most part, however, the governing authorities have respected the modern sentiment, and hence have instituted systems of controlling the enlistment of laborers and supervising the conditions of work. On the whole, it has been found that such native groups as the Polynesian, Melanesian or Malay have not become adjusted easily to plantation work either in their own or in other areas, so that Chinese, East Indian, and Philippine peoples have been introduced or admitted either permanently or temporarily into many regions. In some parts, as a result of rising standards of living among such groups and of other factors, it is now proving more satisfactory to replace direct employment by various forms of peasant proprietorship.

In addition to these basic questions of land and labor, the different governing authorities have interested themselves in other phases of economic development, as the provision of capital, marketing, and scientific experiment and research; sometimes by encouraging private enterprise, sometimes by limiting it or by initiating certain forms of public enterprise. In recent times there has been special emphasis in this connection on an intermediate type of organization — namely, that of self-governing co-operative organizations for credit and marketing with government aid — a movement which some administrators consider the most effective to dynamize native society.[11] One special type of development that usually falls within the sphere of the administration is the establishment and maintenance of communications and other public works and services.

b) The Labor Resources of Pacific Dependencies [12]

The economic development of the Pacific Dependencies consists primarily in the exploitation of their agricultural resources, with industrial processes of more or less complexity arising therefrom, of their forest resources and of their mineral resources. The more elaborate branches of manufacturing production, though they exist and will certainly develop, are not yet of comparable importance. So far as it has yet gone, the economic development of the Dependencies does not always entail a high proportion of wage-earning labour and in agriculture, at least, considerable development may be possible without the use of wage labour.

The volume of independent agricultural production by natives is already considerable and is increasing. In the Netherlands Indies the proportion of the export trade in agricultural produce attributable to native agriculture rose from 11 per cent in 1894 to nearly 35 per cent in 1928. While sugar, tea, cinchona, oil-palm, agave and cocoa were raised entirely or mainly on estates, the native export of coffee exceeded the estate export, pepper and kapok were supplied largely by natives, native coconut cultivation far exceeded estate cultivation, cassava cultivation was almost entirely in the hands of natives, over one-fifth of the European production of tea was obtained from natives growing but not preparing the leaf, and there was an important native cultivation of tobacco. In the case of rubber, the export of native

---

[11] See A. D. A. de Kat Angelino, *Colonial Policy*, Vol. I, chap. viii.
[12] International Labour Office, *Some Labour Problems in Pacific Dependencies*, pp. 3–5.

produce, which was only 13,000 tons in 1919, rose to over 91,000 tons in 1928. . . . .

The development of native agriculture, however, calls for persistent activity on the part of governments in land settlement, education, scientific research and the development of methods of co-operation. Notions of agriculture among the primitive peoples are extremely elementary, and some Administrations have thought fit to enforce compulsory cultivation ordinances (e.g., in New Guinea, Papua, Western Samoa, Fiji and Tonga). The bulk of agricultural production for export remains, however, in the hands of undertakings employing labour, and the methods of recruiting and organising this labour form the biggest single labour problem in the Pacific.[13]

But although agriculture remains the predominant activity in the Pacific Dependencies, mining and industrial development has already gone far and will certainly go much farther, bringing with it an increase in wage labour. A few facts will serve to indicate the lengths to which development has already gone. British Malaya produces nearly one-half and smelts more than one-half of the tin supply of the world. There are important tin mines in the Netherlands Indies (two of which employ respectively 20,000 and 18,000 workers). In Indo-China the number of native workers engaged in mining rose from 28,630 in 1924 to 54,856 in 1928. The phosphate deposits of Nauru, Angaur, Ocean Island and Makatea each employ several hundreds of workers. The factories and workshops of the Netherlands Indies coming under the Safety Ordinance numbered in 1929 nearly 5,000 and employed 143,330 non-European workers. In 1928 an industrial census in Indo-China revealed 220,000 wage-earners in a wide range of industries. The tobacco factory workers of the Philippine Islands numbered 15,000 in 1927. In Hawaii seven pineapple canneries employed in 1928 over 9,000 workers, half of whom were women. Fiji has a biscuit factory and a meat cannery. New Guinea has five sawmills. It may be said that almost everywhere in the Pacific Dependencies there are at least the beginnings of mining and industrial production.

V. PROBLEMS OF CULTURAL ADJUSTMENT

a) " Museum Policy " or Assimilation? [14]

" The mere presence of a white man," says Sir Hubert Murray, " even of the most enthusiastic supporter of native custom, brings with it an influence which works silently for the disintegration of native society."

Some people appear to regard the changing of native ways as " contamination "; they look, from a present marked usually by disruption of the old life and a struggle — not always very successful — to adjust to the new, back to a past that is perhaps often idealized by distance. At least, many feel

---

[13] [For a discussion of the problems arising from contract labor with penal sanction, see chap. xiii, pp. 451 ff.; also De Kat Angelino, op. cit., Vol. II, chap vii — EDITOR.]

[14] Syllabus on Dependencies and Native Peoples of the Pacific, pp, 35–39.

that in areas where resources are not great and there is little to attract settlement, as in Tonga, Eastern Polynesia or much of Micronesia, it is unfortunate to disturb the old order any more than is necessary. Others, however, raise the question as to whether any kind of " museum policy " is desirable in a world of rapidly increasing communications, or even possible in view of the intrusive influences that have already penetrated They would say that change is inevitable, that to delay native adjustment to the new conditions may make the position of the native more difficult later, hence that a steady pressure should be brought to bear in order to modify the native life and ideas as quickly as possible. That is, however, a difference of opinion as to whether the ultimate aim of change should be assimilation into the dominant group or some form of cultural autonomy. Already in some areas the first of these aims is being tried; the question emerges, however, as to whether, even should the native become culturally prepared for assimilation, which some doubt, the dominant group would be willing to accept him without discrimination. Hence there are those who say that the native identity should be preserved, that a fusion of the best of the old culture with the best of the new is the more desirable end.

Much of the cultural transition proceeding in the differing areas can be seen as due to informal and uncontrolled influences. Nevertheless, from early times the governing authorities have sought in various ways to manipulate native life and control adjustment. Unfortunately, so far comparatively little is known of what is involved in culture change, and such interference has proved a somewhat hazardous affair. It has been clearly demonstrated that the modification of an established system of life at one point may produce a set of entirely unexpected and perhaps undesired results at another point; again different aspects of a culture appear to show varying degrees of tenacity, resiliency and mobility. Even where administrators, as also missionaries, may have clear ideas of what they think desirable to preserve, modify or suppress in native life, it may be difficult to put these into effect. Thus they might wish to keep old styles of native costume or housing and at the same time to educate the native or lead him into the new economy. Yet in experience it might be found that the two are not compatible, that the native before long takes to trousers and a bungalow as a mark of his educational or economic progress.

The most casual observer today can see a changing of native life all over the Pacific; in its material forms, in social systems, in the use of leisure and the like. Throughout some areas it would seem that serious maladjustment and unrest is being produced in group and individual as a result of such transition. While it must be recognized that similar manifestations can also be observed in other communities the world over as a result of changing conditions, it would seem that among native groups it has been easier for " deculturation " to be caused than for any new and stable reintegration to be achieved. In fact, the sociological and psychological results have sometimes been so serious that students have cited them as a primary cause of depopulation. The problems here involved have led certain administrations to formulate measures definitely aiming to stabilize the native society once more and to provide positive outlets that may stimulate an " interest in life." These may take such forms as the encouragement of non-harmful elements of the old culture, the introduction of sports, or co-operation with welfare organizations, but sometimes aim more seriously at re-establishment of the traditional functions inherent in village autonomy — including the local administration of justice. In other areas the problem of culture change has not proved quite so serious. Thus some communities have achieved more or less effective readjustment on a basis of religion, either as initiated by mission bodies or else under native leadership. Again, there have been movements for cultural self-determination, usually allied to those aiming at political autonomy, that have sought to re-fashion native life. Yet even here the attitude of the governing authority is of profound importance. It may be noted, finally, that the administrator who seeks to mold and guide the changing culture in accordance with whatever aim he may have in view has not usually the advantage of being able to claim such a divine or patriotic authority for his plans; he must therefore depend either upon force, apparently a doubtful aid, or else upon such less direct means as education, co-operation with the native leadership, and the production of confidence through sympathetic understanding.

So far we have been outlining the problems of native adjustment. It may be said that very similar problems emerge as a result of the presence in the areas of immigrant groups other than of the dominant culture. There is, however, a contrast in that such peoples are usually active and aggressive, having the stimulus of a " struggle for status " that is largely missing in native groups.

b) Cultural Revolution [15]

The process that the world is witnessing today, not only in the Pacific but equally in Asia and Africa and in the conservative sections of Europe and America, is one of abandonment of traditional heritages in favor of participation in, or imitation of, Euro-American industrialism.[16]

The condition and history during the last century of the native peoples in Hawaii, the Society and Marquesas Islands, seems to indicate the danger of attempting too sudden a transition. The decay and suffering of the native populations in these islands may be significant for and worthy of study by the more radical and youthful leaders in India and China who favor cultural revolution and abandonment of traditional heritages for the sake of imitation of Western industrialism, republicanism, bolshevism, or some foreign mode and pattern of life and thought.

The native populations in Polynesia who are tenacious of their own herit-

---

[15] E. S. C. Handy, *Cultural Revolution in Hawaii*, pp. 36–37.

[16] It was pointed out in the Conference that " industrialism " does not completely express the contrast — which is, rather, with the whole socio-economic dynamism of what we call the modern world.

age — namely, the Samoans, Tongans and coastal Fijians — like the Pueblo Indians in America, thrive and prosper. The same may be said of the two Asiatic nations that have most thoroughly maintained the integrity of their traditional civilizations in the face of Western contact — Japan and Siam.

The question of the value of heritages is not a simple one, however. It may be said that the course of events in the Pacific indicates the advisability of cultural revolution. The Polynesians who have attempted drastic change, though they have suffered most, have in a sense progressed most. Certainly the Hawaiians are taking a place and playing a rôle in the world today. This is, of course, in part, but probably not entirely, due to circumstance of location. But it was not owing to geographical position that they made the extraordinary gesture of abolishing their own religion before any missionary set foot on their islands. The Maoris of New Zealand, who have suffered as have the Hawaiians, though from a different cause — through fighting for their rights — are today, like the Hawaiians, coming abreast of the times and taking their place in the forward march of peoples. The conservative Samoans, on the other hand, or the Tongans, though prospering comfortably, are living strictly unto themselves and playing no part in the unfolding drama of humanity. Possibly it is those peoples who can make the break and, by taking a great leap and suffering the consequences, can come into line with modernity, who, while seeming to plunge into the ocean of oblivion, actually have been swept into the stream of life.

c) Nationalism and Cultural Change [17]

I, for one, do not believe in the wisdom of attempting to conserve in their purity our native customs, manners and institutions. As a matter of fact, the changes in the manners, in the customs and the spirit of our people cannot be prevented as long as our people are not isolated from the rest of the world, and continue to have contacts and relations, material and spiritual, with them.

There is no doubt that changes have taken place in the nature of our life, both individual and social. For we have indeed changed our responses to the different situations and problems of life. The only question now is whether on the whole the changes that have taken place in our country and in our people in the last twenty-five years have been for the better rather than for the worse. If we examine the material and spiritual and moral changes that have taken place in the last quarter of a century, we shall be convinced that most of them are desirable not only from the point of view of individual efficiency and happiness but also from the point of view of national solidarity and progress. It seems to me that it is precisely in those changes that we find the foundation of our present national consciousness and solidarity.

[17] Francisco Benitez, *Educational Progress in the Philippines*, pp. 13–14.

QUESTIONS FOR ROUND–TABLE DISCUSSION

The following questions were recommended by the Program Committee as an outline for discussion:

1. How have modern influences affected native peoples? Special problems are:
   a) Depopulation and overpopulation
   b) Race mixture
   c) Cultural disintegration and transition

2. What are and should be the policies of governments, particularly as regards
   a) Preserving, developing, and utilizing native leadership and institutions?
   b) Education?
   c) Isolation or assimilation of the native, status of the mixed blood?
   d) Labor and economic development?

3. To what extent can systematic anthropological and other scientific research and training help in solving difficulties, how far is it already being used, and along what lines should further research be organized?

SUMMARY OF ROUND–TABLE DISCUSSIONS

The discussion began with a preliminary definition of the geographical areas included within the subject.[18]   It was recognized that in some instances a distinction between dependent and independent regions and peoples is hard to make.   As, however, the term " Dependencies " has no exactly defined connection in international law, but is applied variously to protectorates, colonies, insular possessions, territories, and mandates, it is a convenient term to cover those areas, and their human groups, that are still controlled by an alien political authority.   Again, the addition of " Native Peoples " had been made to the name of the round table so as to include within the scope of the discussion certain indigenous peoples, such as the Ainu in Japan or the Australian aborigine, who, though not actually dominated in this way, nevertheless have had much the same experience in modern times, and face today similar problems of adjustment.

I. MODERN INFLUENCES ON NATIVE PEOPLES

DEPOPULATION

The chairman then introduced the first question on the agenda.   It was pointed out that Western influences had apparently in all instances disturbed the older balance of population throughout the Pacific; all were familiar with some areas where serious depopulation had resulted, in fact still continued, and with others where overpopulation had become a major problem.   Regional statements of great interest were then made by members with a view to getting behind the statistical facts to the underlying causes of great changes in population.   A Japanese member showed how difficult it would

[18] See p. 377.

be to give exact information regarding the South Sea Island mandated territory controlled by his country, where depopulation is in general still proceeding:

" The islands are extremely small and spread over a great area, the whole land area equalling only a small province in Japan. In visiting them I have been struck by the divergence of physique, ways of life, language, and stages of development. Some are still isolated and primitive; others are under the influence of missions and schools. In the days of German control a survey was made which showed that the population was decreasing rapidly."

He was asked whether any investigation had been made, as requested recently by the Mandates Commission of the League of Nations, to discover whether this depopulation was due primarily to health factors or rather to cultural disorganization resulting from the effects upon the natives of successive influences from outside — first Spanish, then British and German, and now Japanese. He replied that, to his knowledge, nothing adequate had been accomplished so far. In his opinion, a main cause had been the introduction of venereal disease, which also had affected other areas in the Pacific, but no doubt it was the result, too, of cultural disorganization in some of the islands.

The position of Polynesia and Melanesia was then discussed. A British member asked whether the evidence on depopulation did not suggest that in Polynesia, after an initial great decrease, something approaching equilibrium had now been attained, whereas in Melanesia, where contact had come later, depopulation still continued. An anthropologist pointed out, however, that such generalizations were likely to be misleading. Thus in Polynesia the people of the Marquesas islands are decreasing in number, largely it would appear through the absence of prophylactic and medical work; on the other hand, those of Samoa are increasing rapidly; such a condition shows anything but stability.[19]

The question was then raised as to the circumstances underlying the great population increase in the Netherlands East Indies, especially in Java, and also in the Philippines. One main factor, it was found, was undoubtedly the introduction of modern health measures. This became particularly clear when a Filipino member reviewed how the increase of population in the Philippines was distributed among the different groups:

" It is the most primitive and isolated tribes, such as the Negritos, who are decreasing; they are trying to keep to themselves, to avoid government control, and are unwilling to accept supervision. Those other non-Christian tribes who are co-operating with the government health activities and living less apart, as for instance the Igorots, are increasing." [20]

A tentative generalization seemed to be reached that it is apparently the peoples who withdraw themselves from the shock of contact and refuse to

[19] In this connection see De Kat Angelino, op. cit., I, 355–56; also Keesing, Memorandum on Western Samoa and American Samoa, p. 45.

[20] See also José G. Sanvictores, The Administration of Minority Groups, p. 6; and B. Lasker, Filipino Immigration, pp. 113 ff.

adapt their lives or co-operate with the outside world who decrease. Also it appeared that such peoples were in most cases culturally very specialized, hence perhaps incapable of assimilation, besides being racially specialized and also isolated. However, the members present felt that further research was needed in areas of depopulation to weigh more closely the causes behind the physical factors of disease and the unwillingness to submit to health and other control.

RACE MIXTURE

The question whether racial exclusiveness is a factor in depopulation brought the round table to the next sub-topic on the agenda, " Race Mixture and Its Results." A member from Hawaii, in response to a question, stated that the increase of the native Hawaiian group represented an increase of those of mixed blood; it was added, however, that the decrease in the full Hawaiians did not necessarily mean the passing of the Hawaiian people, for today "anyone who has even a little Hawaiian blood calls himself a Hawaiian." A New Zealand member spoke of population trends among the Maori people, indicating that a large increase which has taken place in modern days is also on a mixed-blood basis: the white strain is spreading widely through the race. Another member from Hawaii pointed out that the significance of the fact that the mixed bloods are the ones increasing depends on whether they or the full-blood group are better adapted to conditions of modern life. Studies conducted by Dr. Romanzo Adams and others of the University of Hawaii, he stated, have proved that the mixed blood fits more successfully into the social, economic, and intellectual life of the territory. There is naturally some divergence of opinion as to whether this is due to purely biological factors or to a combination of these with social circumstances which produce psychological and other differences.[21] But such matters of interpretation hardly affect the fact that under conditions existing in Hawaii the mixed blood is better able to achieve success than is the full Hawaiian. The hope was expressed by the speaker that parallel studies along these lines might be made in other areas.

The need of distinguishing between biological and cultural factors was again emphasized as the result of a statement made by a Japanese member to the effect that, on the whole, the Japanese who had emigrated to Hawaii were of a poor type. A member from the University of Hawaii pointed out that, while the bulk of both Chinese and Japanese emigrants were drawn from supposedly low classes, experience in Hawaii has proved that, given the opportunity, their children rise to equality with those of supposedly better stock of the same and of other racial groups. This, he thought, showed that capacity was there, even though previously stunted by poor social and economic conditions. Similarly, so-called biological inferiority in any other group or race might prove to be merely lack of social opportunity or stimulus.

Further discussion of different types of race crossing was based on an

[21] See Alexander Goldenweiser, *Race and Race Relations*, Part V.

exchange of information from the various countries represented. The studies conducted in Hawaii again proved helpful; [22] it was shown how a belief long current there to the effect that the cross between the Chinese and the Hawaiian was more vigorous than, and superior to, that between the Caucasian and the Hawaiian, owing to the inferior type of whites who had come to the islands in early days, had now been disproved. The results showed if anything that the latter is rating a little higher than the former, though, interestingly enough, it had been found that a cross including all three stocks rated above either. In general, however, research indicated that the results of mixing depend not so much on the race as upon the kind of people who cross. A Filipino member stated that in the Philippines it has been found that the admixture of either Chinese or white blood is an improvement, and that the *mestizos* are the most progressive element in the community. In New Zealand, it was said, " the cross between the Maori and the European is in every way successful, but the cross between the Maori and the Chinese is stigmatized; in the mandated territory of Western Samoa the marriage of Chinese laborers with Samoan women is forbidden by law, though admixture is going on."

Great interest was expressed in the experience of the aboriginal inhabitants of Japan, the Ainu. A member from that country stated:

" In recent years the Ainu do not seem to be mixing much with the Japanese settlers who are pushing northward, and are actually decreasing as a group; but in earlier times a fusion of the Ainu with the immigrant stock evidently took place, so that Ainu blood permeated the Japanese people. Today many Japanese faces have Ainu characteristics, and there are prominent Japanese who are known to be of Ainu descent. To my knowledge there is no racial discrimination against the Ainu mixed blood."

It was noted particularly that Japanese who go to other countries mix very little with their native peoples, as in Formosa, the mandated islands, and Hawaii; it was suggested that this might indicate a " strong feeling for racial purity " which many other peoples did not share.

While it was thus becoming clear that the results of miscegenation did not depend solely on racial, that is biological factors, it was felt that much had still to be learned about the results of crossing between the more extreme racial types, as for instance the white and aborigine in Australia. An Australian member stated that apparently there had been no studies dealing with either the biological or the social results of such mixture, which had now proceeded to a considerable degree, as also crossing between Chinese and aborigines. It appeared, however, that social discrimination against the white-aborigine was very strong, even more so than against the Chinese-aborigine.

At this point the discussion was launched into the wider consideration of what all these examples of miscegenation really mean. It was realized that mixing seemed to be an inevitable process which under modern conditions must take place increasingly. The question arose as to whether or not this

---

[22] The data paper by H. L. Shapiro on *Chinese Population in Hawaii* represents one of a number of such research projects.

indicated that specialized racial groups as entities must ultimately disappear. A member pointed out that this hardly described what was happening:

" While in some cases complete absorption may take place in the future, another process is at work which must be taken into account: there is a strong tendency for mixed-blood groups to become racially stabilized. This has already happened in most of Central and South America where the Latin-American is a product of mixture between Indian and Spanish. While the infusion of alien blood spreads quickly through a native group, so that in some areas already the full blood has all but disappeared, the mixed-blood people through race pride, because of discrimination by other groups or for other reasons, tend to marry back into their own mixed-blood or into the native group. Such a process is to be seen at work even in Hawaii where conditions for assimilation of the native Hawaiian are most favorable. As a result, there are forming what may be called new mixed-blood peoples, some of which will have to be reckoned with long after the last full blood is gone, perhaps indefinitely. It is this fact which makes questions relating to the mixing of races and the political, intellectual, economic, and social status of the mixed blood both a practical and an international problem."

There was general agreement that here was a field in which research was urgently needed and likely to produce valuable results.

A Canadian member here voiced a popular view that certain race mixtures invariably produce bad stock. He instanced a belief in Canada that the French-Indian mixture was less successful than that between the Indian people and Scotch or English immigrants. A Hawaiian member observed that this sounded like the parallel belief that had been proved a myth in Hawaii. Again it was pointed out that it would be practically impossible to prove any great racial differences between the French and British stocks; if true the unfortunate result of miscegenation must be due to cultural causes. One member present who had done research in the experience of the American Indian in modern times asserted that the reasons for any differences that might exist would in this case probably be traceable to the peculiar patterns of relationships built up from the early sixteenth century on between the French and the Indians as compared with those of the British settlers who came later. In this connection, too, a member familiar with conditions in French Oceania made an illuminating statement:

" In Tahiti the French-Tahitian mixed bloods as a rule run wild, but this is distinctly due to the fact that neither parent takes any serious responsibility for them. Usually they do not even know their fathers, and grow up as best they can around the native settlements and among various relatives, really belonging nowhere. They rarely become a significant factor in their communities. A few American and English fathers, on the other hand, have assumed responsibilities for their mixed-blood families, established homes and given them an education. The results of intermixture in these cases have been all that could be desired, and this group of mixed bloods are becoming useful and progressive citizens."

A Filipino member agreed that the same was true in his country. In the early days there were many of these casual cross-matings with Spanish and other visitors, and the children showed unstable characteristics; as a more permanent type of intermarriage took place, however, and homes were established, the results of intermixture had proved successful.

It thus became apparent that social factors were of primary importance for an appreciation both of population trends and of the results of intermixture; so that the discussion passed naturally to the next question on the agenda.

CULTURAL DISINTEGRATION AND TRANSITION

A member from the Philippines pointed out that his country, perhaps even more than Hawaii, was a significant experimental ground in the matter of cultural fusion. There the native cultures had been merged both with various types of Oriental culture and with the two main forms of Occidental culture, the Latin and the Teutonic or Anglo-Saxon. The older native ways, by a gradual process, had been almost entirely supplanted by Spanish ways, particularly through the wiping-out of the basically important old religions and their replacement by Christianity among the great majority of the population. This had paved the way for successful and rapid Americanization. He asserted that except among the non-Christian tribes, the original native cultures have been completely submerged by the more modern influences, and that such successful cultural fusions in the past are making it easier for the Filipino people nowadays to share in the world-civilization as developed both by the East and by the two great branches of the West.[23]

Asked what the Japanese policy was as regards the cultural development of the mandated islands, which had experienced similar waves of influence, a Japanese member stated that his people were not trying to superimpose Japanese customs, but by gradual education to cultivate the native interests:

" We learned a lesson from the experience of the German governor in the revolt of the Ponape islanders. His efforts to improve conditions by making the natives work harder produced only trouble. We try, therefore, not to force anything on the natives. Nevertheless, cultural disorganization is taking place rapidly in many of the islands and is producing difficulties."

In this connection it was pointed out that the experience of the Netherlands in guiding cultural transition among the native peoples of the Dutch East Indies so as to avoid a too sudden disintegration of the indigenous cultures and to promote instead an ordered transition based on growth from within is particularly interesting and instructive.[24]

A British member remarked that in this process of cultural transition, which was now at different stages in the various areas of the Pacific, the Philippines appeared to stand at one extreme, with something approaching a complete blend of cultures. He asked whether there was any area at the other extreme where even after long contact the native culture was being maintained. Could the Tonga Islands protectorate be given as an example of

[23] See also, to the same effect, Sanvictores, *op. cit.*, p. 6.
[24] See De Kat Angelino, *op. cit.*, Vol. I, especially chaps. vii and viii; also for the Hawaiian people Handy, *Cultural Revolution in Hawaii*.

this? It was pointed out in reply by a student of the island region that even in areas such as Tonga the native cultures were not preserved intact but that, as a result of influences brought by missionaries and traders, including various political ideas of the West, the original cultures had been greatly modified from the first days of contact:

" The present life of the Tongan people might well be called a Polynesian-mission-trader culture, very different from that existing before Whites arrived. It became stabilized in earlier days, and as a result of comparative isolation and lack of penetration by other revolutionary influences has been maintained. We may note, however, that in the last few years, with increasing communications, modern educational and other influences are penetrating, and these promise in turn to upset this earlier cultural equilibrium with possible consequences in more or less serious cultural disorganization." [25]

A New Zealand member here raised the important issue as to whether complete absorption of the native cultures into the dominant civilization was the inevitable end of these processes of cultural change. In his own country the Maori had not submitted easily to such cultural conquest, and in recent times had been developing a new culture, based on his own but adapted to modern conditions. This appeared to be maintaining itself alongside that of white New Zealanders:

" We began by trying to make the Maori into a white man, and our native education system was planned with this in view. It was the same in our early land dealings: There was no attempt to understand and develop native land tenure. A Maori had to sell his land and live like a landless white man, or else remain in his communal Maori settlement. The result of all this showed itself in decreasing numbers and cultural disintegration. Those Maoris, however, who won through to a thorough European education, instead of throwing in their lot with the whites, voluntarily turned to their own folk; and near the end of last century a group of them, calling themselves the Young Maori party, set out to save and reorganize their people. They entered various fields: politics, law, medicine, education and the church. Most prominent among them was the Honorable Sir Apirana Ngata, now a Cabinet member in the New Zealand Parliament holding the portfolios of minister in charge of Maori affairs and also of the Cook Islands.

" Under the leadership of this group, Maori village councils were formed under a system of local self-government, dealing with matters of health, sanitation, and the like. From doing things *for* the Maori, the Government has come to learn to do things *with* the Maori, and such co-operation has now become the basis of a new native policy. As a result, a remarkable Maori renaissance has come about. With better health measures and new interest in life, Maori numbers have greatly increased; on the initiative of Maori leaders, adjustments in land tenure and land utilization have been made, harnessing the old communal spirit to the modern economy, thus stabilizing Maori farming effort; the Maori language and literature, arts and crafts, are being preserved and even taught. Thus today the race is accepting all they find good in the white civilization but adapting it to their own genius and at the same time retaining some of the best things from their old culture." [26]

[25] For the somewhat similar case of Samoa see F. M. Keesing, *A Memorandum on the Mandated Territory of Western Samoa and American Samoa,* particularly pp. 7–23, 37–51.

[26] See Sir Apirana Ngata, " Anthropology and the Government of Native Races,"

In the discussion that followed it became clear that this renaissance was not a restoration of the old culture but rather of race pride and of certain idealized aspects of the old, adapted to modern conditions which were a basis of the new integration and of transition to Western forms. It was essentially a practical rather than a sentimental movement and, no doubt, would be instructive as a guide to areas where cultural change has not yet proceeded so far. According to a British member, this also illustrated the fundamentals of British native policy generally, namely, to aim at the development of native individuality rather than at fusion and assimilation.

II. ADMINISTRATIVE POLICIES

With this understanding, then, it was possible to proceed to a consideration of the ways in which various administrations were actually dealing with the problems that had been raised. A statement made by Dr. de Kat Angelino at one of the committee meetings may fittingly introduce this section:

" Our colonial governments everywhere find themselves faced by the same necessity: All these native peoples have to follow the line of world-development. Their traditional systems are being overturned because they were based on isolation, and this disintegration of the old cultures is the basis of all the problems in dependencies. For this reason, the governments are there essentially to protect them from being too suddenly overwhelmed, to prevent complete disorganization, alienation from the land, and eventual extinction. It is impossible to stop the process of change; but it is possible to shelter such isolated communities, to allow a period of transition. At the same time, there must be a policy of development to prepare as quickly as possible for the removal of this protection. The most important factors in such development are, first, the spread of communications; second, what really amounts to the same thing, education, including the teaching of a world-language; and, third, the development of larger loyalties.

" We must educate from the clannish co-operation of the small relationship group to the very different kind of co-operation required for a national, democratic form of government."

It is not surprising, perhaps, in view of the discussion that had preceded and of the data papers and other literature before this round table, that the problems of dependency administration were seen almost entirely as educational problems. Educational policy, however, has many different aspects; and on this occasion it was found expedient to consider it, first, from the point of view of the creation of a native leadership during a period of gradual or revolutionary social change; second, from that of training the foreign administrative personnel for a new type of official responsibility; and, lastly, in more general terms as a means toward the larger objective of enlightened and adaptable living in a world of change.

---

op. cit.; also F. M. Keesing, *The Changing Maori* (Maori Board of Ethnological Research, Wellington; data paper, 1929 Conference), and " Maori Progress on the East Coast of New Zealand," *op. cit.*

NATIVE LEADERSHIP

The development of native leadership and institutions was felt to be of fundamental importance. The experience of the Maori, previously reported (see p. 397), was confirmed by similar situations and experiences in other dependencies. Everywhere the recognition was gaining ground that the co-operation of the people can be obtained only through the development of native leadership. Disregard of the possibilities of such co-operation in efforts to make complete the rule of alien laws and alien institutions had led, in some areas, to revolt, in others, to social disorganization and physical decline. Attention had been drawn to the extraordinary change in the effectiveness of government when various authorities in the Pacific area began systematically to foster and develop that co-operative relationship. On this matter also the distinguished observer from the Netherlands was able to speak with special authority, since the colonial history of that country has been particularly rich in contrasts. Indirect rule, he said, had been adopted from the first, as a sheer necessity, to rule the vast colonial empire of the Netherlands, but only in recent times had become a matter of conscious policy:

" The preservation of native leadership is essential for native progress, even though weaknesses and abuses are inherent in it; for through it are focused all the loyalties of the population. There can be healthy development only as these loyalties are nurtured and widened. The Dutch Administration therefore has maintained the Sultanates and similar organizations of native leadership. But it has not been content merely to preserve: Dutch advisers, equipped with a thorough education and special training, stand back of the native leader. They are kept in the background, so that the population does not see the official but respects and follows the traditional leader. Thus unobtrusively the old traditions are tempered with new influences, and the old loyalties developed, not destroyed. There is a steady evolution. Native leaders become more enlightened, and the people are led to a stage where they can participate in a more democratic form of government." [27]

Asked if the people, as they become better educated, resent the fact that their leader is to that extent the tool of the Dutch officials, he replied that ideally this is met by educating the leaders far ahead of the population, so that before this attitude arises the former can stand by themselves. However, there is always a tendency for the desire for autonomy to mature earlier than the capacity for it. The essential thing is to have administrators sufficiently trained and experienced to appreciate the situation.[28]

Since the round table had before it the results of a recent study of Maori progress in New Zealand, the experience of that people again was drawn upon to furnish illustrations of the problems faced in the development of native

[27] See also De Kat Angelino, *op. cit.*, Vol. II, chaps. i and v, especially pp. 80–129, 358–65.

[28] The policy, essentially similar, of the British administration of the Federated Malay States is described in R. O. Winstedt's data paper on their constitution, especially pp. 9–10. Other relevant information will be found in the series of " Studies in Comparative Colonial Government," published by the Royal Institute of International Affairs (see p. 375).

leadership. In this connection, it was noted particularly that, in addition to local autonomy in village matters, the Maoris have for decades had a direct representation in the New Zealand Parliament. The Maori people are divided geographically and tribally into four electorates each of which sends one of their race to the House of Representatives, while other Maoris have been granted permanent seats in the Legislative Council or Upper House. This enabled them to have a direct say in the government of New Zealand; and more particularly their influence on all matters affecting their people has given excellent training in political leadership. Maori members have held high positions, and there have been occasions when one has been acting prime minister of the country.

One member contrasted the position of the Maori, in thus not being politically swamped by the dominant group, with that of the American Indian. The Indians in the United States, enfranchised in 1924, vote along with all other citizens; on one reservation, at least, it had been observed that the tribal leadership, since it received no constructive outlet, tended to express itself in agitation, with resulting discontent and obstruction of government activities.

The experience of the Netherlands East Indies was again requested. It was explained that there is no official discrimination between the Dutch and the Indonesians. All positions are open to those qualifying, and native leaders, some elected, some appointed, sit in the legislature on an equal basis. The deliberations of that assembly are bilingual in order to enable all to take part.

The Japanese reported that their difficulty in introducing democratic devices come from the fact that native peoples in the mandated territory and Formosa are still not sufficiently civilized to be given responsible status, though they are being educated with this object in view. Native Formosans are sometimes given official employment; but since the population is without any widely developed loyalties, the task of government is not by any means easy.

The Netherlands representative at this point reminded the members of the close relation between a successful education of native leadership and close attention to the training of administrative officials. Unless these are sensitive to the actual and latent abilities and desires of the people among whom they work, the nature and origins of their institutions and customs, and the strength of existing ties and loyalties, serious misjudgments must occur. It is for these reasons that the scientific training of the administrative personnel, he thought, was not a matter of technical interest only but one of great importance. As such it was scheduled for later, separate consideration (see below, pp. 401–3). But at this stage of the discussion another fundamental and seemingly increasing difficulty was brought forward as blocking an effective way of harmonizing native forms of social organization with modern systems of dependency government. Just at the crucial time, it was said, when the established native leaders are most needed to help construct a bridge from the old to the new, their authority is likely to crumble, and the native institutions are likely to disintegrate under the impact of Western influences. It is frequently in this difficult period that education leads to a desire for freedom of choice; a new individualism runs counter to the old unified spirit of the group; commoners, younger people, and women begin to assert themselves instead of continuing the old obedience to their superiors.

" All these are movements in line with modern world-tendencies, the products of widening horizons and of the new education. The problem is how to hold on to the old so as to avoid too rapid a disintegration and its disastrous results, yet at the same time to nurture the new and not to crush developments or permanently to retard growth through overemphasis of conservative ideas."

This need for a careful replacement of disintegrating institutions was illustrated by a British member who referred to the fact that, while in Fiji and Tonga there is still indirect rule through the hereditary chiefs, the old chieftainship in the Gilbert and Ellice islands has already had to be replaced by a system of native magistrates.[29] A member familiar with conditions in the Samoan Islands told how nowadays

" the pressing problem is no longer the maintenance of old political institutions, but the development of adapted forms to satisfy new needs and aspirations. Educated leaders are demanding democratic organizations; the body of the native people rally readily to their appeals, though they are unprepared for, and have only vague ideas about, the desired changes; and pressure from democratic public opinion outside of Samoa complicates the difficult task of evolving a system that will at once satisfy the aspirations of the leaders and the more educated people and be close enough to the life and ideas of the greater number of Samoans." [30]

Is it inevitable, then, that the old local political institutions give way before new ideals? A British member suggested, on this assumption, that the aim of administration might be stated as being, not preservation of native institutions, but their use in an ordered, gradual transition to more democratic government.

TRAINING OF ADMINISTRATIVE OFFICIALS

There was general agreement that, with such an aim, it is essential to have a staff of administrative officers capable of understanding intimately both the old native life and modern conditions and trends. These men should, therefore, be trained not only in anthropology but also in other subjects that bear on human growth — specific mention being made of sociology, economics, psychology, and human geography. Moreover, and this was considered at least equally important, they should be given a progressive practical experience — if possible distributed over several areas with different situations — to enable them to gain a more balanced judgment. A New Zealand member remarked that in the British dependencies of the south Pacific this might perhaps be achieved better if co-operation could be developed between New

---

[29] See Sir Eyre Hutson, *op. cit.*

[30] See also F. M. Keesing, *A Memorandum on the Mandated Territory of Western Samoa and American Samoa,* pp. 10–17 and 56–60.

Zealand, Australia, and the British Colonial Office. Without such co-operation, both New Zealand and Australia faced serious limitations of facilities, finance, and personnel.

Asked what training is given in the Dutch East Indies, the Netherlands observer explained that officials had to be men with a thorough university education of at least five years. They must study not only anthropology but other essential subjects. Thus they go with trained minds to their positions in the field. Within a stated time they have to be proficient in the language and dialects of their district and are expected from the first to make a special study of its peculiarities. They are encouraged to make the best use of their unique opportunity to carry on original research which may be of practical value in administration. At the end of some six years they go on furlough back to Holland where they may take a doctorate on the basis of this work, and on their return may receive a higher position. Various publications in Holland and in the Dutch East Indies, in which the results of research work and also other useful information are published, show to what extent the colonial administrative officials are contributing to the development of scientific research. Thus the officials are encouraged to keep in touch with new thought. The results of this combination of research and administration so far are proving excellent.

Several members then briefly described the training given to prospective officials in their own countries. In Australia, excellent results have been achieved in the last few years, it was learned, with a period of study in the Department of Anthropology of Sydney University for cadets in the administrative services in Papua and the mandated territory of New Guinea. A New Zealand member confessed that lack of knowledge concerning the native people and lack of training for officials had been the chief causes of failure in the administration of the mandated area of Samoa. This recognition, in fact, accounted for the special interest of the New Zealand representatives at the round table in this phase of its subject. In the Japanese and French Oceania territories, and in those of the United States, likewise, no developed system of special training for officials appeared to exist. A Japanese member evoked sympathetic assent when he said that " lack of knowledge of native life is at the root of almost every administrative problem."

The more specific question was then considered, what kind of research was most needed to prepare administrators and enlighten governments. The thought was expressed that the word " anthropology " tended to be overused in this connection, with no very precise definition as to how that science may best be related to problems of administration. A British member submitted some suggestions on this subject made by a British anthropologist, Professor H. J. Fleure: with a view to the future, better studies of race are much needed; of more immediate importance would be studies of (a) varieties of usehold land systems and their reactions to the introduction of new types of production for export, (b) the seasonal cycle of native activities in relation to the ceremonial and mental life — that is, studies of native communities in action, (c) the results of miscegenation. A Filipino member emphasized the need for studies of customary law, particularly as regards land tenures, " because this is the very essence of the culture of a people." The Netherlands representative stated that much work in these fields had been done in the East Indies and was at present going on, particularly in Sumatra and the Celebes.[31] (A student from the latter area has recently gone to the Philippines to make a comparative study of native customary law.) He agreed that agrarian policy can be intelligent only when the relation between the soil and the character of the local social unit is understood; but in his opinion there was even greater need for a series of studies of sample units in all their aspects as " living organisms " — whether they be tribes or specific communities. It is useless, he held, to preserve native forms of leadership or any institutions, except as functioning parts of an integrated culture; hence the life of a group must be studied as a whole. Others heartily agreed with this statement which, they said, was also the conclusion reached by many students in related fields. An American member reported that a distinguished scientist and administrative official in Melanesia had recently emphasized to him the need for just such complete, detailed studies. He added:

" Perhaps Americans have gone to the extreme in the matter of conducting areal surveys; but in this case it seems essential to get out detailed regional information for the whole Pacific. It should be possible to make studies in a form that is of practical use to the administrator without sacrificing the scientific approach."

It was pointed out by another member that general studies were not enough:

" While an understanding of the usual cultural patterns of a people is useful to an administrator, what really counts for practical purposes is an intimate understanding of all the local variations of behavior and custom within the general patterns."

The question was then discussed as to what rôle the Institute of Pacific Relations might have in this enormous field of potential work. A member of the Pacific Science Congress was of the opinion that the detailed scientific study of native backgrounds involved should fall within the scope of that body which had a committee studying the " utilization of anthropological knowledge "; as yet, however, little had been done in this direction. He suggested that the emphasis of the Institute might be on those situations requiring the more sociological approach: the changes of the modern period, the possibilities of intelligent control, and the actual problems of administration. The matter was referred to a subcommittee on research.[32]

EDUCATIONAL OBJECTIVES

The round table now returned to the larger problems of cultural interaction and their significance for general educational aims and policies.[33] This

[31] See De Kat Angelino, *op. cit.*, I, 147–48; II, chap. vi, especially p. 447.
[32] See below, pp. 408 ff.
[33] For an analysis of the whole problem refer to the first volume of De Kat Angelino,

section may perhaps, best be introduced by a quotation from the principal work of reference before the round table:

Education has to fulfil a duty in different territories with very different groups and sub-groups of population. . . . Just as the administration of justice among the indigenous population must satisfy, as far as possible, its sense of justice, and must answer to its legal needs, education must adapt itself to the social environment from which it receives its pupils.

But as administrative policy and administration of justice have a higher task than merely to adapt themselves like a chameleon to existing circumstances, which are not always in agreement with the universal criterion of human dignity, education also has to do more than be satisfied with the passive rôle of adaptation. It must not estrange the rising generation from an environment which can only be improved through the activity of these younger people. It must teach them to look a little beyond their immediate environment. It must also attempt to lift them up a little above what they see every day, in order that, without sterile self-elation, they may acquire the capacity of seeing the faults and limitations of their familiar circle. Only if they satisfy this double condition can they maintain equilibrium and be able to take part fruitfully in the many-sided development which the spirit of the time demands. . . .

In the East, education has to do almost by itself all that in our countries is done by the influence of the independent monogamous household, religion, tradition, public opinion, social institutions, societies of all kinds, all of them generators of dynamic forces which would continue to radiate even if education were sterilized into an intellectual nourishment alone; in the East, education is almost the only force, because environment often counteracts with dull inertia and uncomprehending traditionalism the other forces which might help to develop a wider social consciousness. In such an environment the task of the teacher is really entirely different from what it is in the West. . . .

We stand here before a social vacuum, before a lack of wide civic sense without which all construction on a large scale must be considered altogether impossible. Just as Western authorities embody the idea of unity in tangible forms of organization, especially through their administrative services, in the same way education has also to be more than an instrument for intellectual nourishment. It has also to fill lacunae which are due to the existing social vacuum. Above all, the school must see its task as a social centre and as a nursery of social feeling. The smallest results which it can achieve in this direction amount to giant strides from the point of view of evolution; while a mechanical change from illiteracy into elementary knowledge does not carry society forward by one step.[34]

The general problem of education was to be discussed, then, not as the problem of how a smattering of knowledge might be imposed upon communities but recently without schools, in the Western sense; nor as the problem of training native populations to the use of modern methods of survival in a world-wide economy. It was seen, rather, as the problem of fostering in the very heart of a disintegrating social system the will to live and the most elementary attitudes and skills toward its realization. The criticism implied in the passage just quoted was taken up by an American member from Hawaii who asked:

op. cit. (data paper), which outstanding authorities in other countries have declared to be the most important recent contribution on this subject. For a brief summary of the essential aspects see also Robert E. Park, *The Problem of Cultural Differences.*

[34] De Kat Angelino, *op. cit.*, II, 194–96.

"Must Hawaii be regarded as a horrible example of how a native people has been sacrificed to economic development? Or can we look upon it as an area that has achieved rather remarkable educational results in welding differing racial and cultural groups into a satisfactory co-operative life — perhaps blazing the trail which, sooner or later, all must follow?"

The following is a more or less verbatim report of a dialogue that followed this key question:

BRITISH MEMBER: "What exactly are the objectives of the Hawaiian policy? Is it different in conception from the British?"

HAWAIIAN MEMBER: "The aim has been the organization of native government on the basis of a modern system. The land law was changed; and the native system was replaced by one of individual landholding. The Hawaiian king gave up voluntarily his arbitrary authority, and a limited monarchy was developed. In more modern days all peoples in Hawaii have an equal position under the Government. In other parts of the Pacific the natives are subsidiary. This American policy has been criticized, but I think it wonderful. Should backward peoples be kept back, or should they be brought into relation with civilization?"

BRITISH MEMBER: "Is Euro-American civilization the best?"

HAWAIIAN MEMBER: "It is a development of democracy."

BRITISH MEMBER: "In Fiji and other parts under British rule, the aim is to preserve the old ideas and to adapt them to modern ideas, keeping the native individuality."

HAWAIIAN MEMBER: "Are the natives happier?"

BRITISH MEMBER: "To us the idea of one standardized culture is repulsive. We feel that every chance should be given to the natives to adapt their cultures, while keeping their roots in the old ways."

HAWAIIAN MEMBER: "Do you accept them on equality?"

BRITISH MEMBER: "Yes. But it is felt that they are weaker peoples, and that they should be protected."

This clash in the fundamental aims regarding native policy produced a spirited discussion. It was pointed out that the geographic location of Hawaii and other factors had enabled it to undergo development "during an expansive economic period" that did not mark the occupation of other islands; it was doubtful whether conditions would ever be such as to enable Fiji and other groups to develop similarly, so that perhaps each policy was best in its own area. Another Hawaiian member pointed out that the Hawaiian experience had been essentially pragmatic, not consciously experimental, and that while in political terms the statements of his colleague had been true, the Hawaiian people had by no means been assimilated culturally: they are still clinging tenaciously to elements from the past.

In answer to a question, the modern rehabilitation schemes being tried in Hawaii to get the Hawaiian people back on the land were described; it was said that while there were all kinds of opinions expressed locally as to the success of this move, by which people of native and part-native Hawaiian blood were helped financially to settle and develop farms in chosen areas, it had been on the whole satisfactory — more especially in demonstrating that the Hawaiian may be interested in agriculture and is able to develop a homestead.[35]   Another member commented on this:

" In part I agree with the last speaker, only there aren't any Hawaiians.   In the American experiment the Hawaiian was swept up like chaff, and had to adapt himself as best he could.   I doubt if there are more than a handful of pure Hawaiians, and in a few years there will cease to be any.   At present, they are a political factor as they and the mixed Hawaiians gather together to resist being engulfed.   As I see it, the Polynesian is really an agent of his own destruction; the real rulers of the Pacific are Gandhi and the other racial and nationalist leaders of modern thought.   Their ideas permeate so that even in distant Samoa we hear of self-determination, non-co-operation, boycott.   A native intelligentsia is becoming Europeanized, hence ruined.   I consider the Hawaiian experiment important as revealing that what has encompassed the Hawaiians will in time overtake the Polynesians and Melanesians as a whole; only those peoples with immense vitality and cohesion, such as the Javanese, will escape."

Asked whether he considered that the Hawaiians are being destroyed or assimilated, he replied that they are being assimilated, but that this amounts to the same thing.   An American member strongly disagreed with this interpretation.   He considered that assimilation does not mean the loss of the cultural and ethnic contribution of a group.   Thus, along with mixture of blood that is leaving its mark, certain Hawaiian characteristics survive. These are especially notable in the mixed-blood group which is not dying out.

" We do not think of this as killing off a race but rather as the kind of fusion out of which civilization has grown and become enriched.   There is more liberality in the Hawaiian experiment, it seems to me, than in situations where the native culture tends to be kept as in a museum; there is more chance of a perpetuation of the best of the native in the world-civilization."

Another member from Hawaii pointed out that the native people in Hawaii were playing the part of an amalgam, and had exercised a tremendous influence in producing the comparative freedom from caste that exists in the modern Hawaii.

In a more general frame of reference, this subject was also discussed by the member from the Netherlands who endeavored to answer the question: Should administrative policies aim at accelerating or at retarding the process of assimilation?   He said:

" The answer depends on what should be understood by assimilation.   If it means an artificial and often forcible introduction of foreign forms into the native cultural organization, results cannot be very satisfactory, because cultural forms are not a matter of accident, but the expression of life, of the spirit of a people. If the leadership of a people sees the need of stronger or different organizational forms in social, economic, intellectual, or political life, it should then not concentrate its attention on the introduction of new forms from outside, but rather try to influence the native or national *spirit*, which created the older social organisms, so as to develop a new vigor and to choose a new direction for development.

" Now colonial governments, and also leadership in independent Eastern

[35] A description of this homesteading movement in Hawaii is given in *Filipino Immigration*, pp. 178–80.

countries, have often felt inclined to try the short cut toward development by simply ordering the introduction of foreign institutions, methods, and customs. The older type of missions also have too often insisted on the adoption of Western ways. Although the spirit of Christ is universal, it should be distinguished from the cultural forms Christianity has adopted in the West. And, generally speaking, every one of us is likely, in his attitude toward foreign cultures, to commit this mistake. In independent Oriental countries one sees often enough a similar preference, for instance, for modern political and social institutions, while the question is neglected how the spirit that elsewhere produced these forms might be enabled to animate or to dynamize the native soul. In such cases, the results cannot be good, because procrustean methods of adapting a living cultural organism to a dead instrument have been used.

"For these reasons, my answer to the question regarding a policy of assimilation is that such a policy should not consist in merely trying to adapt native life to extraneous forms, but rather in directing wholesome influences toward the spirit that so far has animated that native life. The principal methods to be used nowadays in the execution of such policy in the dependencies and in the East generally are: the building up of a satisfactory system of communications; popular education; the co-operative movement; and the growth of political forms of a democratic nature, starting from the bottom up in villages and districts."

The attempt of a member to summarize the agreement so far reached by the round table as to major educational objectives further sharpened the main outlines of a desirable policy:

"Looked at from the perspective of time, the idea of preserving a racial and cultural group seems both impossible and not worth the effort.

"'Fusion' seems a happier term than 'assimilation,' because it is doubtful if any group is ever entirely lost, and all history is made up of such fusions. Only complete isolation can prevent reciprocal influences and changes.

"The real question, therefore, seems that of the welfare of the various human groups concerned, and how changes may be prevented from being too violent for their good. This is a problem by no means always related to race."

It was further pointed out that, as was seen earlier, the alternatives were not preservation or assimilation, even if both these terms were modified. For a long period, perhaps indefinitely, mixed-blood groups will continue in existence after the full bloods pass. Like the part-Hawaiians, they will work out types of cultural life, no doubt containing much from the old ways. The problems in this connection are: first, how far we can guide the transition and possible restabilization of the life of such mixed-blood groups, so as to minimize difficult experiences; and second, how we can educate our own dominant peoples to be ready to accept these folk into the wider civilized life with less discrimination than at present, as they become able and desirous to participate in it. A Filipino member agreed with this statement; he felt that the real colonial problem, now being seriously tackled in his country through schools and other means,[36] is how to educate backward and specialized peoples to become a part of the general scheme.

[36] See Paul Monroe, *Education in the Philippines*, "Studies in Comparative Colonial Government."

In summarizing the work of the round table, the chairman expressed regrets that time did not permit a discussion of the final item on the agenda, " Labor and Economic Development," particularly as it involved the major interest of Chinese members present: the position of Chinese abroad.[37]

III. RESEARCH AND CO–ORDINATION

After two sessions of the round table on " Dependencies and Native Peoples," a number of the most interested members continued to meet in three further sessions and several less formal group meetings to consider possible ways and means of co-operation in a consistent program of research. In the round-table discussion itself, seven major types of study had been mentioned as desirable:

1. Population trends and their causes, especially as regards depopulation
2. Miscegenation and the position of the mixed-blood
3. Biological and cultural factors in the adaptation of racial groups to modern conditions
4. Native land systems and economic life in relation to modern economic conditions
5. Native customary law as a basis for administration
6. Administrative control of cultural change
7. [and emphasized as important] Specific local studies of tribes and communities as integrated social units

The need disclosed was thus primarily for intensive regional studies. The question was raised, whether an effort should be made to have a standardized framework of reference for all such research, or whether it should be left to the local groups of the Institute to explore the problems which they considered most acute or meaningful in their own areas, or for which students were available. Owing to the largeness of the subject and the lack of resources and workers, it was obvious that the latter would be the only practical method. Nevertheless, representatives of the various countries felt that a general outline of the scope of the problems would be valuable as a guide, and would help to make results useful as a basis for comparative studies. It was decided that an outline published by the director of the Institute's research project in the May, 1930, number of *Pacific Affairs* [38] would serve this purpose, particularly when read together with the *Syllabus on Dependencies and Native Peoples* and the outline of discussion contained in these proceedings. Rough criteria were suggested for deciding which type of situation would provide the best " samples " for study, in the sense of having significance for the whole area, of illustrating well some particular type or types of problem, and for which conditions of co-operation are particularly favorable at the time.

Some felt that a tendency to give attention to friction spots should not

[37] This subject is discussed, however, in the data paper from the International Labour Office, *Some Labour Problems in Pacific Dependencies.*
[38] " Government of Pacific Dependencies," pp. 457–59.

be unduly encouraged, as such situations are not always the most instructive, and the fact that an area is " on the front page " tends to divert the student or to make study difficult; on the other hand, occasions of friction were recognized as important subjects of study in themselves. Again, while recognizing the value of co-ordinating surveys, members deprecated a tendency for institutions and individuals to work superficially over the same body of material: preliminary descriptions, statistics, general statements, and the like. " We need more detailed studies and painstaking investigation of special problems — in a word, real research rather than descriptive essays." Some dependencies or native peoples have already a voluminous literature; yet practically nothing has been written about them that would contribute adequately to the discussion of such problems as those raised in the round table. In view of the fact that certain other organizations and scientific societies are working or have interest in the field, it was felt that the main contribution of Institute research should be upon the modern experience of transition and its possible control by governing authorities.

It was anticipated that a considerably larger body of information relating to the subject will be ready for the next conference. The British group reported that the Royal Institute of International Affairs intends to make studies of the educational policies of the major colonial powers as a continuation of their studies in comparative colonial government.[39] The Australian Institute of International Affairs has in Sydney a committee which is preparing a series of papers dealing with Papua, the Mandated Territory of New Guinea, and the Australian aborigine, covering racial and cultural backgrounds, legal, economic, and educational matters, missions, and the system of administration. Again the Hawaii group of the American Council of the Institute intend to continue their studies of racial and cultural interaction. A combined white and Maori committee in New Zealand is preparing a comprehensive work on the experience of the Maori and other Polynesian peoples controlled by the dominion, in which an interpretaton will be made by members of both races.

The Japanese and Philippines representatives who attended the round table showed great interest in regional studies, which to them appeared to open up a new approach even to problems with which they have long been familiar. As a result, Japanese members formulated a research project by which the experience of minority groups in the Japanese possessions and also of the Ainu in Hokkaido will be studied as circumstances permit. Again, the Philippines group decided to explore how best, in the light of the existing problems elsewhere, the extremely interesting racial and cultural fusions of their own country can be examined. The Netherlands observer reported that he intended to seek co-operation in the East Indies in order that further data on the Dutch colonial experiments and other relevant topics might be made available in the English language. The hope was expressed that more detailed material would be forthcoming on the situation of the North American Indian in mod-

[39] See the list of conference reference documents, p. 375.

ern times from both the American and the Canadian Institute councils; [40] also that the new group in the U.S.S.R. might contribute information concerning its exceedingly interesting experiments in the study, education, and government of Siberian and Mongolian tribes. A Chinese member felt that the time was approaching for a general study of Chinese communities overseas, as also of Chinese influence abroad, to be dealt with both historically and in terms of present problems; it was even suggested that a beginning might be made by bringing together for comparison and analysis the material that is already available on the Chinese in many Pacific dependencies.

A number of possible forms of co-ordination among the national groups was discussed of which only a few need be mentioned here. It was felt that the international character of the project, together with the scattered nature of the subject matter, called for a special degree of co-operation to secure a profitable exchange of ideas and of results. In illustration, it was pointed out that so far there had been little if any attempt of such co-operation between the Dutch and the Australians to share the problem of governing their respective halves of the great island of New Guinea, though nothing but an imaginary line separates their spheres of administration.

Ways and means were explored of bridging the language problem, especially as between the English and French languages and the Dutch, Japanese, and Chinese. Since the peoples speaking these latter tongues had been much more enterprising in learning the former than vice versa, it was felt that they would contribute greatly to the understanding of the subject if significant publications or articles, or at least abstracts, and brief selected bibliographies with annotations could be translated into English. The possibilities of *Pacific Affairs* as a medium for exchanging information was discussed, and it was felt that correspondents in the various countries might be asked to forward material from time to time to the editor, also notification of current publications, if possible with reviews. The issue of abstracts or of an annotated bibliography, separately or as a supplement to the magazine, was considered rather ambitious for the present; such form of publication, together with translation on a more elaborate scale, might well come in the future, either under Institute auspices or otherwise.

One special form of desirable co-operation noted was the greater standardization of statistics and of the means by which they are gathered.

Again, while it was recognized that all initiative of study would fall upon the local groups, it was believed that a more frequent exchange of students might be made between Pacific countries. Members familiar with different regions emphasized the peculiar value of the fresh and objective point of view often displayed by an outsider; thus a Filipino student might survey the position of his people or of other groups in Hawaii, while a student from Hawaii might explore the social backgrounds, especially of those Fili-

[40] The latter council presented a general survey of *Indian Affairs in Canada* as a data paper for this Conference (*op. cit.*).

pino groups and communities from which large numbers of emigrant plantation workers are drawn.

Finally, it was felt that the proposed co-ordinating study, to be made by the director of the project, should serve as a link between the work in the different countries, and thus fulfil the need for a summary of existing information and a formulation of the problems for future research.

CHAPTER XIII

PROBLEMS OF MIGRATION

DATA PAPERS

1. *Syllabus on Migration in the Pacific* (International Secretariat).
2. *Migration in the Pacific Area* (International Labour Office).
3. K. H. BAILEY. *The Legal Position of Foreigners in Australia* (mineographed, Australian Council).
4. G. L. WOOD. "Growth of Population and Immigration Policy," *An Economic Survey of Australia* (Australian Council).
5. RALPH ARNOLD. *The Status of Aliens in Great Britain* (mimeographed, British Group).
6. RALPH ARNOLD. *The Status of Aliens in China* (British Group).
7. GORDON LINDSAY and D. R. MICHENER. *Legal Status of Aliens Resident in Canada;* H. F. ANGUS, *The Legal Status in British Columbia of Residents of Oriental Race and Their Descendants* (Canadian Council).
8. MINGCHIEN JOSHUA BAU. *The Status of Aliens in China* (China Council).
9. FRANKLIN L. HO. *Population Movement to the North Eastern Frontier of China* (China Council).
10. CHEN HAN-SENG. *Notes on Migration of Nan Min to the Northeast* (China Council).
11. SABURO YAMADA. *Legal Status of Aliens in Japan* (Japan Council).
12. T. D. H. HALL. *Status of Aliens in New Zealand* (New Zealand Council).
13. T. D. H. HALL. "Asiatic Immigration," *New Zealand Affairs* (New Zealand Council), chap. v.
14. HERMENEGILDO CRUZ. *Emigration of Filipinos to Hawaii and the United States* (Philippine Council).
15. J. P. CHAMBERLAIN. *Aliens in the United States* (mimeographed, American Council).
16. BRUNO LASKER. *Filipino Immigration to Continental United States and to Hawaii* (American Council).
17. A. D. A. DE KAT ANGELINO. *Colonial Policy* (American Council), Vol. II, chap. vii.
18. *Census Statistics of Oriental Residents in Continental United States* (mimeographed, American Council).
19. H. L. SHAPIRO. *Chinese Population in Hawaii* (American Council).

REFERENCES

1. J. B. CONDLIFFE (ed.). *Problems of the Pacific, 1929,* chap. ii, Docs. X, XI, XIII.
2. CHARLES P. HOWLAND. *American Foreign Relations, 1930,* chap. vii.
3. CHENG TIEN FANG. *Oriental Immigration in Canada.* Shanghai, 1931.
4. SIR WILLIAM HARRISON MOORE. *The Dominions of the British Commonwealth in the League of Nations* (Australian Council).
5. HAROLD S. QUIGLEY. *An Introductory Syllabus on Far Eastern Diplomacy,* secs. I, xiv; II, iv (American Council).
6. *World Social Economic Congress, 1931, Section 1: Reports of Fluctuations in Unemployment* (International Industrial Relations Association, The Hague).
7. SHUHSI HSU. *Questions Relating to Manchuria* (China Council).
8. J. B. CONDLIFFE. *New Zealand in the Making.* London, 1930.
9. HAROLD G. MOULTON. *Japan: An Economic and Financial Appraisal* (Brookings Institution, Washington, D.C., 1931), chap. xx.

10. *Some Labor Problems in Pacific Dependencies* (International Labour Office).
11. ETIENNE DENNERY. *Asia's Teeming Millions and Its Problems for the West.* London, 1931.
12. *Annual Report of the Health Organisation of the League of Nations,* III (1931), iii, 3.
13. P. M. ROXBY. *A Plea for the Systematic Study of the Chinese Population Problem as a Whole* (mimeographed, British Group).
14. *Syllabus on Problems of Food and Population in the Pacific Area* (International Secretariat).
15. AMRY VANDENBOSCH. "A Problem in Java; the Chinese in the Dutch East Indies," *Pacific Affairs,* November, 1930, pp. 1001–17.
16. SEISHI IDEI. "Japan's Migration Problems," *International Labour Review,* December, 1930.
17. *International Migration,* I: Statistics, II: Interpretation (National Bureau of Economic Research, New York, 1931).
18. *Migration Laws and Treaties* (3 vols. International Labour Office, 1930).
19. *Report on Forced Labour* (International Labour Office, 1929).

INTRODUCTORY NOTE

In the tentative agenda for the 1931 Conference, a technical round table was scheduled on the subject of " Migration and Race Problems." This combination of two seemingly different subjects had its origin in past discussions of migration problems by the Institute in which a consideration of migration and of its economic and social consequences invariably led to questions that have little to do with the process of migration itself. Conflicts arise from attitudes and interests previously formed that now express themselves in the relations of groups newly brought into contact. They are often transferred bodily from one social situation in which only relations between nationals are concerned to another situation in which those between old residents and new, or between one " race " and another, disguise the original issue. Thus, competition for land or for labor, as immigrants of distinct appearance or language enter the scene, no longer remains a subject of economic strife but becomes the occasion for " racial " discord. Thus, also, difficulties arising from many types of contact between members of groups diversified in themselves — " Orientals," " Occidentals " — in the emotional fervor of aroused race consciousness coagulate into one major, seemingly racial conflict, and we speak of the " color question," the " yellow peril," and the " white man's burden." Specifically, migration problems in the Pacific area were seen, in these earlier conferences, to be inseparable from the problems confronted also in the relations between natives and resident aliens and residents of foreign descent.

Of late, the habit of lumping together all sorts of difficulties in group relations and talking of them as problems in " race " relations has become discredited. In the present Conference, as the following account will show, a realistic grasp of the international problems raised by migrations in the Pacific area gave its own clues as to which aspects of them are racial in origin and as such require appropriate treatment; there was no separate discussion of race problems.

International controversies arising from migration across parts of the Pacific Ocean were among the first subjects featured in Institute programs and may, indeed, be said to have been one of the principal causes of its inception.

The First Conference met in 1925 in an atmosphere of great tension, not long after the passing of the American Immigration Act of 1924 which was deeply resented by Japan. . . . The conference plunged immediately into the discussion of these problems and their underlying causes. It emerged with a program of research into the basic underlying social problems, such as the food and population question in the Pacific.[1]

The Fourth Conference, held six years later, confronted a world-situation as regards international migration in which its bearing upon basic economic and social problems is better understood. International conferences and research work carried on in many countries have revealed " good reasons for considering migration never as a problem in itself but always as a symptom or a by-product of some more elemental process." [2]   The subject had last been fully discussed in the 1927 Conference,[3] while in 1929 a smaller number of data papers under this heading revealed the continuing interest of scholars in different Pacific countries [4] and also the emergence of at least one important new set of problems.[5]   It seemed wise, therefore, in order to make the best possible use of the short time available for this subject in the 1931 Conference, to limit the discussion of Pacific migration as much as possible to new developments in the last four years.

In one way, this special round table merely served to approach from one standpoint problems that were faced also by a number of other round tables — for example, those on international political relations, on labor problems and the standard of living, on the dependent peoples of the Pacific Islands, and on cultural relations. As a " technical " round table it had the function of reviewing its subject matter in the light of scientific research, already accomplished, incipient, and yet to be promoted. In this connection, particular significance was attached to two types of inquiry: (1) the nature, causes, and consequences of new migration movements in the Pacific; and (2) comparative studies that illumine the process of migration in relation to social and economic change.

It had been felt in former discussions that the relationship between present migration and the deposits of past migrations in social institutions and attitudes had not been sufficiently explored; and that studies of the status of aliens in the different Pacific countries, apart from their intrinsic

---

[1] *Handbook,* p. 21.
[2] *Syllabus,* p. 6.
[3] *Problems of the Pacific, 1927,* II, 7 and docs. 22–24.
[4] Notably a collection of papers on " The Peopling of Australia."
[5] Chinese colonization in Manchuria.

interest, might be expected to throw light on the nature and directions of present migration movements and on the problems occasioned by them. A recommendation to this effect was made by the Japanese Council, adopted by the International Research Committee of the Institute at the Kyoto Conference, and subsequently translated into a co-operative research project, first as to its more formal aspect — the legal status of foreign residents.[6] The scope of this project was defined as follows:

A study of the disabilities of or the discriminations applied against resident aliens or immigrants, or naturalized aliens, or the descendants of any of them, whether general or directed against particular races, nationals or groups, established by national or dominion or state or provincial legislation, or by municipal ordinances or regulations, or by judicial or administrative application or enforcement of any of them, in any of the Pacific countries.

It is intended to cover disabilities or discriminations, personal, political and economic, such as but not limited to the subjects of land ownership, leasing, trusts, etc., the doing of business by foreign companies, the holding of shares in domestic companies, trade, occupations, residence (not including the individual right of entry), and schooling.

The appeal of this project to the constituent groups is shown by the fact that at the 1931 Conference every one of the national councils of the Institute (except those newly created) was able to present a report on this subject, in the form of a data paper.

A subcommittee of the International Research Committee appointed to consider these papers reported to the effect that, partly owing to the limits set by the earlier definition of scope, the set of papers dealt only in part with what, they suggested, might be conceived of as a more comprehensive inquiry:

1. Immigration and deportation laws and practice.
2. The legal status of resident aliens in each country, involving incidentally such explanation of the origin and purposes of any particular legislation as may be considered necessary and the consideration of restrictions imposed upon persons of any particular race (whether aliens or not) so far as it may be germane to or explanatory of this branch of the subject.
3. The treatment of foreigners generally, both from a legal and from a sociological point of view, cutting across both the legal and the cultural contact aspects.

While the papers received covered in varying degree the subject indicated in the second paragraph, the committee desired that before their publication they should be revised so as to make them as complete as possible and to permit comparison. For this purpose it drafted more detailed specifications of the information desired than had previously been supplied. At the same time, it also recommended that comparative surveys of the immigration and deportation laws and practices in the various Pacific countries also be initiated without delay, so as to have the results of both studies available for early publication in one volume. The third subject, calling for both legal and sociological treatment, would require separate investigation.

[6] *Problems of the Pacific, 1929,* pp. 45 and 655, and *Report of International Research Committee, February 12, 1930,* Appendix H (mimeographed).

With the acceptance of these recommendations by the International Research Committee, the round table on " Migration " preferred to devote its time to aspects of its subject on which systematic comparative study is less advanced. Although there had been no consultation on this matter, its agenda actually took place, for the most part, within the limits of the third of the three items in the recommended program for special study. On this more general topic, a number of suggestive data papers had been prepared, and other recent publications could be referred to for supplementary information.[7] Unfortunately it is not possible in the space available in the documentary section of this chapter to present descriptive data for more than two of the newer migration movements listed in the round-table agenda (p. 445).

[7] Particularly data papers Nos. 1, 9, 10, 16, and reference papers Nos. 7, 10, 15.

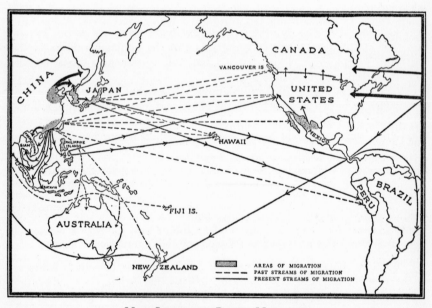

MAIN STREAMS OF PACIFIC MIGRATION

EXTRACTS FROM SYLLABUS [8]

I. THE MAIN CURRENTS OF MIGRATION IN THE PACIFIC

Migration in the Pacific countries is not confined to the Pacific area. On the one hand, the English-speaking countries of North America and Oceania receive most of their immigrants from Europe, and on the other, Japan's largest stream of emigration now flows beyond the Pacific Ocean to Brazil. With this qualification in mind, however, it is possible by a feat of imagination to see the migration movements of the Pacific area as ocean currents flowing in fairly well defined courses, but with this difference that the currents change their direction and intensity with the passage of years and with the waxing and waning of economic cycles. On the accompanying map, therefore, the main streams of migration are no longer the same as those of twenty, thirty and fifty years ago, which are indicated on the map by faint dotted lines. With the passage of immigration restriction laws in the English-speaking countries of the Pacific, the main pre-War streams of migration from South China to British Columbia, California, Hawaii and northern Australia, and from Japan to Hawaii and the Pacific Coast of North America, have dwindled until the present-day movement is largely composed of temporary visitors and returning nationals, and the direction of the flow has so changed that there is often a net emigration of these Oriental migrants from countries which are characteristictically regions of immigration.

At the present time the migration currents are clearly defined. The greatest in volume is the movement of European immigrants into Canada and the United States and the related ebb and flow of migration across the frontier between the two countries. Next in magnitude is the more recent and primitive emigration of peasants from North China into northern and eastern Manchuria and in smaller volume into Siberia. Rivalling it and resembling it in its seasonal emigration and immigration is the flow of laborers from the south coast of China into Indo-China, Siam, British Malay, and the Netherlands East Indies, and the smaller clandestine movement into the Philippine Islands. It mingles in the Malay Peninsula with an influx of laborers from India and Burma. Into Australia and New Zealand there is a steady flow (for the present greatly restricted) of European immigrants, nearly all of them from the British Isles. From Japan the only considerable movement of emigrants is to Brazil where the Japanese communities in the region of São Paulo now comprise about 80,000 people. Across the Mexican border there is a steady inflow of laborers into Texas and California. Plantation laborers come and go regularly between the Philippines and Hawaii, and in recent years they have proceeded a step farther into California. Korean farmers and laborers have migrated year after year northward across the Yalu River, till nearly 800,000 of them now reside in Manchuria on Chinese soil; and simultaneously there has been a perceptible though carefully re-

[8] Conference *Syllabus on Migration*, pp. 11–13, 14–20, 20–23, 24–25, 26–30.

stricted flow of labor across from southern Korea into Japan proper, under the stimulus of higher economic standards in the latter country.

Few of these currents flow solely in one direction. In many instances they represent seasonal migrations not of settlers but of laborers who later return home. Nevertheless, in most of the movements just listed there is an appreciable residuum of net emigration. In most of the remaining migration currents, such as those between Japan and Hawaii or the American Pacific coast, between South China and the same area, between China and Australia or New Zealand, and between the English-speaking countries of the Pacific, the outward and inward movements either balance approximately or there is a net repatriation of nationals. We may conclude by saying that the emigration sources in the Pacific are the provinces of Shantung, Hopei and Honan in North China, the provinces of Fukien and Kwangtung in South China, the southern regions of Japan, India, Mexico, and, to a lesser extent, Korea and the Philippines. The characteristic areas of immigration are Canada, the United States, Australia, New Zealand, British Malaya, the Netherlands East Indies, northern and eastern Manchuria and the Russian Far East.

II. CHINESE CONTINENTAL MIGRATIONS

The figures in Table I show approximately the volume of migration, chiefly from Shantung and Hopei, to the Four Eastern Provinces.

TABLE I

ARRIVALS AND DEPARTURES AT MANCHURIAN PORTS

Year	Arrivals *	Departures	Net Immigration
1923	433,689	....	....
1924	482,470	....	....
1925	532,770	215,000 †	318,000 †
1926	607,352	297,000 †	310,000 †
1927	1,178,254	341,599	836,655
1928	938,472	394,247	544,215
1929	1,046,291	621,897	424,394
1930	748,213	512,793	235,420

* The figures are those compiled by the South Manchuria Railway Company. Other estimates differ slightly. The figures for 1930 were kindly supplied by Mr. Henry Kinney of the S.M.R. office at Dairen.
† Approximate figures from Hsiao.

While the economic and political consequences of this immigration into Manchuria are far-reaching, the social and racial complications that ordinarily attend large population movements are less important, for the newcomers have entered a country which is under the same flag as their home provinces and which has no large element of native people inhabiting it. The influence of Russians, Koreans, Manchus and Mongolians will no doubt be perceptible in the new social order which evolves in Manchuria, but for the moment their effect is practically negligible, and in language and customs the new land differs but little from the provinces of Shantung and Hopei.

This is not true of the southward emigrations from the provinces of Fukien and Kwangtung. Here is an enterprising sea-faring people who, many decades ago, plied a trade with the neighboring islands of the Philippines and the Malay Archipelago, had colonized the island of Formosa, and steadily penetrated across the northern frontiers of Indo-China and Siam. It was from these provinces that shipowners in the nineteenth century recruited or kidnapped their cargoes of the Chinese laborers who have been employed from South Africa to Hawaii and from Queensland to Peru in the pioneer work of opening up new lands for development. From this same area come the traders who are to be found in almost every island group of the Pacific and who form the commercial backbone of Indonesia and Malaysia. The historical side of these migrations has formed the subject of several books,[9] and a study of their influence in British Malaya and neighboring territories was made available at the Kyoto Conference.[10] Obviously, however, a great deal of necessary knowledge on the social and economic effects of Chinese migrations into these regions of southeastern Asia still remains to be brought to light — especially on such questions as the social and biological effects of Chinese intermarriage with native races, the influence of Chinese immigrants on the economic, commercial and educational development of these areas, the use of forced or recruited Chinese labor on plantations and public works in certain regions. Little is yet known of these matters, but the statistics which are presented in Tables II–VI at least indicate something of the opportunity and demand for Chinese brawn and brains in these countries.

The statistics are incomplete, for there is known to be a considerable amount of unrecorded and illegal migration. A useful indicator of the volume of the movement is Table II [11] (p. 420), showing the number of Chinese passing through Hongkong, most of them on their way to or from British Malaya.

These figures, however, represent only a part of the total migration. This can be seen from the statistics of arrivals and departures in the Straits Settlements ports, chiefly Singapore and Penang. These include immigrants from all Asiatic countries, but predominantly they are for Chinese.

Not all those Chinese who arrive in the Straits Settlements can be called immigrants, and even the net immigration figures are increased by the existence of a considerable movement between the Straits and the Netherlands East Indies. It is therefore of interest to glance at Table IV, which shows the migration of aliens in the Netherlands East Indies and Indo-China.

[9] In particular Ta Chen, *Chinese Migrations with Special Reference to Labor Conditions* (U.S. Bureau of Labor Statistics, 1923); Campbell, *Chinese Coolie Emigration in the British Empire* (London, 1923); and Morse, *International Relations of China* (London, 1914), Vol. II.

[10] Hinton, *Government of Pacific Dependencies: British Malaya*. Honolulu: Institute of Pacific Relations, 1929.

[11] Compiled from statistics collected by the International Labour Office in *Migration Movements* and elsewhere.

TABLE II

CHINESE MIGRATION THROUGH HONGKONG

Year	Emigration	Returning	Net Emigration
1920	105,258	122,438	.....
1921	156,011	159,164	.....
1922	98,393	143,547	.....
1923	120,224	121,102	.....
1924	129,859	?	?
1925	140,534	91,662	48,872
1926	216,527	128,661	87,966
1927	285,593	181,100	104,493
1928	257,162	187,847	69,315
1929	227,523	185,390	42,033

TABLE III *

STRAITS SETTLEMENTS — CONTINENTAL MIGRATION OF ALIENS

Year	Immigration	Emigration	Net Immigration
1920–24	1,101,712	404,745	696,967
1925	305,400	121,064	184,336
1926	523,388	186,472	336,916
1927	515,394	243,916	271,478
1928	358,772	240,606	118,166
1929	407,419	216,616	190,803

* International Labour Office, op. cit. For earlier migrations to Singapore and Penang from 1881 to 1915, see Ta Chen, op. cit., p. 84.

TABLE IV

MIGRATION OF ALIENS

YEAR	INDO-CHINA			NETHERLANDS EAST INDIES *
	Immigration	Emigration	Net	Immigration
1920–24	283,420	159,030	124,390	....
1925	45,774	29,335	16,439	46,670
1926	55,996	36,055	19,941	32,263
1927	63,888	30,918	32,970	45,566
1928	81,895	50,842	31,053	50,965
1929	87,311	57,907	29,404	52,923

* Emigration usually less than 3,000 annually.

Finally, it is necessary to take into account the steady but seldom recorded infiltration of Chinese from Yunnan Province across the borders of Indo-China, Burma and Siam, and the fluctuating movement of Chinese labor back and forth between Malaya and Siam, a movement which, as Mr. Hinton points out, is largely determined by changes in the price of tin.[12]

[12] Op. cit., Appendix A, p. 52 (from Survey of International Affairs, 1926 [London, 1928], Part III).

The volume of Chinese immigration into Siam by sea may be judged from Table V, showing deck passengers most of whom are Chinese arriving and departing at the port of Bangkok.[13]

TABLE V

DECK PASSENGERS (MAINLY CHINESE) AT BANGKOK

Year	Arrivals	Departures	Net Immigration
1920–21................	70,252	37,583	32,669
1921–22................	75,242	46,777	28,465
1922–23................	90,508	62,494	28,014
1923–24................	109,372	62,110	97,262
1924–25................	85,768	58,260	27,508
1925–26................	87,717	56,362	31,355
1926–27................	100,000 *	60,000 *	40,000 *
1927–28................	140,102	63,765	76,337
1928–29................	115,324	54,740	60,584

* Estimates.

As a result of these regular migrations from South China the number of Chinese nationals living abroad in southeastern Asia at the present time must be very nearly nine and a half millions. The estimate is necessarily subject to a great margin of error, for even where census figures are available, they usually relate to 1920 or 1921 since when the inflow of immigrants has reached its greatest volume. By taking these census figures and adding such figures of subsequent net immigration as are available, we obtain Table VI. It will be seen that the largest Chinese group overseas is in Formosa where, of course, they cannot be regarded as immigrants in the ordinary sense of the word. The same qualification is partly applicable to Siam also where a minority of the Chinese are recent immigrants.

TABLE VI

CHINESE ABROAD IN SOUTHEASTERN ASIA

Country	Census or Estimate	Estimate for 1930
Netherlands East Indies (foreign Asiatics, 90 per cent Chinese in 1927)............	1,053,120	1,000,000
British Malaya (1921)....................	1,174,777	1,800,000
Burma (1921)............................	1,149,060	180,000
British North Borneo (1921)..............	37,900	50,000
Indo-China (1926).......................	615,000	700,000
Siam (1909).............................	700,000	1,100,000
Philippines (1925, *Governor's Report*).......	65,000	70,000
Formosa (1926, natives excluding aborigines)	3,923,752	4,300,000
Total..............................	....	9,200,000

[13] Figures from the *Statesman's Year Book* (1921–30).

III. MIGRATIONS TO THE PACIFIC ISLANDS

The same urge which brought the enterprising Cantonese into Malaya and the Netherlands East Indies later drove them farther afield into the scattered islands of the Pacific. Today it is rare to find any of the larger island groups which has not its little colony of Chinese merchants or tradesmen. Although this migration is numerically small, especially in comparison with the movements described in the section above, and although the number of Chinese in the islands is probably under 50,000 even when the 25,000 living in Hawaii are reckoned in,[14] the influence of these people on the commercial development of the islands has been important and out of proportion to their numbers. At the present time, however, it happens that most of the island territories where Chinese reside, or to which they might continue to migrate, have enforced restrictive measures against them, so that the characteristic problems are not so much problems of immigration as of race mixture and of social or legal status. This is likewise true of the Japanese living in Hawaii and the south Pacific, and of the Hindus who were formerly recruited for labor in Fiji and now form an exiled group of some 70,000 people.

For the student of anthropology and race relations the presence of these isolated and semi-isolated groups of immigrant peoples set down in new physical and social environments is a fact of great scientific significance and a fact which has begun to challenge attention. As might be expected, Hawaii with its unusual succession of immigrant invasions has thus far provided the chief laboratory for these investigators.

Nowadays the only migration of importance to the Pacific Islands is the movement of plantation workers back and forth between the Philippines and Hawaii. The movement is important in many ways: first, because the two main industries of Hawaii are dependent on it for their labor supply; second, because it is part of the same general movement which in 1929 and

TABLE I*

FILIPINO MIGRATION TO THE UNITED STATES

YEAR	PHILIPPINES TO HAWAII		HAWAII TO MAINLAND	
	Arrivals in Hawaii	Departures from Hawaii	Departures to Mainland	Arrivals from Mainland
1907–19.............	28,449	4,336	2,382	47
1920–24.............	29,226	8,177	3,654	83
1925–29.............	44,404	17,972	9,786	689
1907–29.............	102,079	30,485	15,822	819

Net excess of arrivals in Hawaii from Philippines.................... 71,584
Net excess of departures to mainland from Hawaii.................. 15,003
Net gain for Hawaii... 56,581

* *Filipino Immigration* (American Council), Appendix.

[14] For detailed statistics see the *Syllabus on Dependencies and Native Peoples of the Pacific* (Statistical Appendix).

1930 evoked much alarm and some violence in some regions of the American Pacific coast; and third, because the political relation of the Filipino people to the United States raises a number of far reaching and complicated problems relating to nationality laws and the status of aliens.

IV. MIGRATION IN KOREA AND JAPAN

Although the volume of the movement is small, the problems of Japanese migration have in the past aroused so much international controversy and misunderstanding that they take on greater significance than the statistics alone would suggest (Table I).

TABLE I *

MIGRATION TO AND FROM JAPAN

Year	Emigration Permits Issued	Nationals Returned to Japan	Net Emigration
1920–24................	61,287	77,406	−16,119
1925....................	10,696	13,918	− 3,222
1926....................	16,184	14,549	1,635
1927....................	18,041	14,735	3,306
1928....................	19,850	15,004	4,866

* *Résumé statistique de l'Empire du Japon* (Tokyo, 1929).

Contrary to popular impressions, Japan has during the decade following the War had a net immigration of nationals. Only from 1926 has the outflow of emigrants exceeded the number of returning Japanese. The reasons for this become apparent when the countries of origin and destination are studied. In Table II it is shown that the net excess of returns from Hawaii and North America was over 10,000 for the year 1928, a figure which about counterbalances the annual departures to Brazil, now the chief outlet for Japanese emigrants.

TABLE II *

JAPANESE MIGRATION IN 1928

Country	Emigrants To	Nationals Returning From
Brazil......................	12,002	903
Philippines.................	2,007	.....
Peru.......................	1,410	578
Canada.....................	1,050	1,559
U.S.A. (mainland)..........	306	7,970
Hawaii.....................	265	3,839
U.S.S.R....................	870	.....
Malaya.....................	420	.....
All countries............	19,850	15,004

* *Résumé statistique de l'Empire du Japon* (Tokyo, 1929).

The statistics of returning nationals from Canada, the Continental United States, and Hawaii provide interesting evidence of the tendency for Japanese (and Chinese) who have grown up abroad and received a western education to return to their native land where they are able to occupy relatively important posts from which they would ordinarily be debarred in western countries.

Not only does Japan fail to send more than a handful of her people abroad, but she is increasingly coming to be regarded as a country of immigration, as her economic standards rise above those of other Far Eastern countries. Despite the enforcement of administrative restrictions against other Asiatic immigration, she now has some 25,000 Chinese and 15,000 Filipinos within her gates. The entrance of Koreans into Japan has proved less easy to control on account of the constitutional position of Korea in relation to Japan; and there is regularly a large net influx from Fusan into the south of Japan. Mr. Idei has estimated that of the 1,186,000 Koreans who entered Japan between 1917 and 1929 about 338,000 remained permanently.[15] Their presence in Japan has seriously aggravated the unemployment among unskilled workers.

V. MIGRATION IN THE ENGLISH-SPEAKING PACIFIC COUNTRIES

Thus far we have dealt almost solely with migrations of Asiatic peoples. We turn now to four countries all of which have a characteristic net immigration of persons from the British Isles and other countries of Western Europe. Each of these countries, it is true, contains small groups of Oriental people, mainly Chinese or Japanese; but the immigration restriction policies enforced by each of them now exclude practically all immigration of Oriental laborers, and in some of them there is a net outflow of Oriental people. If exception be made of the relatively small influx of Mexican and Porto Rican workers into the United States, we can say that the immigration into the four countries is of European, and mainly northern European, people, while in the three British Dominions it is predominantly of people from the United Kingdom. For this reason, immigration into these countries is ordinarily not attended, or at any rate less attended, by the race problems and cultural clashes which are typical of the other Pacific migrations and typical of Asiatic migrations into these countries. This, however, is not to overlook the fact that the assimilation of various groups, such as Jewish and Central or Southern European people, has often proved to be slow and difficult, and that many of the popular prejudices and charges against Oriental immigrants on the Pacific coast differ very little from those held at one time against German or Italian communities in the eastern parts of America.

The problems arising from the immigration of Europeans into Canada and the United States have only an indirect bearing on Pacific migration ques-

[15] " Japan's Migration Problem," *International Labour Review*, December, 1930. The article also gives an account of emigration to Brazil.

tions, and we consequently confine ourselves to presenting merely the figures of entrances and departures. First is shown in Table I the immigrant arrivals in Canada from the United Kingdom, the United States, and, for purposes of comparison, from China and Japan.

TABLE I*

IMMIGRANT ARRIVALS IN CANADA

Year	U.K.	U.S.A.	China	Japan	All Orientals	Total Arrivals
1913.............	150,542	139,009	7,445	724	8,174	402,432
1920–24.........	280,312	169,558	6,110	2,531	8,725	577,259
1925.............	53,178	15,818	....	501	547	111,362
1926.............	37,030	18,778	....	421	483	96,064
1927.............	49,874	21,025	....	475	535	143,991
1928.............	50,872	25,007	3	478	537	151,597
1929.............	59,497	30,560	....	445	497	167,722
1930 †...........	......	......	....	....	....	104,806

* *Canada Year Book* (1930). Fiscal year ends March 31.
† *International Labour Review*, May, 1931.

Table II gives the admittances and departures of aliens for all the United States (including Hawaii and Alaska), after which the figures are classified according to countries of origin and destination. It is interesting to observe that the last five years have seen a net emigration of Chinese and Japanese people from the country.

TABLE II*

UNITED STATES MIGRATION OF ALIENS

Year (Fiscal)	Immigrant Aliens Admitted	Emigrant Aliens Departed	Immigrant Excess
1913...................	1,197,892	308,190	889,702
1920–24..............	2,774,600	892,984	1,881,616
1925..................	294,314	92,728	201,586
1926..................	304,488	76,992	227,496
1927..................	335,175	73,366	261,809
1928..................	307,255	77,457	229,798
1929..................	279,678	69,203	210,475
1930..................	241,700	50,661	191,039

* *Annual Reports, U.S.* Commissioner General of Immigration.

The figures for both Canada and the United States are based on the fiscal years, and they consequently do not show the drastic reduction of immigration which has taken place in the latter part of 1930 and the first part of 1931. As a result of the economic depression, administrative restrictions have been tightened up in the United States, and deportation laws have

TABLE III *

United States — Origin and Destination of Alien Migrants

COUNTRY	1920–24		1925–29	
	Admitted	Departed	Admitted	Departed
Canada and Newfoundland..	526,853	22,980	422,433	13,655
Mexico....................	255,774	23,182	243,171	20,261
Australia and New Zealand..	6,458	2,804	2,881	2,188
China.....................	22,723	22,477	7,925	18,570
Japan.....................	38,636	18,016	3,421	5,655
All Europe................	1,787,303	758,619	789,407	294,972
All countries...........	2,774,600	892,984	1,520,910	389,746

* *U.S. Statistical Abstract* (1930). Fiscal year ends June 30.

been more stringently applied, so that in January, 1931, it was reported that, for the first time since 1919, more aliens departed than arrived, and the net outward movement of all passengers was still more marked. Despite the resolutions introduced in both houses at the end of 1930 to suspend all immigration for two years, the United States has not yet followed the example of Australia in barring all alien immigrants during the depression. The figures in Table IV reveal how the decline of migration into Australia has proceeded so far that the year 1930 saw a net loss of 10,000 persons.

TABLE IV *

Immigration into Australia

Year	Net Immigration	Assisted Immigrants
1861–1929..............	1,313,707	1,073,962
1911–20................	207,571	....
1921–24................	134,966	90,621
1925...................	37,357	24,827
1926...................	42,220	31,260
1927...................	48,924	30,123
1928...................	27,232	22,394
1929...................	8,963	12,943
1930...................	−10,228 †	....

* *Commonwealth Official Year Book* (1930).
† *International Labour Review*, May, 1931. Net emigration.

In New Zealand, where the usual policy of Government assistance to selected immigrants from the British Isles has been temporarily suspended, the decline in immigration, if less precipitate than in Australia, is still considerable, as the statistics in Table V bear witness.

TABLE V *

IMMIGRATION INTO NEW ZEALAND

Year	Immigrants Intending Permanent Residence	Residents Departing Permanently	Net Increase
1924...................	14,314	2,256	12,058
1925...................	15,704	1,946	13,758
1926...................	17,868	2,581	15,287
1927...................	11,327	4,145	7,182
1928...................	6,339	3,954	2,385
1929...................	6,343	3,093	3,250
1930 †...............	6,917 †	2,449 †	4,468

* *New Zealand Official Year Book* (1930). Year ended December 31.
† *International Labour Review*, May, 1931. Figures do not include movement to and from other countries in Oceania, e.g., Australia.

EXTRACTS FROM DATA PAPERS

I. THE RECRUITING AND PLACING OF ASIATIC MIGRANTS [17]

Before an attempt is made to describe various methods of introducing foreign workers employed in some important emigration and immigration countries, a word must be said about the restrictions imposed by many Asiatic countries on the emigration of their working class. The development of plantation enterprises and the abolition of slavery throughout the British Empire in 1833 were the direct causes of the large-scale emigration of Asiatic workers during the nineteenth century. The emigrant laborers were mostly introduced as indentured laborers, and were bound by a long-term contract which was enforcible by the criminal code. Aggressive recruitment, suffering in transit and ill-treatment at work were often unfortunate consequences of this form of migration. From the necessity of protecting the interests of the workers from the unscrupulous conduct of some recruiting agents and employers, various countries have taken measures restricting or prohibiting the emigration of workers. For instance, China has adopted a policy of closing her ports for indentured emigration. The Indian Act of 1922 prohibits emigration of unskilled workers except to those countries for which the Government gives a special sanction. Without special permission from the Government authorities no one is allowed to recruit laborers of the Dutch East Indies for foreign employment. In Japan, the Government gives a permit to emigrate only in case an intending emigrant has responsible sureties for his living condition abroad. In this connection it may be mentioned that Australia decided in 1901 in accordance with the " white Australia " policy, to prohibit the recruiting of Kanakas (Pacific Islanders).

China seems to have no well-developed system of recruiting and placing her emigrants. A considerable part of those who emigrate to continental

[17] *Migration in the Pacific Area* (memorandum prepared by the International Labour Office, data paper), pp. 16–23.

destinations depend on help from their relatives and friends who have already established themselves there. Besides these emigrants there are also many laborers who proceed to oversea countries and continental countries through the hands of emigration agents. These agents recruit Chinese laborers for foreign employers charging a certain fee, and in many cases they make advance payment of passage money to the emigrants. The Hongkong Government authorities inspect the health and willingness of these assistant emigrants on board ship when calling at the port. In 1929 the total number of such emigrants examined was 16,988, consisting of 508 for oversea destinations and 16,480 for continental destinations.

Once many Chinese workers emigrated under what is known as the "credit-ticket" system of which a description will be given a little later when the recruiting organization in British Malaya will be discussed. Towards the end of the nineteenth century the Chinese authorities prohibited this form of migration from her ports, but after such action was taken indentured migration continued to take place from foreign settlements. However, public opinion was strongly roused against the abuses of such migration, and measures adopted by the Governments of Hongkong and Macao between 1868 and 1873 put an end to the greater part of this form of emigration.

Chinese emigration to the Transvaal and to France during the early part of this century took place under governmental supervision; in both cases contracts were signed between contracting governments, specifying the period of engagement and the working conditions, etc. More recently, Chinese indentured laborers were introduced to Western Samoa (under the mandate of New Zealand), but the system was abolished in 1923. Since that time Chinese laborers have been introduced under a different system laid down in Ordinance No. 10 of 1923. Chinese labor can be imported only by the Samoa administration, and the Chinese Commission is appointed to watch the interests of the laborers. The administration undertakes to pay the cost of passage to and from Western Samoa. There are some 60,000 Chinese working under the indenture system in the Dutch East Indies, but we are little informed of the method of introducing these workers.

The system of introducing labor from French Indo-China to the French Colonies in the Pacific was formulated in a decree issued in 1922 by the Governor-General, but it did not come into practice until 1925. The outline of this system may be described as follows: Only with the consent of the Government authorities, recruiting may be undertaken by private persons. Application for permission must be addressed to the Governor at least three months in advance and must mention the name of the employer and the recruiting conditions, especially those relating to the journey and the contract of employment. A deposit equal to one month's wages for every worker engaged is required for all persons who want to employ foreign workers. This deposit is returned to the employer on the expiration of the contract of employment, provided he does not fail to observe his various obligations. Further, the employer cannot refuse to engage the emigrants imported at his request, and if such immigrants cannot find employment in the colony he will have to bear all expenses incurred until they are re-established in their country of origin.

The regulations on recruiting in Indo-China have been strengthened by decrees recently issued by the Governor-General. Besides, an Emigration Control Office was set up at Haiphong in 1928, and this office under the direction of a civil officer is engaged in recruiting emigrant laborers in Tonkin and the northern part of Annam.

The emigration of Japanese workers has been largely in the hands of private agencies. By passing the Emigration Protection Act in 1895, the Japanese Government regulated their method of recruiting and transporting emigrants, but the Government, recognizing the difficulty of preventing various abuses of this form of recruiting carried on by numerous private agencies whose purpose is to make profit, brought pressure to bear upon the smaller emigration companies and compelled them to combine in one large organization. It was due to this governmental action that the International Development Company (Kaigai Kogyo Kaisha) came into existence in 1917. The company, having a capital amounting to nine million yen, now monopolizes the whole business of recruiting and placing of Japanese emigrants going to Brazil and other countries. The company has also a plantation in Brazil under its own management. It has some forty representatives in different parts of the country who do the actual recruiting by means of lectures or pamphlets. The Japanese Government grants to the company a subsidy amounting to 100,000 yen per year, and in turn the company does not collect a fee from the emigrants. The Japanese Government gives financial assistance equal to the cost of the passage to most emigrants who embark for Brazil. The representatives of the company also undertake to place these emigrants in suitable employment. The Japanese immigrants in Brazil work generally under contract of a term of three years. Generally they do not receive advance money. Their position is, therefore, different from that of contract labor in the usual sense of the term, but attention should be drawn to the fact that these emigrants have no promise to get their return passage paid by the employer after the termination of their contract, and there seem to exist no supervisors who look after the interests of both contracting parties impartially.

The Overseas Emigration Societies Act of 1927 provides for the establishment of co-operative societies for the purpose of purchasing land in overseas countries with the funds contributed by the society's members. Under the Act, Government assistance may be granted to those members and their families to facilitate their emigration. About three thousand persons emigrated to Brazil under the scheme, but the real value of the system cannot yet be estimated.

British Malaya absorbs a large stream of immigration from China and India. It is desirable to give some historical account of the method of receiving these foreign laborers as well as to explain the system now in force.

In British Malaya, as the native workers are not willing to work in plantations or in mines, the industrial development of the colony must depend on immigrant workers from other countries. Chinese traders have long been settled in Malaya, and during the previous century more and more Chinese workers began to flow into the peninsula, some independently and some under contracts controlled by recruiting agents. There were Chinese agents in Singapore and Penang who worked in co-operation with the Chinese agents at Swatow, Amoy, Hongkong and Macao who recruited labor and arranged for the passages to Malaya. On arrival in port, these agents looked for employers who wanted labor, and the laborers were transferred from the former to the latter who had the power to keep back part of their wages until the expenses of the recruiting and lodging in China and transport were recovered. This " credit-ticket " system was accompanied by serious abuses. The sanitary conditions of the immigrant ships were bad. The workers were forced to accept working conditions under which they became practically slaves. In view of these facts, an ordinance was passed in 1877 requiring all vessels arriving with Chinese passengers at Malayan ports to be inspected, and the registration of all labor contracts made by the Chinese emigrants. From this time on many steps were taken by the Government to improve the system, but in 1911 the British Government took the decision to terminate the Chinese indentured labor in the Malay States, the Straits Settlements and British North Borneo, on June 30, 1914, with the exception of Kelentan, where the system was allowed to exist until June 30, 1916. With the abolition of the Chinese indenture system the " credit-ticket " system came to an end. The recruiting of Chinese immigrants by giving advances still remains in practice, but conditions of work are examined by the Government officials, and breach of labor contract cannot be prosecuted by criminal law.

The industrial development in Malaya caused also Indian immigration on a considerable scale during the last century. The evolution of the methods of recruiting of the Tamils (South Indians) makes a significant contrast with what we have just seen with regard to the Chinese. The Indian immigrants entered the colony both on their own account and under the indenture system. The main features of the indenture system of the Indians were very much like those of the Chinese. The contract of labor was mostly for a term of three years, the cost of recruiting and transport was subtracted from the wages, and breach of contract was punished by the criminal-law penalty. In spite of a series of regulations to control the system, the various evils did not cease to manifest themselves. In 1910 recruitment by indenture was prohibited, and punishment by criminal law in labor offenses was repealed by a series of enactments passed between 1921 and 1923.

The problem of Indian indentured labor in various parts of the world led to the passing of the Indian Emigration Act of 1922 which prohibits the emigration of Indian unskilled laborers, except to such countries and on such terms as the Government may specify. Shortly after the law was passed, the Government of India and several colonial governments entered into negotiations, and emigration to Ceylon and Malaya was sanctioned. The Governments of the Straits Settlements and the Federated Malay States have adopted a Labour Code abolishing penal sanctions, and in various ways the conditions of the Indian workers have been improved. The present system of recruiting Indian emigrants is carried out under the co-operation of the Governments of India and Malaya. The migration of Indian workers in Malaya is placed under the control of the Immigration Committee, having the Controller of Labour as chairman. The Committe levies a certain assessment on all employers of Indian labor. The fund thus contributed is used for defraying expenses of recruiting, repatriating the workers, and the welfare of the workers. The committee has its special agency in India, whereas the Government of India maintains its representative in Malaya, so that constant co-operation in looking after the interests of migrants is insured.

The Kanganis are the instruments for carrying out the actual recruiting of Indian migrants. They are experienced workmen, selected and sent to India from plantations which need new labor, with a license to recruit. They are allowed to recruit only a certain limited number of emigrants with the approval of the village chiefs. Intended emigrants are brought to either Madras or Negapatam where they are examined carefully as to their willingness and health before embarkation to Malaya. During 1929 the total number of Kangani licenses registered at Negapatam and Madras was 2,578 and 1,115 respectively. Of the total number of 75,611 emigrants who proceeded to Malaya, 23,533 embarked from Madras and 53,078 from Negapatam; and the last figure consisted of 32,264 who were recruited by Kanganis while the remaining 20,814 were " voluntary " — that is to say, they came forward on their own initiative and were not recruited by Kanganis. The proportion of emigrants seems to be growing in recent years, and such a tendency may be due to the satisfactory working conditions in British Malaya.

II. PROBLEMS OF FILIPINO EMIGRATION [18]

By HERMENEGILDO CRUZ
Director of Labor, Philippine Islands

a) WHY FILIPINOS GO ABROAD

There are several factors which combine to induce Filipino laborers to emigrate abroad. Among the most important are the following:

1. The school system is considered the main instrument of Americanization in the Islands. In the schools the Filipino youth has learned the great achievements of America, its economic prosperity, its gigantic industrial institutions, the high wages paid, its beautiful cities, its big buildings and skyscrapers and other wonders and opportunities. All of this fires the imagination of the Filipino youth and creates in his mind the love of adventure, to see

[18] Abbreviated sections from *Emigration of Filipinos to Hawaii and the United States* (Philippine Council).

these wonderful creations of American genius. The education he receives in school has increased his wants. To satisfy these wants he seeks a white-collar job. He fails to get it. Manual labor is out of the question. He becomes dissatisfied with the limited opportunities at home. For him, America is the land of promise.

2. The small farmers and tenants earn barely enough to support and maintain their families from the share of their products. It is said that the tenancy system as practised in the Philippines does not give enough return to the average tenant. In the words of Ex-Senator Sumulong " the tenancy system in the Philippine Islands as enforced at the present time takes little account of the condition and interest of the tenants, and all of the benefits that accrue from the land go to the landlord." He believes that the recent agrarian troubles in the rice-producing provinces are due in a large measure to dissatisfaction among hired hands because they get so little of the fruits of the land while the landlord gets almost everything. Ex-Senator Sumulong hits the system that enables the landlord to get the greatest amount of profit through a system of financing that leaves the tenant in the lurch when the crops have been harvested. Continuing he says, " The easiest converts to the principles [of Bolshevism] are the people who have no hope of improvement and who feel they are the victims of an unjust social arrangement. It is high time for Filipino landlords to let their tenants share a greater portion of the profit of the land which they helped materially to make productive, both as a measure of justice to the tenants and as a preventive to the growth of socialism in the Philippines." He points out further that the social unrest in many sections of the Islands is a danger signal which must be met by measures like readjustment of the tenant and landlord relations.

3. Unemployment in large urban centers such as Manila and other large cities is a factor predisposing the emigration of Filipinos abroad. The present tendency of our population, particularly the young generation, is to move toward the cities and big towns, a fact which may be attributed to the comparatively better wages prevailing in industries than in the farms. In the former there are regularity of employment and more conveniences and attractions than in rural communities. On the other hand, this cityward movement aggravates the employment situation in industrial centers, since existing industries cannot readily absorb the constant influx of unskilled hands from the farms. Failing to secure employment they have no other alternative but to emigrate to Hawaii and the United States.

4. The seasonal character of our crops occupies our farm hands for only a limited period during the year. This enormous man-power remains idle during the off-season. And due to the lack of local industries in which they could be profitably employed, they can only eke out a hand-to-mouth existence. Under the circumstances, a little amount of propaganda to induce people to emigrate abroad meets with instant success, as we see in the Ilocos provinces.

5. The absence of any concrete plan to develop the virgin resources of

Mindanao in order to absorb surplus labor from other parts of the Islands is indeed to be deplored. With the limited amount of money appropriated to encourage migration to Mindanao no substantial progress can be expected. The facilities to be found in Mindanao at present, with its wild lands, are not attractive incentives to our pioneers. To pioneer under these conditions is a great sacrifice. Our countrymen therefore must try their luck elsewhere. In explaining the absence of a definite program to solve the Mindanao problem, Senator Osmeña declared that there were many Filipinos who did not believe the time was ripe for executing a policy of general opening of Mindanao and laying it open to exploitation, on the ground that the people were not ready to take advantage of the opportunities offered. He said that the urgent needs of the people of Mindanao would be met as they arose, and that the best would be done under the circumstances.

6. The unevenness of the distribution of population in the Philippines is another predisposing factor. Labor supply in one region is plentiful while in others it is scarce. This condition creates a situation for surplus labor to seek for opportunities elsewhere, and the opportunities offered in Hawaii and the United States are more inviting than those obtainable in the Islands. The possibility of higher wages is not in sight here.

The population per square mile in the provinces from which the largest numbers of emigrants have gone, according to the last census (1918), was:

Ilocos Sur	492
La Union	459
Cebu	458
Bohol	233
Ilocos Norte	169
Tarlac	146

Ilocos Sur was the most densely populated province in the Philippines, excepting, of course, Manila. The average for the islands was ninety persons per square mile. The rich island of Mindanao, second largest in the archipelago, averaged about twenty-five persons per square mile.[19]

7. Letters to relatives at home relating to labor conditions in Hawaii, such as high wages, good working conditions, abundance of work, and the thousands of pesos in money orders exchanged in post offices of the Ilocos provinces serve as potent promoters of the present exodus.

8. The efficient recruiting system built up by the Hawaiian Sugar Planters' Association is also a great factor in encouraging Filipinos to leave the Philippines.

9. The same is true of the activities of steamship companies to encourage travel abroad.

b) PROBLEMS IN THE PHILIPPINES

In this country where the surplus labor is not so plentiful, this constant drain of Filipino man-power cannot but produce a retarding influence on the

[19] *Census of the Philippine Islands,* II, 28.

economic development of the Islands. Public lands which are lying idle can be had for the taking, and yet our laborers are emigrating abroad and spending their energies for the benefit of other nations. Local conditions seem to offer no encouragement, and our laborers' increasing wants must be met by better incentives from some other quarter. Our leaders of thought are unanimous in deploring this anomalous situation. The Honorable Manuel L. Quezon, President of the Philippine Senate, made the following comment regarding the exodus of Filipinos abroad:

I do not blame our laborers for leaving the Philippines if they think they can find better wages in other countries, but I regret the fact that they are leaving.

I hope that conditions here will become such as to offer better opportunities to our working men and give them a better inducement to stay. Our country needs the combined efforts of all to foster its economic development.[20]

Governor Davis has on various occasions taken cognizance of the necessity of retaining our man-power to develop our resources instead of spending it to enrich other nations. He recommended that every encouragement be given to our laborers in order to keep them here. In his message to the Ninth Philippine Legislature, July 16, 1931, he said:

Lack of economic development deprives our labor of the opportunity to build up their country. It drives them to emigrate to other countries which offer greater apparent incentives.

Due to the present business depression, the condition of some Filipinos in the United States is pitiable. Further emigration should be discouraged, both for the sake of the laborer himself and for our own benefit. I recommend that every encouragement be given to Filipinos to build up the Philippines, and that emigration to build up other countries be discouraged.

The fact that only the physically fit after rigid physical examination are selected shows that the best of our manhood is subtracted from our potential producers. In the Ilocos provinces the effect is becoming serious. A good portion of work formerly performed by men in the fields and in private and public works is now being done by women. It will not be long before we hear of women in this region who work as carpenters and in other occupations for men. Moreover, as already stated elsewhere in this paper, the unbalanced proportion of the number of men and women leaving the Philippines creates a social problem of great significance.

As a result, both marriage rate and birth rate in the Ilocos provinces have registered a decrease during the last few years.[21] Furthermore, as a natural consequence of the diminution of man-power, an appreciable decrease has also been noted in the number of hectares cultivated for three important agricultural crops, palay, sugar cane, and tobacco.[22]

Another social evil created by the exodus of married men is the numer-

[20] *Philippines Herald,* June 29, 1929.

[21] *Annual Report of the Philippine Health Service,* II (1928), 102.

[22] Bureau of Commerce and Industry, *Statistical Bulletin* (1928), p. 38, and *ibid.* (1929), pp. 47–48.

ous cases of abandonment of wives and children which come to the knowledge of the Bureau of Labor and which require some action by both the Bureau and the Labor Commissioner in Hawaii in order to find out the present whereabouts of the persons concerned. For the first year, sums of money are regularly received by the wives left behind, but the remittances not only become too far apart but often cease entirely. Cases are not wanting where married men with families in the Philippines contract another marriage in Hawaii or in the United States. On the other hand, not a few cases have been registered in which the wife in the Philippines has maintained amorous relations with another, resulting in serious trouble upon the return of the husband.

c) PROBLEMS IN HAWAII

Recent reports indicate that unemployment is not a problem among the Filipinos in Hawaii who are willing to work on the sugar plantations. In the cities the situation is different on account of the keen competition offered by other nationalities, particularly the Japanese and Chinese. Yet in spite of the presence of a number of Filipinos unemployed in the cities they seldom become public charges in view of the willingness of the Filipinos to take care of their countrymen who are out of work.

One of the most serious problems of the Filipinos in Hawaii is the absence of women of their own race. Many crimes committed by Filipinos can be traced to it. In order to remedy this anomaly, the Hawaiian Sugar Planters' Association has adopted the policy of permitting laborers with families in the Philippines to bring in their wives and children at the expense of the association. It is believed that through this policy the problem of lack of women will be overcome in the course of a few years.

Another problem which is watched with considerable concern by plantation managers is the propensity of Filipinos to indulge in gambling, which not only results in the loss of hard-earned money but also is considered the largest cause of assault among Filipinos. However, recent reports indicate that criminality among Filipinos is decreasing.

d) PROBLEMS IN CONTINENTAL UNITED STATES

As already mentioned elsewhere in this report, there are 45,000 Filipinos in the United States, the majority of whom are found in the State of California where opposition among American labor organizations and other civic bodies is intense on the ground that the Filipinos are a social and economic menace. The opposition of American laborers is accentuated by the acute unemployment situation in the United States. Several bills have been introduced in the United States Congress for the purpose of restricting the immigration of Filipinos to America.

In opposing the attempts to exclude Filipinos from the United States, the sentiment of the Filipinos was expressed by Resident Commissioner Guevara when he said:

If excluded from the United States Filipino citizens who are not eligible to American citizenship are placed on the same level with the Japanese and other peoples of the Orient; and permitting them to enter only for a temporary sojourn or for permanent residence in cases wherein they are members of the classes exempt from limitation under the Reed-Johnson immigration law of 1924, the bill deserves an energetic condemnation on the part of sensible Americans.

The Filipinos were placed under the American flag and sovereignty against their will, and up to the present they continue struggling to become independent and free from the control of the United States. If Representative Johnson believes that the Filipinos would compete with the American laboring class, he should concentrate his efforts on persuading the United States to grant the Filipinos complete and absolute independence, just as Congress has promised. I say this with an absolute frankness, but without rancor or prejudice. The Filipinos have nothing to say regarding the bill introduced by Representative Johnson, but while the Philippines are still under the American flag and protection, there is nothing that would justify even a mere suggestion of a legislative measure against the Filipinos.[23]

There are several problems which affect the Filipinos in the United States, namely: dance halls, gambling dens, self-appointed leaders, absconding labor contractors and fake promoters.

1. *Dance halls or cabarets.* — This kind of recreation, where money accumulated at great sacrifice is dissipated, is one of the sources of evil which ruins many Filipinos. This is particularly true in Los Angeles where fighting often occurs, at times resulting in deaths — which accounts for the fact that dance halls patronized by Filipinos in San Francisco, Seattle and Los Angeles have been closed.

2. *Gambling dens.* — What is considered a worse evil than dance halls is gambling dens, which abound in centers of Filipino population on the Pacific Coast, particularly in Stockton, Walnut Grove, Maryville, Isleton, Salinas, El Centro, Seattle and Portland. There are many cases where Filipino boys after the asparagus season lose their earnings of $400 and after a few days in these gambling dens are rendered practically destitute. It is estimated that half of the earnings of Filipinos in California — which amount to about forty million dollars a year — are lost across the gambling tables of the Chinese.

3. *Divided leadership.* — One of the evils that affect the Filipinos in California is the self-appointed leaders who live at the expense of their countrymen. Promotions for the celebration of patriotic movements, where thousands of dollars are collected by several organizations of Filipinos in California, are indeed a cause of drain on the pockets of the Filipinos.

4. *Absconding labor contractors.* — Farm work in California is done by contract, and most of the Filipinos work under this system. The contractors, many of whom are Filipinos, after receiving money from the employer, get away with the money, leaving the laborers without their wages. This is especially true when the men under the contractors are mostly uneducated.

[23] *Tribune* (Manila), January 20, 1929.

When they escape they usually use fake names in order to evade capture after misappropriating the money of the workers under them.

5. *Fake promoters.* — Another evil which affects the pockets of the Filipinos on the Pacific Coast is the fake promoters who invent doubtful schemes for get-rich-quick purposes.

The seriousness of the situation of Filipinos in the United States is such that Philippine sentiment is widespread in favor of immediate investigation of the matter in order to formulate proper remedies. However, no action has as yet been taken regarding the matter, by either the legislative or the executive departments of the Government.

e) CONCLUSIONS AND RECOMMENDATIONS

The presence of Filipinos abroad is indeed to be deplored, but since local conditions do not offer the necessary incentives they cannot be forced to remain at home unless the attractions in other lands, that is, the returns for their labor, are found here. As a matter of fact, the consensus of opinion of those who have looked into the problem is that the economic motive excels all other causes which impel Filipinos to leave their homes. Our contact with American civilization and the influence of the public schools have increased our wants, which must be satisfied here or elsewhere. If we desire to keep the Filipino laborer to help develop our natural resources instead of enriching other nations, he must be given attractive inducements compatible with his increasing wants.

In our opinion, the emigration problem may be solved by adopting the following propositions:

1. That our rural communities be made more attractive by the introduction of household industries that will occupy our rural population after the busy season in agricultural pursuits, thereby increasing their purchasing power and putting within their reach those facilities and conveniences which make for progressive communities.

2. That a liberal appropriation be made to foster the acquisition of homesteads by the laboring mass, not only by affording free transportation facilities but also by giving such other financial aid as would insure the success of homesteaders in their new homes.

3. That attractive inducements be offered to the laborers in order to keep them here instead of helping enrich other nations.

4. That the diversification of crops which have local as well as foreign demands be encouraged.

5. That steps be taken in our major agricultural industries, particularly sugar, with a view to stabilizing the employment of laborers all the year round as in the sugar industry in Hawaii.

It is hoped that with the carrying out of these recommendations, the problem of the exodus of Filipinos abroad will to a great extent be solved. At the same time our economic status will be placed on a firm basis for the benefit of the country as a whole.

III. CHINESE MIGRATION TO MANCHURIA [24]

By FRANKLIN L. HO

a) MAGNITUDE OF THE MOVEMENT

Though the movement of population from other parts of China to Manchuria on the Northeastern frontier had grown steadily since the beginning of the Tsing Dynasty,[25] no systematic statistics, whether official or non-official, relating to the extent of such movement, had been compiled until 1923. In this year the Research Department of the South Manchuria Railway Company began the publication of annual statistics on the total volume of Chinese immigration into Manchuria. These statistics, which are given in Table I, indicate that more than five million Chinese immigrants have entered Manchuria during the period of eight years from 1923 to 1930. Of these, less than two million arrived between 1923 and 1926, while over three million have arrived since 1927. Indeed, previous to 1925 the Chinese immigration into Manchuria never exceeded half a million. In 1926, about

TABLE I

VOLUME OF CHINESE IMMIGRATION INTO MANCHURIA, 1923–1930

Year	Volume of Immigration	Relatives 1923 = 100
1923.................	342,038	100
1924.................	376,613	110
1925.................	491,949	144
1926.................	572,648	167
1927.................	1,016,723	297
1928.................	938,472	274
1929.................	1,046,291	305
1930 *...............	653,000	191

* Provisional figures.

573,000 came by land and sea from other parts of China; but in 1923, 1924 and 1925 the annual arrivals numbered only 342,000, 377,000 and 492,000 respectively. In 1927, however, the tide changed; over one million Chinese immigrants arrived, showing an increase of 77 per cent above that of the previous year and an increase of 197 per cent above that of 1923. The volume of immigration in the subsequent two years of 1928 and 1929 remained almost stationary, averaging approximately one million per year; but, in 1930, it fell off greatly. According to a provisional estimate, only 653,000 arrived in

[24] First section of *Population Movement to the North Eastern Frontier in China* (abbreviated). Lack of space prevents reproduction in the present volume of the graphic description of this movement in its social aspects — including the conditions in the sending and receiving areas and the experiences of emigrants on the way — given by Chen Hanseng in the data paper, *Notes on Migration of Nan Min to the Northeast*.

[25] An excellent review of the early history of Chinese migration to Manchuria may be found in Dr. Hsu Shuhsi's *China and Her Political Entity* (1926) pp. 1–102.

Dairen, Yinkow, Antung and Mukden, showing a reduction of almost 40 per cent below that of the previous year. This is partly due to the relatively improved conditions in the districts of origin, but principally because of the disastrous effect of the Sino-Russian conflict in the winter of 1929 upon the frontier population and of the overwhelming depression in Manchuria caused by the fall of the bean market and the phenomenal depreciation of silver.

An analysis of the statistics on the Chinese population movement to Manchuria reveals a strong tendency of seasonal variation. Monthly statistics on the number of arrivals and returns of Chinese immigrants in Dairen are available for the period 1923–1929. The arrivals of Chinese immigrants always clustered in the months of March and April. Indeed, in none of the years during the period under review did the number of arrivals of Chinese immigrants in March and April in Dairen constitute less than one-third of the total number of arrivals for the year. The return movement of Chinese immigrants, however, concentrated usually in the months of November, December and January. This is partly due to the seasonal character of the employment of the Chinese immigrants in Manchuria, but principally due to their desire to spend the Chinese New Year with their families.

b) CHARACTERISTICS OF THE MOVEMENT

The migration of the Chinese in Manchuria in the early days had been predominantly in the form of a temporary labor movement. Previous to 1927 only about 20 per cent of the total volume of immigrants stayed as permanent settlers in Manchuria, while the remaining 80 per cent were engaged as casual laborers.[26] The demand for labor in Manchuria comes not only from industries but also from agriculture which is characterized by larger land holdings than those in other parts of China. The chief source of labor supply is, as it always has been, the over-populated provinces of Shantung and Hopei. Table II gives the nativity of laborers in the Kwantung district

TABLE II *

NATIVITY OF LABORERS IN KWANTUNG DISTRICT AND THE SOUTH MANCHURIA
RAILWAY ZONE IN MANCHURIA, 1929

NATIVITY	MANUFACTURING LABOR		MINING LABOR		"COOLIES"	
	Number	Per Cent	Number	Per Cent	Number	Per Cent
Three Eastern Provinces.............	19,976	47.4	10,845	20.4	128	1.6
Shantung..........	17,441	41.4	28,769	54.2	7,311	90.4
Hopei.............	4,512	10.7	12,783	24.1	525	6.5
Other.............	247	0.5	690	1.3	123	1.5
Total..........	42,176	100	53,087	100	8,087	100

* Kiko Yamamoto, *Chinese and Japanese Laborers in the Kwantung District and South Manchuria Railway Zone*, pp. 64–68. (In Japanese.)

26 Soichi Nakajima, *Migration to Manchuria in the 16th Year of the Chinese Republic*, p. 141. (In Japanese.)

and the South Manchuria Railway Zone in 1929. It may be noted that 97 per cent of the coolies, 52 per cent of the laborers in the manufacturing industries and 78 per cent of the laborers in the mining industries came from Shantung and Hopei. These immigrant laborers usually leave their families behind them. When winter comes they begin to return to their home districts across the Gulf of Pechili with such savings as they have accumulated. The length of their stay in Manchuria varies with individuals, depending in most cases on occupation, facilities for remittance in the place where they work, and peace and security in their native districts. The majority of them (40 per cent) stay for three years. Those who stay for two years come next in importance (20 per cent), while those who stay for four years rank third (15 per cent). The so-called " Spring come and Autumn go " laborers and those who stay for more than seven years are comparatively insignificant in number.[27]

A change in the character of the movement from the predominance of casual labor-migration to that of permanent settlement seems to have taken place since 1927. The balance between the volume of immigration to Manchuria and that of emigration from Manchuria each year may well serve as an index of the trend of change in the character of the movement, although it cannot measure quantitatively the exact extent of permanent settlement. In 1926, 572,648 Chinese immigrants arrived but 323,566 returned, thus leaving a residuum of 249,082 which is approximately 43 per cent of the total number of arrivals of the year. In 1927, however, when the total volume of immigration exceeded one million, the residuum amounted to 678,641. The residuum in 1928 was 544,225, and that in 1929, 424,394. Taking 1923 as the base equal to 100, the residuum increased 74 per cent in 1924, 149 per cent in 1925, 145 per cent in 1926, 569 per cent in 1927, 436 per cent in 1928 and 320 per cent in 1929.

Another evidence of the change in the character of the movement from seasonal migration to permanent settlement is the increase of women and children immigrants since 1927. . . . . Of the total number of immigrants arriving at Dairen in 1925, 22,659 were women and children. In 1926, the number of women and children among the immigrants arriving at Dairen increased to 30,448. The most significant change occurred in 1927 when a total number of 118,421 women and children immigrants landed at Dairen from Tsingtao, Chefoo, Kunchow, Tientsin and other minor ports. This represents an increase of 290 per cent over that of the previous year and above 400 per cent over that in 1925. In 1928 and 1929 the number of women and children immigrants landing at Dairen declined somewhat, but still amounted to 87,593 and 79,170 respectively.

A third indication of the increasing tendency toward permanent settlement may be found in the change of the occupation of the Chinese immigrants. Previously, Chinese immigrants in Manchuria were principally mining, rail-

[27] Soichi Nakajima, *Migration to Manchuria in the 16th Year of the Chinese Republic*, p. 148. (In Japanese.)

way, timber and wharf laborers. In 1927, however, it was found that a majority of the Chinese immigrants were farmers and farm hands who left their home districts across the Gulf of Pechili intending to colonize. They migrated to Manchuria with their families, and carried with them, in most cases, such little articles of wealth as they possessed, including agricultural implements or part of them. The Local Relief Organization in Mukden reported that of the total number of 25,835 Chinese immigrants who received assistance in the two months of April and May, 1927, 20,191 (78 per cent) were farmers and farm hands. During the same period, the Changchun Local Relief Organization reported a total number of 12,253 Chinese immigrants receiving assistance. Of these 9,284 (76 per cent) were farmers and farm hands. On the basis of the returns to the inquiries in the different districts in the provinces of Liaoning, Kirin and Heilungkiang, the Research Department of the South Manchuria Railway Company estimated that of the total number of 630,000 Chinese immigrants arriving in Manchuria, from January to July, 1927, 71 per cent were farmers and farm hands. Of these 64 per cent went to North Manchuria, while 36 per cent remained in South Manchuria.[28] Statistics on the occupations of the Chinese passengers landing in Dairen are available since 1928. On the basis of these statistics I have made an estimate . . . . that of all the Chinese immigrants arriving in Dairen in 1928 and 1929 the number of farmers represented 24 per cent and 21 per cent respectively, ranking only next in importance to that of the class of "other occupations." Presumably, the latter includes mostly coolies and farm hands.

c) CAUSES OF THE MOVEMENT

The migration movement to Manchuria from other parts of China is the product of two causes which are opposite in character but concurring in tendency, namely, repulsion from the emigrating districts and attraction to the immigrating country. A recent study on the nativity of the Chinese immigrants into Manchuria reveals that, on the average, approximately 80 per cent of them are from the province of Shantung.[29] Under the present economic and technical development of the province, the population of Shantung has probably reached the point of over-saturation. With the density of population (470 to the square mile) only second to Kiangsu (800 persons to the square mile) among the six industrialized provinces, namely: Kiangsu, Liaoning, Hopei, Kwangtung, Shantung and Hupeh, Shantung occupies the fifth position in China's industrialization. It has only 4.6 per cent of China's

---

[28] *Ibid.*, pp. 142–44.

[29] Of the total number of arrivals in 1927, 87 per cent came from Shantung, 12 per cent from Hopei and 1 per cent from Honan. In 1928, the distribution of the immigrants by nativity remained substantially the same as that for the previous year; Shantung occupied 86 per cent, Hopei 13 per cent and other provinces 1 per cent. A change occurred in 1929 when Honan for the first time sent 11 per cent of the total number of immigrants to Manchuria; Shangtung, 71 per cent; Hopei, 16 per cent; and other provinces 1 per cent (Toyo Kurimoto, *Condition of Immigration to Manchuria in the 18th Year of the Chinese Republic*, p. 13). (In Japanese.)

silk industry, 0.3 per cent of China's bean industry, 3.9 per cent of China's electric power capacity, 5.7 per cent of China's whole trade, 4.1 per cent of China's foreign trade, 1.6 per cent of China's transit trade, 6.7 per cent of China's railways, 11.2 per cent of China's motor roads and 9.5 per cent of China's telegraphs.

Industrialization in Shantung has apparently not progressed far enough to bring about any appreciable change in the situation. In common with that of China as a whole, the population of Shantung has to depend almost entirely on agriculture for a bare livelihood. Furthermore, the size of cultivated land per capita in Shantung is extremely small, as the average density of agrarian population to the square mile of cultivated land exceeds 900 persons, which may be compared with Denmark having 77 persons per square mile of cultivated land and with the United States having 48 persons per square mile of cultivated land. Land in Shantung is scarce, and the price of land is high, varying from $450 per acre in Ichow in the southern part of the province to $546 per acre in Laichow in the Eastern section of the province.[30] Wages paid to farm laborers employed by the year average only from $25 to $37 per annum. Those hired by the day earn approximately $0.40 during the harvest time, but only half as much in the ordinary season.[31] Under such circumstances, the struggle for existence in Shantung is indescribably hard for the mass, particularly for the landless class. Because of the small land holdings which characterize the farm economy in Shantung, especially the eastern section of the Province, and because of the large-family system that prevails in China as a whole, even landowners live on a very narrow margin. . . .

War and famine have lately aggravated the social and natural handicaps of existence in Shantung. The traditional attachment of the Chinese to their ancestral soil which tends to make them somewhat reluctant to migrate can no longer triumph over the unbearable misery and poverty. The latter, more than any other single factor, accounts for the magnitude of the migration movement since 1927. Shantung is noted for the frequent occurrence of famines, due primarily to drought, floods and the ravage of locust pests. Recent famines have occurred in North China, particularly in Shantung, in 1919, 1920–1921, 1926, 1927 and 1928. The famine in 1927 affected 56 districts or hsien in Shantung and 20,861,000 people or 60 per cent of the entire population of the province.[32] The famine in 1928, which centered around Hsiachin, Tungchangfu and Kwanhsien in Western Shantung and around Kufow in Southern Shantung, was more intensive than that of the previous year, though not so widespread. In a number of districts affected by the famine 60 per cent to 70 per cent of the population was in destitution, with

[30] Moichi Kozawa, *Shantung Immigrant Refugees in Dairen*, pp. 23–27. (In Japanese.)

[31] *Ibid.*, p. 27.

[32] Moichi Kozawa, *Civil War and the Rural Districts in Shantung*, p. 64. (In Japanese.)

crop harvests which were less than 10 per cent of the normal.[33]   The situation
was made worse by the constant ravages of soldiers and bandits who infested
the entire province and took away whatever the famine-stricken people might
still have possessed.   The increase in military expenditures, as a result of the
civil war, entailed a proportionate increase in the burden of taxation on the
public.[34] . . .

All that has been said of Shantung applies, to a less degree, to Hopei and
Honan.   The migration from Honan, however, differs somewhat from that of
Shantung and Hopei.   People from Shantung and Hopei migrated, voluntarily
and by themselves, to Manchuria, about which they are more or less familiar,
partly because of geographical proximity but principally through the information furnished them by their friends or relatives who had been there
before as seasonal laborers.   The immigrants from Honan, on the other hand,
were all sent over by groups and as an organized measure of famine relief
through the efforts of the Honan Relief Commission in Peiping, which gathered the destitute from all parts of Honan, furnished them with provisions,
free transportation, and necessary protection on the way, and through previous arrangements, distributed them to the landlords upon their arrival in
Manchuria.

Emigration commonly begins in repulsion, but goes on with attraction.
The attraction of Manchuria consists principally of the availability of arable
land, high wages and facilities for transportation.   The average density of
population in Manchuria in 1929 was 73 persons to the square mile; whereas
that of Liaoning was 210 persons to the square mile, that of Kirin 88 persons
to the square mile and that of Heilungkiang 23 persons to the square mile.
Shantung, the principal source of migration, is, therefore, nearly seven times
as densely populated as Manchuria, more than twice as densely populated as
Liaoning, over five times as densely populated as Kirin, and approximately
twenty times as densely populated as Heilungkiang.   Indeed, 30 per cent
of the arable land in Liaoning, 55 per cent of the arable land in Kirin and
70 per cent of the arable land in Heilungkiang is still available for cultivation.[35]   Liaoning, though with the least arable land available, is, however,
the most industrialized of the three provinces in Manchuria, more so than
Shantung and only second to Kiangsu which is the most industrialized province of China as a whole. . . . .

As a distinct pioneer belt and with the growth of industrialization, Manchuria is in need of more laborers . . . . for the development of industry,
mining and agriculture.   Opportunities for employment are plentiful, and
wages are relatively high.   In Kirin and Heilungkiang, for instance, an assistant farm hand, usually recruited from the new arrivals from Shantung,

[33] *Annual Report of the China International Famine Relief Commission, 1928,*
pp. 25-26.
[34] Moichi Kozawa, *Civil War and the Rural Districts in Shantung* (in Japanese);
Famine Commission Bulletin, Vol. V, No. 4.
[35] *Statistics of Production in Manchuria* (1929), compiled by the Research Department of the South Manchuria Railway Company.

receives about $130 Harbin currency a year, or almost three to four times as much as he can earn in his native district. Even a young immigrant can work as a sub-assistant farm hand, and a boy of 15 to 16 years of age can serve as an apprentice on the farm for an annual wage of $80 and $50 Harbin currency respectively.[36] The abundance in transport facilities in Manchuria, such as navigable rivers and railways, has not only furnished the most ready access, but has also contributed much to the development of an outside market for the cash crops of the farms settled by the immigrants. Manchuria possesses at present approximately 3,870 miles of railways, or nearly one-half of the total mileage of railways in China as a whole. Indeed, the most complete agricultural development of Manchuria is now confined to a belt from 100 to 150 miles wide stretching from the gulf of Liaotung northeastward to Hailun, the terminus of the Hulan-Hailun railway, an area that is crossed throughout almost its entire length by an excellent railway system. Among the rivers, none is more important than the Sungari which furnishes a convenient transportation route to attractive settlement areas below Harbin and north of the Chinese Eastern Railway.

[36] S. Y. Wu, "A Study of Immigrants in Kirin and Heilungkiang," *Economic Monthly of the Chinese Eastern Railway, Special Suppl.,* March, 1930, pp. 36–37. (In Chinese.)

QUESTIONS FOR ROUND-TABLE DISCUSSION

The Program Committee recommended the following questions as an outline for discussion:

1. What significant changes are discernible since 1927 in the social status of aliens resident in Canada, the United States, Australia, New Zealand, British Malaya, and other countries of the Pacific?
   To what extent have these changes been brought about by (a) new trends in public opinion; (b) legislation?
2. What is the influence of immigrant communities on the political and economic relations between Pacific countries, e.g., the influence of Chinese communities in British Malaya on the political and economic relations between Great Britain and China?
3. What problems are involved in recent migration movements in the Pacific, such as
   a) Koreans to Manchuria?
   b) Filipinos to Hawaii and Continental United States?
   c) Chinese to British Malaya and the Netherlands East Indies?
   d) Japanese to Brazil and other South American countries?
   e) Javanese to other parts of the Dutch East Indies?

Incorporated in the present chapter is part of the records of the round tables on standards of living, held earlier during the Conference (see chap. II), in so far as they dealt with the following questions:

1. To what extent is migration a means of raising the standard of living? Consider in its temporary and permanent aspects.
2. What validity is there in the popular argument based on standards of living which is made the basis of . . . exclusion policies?

SUMMARY OF ROUND-TABLE DISCUSSIONS

After a brief historical introduction on the part of the chairman in which he sketched the developing interest of the Institute of Pacific Relations in problems of migration, statements were invited as to significant changes, particularly in the receiving countries, during the last four years. It proved difficult to isolate so short a period for reports on developments which, in some cases, had their beginnings in earlier years though they may be thought of as having matured in the period under review; for this reason, it was agreed to include in the brief oral surveys not only definite events — such as passage of laws — but also discernible tendencies and trends in movements that had been in existence before. It also was seen to be difficult to answer the question on the agenda concerning the " social status " of aliens without at the same time referring to changes in the currents of migration themselves whose ebb and flow so vitally affects the fortunes of those who already reside in a foreign land. The major statistical facts contained in the syllabus and in various data and reference papers before the round table were referred to from time to time.

I. RECENT TRENDS

AUSTRALIA

An Australian started the discussion by drawing attention to an outstanding fact in recent developments which proved to be a keynote throughout the session: the marked way in which the economic depression had affected both the current of migration and the attitudes of the established communities toward aliens in their midst. He said:

" With the deepening of the economic depression that set in earlier in Australia than in most countries, we have experienced a sharpening of opinion in the industrial classes as to who should have the first chance to work. There have been demands both from labor organizations and from political associations that Australians should be given preference — in private employment as well as in employment with public funds. Then the question arose: Who is an Australian? This was found to be an indefinite term. Usually those who make these demands do not analyze it. They do not consider whether only those born in Australia should be considered Australians, or whether those who have been in the country for a long time should have preference over immigrants of recent years.

" All we know is that these demands are made; we do not know the actual strength behind them when made in resolutions passed by parties, trade-unions, and other organizations. We cannot even state positively that all industrial organization share this feeling; it may be only one phase of public opinion that has made itself heard at this time. We do know, however, that the claim varies in vigor from different parts of the Commonwealth. It is strong in Queensland and Western Australia. In Queensland it takes a form directed against Italians — not from any special hostility toward that people but because it so happens that in parts of that province many Italians compete with native-born Australians.

" There is not in any part of Australia a wide spread of any distinctive antinational or anti-racial feeling. The so-called ' White Australia ' policy [37] is a different thing. It relates to legislation, not to the treatment of resident aliens. Opposition to foreigners is entirely on the ground of competition. Since the depression, the Government has had to abandon state-aided immigration [38] and to close down entirely on immigration of people of Eastern Europe. The Gentlemen's Agreement with Italy [39] has been suspended. We have actually lost six or seven thousand people to Great Britain in the last few months.

" There has been no legislation to bar aliens from public works. But such restrictions have been inserted in some public contracts.[40] Our postal law, which was adopted a generation ago, requires that all contracts for carriage of mails must be for ships run entirely by white labor; and there are a few other such old restrictions; but I do not know of any that have been introduced by the Australian Government as a result of the present economic situation."

A Chinese member asked whether a recurrence of animosity toward Asiatic labor in Australia was not evident in recent controversies with the Chinese Government. This was emphatically denied. One of these dif-

[37] See G. L. Wood, " Growth of Population and Immigration Policy," *An Economic Survey of Australia; Annals of the American Academy of Political and Social Science,* November, 1931, p. 14; K. H. Bailey, *The Legal Position of Foreigners in Australia,* p. 12.

[38] Bailey, *op. cit.,* p. 15.

[39] *Problems of the Pacific, 1927,* p. 487.

[40] Bailey, *op. cit.,* p. 8.

ferences was of special interest to American members of the round table since it was on a matter that has its counterpart in an agitation for and against alien registration in the United States. The Australian Government, it was said, had introduced a system of finger-printing to identify Chinese residents leaving and returning to Australia. This method had been resented by the Chinese who called it an indignity because of the association of it in the public mind with criminal procedure. The Chinese Consul-General, it was reported, had offered to substitute for this obnoxious method a system of registration at the Chinese consulates and of issue of identification certificates by Chinese consular officials. This, the Chinese Government held, should provide a sufficient guaranty. The outcome of this correspondence was not yet known.

The other question concerns the Chinese Government's claim to the right of protection over Chinese born in Australia, that is, the children of Chinese parents born in the Commonwealth. This is essentially the same conflict between the *jus sanguinis* and the *jus soli* which, as has been seen in an earlier chapter,[41] has arisen between China and Japan over their respective claim to jurisdiction over Korean residents in Manchuria. Under the Chinese Law of Nationality of 1929, all persons of Chinese blood are claimed as nationals; Australia, like the rest of the Western world, assumes that the place of birth determines nationality. On this matter, an Australian jurist informed the round table, his Government was not likely to give way. International law, he held, would certainly support the Government's right to govern those born in the Commonwealth. Neither country could claim extraterritorial recognition of its nationality law. Chinese members assented to this view but hoped that in the matter of finger-prints the Australian Government would see its way to act upon a protest which was very strong on sentimental grounds even though it might not have a clear legal basis.

The absence of indentured Chinese labor from any part of Australia or its mandated territories was welcomed by representatives of both countries as a solution for many conflicts in the past.

BRITISH MALAYA

From British Malaya no report was available to amplify the information presented by W. J. Hinton at the Kyoto Conference.[42] Many rumors had been current during the summer months concerning differences between the Administration of the Straits Settlements and the Government of China concerning the Chinese population of that colony who outnumber the Malays. Although on the surface the difference was one concerning the right of these immigrant and foreign-born Chinese to join in Kuomintang activities — again involving the nationality issue mentioned above — the particular occasion for unrest was the world economic depression. According to one informed member of the round table, large-scale immigration had entirely ceased be-

41 See p. 286.
42 *Op. cit.*

cause of unemployment, and there were almost as many Chinese leaving as were coming in.[43]   There had, according to a Chinese member, been conflict with natives in competition for work, rather serious in the federated Malay States and less so in the unfederated Malay States.[44]   But there were no legal restrictions upon the status of the Chinese who, indeed, recognize the unusual opportunities offered their nationals in British Malaya (see below, p. 459).

(see below, p. 459)

DUTCH EAST INDIES

These great Dutch dependencies, according to one spokesman from that region, are without restrictive laws as regards immigration.[45]   In spite of this, there has been no considerable fluctuation of immigration in recent years to reflect changes in world economic conditions.   The figures have remained around 50,000 a year.

There has been a complete absence, for some time, of discriminative legislation against aliens.[46]

There is but little regulation of Javanese migration to areas outside the Netherlands East Indies, but although the Government does not interfere with their liberty of movement, it has made some provision for protecting them, both against unscrupulous methods of recruiting and against exploitation after they have left, which has won high praise from the Director of the

[43] The situation is made serious by the fact that most Chinese immigrants have the right to repatriation at the expense of the various Malayan governments.   In August and September, 1931, the number of Chinese laborers landed under the quota was 9,007 in August and 18,567 in September, 1931, while 4,366 were repatriated in August and 12,360 in September.

[44] According to an address made in Singapore on October 13, 1931, by the acting Secretary for Chinese Affairs (who recommended a further drastic cut in the quota of Chinese immigrant labor, which was subsequently adopted by the legislature), the chief source of difficulty are the tin mines of the Federated Malay States, the output of which has under a recent act been reduced by 60 per cent.   The repatriation of large numbers of Chinese was due to a special offer of the Government to pay the fares home for those discharged as a result of this new production policy.   As a result of the general situation, the quota of Chinese immigrants actually was reduced to 2,500, or about one-half of that which had obtained in the previous year.

[45] Vandenbosch, on the contrary, declares that a tax of 100 florins imposed on all immigrants is " in part aimed at controlling foreign Asiatic immigrants and at protecting the natives from too great an influx of labor and small tradesmen immigrants."   This tax, he says, has recently been increased to 150 florins (op. cit., p. 1016).   In recent months repeated requests and petitions have come from the Chinese in the Dutch East Indies to the Ministry of Foreign Affairs in Nanking for aid in their protest against this tax.

A Chinese authority writes: " In addition, the restrictions on the traveling privileges of the Chinese in Java may be mentioned.   Before leaving a town, the Chinese must apply to the resident office for a pass for the intended trip.   While traveling, if he wants to stop over at some place for a period longer than twenty-four hours, he must show the pass to the local authorities in order to be granted the privilege.   On reaching his destination, he must again show the pass at the local office."

[46] Under the penal code, in matters of education, taxation, etc., there are broad distinctions on racial and cultural grounds which, however, are not directed against alien residents or their descendants (see A. D. A. de Kat Angelino, Colonial Policy, II, 164, 248, 280).

International Labour Office who, accompanied by an expert, visited the Dutch East Indies in 1929.[47]

CANADA

Since 1930, it was reported, this Dominion had raised her barriers against every country, including Great Britain:

" Owing to the severity of the depression which set in in 1930, aliens are now admitted only if they have resident friends willing to guarantee that they will not become a charge on the community; and even then admission is only temporary. A certain amount of aided immigration of minors from Great Britain is going on, however."

Restrictions against Oriental immigrants have been somewhat sharpened, not by a passage of new laws but by a stricter interpretation of existing statutes.

" The number of deportations has been increasing. The legal discriminations against residents of Asiatic race — which are frankly on racial grounds — are set forth in the Canadian data papers; [48] in British Columbia, exclusion of Oriental residents from public provisions for the relief of unemployment has in many cases led to deportations on the ground of lacking self-support."

There was some discussion of an unfortunate incident that had recently occurred. A group of young New Zealanders, with only a moderate amount of capital, had sailed from New Zealand to settle in Canada. When they arrived at Vancouver, they found that during their passage a new law had been passed under which they could not be admitted; and after confinement they were deported. This incident, which led to considerable resentment in New Zealand, was quoted as one of the hardships that must be expected to occur when immigration laws are changed without adequate provision for the exercise of administrative judgment. A Canadian member explained that temporary lack of employment in itself is not considered a sufficient cause for deportation; there is always some other reason for deciding that an alien is likely to become a public charge.

NEW ZEALAND

This commonwealth, it was reported, had adjusted its immigration policy to the economic depression even earlier than Australia.

" Although there has been no significant change in the basic immigration law, the Minister of Customs has discretion to grant or withhold permission to enter; and of this provision the strongest possible use has been made when it became apparent that the inflow of new migrants, even from the British homeland, would be likely to create more unemployment. Except for the admission of boys and domestic servants in certain restricted areas, the organized movement for assisted immigration was practically canceled. Even individual immigration of British subjects was now discouraged though it could not legally be banned altogether. While at one time New Zealand paid as many as ten thousand passage fares for

[47] *Ibid.*, p. 562.
[48] Lindsay and Michener, *op. cit.*; Angus, *op. cit.*

'assisted' immigrants to settle sparsely populated regions, this movement is now entirely discontinued; and the three thousand now admitted annually are usually relatives of persons already resident."

As regards the social status of resident Orientals, there had been no change since 1927. The new policy still was, the New Zealand spokesman said, for a " white New Zealand — if possible 99 per cent British." [49]

" With the general apprehension of an influx of unemployed Australians, there has been less public interest of late in the Orientals. With only about three thousand Chinese in the Dominion, almost no Japanese, and only a few Hindus and Syrians, mostly engaged in the fruit trade, there is obviously no serious problem."

A recent law, passed under the stress of unemployment, to give the Government power by an order in council to prohibit immigration of any particular class of persons was not, then, directed against Orientals but against certain types of immigrants from Australia. On the contrary, the speaker thought that the popular attitude toward Oriental residents and their children was improving — as evidenced by the growing feeling that the special poll tax of £100 levied on Chinese residents, a relic of the old mining days, constituted an unjust discrimination and should be removed.[50]

UNITED STATES

Although the United States had been affected later than most countries by the depression in an acute form, there had been a growing intensity in the popular anti-immigration movement, it was reported.

" Not only organized labor but other groups also are practically united behind every legislative proposal that promises, even indirectly, to reduce the number of newcomers from all parts of the world. Under this pressure of public opinion, the Government has taken a number of extralegal measures, on the one hand to speed the deportation of aliens who cannot prove legal entry, and on the other to stop the flow at the source by withholding visas on passports issued to intending emigrants by their respective governments. While the quota of immigration is fixed by law for the nationals of each foreign country, the consular officers have discretionary powers to withhold a visa in case they have reason to believe that an applicant may shortly after his arrival become a public charge. This power has now been interpreted as permitting these officers to take into account not only personal disqualifications but also the general state of the labor market in the United States — an interpretation the validity of which has not been, and perhaps could not be, tested in the courts. Thus, the actual volume of immigration has been greatly reduced. Other important elements in this are the voluntary withdrawal from American territory of many thousands of Mexican seasonal workers and, of course, the inability of residents of foreign birth at a time of widespread unemployment to send money to pay for the passage of relatives."

As regards the status of Oriental residents in the western states of Continental United States, it was reported that there had been no significant

---

[49] He did not, of course, have in mind the native Maoris, now making up about 4 per cent of the population.

[50] See *New Zealand Affairs*, p. 92.

legal change since this subject was last reported upon to the Institute in 1927.[51] But there had been a growing friendliness in the popular attitude toward Chinese and Japanese residents, since fear of a large-scale immigration of either group had been removed. This would be likely to be further reinforced by the realization, on the ground of the 1930 census, that earlier apprehensions concerning an abnormally high birth-rate in these two foreign groups had been unjustified. The growth of this racial population through natural increase was not abnormal.[52] At the same time, an American member said in answer to a question, the problem of the social status of American-born persons of Oriental race is becoming more difficult; it is now no longer a question of a " second generation " with more or less definite connections with the Far East, but of Americans born and brought up in American homes who nevertheless find themselves treated as though they were aliens.

The special problems surrounding the immigration of Filipinos were deferred for later consideration (see below, p. 460).

II. CONTRACT LABOR

During the discussion of recent changes in the status of immigrants and resident aliens, several questions came up concerning contract and indentured labor which proved of interest because the recruiting and transportation of labor from one part of the Pacific to another still is a serious threat to the standards of labor and, as such, affects attitudes toward immigration generally. Unfortunately, neither the information given at the round table nor that found in data and reference papers distinguished clearly between forms of contract that obtain specifically in areas that rely upon immigrant labor and forms that are resorted to with the aim of making native labor contributive either to public works or to the development of the home country.

The question came up, first, in relation to the employment of Chinese indentured labor in the British dominions and mandated areas. It was reported that in Australia and New Zealand and their dependencies this form of contract labor was no longer in existence, though in Papua indigenous labor is, under proper safeguards, indentured to public works.

In Western Samoa a modified " fee labor " system has replaced the indenture system of the former German administration. The supply of Chinese laborers for plantation work is organized by the administration:

The laborer enters into a binding agreement with the Government and with the employer to whom he is assigned. The Government undertakes to find continuous employment for three years for the worker as an agricultural laborer, domestic

---

[51] Eliot G. Mears, *Resident Orientals on the American Pacific Coast;* R. D. McKenzie, *Oriental Exclusion* (American Council). The comment was made, however, that recent drastic administrative interpretations of the immigration laws — particularly in reference to deportation — practically amount to a change in legal status. See Jane Perry Clark, *Deportation of Aliens from the United States to Europe* (New York, 1931).

[52] *Preliminary Census Statistics of Oriental Residents in Continental United States, 1930* (mimeographed).

servant, or otherwise, at a wage of three shillings a day or such other wage as may be agreed upon with the worker, and to repatriate the worker at the end of his service.

The worker has not an absolute right of choice of employment, but his wishes are consulted. . . . Task work is to be practised wherever possible. Sundays and ten Chinese holidays are normally free. . . . In the event of permanent incapacity or of fatal injury arising out of or directly attributable to the employment, the employer must pay a sum of thirty pounds as compensation. Penal sanctions for the breach of a contract by the worker are expressly abolished.[53]

This direct responsibility to the Government is different only in degree but not in principle from that of the Hawaiian employer for the welfare of his Filipino plantation workers, it was reported. Although the Philippine Government is not directly a signatory to the individual labor contract, nevertheless it exercises control over the conditions imposed and maintains a representative in Hawaii for the express purpose of supervising the fulfilment of its contractual obligations on the part of the inclusive employers' association.[54]

In the Philippine Islands themselves, it was said, contract labor on plantations does not affect immigrants who fulfil a commercial rather than a productive function.[55]

The Government of the Netherlands East Indies, it was explained, permits in its own territory indentured labor only under conditions of strict control. When labor is indentured for service abroad, an official of the Labor Inspection Department must be permitted to look after the welfare of the workers; and there must have been no previous complaint as regards the treatment of contract labor. A special license is required for contracts that run from two to three years. There is a penalty for non-fulfilment of contracts on both employers and laborers.[56]

Although primarily concerned in the gradual but complete abolition of the penal sanction in the indenture of domestic labor and inter-island migration, the Government also desires to abolish as speedily as may be the penal sanction where it is yet current in the contract labor of Chinese immigrants.[57]

The present complicated situation in the Netherlands East Indies, with

[53] *Some Labour Problems in Pacific Dependencies,* pp. 20–21.

[54] See Cruz, *op. cit.,* p. 2; and B. Lasker, *Filipino Immigration,* pp. 386–88.

[55] Lasker, *op. cit.,* pp. 235–37.

[56] " The principle of eventual abolition of the penal sanction had been generally adopted (in 1924), and provisional continuation was to last no longer than proved absolutely indispensable. Meanwhile, every effort was to be tried to perfect this labor law in itself, as well as the supervision of the Labor Inspection. It is in the light of these intentions that we must look upon the measures of the years since 1925, and of those still to come. . . . The five-yearly revision of the sanction contained in the coolie ordinance, starting from 1930, has become a fact " (De Kat Angelino, *op. cit.,* II, 549).

[57] Vandenbosch states that " coolies are still recruited in China for the tin mines in Banka and Billiton, and for the plantations on the East Coast of Sumatra. These are mostly under contracts with penal sanction, and most of them return to China upon expiration of these contracts " (*op. cit.,* p. 1017). See also De Kat Angelino, *op. cit.,* II, 502 ff.

this conflict of traditions and intentions under the more recent laws, is described in one of the data papers as follows:

> Under a new Coolie Ordinance which came into force in 1931, employers are required to engage a certain percentage of free workers, rising over a period of years, so that normally the older existing plantations will be required to have at least 50 per cent of free workers by 1936, and those opened in 1935 and 1936 must have at least 25 per cent of free workers by 1942. Registration machinery, maintained by compulsory contributions from employers, has been established to register immigrant workers and prevent the enticement of labor from one employment to another. . . .
>
> In the Netherlands Indies, efforts have been made over a number of years and at considerable expense to settle in the Outer Provinces Javanese laborers whose contracts have expired or who have been brought in as free laborers. It cannot be said, however, that these efforts have yet had, or can be expected in the near future to have, much effect either upon the density of population in Java or upon the labor supply in the Outer Islands.[58]

In Indo-China very stringent conditions accompany the issue by the administration of books of identification that practically constitute the contract. However, the system applies entirely to natives.[59]

In British Malaya, the majority of contract plantation workers are Tamils, recruited in British India. Here a very close co-operation between the Malayan administration and the Indian Government, which exchange officials, characterizes the system of control.[60] The control of Chinese immigration in British Malaya was described at the Kyoto Conference.[61]

The possibility of permanent settlement for immigrant contract workers — one of the main problems as viewed from the standpoint of population policy — depends, of course, on the definiteness and maximum terms of the contracts as regards the period of employment. A comparison of such statements as were available from different parts of the Pacific area indicated that a period of three years is usual where workers are transported over a considerable distance. For work in mining and other non-agricultural occupations, the terms tend to be shorter; where experience is an asset, as in certain types of plantation work, there tend to be provisions for re-employment — usually for one year, as in the case of the Netherlands Indies, Fiji, Gilbert, and Ellice islands. In Hawaii, a second contract is for another three-year period if the worker has in the meantime visited his home in the Philippines; but if he stays on, the duration of his continued service tends to be indefinite. Similarly, there seems to be no limitation on re-engagement in Indo-China.

In all these matters there appeared to be some uncertainty, both as regards the legal provisions in the various Pacific countries and also as to the actual practice where such provisions are flexible enough to permit a free adaptation of employment conditions to particular needs. It was informally suggested by interested members, after the round-table discussion, that a

---

[58] *Some Labor Problems in Pacific Dependencies*, pp. 24, 25.
[59] *Ibid.*, pp. 19–20; *Migration in the Pacific Area*, pp. 18–19.
[60] *Some Labor Problems in Pacific Dependencies*, pp. 22–23.
[61] Hinton, *op. cit.*, Appendix A.

rather comprehensive comparative study of all forms of contract and indentured labor in the Pacific area — especially those which affect migration
and the status of alien residents — would be desirable. Some of the members,
in this connection, were more especially interested in methods of labor
recruiting and its control.

III. THE ECONOMIC EFFECTS OF MIGRATION

1. ON THE HOME COUNTRY

At an earlier session in which four round tables concerned themselves
with influences on standards of living in Pacific countries, a large part of the
discussion was devoted to the question, often raised before, whether emigration really provides a relief for overpopulated areas. The case of Ireland
served as a historical introduction to this theme and incidentally showed how
difficult it is to isolate one causative factor in the complex process of economic
advance. One member took it as a matter of course that large-scale emigration to North America had been the cause of Ireland's rise from abject
destitution. Another thought it had very little to do with it: the country's
rising prosperity had been due chiefly to enlightened economic and political
leadership. Another student of European emigration stated that in Italy the
districts from which there was the largest emigration did not benefit permanently: rents fell, wages rose, conditions of life generally improved; then
the death-rate decreased, and gradually the balance between deaths and
births filled the homes until there was as much pressure as before. In the
meantime, these districts had suffered the loss of a considerable proportion of
their young manhood and womanhood at the age of maximum productivity,
to another country. This statement, however, in so far as it was advanced
in illustration of an inevitable sequence of cause and effect, did not remain
unchallenged. It was usually true, a Japanese member suggested, only of an
early stage in an emigration movement. At first, a temporary relief of population pressure makes possible a rise in living standards; then the lessening
death-rate may in part make up for the loss of population. But the spell
of prosperity may and often does also produce a decreasing birth-rate. Japan's
emigration, he thought, had not yet reached this third stage, so that it up to
the present emigration has not created a more favorable relation of population to the existing resources.

Since no figures were given concerning either Italy or Japan, the assertions made could not be disputed. However, support for the contention that
emigration does not relieve population pressure came from a Chinese member
familiar with the effect of the exodus of farmers on the northeastern provinces
of China. He stated that the vacancies in population created by the migration
movement were rapidly being filled by new births, and that the remittances
received from successful emigrants both stimulated the birth-rate and helped
to conserve child life. On the other hand, a Chinese member stated from
intimate personal knowledge that in southern Anhwei, where the conditions

of life have been very severe for some years, steady migration to Manchuria has produced a noticeable betterment of conditions. He thought that this effect was produced not only through the rising prosperity made possible by home remittances of emigrants but also by declining marriage- and birth-rates, because young male emigrants return at infrequent intervals. This was also the view of yet another Chinese member who has studied conditions in the frontier districts and found there an atmosphere of rising prosperity, in spite of the disruptive effects of large-scale emigration. He agreed, however, that it was too soon yet since the onset of this movement to discern whether the permanent effects would be favorable.

More unanimous was opinion on the influences produced by Chinese emigration toward the south. In the Canton and Swatow districts, emigration had undoubtedly produced a rise in the standard of living that seemed to be permanent. Places like Amoy would have become completely bankrupt in recent years had it not been for the remittances of emigrants. A town in Kwangtung was quoted in this connection which received a maternity hospital from one of her sons who had prospered in Hawaii. Incidentally, an American member reminded this round table, one of the chief arguments for Chinese exclusion in the old days had been that their earnings were not spent in the United States but remitted home to enrich their home communities.

After more testimony to the same effect, it was agreed that it depends entirely on the surrounding conditions whether emigration permanently benefits the sending country or not. The composition of the emigrant group, the volume and duration of the emigration movement, the fortunes of the emigrants, and, not least, the relative permanency of their separation from the homeland all tend to vary the net result for the standard of living of those who remain behind. In the Philippines, the combined effect of remittances sent home by absent sons and husbands and of their return, after a few years' absence, to bring new ideas to the old homestead and village, had unquestionably created a permanent relief of local population pressures — though in some cases these advantages had been offset by a rise in land values due to new competition for farms. In Japan, the personal influence of returned emigrants upon standards of comfort had been notable because they reinforced other influences that make for progress. In contrast, successful emigrants returning to China frequently seek an urban life, as small tradesmen, and so do not enrich the countryside with new ideas or good examples of more effective husbandry. In illustration of this, a small town near Nanking was mentioned in which emigrants returned from the United States have produced a sort of model community for themselves instead of returning to their old homes. In Southern China, where often relations with emigrant communities in Malaya, the South Seas, and the Philippines have continued over a long period, and especially in districts where the exodus has been considerable, both the new capital and the new methods have been more widely diffused to improve standards all around.

In Japan it has been observed, according to well-informed members from that country, that even when there is no decrease in the birth-rate, never-theless a standard of living raised by new contacts with the outside world remains higher than it was before; the influence of emigration in this respect tends to be similar to that of having a considerable proportion of young people go to work in the cities. In all these cases, however, there is a pre-existing ambition for better things, stimulated in part by education. A doubt was ex-pressed whether Japanese emigration to Manchuria had the same effect: here the large majority of emigrants are women and children, and the families move away permanently; also they are from somewhat different types of com-munities, so that their relation with the home community is different from that of Japanese emigrants to other parts of the Pacific area. These are generally not agriculturists but small tradesmen; when they return they tend to introduce innovations at home, especially of a sanitary character, that set new standards. A student of rural conditions in Japan stated that a temporary relief through lessened competition for land or rising wages resulting from emigration often provides the occasion for other, more permanent, helpful influences to become operative. The theoretical objection that eventually the vacancies created will be filled again by new births and a lessened death-rate should not, he held, be allowed to obscure this important fact. It is difficult, he said, for the wages to fall again once the level of well-being has been fixed in accordance with a higher wage standard.

It was recognized, then, that the effects of an emigration movement on the social welfare cannot be expressed in purely economic terms but must be studied in relation to the composition of the emigrant group and other condi-tions in each specific case.

2. ON THE RECEIVING COUNTRY

This recognition also arose from a less extensive inquiry into the effect of immigration on the standards of living in the receiving country — only that here the influence is reversed. For example, the actual fall in wages as a result of increased competition is likely to be less than might be expected because of the defense reactions of the workers whose standard of living is threatened. This does not mean, of course, that immigration has not actually undercut wages and standards of living where the impact has been sufficient to have any effect at all. Testimony substantiating this point was given by Australian and American members. Oriental labor in the United States, one member stated, while it was employed in building railways and in reclaiming land, even in the earlier stages of a developing truck-gardening industry on the Pacific Coast, undoubtedly had helped to raise standards of living.[62] But eventually the saturation point was reached, and the effect of such labor in lowering wages and raising land values outbalanced its effect in lowering living costs. One member suggested that, so long as America has much unused land,

[62] See George T. Renner, "Chinese Influence in the Development of Western United States," *Annals of the American Academy of Political and Social Science*, CLII (November, 1930), 356 ff.

a better distribution of population rather than increasing restrictions of immigration would be to the greatest advantage of all the workers. A Canadian member pointed out, however, that questions of national development — with or without the aid of immigrant labor — cannot be divorced from the whole world economic situation, since each country's prosperity is so largely dependent upon its export trade.

There was a brief but lively interlude, at one of the round tables, in which members debated whether distribution of population to meet the diverse economic needs of a country can be looked upon as a practicable measure. An American member stated that in the United States many of the ill effects of immigration have been due simply to the natural tendency of immigrants, when undirected, to drift into concentrated colonies and thus create local depressions in the wage levels. But even for industrial workers there still are ample opportunities in relatively undeveloped states. But how, he was asked, could legislation or administrative machinery prevent a subsequent drifting back of immigrants thus decentralized into the larger population centers? As a concrete example of the problem, a Canadian member gave the recent experience of the Dominion: here agricultural immigrant workers had carefully been directed to the prairie provinces which had no difficulty in absorbing them. But with the economic crisis in Canadian agriculture, this new population had merely increased the drift to the towns and there sharpened the unemployment problem.

In Australia, according to one member conversant with the country's economic statistics, while immigration was not permitted to lower wages, nevertheless the increase in population has been followed by a rise in the cost of commodities, so that the real income level is not higher today than it has been ten years ago. Another Australian thought that the experience of his country with immigrant labor from countries with low wage levels has been similar to that of the United States. For example, Italian labor on sugar plantations at first made possible the growth of an important industry, without detriment to anyone; that industry has helped to raise the standard of living; but as the Italians did not assimilate with the British population and sent a large part of their earnings out of the country, it is now doubtful whether in the long run their presence has proved beneficial to the country's economic life. In contrast, the migration of Cornish miners to South Africa — another example quoted — has raised standards of living because the immigrants brought with them special skills necessary to utilize the natural resources of the country. Again, a Canadian pointed out, what may represent a large improvement of conditions for the immigrants may nevertheless fall far short of the native population's standards. Thus, there is a potential if not an actual conflict in times when the immigrant group acts as a drag upon the older resident group's ability to achieve a substantial advance in its mode of life — as has been the case in Canada and the United States during the recent period of prosperity. " Oriental residents were found to be less eager to buy radios and refrigerators than the residents of older stocks who resented the slightest break in the pace of their progress toward a mode of life never previously achieved by wage-earners." A Japanese retorted that such resentment frequently is the result of misunderstanding. Thus, while during this period the Japanese in North America did not go in heavily for motor cars of the better makes, they spent an astonishing amount of their income on education, quite unknown to their fellow-citizens. In such a matter as the proportion of income spent on books, for example, their standards are actually higher than those of American workers.

An Australian at this point gave it as his opinion that the increasing mechanization, both in industry and in agriculture, has given a new turn to the whole question of the economic effects of immigration:

" In South Australia it was common for one farmer to do all the work on a farm of two or three, or a maximum of four acres. Today, with the use of machinery, the labor of three men is sufficient to do all the work on a farm of 40 to 45 acres — including every operation, from plowing to getting the crop to market. With this reduction in the man-power required, what is going to happen to the displaced? "

Thus discussion, in several of the round tables, turned to the question of immigrant selection as an important factor in the economic consequences to both the sending and the receiving countries. A British member thought that the recognized desirability of British immigrants, as compared with that of other European immigrants, within the Empire was not due only to the advantages of cultural homogeneity but also to the fact that in much larger proportion they represent sons and daughters of the best social classes, who in the new country show initiative and adaptability. A New Zealander testified to the truth of this statement, even in recent times: British emigration does not represent only labor but consists largely of a selected group that has provided social leadership. A Japanese pertinently remarked that one complaint against the exclusion law of the United States is precisely that it prevents Oriental intellectual leaders from settling among their countrymen on the Pacific Coast.

At least one of the round tables in the end arrived at the conclusion that, before it is possible to speak with certainty in general terms of the effects of immigration upon social conditions in the receiving countries, there is need for more careful comparative studies. If more were known of the actual experiences with concentrated and decentralized settlement, with selection other than broadly by nationality or race, with the continuation or absence of strong home ties, with rapid or more gradual infiltration, well-considered immigration policies would be more possible. Again, a comparative study might take into account differences in experience due to the economic situation at the time of the influx of a particular immigrant group and the particular labor demands and opportunities in different receiving countries. Statements made and refuted, that additions to the population from immigration take the place of indigenous population by reducing its birth-rate, also, it was thought, require more corroborative statistical studies before any generalization could be accepted in different areas with different conditions. At one round table, therefore, a definite request was made that the International Research Committee appoint a subcommittee to frame questions for further studies by the national groups.

IV. THE INFLUENCE OF ALIEN COMMUNITIES ON POLITICAL AND TRADE RELATIONS

The second of the main questions on the agenda was discussed only briefly and almost entirely in relation to two groups, the Chinese in British Malaya and the Filipinos in Hawaii and Continental United States.

A Chinese member spoke appreciatively of the rôle played by returned emigrants to British Malaya:

" In contrast with the experiences of Chinese coolies in almost every other part of the Pacific area, they are here receiving practically full equality of treatment. They are free to hold Government offices. They sit with British members on Government commissions and have seats in the Legislative Councils. There are no laws discriminating against them on racial grounds. The training in political responsibility received in British Malaya has enabled returned Chinese leaders to make important contributions to the modernization of China. Some of them became leaders in the Kuomintang movement in the days when it was a secret revolutionary party. There has been a stream of such men equipped for an active part in public life ever since. In addition, Chinese leaders residing in Singapore and other cities of the Straits Settlements, through their contacts with organizations for civic and political purposes, are exercising a similar influence from a distance.[63]

" Economically also the opportunities enjoyed by the Chinese in British Malaya have been an important factor. The Administration is realizing in a fair degree its responsibility to Chinese residents; and while in the earlier days they have come into conflict with the nationals through competition in sugar plantation work, they now have made largely a place for themselves in mining and the rubber industry. There is thus an actual increase in the prosperity of this Chinese community which is only temporarily interrupted by the present difficult economic situation." [64]

Other Chinese members felt that the picture presented was a little too rosy: After all, the number of Chinese in higher governmental positions is exceedingly small; moreover, there is the continuing resentment of the Chinese community against the Government monopoly on opium of which it is the principal victim.[65]

A more general account of the part played by southern Chinese emigrants, especially in the foreign trade relations of their home country, was

[63] Vandenbosch points out that these Chinese colonials, in spite of their nationalistic tendencies and political affiliations, are too practical-minded to constitute a political danger to the colonies where they find themselves (*op. cit.*, p. 1016).

[64] See also Etienne Dennery, *Asia's Teeming Millions,* chap. vi.

[65] Since 1910, according to one Chinese authority, the Straits Settlements Government has derived about one-half of all its annual revenues from the opium monopoly. The opium smokers are almost all Chinese, and the intelligent Chinese feel that the colonial Government should take immediate and effective steps to discontinue this immoral traffic. The difficulties in the way of prohibition, or even of drastic reduction, were stated at the Kyoto Conference in Hinton's paper, *op. cit.,* pp. 35–37.

found in a Japanese data paper.[66] The writer takes the view that the very precariousness of Chinese capitalist enterprise at home has created a strong Chinese business and banking group in the countries to the south. Because of a low standard of living in such countries as French Indo-China, British Malaya, and Siam, it was possible for clever Cantonese and other Chinese emigrants to acquire wealth and to make themselves indispensable in certain lines of business, not only in the trade relations between these countries and China but also often as middlemen between Europeans and natives. In some cases this functioning of the Chinese has led to popular resentment, not because of their competition with Occidental business — though this in some cases extends to banking and insurance as well as trade in commodities — but because of the obstacle it places in the way of the rise of an indigenous middle class. This has led to restrictive legislation in the Philippines, where the greater part of the retail trade is in the hands of the Chinese.[67]

A Filipino member reported on the political reactions of the movement from the Philippines to the mainland of the United States, and thus led the discussion to the next subject on the agenda:

V. NEW PROBLEMS OF MIGRATION IN THE PACIFIC AREA

I. FILIPINO MIGRATION TO HAWAII AND CONTINENTAL UNITED STATES

The main facts concerning this movement were before the round table in two data papers, one of them the result of a study undertaken by the American Council after informal discussions between Filipino and American members at the Kyoto Conference; [68] the other a statement from the Philippines Government official in direct charge of the administrative control of this movement.[69] These two documents, a Filipino member stated, amply provided all the necessary data for understanding the situation. While there had long been an inter-island migration of Filipinos, their migration to Hawaii, beginning in 1907 but not assuming large proportions until about 1925, had been brought about by the encouragement of Hawaiian sugar planters. The Philippine Government had abstained from interfering with this outflow of labor but had been active in protecting its emigrant workers against exploitation. Only since migration to Hawaii had assumed large proportions had a considerable movement to the Pacific Coast of the United States set in. This had at first been for the most part a re-emigration of Filipinos from Hawaii to the mainland but later in larger part a direct migration movement. In the Philippines, popular opinion was on the whole favorable to such emigration which was not for the purpose of permanent settlement abroad but for a temporary residence during which the emigrant learns new methods, saves money, and

[66] Akira Nagano, *Development of Capitalism in China*, pp. 128–31.
[67] *Filipino Immigration* (American Council), pp. 235 ff.
[68] Lasker, *op. cit.*
[69] Cruz, *op. cit.* See extracts, pp. 431–37.

generally prepares himself for an improved economic and social position upon his return. On the other hand, there was much opposition to Filipino immigration in Continental United States because there they were in competition with other wage-earning groups. A tense feeling on this matter had led to a number of unfortunate incidents. Nevertheless, so long as the Philippines were part of the United States, the Philippine Government did not feel called upon to restrict the travel of its citizens to any part of that country they wished to visit.

At this point a discussion developed on the question how the very real apprehension of people on the Pacific Coast in the face of what they could only regard as another threat of an " Oriental invasion " might be allayed. In reply to a question whether public opinion in the United States would be content with a restrictive measure, it was said that the demand from the Pacific Coast was entirely for exclusion, but that the rest of the country had not as yet shown much interest in the question. It was further stated that in the last year or so, with the possibility of influential support for a Philippine independence measure, there had been a change in the method advocated by responsible leaders to obtain exclusion of Filipinos. While they still supported the exclusion bill, first introduced in 1928, they would prefer to have the Filipino immigrants barred automatically by an independence law giving them the status of aliens.[70] Since the passage of such a law did not seem immediately probable, however, Filipino members were asked whether their own Government would not impose some restrictions or effective discouragements which would greatly reduce the number of migrants to the Pacific Coast while this larger solution was under consideration. To this a Filipino member replied that, as far as he knew, his Government would not, as a matter of principle, adopt voluntary measures to restrict the right of their nationals to make full use of their present legal status under the flag of the United States. This was also, he said, the attitude of the Legislature.

In the meantime, however, the present economic depression already promised to accomplish at least temporarily a falling-off in the number of Filipino newcomers to the American mainland. As Mr. Cruz had pointed out in his paper (see above, p. 434), the migration had not been primarily due to population pressure but to the attraction of better opportunities; if these opportunities failed to materialize, there was every reason to believe that the impetus of the movement would die down.

2. KOREAN MIGRATION TO MANCHURIA

This was the one migration movement in the Pacific area to which considerable attention had been given at the Kyoto Conference. Hence speakers were able to count on a certain familiarity with the major facts, especially since these had entered into the other phases of the Manchurian problem discussed at earlier sessions of the present Conference and were presented in

[70] Under the present immigration law, they would then be entitled to the annual minimum quota of 100, which in their case would also be the maximum.

some detail in several data and reference papers.[71] According to figures quoted by the International Labour Office, the net balance of Korean arrivals in Manchuria over departures in the nine years, 1920–28, amounted to 53,523; but the total number of Korean settlers in different parts of Manchuria is about 800,000. This is also the estimate of the Governor-General of Korea, in his report for 1930. This figure, of course, includes those residents of Korean origin whom the Chinese Government claims as citizens.

A Japanese member of the round table, taking roughly one million as the total number of Koreans in Manchuria, stated that about one-half of these reside in Chientao and enjoy extraterritorial rights under the Sino-Japanese Treaty of 1905 and that of 1915. Difficulty had arisen, however, over the interpretation of some of these rights — from two causes: first, some legal doubts as to the extent to which earlier treaty rights might have become superseded by later agreements; and second, the reluctance of China to fulfil these particular treaty obligations. In this latter connection, he singled out the refusal on the part of Chinese authorities to recognize the validity of the right of Japanese subjects to lease land and conduct business, granted them under articles 2 and 3 of the Treaty of 1915. Moreover, under the agreement regarding Chientao, of July, 1909, Koreans were to receive equal treatment with Chinese in the matter of taxation and other obligations and privileges of citizenship. This agreement was signed at a time when, apparently, China desired to encourage immigration; but more recently there were many indications that the authorities had changed their mind, and the provisions of the 1909 agreement were kept neither in letter nor in spirit.

Another Japanese speaker endeavored to fill in this legal outline of the major problems with a more concrete picture of their human reality:

" Most of the recent difficulties have been about the Koreans who are in South Manchuria farming rice fields. The native Chinese there do not like this kind of work; they do not understand paddy farming, though there is much of it in South China. So the Koreans began rice cultivation in Manchuria. Many of them leased land from Chinese owners. They prepared the land with great labor and then found, a year or two later, just when they were ready to reap a little profit from their effort, that the landlords would not renew the lease but wished to take over the improved land and work it themselves. This is the main source of dispute.

" The most serious aspect of the matter is, however, that this difficulty is aggravated by orders from the Government. The Chinese authorities are afraid of having so many Koreans in this territory and are practically ordering the Chinese landowners to terminate their leases and let these immigrants leave Manchuria.

" We believe that this policy derives, perhaps, from a misunderstanding of the situation. There was not, before the Chinese authorities intervened, much dispute between neighbors; most of the trouble has arisen from the background generally of the bad feeling between China and Japan. In Chientao, especially, Koreans are

[71] Syllabus, sec. V; Migration in the Pacific Area (International Labour Office), pp. 12–13; Shuhsi Hsu, Questions Relating to Manchuria, pp. 19 ff.; Harold G. Moulton, Japan, p. 394; South Manchuria Railway, Second Report on Progress in Manchuria — to 1930, pp. 161, 206. For a discussion of the nationality problem occasioned by Korean migration to Manchuria see pp. 282 ff. in the present Proceedings.

often in a majority in these rice-growing communities and own land. But because they are Japanese in nationality, the Chinese authorities want to get rid of them.

"The Central Government of China should not rely too much on these local authorities but study the conditions as they actually are. It is wrong for Korean farmers so often to be expelled after they have done the hard work. Their discouragement is of no advantage to that region; and their hardship becomes a new source of dispute between the two countries. Both Governments should know the actual conditions."

A Chinese member, very familiar with that region, asked why Koreans go to Manchuria if there is so much oppression as has been alleged. He thought that perhaps there was not so much of the hardship that had been described as a desire to make the most of it to press political demands. There certainly was no Chinese policy of oppression.

"To have the Korean immigrants cultivate the paddy fields of that region is recognized as a good thing. The Chinese migrants from the northern provinces would not be able to do that work. The Koreans thus are an asset to Manchuria and not a liability.

"Thirty or forty years ago, the local Chinese authorities had no policy of exclusion. But in recent years they have tried to check immigration from Korea. Why? Under the terms of the Twenty-one Demands, these immigrants bring extraterritoriality to Manchuria. There is as much objection to that there as there is in China proper. A second reason is that these Koreans stay permanently Japanese subjects because Japan refuses to recognize their naturalization in Manchuria (yet they allow Japanese subjects to naturalize in South America). Thirdly, most of these Koreans are poor; they go to Manchuria to better themselves, but large Japanese development companies exploit their labor in large-scale farming enterprises. This is bad for the development of Manchuria. The political power which these large organizations acquire also is dangerous. Naturally, then, the Manchurian authorities are opposed to all this development."

This statement was challenged by several Japanese speakers. One of them emphasized that Korean immigrants pour into Manchuria of their own will and driven by poverty; there was no evidence whatever, he held, for the allegation that they were brought there or driven out of their former homes under any organized direction. Another thought the main difficulty arose from the fact that the Chinese authorities either could or would not give these immigrant farmers the protection to which they were entitled under existing treaties. A third refuted the statement that Japanese land companies were sending Koreans into Manchuria. Why should such companies want to settle Koreans in Chientao rather than Japanese? It was entirely a matter of population pressure.

"Six hundred years ago the present Fushun mine was worked by Koreans. South Manchuria belonged to Korea. It was later excluded. About twenty years ago, the Tartar general in Mukden encouraged the migration of Koreans to Manchuria, and the whole population benefited. In 1906, there were nine million Koreans; today there are thirty million — is it any wonder that they find themselves compelled to leave their beloved land?"

The Chinese spokesman again remarked that the policies pursued by Japan on behalf of her emigrant Korean subjects are not consistent with the policies pursued by her elsewhere.

" There are just as many restrictions against foreign residents in Canada; but the Japanese do not employ the same policies against Canada. The Chinese have been forced to change their attitude toward Korean immigration because Japan would not recognize naturalization. We should be glad to have the Koreans come if they are not used as an instrument of Japanese policy against us.

" As for the charge of exploitation, it is probably quite true that the Japanese Government does not encourage the movement, but Japanese capitalists do. They have practically driven the Koreans out of their own country." [72]

As will be seen from this record of a discussion almost entirely carried on between Chinese and Japanese members of the round table, there was no opportunity to come to any agreement on those questions that were essentially germane to the general topic under consideration: The atmosphere was charged with political tension, and so the economic and social factors in this Manchurian situation were obscured. The discussion threatened to cover the same ground as that plowed open in the round tables on extraterritoriality (see pp. 290 ff.).

3. OTHER NEW MIGRATION PROBLEMS

The three other special topics named in the agenda remained unexplored, largely owing to lack of reliable first-hand information. Chinese migration to British Malaya and the Netherlands East Indies had been referred to in connection with the general survey of recent trends; but it was not possible to follow up the suggestion of a subcommittee of the Program Committee that an attempt be made " to arrive at a more detailed estimate and analysis than have yet been made of the economic and cultural relationships of the Chinese in Southeastern Asia with China itself, and the influence which this relationship may be expected to exert in the future." Nor was it possible to follow up the clue given in one of the data papers as to the increasing importance of the migration from Java to other parts of the Dutch East Indies. The migration of Japanese to Brazil and other South American countries, according to Japanese members, was too recent to have resulted yet in careful studies and reports. Regret was expressed also that there had not, apparently, been any recent study of the agitations against Japanese landowners and against Chinese tradesmen in Mexico.

[72] This statement was later amplified as follows: " Recently there has been a steady increase of Japanese emigrants to Korea. For several years the increase of the Japanese population in Korea has been at the rate of 20 per cent or more per annum. The declared policy of the Government of Korea is to encourage Japanese immigration in order to alleviate the population pressure in Japan, and also to develop agriculture along modern lines in rural Korea through the increase of Japanese farmers as permanent settlers. For every Japanese who moves into Korea, at least five Koreans are forced out of Korea, for, the average size of the Korean farm is about two and a half acres, whereas the land granted to the Japanese settlers, as an incentive to emigration, is either ten or twenty acres per family." This interpretation (which coincides with that given by Professor Ta Chen, of Tsing Hua University, in the *U. S. Monthly Labor Review* for November, 1930, pp. 35 ff.) perhaps assumes too readily that the increase in Japanese farm occupancy in Korea necessarily deprives the native population of an equivalent acreage.

At the suggestion of an Australian member, the round table concluded with a recommendation to the Program Committee that these special problems be prepared for future round-table discussion by a smaller group.

VI. OTHER RECOMMENDATIONS

The subcommittee mentioned above also recommended that there be further consideration of the question: To what extent and in what ways could personal criteria be substituted for national or racial criteria in the framing of regulations governing the admission of aliens? And it tentatively suggested to the International Research Committee that it consider the possibility of paralleling a proposed study of the biological and social consequence of race mixture in the Pacific islands with similar studies on the Asiatic mainland — especially in Siam, French Indo-China, and British Malaya.

CHAPTER XIV

EDUCATION FOR INTERNATIONAL UNDERSTANDING

DATA PAPERS

1. *Syllabus on Cultural Relations.*
2. Thomas Ming-heng Chao. *The Foreign Press in China* (China Council).
3. Sophia H. Chen Zen (ed.). *Symposium on Chinese Culture* (China Council):
    I. V. K. Ting. "How China Acquired Her Civilization"
    II. Hu Shih. "Religion and Philosophy"
    III. Tsai Yuan-pei. "Painting and Calligraphy"
    IV. Y. R. Chao. "Music"
    V. Chu Chi-chien. "Architecture"
    VI. Yui Shang-yuen. "Drama"
    VII. Hu Shih. "Literature"
    VIII. H. C. Zen. "Science"
    IX. A. W. Grabau. "Palaeontology"
    X. W. H. Wong. "Geology"
    XI. Chi Li. "Archaeology"
    XII. C. Ping and H. H. Hu. "Biology"
    XIII. King Chu. "Education"
    XIV. R. Feng. "Agriculture"
    XV. Franklin L. Ho. "Industries"
    XVI. Pao Swen Tseng. "The Chinese Woman, Past and Present"
    XVII. L. K. Tao. "Social Changes"
    XVIII. Sophia H. Chen Zen. "Concluding Remarks"
4. Kyoshiro Nakayama. *Sinological Researches in Contemporary Japan* (Japan Council).
5. Unokichi Hattori. *On the Convenience and Inconvenience of Chinese Characters* (Japan Council).
6. Soichi Saito. *A Study of the Influence of Christianity upon Japanese Culture* (Japan Council).
7. J. E. Strachan. "Amateur Radio," *New Zealand Affairs* (New Zealand Council).
8. Francisco Benitez. *Educational Progress in the Philippines* (Philippine Council).
9. Cecilio Lopez. *The Language Situation in the Philippine Islands* (Philippine Council).
10. Robert E. Park. *The Problem of Cultural Differences* (American Council).
11. Ping Chia Kuo. "Canton and Salem," *Some Oriental Influences on Western Culture* (American Council), Part III.
12. Edward C. Carter. *American Research Fellowships and the Far East* (American Council).
13. Edward C. Carter. *College Entrance Credit in Chinese and Japanese for Occidental Students* (American Council).
14. *Progress of Chinese Studies in the United States of America* (a report of the American Council of Learned Societies, American Council).
15. A. D. A. de Kat Angelino. *Colonial Policy* (American Council), Vol. I.

REFERENCES

1. J. B. Condliffe (ed.). *Problems of the Pacific, 1929,* chap i.
2. *Handbook of the Institute of Pacific Relations.*
3. Meng Chih. "Returned Students in China," *Pacific Affairs,* January, 1931.

4. DANIEL H. KULP II, " Chinese Continuity "; WILLIAM JAMES HAIL, " Education — Past and Present "; ARTHUR W. HUMMEL, " The New-Culture Movement in China "; KENNETH SCOTT LATOURETTE, " Christianity in China," *China: Annals of the American Academy of Political and Social Science*, Vol. CLII (November, 1930).
5. JEROME D. GREENE. Opening Address, *Pacific Affairs*, December, 1931, pp. 1089 ff.

INTRODUCTORY NOTE

The title of this chapter requires an explanation. It represents not the subject of a round table at the China Conference but the emphasis of several discussions in the field of cultural relations. At previous conferences, three types of interest had been considered under that inclusive heading: first, those imponderables in every problem of international relations that have to do with the diversity of experience, traditions, and social institutions of the peoples in contact; second, the problems of those agencies that exist primarily to affect the opinions and attitudes of peoples across national boundaries — schools, missions, the press, and the like; third, the cultural heritages of peoples as precious possessions that must be protected against the destructive impacts of uncontrolled forces from alien cultures.

At both the Honolulu conferences of the Institute, the first two of these considerations were prominent; at Kyoto, discussions of the impact of modern industrialism upon social organization moved into the forefront of the scheduled round-table program.[1] But already doubt was raised as to the advisability of continuing to recognize cultural relations as a subject sufficiently definite in outline for inclusion in future conference agenda.[2] At the December, 1930, meeting of the International Program Committee, this feeling found expression in a resolution to the effect that, until more fundamental work was done to clarify the major problems of cultural relations, it was better not to have a general round table for the discussion of specific topics in that area. Instead, the recommendation was made that one technical round table be set up at the China Conference at which a few highly qualified members representing different nations and races might formulate cultural subjects for future study, exchange of information, and eventually conference discussion.

During the preparatory session of the International Program Committee in October, 1931, all recommendations received for the conference agenda on cultural subjects — including far more positive suggestions than negative opinions of the kind just mentioned — were referred to a subcommittee at which every national council was represented. The deliberations of this committee started from the obvious fact, amplified by many new suggestions made orally, that there was a considerable demand for a continued discussion of cultural relations on the part of the Institute membership. But at the end of a long and strenuous session, it seemed that the most influential of these

[1] *Problems of the Pacific, 1929*, chap. i.
[2] *Handbook*, p. 23.

recommendations — that is, those backed by special knowledge and experience — were mutually irreconcilable. For example, it had been urged that a conference round table concern itself with the disruptive influence of Western moving pictures upon the morals and manners of Oriental peoples. But it was pointed out that no studies had as yet been made of the exact nature or strength of that influence; and that possibly effects were attributed to it merely because it was the most visible and, indeed, spectacular of many forms of foreign influence upon the indigenous culture. Exactly how could such influences be isolated, measured, and brought into enlightened comparison with other influences, similarly studied on the basis of accurate data? [3]

Others suggested the discussion of more inclusive topics — such as the differences between Orient and Occident in the part played by the family as a social unit, or the differences in the concept of justice.[4] But again, it was felt that there was need for sharper definitions, for more incisive studies, for more extensive information on the historical roots and the economic implications of present social institutions and attitudes before such matters as these could be profitably discussed — either by laymen or even by professional students of society. The committee, therefore, recommended that there be no round table on cultural relations, but that a group of sociologists and of representatives of allied sciences be started in research that would lay the necessary foundation for group discussion. A recommendation to this effect was made to the International Research Committee.

However, a suggestion arose that a number of specific problems dealing with educational rather than sociological interests could profitably be discussed by a technical round table; this met with the approval of the Program Committee, and the subsequent session dealing with these matters is reported below.

In this place it is necessary to record an instance of insubordination on the part of conference members. As will be seen by reference to the list of data papers, considerable work had been done in several countries, and particularly in the Far East, during the last biennial period to prepare information concerning the international impact of cultures in modern times. Some keenly interested members felt that they should have a right to help in formulating the problems for future research; and that there was danger of many urgent questions for social action and educational practice being postponed indefinitely if the results of fundamental studies had to be

[3] As an illustration of the progress actually made in recent years with the development of a suitable methodology for measuring the effect of cultural influences, see Soichi Saito, *A Study of the Influence of Christianity upon Japanese Culture* (Japanese Council).

[4] A preliminary discussion of this subject has been initiated with Professor Kenzo Takayanagi's paper on " Occidental Legal Ideas in Japan — Their Reception and Influence," *Pacific Affairs*, August, 1930, pp. 740–53; Werner Vogel, " Modern Chinese Law and Jurisdiction," *ibid.*, November, 1931, pp. 975–79; and an unpublished paper by Professor James T. Shotwell on " Justice, East and West." See also the discussion of this subject in the round tables on " Extraterritoriality," pp. 308 ff.

awaited before they could even be discussed. On the plea of these insurgents the Program Committee decided to arrange for an informal afternoon session on the more immediately practical questions of cultural contacts in the Pacific area. This meeting also was well attended and is reported below. The point of most interest here is that its practical approach had the effect of emphasizing the promising educational aspects of almost every topic raised.

A number of the topics considered at this meeting were brought up again later, in the form of more definite proposals, at a round table arranged by the International Program Committee for the specific purpose of considering " suggestions received as to ways in which the Institute might more fully contribute toward international understanding in the Pacific area through the use of its own and other available educational resources." For the sake of avoiding duplication, some parts of this later discussion have been incorporated with the earlier informal discussion of the same topics. The actual character of these three meetings, therefore, together with the other materials included, justify the title of this chapter: " Education for International Understanding." The following quotation from the opening address by the chairman of the Pacific Council, Jerome D. Greene, indicates the part played by these considerations in the total program of the Institute:

The primary object of the Institute is the improvement of our mutual relations. To do that we do not shrink from attacking the most delicate and controversial questions. For that audacity we make no apologies. By the very definition these are subjects that stir the nationalistic emotions of our respective peoples; and if we have any function at all it is to see that when national attitudes crystallize into national policy it is on the basis of knowledge rather than of ignorance. But controversy is not a good object in itself, and its causes often lie deep in cultural factors the better understanding of which would go far to forestall international friction.

Every great civilization has contributions of art, literature, and general culture which are its free gift to the world. To be availed of this gift requires an interchange of contact, study, and graphic materials between countries on a far larger scale than has yet been realized. As regards the function of the mere collector of paintings, sculpture, and objects of art, the balance is perhaps in favor of the Western countries, which now possess many of the finest examples of Eastern art, whereas but few examples of the best Western art have found their way into the hands of Eastern collectors. This disequilibrium has, however, been somewhat redressed by the far greater resort of Oriental visitors and students to Europe and America than of Europeans and Americans to the East.

Leaving out of account the exchange of artistic materials, the gross discrepancy between Western scholarship in the culture of the Orient and Oriental scholarship in the culture of the West is a profoundly humiliating fact. Europe has a handful of first-rate scholars, but it is doubtful whether there is in America one native-born scholar in the fields of Oriental literature, linguistics, philosophy, religion or art who is capable of engaging in original studies in any of these fields with a knowledge of the linguistic tools such as would be an elementary requisite to a study of the ancient or modern civilizations of Europe or such as could possibly be compared with the equipment of a Chinese or Japanese scholar. The language barrier is, of course, formidable, one that we could hardly expect to see surmounted by more than a select few; but those few are sorely needed to discover and interpret the vast treasures of art and learning which China and Japan are ready to disclose.

Is there room for doubt that if the literary culture of the East were half as accessible to us as is that of Greece or Rome, many of the mysteries and obscurities that now block our mutual understanding would be dissolved? Such institutions as the American Council of Learned Societies, the China Institute of America, and the Society for the Promotion of Japanese Studies are making an attempt, as yet feeble but not without promise for the future, to attack this formidable task by encouraging publication, and by enticing into the field of Oriental scholarship at least a small number of competent young persons.

Some doubts have been expressed, based upon the experience of former conferences, as to whether the subject of cultural contacts and exchanges lends itself to round-table discussion so much as to an expository form of treatment less appropriate to such meetings. I dare say there is a basis for such doubts. Yet there is surely room for discussion regarding the ways and means of promoting cultural interchange, the extent to which the overcoming of the language barrier is practically feasible, and the extent to which, owing to that barrier, temporary or permanent reliance must be placed upon the mediatory and interpretive rôle of Chinese, Japanese, and a few Western scholars or writers, through lectures, translations or the creation, at second best, of a new literature of the East in the vernacular of the West.

While there may be difficulty in finding the solution of this problem of cultural interchange, in the measure that our efforts enable us to understand each other's character and motivation the problem goes to the very vitals of international relations. We cannot possibly afford to ignore it.

ADDRESSES

I. CONFLICT OF CULTURES

By Hu Shih

I have taken for my subject the cultural conflict in China. May I begin by telling a little story of the Siccawei Observatory which you visited this afternoon? As you know, this observatory of Siccawei had its historic origin in the Jesuit Movement of the seventeenth century. The Jesuits, amongst whom the most prominent was Matteo Ricci, first arrived in China about 1600 A.D. and brought with them three things.

They found out that the best way to approach those powerful eunuchs who were controlling the Government was through the offering of clocks, the newest then made in Europe. These exquisite mechanisms were regarded as great inventions of the time and were readily accepted by the Chinese. That was the first thing.

Next they learned that in order to conquer the resistance of the intellectual class, they must convince it of the superiority of their own learning; so they brought with them the best trained scientists. Among these were included especially astronomers, because at that time the whole Chinese nation was engaged in a controversial discussion of the reform of the calendar which had been in use for 270 years and was no longer accurate in the prediction of the eclipses or other stellar phenomena. So the first Jesuits were all trained in the astronomical science, and Matteo Ricci, the greatest of them, was the favorite pupil of Father Clavius, who was one of the chief authors of the Gregorian Calendar.

Thirdly, they wanted, of course, to proselyte the Chinese to Christianity.

So we have first, mechanical invention; second, astronomical science; and third, the Christian religion. The fate of these three gifts will illustrate the thesis I am going to present today. The eunuchs were very much pleased with the clocks which they regarded as tributes to China from these foreign nations. But it took the Jesuits many years before they succeeded in convincing the Chinese scholars of the time that they were in possession of a new astronomical science which could assist China in the reform of the calendar. At that time there were four groups of astronomers in this country: first, there were the Imperial astronomers in charge of the old calendar; second, a Mohammedan school had become established whose principles were recognized as useful supplements to the astronomical science, and who had had a separate observatory; third, one native scholar, Wei Wen-kwei, had offered a new system of calendar reform and had been given an independent observatory; and lastly there was introduced this new school of the West. These four schools were fighting for ascendency, and the Government adopted a wise policy of assigning to them four different offices or observatories with the aim of letting their actual results be the basis of judgment. So from 1629 to 1643, a period of about fifteen years, these four schools of astronomy were subjected to careful examination as to their relative merits in the prediction of sun and moon eclipses, and other heavenly phenomena.

On all occasions, the Jesuit Fathers were the most accurate. All the astronomical offices tried to prepare tables for the prediction of eclipses, and the results showed the methods of the foreigners to be the most exact. Sometimes, these Jesuit astronomers feared that clouds might spoil the test, so they made predictions of eclipses in Peking, Szechuan, Honan, and Shansi, and asked the Emperor to send out special observers to such stations to time the occurrence of the eclipses. In the case of one moon eclipse on February 22, 1636, all three provinces reported that the Jesuit prediction was exact to the second, while the forecasts by the other astronomical observatories all proved to be inaccurate. Such keenly competitive tests went on and, in every case, the scientific triumph of the Jesuits over the other schools was complete. After fourteen years of careful observation, the science brought by the Jesuits was finally recognized by the Government, and a new calendar worked out by these Jesuit astronomers was in 1643 officially proclaimed the calendar of the Ming Dynasty. The Ming Dynasty fell in 1644; but the Jesuit calendar was adopted by the Manchus and became the official calendar of the Manchu Dynasty. A monument of that victory for scientific astronomy has remained to our days in the form of the Siccawei Observatory.

But the third gift, the religion of these Westerners, was accepted only by the few — only those who came into contact with that remarkable leader, Matteo Ricci, and his associates. These few later succeeded in converting large numbers of people and almost converted one emperor. But opposition soon arose, and it was largely this opposition on religious grounds that caused the decline of the Jesuits' influence. So, out of three things they brought to China, mechanical invention was the most readily accepted; science was accepted when its accuracy had been demonstrated; and religion was the last to be accepted, and only within the narrowest limits.

When we talk about a cultural conflict it always means a graded absorption of the various elements of cultural impact; some are more readily accepted, some are accepted after hesitation, and some are never accepted. Cultural change or growth is the natural result of a contact of peoples. When nations come together it is the most natural thing for one to take from the other those elements that are most advantageous to its own culture. Historically, the invading people as well as the invaded usually took those elements which they needed most. The exchange was usually beneficial to both sides. There is no conflict when a people freely chooses from a visiting culture those elements which it wants.

A cultural conflict occurs only where the native culture offers resistance to an invading culture; and the intensity of the conflict is in direct ratio to the strength of the resistance on the one hand and the force of the invasion on the other. The Jesuit movement in China is a good illustration. The resistance to the Western science of astronomy was overcome after 15 years of competitive tests in accuracy and exactness. The resistance is weakest in the case of a mechanical invention, as in the case of the clocks, which promises an immediate, tangible improvement. But the contact of the Christian religion with the native beliefs of China produced the strongest power of resistance to which the new religion finally succumbed.

Resistance occurs only when there is a counterpart in the native civilization that is good enough for the particular people at the particular moment. Some years ago, when I was a student in America, I visited in the home of an American friend who was working in the laboratory of a great chemical plant at Niagara Falls. One day he said to me, " The director of our laboratory is a real pragmatist. He has a great formula for dealing with new inventions. Suppose a new method is invented by some unknown scientist for the manufacture of the same kind of chemical product that we manufacture, and a patent is granted, then it is to the interest of our laboratory to buy the patent rights. If the new method can easily be put into operation the existing processes will be abandoned; but if the new process is too expensive for us to take over, then we are justified, he says, to shelve it after having paid for the patent rights. He justifies this practice with the formula, " The better is the enemy of the good." I was horrified by this interpretation of pragmatism, but this formula amused me, because it is exactly that of cultural resistance. It is the opposite way of putting the usual formula, " The good enough is the greatest enemy of the better." In all cases of cultural resistance we meet this element of the good enough — good enough for us, for our fathers, for our country; why should we give up the good enough for something that in the long run may turn out no better, after all? That philosophy is not applied, of course, in those cases where there is no " good enough " counterpart in a native culture.

This general formula of cultural conservatism, while it explains much of the long resistance on the part of China to the civilization of the West, is not adequate when we look back into Chinese history. China did accept a great many cultural elements from her neighbors. She did accept a religion from a neighbor and made it one of her three great religions. If China could be so generous and big-hearted as to accept a religion which penetrates every phase of life and which is opposed to the ancient culture of the country, how is it that she so long resists a civilization which is certainly far more useful than Buddhism? There must be something deeper than the general inertia of cultures.

A friend of mine recently published an article in which he tried to offer a suggestion which is illuminating on this point. He said that although in the past China had more than once been conquered by the barbarians of the North, somehow those conquests were never accompanied by cultural conquests. Those barbarian invaders were soon absorbed by the civilization of ancient China. Then, when China did accept the Buddhist religion from India, together with all its art, ritualism and philosophy, that religion was not thrust upon us by a big army or a big navy. Not a single soldier crossed the border. China was willing to accept a great religion and a great philosophy without fear of military invasion behind it. But today for the first time we have been forced to face a new situation. We are facing a race which combines mechanical, scientific, technological invention with superior military strength. A great civilization is behind the military strength, and the great military strength is behind this apparently highly advanced civilization. This is a new situation. We cannot acknowledge the superiority of this culture of the West without at the same time feeling resentment over the necessity of submitting to its military force. The psychology of not being able to swallow this situation is behind all the apologetic reasons advanced against accepting the civilization of the West.

But we may go a step farther and ask, apart from the general explanation on the basis of the natural inertia of civilizations, apart from this historic situation of the fear of the military strength behind the apparently advanced civilization, are there not intrinsic and objective differences between the Chinese and the Western civilization which make the latter difficult for us to accept? I think there are, and I shall outline only a few.

In the first place, this new civilization from the West has brought to us an entirely new conception of economic life — the conception which elevates the position of the merchant. That was the first thing the Chinese could not swallow. In the past, our own traditional place of the merchant has been very low — higher only than that of the soldier. The mechanic and the farmer were above both. The merchant who does nothing but reap unearned increment, through usury and commerce without labor, found his position almost the lowest in society. Here in the new civilization, the merchant was seen to be elevated almost to the highest position; usury, commerce and business in this system are regarded as legitimate and respectable. That was one of the first shocks to the Chinese. It would take a long time for the Chinese to acquire a new conception of this economic situation, a long time to appreciate the function of the merchant and business man in society, the function of transporting goods from the place of production to those places where it is needed most. The utility of exchange, transportation, communication, the idea of creating new wants as an element in civilization, almost never occurred to economists of ancient China, which was chiefly agricultural. Usury was condemned because farmers suffered from it; commerce for the same reason. Agriculture had been the only orthodox economic system. This, then, has been one of the chief obstacles to the ready appreciation of this new civilization. It will take a long time to make the people realize that this new civilization which elevates the merchant and recognizes usury has also made it possible to lower the interest on money loans from 50 or 100 per cent down to 3 per cent. It will take a long time for this people to appreciate the aid which this civilization can render to the agricultural population.

There is also a fundamental difference in the conception of law, of government. It has been said in this Conference that the Chinese are governed by the concept of justice, while the West is governed by the concept of law. Law as the West understands it has practically no place in this country. When the first coded law was published in the fifth century B.C., Confucius, the founder of orthodox moral and political philosophy in this country, opposed it because he was very near the feudal system under which the upper classes were governed by a code of honor and the masses were governed by penalties. It would have been a degradation to subject the upper classes to law. The concept of law itself was opposed to their thinking. Although there was a time when Chinese philosophers were trying to idealize a government by law, it was never accepted by orthodox thinking. So the whole system in orthodox China still is to regard law as something good only for the punishment of law breakers and evildoers; and if that is the purpose of law, it has nothing to do with the upper classes, the gentlemen. It should be allowed to stand as a guidance only for the punishment of the evildoers. And since it is only for the evildoers, we should apply the most drastic measures for the detection of crimes and for their punishment, while a gentleman must be governed by consideration for others, the code of honor and morality.

Law was never accepted by orthodox thinkers in China. The professional lawyer was never legitimately recognized until recent decades. Law was never taught in the Chinese schools of old. Lawsuits were tried by magistrates trained in a purely bookish classical education. They had no idea of a legal procedure based on evidence. If the law were only meant for evildoers and law breakers, why should one refrain from using torture to obtain a confession? The absence of carefully trained judges who would go out of the way to seek evidence and justice, the absence of scientific detection systems, the absence of public defense by trained lawyers, and the prevalence of torture, lynching, etc., to force a confession from the criminals — all these naturally made law a horror in the eyes of the people. And all these made it very difficult for the people to acquire the conception of government by law as a necessarily slow and painstaking process of presentation of evidence and judgment on the basis of evidences proffered.

So there has grown up a reliance on the primitive sense of justice, but not on law, because we all know that law is no sure way of securing justice. At least it is the last method to secure speedy justice. This desire for speedy justice has made many people, including the Chinese, tend to disregard the regular procedures of the law and seek other means of gratifying their desire for justice. A recent case will illustrate: there was a case of suicide of a young woman who was living in the home of an official, but her family suspected that it was not suicide. Suit was brought by her relatives against the official on a charge of murder. It got into the newspapers and was quite a sensational case for weeks. Then public opinion began to demand justice. The military governor thought it was his duty as the Governor of the Province to take up this matter of justice; so he disregarded all regular procedure of the courts and summoned a trial in his presence. He was criticized by the newspapers and by those who thought a military governor should not interfere with the law courts; but somehow he became very popular among the people who had no use for this slow process of appealing and re-appealing.

This primitive sense of justice coupled with a traditional suspicion toward the law is, I think, one of the basic obstacles which China has had great difficulty in overcoming in her efforts to bring about a modern government by law. It will probably take a long time for the people to acquire the patience necessary to wait for a court to go through the all too slow processes of law.

The third obstacle is probably a fundamental intellectual difference. It seems that these two peoples, the Chinese and the Europeans, have from very early beginnings been quite different in the direction of their intellectual development. You will remember the early Egyptian mathematicians; Plato, writing on his door, " One who knows no geometry is not educated "; Euclid, almost a contemporary of Mencius, who perfected geometry; and Archimedes who laid the foundation for mechanics at about the same time. If you seek the Chinese contemporaries of Archimedes, Plato and Euclid, you will find that even in those days they were already working in different intellectual spheres — one in social philosophy and political systems, the other playing with figures, tools, mechanics and machines.

We are proud of the scientific development of scholarship during the seventeenth century in China. Yet when we compare the work of that century in China and the intellectual work of the same period in Europe, we find a fundamental difference. While Chinese scholars were trying to reconstruct the ancient pronunciation of a word by really scientific methods — one man gave one hundred and sixty-two evidences to prove the ancient pronunciation of one word — Galileo was using the telescope to discover new stars in the heavens. And while another Chinese was trying to demonstrate scientifically which chapters of the Book of History (*Shu King*) were forgeries, in Europe van Leeuwenhoek with his microscope marked two great advances in that century and helped to lay the foundation for the new science of Europe. It was the same period which laid the basis for a scientific scholarship in China. But you will find that, while one people was working with objects of nature and with mechanical aids to the senses, the other was working on paper, on literary documents. This, I think, is another fundamental difference. We have been laying stress on literary education, which has practically disabled us from taking an interest in objects in nature. We have failed in conquering nature because we have paid too much attention to documents. Literary education versus natural science — this sharp distinction between the two cultures makes it difficult for those trained in the old literary education to accept this new education, to look at test tubes, to boil unpleasant liquids, and the like. The method of " going to things " was advocated by some of our philosophers but was never seriously put into practice. So here we have a third difference — the difference in intellectual life, which may be traced back to those early days of Democritus and Confucius and Mencius. It will take us a long time to get away from the books and documents and acquire an aptitude for work on objects and machines.

I have tried to explain this resistance of a culture from a historic point of view. After all this explanation, the cultural conflict is still there. What are we to do about it? There are only three roads open — to resist it, to adopt it whole-heartedly, or to take a middle course — what is called " selective assimilation." Resistance is no longer talked about today, because for the last eighty years we have learned the futility of resisting Western civilization; but there is still a great deal of talk about this attitude of selective assimilation. It sounds the most reasonable of all: we ought to select those elements which are useful and reject those elements which are harmful. This seems the most reasonable attitude; and yet when you come to analyze it, it is a subterfuge, a refuge behind which the old resistance shelters itself, a new disguise for the same old conservatism. After all, culture is usually one, is a whole; and if you take this attitude — as has been proposed by some Chinese statesmen — namely, that Chinese learning must be the basis on which the useful learning of the West may be made to function, on the theory that Western civilization is materialistic and Chinese culture is spiritual, you will be compelled to drop all steps of modernization; for, when you assign all the basic functions in the social and cultural life to the old and allow only the superficial external things to this invading civilization, you are really taking the same attitude as those old reactionaries who resisted this new civilization *in toto*.

My own attitude is that we must unreservedly accept this modern civilization of the West because we need it to solve our most pressing problems, the problems of poverty, ignorance, disease and corruption. These are the real enemies we are facing, and none of these can be subjugated by the old civilization. After all, we do not reject a precious stone simply because it comes from the quarries of Italy or Greece; so the social thinkers must not reject any element of culture because it comes from an invading race. We need every stone from every quarry to build. Japan, in the early days of the reform, took over Western civilization whole-heartedly; and Japan has no reason to regret it, because in that short period of whole-hearted modernization she has succeeded in solving some of the most serious problems of national defense and economic poverty. When we have health and wealth and leisure, then we can talk about the preservation of our old traditions. And I am convinced the old traditions will not be lost even when we take an extreme view of the need for modernization, because civilizations are conservative, by their nature. By the natural inertia of cultures, the vast majority will take good care of those traditional values. But it behooves the leaders to go as far as they can in order that they may bring the masses to move a few steps farther in the direction of solving the most urgent problems of the nation by means of every instrumentality which this new world civilization can offer.

II. CULTURAL IMPACTS — OLD AND NEW

SUMMARY OF AN ADDRESS BY INAZO I. NITOBE

The contact of nations means not only the coming together of different cultural systems; it means also the contact of people with different mentalities, resulting from years of life under variant conditions. History shows that until recently such contact has nearly always been forced rather than voluntary. Peoples in olden times were usually self-contained and isolated; they did not care to mix with other peoples, even looked upon them as barbarians. This is well known in Chinese history, and also in that of our own country, Japan. But even the European peoples, occupying that relatively small area which we call a continent, are still divided today into thirty-three nationalities. Modern inventions, however, no longer allow us to be content with this old exclusiveness which was satisfactory for sedentary agricultural communities. We must learn to increase and enrich voluntary contact, or we run the risk of being brought into closer contact by outside force, against our will.

Professor Flinders Petrie, the great Egyptologist, in a little book called *Revolutions of Civilization,* has shown the differences in the longevity of civilizations. His theory is that each system has its own definite length of time to live. . . . . Now a progressive civilization usually, not necessarily, expands, and in this expansion may hit another one near by. Throughout history we have had these great conflicts of cultures when a young, expanding civilization came in contact with an older, declining one.

With the intimate contacts which modern mechanical invention has forced upon us, we may dread such crossing of cultural trends, in different stages of their evolution, as they must still happen now and in the future. But we can also look toward it with hope. Just now, the Chinese and Japanese nations are at odds, and their dispute over Manchuria has absorbed much of our time at this conference. But compared with the march of cultures, sometimes covering more than a thousand years, and with the problems of cultural conflict, such national differences seem a small thing. Perhaps, in twenty or thirty years from now, China and Japan may not only be shaking hands with each other but, forgetting their controversies as rapidly as we have forgotten others in recent history, face together a new cry of " Yellow Peril " in the West.

The outstanding question for us to consider in this Institute is this: as Occident and Orient come into ever closer contact, must they clash or will they integrate?

Let me speak for a moment of one of the practical ways in which all of us individually can contribute toward making this new, close contact of cultures and civilizations a real blessing for mankind instead of letting it become a threat to their very survival: there is one humble process in which we can all take part; we can seek to learn from other peoples instead of finding fault with them; we can disregard the counterfeit in human ambitions, if there be such, and put our mind on the genuine coin of what is fundamentally good in all peoples.

Let me illustrate this opportunity with one simple but remarkable set of figures: during the decade of 1840 to 1849, only nine international meetings were held in the whole world, and not very important ones either, for the most part. These people came together from within a circuit of a few miles, as distances are now counted, one or two from Belgium, a few from Holland, from France and other nearby states, not more than a score or so altogether. But even counting such small meetings as these, not more than nine organized international meetings are known to have been held during that decade in the middle of last century. In the next decade, 1850 to 1859, there were twenty international gatherings, an annual average of two. In the next ten years, 1860 to 1869, there was an annual average of seven; in the next, from 1870 to 1879, an average of seventeen; from 1880 to 1889, an average of 31; from 1890 to 1899 each year 53, or one a week. Then in the decade 1900 to 1909, there was an annual average of 115 such meetings; in the next decade, 1910–1919, the annual average was 120 — that is, ten a month; and beginning with the three years 1920 to 1923, no less than one international meeting for every day of the year. In the League of Nations building you may often find three or four meetings going on at the same time now; and there are other international gatherings of every sort all over the world.

Any common interest between people may become the concern of a permanent international organization. There are such associations of dancing masters, of bicyclists, of teachers of all kinds — in fact, of every profession. (In looking for a certain organization in Paris once I came upon the office of an international association for the rational eradication of rats.) And these permanent organizations, as well as the number of international meetings, are constantly increasing. In this way, contacts between nations are growing from year to year; and they represent efforts in which the humblest private individual can take part. The sum total of these activities constitutes a new form of contact between cultures; they bring people of all sorts into the habit of regularly meeting and conferring with those who share their interests, irrespective of their national affiliations and cultural backgrounds. And so if the time should come for a new crossing of the curves between great ascending and descending civilizations, we can hope that it will not bring with it catastrophic destruction but a common blessing.

Some may think that in holding up as an ideal this concept of world union and co-operation we must needs be traitors to our own culture and to our own nation. But I believe that internationalism of this sort is an extension of patriotism — indeed, that in our time no one can be really patriotic without also being an internationalist. Isolation can never again be a practical national policy: we cannot but be ever mindful of the actual co-partnership of the whole world. Without belonging to the world, we cannot in the best sense belong to our own small country.

QUESTIONS FOR ROUND–TABLE DISCUSSION

The following questions were recommended by the Program Committee as an outline for discussion:

1. How can a healthy interchange of culture between East and West best be promoted — with special reference to the educational sphere?
   a) What can be done through an interchange of lecturers?
   b) What are the problems involved in the visits of Oriental students to the universities of America and Europe? How can they be given opportunities of seeing the best side of the civilizations of the countries which they visit? Can they be guided as to their choice of university courses, etc? Is the present system very haphazard?
      i. What are the problems involved in their vocational training? (E.g., it is contended that Chinese engineering students do not get access to Western works and factories, so that they return without having had sufficient practical experience.)
      ii. What are the practical problems of returned Oriental students in adapting themselves to the practical requirements of careers in their home countries, and what steps may be taken to assist in such adaptation?
2. To what extent is it desirable to increase the number of Western students in adapting themselves to the practical requirements of careers in their home countries, and what steps may be taken to assist in such adaptation?

SUMMARY OF ROUND–TABLE DISCUSSIONS

I. UNIVERSITIES AND THE INTERCHANGE OF CULTURES

The large attendance of university teachers at this round table during an hour usually given up to recreation was the best answer that could have been given if the relevancy of its subject to the major purposes and interests of the Institute of Pacific Relations had been questioned. There was no need to ask whether the part played by interchanges of teachers and students between East and West is an important element in the machinery for international understanding. There was, however, considerable diversity of opinion as regards desirable methods.

INTERCHANGE OF LECTURERS

The current term " exchange professorship " was criticized as hardly describing the actual process that usually obtains when institutions of learning arrange for courses or lectures by visiting teachers. In practice, a direct exchange does not often work well because it is a rare coincidence that an institution in the East and one in the West are in a position to exchange faculty members in such a way as to meet actual needs at both ends. There is the further difficulty that Eastern institutions are rarely in a position to pay the salaries to which Western teachers are accustomed and therefore are obliged to limit their occasional engagements of Western talent to men and women who desire to visit Oriental countries anyhow for purposes of study — usually during a sabbatical leave — and who are willing to serve for a much smaller compensation than they could accept at home.

There was the further distinction between occasional lecturers and full members of the faculty — the former without executive responsibilities, the latter fully taking the place of a " member of the family " with all its general and special responsibilities to the institution.   There was no dissent from the opinion that foreign lecturers are of great assistance to any university, as they bring to bear upon both students and faculty members the impact of a new approach and point of view.   Such lecturers have been found particularly helpful not only because of the often provocative content of their teaching but also because they frequently make useful suggestions on teaching methods.   It was further stated that the value of such occasional lectureships is greatly enhanced if some of their time is given to conferences and seminars, permitting a free exchange of experience and information, instead of devoting all of it to formal courses of lectures.

As to the interchange of faculty members, it seemed evident to the members with the largest experience in this matter that a broader basis for choice must be developed than direct exchange between two institutions. Exceptions to this agreement were found to exist, however, in some of the smaller colleges which see special advantage in a rather close association with individual institutions of similar character and interests overseas.

The round table regretfully found itself without exact information on the number of faculty positions held either in the East or in the West by foreign professors and lecturers, their distribution as to locality, nationality, and subject, and similar matters of interest.   The general impression was that as yet the whole process is a somewhat unilateral affair.   Some Oriental scholars of distinction have served or lectured at practically all the greater universities of Europe and America; but their number has been small compared with that of Occidentals who like to compensate themselves in part for a sojourn in the Far East by taking on some such assignment for a semester or a term.   Considerable doubt was expressed as to the effectiveness of these arrangements.   University administrators in the Far East gave it as their opinion that it takes a foreign teacher no less than a college year to become thoroughly adjusted to the atmosphere of the institution he is serving and, in his turn, to be fully understood by the students attending his classes. There is not only the language difficulty, which is shared to a large extent by permanent foreign members of a teaching faculty, but also, and perhaps a more serious obstacle, a psychological difficulty that arises from unfamiliarity with social and intellectual backgrounds.   This problem, it was agreed, does not seriously impair the value of an occasional foreign lectureship when the main purpose is stimulation; but it is a decided argument in favor of extending engagements of foreign faculty members over longer periods whenever that is practicable.   " Resident teachers," said a university president in China, " can do more for the students."

With these preferences in mind, the question was discussed at some length how this educational demand and supply might be brought into a more effective relationship.   One foreign university teacher spoke from personal experience when he said that there is not now in existence any inclusive organization to which he could turn for information as to where in the Far East his services might be welcome as a lecturer on a relatively popular subject which he was willing to offer in exchange for living expenses and the opportunity of spending his sabbatical year in an Oriental community. The Institute of International Education was mentioned as an agency engaged in this field of effort, as between Europe and America; but its activities had not yet penetrated very far into the East. The China Institute also was mentioned as interested but so far with limited resources. There was little contact with British universities. Here a special difficulty was mentioned, as regards the employment of foreign professors, to consist in their unfamiliarity with the tutorial system; but this did not, it was held, affect the usefulness of a greatly increased exchange of occasional lecturers. Both in England and in Canada, it was reported, there was considerable hospitality to the idea of a larger program of this sort; but the necessary information to guide those lecturers willing to go abroad and those institutions willing to place visiting lecturers from abroad was lacking.

Under the provision recently made in the agreement between the Chinese and British governments for the administration of a grant of £200,000 from the China indemnity fund to promote cultural relations between the two countries, there is likely to be a considerable development of such exchange of lecturers, it was reported. A Universities China Committee was formed, consisting of the vice-chancellors of the universities in Great Britian and Ireland, together with other interested men and women, to administer this fund when it becomes available. The first of its purposes, as defined by Act of Parliament, is " to arrange for such Chinese men and women to visit and lecture in the United Kingdom and for such British men and women to visit and lecture in China as may seem to them suitable."

Another purpose, perhaps even more far-reaching for the future growth of cultural relations between the two countries, is " to encourage and facilitate the teaching of the Chinese language and literature at the Universities of the United Kingdom by the endowment for those purposes of professorships and lectureships, or otherwise."

The Committee had not yet received its grant but already had made preliminary studies of the task that lies before it.

There was a division of opinion as to whether existing agencies in the various countries that already are interested in this matter could be brought into a more effective co-operative relationship or whether it was necessary to create a new international agency in direct touch with the institutions of learning throughout the Pacific area. A suggestion that the Institute of Pacific Relations itself might be that agency did not, however, seem to appeal to many members, who saw the task as a specialized one and outside the scope of the Institute's functioning. It was finally agreed to recommend further study as to the organizational needs and possibilities of an inclusive agency, with a view either to a linking-up of existing agencies or to the creation of an entirely new one under suitable auspices.

ORIENTAL STUDENTS AT WESTERN UNIVERSITIES

A member from one of the municipal universities in England drew attention to the difficulties faced by foreign university authorities when asked to recognize Chinese degrees. Obviously, with the differences in grading, such credentials as these students bring with them do not on the face indicate for what studies they are sufficiently equipped. Consequent misplacements mean not only trouble for the faculty but, and this is much more serious, disappointment and discouragement for the students, or unforseen expense for special tuition. How are the students in the Far East, and particularly in China, informed of the requirements and facilities of the different institutions in Europe and America?

A number of organizations were named that try to fill this obvious need for information. But on examination each of them was found to be limited in its operations. There is no recognized center to which students or their advisers in China can turn for the exact knowledge they should have before making a decision as to the choice of a foreign university. According to their opportunities, they will turn to representatives of the China Foundation, the Institute of International Education, some missionary body, the Y.M.C.A., individual foreigners in China, or students recently returned from abroad. One member suggested that, with such general sources of information, after a preliminary choice students could always get the printed catalogues of the universities and colleges they had in mind for a final choice; but it was pointed out that the formal information given in these catalogues does not suffice; it is desirable that the students should learn a great deal more as to expense and social advantages or disadvantages, opportunities for vocational experience, and other such matters, before enrolling in a foreign institution. In this connection, an Indian bluebook, published annually to give Indian students full information about British universities, was praised by several speakers as a model. An American member reported that there was in preparation such a handbook for the American colleges and universities, which would give full information about courses, facilities, available scholarships, and other matters for each institution. (A *Guide Book for Foreign Students in the United States* was published by the Institute of International Education, New York, in 1931.) But a more personal service is needed, many felt, because students differ greatly in individual qualifications and purposes. The institution or course of study most suitable for one student is not necessarily suitable at all for another with the same equipment. As a considerable advance toward filling this need, at least in one area to which Chinese students are going in increasing numbers, members of the round table welcomed the newly organized Office for Chinese Students of the British Universities China Committee. This Committee, in addition to the purposes mentioned on page 482, also endeavors " to assist Chinese students coming to the United Kingdom to find hospitality and suitable living accommodation; to advise Chinese students as to their course of studies in the United Kingdom and as to other matters connected therewith."

Although set up only very recently, this office, in co-operation with the Chinese consul-general in London and the Chinese Students' Central Union, already has invited students who are enrolled in British universities and also those desiring to enrol to consult its secretary as to lodgings, tutoring, introductions to factories, university entrance requirements, as well as choice of institutions and courses. The Committee particularly desires to hear in advance of new Chinese students arriving from overseas, to assist them in their first contacts.[5]

A Chinese member thought that one of the chief difficulties arises from the possibilities open to those students who have not finished their studies in the government and provincial colleges in China to go abroad for the purpose of securing a foreign degree. Responsible educators in China do not encourage that practice but agree with foreign faculties that normally only those students should go abroad who are equipped for graduate work.[6] The Chinese institutions can take care of all undergraduate work and also of many types of graduate work. The Government now requires a special certificate before it will issue a student passport. But there still are cases in which students get overseas on an ordinary traveler's passport and then try to get into a university.

In this connection the question was raised whether the American regulation that a student must be enrolled in an American college or university before he can obtain a student visa is advantageous or not. It was reported that more Chinese students are now going to England, partly as a result of the strict application of this regulation. Other speakers refuted this statement, saying that in Canada, for example, the system is more severe than in the United States, and that in England the foreign student faces the double handicap of university and college entrance requirements. Chinese educators, it seemed, were not opposed in principle to the restrictions in Canada and the United States because in practice they have proved an advantage by saving the students anxiety and risk. One way of avoiding the present difficulties, it was suggested, would be to have the foreign consuls insist on a certificate from the Chinese Ministry of Education before issuing a visa to a student; but other members objected to any introduction of new machinery that would overformalize the process. In some cases, men going abroad to study on their own responsibility, without the blessing of their college authorities, it was said, have done very well, and the existing freedom to do so should not be restricted.

The practical problem at the present time does not, then, lie in any widely recognized deficiency of the systems of admission or passport require-

[5] Brief reference was made to the excellent work done in this field by the Committee on Friendly Relations among Foreign Students in the United States.

[6] On this point see *Filipino Immigration*, p. 311.

ments, but in China itself: the lack of uniform grading by Chinese institutions, and the absence of an adequate machinery of information. As to the former difficulty, members of the round table did not feel competent to offer advice; the Chinese universities had been handicapped, it was felt, by many difficulties not shared in other countries with more developed communications; and the need was for careful committee work on a delicate situation. In the meantime, some of the Western universities have adopted the practice of admitting Oriental (and sometimes other foreign) students on an unclassified basis for one semester's work, after which their standing is judged by the record they have made in that time. As to sources of information on the opportunities for study abroad, it was agreed that the existing channels do not suffice: there is no one agency that really has access to all the facts which in many individual cases should be known before a student makes his decision to enrol in a particular foreign institution. For this, the lack of concise published data in the foreign countries themselves is partly responsible; but the special need is for the establishment of some bureau — perhaps jointly by the interested organizations — in China to collect and make available what information there is.

The need for some supervision over Oriental students in foreign colleges and universities was mentioned as a subsidiary problem. Often such students need advice from someone they trust after they have entered upon their foreign studies. A Philippine member reported that there is an officer especially charged with this responsibility in the United States, and that his activity has proved of great benefit to the Filipino students there. Attention was drawn also to the admirable services in this direction rendered by the Y.M.C.A. and the Y.W.C.A., by the China Institute, by local societies at different colleges and universities to befriend Oriental students, and in America by International House — soon to be represented also in Paris. There was recognition, on the part of Chinese members of the round table, of the friendly spirit in which Chinese students abroad are usually accepted by both faculties and fellow-students; so that the need for any special machinery of counsel and advice from a representative of their own Government did not seem urgent.

Special problems, however, are frequently encountered in the desire of Oriental students to acquire vocational training along with their academic studies. There is much complaint in China, it appeared, that returned students are not practically equipped for the professions they seek to enter.[7] The major cause of this, it was explained, is twofold: on the one hand, the nature of the legal restrictions imposed upon wage-earning activities of persons admitted under student passports in such countries as the United States and Canada; on the other, the reluctance of employers in these countries to accept foreign apprentices. As to the former, no early modification of the present status could be hoped for with the general trend for even greater discouragement of any form of immigration that would introduce competi-

7 See below, p. 487.

tion for jobs.[8] Attention was directed, however, to a series of treaties signed in recent years between various European powers for the exchange of apprentices.[9] It was suggested that under the provisions of these agreements it might be possible for students admitted under a student visa to continue their efforts to gain practical experience in industry and business under the provisions of special agreements, to be concluded between China and the foreign powers in application to limited numbers and for limited periods.

The reluctance of foreign employers to give such experience to foreign students was explained with the fact that obviously their purpose in training apprentices is to assure themselves of a continuing supply of skilled workers acquainted with the processes of their own works. If they were to be induced to increase the employment given to foreign students, a purely philanthropic motive would have to be appealed to. It was stated that in certain types of enterprise there was less difficulty because of a relationship of co-operation rather than of competition between employers in the West and the East. Thus, banking institutions are more likely to accept responsibility for the training of young men recommended by their foreign correspondents than, for instance, engineering works.

This introduced the next topic for discussion, the part played by returned students in the vocational life of the Orient.[10] " The chief trouble," said a Chinese member, " is that they cannot apply what they have learned." Both native and foreign residents in China seemed to agree with this to some extent. The difficulty, it was recognized, lies largely in their lack of practical training for the reasons just explained. There was much agreement with the view that this problem might best be solved if students did not immediately proceed to the West upon graduation but first entered such positions as they might be able to secure in their chosen line of work, to be sent abroad later by their employers for graduate study on the understanding that they will be taken back. A young foreign resident in China made

[8] In the spring of 1931, the United States Secretary of Labor suspended for the time being the admittance of foreign industrial students, about two hundred of whom had annually entered under reciprocal arrangements with other countries to gain experience in industry. (In practice, only very few American young men had availed themselves of this privilege.) The order does not extend to industrial students sent to the United States by foreign governments or by American business houses desirous to train foreigners in their employment abroad (*Industrial and Labour Information* [International Labour Office, May 18, 1931], p. 257).

[9] Typical of such agreements, of which there are many, is the following between France and Germany of August 13, 1928: Student employees of either sex, as a rule not over thirty years of age, to a number not exceeding 500 a year, are granted permission to take up employment in an industrial or commercial establishment in the territory of the other state to perfect their vocational and linguistic knowledge. As a general rule, permission shall be given for one year; in exceptional cases it may be prolonged for six months. At the initiative of Denmark, similar agreements between several states have been extended to young agricultural workers. For a general account of this interesting development, see *International Labour Review*, August, 1930, pp. 199–208.

[10] For a preliminary survey of " American Returned Students of China " see an article with that title by Chih Meng in *Pacific Affairs* for January, 1931.

a strong plea for the assistance of foreign business houses in dealing with this problem:

" The family basis on which Chinese business is carried on offers no opening for outsiders. Many of these students find on their return that the high motives with which they have equipped themselves to help advance Chinese commerce and industry are unappreciated. Unless their own family has use for their services, they find themselves out of work.

" Foreign business is prejudiced against the employment of these young Chinese and does not co-operate with those who are trying to place them. It is probably just a matter of conservatism. Instead of being unemployed, embittered, and a source of antiforeign feeling, these returned students could serve as a most valuable liaison between foreign business and Chinese markets."

A Chinese member thought that the fault lies to some extent with the students themselves or with those who are training them:

" We have a vocational bureau for returned students in Shanghai, and we need more such bureaus in other parts of China to deal with this rather serious problem. But lack of such guidance is not the only difficulty. Too many students come back from abroad with wrong impressions. They demand too much, are not willing to start from the bottom. Foreign business firms would take these men as assistants; but they will not accept the rather humble positions they are offered. There is, in fact, quite a demand for assistants who speak Chinese. But when the returned students insist upon being employed in more responsible positions, I am afraid the trouble is that too many of them ' do not have the goods.' "

In spite of this diversity of views, there was agreement with the practical suggestion that the value of foreign graduate study for Chinese students could be greatly enhanced if foreign firms in China were to offer more frequently scholarships of their own to promising young Chinese in their employment with the understanding that they will be re-employed upon their return.

II. EDUCATIVE CULTURAL CONTACTS

This meeting, at the request of the Program Committee, endeavored to avoid topics that would conflict with the subjects already scheduled for consideration by special, technical groups and for future research, and limited its scope to " suggestions for increasing cultural contacts in the Pacific area on the higher levels." After a number of such suggestions had briefly been made by members, it became evident that, in the main, they grouped themselves under three major headings — each of them dealing, as it happened, with one distinctive phase of the task represented by the general desire to further international understanding. They will therefore here be considered under appropriate subheadings.

APPRECIATION OF THE ARTS AS AN ELEMENT IN INTERNATIONAL UNDERSTANDING

An Australian member invited international co-operation in efforts to record aboriginal music in different parts of the Pacific area. The University of Adelaide, she reported, had made a promising beginning; but the work was held up through lack of funds. Anthropologists and musicians working together were needed to preserve valuable material and make it accessible to the world. It appeared that in China and elsewhere an interest was developing along similar lines;[11] and the suggestion was made that the Institute of Pacific Relations itself promote a research project in this field. However, after further discussion it was agreed that for the present the national councils particularly interested must be content with a knowledge of the genuine interest in this type of study by scholars and musicians throughout the world.

Another suggestion was for an inclusive study, by the Institute, of the question: " How may native forms of architecture be preserved with modern forms of building construction, and in keeping with the requirements of modern town planning? " The member who suggested this study had in mind not so much the archaeological interest in the preservation of ancient buildings as the enhanced appreciation for the culture of a foreign nation that comes with a knowledge (from travel or from pictures) of its native architecture in its most developed forms. He said:

" There are really two aspects of this matter: the preservation of historical remains that threaten to be destroyed by neglect, and the embodiment of traditional building forms in the new construction enterprises that are necessarily influenced by modern requirements. Of the first, such work as that now carried on by the Chinese Government, by the Japanese Government in Korea,[12] and by the Dutch in Bali and elsewhere [13] may be taken as examples. Of the second we have interesting examples in both China and Japan, and also in many other parts of the Pacific area, including the Philippines, French Indo-China, Hawaii, and the national parks in Continental United States. The difficulties have been set forth in one of the data papers before this Conference,[14] and several of the national and local governments in the Pacific area have given evidence of their interest in this phase. What is needed is a correlative survey of what is being done in this matter in the different countries."

Several members referred to existing literature and to the increasing attention given by architects to the problem under discussion. It was thought that some architectural organization or one of the research foundations might be interested in such a study.

The possibilities of various educational enterprises with the aim of making the peoples of the Pacific better acquainted with each other's artistic endeavors were briefly mentioned. It was suggested that the East is as much in need of exhibitions of the best modern work in the Occident as the West

[11] See, e.g., the chapter by Y. R. Chao in the *Symposium on Chinese Culture* (China Council) and the chapter by Hisao Tanabe in the Japanese symposium presented at the Kyoto Conference. *Western Influences in Modern Japan* (University of Chicago Press, 1931).

[12] See Tadashi Sekino, *Ancient Remains and Relics in Korea* (Japan Council).

[13] A. D. A. de Kat Angelino, *Colonial Policy*, II, 345–47.

[14] Ino Dan, *The Reconstruction of Tokyo and Aesthetic Problems of Architecture* (Japan Council).

is in need of more frequent and more comprehensive showings of the work of living Oriental artists. An American member reported that it was hoped in the United States to follow up the recent survey of Far Eastern art in the public collections of that country [15] with some study of the methods used in making these collections effective instruments of education.

TRAVEL AS AN EDUCATIVE EXPERIENCE IN INTERNATIONAL UNDERSTANDING

Members from several countries commented on the large part played by tourist and other travel in the creation of cultural contacts and offered practical suggestions for making these contacts more valuable. A Chinese member regretted that it was no longer the practice in his own country to provide travelers with educated guides. Owing to commercial propaganda, shopping had asumed too large an importance in the time-table of foreign visitors. But persons with genuinely intellectual and aesthetic interests also found it hard to obtain accurate information. Others testified to the fact that even experts, unless they have much time at their disposal, find it exceedingly difficult to carry on serious studies in the museums of China and Japan; with stimulation from the right sources, they thought, the authorities might be induced to give more attention to provision of labels or descriptive leaflets (if not complete catalogues) in English or French.[16] Facilities for guidance probably would have to be provided by interested outside organizations. A more active co-operation between the government railways, the commercial tourist bureaus, the travel departments of banks, educational institutions, and international associations might result in the creation of better opportunities for intelligent sight-seeing and study. In some cases, it was suggested, national councils or local groups of the Institute itself might function as the co-ordinating link in such efforts by appointing committees to look into this matter and to keep in touch with other committees and agencies having the same object at heart.[17]

But even such formal organization if it could be effected would not suffice, one member suggested, to meet the entire need. Even with excellent guidance through the museums and places of historical and artistic im-

[15] Benjamin March, *China and Japan in Our Museums* (data paper, Kyoto Conference) ; see also the continuation of that study in *Progress of Chinese Studies in the United States of America* (American Council).

[16] Even more ambitious plans to provide students with facilities for museum study are on foot in Peiping, where a special building for this purpose is under consideration.

[17] At the later meeting, scheduled to consider practical activities to promote education for international understanding, the suggestion was made that greater effort might be made to secure organized travel of an educational character in the Pacific area. An Australian member mentioned in this connection the student tour of the Far East organized by Sydney University; an American member, various student parties to the Far East arranged by universities in California and Oregon. Debating teams also served a useful purpose if they were used to further international understanding. Grateful allusion was made also to an organized effort on the part of Peiping members of the China Council to help members of the present Conference in making their visits to North China worth while in furthering their various personal and group interests.

portance, travelers could not come close to the culture of the country visited unless they had access to its homes. Both in the West and in the East, visitors desire above all, he said, to enjoy personal relations with their intellectual equals. Efforts to help bring about such contacts are already in some instances successfully made by such organizations as branches of the English-speaking Union, International House, and various special committees for fostering international friendship, both in the East and in the West. The hope was expressed that the national councils of the Institute would co-operate with such agencies and inquire how such facilities might be extended where they are most needed — that is, primarily in localities where there are many students from other Pacific countries.

LITERATURE IN ITS EFFECT ON MUTUAL UNDERSTANDING

Under this heading suggestions ranging all the way from books for children to reference materials for scientific research workers were made. One member gave a brief description of the present status of the movement to make the folklore of all peoples available to the children of the world. While samples of Oriental folklore are to be found in the children's literature of many lands, she said, the distribution is quite uneven; and many treasures of folklore which might help to interest children in other peoples and races so far have remained unexplored. The suggestion was made that each national council appoint someone (or request some agency) in its country to make a list of published folklore available for translation and popular adaptation.

Several members of the group referred to the importance of early reading and story-telling upon the formation of appreciative attitudes toward foreign cultures.[18] No agreement was reached, however, as to practical ways in which the translation and production of suitable books might best be stimulated; this, it was felt, required further inquiry. Even greater was the concern expressed over the prejudicial tone of the information about Pacific countries to be found in school textbooks. An impetus had been given to this discussion by the publication in a Shanghai newspaper, a few days previously, of charges contained in a Japanese study of Chinese school textbooks. Both in Occidental and in Oriental schoolbooks, it was revealed, misinformation about other Pacific countries is given, not necessarily with the aim of creating animosities, but often from mistaken patriotic zeal or simply from lack of knowledge.[19]

An animated discussion developed at the later meeting between Chinese members on the question whether the antiforeign expressions contained in Chinese books and posters represent only a passing phase or must be con-

[18] See *Race Attitudes in Children,* data paper before the Kyoto Conference (American Council).

[19] Conversation between interested members outside the round-table meetings revealed that misinformation and animus against other Pacific countries may be found also in other forms of literature for children and adults and has, in some cases, been corrected after protests to the publishers. In this connection a guidebook, an encyclopedia, and a camp-craft handbook were mentioned.

sidered a permanent danger to the creation of realistic attitudes on international affairs.   Foreign members explained that, in varying degrees, they all faced this difficulty.   It was finally decided that the examination of the teaching about other countries, more particularly in school textbooks, be made the subject of a joint project of inquiry by the various national councils; and the International Program Committee was requested to appoint a small committee to draft such a project which was visualized more in the nature of an initial general survey rather than a deep-going scientific analysis, such as would have to be made by specialists in educational psychology.[20]

Yet another side of the problem of making reading a more effective means of international understanding was seen in the relative paucity of well-translated current fiction and *belles-lettres* that permit an insight into the contemporary life and thought of culturally distant peoples.[21]   The novel, it was explained, is an ancient but undeveloped medium of literary expression in the Far East.   An Occidental member who had recently inquired into the availability of such literature in Japan that might be suitable for re-publication in the Occident had tentatively come to the conclusion that possibly the short story and a certain type of newspaper " feature story " are more characteristic and informing of contemporary expression in that country than the novel.[22]   The question was raised whether Oriental readers are not, perhaps, equally in need of translations of books permitting an insight into the national psychologies of the West that cannot be gained from either translated newspaper articles or the more specialized literature available to the scholar.   The appalling cost of Western books and periodicals in China, owing to the present exchange rate, was also mentioned as a difficulty.

This led to a general discussion of the part played by the press as a means of acquainting peoples in different countries with the real sentiments and attitudes of citizens,[23] and of possible means of supplementing this

[20] Shortly after the Conference the subject came up strongly in the Shanghai Municipal Council, apropos of grants in aid recommended to be given to Chinese private schools in the International Settlement.   The Education Board recommended a condition to the effect that " patriotism and good citizenship should be encouraged in all schools, and no instruction likely to offend national susceptibilities or to create interracial animosity shall be permitted."   Allotments of the grants will be made on the advice of a Chinese Committee of the Board, and the co-operation of the Mayor of Greater Shanghai was invited to see that the Chinese schools, while conforming to the regulations and requirements of the Chinese Government, also adopt such changes as might be necessary to bring them within the scope of the conditions set for the allotment of these grants (*North China Daily News,* December 7, 1931).   See also *Feetham Report,* II, 206.

[21] See Pearl S. Buck, " China in the Mirror of Her Fiction," *Pacific Affairs,* February, 1930, pp. 155–156.

[22] Both in China and in Japan there is criticism that modern novelists are too much influenced by Western models and so, both in form and in content, fail to represent the essential traits of their own people.   There are schools in both countries, however, which cultivate a modern literature in direct continuation of the national traditions and in keeping with the prevailing national psychology.

[23] See the data paper by Thomas Ming-heng Chao, *The Foreign Press in China* (China Council).

source of information. The discussion of Manchurian problems during the previous days of the Conference had given the members an appreciation for the devastating effect which misleading news dispatches and articles can produce upon public opinion. Members of the Institute's international secretariat described efforts under way to secure more and better translations from the Oriental press for Occidental readers who so far do not have even as much direct contact with public opinion in China and Japan, through their newspapers, as readers have in the Far East with public opinion in the West.[24] The part played by *Pacific Affairs*, the Institute's own journal, as a means of supplementing in this respect the press in the different Pacific countries was appreciated; and suggestions were made as to ways in which this service might be further enlarged if the Institute's resources should permit.[25]

Lastly, various suggestions were reviewed that aimed at increasing the literary resources of those professionally concerned in the study of Pacific problems. One of these was to the effect that scientific periodicals should provide at least the titles if not abstracts of their principal contributions in several languages. It was recommended that in Japanese, Chinese, and Dutch periodicals, in addition to such aids, the captions of tables and graphs be given in English as well as the original language. A need was also expressed for more reading lists and study outlines to stimulate a wider use of existing literature on Pacific subjects among different types of readers. It was thought that a report on what is already being done along this line in the various countries might be helpful in suggesting further activity. The possibility that the Institute itself might establish circulating libraries for use by national councils and associated groups in the Pacific countries was briefly mentioned.

MISCELLANEOUS SUGGESTIONS

The Subcommittee on Cultural Relations of the International Program Committee had reported in favor of a survey of research institutions and organizations in China and Japan, and of the projects on which they are engaged. The suggestion was made at the round table that such a survey should also include groups and institutions, other than those primarily engaged in research, that have the purpose of fostering international cultural relations in the Pacific area, and of their periodicals and other publications.

There was a general recommendation, not discussed in detail, for a joint study by the various national councils of the two great modern mediums of popular education, the motion picture and radio, in their influence on mutual understanding between peoples of the Pacific. The subject of the effect of

---

[24] A special committee was appointed by the Pacific Council to consider the subject of translations and recommended that the Central Secretariat be authorized, in cooperation with the national councils concerned, to take measures for extending the translation service of the Institute.

[25] The Pacific Council subsequently considered at length proposals for extending the usefulness both of *Pacific Affairs* and of other Institute publications.

motion pictures on international attitudes again came up prominently at the later meeting on the educational functioning of the Institute itself. Instances were given of misinformation disseminated in both directions: Oriental members of the meeting stated that it was almost necessary to visit the Occident to overcome the persistent direction of attention by American moving pictures to aspects of Western life that are non-typical, derogatory of the finer side of life, and making for wholly false impressions. On the other hand, the complaint was made that Orientals in Western moving pictures are rarely depicted in rôles creditable to their race and country. The American Council, it was stated, already has devoted considerable attention to this matter and is glad to receive further concrete suggestions as to possible ways of dealing with this difficult problem.[26]

The changing position of woman and the change of moral standards in the East under the impact of the West were briefly suggested as in need of comparative studies.

A memorandum submitted by the British group on the *Cultural Relations Syllabus* contained several suggestions by C. Delisle Burns bearing upon the special concern of the present meeting. One of the outstanding causes of misunderstanding between East and West, one of the members suggested, had been indicated by Professor Burns in his reference to differences in manners. While not necessarily requiring profound research, a study of this subject, he thought, might contribute toward the improvement of the mutual impressions gained in personal contact.

The meeting ended with expressions of the hope that many of the topics which it had been possible to review only very briefly might become the subjects of more thorough inquiry on the part of the appropriate committees of the Institute and of the various national councils.

III. THE EDUCATIONAL FUNCTIONING OF THE INSTITUTE OF PACIFIC RELATIONS

As has already been explained in the introductory note to this chapter, the third round-table meeting included in its scope was held toward the end of the Conference for the purpose of considering what practical action might be taken on specific suggestions made throughout the various sessions to improve or enlarge the educational functioning of the Institute. The suggestions considered were not limited, however, to recommendations for international action through the central organization. On the contrary, emphasis was laid at this round table upon experiments and studies that might during the next biennial period be initiated by the various national councils. Some of the topics considered by this meeting represented the practical aspects of

[26] An American foundation has recently initiated a comprehensive project of research in this field and, in an initial study, has experimented with new and promising scientific methods of research to evaluate the actual impressions produced by moving pictures upon the attitudes of children, as regards both the immediate impact and the more lasting influences.

subjects previously considered in other round-table meetings and have, for the sake of conciseness, been added to the reports on their proceedings. Others emerged for the first time at this later meeting. The first of these was the fundamental problem of language.

THE LANGUAGE OF THE PACIFIC

The round table had before it the following memorandum from two members of the American group on this problem as it affects the practices of the Institute itself:

It is only through the courtesy of the non-English-speaking members of the Institute that all its proceedings have so far taken place in English, without the use of interpreters. To continue this arrangement indefinitely is undesirable for the following reasons:

1. It places one of the most essential features of the Institute's effort to produce international understanding on a basis of sacrifice and privilege rather than of mutuality.
2. It entails concrete limitations upon the functioning of the non-English-speaking groups in the Institute, by
   a) Burdening them with the expense of translation, and
   b) Preventing them from co-opting for personal participation in Institute conferences and committee work persons of outstanding competence and learning who do not happen to possess a fluent command of the English language.
3. It deprives the Institute members of the wholesome experience of having personally to meet one of the greatest difficulties in the way of international understanding the world over and thereby makes many problems under review by the Institute appear easier of solution than they actually are.

We suggest that the Pacific Council appoint a committee composed of one member of each of the component national councils:

1. To inquire into and evaluate the methods by which other international bodies are endeavoring to deal with the problems of diversity of language among their constituents;
2. To report on other possible methods that may have been suggested by various people and groups, as regards
   a) Methods of mutual interpretation,
   b) The uses of auxiliary international languages;
3. To report on the progress made in different Pacific countries with efforts to spread a knowledge of the languages spoken in other Pacific countries;
4. To review, more specifically, the efforts made by the different national councils of the Institute to stimulate the provision of facilities for such language study;
5. To consider possible ways in which the Institute might best meet its own immediate language problem while larger efforts to overcome the inequalities inherent in its present reliance upon the use of English are under way.

While there was sympathy at the round table with the proposal to set up a committee of inquiry into this question, the discussion disclosed an even greater complexity of the problem than this brief memorandum conveyed. Doubt was raised as to whether it was profitable to look into the auxiliary language question at all. A seeming implication that Western members might in large degree equip themselves with a knowledge of Eastern languages also was considered by some as impracticable.[27]   Oriental members of the round table seemed to be less conscious of the problem than Western ones because those in the Far East who are interested in international affairs have long been in the habit of looking upon English as their second language.   It was said that frequently there was a *sotto voce* interpretation going on at the round tables for the benefit of members who did not feel sure that they thoroughly understood what was being said.   It was also revealed that frequently an Oriental member will ask some other member of his group to make the oral comment for him that he desires to contribute.   This expedient was regarded as not altogether satisfactory because it gives an impression of solid group opinion in discussion groups that are intended to provide for an exchange of individual opinion.[28]   It was admitted that fluency in the use of English does enter somewhat into the selection of the Far Eastern conference membership.   An American member reported that the Institute had been criticized in Europe for taking no cognizance of the large number of Orientals who are more familiar with French or German than with English.[29]   It was stated that other international organizations, such as the International Federation of University Women, do not find themselves unduly hampered by permitting members to speak in their own language and by having interpreters provided for them.   It was recommended that the Program Committee appoint a subcommittee to study the whole situation and make a report.[30]   Several members thought that the problem involved in making the results of Institute conferences and research available to interested groups that do not read English was equally important; and the need was emphasized for a concerted plan to have translations made available.[31]

EXCHANGE OF EDUCATIONAL EXPERIENCE

Under this heading the Program Committee had suggested for discussion the following questions:

[27] Yet missionary conferences in China are frequently held in Chinese even when half the members are from the Occident. The use of English is more common at mixed conferences in China when a majority of the members are university graduates or when there are Chinese representatives in about equal numbers from the south and from the north who find English the easiest medium of communication between themselves.

[28] At several round tables in the present Conference this appearance of national group solidarity led to unfortunate misunderstandings.

[29] An illustration of this failure was given by the formal Conference procedure at Hangchow, where prominent provincial and municipal officials addressed the members through English-speaking interpreters although they spoke French fluently. The formation of a Soviet Union council of the Institute also is introducing a new complication for future meetings.

[30] This task was subsequently remitted by the Pacific Council to the International Secretariat.

[31] Both the Chinese and the Japanese councils are publishing reports on the Institute's conferences in the languages of their own countries; but the complete translation and publication of official Institute publications in these languages have hitherto proved prohibitive in cost.

a) How may the educational activities and methods of the different national groups, and the results obtained, most effectively be used to help other member groups enrich and improve their activities in this field?

b) What types of educational activity carried on or contemplated by national councils are most in need of international co-operation? How may such co-operation best be effected?

A Chinese member suggested as a first answer that the Institute, through its official journal, *Pacific Affairs*, contribute more frequently accounts of interesting national or local experiments and achievements in the general field of education for international understanding. He also drew attention to the need for local units if the study of Pacific problems was to be more widely diffused. In this connection he gave an account of an experiment carried on at Shanghai University after the second Honolulu Conference of the Institute, to stage a similar conference for faculty and students. One outcome of this experience had been the formation of an International Relations Library and Club at that institution. The holding of the next World Student Federation at Honolulu, in 1932, might provide for an experience of this sort on an international scale. Fellowship groups in California and elsewhere also had shown that conference and discussion need not be limited in the Institute's program to its formal biennial sessions, but that much useful educational work could be done through co-operating with other conference organizations.[32] A member of the New Zealand group, which at this Conference happened to consist almost entirely of educators, explained this fact with the circumstance that in his country the interest in Pacific affairs is most strongly represented in the educational organizations and institutions.

"In the Workers' Education Association, lectures and discussions of international problems by qualified university tutors are frequent; and many of them use materials prepared by the Institute. In the secondary schools many teachers aim at the creation of tolerant international attitudes on the basis of knowledge. Institute literature and methods have shaped a course on current history in my own institution, which proved an unqualified success. In fact, the interest aroused by this course among faculty and students is largely responsible for my presence at this Conference. They decided that I should go to China to bring back to them all possible information. Many other schools are equally interested. We must bring all this information to bear upon the ideals and motives in our school systems if we are going to build a new social order around the Pacific in which acquisitiveness will give way to co-operation. Only the schools can bring about new attitudes based on fuller knowledge. We should, therefore, more and more think of ways

[32] At a later session, reviewing the Conference procedure, it came out that opportunities for such participation of the national councils in the educational activities of other organizations are particularly strong immediately after one of the biennial conferences of the Institute, when interest has been aroused in the press, and members return equipped with new information. The suggestion was made that it would be helpful for the purpose of such diffusion of knowledge if members could have, in addition to the data papers, a preliminary brief summary account of the conference to aid their memories. In response to this suggestion, the Institute's publicity director prepared a mimeographed edition of his press releases and general review articles in time for members to take with them at the end of the conference.

in which these problems can be brought closer to the understanding of boys and girls through our schools."

Another member of the New Zealand group said that there are in New Zealand four such clubs or study groups organized directly through the New Zealand Council of the Institute; and they are doing excellent work.   In addition to Institute literature, the publications contributed by the Carnegie Endowment have been found helpful.   But apart from opportunities of stimulating and aiding such efforts as these, the Institute would sooner or later have to concern itself more thoroughly with the part played by education in international relations:

" To ' help the individual find his best possible adjustment to the environment into which he is coming ' is the aim of all education.   But it has not yet been thoroughly applied internationally.   The League of Nation's Committee on Intellectual Co-operation is facing this problem.   It has been expounded by Professor Alfred Zimmern in his *Learning and Leadership,* by Raymond B. Fosdick in *The Old Savage and the New Civilization,* and again, most recently, by Arnold J. Toynbee.[33] We have learned that our social sciences are far behind the need of the times. Dr. Zimmern has told us that the League cannot properly function because the intellectual foundations have not yet been laid.   We have yet to build the fundamental attitudes for world-peace."

A member of the Hawaii group gave it as his growing conviction that the Institute should provide the machinery for the correlation of the needed educational materials in the same way as it is providing for that of research work carried on in the Pacific area.   Other members thought that progress could be made if the Institute were to devote more time to educational problems at future conferences.   A member of the Research Committee pointed out that no sufficiently definite project in the educational field has yet been brought before it to enlist its co-operation in the study of one or more of the scientific aspects of the subject before this meeting.   A recommendation was, however, adopted and later transmitted by the Pacific Council to the international secretariat that every national council of the Institute which had not yet done so be urged to set up a committee on education further to explore the questions raised at the round tables here reported.   And it was further recommended that reports on the educational activities of the national groups be made the basis, at the next biennial conference, for a program of joint action by an international education committee of the Institute, to parallel the existing International Research Committee.

INSTITUTE LITERATURE

Other questions suggested by the International Program Committee were:

[33] *World Sovereignty and World Culture — the Trend of International Affairs since the War,* a paper read at the Fourth Conference of Institutions for the Scientific Study of International Relations, Copenhagen, June, 1931; reprinted in *Pacific Affairs* for September, 1931.

a) To what extent have the publications of the Institute and of the various national councils been found useful for educational purposes other than adding to the knowledge of specialists? How may such usefulness be increased?

b) What types or forms of publication may be recommended to the Institute councils for experiments in popular education?

To some extent the first of these questions has already been dealt with in the previous section. Unfortunately, lack of time did not permit a close scrutiny of the part played by Institute literature in the more popular educational activities of its own national councils or of allied organizations.[34] Attention was drawn to the opportunities which individual members of the Institute have to make their sets of Institute publications accessible to a larger public by depositing them in libraries. It was suggested further that national councils might take further steps to get a wider circulation in their respective countries for those data papers that are of general interest. There are two ways of doing this: their re-publication in local periodicals, and the printing of a somewhat larger edition than is needed for Institute purposes to have copies available for distribution at low cost. One member suggested that national councils might prepare lists of libraries and institutions to which sets of these documents should be sent. One of the national councils had already, before the present Conference, circularized such a list and taken orders for complete sets at an inclusive price.

The two symposia on national cultures, the Japanese and the Chinese, were singled out for mention as likely to appeal to a wide audience and therefore justifying publication through commercial channels, which, in fact, had already been arranged for. The Philippine group had already started such a survey, sections of which had been contributed to the present Conference in the form of data papers on specific cultural topics. It was suggested that there would be a market for a smiliar comprehensive survey by specialists on the more important aspects of the present cultural status of the Occident. The newly created Soviet Union Council, it was stated, had already expressed its special interest in this aspect of the Institute's work.

A Japanese member suggested that a second series of symposia might take for its theme the cultural debt that each of the Pacific countries owes the

---

[34] At a general session reviewing the conference as a whole, one of the Canadian members made the following suggestions: " Conference papers seem to divide themselves into four categories: (1) those prepared by national groups for the education of their own members; (2) those prepared as part of the continuous and fundamental research work of the Institute; (3) those that have a direct bearing on the program of the conference itself, submitted either by the central secretariat or by national groups; and (4) those that a national group has submitted because it has some interest on a subject bearing on the problems of the Pacific and has a contribution to make upon it. Either the central secretariat or the Program Committee should direct the members who are likely to come to the conference as regards the emphasis to be placed on the respective data. Perhaps a selection could be made so that members could concentrate on those papers that would be most helpful to prepare them for intelligent participation. But this would mean that the papers must be in hand some three or four months before the conference convenes."

other countries. Japan, for example, might thus acknowledge its indebtedness to Chinese literature, to the development of modern education in Germany, to the reinterpretation of world-history by American scholars, and so on. There was agreement that such literary contributions, to help the peoples of the Pacific realize their interdependence, would have to be planned over a longer period than merely in preparation for a particular conference; but that there was no need for complete uniformity if any of the national councils saw their way to do something in this matter at once.

CONFERENCE AND EDUCATION FOR INTERNATIONAL UNDERSTANDING

This chapter, and with it our account of the round-table proceedings of the Fourth Conference of the Institute of Pacific Relations, may fittingly be concluded with the following extracts from an address by the president of the Conference, Dr. Hu Shih:

" I believe the greatest significance of a conference of this kind lies in its educational value. There are three things which are valuable in this connection: First there are the data papers. . . . The second thing is the personal contact, made not only during the progress of the conference but to last all our lives. Last, but not least, is the conference itself. To attend a conference of this kind, to think for nations and for peoples, to listen to the grievances and explanations from all sides, to try to see a national issue in the light of its international significance — in the light of the difficulties of the various peoples themselves — so seek solutions for these problems, to see that those who hold opposite views from our own are not necessarily stupid or evil-minded — these experiences can only be gained through attendance of a conference of this kind. . . .

" All forms of education have to confront three classes of people: First, those who can be educated without much effort — the best students; second, those who cannot be easily educated, whose minds are set, either through prejudice or through mental senility; third, the middle class between these two — those who can be educated for better or for worse. This is the class for which education is most needed. After all, we cannot, all of us, be expected easily to give up our prejudices and habits long formed. We must recognize that each of us has these three possibilities in him: he may be very liberal on certain things, very conservative on other things, and easily influenced one way or the other in yet other things. So, these three degrees of teachability are present not only in any large group of men and women but in every one of us. Through a conference of this kind, through reading documents prepared by opposite camps of thought, and through coming into direct contact with people — arguing with them, listening to their arguments, trying to think well of our opponents — through all these processes we hope to remove in ourselves those long-formed habits and prejudices. So, I believe, education is the keynote for all of us at this Conference."

APPENDICES

APPENDIX I

LIST OF CONFERENCE MEMBERS, OBSERVERS, AND STAFF

AUSTRALIA

† TRISTAN BUESST, Writer, Melbourne
†H. W. GEPP, Chairman, Development and Migration Commission, Macleod, Victoria
*† MISS ELEANOR HINDER, National Committee of the Y.W.C.A., Shanghai
MISS JANET MITCHELL, Journalist, Sydney
* SIR WILLIAM HARRISON MOORE, K.B.E., C.M.G., Professor Emeritus of the University of Melbourne, Australian Delegate to the League of Nations Assembly, 1927–29 (*Chairman of the Group*)
MRS. ERNEST SCOTT, Melbourne
DR. E. J. STUCKEY, Community Hospital, Tientsin
MRS. E. J. STUCKEY, Community Hospital, Tientsin
MISS MURIEL SWAIN, Labor Statistician, Sydney

CANADA

* J. MACKINTOSH BELL, Mining Engineer, Almonte, Ontario
W. M. BIRKS, Henry Birks & Sons, Montreal, Quebec
C. A. BOWMAN, Editor, *Citizen*, Ottawa, Ontario
C. J. BURCHELL, K.C., Barrister, Halifax
* THE HON. VINCENT MASSEY, former Canadian Minister to the United States of America, Port Hope, Ontario (*Chairman of the Group*)
NORMAN MACKENZIE, Professor of Law, Toronto
DR. ROBERT McCLURE, Medical Missionary, Honan, China
† MRS. R. F. McWILLIAMS, Writer, Winnipeg
ADJUTOR SAVARD, Journalist, Montreal
† GEORGE SMITH, Professor of History, University of Alberta, Edmonton

SECRETARIES

GEORGE FULFORD   GUY ROGERS
† ALAN O. GIBBONS   MISS B. WINTERS

CHINA

* CHANG POLING, President, Nankai University, Tientsin
T. B. CHANG, General Manager, Shun Pao, Shanghai
*† L. T. CHEN, Director, Extension and Research Department, Kincheng Bank, Shanghai
R. C. CHEN, Bank of China, Shanghai
TA CHEN, Professor of Sociology, Tsinghua University, Peiping
† FRANKLIN L. HO, Director, Committee on Social and Economic Research, Nankai University, Tientsin
* C. L. HSIA, President, Medhurst College, Shanghai

* Chairmen of round tables.   † Secretaries of round tables.

503

Hsu Shuhsi, Professor of Political Science, Yenching University, Peiping

Hsu Singloh, General Manager, National Commercial Bank, Shanghai (*Chairman of the Group*)

*Hu Shih, Educational Director, China Foundation, Professor of Philosophy, Peking National University (*President of the Conference*)

T. K. King, China Merchants Steam Navigation Co., Shanghai

†T. Z. Koo, London Mission, Peiping

Y. C. Koo, Manager, Chang Foo Bank, Shanghai

O. S. Lieu, General Manager, Shanghai Portland Cement Company, Shanghai

C. S. Liu, President, Asiatic Trading Corporation; former President, Chinese Eastern Railway, Shanghai.

Herman C. E. Liu, President, University of Shanghai

Mrs. Herman C. E. Liu, General Secretary, W.C.T.U., Shanghai

S. Francis Liu, Attorney, Shanghai

S. Y. Liu, Bank of China, Shanghai

C. H. Lowe, Industrial Secretary, Y.M.C.A., Shanghai

E. C. Ning, Vice-President, Northeastern University, Mukden

Quentin Pan, Editor, *China Critic*, Shanghai

Mrs. J. H. Sun, Instructor, Kwang Hua University, Shanghai

*L. K. Tao, Director, Institute of Social Research, Peiping

*V. K. Ting, Director, Geological Survey of China, Peiping

Miss P. S. Tseng, Principal, Yih Fang Girls' School, Changsha

D. C. Wu, Director, Bureau of Statistics, Nanking

Miss Yih-Fang Wu, President, Ginling Girls' College, Nanking

Paul Yen, General Secretary, Y.M.C.A., Mukden

Stewart Yui, University of Shanghai

* Mrs. Sophia H. Chen Zen, Writer, Peiping

SECRETARIES

Mrs. C. Chen
Joseph Chow
Mrs. Y. O. Lee

Wellington Liu
Philip Wang
W. C. Wang

GREAT BRITAIN

*W. G. S. Adams, Professor of Politics, Oxford

Miss Cecil Alexander, London County Council

Dr. H. Chatley, Director, Whangpoo Conservancy Board, Shanghai

C. I. Cooks, Hongkong and Shanghai Banking Corporation, Shanghai

W. C. Costin, Lecturer in Modern History, Oxford

Dame Rachel Crowdy, former Head of Social Questions Section, League of Nations Secretariat

Lionel Curtis, Fellow of All Souls College, Oxford

Mrs. Lionel Curtis

F. A. Firth, British-American Tobacco Co., Ltd., Swatow

Miss Marjorie Giles, Tientsin

E. W. Grey, Hongkong and Shanghai Banking Corporation, Shanghai

*G. E. Hubbard, Diplomatic Adviser to Hongkong and Shanghai Banking Corporation, Shanghai

* Sir Reginald Johnston, former Administrator of Leased Territory of Weihaiwei

JOHN KESWICK, Jardine Matheson & Co., Shanghai
*† ARCHIBALD ROSE, British-American Tobacco Co., Ltd., London (*Chairman of the Group*)
* P. M. ROXBY, Professor of Geography, University of Liverpool
COLIN SCOTT, Butterfield and Swire, Shanghai
W. E. L. SHENTON, Legal Adviser to Executive and Legislative Councils of Hongkong
N. L. SPARKE, Shanghai

SECRETARIES

† PETER FLEMING   † A. D. MARRIS

JAPAN

MITSUTARO ARAKI, Professor of Economics, Tokyo Imperial University
TATSUICHIRO FUNATSU, Member, Shanghai Municipal Council
ZENICHI ITANI, Professor of Economics, Tokyo University of Commerce
KIYOSHI KANAI, Railway Expert
† SHIGEHARU MATSUMOTO, Tokyo Institute of Political and Economic Research
TAMON MAYEDA, Editorial Writer, *Tokyo Asahi Shimbun*
* SHIROSHI NASU, Professor of Agriculture, Tokyo Imperial University
* INAZO NITOBE, Member, House of Peers, Tokyo (*Chairman of the Group*)
TOKUSUKE SAHARA, President, Chengching Shihpao, Mukden
* SOICHI SAITO, General Secretary, Tokyo Y.M.C.A.
MAJOR-GENERAL YASUNOSUKI SATO (Retired), former Member of House of Representatives, Tokyo
JUMPEI SHINOBU, Professor of Law, Waseda University, Tokyo
BUNJI SUZUKI, former President, Japanese Federation of Labor, Kamakura
* KENZO TAKAYANAGI, Professor of Law, Tokyo Imperial University
YUSUKE TSURUMI, Writer, former Member of House of Representatives, Tokyo
KATSUSHI UCHIDA, Managing Director, East Asia Industrial Co., Ltd., Tokyo
KISABURO YOKOTA, Professor of Law, Tokyo Imperial University

SECRETARIES

MRS. ETHEL L. MARTIN   SHUJI SUZUKI
YOSHITAKA SAKAMOTO   † SAMITARO URAMATSU

NEW ZEALAND

* W. T. G. AIREY, Lecturer in History, Auckland University College
H. F. VON HAAST, Barrister, Wellington
R. G. HAMPTON, Secretary, Christchurch Branch, New Zealand Council
MISS A. VERA HAY, Secretary, Auckland Branch, New Zealand Council
J. E. STRACHAN, Headmaster, Rangiora High School (*Chairman of the Group*)
H. C. TENNENT, Accountant, Honolulu

PHILIPPINES

JUAN M. ARELLANO, Consulting Architect, Bureau of Public Works, Philippine Government, Manila

Francisco Benitez, Dean of College of Education, University of the Philippines, Manila

Harold Fey, Professor of Sociology, Union Theological Seminary, Manila

Rafael Palma, President, University of the Philippines, Manila (*Chairman of the Group*)

N. Maronilla Seva, President, Far Eastern College, Manila

SECRETARY

Miss Alice B. Norwood

UNITED STATES

Willis J. Abbot, Editor, *Christian Science Monitor,* Boston

M. Searle Bates, Professor of History, Nanking University

C. R. Bennett, National City Bank, Shanghai

J. Lossing Buck, Professor of Farm Management, University of Nanking

*† E. C. Carter, Secretary-Treasurer, American Council, New York

Everett Case, General Electric Company, New York

Mrs. Everett Case

† J. P. Chamberlain, Professor of Public Law, Columbia University, New York

* Miss Ada L. Comstock, President, Radcliffe College, Cambridge, Mass. (*Vice-Chairman of the Group*)

* R. J. Corbett, Standard Oil Company of New York, Shanghai

David L. Crawford, President, University of Hawaii, Honolulu

Miss Margaret Elliott, Professor of Economics, University of Michigan

Wallace R. Farrington, Publisher, *Honolulu Star-Bulletin,* former Governor of Hawaii

* Jerome D. Greene, Lee, Higginson & Co., New York (*Chairman of the Pacific Council; Chairman of the American Council*)

* E. S. C. Handy, Ethnologist, Bishop Museum, Honolulu

Paul Hopkins, Shanghai Power Company, Shanghai

Theodore J. Kreps, Professor of Economics, Stanford University

Bruno Lasker, New York

Mrs. J. W. Morrisson, League of Women Voters, Groton, Conn.

† Harold S. Quigley, Professor of Political Science, University of Minnesota

Chester H. Rowell, Journalist, Berkeley, Calif.

* Paul Scharrenberg, Secretary, California Federation of Labor, San Francisco

Corwin S. Shank, Lawyer, Seattle

Mrs. F. Louis Slade, League of Women Voters, New York

Mrs. Sarah Bixby Smith, Writer, Los Angeles

J. Leighton Stuart, President, Yenching University, Peiping

SECRETARIES

† Joseph Barnes † Frederick V. Field
† E. C. Carter, Jr. Miss Elizabeth Miner
Miss Edith Chamberlain Miss Catherine Porter

OBSERVERS

Arnold D. A. de Kat Angelino, Netherlands

Dame Adelaide Anderson, International Labour Office, Geneva

* IWAO F. AYUSAWA, International Labour Office, Geneva
JENNINGS WONG, International Labour Office, Geneva
* CAMILLE PONE, International Labour Office, Geneva
PAUL LANGEVIN, League of Nations, Geneva
FRANK G. WALTERS, League of Nations, Geneva

ROUND-TABLE RECORDERS

W. G. S. ADAMS	BRUNO LASKER
MISS CECIL ALEXANDER	MRS. Y. O. LEE
JOSEPH BARNES	MISS RUTH LI
MRS. EVERETT CASE	W. W. LOCKWOOD
MISS EDITH CHAMBERLAIN	C. H. LOWE
W. C. COSTIN	MRS. NORMAN MACKENZIE
HAROLD E. FEY	A. D. MARRIS
FREDERICK V. FIELD	SHIGEHARU MATSUMOTO
PETER FLEMING	MRS. R. F. MCWILLIAMS
GEORGE T. FULFORD	MISS B. METZGER
A. O. GIBBONS	MISS ELIZABETH MINER
MISS MARJORIE GILES	MISS ALICE NORWOOD
W. LEON GODSHALL	MISS CATHERINE PORTER
MISS ELIZABETH GREEN	J. G. SAKAMOTO
R. G. HAMPTON	SHUJI SUZUKI
MISS A. VERA HAY	TANEO TAKETA
E. M. HAYES	P. Y. WANG
MISS RUTH HILL	MRS. P. Y. WANG

† MRS. FELIX M. KEESING

CENTRAL SECRETARIAT

CHARLES F. LOOMIS, Acting General Secretary
† ELIZABETH GREEN, Editor, *Pacific Affairs*
CHESTER H. ROWELL, Director of Publicity
† WILLIAM L. HOLLAND, Acting Research Secretary
† FELIX M. KEESING
MRS. MARGUERITE C. MILLER, Office Manager

SECRETARIES AND CONFERENCE STAFF

CORA HARTDEGEN
LUCY KNOX
KATHLEEN MUIR

ELIZABETH BARNES	RUTH MILLER
ELEANOR D. BREED	OLIVE MORGAN
BERTA METZGER	JANET MCTAVISH

APPENDIX II

DATA PAPERS PRESENTED TO THE ROUND TABLES

AMERICAN GROUP

AMERICAN COUNCIL OF LEARNED SOCIETIES. *Progress of Chinese Studies in the United States of America* (102 pp.).

EDWARD C. CARTER. *American Research Fellowships and the Far East* (33 pp.).

EDWARD C. CARTER. *College Entrance Credit in Chinese and Japanese for Occidental Students* (66 pp.).

JOSEPH P. CHAMBERLAIN. *Aliens in the United States* (mimeographed; 16 pp.).

JOSEPH P. CHAMBERLAIN. *Foreign Flags in China's Internal Navigation* (36 pp.).

FREDERICK V. FIELD. *American Participation in the China Consortiums* (198 pp.).

FREDERICK V. FIELD. *A Preliminary Collection of Maps of the Pacific Area.*

ALEXANDER GOLDENWEISER. *Race and Race Relations* (31 pp.).

E. S. CRAIGHILL HANDY. *Cultural Revolution in Hawaii* (40 pp.).

A. D. A. DE KAT ANGELINO. *Colonial Policy* (2 vols.; 530 and 674 pp.).

PING CHIA KUO. *Canton and Salem* (" Some Oriental Influences on Western Culture," Part III; 40 pp.).

BRUNO LASKER. *Filipino Immigration to Continental United States and to Hawaii* (University of Chicago Press; 445 pp.).

LEWIS L. LORWIN. *The Need for World Economic Planning* (16 pp.).

W. H. MALLORY. *Extraterritoriality in China* (mimeographed; 8 pp.).

ROBERT E. PARK. *The Problem of Cultural Differences* (16 pp.).

HAROLD S. QUIGLEY. *An Introductory Syllabus on Far Eastern Diplomacy* (University of Chicago Press; 40 pp.).

H. L. SHAPIRO. *The Chinese Population in Hawaii* (29 pp.).

PHILIP G. WRIGHT. *The American Tariff and Oriental Trade* (177 pp.).

Preliminary Census Statistics of Oriental Residents in Continental United States, 1930 (mimeographed; 5 pp.).

AUSTRALIAN GROUP

K. H. BAILEY. *The Legal Position of Foreigners in Australia* (mimeographed; 13 pp.).

D. B. COPLAND (ed.). " An Economic Survey of Australia," *Annals of the American Academy of Political and Social Science*, Whole No. 158, (November, 1931; 281 pp.).

A. S. KENYON. *The Subjugation of a Province — the Story of the Mallee Country of Victoria* (mimeographed; 20 pp.).

SIR WILLIAM HARRISON MOORE. *The Dominions of the British Commonwealth in the League of Nations* (reprinted from *International Affairs*, X, No. 3 [May, 1931]; 20 pp.).

G. L. WOOD. *Memorandum on the World Depression and the Australian Standard of Living* (mimeographed; 21 pp.).

Trade in the Pacific (reprint of five articles from the *Argus*, Melbourne, June, 1931).

BRITISH GROUP

RALPH ARNOLD. *Notes on the Status of Aliens in Great Britain* (mimeographed; 9 pp.).

C. DELISLE BURNS. *The Standard of Living in China and Japan — an Essay on Policy* (mimeographed; 22 pp.).

P. M. ROXBY. *A Plea for the Systematic Study of the Chinese Population Problem as a Whole* (mimeographed; 12 pp.).

W. F. SPALDING. *The Position of Silver in the Far East* (mimeographed; 8 pp.).

G. WARREN SWIRE. *The Coast and River Trade of China* (mimeographed; 22 pp.).

A. TOYNBEE. *Survey of International Affairs, 1930* (28 pp.).

R. O. WINSTEDT, C.M.G. *The Constitution of the Colony of the Straits Settlements and of the Federated and Unfederated Malay States* (20 pp.).

The Status of Aliens in China (27 pp.).

CANADIAN GROUP

R. K. FINLAYSON, K.C. *The British Commonwealth and Its Relation to Pacific Problems* (9 pp.).

GORDON LINDSAY and D. R. MICHENER. *Legal Status of Aliens Resident in Canada;* H. F. ANGUS. *The Legal Status in British Columbia of Residents of Oriental Race and Their Descendants* (16 pp.).

NORMAN MACKENZIE. *Canadian Tariff Policy — Its Effect on Pacific Trade* (17 pp.).

DUNCAN CAMPBELL SCOTT. *The Administration of Indian Affairs in Canada* (27 pp.).

CHINESE GROUP

MINGCHIEN JOSHUA BAU. *Foreign Navigation in Chinese Waters* (29 pp.).

MINGCHIEN JOSHUA BAU. *The Status of Aliens in China* (36 pp.).

C. C. CHANG. *China's Food Problem* (29 pp.).

THOMAS MING-HENG CHAO. *The Foreign Press in China* (115 pp.).

CHEN HAN-SENG. *Notes on Migration of Nan Min to the Northeast* (31 pp.).

H. D. FONG. *China's Industrialization, a Statistical Survey* (46 pp.).

FRANKLIN L. HO. *Population Movement to the North Eastern Frontier* (51 pp.).

HOU SHU-T'UNG. *Japanese Bank-Notes in Manchuria* (28 pp.).

C. Y. HSIEH and M. C. CHU. *Foreign Interest in the Mining Industry in China* (66 pp.).

SHUHSI HSU. *The Manchurian Dilemma — Force or Pacific Settlement?* (88 pp.).

SHUHSI HSU. *The Manchurian Question* (rev. ed.; 120 pp.).

SHUHSI HSU. *Questions Relating to Manchuria* (30 pp.).

D. K. LIEU. *Foreign Investments in China* (53 pp.).

L. K. TAO. *The Standard of Living among Chinese Workers* (37 pp.).

SOPHIA H. CHEN ZEN (ed.). *Symposium on Chinese Culture* (373 pp.).

 I. V. K. TING. Introduction: " How China Acquired her Civilization."

 II. HU SHIH. " Religion and Philosophy in Chinese History."

 III. TSAI YUAN-PEI. " Painting and Calligraphy."

 IV. Y. R. CHAO. " Music."

 V. CHU CHI-CHIEN. " Architecture: A Brief Historical Account Based on the Evolution of the City of Peking."

 VI. YUI SHANG-YUEN. " Drama."

 VII. HU SHIH. " Literature."

 VIII. H. C. ZEN. " Science: Its Introduction and Development in China."

 IX. A. W. GRABAU. " Palaeontology."

X. W. H. Wong. "Chinese Geology."
XI. Chi Li. "Archaeology."
XII. C. Ping and H. H. Hu. "Recent Progress of Biological Science."
XIII. King Chu. "Education."
XIV. R. Feng. "Agriculture."
XV. Franklin L. Ho. "Industries."
XVI. Pao Swen Tseng. "The Chinese Woman, Past and Present."
XVII. L. K. Tao. "Social Changes."
XVIII. Sophia H. Chen Zen. "Concluding Remarks."

JAPANESE GROUP

Mitsutaro Araki. *Report on the Currency System of China* (94 pp.).

Junshiro Asari. *Development of the Cotton Spinning Industry in Japan* (21 pp.).

Ino Dan. *The Reconstruction of Tokyo and Aesthetic Problems of Architecture* (15 pp.).

Unokichi Hattori. *On the Convenience and Inconvenience of Chinese Characters* (18 pp.).

Zenichi Itani. *The Export of Japanese Capital to China* (36 pp.).

Masutaro Kimura. *Problems of Financial Reforms and Readjustment of Public Loans in China* (25 pp.).

Member of the Japan Economic Committee. *The Recent Customs Tariff Revision in Japan* (9 pp.).

Kokichi Morimoto. *The Efficiency Standard of Living in Japan* (76 pp.).

Akira Nagano. *Development of Capitalism in China* (139 pp.).

Kyushiro Nakayama. *Sinological Researches in Contemporary Japan* (31 pp.).

Shiroshi Nasu. *A Study of Correlation between Factors of Production and the Yields of Arable Land* (15 pp.).

Inazo Nitobe. *Japan's Public Economy and Finance* (42 pp.).

Soichi Saito. *A Study of the Influence of Christianity upon Japanese Culture* (71 pp.).

Major-General Yasunosuke Sato (retired). *Sino-Japanese Problems* (48 pp.).

Tadashi Sekino. *Ancient Remains and Relics in Korea: Efforts toward Research and Preservation* (31 pp.).

Tetsujiro Shidachi. *The Depression of 1930 as It Affected Japan* (28 pp.).

Kenzo Takayanagi. *A General Survey of the History of the Japanese Commercial Law* (35 pp.).

Katsushi Uchida. *The Problem of China's Loan Readjustment* (21 pp.).

Saburo Yamada. *Legal Status of Aliens in Japan* (61 pp.).

NEW ZEALAND GROUP

Sir James Allen, W. N. Benson, Walter Nash, G. H. Scholefield (ed.). *New Zealand Affairs* (L. M. Isitt, Ltd., Christchurch; 241 pp.).

I. W. N. Benson. "Geographical Environment, Population and Resources of New Zealand."
II. Sir Apirana T. Ngata. "Anthropology and the Government of Native Races."
III. G. H. Scholefield. "The People of New Zealand."
IV. H. Belshaw. "Farm Production and Population in New Zealand."
V. T. D. H. Hall. "Asiatic Immigration."

VI. Lloyd Ross. " The Absorption of Immigrants."
VII. E. P. Neale. " New Zealand's External Trade."
VIII. A. H. Tocker. " The Balance of Trade."
IX. Walter Nash. " New Zealand Labour and the Pacific."
X. W. H. Cocker. " The Mandate for Samoa."
XI. G. H. Scholefield. " Japan and New Zealand: An Interesting Trade Agreement."
XII. J. E. Strachan. " Amateur Radio."
T. D. H. Hall. *Status of Aliens in New Zealand* (13 pp.).
Downie Stewart. *New Zealand's Pacific Trade and Tariff* (29 pp.).

PHILIPPINE GROUP

Francisco Benitez. *Educational Progress in the Philippines* (18 pp.).
Hermenegildo Cruz. *Emigration of Filipinos to Hawaii and the United States;*
José G. Sanvictores. *The Administration of Minority Groups* (11 pp.).
Mariano D. Gana. *Social Legislation in the Philippine Islands* (37 pp.).
Maximo M. Kalaw. *The Philippine Question — an Analysis* (90 pp.).
Cecilio Lopez. *The Language Situation in the Philippine Islands* (47 pp.).
Maria Paz Mendoza-Guazon, M.D. *The Status of the Filipino Woman* (5 pp.).

DOCUMENTS ORIGINATING WITH THE CENTRAL SECRETARIAT
A. DATA PAPERS

International Labour Office:
   Migration in the Pacific Area (28 pp.).
   Some Labour Problems in Pacific Dependencies (35 pp.).
   *The Possibilities and Limitations of International Comparisons of Cost of
      Living and Family Budgets* (20 pp.).
Felix M. Keesing. *A Memorandum on the Mandated Territory of Western Samoa
   and American Samoa* (60 pp.).
Carl F. Remer. *Foreign Investments in China* (mimeographed; 49 pp.).
R. H. Tawney. *A Memorandum on Agriculture and Industry in China* (128 pp.).

B. CONFERENCE SYLLABI

Handbook of the Institute of Pacific Relations (55 pp.).
Trade Relations in the Pacific (48 pp.).
China's Economic Development (87 pp.).
Problems of Food and Population in the Pacific Area (37 pp.).
Diplomatic Machinery in the Pacific (by Stephen A. Heald; mimeographed;
   34 pp.).
China's Foreign Relations (51 pp.).
Dependencies and Native Peoples of the Pacific (65 pp.).
Migration in the Pacific (40 pp.).
The Cultural Relations of Pacific Peoples (30 pp.).

APPENDIX III

THE CONFERENCE PROGRAM [1]

9:00–10:45. Trade Relations in the Pacific
Four round tables [2]

11:15–12:15. Continuation of round tables

12:45–2:15. Luncheon and reception for members of the Conference, given by the China Council [3]
Greetings: Hsu Singloh, Chairman of the China Council
Response: Jerome D. Greene, Chairman, Pacific Council
Messages of greeting from Governments [4]
Inaugural address: Hu Shih, President of the Conference
Conference announcements: Charles F. Loomis, Acting General Secretary
Official conference photograph

2:15–2:45. National group meetings [5]

8:30–9:45. General conference session: Symposium on Possibilities and Tendencies of China's Economic Development:

P. M. Roxby. The Geographical Background C. C. Chang. Agriculture
V. K. Ting. Mineral Resources O. S. Lieu. Industrial Growth

THURSDAY, OCTOBER 22

9:10–10:45. China's Economic Development
Four round tables

---

[1] The program here given is that which actually took place as a result of daily, and often more frequent, decisions of the International Program Committee in consultation with the officers of the Conference and the round-table chairmen. In its main lines this program adhered to the agenda worked out in a week's preliminary sessions of the International Program Committee, assisted by subcommittees composed of members especially interested in the different subjects. It has been the general testimony that this elaborate procedure, aided by the presence of a majority of the Conference members in the week preceding the formal opening (owing to the situation explained by the acting general secretary in the Preface), resulted in an unusually careful selection of topics and formulation of questions for discussion. For the sake of readers interested in conference procedure, the exact time schedule is here presented.

[2] Except where especially indicated, both round-table and general meetings of the Conference were open only to Conference members and formally invited guests (the latter only on a few occasions when the presence of available specialists, not members of the Conference, was felt to be desirable).

[3] Through the hospitality of the China Council, a luncheon was given at the same time on each day of the Conference sessions in the International Recreation Club.

[4] See Preface, pp. vi–viii.

[5] This period was reserved for national group meetings on each day of the Conference, when called by national chairmen.

512

11:15–12:15. Continuation of general session: Symposium on Possibilities and Tendencies of China's Economic Development:
HSIA PIN-FANG and G. E. HUBBARD. Finance

8:30–9:45. General conference session: The Feetham Report and the Future of Shanghai
Address by C. L. HSIA
Discussion

FRIDAY, OCTOBER 23

9:00–10:45. China's Economic Development
Continuation of four round tables

11:15–12:15. Continuation of general session: Symposium on Possibilities and Tendencies of China's Economic Development:
C. S. LIU. Transportation
FRANKLIN L. HO. Industrialization
Discussion

8:30–9:45. Continuation of general session: Symposium on Possibilities and Tendencies of China's Economic Development:
P. M. ROXBY. China's Population Problem

SATURDAY, OCTOBER 24

9:00–10:45. China's Economic Development
Continuation of four round tables

11:15–12:15. General conference session: China's Economic Development
Summary reports of round tables
Discussion

Evening: Reception and banquet offered to Conference members by the provincial and municipal authorities of Hangchow

SUNDAY, OCTOBER 25

9:00–9:30. Address by DR. HU SHIH: Hangchow in Chinese History and Literature [6]

MONDAY, OCTOBER 26

9:00–10:30. Labor Problems and Standards of Living
Four round tables

10:50–11:45. Continuation of round tables

11:55–12:40. General conference session: Labor Problems and Standards of Living
Summary reports of round tables
Discussion by observers of the International Labour Office: CAMILLE PONE and DAME ADELAIDE ANDERSON

6:15–7:30. Informal round table: Cultural and Social Relations

[6] The Pacific Council of the Institute held an important session at Hangchow, which, together with this and the preceding evening's general conference sessions, to some extent went to justify the name " Hangchow Conference " inscribed on many of the preconference documents in the expectation that the whole conference would be held in this city.

TUESDAY, OCTOBER 27

9:00–10:45. Diplomatic Machinery in the Pacific
Four round tables
Pacific Dependencies and Native Peoples
One round table

11:15–12:15. General conference session: Symposium on Pacific Dependencies and
Native Peoples: E. S. C. HANDY, A. D. A. DE KAT ANGELINO, FELIX
M. KEESING
Summary report of round table: Cultural and Social Relations

6:15–7:30. General conference session: Diplomatic Machinery in the Pacific
KENZO TAKANAYAGI. Manchuria, a Case Problem
FRANK G. WALTERS. The League of Nations and the Pacific

WEDNESDAY, OCTOBER 28

9:00–10:45. Continuation of four round tables: Diplomatic Machinery in the
Pacific
Continuation of one round table: Dependencies and Native Peoples

11:15–12:15. General conference session: Diplomatic Machinery in the Pacific
Summary reports of round tables
Discussion

6:15–7:30. General conference session: Introduction to China's Foreign Relations
SHUHSI HSU and Y. TSURUMI. The Manchurian Situation

THURSDAY, OCTOBER 29

9:00–10:45. China's Foreign Relations
Four round tables

11:15–12:15. Continuation of round tables

2:15–4:30. Round table: Silver and the Currency Problem of China

6:15–7:30. General conference session: International Relations
DR. I. NITOBE. Contact of Nations
DR. L. RAJCHMANN. The Technical Work of the League of Nations

FRIDAY, OCTOBER 30

9:00–10:45. Continuation of four round tables: China's Foreign Relations

11:00–12:00. Continuation of round tables

12:05–12:45. General conference session: China's Foreign Relations
Summary reports on round tables
Discussion

2:15–3:45. Round table: Universities and Cultural Relations

SATURDAY, OCTOBER 31

9:00–10:00. General conference session: The Relationship between the Work of
the International Research Committee and the Conferences and
Other Activities of the Institute

Addresses by W. L. HOLLAND, Acting Research Secretary, and E. C. CARTER, Chairman of International Program Committee
Discussion

10:15–12:00. China's Foreign Relations
The Future of Shanghai
One round table
Educational Aspects of the Institute of Pacific Relations
One round table
Migration and Race Problems
One round table

6:00–7:15. General conference session: Cultural Relations
Address by HU SHIH: Cultural Conflict in China

SUNDAY, NOVEMBER 1

8:00 Dinner to Conference members by the Chairman of the Pacific Council
Addresses by JEROME D. GREENE, HU SHIH, SIR WM. HARRISON MOORE, INAZO NITOBE

MONDAY, NOVEMBER 2

9:00–10:30. Coastal and River Navigation
One round table
International Co-operation in Research
One round table

10:15–11:45. Critique of the Conference
Four round tables

12:00–12:45. General conference session: Critique of the Conference
Symposium by GEORGE M. SMITH, NORMAN MCKENZIE, Y. TSURUMI, MRS. SOPHIA H. CHEN ZEN, E. S. C. HANDY, SEARLE BATES, E. C. CARTER, HU SHIH

2:30–4:00. Coastal and River Navigation
Round table — *continued*

5:00–6:15. Closing session of the Conference: Conference Learnings
Symposium by FRANCISCO BENITEZ, MISS YIH-FANG, WU, S. MATSUMOTO, FRANK WALTERS, CHARLES F. LOOMIS, VINCENT MASSEY, INAZO NITOBE, JEROME D. GREENE, HU SHIH

NOTE. — Many items on the social schedule offered by the China Council to the Conference were important parts of the conference experience, especially for foreign members who were thus enabled to enlarge their circle of acquaintances, to continue informally discussion of conference subjects, and to gain glimpses of Chinese social life and institutions. Included in the schedule of afternoon events were, in addition to several official receptions, visits to local universities, visits to monuments, institutions, and private homes in Hangchow, a reception by national and local Y.M.C.A.'s and Y.W.C.A.'s, a recital of ancient Chinese orchestral music, a reception by the Federation of Colleges and Universities of Shanghai, a visit to Ziccawei Observatory, visits to industrial plants, new housing developments, parks, and municipal improvements.

APPENDIX IV

SUMMARY OF REVENUES AND EXPENDITURES
1929–31

RECEIPTS

GENERAL PURPOSES	1929	1930	Jan. 1–Sept. 30, 1931	Whole Year, 1931*
International contributions:				
Australia...............	$ 723.00	$ 600.00	$ 625.00	$ 415.00
Canada.................	4,950.00	5,000.00	7,990.00	7,990.00
China..................	....	1,695.57	....	1,463.41
Great Britain...........	4,820.00	4,830.00	4,863.13	4,863.13
Hawaii.................	20,000.00	10,000.00	9,900.00	10,000.00
Japan..................	10,000.00	4,915.00	....	4,887.50
New Zealand...........	482.00	483.00	487.00	500.00
U. S. mainland	76,800.00	49,525.00	25,000.00	45,000.00
Other income:				
Subscriptions — *Pacific Affairs*...............	660.64	2,331.33	1,335.46	2,123.24
Miscellaneous...........	543.86	1,244.74	1,337.07	1,321.44
Temporary receipts......	....	....	21.00	....
Surplus................	9,175.24	1,107.67	1,025.62	1,025.62
Total...............	$128,154.74	$ 81,732.31	$52,584.28	$ 79,589.34
INTERNATIONAL RESEARCH FUND	50,000.00	50,000.00	25,000.00	50,000.00
Bank balance at beginning of year................	....	16,500.30	17,957.51	17,957.51
GRAND TOTAL........	$178,154.74	$148,232.61	$95,541.79	$147,546.85

EXPENDITURES

GENERAL PURPOSES	1929	1930	Jan. 1–Sept. 30, 1931	Whole Year, 1931*
Administration...........	$ 40,309.88	$ 37,829.43	$16,650.75	$ 22,856.16
Information — editorial section...................	22,184.16	18,783.85	14,395.08	20,160.43
Research administration...	13,347.90	12,560.69	6,656.30	9,774.03
Library.................	9,805.47	1,659.20	1,197.33	1,726.73
Conference..............	38,480.23	9,379.33	2,090.00	16,510.28
Capital expenditure.......	2,919.43	494.19	54.00	124.38
Total...............	$127,047.07	$ 80,706.69	$41,043.46	$ 71,152.01
INTERNATIONAL RESEARCH FUND				
Expenditure.............	33,499.70	48,542.79	44,707.49	67,952.21
TOTAL EXPENDITURES.	$160,546.77	$129,249.48	$85,750.95	$139,104.22

* Figures supplied by the Honorary Treasurer at the time of going to press.

APPENDIX V

CONSTITUTION OF THE INSTITUTE OF PACIFIC RELATIONS [1]

ARTICLE I. NAME

The name of this organization shall be Institute of Pacific Relations.

ARTICLE II. OBJECT

The object of the Institute is to study the conditions of the Pacific peoples with a view to the improvement of their mutual relations.

ARTICLE III. MEMBERSHIP

1. Subject to the provisions hereof the Institute of Pacific Relations is constituted by the national units, the names of whose representatives are appended to this Constitution, and by such other national units as may hereafter be admitted to membership as provided herein.

2. A national unit as comprehended by section 1 of this Article shall be a National Council organized for the purposes of the Institute, or an organization of similar purposes, in any sovereign or autonomous state lying within or bordering the Pacific Ocean or having dominions, colonies, dependencies, territories, mandated or otherwise, in the Pacific Area, subject to its being approved and admitted to membership by the Pacific Council as hereinafter constituted. Each constituent country shall have one National Council or equivalent organization, hereinafter referred to as the National Council. With the approval of the Pacific Council, independent Local Groups may be organized in an eligible country which has not created a National Council.

3. To encourage at Conferences of the Institute the representation of distinct racial or territorial groups existing within or under the jurisdiction of a country having a National Council of the Institute, the Pacific Council and the Secretariat may, by unanimous vote of the Pacific Council, enter into direct relations with such groups in making arrangements for their representation and participation in Conferences.

4. Each National Council shall determine its own constitution and rules of procedure and shall file with the Secretariat of the Institute a certified copy thereof and of any subsequent amendment.

ARTICLE IV. PACIFIC COUNCIL

1. The Institute shall be directed by a Pacific Council consisting of one member duly appointed by each National Council, together with the Chairman of the Advisory Committee. The members of the Pacific Council shall each have one vote.

2. The officers of the Pacific Council shall consist of a Chairman, a first Vice-Chairman, and a second Vice-Chairman, who shall be, *ex officio,* the Chairman and Vice-Chairmen, respectively, of the Institute. They shall be elected by the Council at a meeting held during the stated Conference, or at an adjourned meeting held thereafter, to serve until the close of the next stated Conference or until their successors have been elected. The Pacific Council shall appoint the General Secretary

---

[1] As amended at the 1931 Conference of the Institute. (Amended clauses: Art. III, sec. 3; Art. IV, sec. 8.)

and the Treasurer of the Institute. The General Secretary shall act as secretary of the Pacific Council.

3. A stated meeting of the Pacific Council shall be held during the period and at the place of the Institute Conference. Special meetings may be called by the Chairman on not less than thirty days' notice by telegraph or ten weeks' notice by post, and they shall be so called at the request of three members.

4. In the event of the inability of a member of the Pacific Council to attend a stated meeting his place may be taken by an Alternate designated by his National Council. In the event of the inability of a member to attend a special meeting his place may be taken by an Alternate designated as above or by a Proxy appointed by the member himself; but the vote of a Proxy shall be valid only as to proposals of which his principal has been informed at least ten days before the special meeting is held or as to which the principal's instructions governing the voting of the Proxy are received before a vote is taken.

5. A quorum of the Pacific Council shall consist of not less than four members including a member or his Alternate or Proxy from each of the following: a member of the British Commonwealth, China, Japan and the United States.

6. A majority vote of the members present shall determine the action of the Pacific Council except as otherwise expressly provided.

7. A copy of the minutes of each meeting of the Pacific Council shall be sent to each National Council.

8. A resolution signed by each member of the Pacific Council as hereinafter mentioned shall have the same force and effect as if it were a resolution passed at a duly constituted meeting of the Pacific Council. For the purpose of this section the General Secretary, on receipt of a proposed resolution signed by two members of the Pacific Council, shall transmit a copy of the same forthwith to each national group, and if within three months of such despatch he shall receive a copy of such resolution signed by each member of the Pacific Council or his alternate such resolution shall be entered in the minutes as a resolution of the Pacific Council.

ARTICLE V. SECRETARIAT

The Secretariat shall be the instrument of the Pacific Council for carrying on the work of the Institute. It shall be directed by the General Secretary who shall be responsible to the Pacific Council for all its activities. The General Secretary shall be assisted by a staff appropriate for the direction, supervision or execution of the several activities of the Institute in accordance with the policies and regulations of the Council.

ARTICLE VI. ADVISORY COMMITTEE

The Pacific Council shall appoint a Committee the advice and assistance of which shall be available to the General Secretary in the discharge of his functions and to which the Council may delegate such authority as shall seem expedient. So far as practicable the personnel of the Committee shall represent the countries having members on the Pacific Council; but at least three of its members shall reside sufficiently near the Secretariat to be able to attend meetings of the Committee and to inform themselves of the condition of the Institute's affairs. The Advisory Committee shall report to the Chairman of the Pacific Council at least once in six months, and at any time upon his request, with regard to the administration and activities of the Institute.

ARTICLE VII.   CONFERENCES

1. Conferences of the Institute shall be called by the Pacific Council at stated intervals, which, however, may be changed from time to time as the Council may see fit.   In addition to such regular Conferences the Council may call special Conferences.   The location of Conferences shall be fixed by the Council.

2. The arrangements for Conferences shall be in charge of the General Secretary acting in co-operation with the Committees concerned with the program and other preparatory work and with the National Council within whose territory the Conference is held.

3. The members of the regular Conferences shall be appointed by the National Councils and independent Local Groups, except as otherwise provided in Article III, section 3 hereof, the quotas whereof shall be fixed by the Pacific Council.

ARTICLE VIII.   FINANCE

1. The expenses of the Institute shall be met by an international budget to which contributions shall be invited from all National Councils and from other sources, but in such manner and to such an extent as to safeguard in the highest possible degree the international character and control of the Institute.

2. The Pacific Council shall fix the fiscal period to be covered by the budget, beginning with the calendar year.   At a suitable time prior thereto, as determined by the Council, the General Secretary shall submit a budget for the following fiscal period; and upon the adoption of such budget by the Council, with any necessary modifications, all expenditures shall be made in conformity therewith subject to any subsequent amendments thereof by, or under the authority of, the Council.

3. The property of the Institute shall be vested in the Pacific Council and the custody and disbursement of its funds and the accounting therefor shall be under the control of the Council.

4. A copy of the budget and of any amendment thereof and a semi-annual statement of receipts and expenses shall be sent to each National Council.

5. Each National Council and independent Local Group shall be responsible for its own expenditures.

ARTICLE IX.   BY-LAWS AND REGULATIONS

The Pacific Council shall have power to make such By-laws and Regulations for the conduct of its business and of the affairs of the Institute generally as are not inconsistent with the provisions of this Constitution.

ARTICLE X.   AMENDMENTS

This Constitution may be amended or repealed by an affirmative vote of not less than two-thirds of the members of the Pacific Council provided that notice of the proposed amendment shall have been given by the General Secretary to each National Council not less than four months if by mail and not less than two months if by telegraph, in advance of the meeting at which the amendment is presented.

ARTICLE XI.   RATIFICATION

This Constitution shall take effect upon its ratification by the several National Councils provided, however, that the failure of any National Council so to ratify it shall not invalidate it as between the other parties thereto. The vote of each National Council ratifying this Constitution shall be attested by a competent officer of such Council and filed with the Secretariat.

SIGNATURES

The undersigned, by authority of their several groups assembled at the Conference of the Institute of Pacific Relations in Honolulu, Territory of Hawaii, U.S.A., hereby approve and adopt the foregoing Constitution of the Institute of Pacific Relations, subject to the ratification of the said Constitution by the full authority of their respective National Councils.

[Signed]   FRED W. EGGLESTON, *Australia*
               A. F. WHYTE, *For the British Group*
               A. W. CURRIE, *Canada*
               DAVID Z. T. YUI, *China*
               A. ISHII, *Japan*
               W. NASH, *New Zealand*
               RAY LYMAN WILBUR, *United States of America*

July 29, 1927

APPENDIX VI

HANDBOOK OF THE INSTITUTE OF PACIFIC RELATIONS [1]

I. THE GROWTH OF AN IDEA

The Institute of Pacific Relations came into existence in July, 1925, at the close of a conference convened at Honolulu by a group of Hawaiian residents and attended by members from China, Japan, Korea, Canada, Australia, New Zealand, the Philippines, and the United States. It has since held three other conferences, at Honolulu in July, 1927, at Kyoto in November, 1929, and at Shanghai and Hangchow from October 21 to November 4, 1931, and it is expected that regular biennial conferences will be held thereafter.

The Hawaiian group which convened the First Conference consisted of business and academic men and women and social and religious workers. They were impressed with the success that had attended the efforts to approach racial and social problems in the Hawaiian Islands by the method of friendly continuous discussion among the interested parties. They regarded Hawaii as a microcosm in which might be seen in miniature all the varied and complex forces of racial and international relationships at work in the Pacific area as a whole. While the impact of controversial political issues, such as immigration restrictions, and of economic problems, such as those presented by differing standards of living, was clearly recognized, considerable emphasis was placed also upon such questions as the biological and social consequences of race mixture, and the possibilities and difficulties of cultural interchange among the different Pacific peoples. The situation therefore was viewed as arising from the contact of different civilizations in all their many-sided aspects; but less stress was laid upon the conflict or clash of political and cultural conceptions than upon the more positive and constructive possibilities of interchange of experience.

The founders of the Institute contemplated one comparatively small conference in Honolulu to discuss the possibility of international organization. The success of the First Conference seemed to warrant some form of continuing organization, so that the Institute of Pacific Relations was established at the close of the Conference. The newly appointed General Secretary, Mr. J. Merle Davis, undertook a tour of the principal Pacific countries, and branches were formed in Japan, China, Australia, New Zealand, Canada, and the United States. At the suggestion of the Dominion groups, an invitation was extended also to the Royal Institute of International Affairs to co-operate on behalf of Great Britain. At the same time liaison was established with the secretariat of the League of Nations and the International Labour Office.

Successive conferences have shown that the idea of approaching international problems through unofficial discussion supported by scientific research has been well received in the Pacific area. The membership of the Third Conference, held at Kyoto in November, 1929, was just over two hundred, made up for the most part of members nominated by the National Councils in the countries named

---

[1] A preliminary draft, edited by Dr. J. B. Condliffe, was circulated before the Fourth Biennial Conference. It is here reprinted, with slight amendments, to give the present report of proceedings a needed background of explanations of the history, purposes, and methods of the Institute.

above.[2] It would not have been difficult to organize a much larger conference, but an effort is made to restrict membership to small, carefully selected and representative groups from each country. In addition to the members from the principal sovereign countries, local groups in Hawaii, the Philippines,[3] and Korea were represented, and observers were present also from Soviet Russia, France, the Dutch East Indies, and Mexico, as well as members of the staff of the League of Nations and the International Labour Office.

In little more than five years, interest in the Institute has spread not only over the Pacific, but also to European countries which have territorial interests in the Pacific. Negotiations are progressing for the formation of groups in France, the Dutch East Indies, and the U.S.S.R.[4] Close touch is maintained with the League of Nations and the International Labour Office at Geneva.

All of these groups are organizations of private individuals, privately financed. There is no connection with, or help from, any of the governments. When the first chairman of the Institute, who was also chairman at that time of the American Council, Dr. Ray Lyman Wilbur, became Secretary of the Interior, he severed his Institute connections. This precedent was followed a few months later when his successor, the Japanese Chairman, Mr. Junnosuke Inouye, became Minister of Finance in the Hamaguchi Cabinet.

Without any governmental backing, and at first indeed with some apprehension on the part of certain of the Foreign Offices — apprehension which has fortunately disappeared — the Institute branches have built up their organization on a purely private and individualistic basis. Each group aims to represent a cross-section of interests in its own country. There are no political affiliations, and an effort is made to include women as well as men, business as well as academic leaders, labor men and capitalists, social workers and men of affairs. That the effort has so far been successful must be set down to the appeal of the original idea for which, it is now evident, the times were ripe and the circumstances particularly propitious in the Pacific area.

That idea is best expressed in the words of the simple constitution under which the Institute works, as the " study of the conditions of the Pacific peoples with a view to the improvement of their mutual relations." In practice the " study " which the Institute carries forward consists of a continuous process of discussion and education supported by research. The biennial conferences form the focusing points of this process which, however, is much more extensive and continuous than the gathering at biennial intervals might suggest. In each of the constituent countries there is a definite organization carrying forward, in the intervals between conferences, research and education as aids to the formation of public opinion. Most of the national groups co-operate with the press, the universities, and the schools, and with women's, business, and labor organizations, in making and sharing the results of studies. There is a steady stream of interchange also between the constituent groups, so that preparation for the next conference goes on side by side with the re-evaluation of experience gained at the preceding meeting. In these ways a co-operative effort is under way, aiming at the elucidation of the main controversial Pacific issues and their backgrounds.

This is an age of scientific research, an age, moreover, when people are becoming increasingly aware of the importance of the psychological factors in international relations and the possibilities of the new methods of conference diplomacy.

[2] The China Conference had a membership of 132.

[3] A Philippine National Council was formed in 1931.

[4] A Soviet Union Council of the Institute was formed in 1931.

The Pacific area seems to be especially suited for experiments in these new methods of international discussion. The most obvious, if not the most important, fact which suggests this is the degree to which the Pacific peoples are being brought into closer contact by increasing communications and trade. The trade of the Pacific has for some years increased faster than that of any other area; shipping is developing rapidly, both east and west, and north and south.

In such contacts the very marked contrasts of economic conditions, cultural conceptions, and social organization present difficulties and possibilities which are only now being fully appreciated.

The contrasts have often been summarized — densely populated countries and relatively under-developed regions, communal island societies, stabilized ancient cultures and new aggressive scientific communities, the lowest living standards confronting the highest, democracies in various stages of development, strong free nations and peoples in tutelage — a veritable conflict of civilizations and cultures. Present economic and political differences, properly analyzed, often prove symptoms of older and more deeply rooted cultural and social differences. There is therefore an obvious need for the mutual examination both of the political contacts and also of the economic relations and the diverse cultural backgrounds of the Pacific peoples.

The Institute of Pacific Relations is an attempt to meet this need — an attempt to apply the methods of discussion and research to an exploration of these differences of outlook and conflicts of understanding. It has been described as an " experiment in diagnosis " or, more precisely, as a means for providing " carefully organized group discussion preceded and followed by a continuous process of study and research."

Its function, however, is one of diagnosis rather than prescription. It has carefully eschewed the recommendation of remedial courses of action. In this it has taken to heart a favorite quotation of Sun Yat-sen — " Action is easy; understanding is difficult." By carefully refraining from even the appearance of action in its corporate capacity, it has been freer to provide the proper atmosphere in which its members may explore the possibilities of understanding. It passes no resolutions, comes to no agreements or conclusions, advocates no policies.

While this attitude has been steadily maintained throughout the Institute's history, it is obvious that such an organization must constantly relate its program to the forces that influence and change international relations. Hence it seeks the services of men and women who are responsibly connected with the shaping of public opinion and the formulation of group policies. And it tries to improve the influence of such persons by enlarging and deepening their understanding of the problems with which they are called upon to deal — particularly in relation to current questions. It enlists the co-operation, for example, of both business and academic groups, and aims to apply scientific method with equal care to its research and to its conference procedures. It chooses by preference controversial issues that are in special need of clarification, and techniques of discussion that ensure full participation.

The very fact of its existence and the continuous attention it gives to important Pacific problems is in itself sufficient to raise those problems more effectively and steadily into the consciousness of its members and of all who know of their interests. The biennial conferences, especially when they are held in the Far East, attract attention; and between the conferences there is a less spectacular but quietly persistent direction of attention to these problems by reason of the group discussions, research work, and individual activities of the members.

Both in the biennial conferences and in the group preparation, there is inevitably a marked tendency for the individual members and the groups as a whole to gain in interest, understanding, and grasp of the problems studied. A recognition of the causes of people's emotional attitudes often is as important as are statistical data. Each member has the consciousness of studying in an international fellowship, and of being able to get accurate and direct reflections of public opinion in other countries as well as his own. The depth and confidence which this gives to individual experience, attitudes, and judgments are of some importance.

While, therefore, the Institute both as an international body and in its national branches scrupulously refrains from any resolutions or corporate actions which might have even the appearance of supporting particular policies or proposals, its activities undoubtedly do contribute toward the formation of an informed public opinion. They emphasize the importance of, and draw more attention to, the problems under discussion and raise into clear relief the agreed facts or the disagreements on issues. They thus substitute a precise educational or scientific approach for the rather hazy appeals to prejudice or partial statements which are only too common in international affairs. The Institute is seeking to substitute scientific educational procedures for biased propaganda in the formation of public opinion; curiosity for the inertia of indifference; and real divergencies of policy for the gusts of emotional prejudice which make these difficult problems so dangerous. Its work is founded on the belief that if the real facts and issues are revealed, they can be dealt with intelligently; but as a body it refrains from any attempt at solution of problems. It concentrates instead upon the revelation of the causes of differences, holding that its renunciation of practical action is an indispensable condition of usefulness in the prior work of understanding.

This attitude is quite consistent with the fact that inevitably there are by-products of action, proceeding from the activities and influence in their private capacities of the men and women who have participated in the Institute's work and come thereby to new points of view or clearer understanding. It is obviously difficult, if not impossible, to ascribe definite events to such indirect influences; but the opinion has been expressed that such developments as the saner handling of the controversy over American legislation for the restriction of Oriental immigration, the improvement of diplomatic relations between Great Britain and China, the adherence of Japan to the Pact of Paris, the better feeling between Japan and China,[5] the lowering of the cable rates between Japan and the United States — were in some degree facilitated by the full and frank exploration of these problems at successive conferences, or even by the preparations for their discussion. For these by-products, however, the Institute takes no responsibility. It merely provides a forum for frank intimate discussion of controversial topics and steadily adheres to its policy of taking no corporate action of any kind beyond the concerted advancement in understanding of the problems. Its membership, indeed, is made up of such diverse elements that the approach to unanimity of opinion necessary for political action would be impossible to achieve. Even indications of majority opinion on policy would, it is believed, do more harm than good.

The secret of the Institute's power to enlist the co-operation of such wide-

[5] [Even in these matters, overshadowed by recent events, it is evident that Institute processes have laid the foundation for a more happy co-operation in the days to come. EDITOR]

spread groups of people must, therefore, be sought elsewhere than in the natural attraction of opportunities for political action.   Little effort has been made to enlist support by such means as publicity or recruitment of members.   The Institute groups in each country remain comparatively small circles of interested people, as yet weak in financial resources, steadily refusing official backing or sanction, and making no effort to build up imposing organizations.

Each group is autonomous and financially independent, receiving its modest funds from private subscriptions, greater or less, according to the financial resources of the country in which it works.   The autonomous groups are linked in a loose co-operative federation with central secretarial headquarters at Honolulu.   Each group has its own research committee, and the more developed groups have education committees seeking to stimulate in existing educational agencies the same process of research and discussion that characterizes the Institute's own program. For the same reason, the research committees work through existing agencies, such as the universities, rather than by setting themselves up as *ad hoc* research bodies. In this way an effort is made to mobilize the widest possible resources of research and education without setting up new ones.   In each of its groups and internationally the Institute has conceived its function as that of a catalyzer bringing into useful action already existing forces.   The peculiar value both of its discussion methods and of its research work in this connection is dealt with in more detail below.

Co-ordination is maintained by linking the various groups in international committees which, however, can meet only at the biennial conferences, and by the work of the Central Secretariat.   The chairmen or other designated representatives of the National Councils form the controlling body, known as the Pacific Council. In the same way, the chairmen of the various research committees form an International Research Committee.   Both bodies delegate to the chairmen and secretaries necessary responsibilities in the periods between the biennial meetings.

The Central Secretariat at Honolulu acts as a clearing house or connecting link between the various groups.   Its functions consist mainly in the interchange of information between the groups, the organization of the conference arrangements and program, co-ordination of research activities, and publication of a monthly journal, *Pacific Affairs*.   As far as possible the organization is decentralized, the ultimate power and initiative residing in the constituent national groups.   Conference programs are built out of an interchange of suggestions between the groups, and research activities are decentralized in the same way.

The journal of the Institute, *Pacific Affairs,* has a steadily expanding circulation and is recognized widely as of increasing value to all students of Pacific problems.   In addition to authoritative articles, it contains each month summaries of important Pacific happenings, extracts from editorial opinion, book reviews, and an extensive review of magazine and pamphlet literature relating to the Pacific.

The Institute has also accumulated at Honolulu a specialized library on Pacific problems which is particularly rich in such materials as pamphlets, magazine articles, government reports, and news-clippings.   As this collection is built up with the co-operation of the national groups, it is increasingly valuable for research students.

To the expenses of the central headquarters and the preparation and conduct of the biennial conferences each of the National Councils contributes in an agreed proportion, the bulk of the funds coming from the larger and richer countries.

There is also a separate International Research Fund provided by the generosity of an American foundation, grants from which, however, are in part conditional upon contributions of a stated amount being raised from local sources in the country concerned.

Such a loose and inexpensive organization is made possible only by the Institute's policy of decentralization. The autonomous National Councils carry the whole burden of its work save for the minimum of co-ordination provided by the activities of the small central staff. In most of the groups the committee and secretarial work of the Institute is undertaken as voluntary service.

How, then, has the Institute managed to enlist and retain the support of busy leaders of thought and action throughout its whole constituency? The answer to this question must be sought partly in the attraction of the Institute's basic idea of applying the methods of scientific research and carefully prepared discussion to the study of international affairs, partly in the caliber of the original leaders of the venture whose names were a guaranty of the character of the Institute, and whose devotion ensured its success in the first critical period, partly in the intrinsic interest of the problems it tackled and the nature of its approach to those problems.

The first chairman of the Institute defined it as an instrument for the discussion of " problems too delicate for discussion by diplomats." The First Conference met in 1925 in an atmosphere of great tension, not long after the passing of the American Immigration Act in 1924 which was deeply resented in Japan, and almost immediately after the incident of May 30, 1925, in Shanghai, which sent a flame of anti-foreign feeling throughout China. The conference plunged immediately into the discussion of these problems and their underlying causes. It emerged with a program of research into the basic underlying social problems, such as the food and population question in the Pacific. The results of this first " adventure in friendliness " proved that frank expressions of opinion on controversial subjects, so far from disrupting the conference, were an essential condition for mutual respect and understanding. As a leading Japanese put it, this " was the first occasion on which the Occident had approached the Orient with nothing to sell, nothing to preach, and nothing to teach."

Ever since, the Institute has lived dangerously, choosing for its main subject of discussion at each conference the hottest and most controversial issue of the moment. In 1927 the presence, for the first time, of a well-informed British group concentrated attention upon the relations of China with foreign powers, particularly with Britain, which was at that time the chief target for anti-foreign agitation. Two years later the conference, meeting for the first time on Japanese soil, did not hesitate to concentrate its attention on Japan's most vital foreign problem, the situation in China's Three Eastern Provinces,[6] with results that were eminently satisfactory in terms of informative discussion and increased understanding. Preparations for the Fourth Conference, to meet in China in 1931, were directed largely to two major topics, the international economic relations of Pacific countries and China's foreign relations.

It is perhaps inevitable that this attack upon problems which are the subject of so much political controversy should lead to some misconceptions of the nature of the Institute's discussions and their purpose. It has been suggested that the Institute is departing from its original purpose of scientific study and becoming a political organization. It has been characterized as " amateur " or " unofficial " diplomacy and even compared with the League of Nations. On the other hand, one observer has confessed himself frankly puzzled by the futility of a conference

[6] Manchuria, now the Four Eastern Provinces.

which, face to face with important political problems, came to no conclusions and did not even attempt the formulation of policies of action.

The fact, however, familiar enough to all who have actually participated in a conference, is that these incidents of political controversy are used merely as entering points for the discussion of the more fundamental problems of which they are symptoms. The atmosphere of the discussions is distinctly non-emotional, oratory is at a discount, appeals to such abstractions as national rights seem out of place, discussion around the table quickly moves from such generalities to practical details. The heat goes out of the controversy, and attention is soon drawn to the more complex and less understood social phenomena which are, after all, the important causative factors. In this development the research work of the Institute is an important influence; but the technique of discussion also is so devised as to discount propaganda and advance understanding. So a controversy about migration leads to research in the field of population, a revelation of the conflict of interests and policies in the Four Eastern Provinces to a study of economic development in that region, a difference on tariffs to research into the nature of Pacific trade. The Institute, in other words, has discovered the value of approaching its problems from the point at which interest has already been created by political controversy rather than from the treatment of those subjects by academic discussion divorced from the practical realities of conflict.

There is one possibility of misconception in this method which deserves passing mention. The misconception is present not so much in the minds of the participants as of those whose interest in the conferences is aroused indirectly. Interest is naturally attracted by such a gathering as that at Kyoto, including many distinguished public men, to discuss what are readily recognized as situations of acute diplomatic controversy. The suggestion naturally arises that there must be something behind such discussions, some effort at concealed diplomacy. The discussions tend to be an anti-climax. No sensational clashes result, no strongly expressed national policies, and still less any definite conclusions or suggestions for action. Instead, there is a rather academic and quite friendly discussion of detailed incidents and underlying problems, all in the nature of sharing information and opinions.

The danger really is that the success that has so far attended the Institute's organization has led outside observers to expect something different from what is actually aimed at. The Institute is an educational not a diplomatic body, engaged in research and discussion, not in the formulation of policy. It prefers to work in privacy rather than publicly, but it has nothing to conceal. Its results are in the realm of education, first of its own members and then of a wider constituency. Any results in the realm of practical politics are merely by-products from the activities of individual members in their private capacities.

II. THE BACKGROUND OF DIPLOMACY

It is unlikely that an unofficial body organized primarily for discussion and research, as the Institute is, would have any great claim upon the time of busy practical people in such widely scattered lands, unless it met a real need. That need would seem to have been created by the changed conditions of international relationships in modern times.

It has long been recognized that the profound economic changes which are generally known now as the Industrial Revolution carried with them the necessity for political and social reorganization. The history of most of the western European countries in the nineteenth century is largely concerned with the national reorganization called forth by the development of large-scale machine industry and transport. Old forms of local government and regulation broke down, despotisms and oligarchies were doomed when wider communications and trade were followed by systems of universal education and political democracy. The advent of parliamentary forms of government, the building up of effective civil services and of new forms of local government were essentially products of the changes brought about by machine industry. Wherever determined efforts were made to preserve the existing régime, the result was revolution.

On the other hand, where the ruling groups assisted in the establishment of democratic institutions soundly based on popular education and free discussion, the transition was peaceful. It is now a truism that national government rests, however imperfectly, upon the popular will. It follows obviously that there must be devices for ascertaining, expressing, and educating the popular will. Party and sectional organizations, journalistic and public discussion, and parliamentary debate are devices common to most countries.

Broadly speaking, it is true to say that no great matter of public policy comes to decision without at least the opportunity for thorough public discussion. Not only is the proposal examined in all its bearings upon different interests, and the will of the people, or at least of interested groups, upon it made clear; but, in the course of the discussion, it is clarified, details are worked out, and adaptations made to suit practical conditions. Not the least important aspect of this preliminary discussion is the educative and preparatory effect it has upon the minds of those concerned.

Popular control over international, as distinct from national, policy has lagged behind. Long after parliamentary control, preceded by popular discussion, had been successfully asserted over domestic affairs, foreign relations continued to be conducted almost as if they were the private concerns of small ruling groups in each country. In the meantime, the machine methods and large-scale organization typical of the industrial revolution had been increasingly extended to commerce as well as manufacture. The whole modern world was becoming knit into economic unity by the railway and steamship, the telegraph and the radio. Interdependence became more and more pronounced, and, after the event, it seems obvious that the survival under such conditions of the earlier systems of diplomacy was bound to result in the cataclysm of war. It was a general if dim realization of this fact which lay behind the popular demand during the war for a League of Peoples rather than a League of Nations. What touches all must be approved by all.

While popular control of anything but the broadest aspect of policy is even more difficult in international than it is in national affairs, there remains a substantial truth in the idea that post-war diplomacy must strive to base itself more firmly upon informed public opinion, and must also contrive in some way to carry this opinion along with the negotiated compromises of experts and statesmen. It would be superfluous to do more than mention the progress made at Geneva toward the establishment of political institutions for international co-operation. It is well to remind ourselves, however, that it is unlikely that these institutions could have come into being if it had not been for the preceding half-century of discussion among international lawyers and statesmen and for the network of treaty commitments by which the statesmen had bound themselves and accustomed their nationals to the rule of law in international affairs.   Nor could they have extended and consolidated their functions as rapidly as they have done if there had not been the consistent effort of many private citizens in every land to explain and support their activities and explore the possibilities of their extension.

It is not without significance that two of the earliest institutions for the scientific study of international affairs had their birth in informal meetings among the British and American experts who were in attendance upon the statesmen who were drawing up the Treaty of Versailles.   The British (now the Royal) Institute of International Affairs and the Council on Foreign Relations of New York were formed to continue in their respective countries the contacts that had been built up between experts and men of affairs.

Since the formation of these bodies, there has been a distinct tendency to multiply the institutions engaged in studying international problems.   Among them the Institute of Pacific Relations holds a unique place.   It is the only unofficial organization in the field of international affairs which is organized on a thoroughly co-operative international basis, being in fact composed of a federation of national institutions, and established for the specific purpose of facilitating co-operation in research and discussion.

Its place in the modern world in which a new diplomacy of discussion and conference is struggling into existence, is assured by the necessity for institutions to investigate international problems in the spirit of detached scientific inquiry, by the urgent need for the exploration of situations in which public opinion in many countries is an important factor, and by the desirability of awakening and informing public opinion upon the important problems of international relations.   In a world where economic progress has pushed across the political boundaries of nationalism to a degree that is constantly increasing the economic interdependence of all peoples, where improving communications are bringing every year a greater number of contacts, and where the scientific mechanization and economic organization of warfare threaten the prosperity if not the life of every member of the community, there is ample reason for directing trained intelligence to the study of international affairs.

The Pacific area is a region peculiarly suitable for an experiment in this direction.   It is the region where economic progress and trade are proceeding fastest and communications are most rapidly improving.   The extension of machine processes to industry has reached the great Oriental countries at a time when the industrial, commercial, and banking organization, particularly of the United States, is capable of transplantation as fast as the economic resources and social conditions of those countries will permit.

The contrasts exhibited by the Pacific countries are sufficiently obvious to warrant investigation now that they are being brought into closer contact.   The differences in population pressure, economic resources, standards of living, industrial and political organization, challenge the imagination.   To many observers they presage conflict resulting ultimately in war, which, if it comes, will be embittered by racial antagonisms.   They imagine again the conflict that Coleridge dreamed:

> And 'mid this tumult Kubla heard from far
> Ancestral voices prophesying war.

To others such a danger appears more remote and not incapable of being averted by intelligent study and wise, constructive statesmanship.   To these also there comes the challenge presented by the possibility of building in the Pacific a new and greater civilization which will not shatter itself upon negative conflict but will build upon the elements of social strength which are present both in the scientific industrialism of the West and in the ancient philosophies of the East.

III. SCIENTIFIC METHOD IN INTERNATIONAL RELATIONS

There is a sense in which practically all international problems can be described in terms of the conflict between the dynamic progress of economic organization and the static conceptions of political sovereignty and cultural organization. Analyzing this conflict in his Lowell Lectures delivered in 1929, Mr. R. G. Hawtrey pointed out the real dangers, particularly of politico-economic relations between the advanced and backward industrial countries:

"The idea that no motive but selfishness ever counts in politics," he writes, "is as baseless as the pretence of a high moral purpose. In the mixed motives of imperialism there is to be found, along with cupidity and ambition, a perfectly genuine desire to help the subject populations, by maintaining law and order and promoting the material welfare of the people. What we need in the future is a little political chemistry to separate the elements which compose the mixture."

It is the elements of precisely this kind of "political chemistry," applicable not only to subject races but also to sovereign peoples at different stages of economic development, which the experimental processes of the Institute of Pacific Relations are designed to investigate. No one would claim that the investigation has as yet gone very far, or indeed done more than experiment with certain scientific techniques. But those who have participated so far have been encouraged to believe that the experiments are promising enough to warrant continuation and extension.

They owe a good deal to the established principles of scientific method which have yielded such striking results in the natural sciences and which, indeed, are the primary cause of the economic organization outgrowing the political and social controls of the modern world. Their translation into the more elusive and less measurable phenomena of social life is difficult; but certain broad principles are useful.

Of these, emphasis upon research is perhaps the most obvious. As soon as the first Institute conference got past generalities to practical details, it became clear that there was a real lack of reliable information on many of the most important subjects discussed. Even a brief discussion of immigration restriction showed that the attitudes taken depended upon economic, social, and biological conceptions for which little scientific evidence could be adduced, and which in fact were nothing more than prejudices rationalized from limited experience. The very definition of "race" is uncertain, and there is extremely little ascertained and verified fact upon which to base conclusions regarding the biological or social effects of race-mixture. In regard to economic and political conceptions, there is surprisingly little accurate information of a descriptive character, and less analysis that has borne the test of observation and experiment. No accurate measurements have been made of standards of living, and the very term is vaguely defined, though it is bandied about freely in discussions not only of immigration restriction but also of tariffs, international labor legislation, and similar subjects of international controversy.

There are even greater and more obvious gaps in our information concerning the most elementary facts of population, food supply, and industrial progress, which underlie and shape practically all the political problems which vex the Pacific area. Deeper still, and more difficult of approach, lie the divergent social and cultural ideals and institutions of the Pacific countries. The first task to be undertaken, therefore, is that of accurate observation and systematic description and classification, to facilitate a charting of social processes and trends. Only a multitude of accurate observations can validate the more imaginative methods of synthesis peculiar to the social sciences.

Scholars have long been conscious of the importance of these problems; but scholars are likely to pursue knowledge for its own sake without paying any great regard to the practical situations of difficulty in which social conflicts come to the surface. Practical men of affairs, on the other hand, dealing in the course of a busy life with a succession of awkward situations, find it difficult to gain and keep an adequate comprehension of the underlying profundity of vast, slow-moving social processes. Yet the solutions they propose for immediate problems will be futile if they do not fit the general trend of social development.

The peculiar value of the Institute of Pacific Relations lies in its attempt to combine both of these viewpoints to their mutual advantage. In attempting this difficult task, the Institute has chosen to work from the surface down rather than from the more remote social processes to the practical situations of politics. It uses political conflict as an entering point for the study not only of the immediate circumstances of conflict, but also of the fundamental movements which create those circumstances. It studies not only the surface currents but also the tidal movements around which they play.

In doing so it has largely discarded the divisions, though not the techniques, of the social sciences. A situation of difficulty, such for example as the problems presented by the Four Eastern Provinces, is viewed in its entirety. Political scientists, historians, economists, psychologists, sociologists are invited to collaborate in its investigation and share in the discussion with business men and leaders of public opinion. Scientific analysis is checked by practical description and observation.

One further experiment of considerable significance and promise is being made in the effort, long since made by the natural sciences, to utilize comparative methods of study upon problems common to more than one country. The rapid advance in recent years of such sciences as physics, has come largely from the fact that there has been a great deal of international co-operation among those engaged in their study. The checking and comparison of results obtained by many investigators in different countries, results that are freely interchanged and discussed, have led to brilliant new syntheses and hypotheses, first in one country then in another, syntheses that immediately become the common property of all workers in the field and the bases for further study.

The Institute has made a modest start in following this method by conceiving its research projects as comparative international studies. The projects are outlined after discussion in the International Research Committee, following which individual investigators are set to work in the different countries concerned; the results of their investigations are brought together later for comparison and synthesis and if necessary for the initiation of further work in the same field. In every case, the research projects are entrusted to already established institutions, such as universities, so that a double purpose is achieved by building up several research centers in the process of securing the needed information.

The processes of research are, however, both laborious and slow. Not only the subjects but the methods of investigation are new, and trained technical investigators are scarce. Research is necessarily a long, cumulative process from which it is unreasonable to expect immediate spectacular results of practical importance. These results will come in time, from the patient, painstaking, and accurate application of scientific methods; but in the meantime there are many situations of present difficulty which cannot await the processes of research and must be studied in the light of the best knowledge at present available. It is primarily for the study of these problems that the Institute of Pacific Relations has developed its biennial conferences, the organization and methods of which are described below.

The existence of these conferences, moreover, provides regular opportunities for considering the longer-term investigations. It has been pointed out that the methods of the natural sciences are not wholly valid for social studies. But the integration of those methods with the psychological processes of discussion appears to promise useful results. The next section therefore attempts to outline the procedures used in conference discussions.

IV. THE PROCEDURE OF CONFERENCE

Like the Institute itself and all its processes, the procedure devised for the conduct of the biennial conference is as yet experimental and subject to change. No one would claim more than that certain new types of preparation and discussion appear useful enough to warrant further trial and development. The biennial conferences are naturally the most spectacular part of the Institute's work. They tend to be regarded as isolated phenomena but can be properly understood only when they are regarded as part of a " continuous process of study, discussion, and research." The larger part of this process does not attract much attention, consisting as it does of a research program entrusted to university institutions scattered over the Pacific countries, and of group discussions carried on even more widely in the various branches of the Institute.

The method of group discussion at the biennial conferences has a direct bearing on the Institute's whole procedure. The actual conduct of conference discussions has been the subject of a good deal of experiment. From the beginning an effort was made to get away from the time-honored method of addresses or papers followed by discussion. However satisfactory this method may be for scientific conferences where information is being shared among experts, it does not carry the processes of group thinking very far in international affairs. The Institute finds expert addresses useful on occasion when, for example, a complicated situation is outlined by someone who has special knowledge of it, in such a way as to make all conference members familiar with the facts necessary for fruitful discussion of the difficulties it presents. Such addresses, it will be evident, are used as preparation, rather than substitutes, for the group discussion which is the most important method used in the conferences.

It has been found that the rôle of the expert, valuable as it is, must be subordinated in a conference which represents one stage in a continuing process shared in by lay members and the general public. The members do not come to hear or to deliver authoritative expositions, but to discuss problems with their equals. Those who have special knowledge share it with the group; but the processes of group thinking are more important than individual lectures. In this respect the round tables resemble a business conference rather than the lecture room of a university.

Some interesting experiments have been made in the direction of securing adequate participation by all members in the discussions, and fruitful interplay of ideas and emotional attitudes, leading to mutual understanding. These experiments are not easy to describe, since they consist only partly of technical devices and depend largely upon the elusive art of discussion leadership with its grasp of opportunities that make for sympathetic mutual understanding. The fact that, whenever possible, conference members are housed together and meet informally in small casual groups further helps to cultivate personal friendships. Such conditions are favorable to the creation of attitudes of mutual consideration, tolerance, and receptivity.

Discussion begins with the interchange of opinions, information, and experience on the subject before the meeting. This in itself is a valuable process since it leads to a rounded, tolerant consideration and often to a surprisingly large measure of common agreement. Differences of opinion are found to be not as irreconcilable as they seemed; one's opponents are found to have " reasonable " points of view. The way is cleared for a renewed effort to appreciate the real issues of disagreement. Even at this early stage there may emerge modifications and enlargements of understanding that go far to offset the variety of previously held opinions and premature conclusions.

The First Conference began with prepared statements on behalf of the National Councils, reviewing recent international developments from the standpoint of their respective countries. While some of these statements were valuable and lucid expositions of national policy, they have seemed less suitable in the light of the Institute's development, which has been toward the discussion of practical details rather than general attitudes. They have therefore been dispensed with at the China Conference.

The Program Committee, working on materials to be described below, selects the main areas of discussion. The agenda for each round table is carefully framed, not in the form of positive statements, but as a series of questions. These questions are designed to elicit the presentation of controversial positions. But the questions are so arranged that they aid the members in discovering what the total situation is, what the underlying problems are, what are the sources of attitudes and emotions, which added facts can be secured immediately and which must await the results of further research. Finally, the questions aim to lead to an objective analysis of all of the various solutions proposed for meeting the situation under discussion. The conference divides into groups, with no visitors' gallery. The groups meet around a table in informal, face-to-face discussion. The round-table chairmen are carefully selected, not as experts, but as discussion leaders. They have a general, but not necessarily or advisedly a specialized, acquaintance with the problem to be discussed. Their function is to draw the whole group into a conversational discussion of a give-and-take, question-and-answer character, while keeping it relevant in the main to the questions which the Program Committee has selected as the agenda.

The best parallel to a round table, therefore, is a meeting of a board of directors where long speeches are not encouraged but an effort is made to exchange information and, even more, to appreciate attitudes and viewpoints in order to arrive at a common understanding. The round tables, however, unlike a directors' meeting, make no effort to arrive at decisions or binding agreement. Yet, a wholly new direction may be given to thought.

A skilful chairman quickly learns how to repress the loquacious and encourage the reticent, to keep his eye open for the niceties of different codes of etiquette, to make sure that language difficulties do not place an undue handicap upon those whose mother-tongue is not English — since the Oriental members have graciously accepted English as the language of the conferences, despite the handicap under which they thereby place themselves [7] — and to balance the ready frankness of Occidental speech against the courteous reserves of Oriental phraseology.   The prominence of the expert tends to disappear when many experts are present, particularly when, as often happens, they disagree, and it becomes evident that the layman has a point of view which is equally important.   Moreover, it has been found that authoritative statements do not enlist effective participation by non-experts in the subsequent discussions.   Such authoritative statements are discouraged and kept at a minimum.

There are disadvantages in the round-table method.   Discussion may wander, a too rigid chairman may sterilize it by keeping it too strictly relevant or by overmuch restatement and recapitulation from the chair.   Not all the members can be expected to have the lowest common denominator of essential information, from which profitable discussion of debatable areas of the subject ought to begin.   The experts may feel that the whole position could be clarified by an authoritative statement of known facts.

But there is a consensus of opinion that with all its disadvantages round-table discussion is an immense improvement on the lecture method.   The very act of participation, the effort to phrase one's own conception of the idea under discussion, is a valuable mental stimulus.   Moreover, not all the problems before the Institute can be resolved by the techniques of specialized research: often agreement depends not on the acceptance of a sound body of data but on the capacity of people to develop sensitivities for values implicit in alien schemes of life.

Preparation for a conference begins with the closing round tables of the previous meeting.   In these discussions the Central Secretariat gathers from the participants any criticisms and suggestions they may have for improvement of method, and for the agenda of the following conference.   New research studies are launched, the conference proceedings are printed and circulated, and the groups are invited to begin consideration of the next conference program.

With stronger group organization and improved understanding of the conference processes, preparation was far enough developed in November, 1930, for a meeting to be assembled in New York at which representatives from the National Councils in Japan, China, Australia, Canada, Great Britain, and the United States made recommendations, later amplified through correspondence, upon the main outlines of the conference to be held in China, October 21–November 4, 1931.

The outline program adopted was then remitted to the National Councils as a basis for their group discussions in the period intervening before the conference met.   In order to facilitate these discussions, the Secretariat prepared draft syllabi which were circulated to the groups for amendment and criticism.   The International Program Committee, meeting during the week before the conference opened, had before it not only these draft syllabi, but the considered opinions upon them of the various National Councils, opinions arrived at after group discussions.   It also had data papers prepared by the National Councils, and digests of the research material

[7] This language difficulty was the subject of earnest consideration at the China Conference.   It was felt that some modification of the present exclusive use of the English language was desirable.   See p. 494.

available.   Each Council nominates a member of the International Program Committee.

The outline program provisionally agreed upon has also been used as a guide to the National Councils in the selection of their representatives at the conference. It need hardly be stated that the discussions are not open to any member of the general public who cares to attend, but are private meetings, invitations to which are in the hands of the National Councils.   An agreed limit is set upon the number of members sent by any Council.

There is one clear disadvantage of round tables, which has offered a conundrum to the Institute.   The essence of round-table discussion lies in breaking up the membership into smaller groups.   Not infrequently there are several such groups pursuing day after day different topics or different aspects of the same topic, some more successfully than others.   The preservation of unity, carrying the whole membership along with a general comprehension of what is happening in every part of the conference, is difficult to achieve.   Various types of plenary meetings or forums of the whole conference have been tried, with varying degrees of success.

The Institute has been rather embarrassed by the success it has so far had particularly in attracting well-known people to discuss topics of considerable public interest.   Both the personalities and the topics seem to offer possibilities of " news " which are not in fact borne out by the character of the discussions.   The interest of the Press has been stimulated, and two points of view have emerged.   There is the natural point of view of the journalist that the public is entitled to know what is said, that the Press is a good agency for the education of public opinion, and that it would serve the best interests of the Institute itself and of the objects it sets out to achieve if the Press were admitted freely to all meetings.   It is clear that the co-operation of the Press is indispensable if the Institute is to hope for any success in that part of its work which aims to secure responsible public participation in the study and discussion of Pacific problems.   It has sought and has obtained a generous measure of co-operation from the journalistic profession in the preparation of its conferences, but has hitherto found no wholly satisfactory means of continuing that co-operation during the actual meetings.   The newspaper men naturally regard themselves as competent to handle the news of the conference with discretion, judgment, and good faith.   As a body they are sympathetic with the Institute's aims but inclined to question the policy hitherto followed of excluding reporters from the actual round-table discussions.   The sole reason for this policy is the desire to obtain the fullest possible freedom of discussion.   It is thought that members should be able to speak freely, to change their opinions, and, for the time being, to forget all about their home constituencies and the newspaper audience to which they might possibly be speaking.

There are many members of the Institute who hold that the meetings are private in character, that their sole purpose is the private purpose of friendly discussion for the exchange of ideas and information, and that this exchange will be greatly hampered and frankness will be impossible if members are conscious that they are speaking not only to their friends in the room but possibly also to a larger audience of newspaper readers at home and abroad, an audience, moreover, which does not fully understand the nature and purpose of the Institute's discussions.

Considerable progress has, in fact, been made toward a resolution of the difference of outlook.   The Institute members are increasingly conscious of the debt they owe to the Press and of the difficulty, if not impossibility, of achieving their purposes without its aid.   It is realized, too, that, as a matter of fact, high cable rates and pressure of news are sufficient to make the problem one of getting adequate, as well as of curbing too great, publicity.

The policy of the Institute so far has been to admit the Press to lectures and general meetings where individual members take responsibility for their words; but to maintain the privacy of the round tables. At Kyoto, and again at Shanghai, well-known journalists arranged daily interviews at which they gave full accounts of all the discussions of that day without mentioning individual names. One of the real difficulties of this process lies in the disappointing dearth of real " news " in the sense of " clashes " or " disagreements." It is difficult for some journalists to accept the fact that individuals known to hold strong views on important controversial topics can and do discuss them without " disagreements " flaring up into sensational " clashes." The explanation is that the conference is unofficial and educational in character, the members are there to gain information and understanding, not national advantage.

The round-table discussions reach their highest level when they most fully utilize the discussion and research which have been carried on in all the National Councils during the preceding biennium. It is difficult to summarize this very scattered process of continuing discussion and research which consists largely of independent group activities in widely separated countries. The methods followed in different countries vary a great deal in accordance with the circumstances. In Japan and Great Britain, for example, there is a comparative concentration of activities, while in China, Canada, and the United States, there is more dispersion over various centers. In every case, however, the National Council of the Institute works continuously through committees which are in touch with local agencies of research and education. Sometimes it is possible to reach a whole people through such national agencies as press associations, in other cases some degree of regional decentralization is necessary.

The research activity of the Institute lies partly in the preparations made by National Councils for successive conferences and partly in the projects entrusted by the International Research Committee to universities in various countries.

The total result of all these various activities is that a fairly considerable number of people of varied interests in widely separated lands continuously devote a good deal of attention to Pacific problems. Moreover, their discussions proceed along an orderly plan, are integrated with those of the other groups, and focused every two years in conference discussions. The result obviously is a steady deepening of interest and knowledge among those most concerned, a result which has emotional as well as intellectual aspects. From these nuclei of interested, informed people, familiar with their own local backgrounds, there naturally radiates an increasing influence upon public opinion.

The preparation of an Institute conference is therefore part of a continuous process. The conferences are not isolated events but maintain a large degree of continuity in their discussions, both with previous conferences and with the interim processes of preparation. Important subjects are not dropped after a few days' discussion at a single conference. They are carried back from the conferences to the research workers and to the discussion groups for further detailed consideration. In this way a wider circle of participants becomes acquainted with and makes its contribution to the discussions.

Conversely, the following conference takes up again from the research workers and the discussion groups the subjects which have been further explored in the intervening period. There is thus a definite thread of continuity running through the biennial meetings, which should be regarded not as isolated conferences but as the focusing points of the whole process of study, discussion, and research, upon which the Institute is engaged.

The venue of the succeeding meeting is fixed at the close of each conference, generally by the acceptance of an invitation from one of the constituent groups. The exact time and place of meeting is fixed by the host group which is responsible also for the general arrangements.   The preparation of the conference, however, is entrusted to the Central Secretariat which assures the necessary accommodation for meetings, clerical assistance, and staff organization.   Each National Council undertakes the cost of preparing its own data material, paying the travel expenses, and defraying the charges of its representatives.   The Central Secretariat later publishes the proceedings of the conferences, with a summary of discussions supported by a selection of the papers presented.   The organization is therefore cooperative, the burden being shared among the host group, the other National Councils, and the Secretariat.

V. THE VALUE OF THE WORK

A careful record is kept, not indeed of the actual words of the round-table discussions, but of the main drift of ideas.   Recorders at each round table take down notes of the discussions which are afterward used as a basis from which the editor writes the proceedings of the conference.   In addition to these records there is always a large number of data papers and research reports.   Some of these have already found independent publication; others are published by their authors in a revised form after the conference.   A limited number of the smaller papers are also published, in whole or in part, in the proceedings, but there still remain a fairly considerable number which are available only to the members of the conference, and to a few libraries particularly interested in securing complete collections of such material.

Apart from the value of the conferences to those who participate in them, it is difficult to estimate the results of such meetings.   Each member on returning home naturally shares his experiences with his own circle, and in some cases this may be a very influential circle.   The considerable volume of addresses, newspaper interviews, and journal articles which follows every conference is an indication that the discussions eventually reach a much wider circle of public opinion.   In the long run, however, it is probable that the most important educational values of the Institute's work will accrue from the use in universities and schools, discussion groups, business and governmental circles, of the research studies which it has promoted and the published reports of its proceedings.   In this as in every other aspect of its work it is to be remembered that the Institute is only at the beginning of its work.   It has set itself a colossal task in applying scientific methods to the analysis and discussion of the difficult problems of a vast and important area of international relations and ought not to be judged finally until it has been at work for a much longer time.   In the meantime, it proceeds with its task in the spirit of confidence which William Morris put into the mouth of the medieval reformer-priest, John Ball, that " he who doeth well in fellowship, and because of fellowship, shall not fail, though he seem to fail today; but in the days hereafter shall he and his work yet be alive and men be holpen by them to strive again and yet again."

INDEX

INDEX